Second Edition

FORENSIC SCIENCE

the basics

About the Cover

Growing rusticles (3, 19-26 RST) became important after researches of the wreck site of the *RMS Titanic* off the continental shelf in the North Atlantic. The exposed steel surfaces of ship appeared to be coated with rusticles. In 1996 and 1998, expeditions recovered rusticles from the ship and by late 1999 methods were found to culture these consormial growths in a laboratory. The picture shows the manner in which rusticle growth may be enhanced using electrically impressed steel plates. In 2000, the technology advanced to the point where an aquarium of cultured rusticles went on tour with the Titanic Science exhibition organized by the Maryland Science Center. Over the next five years, more than 2.5 million exhibition visitors witnessed the growing rusticle consorms that formed in seven distinct growth patterns.

Second Edition

FORENSIC SCIENCE

the basics

Jay A. Siegel • Kathy Mirakovits

CRC Press
Taylor & Francis Group
Boca Raton   London   New York

CRC Press is an imprint of the
Taylor & Francis Group, an **informa** business

CRC Press
Taylor & Francis Group
6000 Broken Sound Parkway NW, Suite 300
Boca Raton, FL 33487-2742

© 2010 by Taylor and Francis Group, LLC
CRC Press is an imprint of Taylor & Francis Group, an Informa business

No claim to original U.S. Government works

Printed and bound in India by Replika Press Pvt. Ltd.
10 9 8 7 6 5 4 3 2

International Standard Book Number: 978-1-4200-8902-8 (Hardback)

Library of Congress Cataloging-in-Publication Data

Siegel, Jay A.
    Forensic science : the basics / Jay A. Siegel, Kathy Mirakovits. -- 2nd ed.
        p. cm.
    Includes bibliographical references and index.
    ISBN 978-1-4200-8902-8 (hardcover : alk. paper)
    1. Forensic sciences. 2. Criminal investigation. I. Mirakovits, Kathy. II. Title.

HV8073.S444 2010
363.25--dc22   2009048855

Visit the Taylor & Francis Web site at
http://www.taylorandfrancis.com

and the CRC Press Web site at
http://www.crcpress.com

Dedication

To my family, Maggie, Paul, and Sam. They are my reason for being. Can any legacy be as important? Thank you all for your love and support.

Jay Siegel

I dedicate this book to my father, Carl J. Busch, who always had faith in my accomplishments. He quietly supported and gently nudged me to push myself to the upper limits of my abilities.

Thank you, Dad. I hope you are smiling and applauding in Heaven.

Kathy Mirakovits

Contents

PART II: Tools of the Trade

PART III: Patterns and Impressions

PART V: Forensic Chemistry

PART VI: Legal Aspects of Forensic Science

Foreword

If you were to ask middle school or high school teachers why they teach science, their answers might not display a specific love for a particular area of science such as physics or biology. The true love of teaching science stems from a thirst for problem solving and answering the questions of *why* and *how*.

When I first began teaching high school students nineteen years ago, I had a predescribed checklist of science knowledge that I thought students had to master in order to succeed in life. Within my first four months of teaching, I realized those factoids didn't matter to most kids. What became most important was the student's attitude toward science. Once students walked through my classroom doors as ninth graders they had already formed their views of science as either boring, fun, or something for boys to do. My goal for my students was to foster a love for problem solving, giving them a foundation of steps to begin to answer the why and how questions with confidence and perhaps a little enthusiasm. I knew I was on the right track when on the last day of school, one of my female students turned to me and said, "Thanks for a great year. For the first time in my life, I actually enjoyed science!"

Traversing through my career of teaching earth science, integrated science, agriculture biology, animal physiology, veterinary science, and now biotechnology, I have solidified my resolve that teaching high school students skills provides them the foundation they need to academically succeed in any content area. Forensic science naturally teaches students skills in observation, documentation, inquiry, literacy, communication, and investigation, all while connecting academics to the working world. Through the television experience of *CSI*, students make direct connections to careers through forensic science. Even though glamorized, they see a range of personalities performing as skilled lab technicians, crime scene investigators, medical examiners, and all areas of law enforcement. They see curiosity in action and the range of skills and aptitudes required to perform the specific duties of the job. *Forensic Science: The Basics* provides a much-needed resource for teachers and students. Each chapter is clearly mapped out with learning objectives and contains a wealth of current content information, examples and illustrations, a useful summary, self-evaluation at the end of each chapter, and additional resources for further comprehension. This book is critical for providing the content background necessary for students to understand before they complete any laboratory experience.

Forensic science is exciting to teach and learn, as it is the realistic application of all areas of science. Jay Siegel and Kathy Mirakovits have created a reliable and fundamental resource to add credibility to real world science in the classroom. I have worked with Kathy as a participant in her forensic workshops for teachers and enjoy her passion for science and applaud the professional commitment she has made to provide teachers with critical content and hands on training. I met Jay as a guest presenter at one of Kathy's workshops. I appreciate his understanding of the need to provide a user-friendly resource connecting the bridge between college level academia and middle and high school education.

Lori Steward
Linden High School science teacher
Linden, California

Preface

Forensic science has changed quite a lot since the first edition of *Forensic Science: The Basics*, was published in early 2007. Media coverage of the successes and failures of the criminal justice system and forensic science continues to increase as does public interest in science and the law. The Innocence Project has helped free more than 200 wrongly convicted people to date. The validity of some traditional forensic sciences such as fingerprints and firearms is being questioned by scientists, judges, and lawyers. The number of high school classes in forensic science as well as college degrees, both undergraduate and graduate, continues to increase. Case backlogs nationwide have risen to more than 500,000 and there is a shortage of qualified forensic scientists that is approaching 2,000. With all of these happenings, there continues to be a need for quality forensic science text and lab materials that provide students in high school and college with a solid education in forensic science that builds upon a firm foundation in the sciences. *Forensic Science: The Basics, Second Edition*, builds on the standard it set for introductory forensic science text books and goes it one better.

Forensic Science: The Basics keeps the basic structure of the book, taking students through the criminal justice and forensic science systems from crime scene to court. It builds a solid foundation of tools such as microscopy, spectroscopy, and separation sciences and then applies them to the analysis of both the familiar types of evidence such as DNA, drugs, and trace evidence, but still covers the not so commonly studied "-ologies"—pathology, anthropology, odontology, and entomology. The book is flexible and comprehensive enough to be used in a one- or two-semester class, giving the teacher maximum flexibility in topics to cover.

Even though the basic structure and chapters have stayed the same, there have been big changes in the second edition. First, there are now two authors. In addition to Dr. Jay Siegel, a forensic scientist and college educator for more than thirty years, Kathy Mirakovits has joined the team. She is one of the most experienced and dynamic secondary school teachers of forensic science in the United States. She not only teaches basic and advanced forensic science classes in Portage, Michigan, she also conducts workshops for teachers all over the country and at national and statewide science teachers' meetings. She is also a consultant for a leading producer of forensic science education kits and has developed many of her own materials. She brings to *The Basics* the secondary school perspective that makes it even more relevant and appropriate for high school, community college, and university courses. She has also taken the best from her workshops and incorporated them into *Forensic Science: The Basics*. Each adopter will get a collection of laboratory exercises from the basic to the advanced, with detailed instructions as well as lists and sources of the materials needed. Other new features of *The Basics* include presentations of real cases that illustrate the various types of forensic evidence, a mini glossary at the beginning of each chapter, Web resources, mini lab exercises in most chapters, up-to-the-minute information about forensic science, many new figures and photos, and expanded questions at the end of each chapter. We are also planning a teacher's edition of the book and access to informative Web resources of Taylor & Francis. We believe that *Forensic Science: The Basics* will meet and exceed your needs and expectations for text material in your introductory or advanced class in forensic sciences. Feel free to contact us with your questions and comments.

About the Authors

Jay Siegel is currently director of the forensic and investigative sciences program at Indiana University–Purdue University, Indianapolis, and chair of the department of chemistry and chemical biology. He holds a Ph.D. in analytical chemistry from George Washington University. He worked for three years at the Virginia Bureau of Forensic Sciences, analyzing drugs, fire residues, and trace evidence. From 1980 to 2004, he was a professor of forensic chemistry and director of the forensic science program at Michigan State University in the School of Criminal Justice. Dr. Siegel has testified as an expert witness more than two hundred times in twelve states, federal court, and military court. He is editor-in-chief of the *Encyclopedia of Forensic Sciences,* author of *Forensic Science: A Beginner's Guide* and *Fundamentals of Forensic Science,* and has had articles and papers published in more than thirty forensic science journals. In February 2009, he was named Distinguished Fellow by the American Academy of Forensic Sciences. In April 2009, he was named the Distinguished Alumni Scholar by his alma mater, George Washington University.

Kathy Mirakovits teaches forensic science and physics at Portage Northern High School in Portage, Michigan. She holds a master's degree in science education from Western Michigan University and a bachelor's degree in science education from Miami University. Kathy has also served as science department chairperson for six years at Portage Northern. She taught at the high school level in Ohio, California, and Michigan for almost twenty years, and during that time taught general science, physical science, chemistry, biology, Earth science, and physics. Additionally, Kathy conducts workshops across the United States for teachers who wish to learn the application of forensic science in a school curriculum. She has developed numerous forensic science educational products for a national science supplier and has led workshops at the National Science Teachers Association (NSTA) in forensic science. Kathy led the teacher steering committee for the Forensic Science Educational Conference sponsored by the American Academy of Forensic Science at Michigan State University in August 2008.

Kathy has served as president of the Michigan Chapter of the American Association of Physics Teachers (AAPT) and as a curriculum writer for the Michigan Department of Education. Currently, Kathy serves as director-at-large for the Michigan Science Teachers Association. She has received the RadioShack Science Teaching Award and was a state finalist for the Presidential Award for Excellence in Math and Science Teaching (PAEMST).

PART I

Forensic Science and Investigation

PART I

Forensic Science and Investigation

1
Introduction to Forensic Science

Learning Objectives

1. To be able to define forensic science and describe its various areas
2. To be able to describe the major events in the history of forensic science and relate them to modern-day practice
3. To be able to describe the duties of a forensic scientist
4. To be able to describe the organization of federal, state, and local forensic science laboratories
5. To be able to diagram and describe the flow of evidence through a crime laboratory
6. To be able to describe the qualifications for becoming a forensic scientist
7. To be able to obtain information on careers in forensic science

Chapter 1
Introduction to Forensic Science

Mini Glossary

Behavioral forensic sciences: Applications of psychology and psychiatry to criminal matters including competency, interrogation, and crime scene reconstruction.

Computer forensics: Applications of computer science to criminal and civil offenses including the use of computers to commit crimes and the use of computers to help solve crimes.

Criminalistics: Analysis of physical evidence generated by a crime scene. Also, the pattern science areas of forensic evidence including fingerprints, firearms and questioned documents.

Forensic anthropology: Analysis of skeletal remains recovered from crime scenes for the purposes of developing a biological profile and identification of the remains.

Forensic engineering: Application of engineering principles in forensic cases including failure analysis and traffic accident reconstruction.

Forensic entomology: Study of insect activity and cadavers assist in the determination of time of death (postmortem interval) and for other forensic purposes.

Forensic odontology: Synonymous with forensic dentistry. Analysis of dentition for the purposes of human identification and examination of injuries. Also analysis of bite marks.

Forensic pathology: Determination of the cause and manner of death in cases of unattended or suspicious death.

Forensic science: Application of science to matters involving the public or applications of science to legal matters.

Forensic scientist: A scientist who analyzes evidence generated by criminal or civil offenses and who can offer expert testimony concerning the evidence in court of law.

Lay witness: A witness to a crime who testifies what she saw or heard. Lay witnesses do not normally give opinions. They are contrasted with expert witnesses who do have to render opinions at times.

Acronyms

AAFS: American Academy of Forensic Sciences
BATF: Bureau of Alcohol, Tobacco, and Firearms
CSI: Crime scene investigation or investigator
DEA: Drug Enforcement Administration
FBI: Federal Bureau of Investigation
FEPAC: Forensic Science Education Program Accreditation Commission
FSRTC: Forensic Science Research and Training Center
FSS: Forensic Science Service (United Kingdom)
FWS: U.S. Fish and Wildlife Service
IRS: Internal Revenue Service
LIMS: Laboratory Information System
PCR: Polymerase Chain Reaction
TSA: Transportation Security Administration
USSS: United States Secret Service

Introduction

Forensic science, forensic computing, forensic art, forensic accounting, forensic psychology. "Forensic" is the buzzword of the twenty-first century. It seems like there is "forensic" everything. More than 150 colleges and universities in the United States and more than 300 in the United Kingdom now offer some type of forensic science degree program. Movies, books, and TV shows about forensic science abound. Everyone is familiar with the sight of a white-robed scientist peering into a microscope, staring at a computer screen, and uttering a dramatic statement about evidence from a crime—the hair came from the victim, the DNA matches the suspect, the white powder is cocaine, and so on. At this writing, the three versions of *CSI* on television are among the most popular shows ever. Why the sudden popularity? After all, forensic science has been practiced in one form or another for over five thousand years. An important reason is that recent serious cases have occurred in the U.S. and elsewhere where forensic science has played a major role. Jon Benet Ramsey, O. J. Simpson, Theodore Bundy, the Green River Killer have all exploded onto the headlines in recent years and forensic science has played an important part of all of them.

People all over the world are fascinated by crime, its investigation, and its solution. People enjoy using clues to solve puzzles and problems. They are concerned with violent crime and want to do something about it. All of these factors feed into the popularity of forensic science. The major impact of this growing field seems to have been on women. Today, more than 75 percent of all students in forensic science education programs in the U.S. are women and this trend seems to be the same in other countries such as Australia and England.

In some ways, for women and men alike, the interest in "whodunit" isn't a new phenomenon. For more than a century, people have been fascinated by the exploits of Sherlock Holmes, the clever detective penned by Arthur Conan Doyle. As far back as the early days of TV and cinema, there have been shows about crime, policing, lawyers, and criminals. In recent years, the focus has shifted to forensic science. Although some people decry *CSI* and other similar shows about forensic science, the fact is that they have raised the public conscience about science and its role in crime solving. Forensic science provides a unique way of teaching students the principles of science as well as problem solving, critical thinking, oral and written communication skills, and the role of bias in the practice of science.

Is the portrayal of forensic science and scientists in the media accurate? What do forensic scientists really do? How is forensic science presented in court and what effect does it have on juries as they deliberate the fate of the accused? This is what this book is all about. You will learn about the various branches of forensic science, how crime labs are organized, how evidence is collected and analyzed, and how scientific testimony is presented in court.

What Is Forensic Science?

In the ancient Roman Empire, the Senate used to conduct its meetings in a public place called the *forum*. Anyone who wanted to could listen to the great debates of the day and watch the government in action. The key here is that the forum was a place where everyone could come and observe. The term "forum" is Latin for "public" and "forensic" is derived from that term. "Forensic science" implies, then, something about science and the public. In the broadest sense, **forensic science** can be defined as the methods of science applied to public matters. By this definition, forensic science doesn't necessarily have to do with crime, but the term has evolved in modern times to refer to the application of science to court or criminal matters.

Most forensic scientists work in the criminal area of the justice system, although civil cases are an important component of forensic science. In this book, focus will be on the applications of science to criminal matters.

Depth and Breadth of Forensic Science

If "forensic science" refers to science applied to criminal and civil law, one may wonder which of the sciences are actually forensic sciences? The answer may surprise you. Any science can be a forensic science if it has some application to justice. Think about how many different areas of science could potentially be brought to bear on solving crimes. Many medical, physical, and biological sciences have forensic applications, as do math, business practices, sociology, and psychology. The list is nearly endless. The most common areas of science that have forensic applications are described below. This will give you an idea of the "big tent" that is forensic science.

Forensic Science v. Crime Scene Investigation

There is a good deal of confusion about the relationship between forensic science and crime scene investigation. Part of this may be due to TV shows such as *CSI* that blur the distinctions between them by depicting the people who collect evidence from a crime scene as the same people who analyze the evidence in the crime lab. In reality, these are different functions, but with some actual overlap. Crime scene investigators are usually, but not always, police officers trained for and then assigned to the crime scene unit. They learn how to recognize evidence, protect it from contamination, collect it properly, thoroughly document its location and condition, and maintain a chain of custody to help authenticate the evidence when it gets to court. Crime scene investigators have a science education background, but many do not. Some are also trained in procedures that could be considered forensic science because they involve preliminary (or complete) analysis of some types of evidence. Examples include preliminary analysis of suspected illicit drugs (called "field tests"), collection and analysis of fingerprints, and documentation and analysis of bloodstain patterns. To the extent that they analyze this evidence and reach scientific conclusions and then testify in court as experts, these investigators would be considered forensic scientists and this part of their job would be forensic science. This type of activity among crime scene investigators is relatively rare but still common enough to bear mention. Under normal circumstances, the job of crime scene investigator stops when the evidence is delivered to the laboratory where the actual work of the **forensic scientist** begins. Most people in the forensic science field do not consider crime scene investigation activities to be part of forensic science in spite of the fact that many crime scene units are administratively within the lab structure and that forensic scientists are increasingly going to some crime scenes to help with investigations.

Criminalistics

The term "criminalistics" was first coined by Paul Kirk, considered by many to be the father of forensic science in the United States. In some quarters, criminalistics is synonymous with forensic science and the two terms are often used interchangeably. In California, forensic scientists are often officially called criminalists. The term can be used to describe the comparative forensic sciences such as fingerprints, questioned documents, firearms, and tool marks. Most commonly, however, criminalistics refers to the myriad types of physical evidence generated by crime scenes. This includes illicit drugs, blood and DNA, fire and explosive residues, hairs and fibers, glass and soil particles, paints and plastics, fingerprints, bullets, and much more.

A Bit of History: Paul Kirk

Paul Leland Kirk was a chemist and forensic scientist. He held a Ph.D. in biochemistry from the University of California at Berkeley. He started his career at Berkeley in the biochemistry department and became interested in forensic science when authorities asked him to examine evidence from a rape case. Because of his interest and experience in microscopy, he was asked to head up the new Berkeley criminology program in 1937. He subsequently worked as a microscopist on the Manhattan Project where he helped isolate fissionable material for making bombs. In 1946, he returned to Berkeley and headed up the technical criminology major program and served as head of the criminalistics department. Kirk is best known professionally for his work in the Sam Sheppard murder case. In this case, Dr. Sam Sheppard was falsely accused of murdering his wife. He escaped from custody and helped the police find the "one-armed" man who committed the crime. This case was the basis for *The Fugitive*, a book, TV show, and movie. Kirk examined bloodstain patterns from the scene and his subsequent report and testimony at the second trial helped free Sheppard. Today, Kirk's legacy lives on in the Paul Kirk Award, the highest award given by the criminalistics section of the American Academy of Forensic Sciences.

Pathology

When some people think of forensic science, they envision dead bodies and autopsies. Not all of forensic science is like this, but **forensic pathology** is. The forensic pathologist is a medical doctor who first specialized in pathology and then in forensic pathology. Forensic pathologists determine the cause and manner of death in cases where someone dies under suspicious or other circumstances as prescribed by state law. Many forensic pathologists work for state or local medical examiners or coroners. These are appointed or elected officials who must decide when a medicolegal autopsy (an autopsy in a case of suspicious death or homicide) is needed and they must sign death certificates that indicate the cause and manner of death. Medical examiners and coroners don't usually perform the autopsies themselves. They employ forensic pathologists to do this. Forensic pathology is discussed in detail in Chapter 10. If you would like to learn more about medicolegal autopsies, check out www.nlm.nih.gov/ex hibition/visibleproofs/e ducation/medic al/index.html.

Anthropology

A Bit of History: An Early Case in Forensic Anthropology

In 1849, a Boston physician named Dr. George Parkman was murdered. The suspect in the case was John Webster, a professor of chemistry at Harvard who was in considerable debt to Dr. Parkman. The modus operandi of the crime was that Professor Webster incinerated Dr. Parkman. When investigators searched through the ashes, they found some remains of skull and some badly damaged remains of dentures. The prosecution retained several experts in osteology and physiology who examined the bone fragments. They determined that they belonged to a white male, about 50 to 60 years of age, about 6 feet tall. Dr. Parkman was 60 years old and 5 feet 11 inches tall. In addition, experts matched the dentures to Dr. Parkman (Berryman, 13 *Crime Lab Digest*, 1986).

Forensic anthropologists work with skeletal remains. They identify bones as being human or animal. If animal, they determine the species. If human, they determine from what part of the body the bone originated. If they have the right bones, gender can be determined as well. Sometimes age can be approximated and racial characteristics determined, and even socioeconomic status may be estimated. If there is an injury to a skeleton or major bones, the anthropologist can help determine the cause of the injury or even death. Forensic anthropologists do other things besides identifying bones. They also work closely with skulls. It is possible to literally build a face onto a skull, using clay and wooden or plastic pegs of various sizes. Using charts that give average tissue depth figures for various parts of a face, an anthropologist constructs a face and then makes judgments as to that person's eye, nose and mouth characteristics. Facial reconstruction can be useful in helping to identify a missing person from the face built around a recovered skull. It is also possible for a forensic anthropologist to superimpose a skull onto a picture of a face to see if they are one and the same person. This is not usually definitive, but can be quite helpful in establishing the identity of a skull. **Forensic anthropology** is discussed in detail in Chapter 11.

Odontology

"Odontology" is a synonym for dentistry. You may be curious about how a dentist could be a forensic scientist, but actually there are several ways. A few years ago in Pennsylvania, a burglar broke into a house and ransacked it for valuables while the owners were on vacation. During his foray, he got hungry and rooted through the refrigerator for something to eat. He found a hunk of Swiss cheese and took a bite. Later, he was arrested, trying to "fence" (sell on the black market) the stolen merchandise. When the police investigated the home looking for clues that would tie him to the scene, they found the cheese. A forensic dentist made a cast of the bite mark in the cheese and matched it to an impression of the burglar's teeth.

The most famous case where bite marks were crucial evidence involved Theodore Bundy, suspected of killing more than thirty young women in his career as a serial killer. He operated first in Washington, Utah, and Colorado and then moved to Florida. During his last homicide, he bit his victim on her buttock after strangling her. A forensic dentist was able to match Bundy's teeth to this bite mark. He was executed in Florida for this murder in 1989.

Key Figures in Forensic Science: Ted Bundy

Ted Bundy was born in 1946 in Vermont in a home for unwed mothers. His father's identity was not conclusively determined and he was raised by his grandparents. He later moved to Washington state where he went to high school. Before he graduated from high school, he was a thief and shoplifter and known for being quite introverted and socially awkward. After graduating from high school, he went to the University of Washington and ultimately earned a degree in psychology. By all accounts, he was an honors student and well liked by his teachers. He subsequently began law school there, but dropped out.

Some experts, including those who knew Bundy, believe that he started his killing spree during his early teens. At one point, he told his attorney that he attempted his first kidnapping when he was in college. The earliest murders that could conclusively be attributed to him occurred when he was 27. He started a string of brutal killings of young, white women in Washington and Oregon and then Utah and Colorado. He was caught in Colorado but escaped twice from jail and fled to Florida where he resumed his rampage after more than two years. His last murders took place in Tallahassee at a sorority house. It was these murders for which he was tried and ultimately executed. Crucial evidence in these murders was a bite mark that he left on the buttock of one of his victims. At his trial, a forensic odontologist testified that he matched the bite mark to a cast made of Bundy's teeth. Several jurors told the media after the trial that this was the crucial piece of evidence against Bundy. This was the first instance in the U.S. where bite marks had been used as evidence in this fashion. It should be noted that, as Bundy's execution date neared, he tried to buy time or get his sentence commuted to life in prison by offering to tell families where the bodies of some of his victims were in exchange for their writing letters to the judge asking for clemency. Not one family agreed to this and he was electrocuted in January of 1989.

Forensic odontologists can also be very helpful in identifying the remains of victims of mass disasters such as airplane crashes. Sometimes bodies are so badly burned or dismembered the only way to identify the remains is by using dental records. Postmortem dental records are taken and matched to x-rays taken before death.

Finally, forensic dentists may play a role in child or other abuse cases. A forensic dentist can often tell whether facial injuries received by a person were the result of falling down a flight of stairs or if they were due to blunt force injury such as striking the person with a fist or other object. **Forensic odontology** is covered in more detail in Chapter 11.

Engineering

Forensic engineers can be valuable in cases where something has gone wrong with a mechanical or structural entity or in cases of automobile crashes. A few years ago, a balcony collapsed in the lobby of a Hyatt hotel in Kansas City. Many people were on the balcony at the time watching a rock concert going on in the lobby several stories below. Questions arose about why the balcony collapsed. Forensic engineers were called in to examine the structural remains of the balcony and the concrete that fell. They concluded that the construction of the balcony was faulty and contributed to its failure. Failure analysis is one of the major contributions that forensic engineers make to the justice system. Figure 1.1 shows the damage to the Hyatt hotel in Kansas City after the walkway collapse.

The majority of the work of forensic engineers is in the investigation of traffic crashes. Accident reconstruction is used to determine speed of travel, direction of impact, and who was driving the vehicle at the time of the crash. Insurance companies and police departments use forensic engineers extensively in traffic incident investigation.

Figure 1.1 Wreckage of the collapsed Hyatt Regency Hotel in Kansas City. Associated Press file photo (with permission).

Entomology

When a person dies and the body is exposed to the elements, who (or what) gets there first? It's not witnesses or detectives, but flies—more specifically, a species called the blow fly. During the bombing of the Murrah Federal Building in Oklahoma City (Terry Nichols and Timothy McVeigh were convicted of the bombing), bodies were buried in the tons of rubble from the collapsed building. Investigators literally followed the flies into the rubble in order to locate many of the bodies. Female blow flies and other insects lay their eggs in decaying flesh and different insects do this at different times. Other insects such as beetles and wasps attack and feed off the insects and the eggs. Depending on temperature and other environmental factors, this parade of visitors takes place at surprisingly consistent time intervals. By inspecting the corpse, forensic entomologists can give a pretty good estimate of the elapsed time since death and determine whether the body has been at a site for many hours or several days.

In addition to the postmortem interval, there is other information that can be gained from studying insects feeding on a corpse. If a person has been poisoned, the flies and other insects will ingest some of the poison. A toxicologist can capture some of these critters, chop them up, and extract the poison and identify it. There are also cases where a person took cocaine and then died. Some of the maggots on the body became abnormally large in size owing to their ingestion of the cocaine. **Forensic entomology** is covered in detail in Chapter 12.

Behavioral Forensic Science

Forensic psychiatry and psychology have been long contributors to the forensic sciences. As long as there has been crime, people have wrestled with the concept of responsibility. Our laws and those of most other countries have long had provisions for how people who commit crimes and have diminished capacity are treated. If a person is truly insane, can she be held responsible for committing a crime? Although the definitions vary as to what constitutes responsibility, insanity, etc., it falls to forensic psychiatrists and psychologists to examine defendants and render expert opinions to courts. There are real differences between psychiatrists and psychologists. Psychiatry is a medical specialty attained by medical doctors. Psychology is a behavioral science that does not involve medical training. Both have a role to play in determining responsibility for committing crimes.

Forensic psychologists play other roles in the criminal justice system. Some crime investigations include a component of psychological crime reconstruction. Serial killers

Figure 1.2 A drawing of a car outfitted so that a sniper can fire a weapon out of the back without being detected. This is similar to the set up used by the DC snipers.

and others who commit multiple crimes develop habits and traits that show up time after time as they commit crimes. Discovering and understanding these patterns can help lead investigators to the right suspect. Specially trained forensic psychologists can examine a series of crime scenes and develop theories about the type of person who committed the crimes. It must be noted that this work is much more of an art than a science and is often fraught with uncertainties. A case in point is the Washington D.C. sniper case of October 2002. Forensic psychologists and criminal investigators initially determined that the killer was a young, white male. As it turned out, the killers were two black males. Such attempts to determine a profile of a serial killer can be very difficult, even if there are many incidents to draw on for data. Figure 1.2 is a drawing of the car similar to the one the killers used when killing their victims.

Psychological profiling has also been used in other criminal and civil areas. For example, the Transportation Security Administration (TSA) uses forensic psychologists to create profiles of what a likely airplane hijacker might look like or behave like so security checkpoint officials can subject people who meet the profile to additional screening. This has been going on for many years in one form or another. The Department of Homeland Security has a similar program for border guards to help spot potential terrorists.

There are other types of behavioral forensic scientists. Some study interrogation and investigation techniques such as polygraph instruments to determine their accuracy and usefulness in criminal and civil investigations. Others do research in developing new areas of interrogation and deception detection.

Computer Forensics

Computer forensics is sometimes called digital forensics as well as by other descriptors. Computers have become very important in crime today, both as instruments of crime and in helping to solve crime. Many criminals and criminal enterprises conduct much of their business and keep their business records on computers. Sometimes these records are highly encrypted. When caught, criminals often try to erase or physically destroy the data to prevent it from being used against them.

Computer forensic scientists and engineers study ways to recover data even from smashed hard disk drives. They also learn how to handle a computer found at a crime scene, especially one that is turned on. Computers are also used to steal identities from people and merchandise from companies. They can be used to disrupt entire networks and hack into otherwise secure, private websites. Computers can also be used to help solve crimes. They can track people down, store incriminating data that can be used against criminals, and help test and improve computer security. Computer forensics is one of the fastest-growing areas of forensic science and will continue to grow in the future.

History and Development of Forensic Science

When did people actually invent forensic science? When was science first applied to answering questions about crimes or civil issues? Some baby boomers remember the *Quincy* TV show as the first time they saw forensic science in action. Twenty- and thirty-somethings think of the O. J. Simpson case as the beginning of the use of science to solve real crimes. Today many people think of *CSI* as the birth of forensic science. In reality, some aspects of forensic science have been at least recognized for centuries. An excellent outline of the history of forensic science in the form of a timeline has been published by Norah Rudin and Keith Inman and can be found on the Web at www.forensicdna.com/Timeline020702.pdf. The earliest milestones in all areas are covered first and then gradually brought up to date. In this chapter, data from the timeline referenced above will be used to illustrate the history of forensic science, highlighting three important examples: fingerprints, crime laboratories, and blood analysis.

As in many other fields of knowledge, the Chinese were the first to discover the value of forensic science in identification. They were the first to use fingerprints to identify the owners of objects such as pottery, but had no formal classification process. In later centuries, a number of scientists, such as Marcello Malphighi, noted the presence of fingerprints and that they had interesting characteristics, but didn't make any connection to personal identification. The first person to recognize that fingerprints could be classified into types (nine major kinds) was Jan Purkinje, a professor of anatomy. In 1880, a Scottish physician named Henry Faulds published an article in the journal *Nature* that suggested that the uniqueness of fingerprints could be used to identify someone. This was quickly followed in the 1890s by Frances Galton, who published the first book on fingerprints; Juan Vucetich, who developed a fingerprint classification system that is still used today in South America; and Sir Edward Henry, who developed the fingerprint classification system that has been adopted in the United States and Europe.

The development of a forensic science infrastructure including crime labs is much more recent and quite interesting. For example, the first detective force was developed in France, The Sûreté of Paris by Eugene Vidocq in 1810. In 1905, President Teddy Roosevelt established the FBI, but the FBI lab was not established until 1932. The first crime laboratory was established in France in 1910 by Edmund Locard, a professor of forensic medicine. He later espoused his famous Locard Exchange Principle, which will be discussed in the next chapter. In the United States, the first crime laboratory was established by August Vollmer, chief of police in Los Angeles. The first journal devoted to forensic science was begun by Calvin Goddard and his staff in 1930 at the newly formed Scientific Crime Detection Laboratory on the campus of Northwestern University. Initially called the *American Journal of Police Science*, the name was later changed to the *Journal of Criminal Law, Criminology, and Police Science*. In 1937, Paul Kirk established the first university-based forensic science program at the University of California at Berkeley. It was called *Technical Criminology.* Dr. Kirk is generally considered the father of modern forensic science in the United States. In 1950, the American Academy of Forensic Science (AAFS) was founded in Chicago. The AAFS is the largest forensic science society in the world and has members from many different countries. The Academy began publication of the *Journal of Forensic Sciences,* the professional journal of forensic science, shortly after AAFS was founded.

The realization that blood and bodily fluids had the potential for being important evidence in criminal investigation is an old idea. Bloody palm prints were used as evidence more than a thousand years ago in Rome. In 1853, Ludwig Teichmann developed the first of a number of crystalline tests still used today in the characterization of blood. His test detected the presence of hemoglobin. The German scientist Schönbein developed the first presumptive test for blood. It takes advantage of the ability of hydrogen peroxide to react with hemoglobin. This was in 1863. In 1900, Karl Landsteiner made major breakthroughs in the analysis of blood when he determined that there are actually four types of human blood. This became the basis for the ABO blood typing system and set the stage for all further work in serology. Landsteiner won the Nobel Prize for his work in 1930. Max Richter took Landsteiner's results and adapted them to blood stains, such as those found in crime scenes. Fifteen years later, Leone Lattes, a professor in Italy, developed a test to determine blood type in the ABO system and wrote a book about how to type dried stains. There were a number of advances over the next thirty years, culminating in the work of Sir Alec Jeffreys of the University of Leicester. In 1984, Jeffreys used a technique called *DNA fingerprinting* to solve a double murder case in England, the first case solved by DNA analysis. The year before, Kary Mullis developed the polymerase chain reaction (PCR), which is the basis for all DNA typing in forensic cases today. He also won the Nobel Prize for his work.

What Is a Forensic Scientist?

Since practically any science can be a forensic science at times, many scientists can be forensic scientists. It is partially a matter of what they do in their jobs, but also a matter of training and education. Forensic pathologists, for example, are educated as physicians and then trained as pathologists. After that, they can get specialized training in the forensic aspects of pathology and become certified as forensic pathologists. This assures that they will have the proper education, training, and licensure to practice pathology on medicolegal cases. There is, however, a critical shortage of certified forensic pathologists in the U.S. and many medicolegal autopsies are performed by pathologists who have no forensic training. Are they forensic pathologists by virtue of their performing forensic autopsies? Most pathologists would agree that they are not. The situation is somewhat different for forensic anthropologists, odontologists, and entomologists. There are a few forensic anthropology degrees, but essentially none in odontology or entomology. There are certifications for all three that result in a designation as forensic anthropologist, odontologist, or entomologist. The fact is, however, that most of what would be considered forensic cases in these areas are performed by noncertified but professional scientists. With increased attention being paid to these forensic sciences, questions of who should be performing forensic analysis become more important.

The majority of forensic scientists work in crime laboratories on the local, state, or national level. Most forensic science laboratories are associated with law enforcement agencies such as the Detroit Police Department Crime Lab, Indiana State Police Forensic Lab, and FBI Lab. Although early in their history most of these laboratories were staffed by enlisted officers, special agents, and the like, today increasing numbers are civilians who have no police duties. One of the reasons is that as forensic science has become more sophisticated and rigorous, it has been harder to find scientifically trained police officers. The other reason is that police departments want to put more officers on the street and are transferring enlisted analysts out of the lab and into law enforcement duty.

In a crime laboratory, forensic scientists have two major duties: to analyze evidence and to testify in court. Forensic science laboratories behave in a reactive role. When a crime is committed, the crime scene unit collects the evidence and turns it over to the police investigators (sometimes detectives) who then bring it to the crime lab. In some cases, the crime scene investigation unit may turn evidence directly over to the lab. The lab scientists then analyze the evidence. They generally do not have much input into what evidence is collected, although there may be occasions where a forensic scientist asks the police to collect additional items of evidence for comparison or further analysis. In recent years, there has been an increasing trend toward having forensic scientists attend at least some crime scenes. For example, the Michigan State Police Forensic Science Division forms teams of forensic scientists that are called on to help process serious crime scenes such as those in which there is a dead body. These scientists work along with the police CSI team to help process the scene and collect evidence.

The other major duty of forensic scientists is to testify in court. In the United States criminal justice system, there are basically two types of witnesses who testify in court: lay and expert witnesses. A **lay witness** is someone who is not an expert but has something to contribute to help the judge or jury determine the guilt or innocence of the accused. This person may have been an eyewitness to a crime, a victim or someone who knows something about the suspect or the crime. Such witnesses are supposed to testify only to what they have perceived with their five senses: touch, taste, smell, sight, and hearing. They are not to give their opinions. It is the jury's job to make conclusions about the evidence presented to them, not the witness. For example, if a witness offers testimony that the driver of a car involved in a traffic accident was drunk, that conclusion would not be permitted in court. Being drunk in the motor vehicle code sense requires an expert finding of sufficient alcohol exceeding the legal limit in the driver's body.

The other type of witness in a court is an expert witness. This is a person who has knowledge and/or skills, derived from education and/or experience, that qualifies him or her to take a set of facts and reach conclusions not attainable by the average person (the judge or jury). Most people think of experts as being Ph.D. scientists or doctors and, although many of them are, other experts may derive their expertise from experience rather than formal education. For example, suppose that a man is driving down a mountainous road when his car's brakes fail. He crashes his car and dies. The police investigator would want to know why the brakes failed. Were they old and in need of repair? Were they installed improperly by a mechanic? Were they tampered with so that they would fail purposefully? Each of these explanations would call for a different response by the justice system. If someone were put on trial for killing the driver, it would not be prudent to have the jury go to the garage where the wrecked car was stored and have the jurors inspect the brakes to see what caused them to fail. Most jurors would not have the knowledge to inspect the brakes (the facts) and draw conclusions (the opinions) about how they failed. An expert brake mechanic should be called on to inspect the brakes and determine the cause of their failure. This individual can give testimony as an expert about the failure of the brakes.

Whether a trial is by jury or judge, it is the judge's responsibility to decide whether expert testimony is needed and who is qualified to offer it. Even if a forensic scientist has testified hundreds of times, he or she must be requalified as an expert for every trial. It is important that the expert explain complex scientific or technical principles in a language that a jury can understand. Forensic scientists must be equally competent in the trial part and the scientific part of their jobs.

So You Want to Be a Forensic Scientist

So now you know what forensic scientists do and where they work, but what does it take to be one? This depends on what type of forensic scientist you want to be and what type of work you want to do. Becoming a forensic scientist requires both education and training. We shall discuss a few of the more common areas of forensic study. Figure 1.3 is a chart that summarizes selected forensic science careers, optimal education, and job markets.

- **Crime lab forensic scientist.** Entry level requirements for a crime lab scientist position are usually either a bachelor's degree in a science such as chemistry, biology, or forensic science with a year or two of experience or a master's degree with less experience. (The job market is very competitive and a master's degree is becoming the preferred degree.) There are more than 100 forensic science education programs in the U.S. today and more than 300 in the United Kingdom—that's a lot Many of these so-called forensic science degrees are not science-based or not rigorous enough to properly prepare students for careers in forensic science. A few years ago, the American Academy of Forensic Science and the National Institute of Justice developed a set of standards for bachelor's and master's degree forensic science programs and created the Forensic Science Education Program Accreditation Commission (FEPAC). Information can be found on the website of the American Academy of Forensic Sciences: www.aafs.org.
- **Forensic pathologist.** To become a forensic pathologist, you first need to graduate from college with an excellent academic record. Then you must graduate from medical school, requiring another four years. After medical school, you complete a residency in pathology, which takes an additional four years. Finally, an additional residency in forensic pathology is recommended in order to become certified. This takes another year to complete.
- **Forensic anthropologist.** Few crime labs can afford to hire a forensic anthropologist full time. If you have another area of specialization such as trace evidence or DNA typing, you may be hired by a crime lab and then handle anthropology cases as they come up. Another way of getting into the field is to obtain a Ph.D. in physical or forensic anthropology and teach and do research at a university; then local crime labs would come to you for your services as needed.
- **Forensic odontologist.** This is similar to the route for a forensic pathologist except that you would complete dental school instead of medical school.

Career	Job Description	Optimal Education	Job Market
Crime Lab Forensic Scientist	Analyze scientific evidence Testify in court	At least a BS degree in science MS degree preferred	Robust but spotty More than 1900 new forensic scientists needed
Forensic Pathologist	Determine cause and manner of death in suspicious or unattended deaths	BS or BA degree + 4 year medical school degree + 3–4 year residency in pathology + 1–2 year residency in forensic pathology	Excellent. There is a nationwide, critical shortage of certified forensic pathologists.
Forensic Anthropologist	Excavate crime scenes and analyze skeletal remains	PhD in physical or forensic anthropology	Most forensic anthropologists teach at colleges and do forensic anthropology on the side. Job market is small.
Forensic Odontologist	Analyze bite marks, facial injuries and identify human remains from dental work	BS or BA degree + 4 years of dental school. No residencies in forensic dentistry	Few people make a living strictly on forensic dentistry. Most have conventional dental practices and do forensic work on the side. Job market is small.
Forensic Engineer	Reconstruct vehicle accidents, structural failure analysis, explosion analysis, electrical systems	PhD in engineering, lots of experience	Most forensic engineers are in private practice. Need for experienced engineers is pretty large.
Computer Forensic Scientist	Determine role of computers in crime Reconstruct media devices and computers Track down criminals who hack into sites and steal identities	PhD in computer science or computer engineering, lots of experience	Some are in private practice. Many work for colleges as teachers/researchers and do forensic work on the side.

Figure 1.3 This chart shows the types of careers and best educational preparation for various areas of forensic science.

There are few (if any) residencies in forensic odontology, therefore you would have to work with police departments on an as-needed basis.

- **Forensic engineer.** This career requires education in engineering—and the more the better. Usually, experts in **forensic engineering** need to have a Ph.D. Most forensic engineers have their own private companies that are hired by prosecutors or defendants.
- **Computer forensic scientist.** There are few education programs that turn out computer forensic scientists. People who work in this area invariably have a strong interest and educational background in computer science and engineering. Their designation as computer forensic scientists arises from the types of cases that they work on or the type of research and teaching they do.
- **Related careers.** Not everyone wants to be a forensic scientist in a laboratory. Some people decide they want to work in a career that makes use of their strong science background and perhaps a forensic science education. There are a large number of related careers one could consider. If you decide to be a lawyer, a science background can be very handy in the field of patent law. Many patents require practice and skill in reading and digesting sometimes complicated journal articles and books. These particular skills are highly developed in a science education. Environmental forensic science is becoming a major area of environmental study. Scientists work for environmental analytical laboratories determining pollution levels in air, water, and soil and can help companies comply with environmental laws or, conversely, help government agencies track down and prosecute polluters. The pharmaceutical industry is very interested in people with strong analytical chemistry backgrounds. Many forensic science educational programs teach the chemistry and analysis of illicit drugs—information that can be valuable in a career in pharmaceutical chemistry. The insurance industry is also interested in employing scientists, including those with forensic science backgrounds. They investigate fires, explosions, traffic accidents, stolen automobiles, and other property incidents to help determine if a crime was committed or a covered loss occurred.

Career Information

The websites of any of the federal agencies listed in the section on the organization of federal forensic science labs will provide information about how one joins that organization as a forensic scientist. In addition, one can check the website of the state or local law enforcement agency where crime labs are housed for information about obtaining employment.

General job and career information in forensic science can be found at the American Academy of Forensic Sciences: www.aafs.org. The Academy is the major national organization for forensic scientists. There is a section on its website that posts job openings in the field. The Academy also provides information on careers in forensic science.

Information about careers in particular areas of forensic science can be found on the websites of the specific association or society. A few of them more common ones are listed below.

- American Academy of Forensic Sciences: www.aafs.org
- National Association of Medical Examiners: www.thename.org

- Society of Forensic Toxicologists: www.soft-tox.org
- American Society of Questioned Document Examiners: www.asqde.org
- American Board of Forensic Anthropology: www.csuchico.edu/anth/ABFA
- Forensic Entomology: www.forensic-entomology.com
- Association of Firearm and Tool Mark Examiners: www.afte.org/index_forum.php
- American Society of Forensic Odontology: www.forensicdentistryonline.org/new_asfo/newasfo.htm

The United States Forensic Science System

There are approximately four hundred forensic science laboratories in the United States. Most of them are public labs supported by a unit of federal, state, or local government. Others are private labs. A laboratory may be full service, running tests in all of the major areas of forensic science. Others may conduct only the most common examinations of evidence such as drugs, firearms, and fingerprints. The federal government and all fifty state governments administer some form of laboratory system or network.

Federal Forensic Science Laboratories

Most people are familiar with the FBI laboratory and many people think that it is the only crime lab run by the United States government. The fact is that there are many federal laboratories and they are located within several cabinet departments. Figure 1.4 is a diagram of how the federal forensic science labs are arranged.

Figure 1.4 An organizational chart of the major federal forensic science laboratories.

Figure 1.5 The new FBI laboratory in Quantico, Virginia.

The Justice Department

Most of the federal crime labs are located within the Department of Justice. They are under the administrative control of the Attorney General of the United States.

The FBI Laboratory

www.fbi.gov

The Federal Bureau of Investigation laboratory is in Quantico, Virginia. It is supported by the Forensic Science Research and Training Center (FSRTC), also located in Quantico. The FBI lab is one of the best known and most prestigious forensic science laboratories in the world. The FBI lab supports the law enforcement and antiterrorism missions of the FBI by analyzing evidence generated by these activities. The FBI lab also processes evidence sent in by state and local law enforcement agencies or crime labs. Personnel from the FBI lab also travel to foreign countries to help indigenous law enforcement agents solve crimes against United States citizens and those with global implications. Figure 1.5 is the FBI Laboratory in Quantico, Virginia.

The Drug Enforcement Administration (DEA)

www.usdoj.gov/dea

The DEA has a network of regional laboratories located in Washington, D.C., Miami, Chicago, Dallas, San Francisco, and New York. They are supported by the Special Testing and Research Lab in Virginia. The DEA analyzes illicit drugs seized by DEA agents and by task forces made up of state or local drug agents working with the DEA. It also works with foreign countries to help eradicate illicit drugs or help prevent their importation into the United States. The DEA shares training facilities with the FBI in Quantico, Virginia.

The Department of the Treasury

Most people are surprised to find that the Department of the Treasury has crime labs, but in fact it has several. These labs have definite areas of responsibility.

The Bureau of Alcohol, Tobacco, and Firearms (BATF)

www.atf.treas.gov

The BATF has a number of missions supported by a network of its three laboratories located in Beltsville, Maryland, Atlanta, and San Francisco. As the name of the agency suggests, agents of the BATF are in charge of making sure that all alcohol produced in or imported into the United States has the proper tax stamp indicating that the correct taxes have been paid. This is a revenue function that explains why the agency is in the Department of the Treasury. Likewise, the BATF has similar functions in the tobacco industry to ensure that the proper taxes have been paid on cigarettes and that contraband tobacco products such as Cuban cigars are not imported illegally. The firearms mission is a bit different. The Bureau is charged with making sure illegal firearms are not produced, imported, or exported and that the proper taxes and duties are paid on legal weapons. In addition to the areas mentioned above, BATF labs employ some of the world's leading experts in fire and explosive analysis who work with law enforcement agencies all over the world. The labs also have expertise in trace evidence, fingerprints, and questioned documents.

The Secret Service

www.ustreas.gov/usss/index.shtml

When most people think of the Secret Service, they picture serious, dark-suited people guarding the president of the United States and other domestic and international VIPs. Certainly the protective function is the most visible part of the Service, but not the only one. The Secret Service maintains a laboratory in Washington, D.C. that has several functions. It supports the protective services of the agency by continuously developing methods that counter attempts to harm the people that the Service is guarding. In addition, the agency is charged with preventing attempts at counterfeiting money and credit cards. This explains why the agency is in the Department of the Treasury. As one would expect, there are leading experts in counterfeiting and questioned documents as well as trace evidence employed in the Secret Service lab.

The Internal Revenue Service (IRS)

www.irs.gov

No discussion of the Department of the Treasury would be complete without mention of the IRS. The IRS is charged with making sure that everyone pays a fair share of taxes according to the law and there are many IRS agents who do that job. They are supported by a laboratory in Chicago, whose major expertise lies in the area of questioned documents. This lab utilizes experts in handwriting, typewriting and printers, inks, and papers. In addition to their analytical work, they carry out numerous training activities for other agencies.

The Department of the Interior

www.lab.fws.gov

Wait, doesn't the Department of the Interior take care of the national parks, forests, and the environment? What do they need with a crime lab? Doesn't the FBI have jurisdiction over the parks and forests? Well, yes and no. The FBI lab has a lot of experts, but none in wildlife biology and animal body parts. So in 1987, the United States Fish and Wildlife Service established the world's first and only laboratory that specializes in wildlife forensic science in Ashland, Oregon. This lab supports the enforcement activities of the fish and wildlife agents who patrol the national parks and forests to help prevent poaching and hunting of endangered species. The lab also supports such efforts worldwide.

The United States Postal Service

www.usps.com/postalinspectors/crimelab.htm

The United States Postal Service has an investigative arm that swings into action when someone uses the mail to commit a crime. Such crimes can include fraud, extortion, mailing anthrax or another dangerous substance to a government official, illegal gambling, and other shady activities such as pyramid schemes, etc. The United States Postal Service Laboratory in Washington, D.C. supports these investigative activities. The emphasis here is on document analysis but other areas of forensic science are also represented. These include trace evidence and fingerprints. The Postal Service is a quasi-governmental agency, meaning that it is private but is also government subsidized.

State and Local Forensic Science Systems

Each of the fifty U.S. states has a public crime lab system. The types and numbers of laboratories depend on the size and population of the state. For example, Montana has one laboratory that serves the entire state, whereas California has more than fifty public laboratories that operate at all levels of government. Every state has at least one publicly funded forensic science laboratory. Governmental units that administer crime labs include the state police, state highway patrol, and Attorney General's office. Some states have a consolidated laboratory division that may also include health department, toxicology and agricultural laboratories, and state medical examiner or coroner. For example, the Michigan State police have seven regional laboratories throughout the state. The headquarters lab in Lansing is considered full-service. It has all of the forensic science services needed in the state including toxicology and behavioral analytical capabilities. The other six labs provide the services that are in the most demand locally such as drug analysis, trace evidence, firearms, and fingerprints. In addition to state-run laboratories, most states have some locally controlled facilities. In Maryland, some of the larger counties have laboratories attached to the county police. In California, the county sheriff in many large counties such as Los Angeles supervises an associated crime lab. Many large cities also have their own crime labs, usually within their police departments. These include Detroit, New York City, and Los Angeles.

Private Forensic Science Laboratories

Besides the federal, state, and local forensic science crime labs, there are numerous private laboratories and their number is increasing. These range from one person "niche" laboratories where one type of forensic science analysis is done, to nationwide networks of labs that may handle several types of analysis. Many of the one-person labs have been started by forensic scientists who retired from public laboratories. They continue to ply their trade using prior contacts and word of mouth or print advertising to build a client base. In the criminal arena, they usually work for defendants. The prosecutor has the use of the local or state public laboratory and in most cases, the defendant cannot have access to the public facilities unless a judge specifically orders it. The private labs perform a service to the criminal justice system by providing resources for defendants of crimes. A few private laboratories operate in the public arena. For example, the Northern Illinois Police Crime Laboratory is a private laboratory that contracts its services to the northeastern areas of Illinois between Chicago and the Wisconsin border near Milwaukee. Another example is Orchid Laboratories, which maintains a nationwide network of private DNA labs that provide paternity testing services to public and private clients. Orchid performs the majority of noncriminal paternity testing in the United States each year. One area where private labs seem to prosper is forensic engineering. Most professional forensic engineers are privately employed. They may work for the prosecutor, the plaintiff, or the defendant. Some are connected with colleges or universities and work as consultants on the side.

Other Forensic Science Systems

There is no standard organizational structure for a forensic science laboratory system. Each country has a system that best meets its needs. Organizational decisions are based on historical precedent, population and its distribution, resources available, and levels and patterns of crime.

The United Kingdom

England and Wales have the Forensic Science Service (FSS) which includes a network of five regional crime laboratories. Originally, the police had access to the FSS for free; the government supported the laboratories. The London police force (Scotland Yard) had its own forensic science laboratory, the Metropolitan Police Laboratory. In 1992, the Forensic Science Service was complete revamped. The system adopted a pay-as-you-go process for all clients, including law enforcement agencies. Access to the system was also given to people accused of crimes at the same costs borne by others. Later, the Metropolitan Police Lab was incorporated into the FSS, making a total of six regional labs. Dire predictions of bankruptcy for the FSS and for police departments that couldn't afford the cost of what had been free forensic science services never materialized. The system adapted to the new technology methods and is prospering today.

Australia

In a country the size of the U.S. but with 10 percent of the population, and where most people live on the coast, one would expect a different type of forensic science system. Each of the seven states in Australia supports some type of laboratory. These range from single, full-service laboratories such as the Victoria Police Science Centre near Melbourne, to the fragmented system in New South Wales, which uses separate laboratories for firearms and fingerprints and for drugs and for chemical evidence. There is also a laboratory within the Australian Federal Police in Canberra.

Colombia

A large South American country, Colombia's judicial system has undergone major changes in recent years. These include development of a forensic science laboratory system. There are four regional laboratories. Three are part of the federal law enforcement system, which includes the Prosecutor General and the national police. The fourth is a medical lab that supports the national medical examiner system.

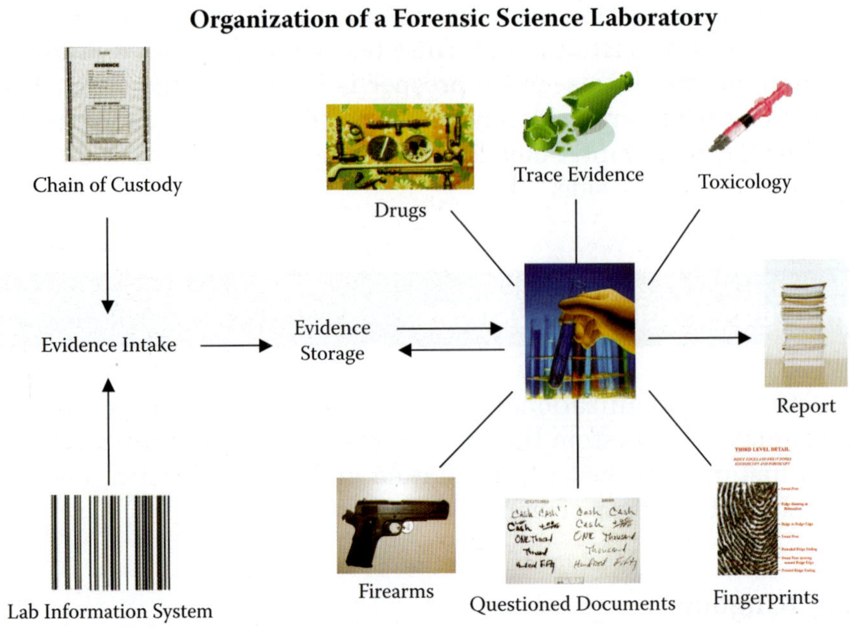

Organization of a Forensic Science Laboratory

Figure 1.6 Various sections of a typical forensic science laboratory.

The Organization of Forensic Science Laboratories

If you were to look at the inside of a forensic science laboratory it would, at first glance, look like any other analytical laboratory. There are lots of instruments, glassware, implements, and scientists in white lab coats and safety glasses. Like most laboratories, forensic science labs are secure facilities that allow only very limited, escorted access to the public. But if you look a little deeper into a forensic science lab, you would see some things that you wouldn't find in other types of scientific labs. Many crime labs have few windows because windows are less secure. On the other hand, questioned document examiners like to have windows in their sections because they like to have natural light for document examination. The common sections of a crime lab are listed below. Figure 1.6 is a chart that shows the major sections of a typical crime lab.

In order for physical evidence to be admissible in a court for a trial, it must be authenticated. That is, there must be proof that the evidence seized at the crime scene is the same evidence that is now being introduced into court. There must be a document that records who was in custody of the evidence at all times. The evidence must be kept in a secure container such that any attempt to breach the seal would be evident. When the evidence container is opened, the person opening it must reseal it with his or her initials and the date and time. All of these procedures and the custody record collectively make up the chain of custody. An improper chain of custody can be grounds to render evidence inadmissible.

Once impounded, the evidence will be put in a locked storage room. At some point, the evidence will be assigned to one or more scientists for processing. Some items of evidence require more than one type of analysis and decisions will have to be made about which section analyzes it first. One of the important considerations here is to make sure that one test done on the evidence does not ruin it for another test. For example, suppose a gun is submitted for evidence containing the suspect's fingerprints on it along with some blood spots. The gun will have to be test fired so a known bullet can be recovered for comparison. The blood will have to be removed and tested for DNA. The fingerprints will have to be carefully lifted and compared with the suspect's prints. The order in which these tests are done is important. When a decision is made, the evidence is turned over to the scientist, who uses a bar code to log possession of the evidence.

1. **The intake section.** This is at the front of the lab. There will usually be an intake officer who will log in the evidence to the *laboratory information system* (LIMS). Typically, a bar code will be affixed to all of the pieces of evidence. Each item will have its own unique identification number.
2. **The analysis area(s).** This is the familiar laboratory setting. In most cases, the scientists' offices are located in a separate place away from the instruments. The area where the chemicals are kept is also isolated from the instruments because chemicals and electronics are not compatible. Each scientist has a dedicated area of the lab for evidence handling. The instruments are used by all of the scientists. In many larger laboratories, each scientist has his or her own safe or other locked storage device for keeping evidence while it is in his or her custody.
3. **Other sections of the lab.** Depending on the size and nature of the lab, other sections are used by scientists from time to time. Some labs have a garage where cars can be kept for inspection and searching. Many firearms sections have huge stainless steel tanks full of water used to test-fire weapons for comparison with bullets or cartridges recovered from crime scenes. Some large labs have collections of seized weapons as well as ammunition. If there is a polygraph section of the lab, there will be one or more interrogation rooms.

Summary

Forensic science is the application of scientific methods to solving crimes. Any science can be a forensic science if it has an application within the criminal justice system. The largest area of forensic science is **criminalistics**, which includes the physical evidence commonly found at crime scenes. There are about four hundred crime labs in the United States. Several departments in the federal government have forensic science labs. These include Justice, Treasury, and Interior. Each state has its own forensic science laboratory system. These include labs run by state or local government.

Forensic scientists analyze evidence and testify in court as expert witnesses. They may also go to some crime scenes where especially serious or notorious crimes have been committed. Crime laboratories must be secure so that evidence can be protected. There are many types of labs, but each has an intake section, an analysis section, and a storage location for evidence.

Test Yourself

Multiple Choice

1. Which of the following federal departments does *not* have a forensic science lab?

    a. Interior
    b. Justice
    c. Commerce
    d. Treasury
    e. All of the above have forensic science labs

2. Which of the following is generally *not* considered to be a forensic science?
    a. Chemistry
    b. Biology
    c. Anthropology
    d. Odontology
    e. Sociology

3. California has about ____ percent of the crime labs in the United States?
    a. 10
    b. 50
    c. 25
    d. 12
    e. 1

4. Which of the following is *not* part of forensic anthropology?
    a. Matching teeth to a bitemark
    b. Identification of skeletal remains
    c. Building a face on a skull
    d. Superimposition of the picture of a face onto a skull
    e. Determining the gender of a skeleton

5. DNA typing is part of:
    a. Forensic pathology
    b. Criminalistics
    c. Odontology
    d. Engineering
    e. Criminal investigation

6. If a forensic science laboratory uses a barcode system as part of its evidence identification, the barcode would be affixed to the evidence when:
    a. The evidence is about to be analyzed
    b. When the final report is written
    c. As soon as the evidence is accepted by the lab
    d. When the evidence is put in central storage
    e. When the evidence is returned to the submitting officer

7. Which of the following is *not* a forensic application of science?
    a. Identification of human remains through dental x-rays
    b. Verifying the composition of an aspirin tablet before it leaves the factory
    c. Identification of a bag of tablets taken from a car when the driver is stopped for erratic driving
    d. Determination of why a Ferris wheel crashed at an amusement park when three people were killed

8. From the time you graduate from high school until you are certified as a forensic pathologist takes about ____ years.
    a. 4
    b. 8
    c. 12
    d. 13
    e. 16

9. Go to the American Academy of Forensic Sciences (www.aafs.org) and look up "Daubert Tracker." This service permits a site visitor to:
   a. Track Dauberts
   b. Keep the forensic scientist up to date on some legal aspects of scientific evidence
   c. Determine when the annual academy meeting is
   d. Keep track of new types of scientific evidence
   e. Tracks dues payments to the academy
10. On the website for the Society of Forensic Toxicology (www.soft-tox.org), the definition of forensic toxicology includes all of the following *except*:
   a. Postmortem forensic toxicology
   b. Analysis of suspected drug powders
   c. Forensic urine testing
   d. Analysis of blood and body fluids for human performance-altering drugs
   e. All of the above are included in the definition of forensic toxicology

Matching

11. Determines cause and manner of death _____   a. Anthropology
12. Identifies people from their teeth _____   b. Pathology
13. Reconstructs hard disc drives _____   c. Entomology
14. Analyzes bone fragments _____   d. Computer forensics
15. Determines competency to stand trial _____   e. Engineer
16. Determines how a bridge collapsed _____   f. Odontologist

Fill in the Blanks

17. The _____ is the United Kingdom national forensic science system.
18. Mail fraud is investigated by the _____.
19. The federal laboratory whose responsibility is the investigation and analysis of illicit drugs is the _____
20. The two major duties of a forensic scientist in a crime lab are _____ and _____.
21. The national "umbrella" organization for forensic science in the U.S. is the _____.
22. When evidence is brought into a crime laboratory it is delivered to the _____ section.

Short Essay

23. What makes a science "forensic"? Give an example of dentistry (odontology) that is forensic and one that is not. Do the same thing for engineering.
24. An increasing trend in crime scene investigation is to have forensic scientists from a crime lab go to some crime scenes and help the crime scene investigators search for evidence. What are the advantages and disadvantages of this practice?
25. Since 1992, the national forensic science system in the United Kingdom now operates on a fee-per-service basis. Everyone, police and defendants alike, is charged for forensic analysis, whereas in the U.S., crime labs are generally units of government for the use of police and prosecutors only. Defendants

have no access to public crime lab facilities. What are the advantages and disadvantages of each system? Why do you think that the U.K. changed to the fee-for-service model?

Further Reading

James, S. H. and J. J. Nordby, eds. *Forensic Science: An Introduction to Scientific and Investigative Techniques.* Boca Raton, FL: CRC Press, 2003.
Saferstein, R. *Criminalistics: An Introduction to Forensic Science. 8th ed.* Englewood Cliffs, NJ: Prentice Hall, 2004.
Siegel, J., ed. *Encyclopedia of Forensic Sciences. Vols. 1–3.* London: Academic Press, 2001.
Thorwald, J. *The Century of the Detective.* New York: Harcourt, Brace & World, 1964.

On the Web

Take an online tour of a real crime lab. www.ok.gov/osbi/Forensic_Laboratory/Virtual_Tour/index.html
Learn all about forensic entomology, including some real cases. http://research.missouri.edu/entomology
You can learn a lot about forensic science and solve a virtual crime at www.virtualmuseum.ca/Exhibitions/Myst/en/game/entry/index.phtml
How does a forensic anthropologist analyze bone fragments? www.anthro4n6.net/forensics

2
Crime Scene Investigation

Learning Objectives

1. To be able to describe the characteristics of a crime scene
2. To be able to list the steps in the investigation of a crime scene
3. To be able to list the steps in the collection of evidence
4. To be able to define chain of custody and describe its elements
5. To be able to list and describe the ways of searching a crime scene
6. To be able to list and describe the ways of documenting a crime scene
7. To be able to complete a rough draft and final sketch of a mock crime scene

Chapter 2
Crime Scene Investigation

Chapter Outline

Mini Glossary

Authentication: Documenting who has possession of crime-related evidence from the point of collection to its appearance in a court of law.

Chain of custody: A physical log for a single piece of evidence that documents who had possession of the evidence and when the evidence was in his or her possession. It is a flow chart of the movement of evidence from collection to processing at the crime lab to presentation in court.

***Corpus delicti*:** The Latin translation is "body of crime." *Corpus delicti* means that it must be proven that a crime has occurred before an individual can be convicted of committing a crime. For example: A death must be ruled a homicide before anyone can be tried for murder or a fire must be ruled as an arson in order for a person to be tried for setting the fire.

CSI: The acronym for Crime Scene Investigation or Crime Scene Investigator.

Documentation: Recording in detail the conditions when the crime occurred.

Druggist's fold (or evidence fold): Small pieces of evidence are packaged in druggist folds (papers) to ensure that they are not lost. They are sometimes also referred to as "evidence folds." The folded paper is then placed in standard evidence packaging.

Exemplars: These are baseline, known evidence such as fingerprints, DNA, hair, or voiceprints collected from suspects or victims in order to compare with evidence taken from a crime scene. Exemplars are sometimes referred to as "knowns" or "controls."

First responder: The initial police officer at the crime scene is regarded as the first responder.

Modus Operandi (MO): The Latin translation means "mode of operation." This refers to the style or method that a criminal uses when committing a crime. For repeat offenders, an MO may assist investigators in locating the suspect due to his or her characteristic way of committing the crime.

Postmortem Interval (PMI): *Postmortem* interval is the length of time from discovery of a dead body to the time the victim died.

Probative: A piece of evidence that tends to prove or disprove a fact or assertion.

Protocol: In criminal investigations protocol is an established, detailed plan or procedure that must be implemented for evidence to be valid.

Search methods: Evidence may be located using a systematic approach to survey the site. These methods employ spiral, grid, line, or zone techniques.

Sting operation: Law enforcement agents stage a scenario whereby criminals are encouraged to commit crimes that they would probably have committed anyway.

Tamper-evident packaging: Specific types of containers or packages for crime scene evidence that have seals that can only be opened by tearing or cutting, thereby giving proof of access.

Introduction

A crime has been committed. It was a recent event, but it happened in the past, therefore a crime scene can be thought of as a piece of history. Like all historical places, the crime scene has a story to tell. Anthropologists and archaeologists investigate places where ancient civilizations once lived. They look for evidence of who lived there and how they lived. Perhaps they will find clues as to the fate of the citizens. Historians examine the site of a Civil War battlefield to learn many things, like how the battle was fought, how many people fought and died, what they wore, and what armaments they used. Crime scene investigators carefully and systematically sift through a crime scene to learn how and when the crime was committed, who committed it and why, and perhaps what items may have been removed from the scene. All of these historical scenes—the ancient village, the hundred-year-old battlefield, and yesterday's homicide scene—contain evidence that, if properly collected, analyzed, and interpreted, tells the story behind the events that took place.

The Crime Scene as Recent History

It is useful to think of a crime scene as history because it has much in common with older historical sites. The proper methods of conducting an archaeological dig and reconstruction of a battle are similar to the methods that should be used to successfully search a crime scene. Some areas of similarity are as follows.

- **Timing.** A historical scene changes all the time, especially if it is outdoors. For ancient ruins, this may not be too important in the short run. A couple of weeks of delay in searching a ten-thousand-year-old village will probably have little consequence. For crimes that occurred only a few hours or days ago, however, *time may be of the essence*. For example, if a burglary isn't discovered and solved within an hour after it occurs, it never will be. The trail gets cold really quickly.

- **Plan of attack**. There must be a plan for *systematically searching the site* that ensures that no stone is left unturned without needlessly covering the same area again and again.
- **Safety issues**. *Safety of the scene searchers* must be considered. Hazards at the ancient remains of a city are going to be different from those at a modern crime scene, although the flooring in a house that had major fire damage may be just as unstable as the ancient ruins of a building.
- Appropriate personnel. Only *highly qualified, trained personnel should conduct the search* of the site.
- **Controlling the scene**. *Contamination must be minimized* by permitting access to the site to as few people as possible. Additionally, those persons at the scene may be asked to give elimination samples if necessary to compare with collected evidence. For example, CSI team members may be asked for samples of their DNA.
- **Documentation**. Every instance of searching an historical site further changes it. Evidence is found and then is moved or removed. Gathering evidence is a vital part of learning the story of the site. Once it changes, it will never be the same again. This is an important concept in searching a crime scene. The *crime scene must be documented thoroughly* so that a record can be made of its condition when the crime occurred. This includes labeling the location of each piece of evidence when it is discovered. Ultimately, the evidence will be useful in establishing that a crime has actually occurred and someone must be prosecuted for it, a process called ***corpus delicti***.

One major difference in the documentation of a crime scene from that of historical sites is that there must be a **chain of custody** for each piece of evidence that is removed from the scene. The chain of custody begins when the evidence is discovered.

In the remainder of this chapter, the crime scene investigation process will be detailed. Evidence collection procedures described are recognizing evidence, documentation of evidence, collection of evidence, and the delivery of evidence to the laboratory for analysis.

Crime Scene Investigation Process

A number of procedures take place at a crime scene. Some procedures are always followed, while others depend on the nature of the scene and the circumstances surrounding the crime. Figure 2.1 shows the overall process that takes place during a crime scene investigation.

A Crime Occurs and Is Discovered

There are three ways that crimes are discovered.

1. A witness sees a crime in progress and reports it to the police.
2. A victim of a crime reports it to the police.
3. The police discover a crime in progress.

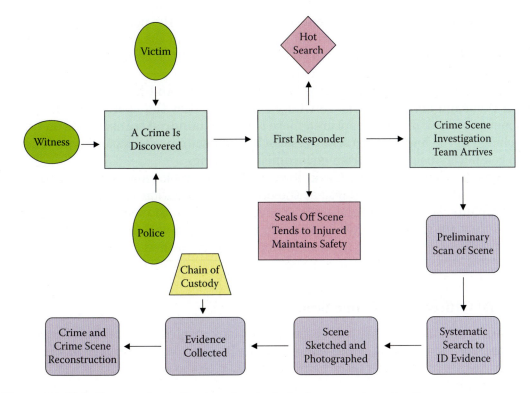

Figure 2.1 This diagram shows the steps in a typical crime scene investigation.

In the first case, someone witnesses a crime in progress. An example of this is when someone is walking down the street at night and sees someone leaving a dark electronics store with arms full of merchandize. Another example is when someone hears what sounds like a gunshot at a next door neighbor's house and runs over to investigate, only to find the owner dead. No one else seems to be around.

In an example of a crime being reported by a victim, the owner of a small business arrives at work one morning and finds that the safe has been opened and money stolen. The owner calls the police to report the robbery and the crime scene investigation begins.

A situation where a police officer discovers a crime in progress is when an officer stops a speeding car and finds a hoard of illegal weapons in the back seat. Police may also "discover" a crime by staging a **sting operation**. These are situations where law enforcement agents set up a scenario whereby criminals are encouraged to commit crimes that they would probably have done anyway.

Example of a Sting Operation

A sting operation is set up by local police and/or federal agents as a type of proactive law enforcement. One of the earliest examples of a sting occurred in Washington, D.C. in the 1960s. This was a joint FBI and Washington, D.C. Police Department operation to combat major theft rings operating in the city. The agents and police set up a storefront operation and put the word out on the street that the store was a well-financed "fencing" operation (a fence is someone who buys stolen merchandise and resells it at a profit). Further, the word was that this operation was being run by "organized crime" (the Mafia). Anyone who had something of value to sell would get top dollar with no questions asked.

The "store" was rigged with a one-way mirror so that the police could videotape the "sales" through the glass without being detected. All the crooks could see was a mirror. To make sure that each seller would look at the camera, a picture of a bikini-clad model was prominently posted.

The sting operation was supposed to last a month and had a budget of several thousand dollars. It was so wildly successful that the operation ran out of money in a week and had captured more than two hundred transactions on tape. Included in the haul were stacks of stolen Social Security checks and typewriters (no computers back then) from government buildings.

So as to avoid having to track down all of the crooks and arrest them, the "owners" advertised a big party at the end of the operation. Virtually all of the participants were invited and were promised a chance to meet the "Godfather." What they got were handcuffs and a trip to jail. Faced with a videotape of their "transactions" every one of the scofflaws pled guilty to theft.

The First Officer at the Crime Scene

Archaeological digs and battlefield reconstructions involve large teams of searchers from the very start. In a crime scene search, however, the discovery of the crime usually results in a police officer being dispatched to the scene. This officer has several important duties:

1. **Ascertain whether the perpetrator is still at the scene.** If so, a hot search for the perpetrator should commence immediately. If this proves futile, later on, detectives or criminal investigators will likely perform a cold search, whereby people in the neighborhood are interviewed to determine whether they saw the crime being committed or saw the perpetrator flee the scene or observed other suspicious events.
2. **Tend to the injured.** If an ambulance is needed, it should be called right away. Waiting can cost lives.
3. **Notify supervisors, medical examiner, crime scene team, or other personnel.** It will take time for requested personnel to arrive at the location. Once the team has arrived, the investigation process can commence.
4. **Secure consent or a warrant to search the scene.** Unless there is an emergency situation, such as threats to someone's life or safety, destruction or removal of evidence, or possible escape of the perpetrator, the officer should obtain the right to enter a crime scene. According to the Fourth Amendment of the United States Constitution, in order for the crime scene search to be constitutional, consent must be given voluntarily by a person reasonably believed by law enforcement officers to have lawful access and control over the premises. In most cases, this will be the person who called police to the scene. If consent is not possible, a warrant or judicial order authorizing a search must be obtained.
5. **Secure the scene.** Contamination of the scene must be minimized. The number of people who have access to the scene must be limited and the entry and exit paths of these personnel should be determined. Initially it is advantageous to make the scene perimeter large to prevent loss of any pertinent evidence. For example, if a crime occurred in a home, consider the entry and exit of the perpetrator as important and secure the outside of the home, too. Footprints and tire tracks are just as important as the physical evidence

found inside a residence. If a body is found in the woods, the potential scene can be quite large and isolating it can be difficult.

6. **Avoid walking through the scene and searching for evidence.** Remember that any contact with a crime scene alters it forever. Searches of even localized crime scenes must be done by professionals who have formulated a search plan. In some cases, what appears to be the scene of the crime may not be. The site may have been set up to look like a crime scene so as to divert attention from the real scene.

7. **Note any obvious safety hazards.** Strange smells could be gas or potentially dangerous chemicals that may pose a fire or poison hazard. Structures may be weakened or rigged to kill or maim. Electrical wires may be exposed. The job of the first officer at the scene is not to remediate these hazards but to protect others from them and to warn personnel who subsequently come to the scene. The 1991 Universal Studios movie, *Backdraft* had a scene that illustrates the situation where a crime scene is rigged to cause harm to investigators. A fire was set in a building that was then completely sealed up. When the oxygen became depleted and could no longer support flames, the fire began to smolder. When the fire department arrived and broke in to the building, the onrush of oxygen into the building caused the fire to explode into flame. Firemen were killed and injured. This also happens in real life fires and may occur naturally as a fire proceeds.

Protocol at the Crime Scene

The examination of a crime scene must follow **protocol** established for the crime scene investigative unit. Protocol is a detailed plan or procedure established by law enforcement that must be implemented for evidence to be valid and admissible in a court of law. Following protocol insures that all crime scenes will be investigated in the same manner by using established guidelines. Following procedural guidelines becomes important when police officers and crime scene investigators must testify in court regarding the validity of evidence.

As soon as possible after the crime scene has been discovered and protected, the **crime scene investigation (CSI) unit** will arrive. If there is a dead body at the scene, someone from the medical examiner's or coroner's office will take charge of processing the body. This person will normally be a forensic pathologist who certifies that the person is dead and makes a preliminary determination of the **postmortem interval (PMI),** or the time since death. This topic will be covered in more detail in the chapter on forensic pathology. If there is a body at the scene, some police departments dispatch a death scene CSI squad to process and remove the body from the scene. This processing includes photographing the body, making sure all trace evidence is protected and gathered, and transporting the body to the medical examiner's or coroner's laboratory.

The crime scene unit, which is usually made up of specially trained police officers, takes charge of the crime scene. Each member of the team has a defined role, such as sketcher, photographer, searcher, or documenter. Fingerprint and blood spatter technicians will also be called to the scene if needed.

The Preliminary Scene Examination

The first duty of the CSI unit is to conduct a preliminary examination of the scene. This is done for a number of reasons. Safety hazards will be promptly addressed and remediated. The boundaries of the crime scene must be ascertained. This may be a simple process if the crime clearly occurred in one room of a house (keeping in mind that routes of entry and escape can be very important sources of evidence). If the crime is outdoors, then fixing the boundaries of the scene can be very difficult. The area where the crime was committed may only be the primary crime scene. Perpetrators often carry evidence away from the scene and there may be one or more secondary locations where important evidence may be found.

Additionally, if preliminary examination of the scene has some aspects similar to other recent crimes in an area, the investigators may look at the **modus operandi** or **MO** of the crime. *Modus operandi* is the pattern or method of operation that a criminal repeatedly uses during an illegal act. A repetitive MO could imply the work of a single criminal in more than one crime.

Systematic Search of the Crime Scene

After the preliminary examination of the scene has been made, systematic documentation and searching begin. This process is carried out in ways that minimize alteration of the scene. It is easily and permanently altered as people conduct their investigations. Photographing the scene is carried out as early as possible. Although regular photography is still widely used in crime scene investigations, the recent trend has been to use digital photography because photographs can be seen immediately. In addition, digital pictures are easily incorporated into computerized crime records and reports. It is also common for the crime scene team to use videotape to complete a walk-through of the scene. This is very effective for the jury in order to get an overall sense of the scene. It is important, though, for the audio of the tape to be silenced so that no comments are inadvertently shared that might influence the jury.

One of the first decisions to be made is the search pattern that will be used at the crime scene. There are four basic types of **search methods** that can be used, depending on the type of crime scene. For example, if the entire crime scene is one room in a house, a search may begin at one end of the room and proceed in a *spiral* fashion toward the center or may be a back-and-forth (*line*) pattern across the room. If the scene includes several rooms, each one is searched systematically using a *zone* method. If the scene is outdoors in a large area, it may be necessary to divide the scene into *grids* and then search each grid. Examples of each method are shown in Figure 2.2.

Sometimes unusual tactics are used to search a crime scene such as those described in the 1984 shooting of police officer Yvonne Fletcher at the Libyan Embassy in London, England. It is seldom necessary to devote the large amounts of investigative resources that were used in this case, but the crime was very serious and had major political implications at the time. Also, the police had lost one of their own and they were eager to find the evidence that would bring the killer(s) to justice. This case illustrates that sometimes unusual methods are needed to effectively search a crime scene.

Yvonne Fletcher

On April 27, 1984, an eleven-day siege ended at the Libyan Embassy in London. The siege was the result of the shooting of a London police officer, Yvonne Fletcher, on April 17. Witnesses saw smoke and flame from a first floor window of the Embassy right before the officer fell. When she was loaded onto a gurney and taken to the hospital, a slug that had hit her fell out of her body and onto the ground. The

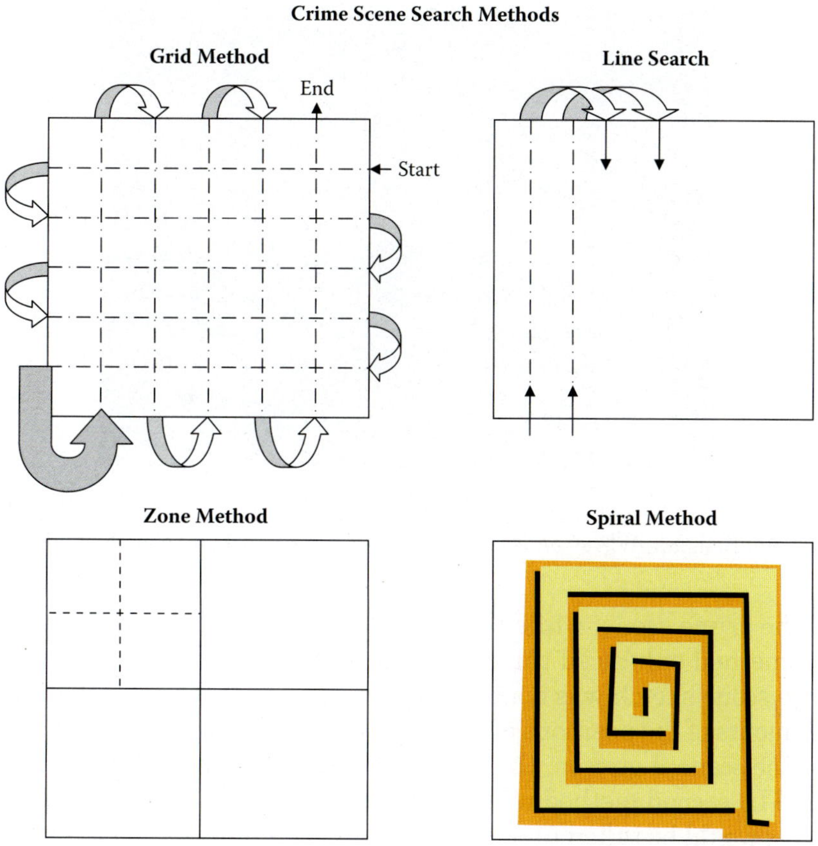

Crime Scene Search Methods

Figure 2.2 Four general methods used to systematically search a crime scene.

slug was missing when the forensic pathologist did the *postmortem* examination. It was very important to find the slug so it could be compared to the weapon if found. The area in question was a large courtyard in front of the embassy. More than fifty police officers gathered in the courtyard and then crawled shoulder to shoulder on their hands and knees all the way across the courtyard in search of the slug. It was found and later matched to the suspect weapon.

Something for You to Do

Go into the largest room in your house (this may be the garage). Ask someone in your family to plant a piece of "evidence" in the room. This could be a small object that could be evidence in a real crime. It could be hair, fiber, or paint chips, or other trace evidence. You should figure out how you would search this scene to make sure you cover the entire scene. You also want to make sure you don't go over the same ground more than once so as to minimize contact and contamination of the scene. Draw a diagram of the search pattern you would use to search this scene.

Now go into the smallest room in your house and repeat this exercise. Next go outdoors to your front yard or back yard or a nearby park and repeat the exercise again. Did you decide to use the same type of search pattern in each case? Why? In which case(s) would you try and get help in searching the scene? After you have developed a strategy for searching each scene, pick one and try to find the object.

See if your strategy works. You may not be able to find the object, especially if you don't know what you are looking for or you may inadvertently step on it or track extraneous material into the scene and mistake this for evidence. This is what crime scene investigators face every day in their work. Crime scene investigation is a difficult process even for experienced investigators.

Recording the Crime Scene

Historically, there have been two basic methods of documenting a crime scene and recording its condition and the locations of all of the evidence. The first was making

Figure 2.3 A shoe print in soil with a ruler. The ruler is used to show the size of the shoeprint. With permission of Bodziak, WT. *Footwear Impression Evidence,* 2d ed., New York: Taylor & Francis, 2000.

a sketch of the crime scene, while the second was using photography to document a scene. Each method enhanced the effectiveness of the other.

The crime scene sketch was done by first making a freehand sketch and then taking measurements of the positions of various objects with reference to at least two fixed positions in the scene. Later on, this sketch would be translated into a scale drawing of the scene. The second method was by still photography (35 mm) using regular film. Many pictures would be taken under various light conditions and at various distances and angles in the hope that some would properly record the scene. Measuring instruments, such as small rulers, would be put in photographs where size perspective was important, as with shoeprints and tire treads. Without a scale to show size for such evidence, it would be difficult to admit such evidence into court as demonstrative evidence. Figure 2.3 shows a picture of a shoeprint. Note the ruler in the picture.

Today, the situation is different but some of the old practices are still used. Hand-drawn crime scene sketches, as shown in Figure 2.4, are still used and measurements taken, but the scale drawings are often rendered on a computer that has specialized crime scene reconstruction software.

Sometimes scale models of crime scenes are made from cardboard, wood, plaster, and the like. An extreme example of modeling is performed at the Federal Bureau of Alcohol, Tobacco, and Firearms (BATF) at its fire research laboratory near Beltsville, MD. In cases where a fire has occurred in an apartment or house, a construction crew builds an exact model of the structure to scale and then re-creates the fire conditions as precisely as possible so the progress and damage caused by the fire can be studied. The BATF laboratory employs professional builders to construct the structures that are then sacrificed to research. The fires are carried out in a huge building equipped with exhaust fans and filters that prevent particulates and harmful gases from escaping.

Today, crime scenes are often videotaped. A crime scene investigator will walk the crime scene with a video camera and take footage from all angles. This can take the place of some of the still photography, but will not replace the crime scene sketch. There is even one company, 3rd Tech, that makes an automatic video system. A camera is set up in a room and it takes thousands of frames of the scene in a 360-degree arc that, when reconstructed, provides unprecedented details about the locations of objects and perspectives at the scene.

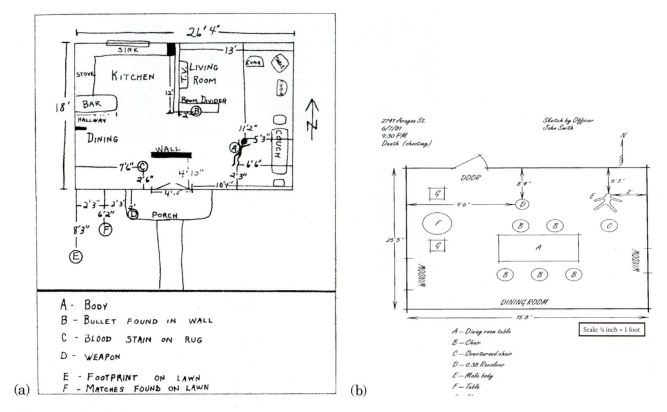

(a) (b)

Figure 2.4 Rough draft (a) and (b) final sketches of a crime scene. From: *www.cool physics.org* /**Crime%20Sc ene%20 05% 20v2.ppt**

The 35 mm cameras are still used at crime scenes to photograph individual objects, but this method of taking photos is rapidly being replaced by digital photography. Advantages to digital photography of crime scenes include the ability to easily incorporate pictures into reports and the ability to examine a photo right after it has been taken so the photographer will know right away if the picture is useable. Digital photographs can also be *enhanced* or touched up using computer software such as Adobe Photoshop®. This is not the same as *altering* digital photos, which would be called into question in a court of law. The forensic photographer must inform the court which photos were enhanced and what was done to enhance them. Enhancement is used only to make the original photo clearer for presentation to the jury, and must never be used to change the photographic evidence or alter it.

Photographs are taken in an organized manner. First the entire scene is photographed from each corner of the structure, room or object. Then the item of interest is photographed from a distance, mid-range, and then close up with and without a scale in the picture. Figure 2.5 shows outside and interior room photography. Figure 2.6 illustrates photography of a victim.

Additionally, it is useful to photograph any bystanders at the crime scene. These photographs can aid in identifying witnesses or in some cases the actual perpetrator, as criminals sometimes like to watch the police process crime scenes.

Collection of Evidence

There is an old saying at crime labs: "You cannot make chicken salad out of chicken feathers." This is a reminder that the results of the scientific analysis of evidence

Distance shot of residence, walkway to entrance, front door entrance

Living room views from all four corners.

Figure 2.5 Crime scene photography. Outside photographs should document the entire residence, the path to the residence and the entrance. Similar shots should be made of the rear of the home. Each room should be photographed entirely and as seen from all four corners.

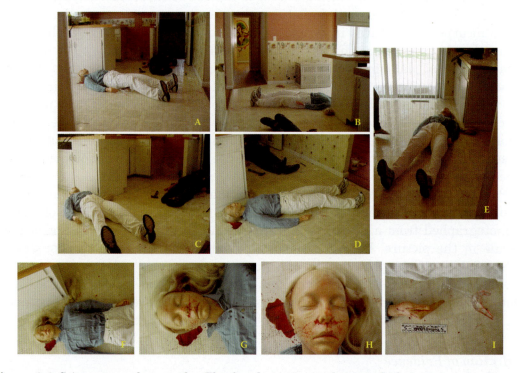

Figure 2.6 Crime scene photography. The female victim is photographed at various locations in the room (A–E). Then close-up shots are captured of her injuries and potentially important evidence (F–I).

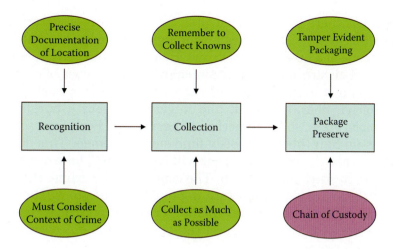

Figure 2.7 The steps in the evidence collection process.

from a crime scene are only as good as the evidence brought to the lab. If evidence is contaminated or degraded or the wrong evidence is collected, the evidence will be of limited or no value. The collection, preservation, and packaging of evidence are crucial to a successful criminal investigation. Under ideal circumstances, crime scene investigation would be done by the forensic scientists who analyze the evidence because they know best how to recognize, collect, preserve, and package it.

Unfortunately, caseloads being what they are, forensic scientists cannot afford the time it would take to process all crime scenes. The trend today, however, is to have a forensic scientist team respond to homicides and other serious crimes and they work with the crime scene investigators to process the scene. A group of forensic scientists usually volunteer for crime scene duty. They form a team of experts whose areas of expertise might be important to the investigation. This would include DNA analysts, serologists (who are experts in locating and collecting small blood stains or other body fluids and who can process blood spatter patterns), and trace evidence scientists (who are adept at recognizing which trace evidence is important and how to properly collect it). Other specialists may be called in from time to time. For example, one or more forensic drug chemists are usually called on to help investigate scenes of clandestine drug activity such as a methamphetamine lab operation. These scenes can be very dangerous because of flammable chemicals and a lack of safety concerns. Clandestine laboratories are discussed in greater detail in the chapter on illicit drugs. When forensic scientist crime scene teams are sent to help local crime scene investigators process complex scenes, there is an agreement in place that establishes when the lab team is sent out and how the chain of command at the crime scene will be determined.

Three major steps in the process of evidence collection are recognition, collection, and packaging/preservation. Each has other considerations that are important for the other steps. Figure 2.7 shows how these steps and their associated processes are related.

Recognition of Evidence

An object at a crime scene must be recognized as evidence before it can be collected. When you did the exercise of searching a room in your house or outdoors for evidence, you had the advantage of knowing what is supposed to be in these rooms. It is easier to recognize something that is out of place or doesn't belong. That advantage is lost at a crime scene. The crime scene investigators do not know what objects belong to that particular location and therefore they don't know what objects may have been left there by the perpetrator. So how do investigators know what *is* evidence and what *is not*? This takes a thorough knowledge of what is likely to be present at the scene of a given type of crime. Homicides, burglaries, sexual assaults, and other types of crimes usually contain characteristic types of evidence that the crime scene investigator would hope or expect to find. For a homicide, this might be a weapon, blood, fiber, and hair, and fingerprints. For a burglary, one might expect to find tools, glass, soil, and perhaps fingerprints. For a rape scene, investigation often turns up hair, fiber, and body fluid such as semen. This doesn't mean, of course, that these are the only items that will be present. These are guidelines that investigators use to start their search. The context of the crime, the type of crime, and the type of scene are very important in providing clues to what evidence should be present. If the crime looks similar to another recent one, investigators might be watchful for evidence that would suggest the same MO (*modus operandi*) and therefore the same perpetrator.

In general, there is no such thing as too much evidence. If an investigator has doubts about whether an object is significant, it should be collected and sent to the lab. As the investigation proceeds and the scene is reconstructed, it will be easier to determine whether the material is actually evidence. Once the crime scene unit is finished with the scene and it is released to the owners, it will not be possible to come back and collect more evidence. For example, suppose an investigator comes upon fibers at a scene and neglects to collect them. Later on, it is determined that these fibers are important evidence, but the owners have taken possession of the premises and have vacuumed the carpets. The evidence is lost forever.

Once evidence is located but before it is collected, its exact location must be recorded. This may be done by photography and/or measurements with respect to a fixed object. This is necessary so that when reconstruction of the crime scene is done, the location of the evidence will be known. After it is moved and taken to the lab, evidence cannot be relocated at the scene. Besides the location of the evidence, other information must be recorded for chain of custody purposes. This will be discussed in more detail below.

Collection

How much evidence should be collected? The short answer is: as much as possible. At clandestine drug laboratories, everything that could have any remote connection with the manufacturing operation is collected. In the case of illicit drug seizures, all of the drugs are collected, even if tons are involved. The forensic science laboratory will sort out the issue of sampling for analysis purposes later. In many cases involving trace evidence, the lack of sample may limit the tests that the scientists can do. In addition, the rules of evidence in the United States require that the defendant be given a fair chance to perform tests on the evidence. If it can be shown that there was more evidence available that wasn't collected or the government crime lab used all that was collected, the defense attorney may be able to have the evidence excluded from the trial on the grounds that the defense didn't have an opportunity to analyze the evidence with its own expert.

Another important consideration in the collection of evidence is the issue of comparison samples, or "knowns." Knowns are also referred to as **exemplars**. Exemplars are baseline, known evidence such as fingerprints, DNA, hair, or voiceprints collected from suspects or victims for comparison with evidence taken from a crime scene. (The concept of known versus unknown evidence is further discussed in the next chapter.) With many types of evidence, the **probative** value or significance in the case can be greatly enhanced if it can be compared with and linked to a known material or object. Fingerprints found on an object have little meaning unless they can be compared to the exemplar fingerprints of a suspect and then shown to have originated from that person. Known evidence may be found at the crime scene or may be taken later from a suspect or another location linked to the primary crime scene. Known evidence (or exemplars) may either link a suspect to the crime or may serve as elimination samples—samples that clear an individual from involvement in the crime.

A Really Big Case

In 1985, the U.S. Coast Guard seized a private boat that was racing up the Atlantic Coast near Virginia. The boat was boarded and 8.5 tons (17,000 pounds) of suspected marijuana was found. This was taken to the Drug Enforcement Administration (DEA) lab in Washington, D.C., where it was identified as marijuana. Then it was transported to the Baltimore garbage incinerator where it was to be destroyed. The defense attorney in the case wanted the evidence analyzed by his own expert prior to its destruction. The expert (one of the authors of this book) went to the incinerator and found hundreds of bales of marijuana, each weighing hundreds of pounds. He took representative core samples from each bale. A DEA chemist followed behind and also took a sample from each bale. After each bale was sampled, it was incinerated. The resulting total sample weighed approximately 5 pounds. This raises the issue of representative sampling of large exhibits of drugs. This topic is covered in the chapter on illicit drugs.

Packaging and Preserving Evidence

Once the evidence has been located and collected, it must be properly packaged. This may not seem too important at first glance, but it can be critical to a case. There are physical, scientific, and legal requirements that determine how evidence should be packaged, and today appropriate packaging is available for all types of evidence.

Attention to detail and following proper protocol are vital when collecting evidence. Only one type of item can be collected per container or package. Crime scene personnel must change their gloves and tools after each item is collected to avoid contamination. These procedural guidelines make collection and preservation a long, tedious process, but they are essential for the proper preservation of evidence.

The chain of custody. Rules of evidence in federal and every state court in the United States require that all evidence be **authenticated**. Authentication requires:

1. A record of *who is in possession* of the evidence from the time it is collected at the crime scene until the time it is delivered to court. This detailed record is called the **chain of custody**.
2. The evidence must also be *uniquely identified* (for example, using a bar code) in such a way so that it cannot be confused with any other piece of evidence and so that it can be shown that the evidence being used in court is the same evidence that was taken from the crime scene.
3. The evidence must also be *packaged* in **tamper-evident packaging**. This is both a document and a process that insures the integrity of the evidence. If the chain of custody has a substantial break—one that would seriously call into question the quality or integrity of the evidence—the evidence may be ruled inadmissible in court.

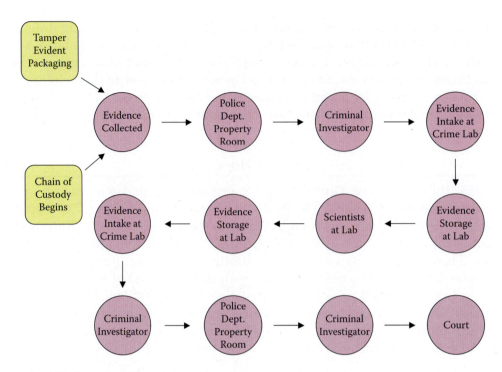

Figure 2.8 The flow of evidence from crime scene to court.

At one time, certain evidence from sexual assault cases was frequently challenged on chain of custody grounds. In cases of sexual assault, the victim is taken to a hospital (or often now to a SANE clinic—sexual assault nurse examiner). The victim's clothing is removed pursuant to an examination by a nurse or doctor. In years past, the clothes might be left in an examining room or elsewhere in the clinic that was not secure from the public. This clothing could potentially be the source of critical evidence of the identity of the perpetrator, especially in these days of DNA typing. Since no one was in possession and in charge of the evidence, the chain of custody might have been seriously damaged and evidence from these clothes might not have been admissible. Today, most hospitals and clinics have doctors and nurses who are trained in the collection and preservation of evidence from the victim. Crime labs or SANE clinics now supply doctors and nurses with "rape kits"—evidence kits that contain packaging for various types of evidence such as hair, vaginal swabs, individual articles of clothing, and so on. The packaging is suitable for the criminal justice system and the chain of custody.

Figure 2.8 shows a typical journey of evidence from crime scene to court with chain of custody considerations along the way. Note how many times the evidence changes hands during its journey. This is why it is so important to maintain a record of who is in possession of the evidence at any given time.

Two of the most important elements of the chain of custody are tamper-evident packaging and the custody form. Tamper-evident packaging is just that. Once the package is sealed, no one can open it without leaving evidence that the package was opened. It must be cut or torn to get inside. This is sometimes erroneously called "tamper-proof" packaging, but there is no such thing. Any package can be opened using whatever force is necessary. In addition, there must be a form, sometimes incorporated in the package itself that has space for whoever has custody of the evidence to sign and date the form. Every time the evidence changes hands, the donor and receiver sign and date the form. This form is kept with the evidence at all times. Figure 2.9 is an example of a chain of custody form.

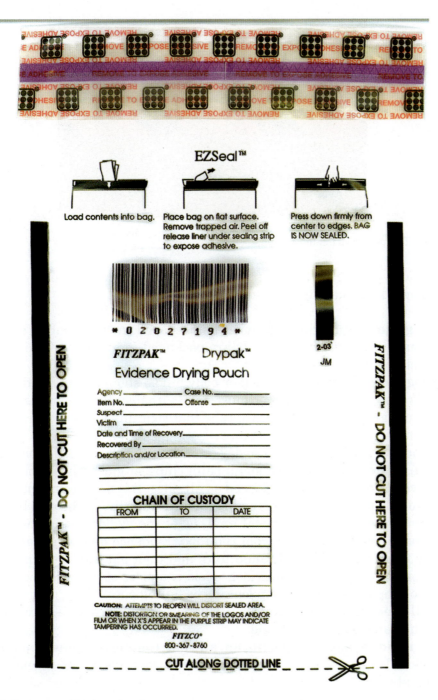

Figure 2.9 Tamper-evident packaging.

An alternative to the tamper-evident container is tamper-evident tape. This can be applied to any bag, box, or pouch. It is very sticky and shreds when removed. Also, some of the glue from the tape is left behind on the package. Figure 2.10 shows one type of evidence tape.

Preserving Evidence

In addition to being tamper-evident, packaging for evidence must also be designed to preserve the evidence to the maximum extent possible. From the time evidence is collected, it may be weeks or months until scientists at the crime lab are able to analyze it (many labs have several months of case backlogs). Different types of evidence

Figure 2.10 Tamper-proof evidence tape.

require unique packaging to preserve it. Some of the more common evidence types that need special packaging are listed below.

- **Living plants (marijuana)** must be packaged in "breathable" containers such as paper bags. If the plants are packaged in airtight containers, they will rot and may become useless.
- **Biological evidence** (wet blood or body fluids) should be allowed to dry or, if packaged wet, the container must be breathable. Blood can also be packaged in a glass or plastic culture tube that contains a preservative, usually ethylenediamene tetraacetic acid (EDTA).
- **Wet paint** should be allowed to dry or packaged in breathable container
- **Trace evidence** (hair, fiber, small paint chips, or glass) should be placed in an envelope or plastic baggie sealed on all sides. It is not recommended to use tape to hold this evidence (commonly called a "tape lift"). The glue in the tape can interfere with the chemical analysis of the evidence and the evidence may be difficult to remove from the tape. Evidence can be put in a **druggist's fold** (also called **evidence fold**) and then put into a tamper-evident envelope. A druggist fold or evidence fold is a piece of paper folded in such a way to keep the evidence from leaking or falling out.
- **Small amounts of powder** should be put in paper with a druggist's fold and then an envelope or baggie.
- **Fire residue** must be put in an airtight container. Unused paint cans are best. If fire residue is put in breathable containers, the accelerant will evaporate.

As a side note, **fingerprints** are typically the last evidence taken at the scene due to possible contamination of fingerprint dust with the other crime scene evidence.

Reconstruction

Remember that a crime scene is a slice of recent history. It has a story to tell and the evidence at the scene helps tell the story. Each piece of evidence contributes to the story. Once the evidence has been collected, analyzed, and compared to known evidence, the criminal investigators, often with the help of forensic scientists, attempt to reconstruct the crime, including the identities of the victim(s) and the perpetrator(s) and the sequence of events that took place leading to the crime. The focus here is, of

PMI	f. Evidence used for comparison, a known sample
Probative	g. Containers for evidence that seal and prevent altering
Protocol	h. Evidence that can prove or disprove
Sting operation	i. Deems it necessary to prove a crime occurred
Tamper-evident packaging	j. Detailed plan or procedure followed in an investigation

Mini Laboratory Activities

MINI LAB 1: MAKING A DRUGGIST (EVIDENCE) FOLD

1. Take an 8 × 10 sheet of paper and fold the upper right edge across the paper until it meets the left edge. The result will be a triangle with an extra edge on the bottom that is untouched.

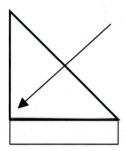

2. Cut off the unfolded edge so that when the triangle is opened the remaining paper will be a square.

3. Re-fold the paper back into a triangle with the base at the bottom and the points at the top and sides. Fold in the sides of the triangle so that you have 3 approximately equal parts as shown below.

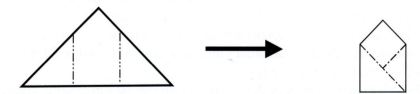

4. The pointed top of the evidence fold can now be opened and serves as a pouch for small pieces of evidence.

5. Evidence placed in the pouch should be positioned to the base of the pouch. Then the evidence fold is secured by making two folds and a tuck. First, fold the top point down so that the remainder of the paper is in the form of a square. Second, fold the square in half horizontally.

6. Open the rectangle. Take the folded top point and tuck it into th bottom where the two pointed end pieces cross. This secures the evidence fold. Next label the folk and place it into an evidence envelope, labeled, and secured with evidence tape.

tuck this inside

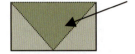

MINI LAB 2: SKETCHING A CRIME SCENE

Once the mock crime scene is set up, your task is to make a detailed sketch of the scene. Follow the steps below to make your rough sketch. Refer to Figure 2.4 in this chapter as an example of what should be included in a crime scene sketch.

Step 1: Locate the direction of north in your room and stand facing that direction as you look into your scene. North should be at the top of your sketch paper, south at the bottom, east to the right and west to the left. Placed the letter "N" on your paper and indicate the direction of north by placing an arrow next to the N that points to the top of your paper.

Step 2: Draw a square or rectangle on your paper to represent the sides of the room. Measure the room dimensions in feet and inches and label the sides of your sketch with the appropriate dimensions.

Step 3: Locate large objects that are important pieces of evidence, such as a table, a couch, a victim, or a bed, and place them in the sketch by taking measurements. Measure a point on the object to two fixed positions (walls, countertops, windows, doors) in the room. (See figure 2.4) On the paper draw a picture of the item being measured and show the dimensional measurements with lines connecting the items to their points of measurement.

Step 4: Give each item that has been measured a number or a letter label and add it to your sketch. Record the label and a description for your Evidence Key. For example, Letter A-victim; Letter B-knife.

Step 5: Sketch smaller items in the scene that might be important. These items do not necessarily have to be measured if they can be easily located in the scene.

Step 6: At the bottom of your paper create an Evidence Key that includes the letter/number labels and a short description of the item.

Step 7: Place a heading on your sketch. Include the date and time, the address, the name of the victim (if any), the type of crime (if known) and your name as the "Officer."

Further Reading

Fisher, B. A. J. *Techniques of Crime Scene Investigation.* 7th ed. Boca Raton, FL: CRC Press, 2004.

Wecht, C. H. *Crime Scene Investigation, Reader's Digest.* New York, 2004.

Grant, S. *CSI: Crime Scene Investigation: Secret Identity.* New York: IDW Publishing, 2005.

On the Web

www.crime-scene-investigator.net
www.mycriminaljustice.com
www.feinc.net/cs-inv-p.htm
http://science.howstuffworks.com/csi.htm
www.ncjrs.gov/pdffiles1/nij/178280.pdf
www.crimeandclues.com/crimescene.htm
www.atf.treas.gov/labs/frl/index.htm

3

The Nature of Evidence

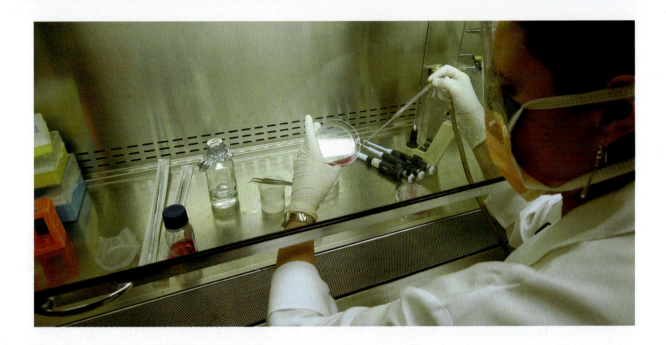

Learning Objectives

1. To be able to describe the difference between real and demonstrative evidence
2. To be able to describe the difference between known and unknown evidence
3. To be able to recognize when evidence is known and when it is unknown
4. To be able to define class evidence and individual evidence
5. To be able to determine whether a characteristic is class or individual
6. To be able to define identification and individualization
7. To be able to define and give examples of positive and negative controls
8. To be able to define false positive and false negative tests

Chapter 3
The Nature of Evidence

Chapter Outline

Mini Glossary

Class evidence: Evidence that cannot be associated with one particular object or person. It can only be put into a group of similar pieces of evidence.

Demonstrative evidence: Evidence that does not arise from the crime itself, but is created to illustrate or explain evidence. Crime scene drawings or photographs are examples.

Evidence: Anything that will make an issue more or less true than it would be without the evidence.

False negative test: A chemical test that turns out negative even though it should have been positive.

False positive test: A chemical test that turns out positive even though it should have been negative.

Identification of evidence: The process of describing and documenting chemical, biological, and/or physical characteristics of evidence.

Individual evidence: Evidence that can be associated with one particular person or object.

Known evidence: Evidence whose source or ownership is known at the time it is collected.

Material: Evidence is material if it pertains to the particular case that is being tried or investigated.

Negative control: A material, usually a matrix, that would be expected to respond negatively to a particular chemical test.

Nonphysical evidence: Evidence such as eye witness or expert testimony or interpretation of an analytical test.

Physical evidence: Evidence that consists of objects, people, or materials.

Positive control: A material or chemical expected to respond positively to a particular chemical test.

Probative: A piece of evidence that tends to prove or disprove a fact or assertion.

Real evidence: Evidence generated directly from criminal activity.

Relevant: Evidence that is both material and probative that pertains to the case at hand and tends to prove or disprove some aspect of the case.

Unknown evidence: Evidence whose source or ownership is not known at the time it is discovered.

Introduction

In Chapter 2, we learned that crime scene investigation is a type of reconstruction. It is somewhat like an archaeological dig where anthropologists painstakingly search through the scene to find **evidence** of who lived at the scene, when they lived there, how they lived, and why and how they left. Sometimes we call evidence clues. Evidence consists of hints or pieces of data that help reconstruct a scene—in our case, a crime scene. Evidence can be thought of as something that supports or rejects a theory about a crime, how it occurred, and who committed it. Evidence is defined in law books as *anything that would make an issue more or less likely that it would be without the evidence.* Another way of expressing this would be that evidence is *anything that tends to prove or disprove something at issue.* So does this mean that a crime scene investigator should seize everything at a crime scene in the hope or presumption that it might help prove or disprove something? More importantly, how does one decide what is evidence and what isn't? This is of course, partly a question of experience but more an issue of context. A crime scene investigator will view the scene carefully to determine what type of crime may have occurred and that knowledge will guide her in determining what may be evidence and should be collected. Interestingly, the popularity of the TV shows such as *CSI* has resulted in a situation where juries often question why some evidence wasn't collected (as it would have been on the show). This has caused prosecutors to direct investigators to collect practically everything—just in case.

Another concept from law also provides guidance as to which evidence should be collected. A rule of law states that evidence must be **relevant** if it is to be admitted into evidence. This means that it must be **material** (it must pertain to the particular crime being investigated and not some previous incident) and **probative** (it must actually prove something). Thus, crime scene investigators are guided by whether a potential piece of evidence passes or is likely to pass the relevance test. For example, at a homicide scene where the victim was killed by being shot with several bullets, what purpose would be served by seizing kitchen knives (assuming they are not bloody or in the victim)? The knives wouldn't be relevant. This concept will be covered in more detail in Chapter 21.

Classification of Evidence

Evidence may be categorized in a number of different ways. At first glance, one may wonder why there should be so many different ways of categorizing it, but as it turns out, the class or type of evidence can be very important in determining what value it has, how it should be collected, what else should be collected (controls, exemplars) and most important, what conclusions can be drawn from a scientific examination of the evidence. There are also legal distinctions among different types of evidence that help determine its admissibility in court. The major classification systems for evidence are listed and discussed below. These schemes apply to all evidence, not just scientific or technical.

- Physical–nonphysical
- Real–demonstrative
- Known–unknown
- Individual–class

Physical–Nonphysical Evidence

Physical evidence consists of objects or things. **Nonphysical evidence** is verbal testimony about a crime, or someone's actions during a crime. If someone is seen running away from a bank robbery holding a bag of money, the action of running away is nonphysical evidence while the bag of money is physical evidence. The reason for discussing this somewhat obvious distinction is to emphasize that not every piece of evidence is an object. Courtroom dramas often focus on motive—why someone would commit a crime. This can be critical evidence. A motive is often required as an element of a crime. Sometimes the distinction can be tricky. If a witness identifies a suspect at the scene of a bank robbery, what is the evidence? The suspect? The witness? The testimonial evidence of the identification? Suppose a polygraph test has been administered to a suspect as a means to detect deception. A qualified examiner interprets the polygraph chart and renders an expert opinion in court as to the truthfulness of the suspect. What is the evidence here? The machine? The squiggles on the chart? The testimony of the expert? Figuring out what is actually the evidence can be tricky but is very important.

Real–Demonstrative Evidence

Real evidence is that generated by criminal activity. It is found at the crime scene or elsewhere and pertains to the crime. It may be fingerprints left at the scene or those obtained from a suspect. It may be drugs, blood, or bullets. Real evidence, however, may not be found at the crime scene. If someone is shot and killed and there is no weapon at the scene, a search of a suspect's house may turn up the gun. It is no less evidence because it wasn't found at the crime scene. Of course, testing will have to be done to prove that this gun actually fired the fatal bullets. The vast majority of evidence in criminal cases is real evidence.

Demonstrative evidence, on the other hand, is created to help explain or clarify real evidence. It is produced after the crime and not by the crime. Crime scene investigators always make sketches or videotapes of crime scenes and sometimes produce scale drawings or physical models if needed. This way, the crime scene is preserved for the jury long after it has been turned back to the owner. Increasingly, computer simulations of events such as fires, explosions, vehicle crashes, structural failures, and so on are produced to help determine how an incident occurred or to reconstruct it for a judge or jury. Demonstrations may be performed to illustrate the value or characteristics of evidence. About twenty years ago, one of the authors of this book was involved in a civil case that involved the issue of whether a certain hair product (a curl activator) could have caused the victim's hair to catch on fire when a lit match accidentally flew into her hair during the act of lighting a cigarette.

In order to answer this question, we tested many samples of hair with and without the product, dropping lit matches into the hair and determining how long it took for the hair to catch fire. The entire process was videotaped and the tape shown to the jury. They were able to see that the hair product actually retarded burning. The videotape is a classic example of demonstrative evidence.

Known–Unknown Evidence

Probably the most important question asked about evidence found at a crime scene is: *Where did this come from?* In other words: *From what person or object did this arise?* The value of every piece of real evidence arises from its association with someone or something that was involved in the crime. Crime scene reconstruction depends on making these associations. **Known evidence** consists of objects whose source or ownership is known at the time it is collected at the crime scene or elsewhere. We use the term **unknown evidence** to refer to evidence discovered at a crime scene that has an unknown origin or source. A bullet found in the body of the victim of a homicide is unknown evidence. The criminal investigator is going to want to know where this bullet came from. What gun fired it? At the time it is discovered as evidence, however, the bullet's source is unknown. Suppose a burglar enters a house by breaking a glass window and climbing through. On his way in, he cuts himself on the broken glass that is still in the window, leaving some blood on the glass. Some of the broken glass from the window falls to the ground where the burglar steps on it and gets some imbedded in his shoe. After the crime is committed, the investigators examine the scene and find the blood on the glass in the window. The blood is an unknown—its source is not known to the police. The glass in the window is a known—it obviously comes from the window. The glass on the floor around the window is an unknown. It would be tempting to say that it must have come from that window, but there is no proof. It could have been there since before the crime was committed. When the suspect is arrested, a search warrant may be obtained to search his house for evidence, especially his shoes. The glass found embedded in his shoes is an unknown. It could have come from anywhere. To find out whether it came from the broken window, it will have to be compared with glass taken from the broken window (known evidence). It is very important to be able to categorize evidence in this way. It guides criminal investigators and forensic scientists in their decisions about what evidence has to be tested and what known evidence must be collected in order to perform the tests.

Something for You to Do

Below is a crime scenario and a list of possible pieces of evidence. Identify each one as known or unknown. If the evidence is unknown, then determine what known must be collected so that it can be compared to the unknown.

A man was walking across a street carrying a load of Christmas presents. A light blue car comes careening down the street and hits the man with the right front fender of the car, killing him instantly. The car sped away from the scene at a high rate of speed without stopping. A witness who saw the crash called the police with a description of the car and a partial license plate number. A few minutes later a car matching the description was stopped by police for speeding and suspicion of vehicular homicide. The car was then impounded. Upon inspection of the car, the crime scene investigator noted that the right front fender was badly damaged and some paint was missing. The right front headlight was broken and part of the glass lens was missing. The damaged area of the fender had some black fibers imbedded in it. Examination of the hit and run scene revealed that the victim's black coat had some light blue paint flecks imbedded in it. There were also a few flecks of glass in the fibers of the coat. The street around the victim's body had pieces of broken glass strewn about.

Possible evidence:

The victim's black coat and fibers taken from it
Fibers found imbedded in the damaged fender of the suspect car
Glass taken from the broken headlight of the suspect car
Glass from the street around the victim
Glass taken from the victim's coat
Paint chips taken from the victim's coat
Paint taken from the damaged area of the car

Individual–Class Evidence

In the previous section, we are asking questions about the origin or source of evidence. Now we must examine what types of answers can be given to these questions. Consider, for example, a fingerprint left on a wine glass at the scene of a crime. This might be evidence of the perpetrator's presence at the scene. It is clearly unknown evidence. If a suspect is identified, a fingerprint examiner can compare the print on the wine glass with fingerprints known to be from the suspect. The question of association now becomes: *With what certainty can we conclude that an unknown print from a crime scene came from a particular finger on a particular person?* For more than a hundred years, fingerprint examiners have testified in court that a latent fingerprint found on an object *definitely* came from a particular finger of a particular person. Fingerprint experts will testify that they are sure of this conclusion to a degree of reasonable scientific certainty. Now consider a case where blue denim fibers (blue jeans) are found on an overturned chair in a room where a dead body is found clothed in white polyester pajamas. Later a suspect is identified who is wearing blue jeans. Fibers from these blue jeans are compared with those from the chair at the scene in order to determine whether the jeans were the source of these fibers. In this case, the fiber expert could only testify that blue denim fibers found at the scene of the murder *could* have come from the pants worn by the suspect. Analysis of evidence of this type cannot support a conclusion that the unknown fibers definitely came from the blue jeans worn by the suspect. There is certainly a difference in the conclusions reached by the scientists in these two cases. In the first case, the examiner has concluded that there is only one finger that could have left the fingerprint on the object at the crime scene. In the other case, the examiner concludes that the fibers are similar to those from the pants worn by the suspect, but they could also be from another pair of pants of the same type, made of the same fibers.

Why is there a difference in the conclusions? The answer lies in the concept of individuality and uniqueness. In the case of fingerprints, there are characteristics of each fingerprint of each person that make that print unique. The argument goes that, if there are enough of these unique characteristics in the pattern of a latent fingerprint found on an object, then that latent print must have come from the one single finger. The underlying principle is that all fingerprints are measurably, demonstrably unique. This will be discussed further in the chapter on fingerprints.

In the case of the blue denim fibers, the examiner was unable to conclude that the fibers from the crime scene definitely came from the pair of pants worn by the suspect. This is because the fibers in a given pair of pants are not unique. Mass production of textiles means that there are sure to be many pairs of pants made from the same batch of fibers and there is nothing unique about any one pair. Even if the unknown fibers from the crime scene had exactly the same characteristics as those from the suspect's pants, it doesn't rule out the possibility that fibers from another pair of pants would also match exactly.

The two examples given above, fingerprints and fibers, are examples of **individual evidence** and **class evidence**, respectively. One way of defining individual evidence is that it could have arisen from only one source, in the case above, one fingerprint. Class evidence could have come from any of several possible sources. In most cases, the number of possible sources is unknown. There is another important concept at work here and that is **probability**. If a fingerprint examiner concludes that the print on the wine glass came from the suspect's right index finger, she is really saying that the probability that the fingerprint came from someone else is negligible. Any chance that the print could have another source can be ignored. On the other hand, the fiber examiner's conclusion implies that there could be other pairs of pants besides those worn by the suspect that could have been the source of the unknown fibers. This being the case, an important question would be: *What is the probability that the fibers came from the pants worn by the suspect?* Certainly a jury that would be considering the guilt or innocence of the suspect would want to know how likely it is that the source of the unknown fibers was his jeans. Unfortunately, in most cases, forensic scientists do not have enough data about the frequency of evidence such as fibers to calculate or even estimate such probabilities. This is a major weakness in the value of such evidence, but at this time, is the state of the science. These concepts are discussed in more detail in the chapters that follow on the various types of evidence.

Identification

When evidence is collected from a crime scene, object, or suspect, what happens to it when it gets to the lab? What types of analysis do forensic scientists perform on evidence? There are two major types of analysis: identification and comparison. The first, identification, is always performed on all evidence, known or unknown. **Identification** is a process of discovering chemical and/or physical properties of a piece of evidence. In the case of the fingerprint on the wine glass, the examiner would visualize the print, remove it from the wine glass, and preserve it. She would then examine it carefully, noting its size and shape and the patterns that the ridges on the print form (level 1 detail). Then there would be further examination to determine exactly what types of ridges are present and their locations relative to each other (level 2 details called **minutiae**). The examiner might even note the presence and positions of microscopic sweat pores and similar features (level 3 detail). All of these details are physical characteristics of the fingerprint. When known fingerprints are obtained and brought to the lab, they too are identified by the same process. Then the prints are compared. The three details from the known and unknown prints are carefully compared. The overall patterns of the prints (level 1) must, of course, be the same. This pattern is a **class characteristic**. It is common to many fingerprints. If there are enough corresponding level 2 minutiae, these are the individualizing characteristics, the ones that enable the examiner to conclude that the unknown and known prints have a common source; they were made by the same finger. If level 3 characteristics are also present, they provide further confirmation. In this case, the fingerprint examiner is able to **individualize** the evidence because of the presence of unique ridge characteristics. Examine Figure 3.1 which shows level 1 and 2 characteristics from known and unknown palm prints and how the prints are compared.

Now consider the blue denim fibers discussed above. The fibers found on the chair will be examined in the laboratory by a forensic chemist. She will note the length and diameter of the fibers as well as their shape. She will also determine their exact color by a spectroscopic technique (see Chapter 5 for a detailed discussion). She will also determine the chemical composition of the fibers (e.g., cotton, wool, acrylic, etc.). These physical and chemical characteristics constitute the identification phase of the analysis of the fibers. When the blue jeans are recovered, representative samples of fibers are collected from them and they are identified in the same way. If all of the physical and chemical characteristics of the known and unknown fibers are

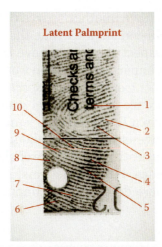 

Figure 3.1 Palm print comparison. The examiner found ten points of identification on the partial palm print lifted from the crime scene and was able to find the ten corresponding points on an inked palm print from the suspect. *Courtesy of* David Zauner.

the same, some of them may be compared side by side under a microscope. Even with all of this testing, the examiner will only be able to conclude that the known and unknown fibers belong to the same class—blue denim. There are no unique characteristics present in these fibers so no conclusion of individuality would be permitted. This is the fundamental difference between class evidence and individual evidence. Individual evidence must contain unique characteristics found only in the known and unknown evidence and not found in any other members of this class of evidence. Side by side comparison must be performed and sufficient unique characteristics must be present in both the known and unknown evidence and there must be no unexplainable differences. What constitutes sufficient unique characteristics is a function of the type of evidence and the experience of the examiner. Figure 3.2 shows a comparison of two fibers under a microscope.

All physical evidence types can be classified as being class or individual evidence.

Table 3.1 contains a list of some evidence types that are considered to be individualizable along with the characteristics that permit this conclusion. There is also a list of some evidence types that are not individualizable along with why they are not. In those cases where individualization is possible, there are a few points that have to be considered and kept in mind:

- There is no set number of unique points that must be present for any of these evidence types. At one time, there were standards for the number of points that had to be demonstrated for fingerprints, but this standard varied from state to state in the U.S. and from country to country, so there really was no standard. Today the standard is that there must be enough points present for the examiner to be sure of her conclusion that the unknown and known have a common source.
- With the exception of DNA, there is no statistical data for any of these evidence types that can support the certainty of a conclusion. There is no data about the uniqueness of a particular fingerprint or shoe print or bullet that would allow an examiner to state that the unknown matched the known to a degree of 90 or 95 or 98 percent certainty. The examiner can only conclude that the fingerprints, shoe prints, or bullets match and have a common source. This has led to some problems with questions of rates of error for

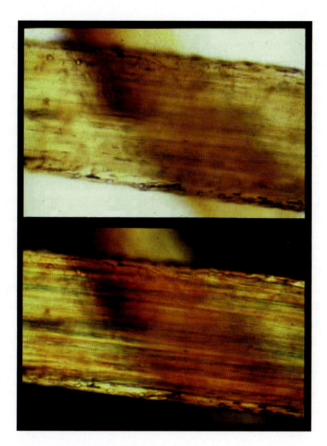

Figure 3.2 Synthetic fiber comparison. The two photomicrographs of these fibers indicate many similarities and no unexplainable differences between them. The examiner can conclude that the fibers could have arisen from the same source. Note the reddish-brown diagonal stripe of the same angle and width through each fiber. *Courtesy of* Max Houck.

TABLE 3.1
Types of Individual and Class Evidence and Their Major Characteristics

Individualizable Evidence	Individualizing Characteristics
Fingerprints	Levels 2 and 3 minutiae details
Handwriting	Individual, unique style and characteristics
Shoe prints and tire treads	Unique characteristics that develop with time, damage and wear
Large pieces of paint or glass or paper, etc.	Fracture or tear match with unique edge characteristics
DNA	Rarity of any DNA type makes probability of two people with same DNA very low

Class Evidence	Why Not Individual?
Tiny glass or paint fragments	Too small to fracture match; no unique chemical or physical properties
Soils	No classification system; too much variability between nearby samples
Hairs and fibers	No unique characteristics; hair can be individualized if DNA present
Illicit drugs, explosives, fire residues, etc.	Can identify all chemical components but no unique characteristics

these types of analysis. Since examiners do not know the certainty of their conclusions, they leave no room for error and cannot explain what the error rate is. Some examiners thus conclude that the error rate is zero, which is, of course, not possible in a scientific examination.

- There has been insufficient rigorous scientific validation of the principles that underlie the conclusions of individuality of these evidence types (except for DNA). For example, when a firearms examiner concludes that a bullet came from a particular weapon, the principle that underlies the conclusion is that each weapon leaves unique markings on the surfaces of bullets that were fired from that weapon. The markings on the surface of such bullets become a sort of signature of that weapon. This principle has not been subjected to the level of rigorous scientific testing that would be needed to firmly establish the conclusions to a degree of scientific certainty. However, this principle has been accepted in courts for many years and there have been few questions raised about it until very recently. There have also been trials where the validity of conclusions of individuality have been challenged for handwriting and fingerprints. Some courts have ruled that handwriting evidence has not been proven to be unique. One federal court questioned the premise that all fingerprints are unique, but admitted the fingerprint. In a recent case in Baltimore, Maryland, the judge ruled that there was no scientific basis for the conclusion of individuality of fingerprints. These decisions may have implications about the admissibility of some or all of these types of evidence in court in the future. We will return to this issue in more detail in Chapter 21 on forensic science and the law.

To summarize so far, all scientific evidence is identified, meaning that relevant physical, biological, and chemical characteristics are described and documented. In order to establish individuality in those evidence types that have this potential, there must be sufficient unique characteristics that are common to the known and unknown evidence. Figure 3.3 illustrates the classification of evidence in general and a specific illustration of the process with glass fragments.

The DNA Typing Situation

The science of DNA analysis has developed to the point that it is usually considered to be individual evidence. Virtually every forensic science laboratory in the world recognizes this. The mode of comparison of known and unknown biological samples for DNA is different from that for other types of potentially individualizable evidence. Recall that the principle for individualization of fingerprint, handwriting, firearms evidence, etc. is that the evidence contains unique characteristics that would not be found in other evidence of that type. The difference with DNA evidence is that the characteristics that are being compared are not unique to that one person. When DNA is typed, comparisons are made between the known and unknown DNA at thirteen locations. The structure of the DNA is determined at each of these locations. These parts of human DNA are not unique, but they are **polymorphic**; there are multiple forms within the human population. Each person possesses one or two forms (depending upon the DNA of his or her parents) of DNA at each location and the status of each location is independent of the others.

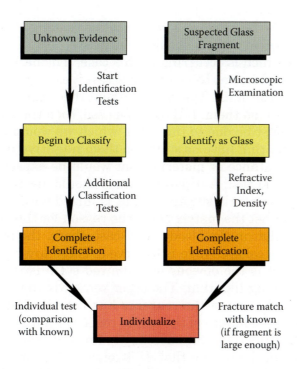

Figure 3.3 A scheme for the analysis of evidence using a glass comparison as an example. First, screening tests are done that show similarities and differences between the known and unknown. Additional classification tests are done followed by a more specific individualizing test, if it exists. This may lead to a determination of the exact source of the unknown glass. *Courtesy of* Meredith Haddon.

There is also reliable data about how common each form is in the human population. We know that if a piece of known DNA and unknown DNA have the same forms at all thirteen locations, then the probability that the two pieces of DNA have the same source is so astronomically high that all other possible sources are essentially eliminated. Thus, what makes DNA different from other types of evidence is that there is quantitative data that helps in making decisions about the association of evidence with a particular source. This topic is covered in more detail in the chapter on DNA typing.

Positive and Negative Controls

Suppose you are a forensic serologist in a crime lab and you receive evidence from a homicide in which the victim was alleged to have been stabbed to death with a knife. You receive a shirt that was worn by the victim at the time of the alleged homicide. The shirt has red stains on it that you are asked to identify. One of the first tests performed on such evidence is a test to determine whether the stains are, in fact, blood.

There are a number of tests that determine whether a red stain is blood. One of the more popular tests is called the phenolphthalein test. If a red stain is blood, it will react with phenolphthalein to give a purple color. There are other substances that will also turn purple, but these **false positives** are well known to forensic scientists. The phenolphthalein test is run by cutting out a few threads of the shirt that have the stain on them and adding the reagent to the threads. If the reagent turns purple, it is possible that blood is present. In reality, this test could produce a positive result for two reasons. The first, of course, is that the stain is really blood. It also could be that the stain isn't blood but that there is something in the fibers of the shirt that causes the test to give a false positive reading. A false positive test is one that comes out positive when it should be negative.

How do we detect which is occurring in this case? The best way is to take some fibers from the shirt that has no blood on it and test it exactly the same way as with the fibers that contain the stain. The fibers without the stain should come out negative when the test is run on them. If that is the case, then the positive result on the fiber with the stain must be due to the stain, which we would then presume to be blood. We call the fibers that have no stains on them **negative controls**. A negative control is a known substance or material that would be expected to yield a negative result to a particular test. A negative control should always be run whenever a chemical test is being run on a substance that is mixed with a matrix such as the shirt. This guards against the matrix being the reason for the positive test.

Now let's suppose that in the bloody shirt case above, the phenolphthalein test comes out negative. No color change is observed. There are two reasons why this could happen. The first is the obvious one; the red stain isn't blood. It is ketchup or beet juice or something like that. The other reason is that the test may not be working properly. Maybe one of the reagents has deteriorated or was improperly prepared. In this case, the failure of the test to react to what is actually blood would be called a **false negative** test. One sure way to find out would be to take a sample of known blood and run the test on that. If it comes out positive, as it should, then we know that the test is working properly. The known blood is called a **positive control**. This is a substance that would be expected to respond positively to the test. Positive controls should always be run any time a chemical test is used to avoid false negative results. The consequences of getting false positive and false negative results can be serious but false positive results are more so. A person can be falsely accused of a crime on the basis of a false positive result. The criminal justice system should always operate in a manner that minimizes false arrests or accusations. Remember also that good science dictates that both false positive and false negative results should be avoided.

Summary

Evidence can be classified in a number of different ways:

- Physical–nonphysical
- Real–demonstrative
- Known–unknown
- Class–individual

If evidence is discovered at a crime scene and its source (the object or person it came from), is not known, the evidence is considered to be unknown. Evidence collected from particular people or objects is known. Unknown evidence is compared to known evidence to help determine the source of the unknown. All evidence undergoes an identification process whereby its physical and chemical characteristics are discovered and described. The evidence is put into successively smaller classes. If the evidence has unique characteristics and can be compared to known evidence with the same characteristics, then the unknown can be put into a class of one and is said to be individual evidence. Individual evidence can be associated with one object or person.

Many analytical tests must be verified to make sure that they are working properly. Positive controls are used to make sure that the chemicals in a test are functioning properly so that there are no false negative results. Negative controls are used to make sure that only the target of the test will react with the reagents in the test and that a false positive reaction will not result.

Test Yourself

Multiple Choice

1. A positive control
   a. If not used, will cause a false positive test
   b. Has an unknown source
   c. Is used in a confirmatory test only
   d. Is a substance that is expected to give a positive result to the test
2. An individual test
   a. Puts the evidence in a class of one
   b. Is run on one piece of evidence at a time
   c. Always gives inconclusive results
   d. Is only run on chemical evidence
3. Identification
   a. Always individualizes evidence
   b. Describes physical and chemical properties of evidence
   c. Always requires a comparison test
   d. Is only done on positive controls
4. Unknown evidence
   a. Means evidence whose source is never determined
   b. Means evidence whose source is unknown at the time it is discovered
   c. Can never be individualized
   d. Is always class evidence
5. The statement in court that "the evidence found at the crime came from the suspect" conveys the meaning that
   a. The evidence is individual evidence
   b. The evidence is class evidence
   c. The evidence is unknown
   d. The evidence is demonstrative
6. Which of the following is demonstrative evidence?
   a. Fibers found on the victim of a homicide
   b. Fibers taken from the suspect in the homicide
   c. A scale drawing of the crime scene
   d. The getaway car used by the suspect to flee the crime
7. Which of the following is an example of demonstrative evidence?
   a. Soil tracked into a kitchen in a burglary case
   b. A gun found in the possession of a suspect in a homicide case
   c. Photographs of the scene of a fatal automobile crash
   d. A plaster cast of a shoeprint recovered from the garden of a home where a burglary took place
   e. None of the above

True or False

8. True/False. For a fingerprint examiner to conclude that a fingerprint on a gun was left by the suspect in a murder case, there must be at least 16 unique ridge details in the known and unknown prints.
9. True/False. The individuality of DNA evidence is based on the probability that no two people have the same DNA type. T
10. True/False. A suspected accelerant (e.g., gasoline) is found at a fire scene in a chair cushion. A sample of the cushion without the accelerant would be a positive control. T

Matching

11. A scale model crime scene drawing d   a. Unknown evidence
12. A blood sample taken from the suspect of a crime e   b. Nonphysical evidence
13. A human hair found on a car seat in a kidnapping a   c. Individual evidence
    case
14. Shoeprints b   d. Demonstrative evidence
15. A polygraph chart d   e. Known evidence

Fill in the Blanks

16. A false positive test can occur when the scientists fails to run the test on a _____control_____.
17. Evidence generated by crime scene activity and that can be found at the crime scene or elsewhere is _____ evidence.
18. _____ is the process of describing and documenting physical, chemical, or biological properties of evidence.
19. Evidence that cannot be associated with one particular person or object is _____class_____.
20. Large pieces of glass can be individualized by a _____ test.

Short Essay

21. Why are some types of evidence individual whereas others are class?
22. How is DNA different that other types of individual evidence?
23. What is demonstrative evidence? Give an example. Of what value is it?
24. What is unknown evidence? How does it become known?
25. What is a false positive test? Why should they be avoided if at all possible?

A Classroom Activity

A man goes into a bank to commit a robbery. He shoves a handwritten note to the teller demanding money. He gets the money and starts to leave the bank, when a guard tries to stop him. The robber shoots and fatally wounds the guard. But, before dying, the guard gets off a shot which nicks the robber in the arm, causing him to bleed. Classify each of the following types of evidence as either "known" or "unknown."

1. Blood spots found on the floor near the entrance to the bank
2. The note demanding money given to the teller
3. A sample of the robber's handwriting
4. A bullet test fired from the robber's gun

Further Reading

James, S. H., and J. J. Nordby, eds. *Forensic Science: An Introduction to Scientific and Investigative Techniques*. Boca Raton, FL: CRC Press, 2003.

Kirk, P. L. *Crime Investigation.* 2nd ed. New York: John Wiley & Sons, 1994.

O'Hara, C. E. and Osterburg, J. W., *An Introduction to Criminalistics,* New York: Macmillan, 1949.

Thorwald, J., *Crime and Science,* First American Edition, Harcourt Brace & World, New York, 1966.

PART II

Tools of the Trade

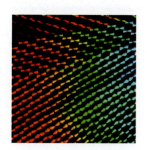

4
Separating Complex Mixtures

Learning Objectives

1. To be able to explain the concept of pH
2. To be able to recognize polar and nonpolar substances and distinguish between them
3. To be able to explain how a liquid extraction of an acid or basic drug is carried out
4. To be able to define and characterize the different types of chromatography
5. To be able to explain the basic principles of gas chromatography
6. To be able to explain the basic principles of high-performance liquid chromatography
7. To be able to explain the basic principles of thin-layer chromatography
8. To be able to explain the basic principles of electrophoresis

Chapter 4
Separating Complex Mixtures

Chapter Outline

Mini Glossary

Adsorption: A process whereby a solid in solution or liquid is attracted to the surface of a finely divided solid such as charcoal.

Analyte: A mixture of substances that are to be analyzed or separated.

Chromatography: A family of separation techniques based on the attraction of components of an analyte by a stationary or mobile phase.

Electrophoresis: A type of chromatography where the mobile phase is an electric current. It is capable of separating substances that are very similar in structure, such as fragments of DNA.

Elution: After an analyte component is captured by a stationary phase in chromatography, it can be washed off with a suitable solvent. This process is called elution.

Gas chromatography: A type of chromatography where the stationary phase is a solid and the mobile phase is a gas.

High performance liquid chromatography: A type of chromatography where the mobile phase is a liquid or liquid solution and the stationary phase is a solid or viscous liquid in a column. The analyte is dissolved and then mixed with the mobile phase and then pumped through the stationary phase.

Immiscible: A condition whereby two liquids will not mix or dissolve in one another. Examples include water and gasoline.

Ionic substances: Made up of ions, which are molecules that have extra electrons (negative ions) or are deficient in electrons (positive ions).

Liquid/liquid extraction: A type of extraction process where the analyte is dissolved in a liquid and then extracted with an immiscible liquid to remove one or more components.

Mobile phase: A liquid solution or gas that carries the analyte over or through the stationary phase in chromatography.

pH: The negative logarithm of the concentration of H^+ (hydrogen ions) in an aqueous solution. A measure of the acidity of the solution.

Polarity: The property of molecules whereby they act like magnets with a positive and negative side. Nonpolar molecules are neutral, having neither a positive or negative side.

Pyrogram: A chromatographic chart of peaks representing fragments of a substance that has undergone. pyrolysis

Pyrolysis: Heating a substance to high temperatures in the absence of oxygen. Instead of burning, the substance decomposes into simpler fragments. Pyrolysis can be carried out with gas chromatography to analyze substances with high boiling points such as plastics, paints and fibers.

Separatory funnel: A piece of glassware that is used to separate two immiscible liquids.

Solid phase extraction: An extraction method whereby a finely divided solid is used to adsorb liquids or solids in solution.

Stationary phase: A solid or viscous liquid that attracts various components of the analyte and separates them.

Thin layer chromatography: A type of chromatography where the stationary phase is a solid that is coated onto the surface of a plastic or glass plate. The mobile phase is a liquid or solution that travels through the stationary phase by capillary action carrying the analyte.

Retention factor: In thin layer chromatography, the retention factor is the ratio between the distance that a given analyte component travels up the plate from the point where the analyte spots are made, to the distance that the mobile phase travels. An Rf is specific to a substance using a particular stationary phase and a particular mobile phase.

Resolution: The ability of a chromatographic system to separate and detect two closely related compounds.

Acronyms

GC: Gas chromatography; same as
GLC: Gas liquid chromatography
HPLC: High performance liquid chromatography
MS: Mass spectrometry
PyGC or PGC: Pyrolysis gas chromatography
TLC: Thin layer chromatography

Introduction

Few substances in our environment exist in a pure state. Air is a solution of many gases including oxygen, nitrogen, carbon dioxide, many pollutants, and other substances. Our drinking water contains many minerals, salts, and, unfortunately, pollutants. The same is true with forensic chemical evidence. In some cases, only one component of the mixture is important. An example of this would be a white powder that contains an illicit drug such as cocaine that has been mixed with other inert powders such as sugars. These are used to dilute the drug in order to maximize profit. In other cases, the entire mixture is the evidence. For example, gasoline is a common accelerant used to start fires. It contains over three hundred separate substances. It is identified as gasoline by separating these substances from each other and examining the separated components. It is the only substance that has these particular hydrocarbons in unique proportions. There are many cases where forensic chemists are called on to identify one or more components of a mixture. Often, it is necessary to separate the mixture into individual substances before identifying them. Sometimes the evidence consists of many exhibits or large quantities of a single mixture. Other times, the mixture occurs in only trace amounts in a particular case. Figure 4.1 shows various kinds of complex mixtures.

Many types of chemical evidence exist as mixtures. There are solid mixtures such as illicit drugs, paint chips containing pigment and polymers, or piles of rubble containing explosive residues. There are liquid/solid mixtures such as soil that contains liquid residues from an accelerant used in a fire. There are liquid mixtures such as gasoline or blood. These different types of mixtures require different methods of handling and analysis, including methods to separate the components of the mixtures. In some cases, we are interested in separating and perhaps identifying most or all the components of the mixture. In other cases, only one component of the

Figure 4.1 Examples of complex mixtures. Milk is both a solution and suspension and is very complex. Soil is a mixture of organic and inorganic solids. Paint is also a both a solution and suspension and is one of the most complex commercial products.

mixture is of interest such as the drug in an illicit drug mixture or the explosive residue in a pile of rubble at the scene of an explosion.

In this chapter, we discuss various types of mixtures and how they are separated into individual components and how they are analyzed. We will consider large and small quantities of mixtures as well as various combinations of solid and liquid mixtures.

Physical Separation of Solid Mixtures

A physical separation is used when one or more of the components of the mixture must be separated from the rest of the mixture and recovered. An example of this is the explosive residue in the pile of rubble mentioned above. Most of this debris is not evidence and thus not important to investigators. But the debris may contain particles of undetonated explosive and/or pieces of the bomb that contained the explosive, or perhaps pieces of a timing device or some tape that held the bomb together. The best method for sifting through this rubble may be where the examiner, using a low-power stereomicroscope, physically sorts through the mixture searching for evidence. The stereomicroscope magnifies objects and allows them to be viewed in three dimensions. This is discussed in detail in Chapter 6. This can be a time-consuming, arduous task and requires a skilled examiner who can identify particles of explosives and explosive devices.

Another example of a physical separation occurs in adulterated products. One of the authors of this book had a case a few years ago in which glass particles had been added to a package of salad mix. The product had to be hand searched to pick out the glass particles from the vegetables.

Sometimes a single sieve or a set of nested sieves can be very useful for physically separating mixtures. If one is trying to find bullet fragments in a pile of sand, a sieve of the appropriate mesh to pass the sand through but trap the bullet fragments can be used. Sometimes soil samples are profiled by separating the soil into particles of various sizes. A set of nested sieves, with each one having successively smaller mesh sizes, can be used. A soil sample is dried and then poured through the nest of sieves. Various size ranges of particles will be trapped in each sieve. The percentage of each size range in the soil sample can then be calculated by weighing the contents of each sieve. This is illustrated in Figure 4.2, which shows a set of nested sieves with soil fractions.

Something for You to Do

You can make your own sieves by purchasing some screen material at a hardware store. You can buy screens of different meshes (the size of the spaces between the screen wires). A sieve can be made by stretching some screen material across a frame made of wood or metal and fastening it with nails or staples. The mixture can be placed in the sieve. Put a bucket or other container underneath and gently shake the sieve. Particles smaller than the mesh size will pass through the screen into the bucket, leaving behind only the larger pieces. Strainers and colanders are kitchen appliances that are also essentially sieves.

For this exercise, you will need a sieve or two and a magnifying glass or other small magnifier. Take some dirt and put it in three small plastic containers. To one, add a penny and mix thoroughly. To the second, add a couple of metal staples. To the third, add some table salt. Now figure out what the best way would be to recover the "evidence" (the penny, the staples, and the salt) from the soil mixture. The best way of recovery for one type of evidence may be different from another type. In determining the best method, consider that you want to get as much of the evidence as possible in the shortest amount of time. You cannot use water or another solvent. Remember to consider some useful properties of pennies, staples, and salt when you design your strategies.

Figure 4.2 A group of nested sieves. Each sieve has a finer mesh than the one above it. The sieves are put in a series and soil or other material is poured through it. After gentle shaking, the soil is distributed throughout the sieves by particle size.

Using Solvents to Separate Solids

In the exercise above, it would be tempting to take advantage of the solubility of table salt in water and just add water to the soil containing the table salt. Then the water could be poured off and evaporated, thus recovering the table salt. This would be acceptable, except for the fact that other substances that are water soluble might also dissolve, and then when the water is evaporated they would recrystallize and mix with the salt, or the components of the table salt (sodium and chloride) would react with other substances in the soil and form new substances.

Separating parts of a mixture by solubility in water or other solvents should only be done when the examiner has a good idea of what else is in the mixture or when the crystal structure of the component is not an issue. Solubility can be a very powerful means of separating mixtures. It is especially effective in cases where the particles are so small that it would be difficult or impossible to physically separate them or when there is only a small amount of material available to process. The proper use of solvents to separate components of a mixture relies on two properties of solids and solvents: **pH** and **polarity**. These are two chemical properties of substances that are determined by their structure. They can often be manipulated and exploited to make them favorable candidates for separation techniques. In the discussion that follows, these properties will be used to illustrate how an illicit drug can be separated from a typical mixture of inert powders that are used as cutting agents dilute the drug.

A typical case involves a baggie of white powder that contains cocaine mixed with sucrose, a common cutting agent for illicit drugs. The chemist's goal here is to separate the cocaine from the cutting agent In these cases the particles of cocaine and sucrose are extremely small and very well mixed so it is not possible to physically separate them even under a microscope. Instead the chemist will rely on pH and polarity to effect the separation. The ultimate purpose of this separation will be to confirm the presence of the cocaine. In order to do this, the cocaine must be pure—completely free of the sucrose cutting agent. The separation method that is employed in these cases is called a **liquid/liquid extraction**. This type of separation involves the use of two **immiscible** solvents. These are liquids that do not dissolve or mix with each other. Cooking oil and water are immiscible solvents. Before discussing the details of the liquid/liquid extraction, we need to look more closely at pH and polarity, the two properties that we will exploit to help separate the two solids.

Polarity

Students in elementary school learn that a magnet has two **poles**, north and south, and that electric charges can be either positive or negative. The same is true with certain kinds of chemicals. Some are **neutral**. They do not have poles. Other molecules are unbalanced, and they have a positive side (deficient in electrons) and a negative side (excess electrons). These substances are called **polar**, whereas the ones that don't have positive or negative sides are called **nonpolar**. There are degrees of **polarity** in chemistry, and it is possible for one substance to be more or less polar than another one. Some can be described as *slightly polar* or *very polar*. The most polar substances have actual, identifiable positive and negative sides. Made up of positive and negative ions, they are called **ionic substances**. They are always solids. Sodium chloride (table salt) is an example of an ionic compound. It is designated as Na^+Cl^-, and it is pretty clear which end is positive and which end is negative. Figures 4.3a and 4.3b show some polar and nonpolar substances. The ones shown in this figure are all liquids and gases. Note that water is included in the polar substances.

A Rule of Thumb in Chemistry

Why is it that some solids or liquids are soluble in certain liquids but others are not? Olive oil and vinegar make a nice salad dressing but the two liquids don't mix at all. Ethyl alcohol is very soluble in water. Add some flavorings and you have alcoholic beverages. Table salt is very soluble in water but not in cleaning fluid.

The reason for this lies in the polarity of the two substances. The substance that is being dissolved is called the *solute*. The substance that the solute is dissolved in is called the solvent. There is a simple yet important rule that pertains to solubility. It is simply stated as follows: *like dissolves like*. This means that if you want to dissolve a solute in a solvent, both should be either polar or nonpolar. If you try to mix gasoline and water, they will not dissolve in each other. Two layers will form, with the gasoline on the top. This is because gasoline and other *hydrocarbons* are nonpolar

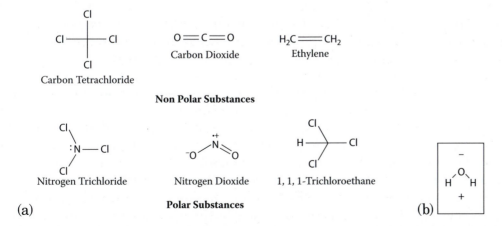

Figure 4.3 Some polar and nonpolar substances. Figure 4.3a shows some nonpolar and polar substances. Polar substances are, in general, asymmetric. Figure 4.3b is the molecular structure of water, which shows polarity.

and water is polar. On the other hand, table salt, Na^+Cl^-, is very polar and will dissolve readily in water. Most organic compounds, but not all, being made of carbon and other elements, tend to be nonpolar relative to inorganic compounds. We would expect most organic compounds to have limited or no solubility in water. Most drugs are organic, and most are not very soluble in water. There are many exceptions, and some of them will be pointed out along the way.

pH

The term **pH** describes how acidic or basic a substance is. An acidic substance is one which, when dissolved in water, contains an excess of hydrogen ions (also called protons), which are designated as H^+. When hydrogen ions are mixed with water, they attach to the water molecules and are designated as hydronium ions or H_3O^+. A basic or alkaline substance is one that has an excess of hydroxide, OH^- ions. In pure water, a few molecules will dissociate, forming some hydronium and hydroxide ions as shown in Equation 4.1.

$$2\,H_2O \leftrightarrow H_3O^+ + OH^- \tag{4.1}$$

This only happens to a very few molecules, 10^{-14} moles per liter, forming 10^{-7} moles per liter of each ion. If an acidic substance is dissolved in the water, it will furnish additional H_3O^+ ions to the solution, making the concentration of H_3O^+ higher than 10^{-7}. Likewise, a basic solution dissolved in water will grab H_3O^+ ions from the water or furnish OH^- ions to the solution, thus increasing the OH^- concentration. Instead of describing the acidity or alkalinity of a solution in terms of these tiny exponential numbers, we use a short hand notation called pH. The p in pH stands for the "negative logarithm of the concentration in moles per liter." We could just as easily describe this as the pOH. In this notation, a concentration of 10^{-7} moles per liter of hydronium ions would be expressed in pH units as 7. An acidic solution has a H_3O^+ greater than 10^{-7} or a pH of less than 7. Likewise, a basic solution has a pH greater than 7. The pH of pure water is exactly 7.

You may be familiar with acids such as hydrochloric acid (HCl) or sulfuric acid (H_2SO_4), or bases such as sodium hydroxide (NaOH) or ammonium hydroxide (NH_4OH), which is also called *ammonia water* or just *ammonia* ($NH_3 - H_2O$). Many other substances are acidic or basic when dissolved in water. This is true even of substances that appear to be neutral but have some acidic or basic character to them. Many drugs fall into this category, including cocaine. This can be exploited in the problem of separating cocaine from sucrose and we will turn to this issue now. The structures of cocaine and fructose are shown in Figure 4.4.

Sucrose, like most complex sugars, is a neutral compound. Also, like most sugars, it is fairly soluble in water, even though it is neutral. The $-OH$ groups that are attached to the carbon atoms in the molecule make it more soluble than one would think, but do not make sucrose basic. The OH groups do not come off the carbon atoms and form OH^- ions in the water. Cocaine is a slightly basic drug. It is basic because of the $-NCH_3$ group in the molecule. It is only very slightly soluble in water, and when it does dissolve, it takes a proton (an H^+ ion) away from some of the water and puts it on the $-NCH_3$ group, making it a $-NH^+CH_3$ group, leaving an OH^- behind in the water so the water has a slightly higher pH. This is shown in Equation 4.2 below. This is why cocaine is classified as a slightly basic drug. Trying to separate cocaine from sucrose by adding water wouldn't work because a little of the cocaine would dissolve and some of the sucrose would also dissolve, so neither

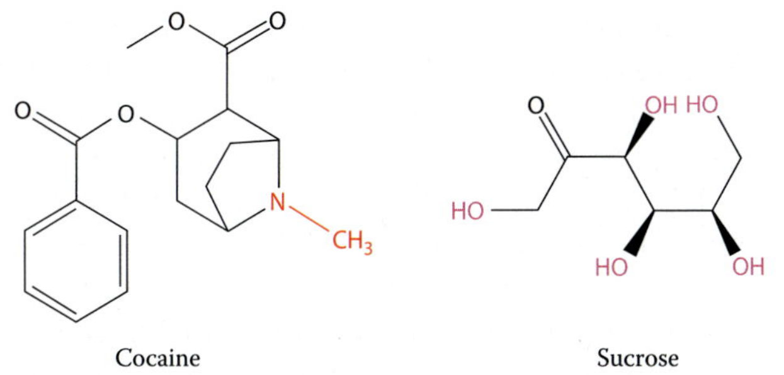

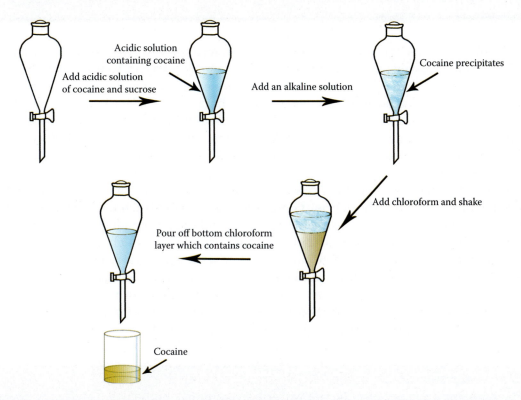

Figure 4.4 Cocaine and sucrose. Cocaine free base is a large molecule that has several polar centers, but overall is considered to be nonpolar. Sucrose is quite polar like most sugars and is very soluble in water, which is also polar.

the water solution nor the undissolved solids would be pure. Remember that the goal of this separation is to obtain pure cocaine.

$$C_{17}H_{21}NO_4 + H_2O \leftrightarrow C_{17}H_{22}NO_4^+ + OH^- \qquad (4.2)$$

Using the polarity and pH properties of cocaine and sucrose, we can now separate a mixture of the two. All that is needed is a dilute acid solution (hydrochloric acid is usually used), a dilute basic solution (ammonium hydroxide is usually used), an immiscible solvent such as chloroform ($CHCl_3$), and an apparatus known as a **separatory funnel**. Follow along using Figure 4.5 below as the process is described.

The cocaine and sucrose mixture is added to the dilute acid solution. The cocaine will become slightly polar as shown in Equation 4.2 above and will readily dissolve

Figure 4.5 Separation of cocaine from sucrose. This process takes advantage of the nonpolar nature of cocaine in its free base state. It can be made more polar with the addition of hydrochloric acid. This makes it soluble in water. After separation, an alkaline substance is added, regenerating the free base, which is insoluble in water and thus, the purified cocaine precipitates. *Courtesy of* Meredith Haddon.

in the acid. Some of the sucrose will also dissolve in the acid owing to its slightly polar nature even though it is a neutral compound. It may be necessary to filter the solution to remove any undissolved sucrose. This is put into a separatory funnel.

The solution is now made basic by adding the dilute basic solution. When this happens, the excess OH⁻ ions will remove the extra proton from the cocaine ion, regenerating the nonpolar cocaine molecule. This is the reverse of Equation 4.2. Since the water solvent is polar, the cocaine is no longer soluble and it precipitates out. The solution becomes cloudy. The sucrose, being neutral, stays in solution.

Now the chloroform is added to the separatory funnel. This solvent is very nonpolar and will not mix with the water. It is more dense than water and will settle to the bottom of the separatory funnel. When the funnel is shaken, the cocaine will dissolve in the chloroform (like dissolves like). The sucrose will stay in solution in the water.

The chloroform layer is now poured out from the bottom of the funnel. It can be evaporated, leaving the solid cocaine behind. The separation has now been accomplished.

Just about any basic drug can be separated from other substances this way as long as only the drug of interest is basic. Cocaine is often diluted with other, cheaper drugs such as lidocaine, which is also a basic drug. It will behave chemically the same way as the drug and no separation will take place. Other means must be used to separate multiple basic compounds in the same mixture. The same kind of process can be used with acidic drugs and neutral cutting agents like sucrose. The solvents are changed, and where acidic solutions are used with basic drugs, basic solutions are used with acidic drugs. Everything is reversed.

Solid Phase Extractions

Some solids such as finely divided charcoal have the ability to grab and hold dissolved solids or some volatile liquids in a mixture. These materials can be directly extracted from the mixture and **adsorbed** onto the surface of the charcoal or other adsorbent. This process is called **solid phase extraction**, because the adsorbent is a solid. One of the most common examples of solid phase extraction in forensic science is the trapping of fuel residues from the debris collected from a fire scene. A finely divided solid, often charcoal, is coated onto a small plastic strip. The strip is then suspended from the inside of the top of a sealed paint can containing fire debris suspected of containing an accelerant such as gasoline. The can is gently heated, driving the gasoline fumes into the air space above the debris. These fumes will then attach to the surface of the charcoal strip. After a time, the strip is removed and the fire residues can be desorbed (removed from the strip) and further analyzed. In addition to charcoal, adsorbents can be made from finely divided particles of several synthetic solid materials and coated on strips or wires. These can be dipped directly into a liquid solution containing a substance of interest such as a drug. The drug will adsorb onto the surface of the polymer and will thus be separated from the solution. Solid phase extraction has become very popular because it is quick and easy and sensitive.

Chromatography

Separation processes such as liquid/liquid extractions, sieving, and physical separations work well when there is a relatively large amount (at least a few grams) of material present. When only very small amounts of chemical evidence are available, these methods are not suitable and others must be used.

Over the past decades, a series of separation methods have been developed that are designed for small amounts of material. These methods can efficiently separate amazingly small amounts of material, as little as 10^{-12}g (picograms). Of course at these levels, the pure substance is not isolated and recovered. Instead, it may be subject to further analysis to confirm its identity.

These evolving methods collectively belong to a family called chromatography. The term **chromatography** means to analyze by color. The original chromatography experiments involved separation of plant pigments. Plants contain many pigments within their leaves, some of which change color with the seasons. Early analytical chemists wanted to separate, isolate and identify these pigments. Some leaves were ground up, and a solvent was added to dissolve the pigments. A large glass column, about 3 cm in diameter and about 60 cm long, was filled with silica (very pure sand) or a similar finely divided solid. The plant pigment containing solution was then poured through the column. As the pigments traveled down the column by gravity, they separated into individual colors, each one becoming affixed to the silica in the column at various points along the way. This separation occurred because each of the pigments differed in its attraction to the solid particles in the column. Some of the pigments were strongly attracted and would leave the solution early in the process. Others were only weakly attracted and would take longer to attach to the particles. The effect was to separate most or all of the pigments into bands of color fixed to the solid bed. Figure 4.6 illustrates how this happens.

After all of the solution has been poured through the column, the various bands of color can be separately removed by several methods. The column could be dismantled, and each area of colored silica could be separated. Solvents would be added to each area to redissolve that pigment, and then the silica would be filtered out. Another way of removing each pigment involves adding a solvent or series

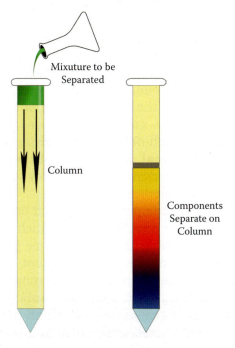

Mixuture to be
Separated

Column

Components
Separate on
Column

Figure 4.6 Separation of plant pigments by column chromatography. The mixture of plant pigments is dissolved in an organic solvent and then poured onto the solid phase column. The pigments are attracted to the column in different degrees and so they separate. *Courtesy of* Meredith Haddon.

of solvents that removes the bands from the column individually. This process is called **elution**. This method of pigment separation was the first type of chromatography. Today this is called *column chromatography*. It requires relatively large amounts of mixture. It also requires that the components of the mixture be soluble in a suitable solvent and that they be colored; otherwise they cannot be detected. The human eye is the *detector* in this instrument. Today there are much better methods of detection that are not based on color and methods that require much smaller amounts of material.

The chromatography family of methods differ in details, but all are based on similar principles. In chemistry parlance, the mixture that is to be separated is called the **analyte**. Every different substance in a mixture is a component of the analyte. For example, a mixture of heroin, procaine, and maltose would be a three-component analyte. Gasoline would be an analyte and each of the more than three hundred different substances in gasoline would all be components of the analyte. All forms of chromatography contain two phases, the **stationary phase** and the **mobile phase**. The stationary phase is the filling in the column, as described above, or it may be a thin coating of a material like silica that is put onto a microscope slide or piece of plastic or may line the inside walls of a very narrow column. It is called the stationary phase because it does not move. It is fixed in one place—the inside of a column or coated onto a plastic or glass plate. Today's columns are very narrow (they can be the diameter of a human hair) and can be very long (some are sixty meters in length). The mobile phase can be a liquid or liquid solution or an inert gas, such as helium. The mobile phase is usually pumped under pressure, carrying the analyte through the stationary phase. The mobile phase does not mix with the stationary phase. They are completely incompatible.

The function of the stationary phase is to act as a carrier or transporter of the analyte. This means that the analyte must be completely soluble in the mobile phase. As the analyte is carried by the mobile phase through the stationary phase, there are interactions between the various components of the analyte and the surface of the stationary phase.

Different components interact differently with the stationary phase. Some components are strongly attracted and others weakly or not at all. The more that a component of the analyte interacts with the stationary phase, the longer it takes for it to make it all the way through to the end. This is how mixtures are separated. When a component of the analyte reaches the end of the stationary phase it interacts with a detector that signals its presence and, in some cases, determines how much of that component is present. Although detectors do not identify substances they can detect very small amounts of material, whether or not they are colored. This makes chromatography techniques very versatile because they can detect a wide variety of substances in very small quantities.

The interaction of the analyte components is based on two factors: polarity and size. Recall the maxim that "like dissolves like," which referred to the ability of polar solutes to dissolve in polar solvents, etc. The same principle holds true for the interactions between molecules of an analyte component and the surface of the stationary phase. If the analyte is polar it will be more strongly attracted to a polar stationary phase. The same holds true with nonpolar analytes and stationary phases. Since few substances have exactly the same polarity, all components of a given analyte would be expected to be attracted differently to a stationary phase and thus would all eventually separate. This is shown graphically in Figure 4.7.

Another mechanism for separating components of an analyte is called mass action. This is simply a recognition that size matters. In the case of chromatography,

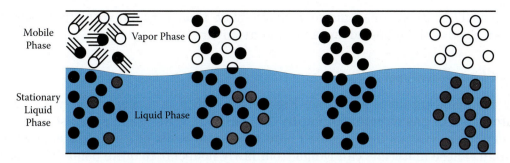

Mobile Phase

Vapor Phase

Stationary Liquid Phase

Liquid Phase

Figure 4.7 Attraction of analyte components to the stationary phase of a column. The two components of the mixture are attracted differently to the stationary phase and thus they separate as they travel through and over the stationary phase. *Courtesy of* Meredith Haddon.

different size molecules move at different rates in a mobile phase regardless of the nature of the stationary phase. Heavier molecules move slower than lighter ones. Consider the Boston Marathon. Thousands of people line up in the same place and then all run twenty-three miles. At the end, they are all separated by their ability to run fast and indirectly by size (lighter people run faster?). The other way that mass enters into chromatography is that the molecules of analyte have to work their way through and around the stationary phase molecules and lighter ones can do that more easily and get through faster. Consider a large leaf and a small leaf floating down a stream. It is easier for the small leaf to float through obstacles such as stones or branches and the lighter leaf generally goes down the stream faster.

Quantitative Analysis

In addition to separating components of an analyte, some types of chromatography are able to determine how much of a substance is present in a mixture. This is often exploited to determine how pure a drug sample is. In those types of chromatography that rely on pushing an analyte mixture through a column containing a stationary phase, the detector signals the presence of a component and plots it on a graph in the form of a roughly triangular shaped peak. The computer that plots the data keeps track of the size of the peak (its area). The area under a peak is directly proportional to the concentration of the analyte component detected. The way that the computer calculates area is by starting a counter when the peak begins and stopping the counter when the peak ends. The area data is stored as "counts."

Something for You to Do

A forensic drug chemist wishes to find out the percent heroin in a small bag submitted to the laboratory. Part of the analysis is a chromatography test. The chemist weighs out 100 mg of the unknown and dissolves it in 100 mL of methyl alcohol and injects 10 ul into a chromatograph. A peak corresponding to heroin emerges and the computer calculates that its area is 10,000 peaks. The chemist then obtains some pure heroin from her standards safe and dissolves 100 mg of that into 100 mL of methanol. She then injects the same amount, 10 ug into the chromatograph. The computer calculates that the area under the heroin peak is 50,000 counts. What is the percent heroin in the mixture?

Types of Chromatography

The family of chromatography techniques is large, so a discussion of all of them is beyond the scope of this book. In any case, only a few types are commonly used in forensic science and we will discuss them in some detail. They are gas (or gas–liquid) chromatography (**GC**), high performance liquid chromatography (**HPLC**) and thin layer chromatography (**TLC**). These types of chromatography differ in stationary phase and mobile phase. GC and HPLC use columns to hold the stationary phase whereas TLC uses a small glass or plastic plate that is coated with the stationary phase. Each of them has advantages and disadvantages.

Gas Chromatography

For the following description, see Figure 4.8, which is a diagram of a gas chromatograph. In **gas chromatography** (GC or GLC), the stationary phase is usually a very thick, viscous liquid coated onto the inside walls of a thin glass or plastic column. These materials can range from fairly nonpolar to quite polar. The mobile phase is an inert gas (vapor) such as helium, nitrogen or hydrogen which is put under pressure. These inert gases are always very nonpolar. Since the analyte must dissolve completely in the mobile phase, it is heated to high enough temperatures to convert at least some of it to a vapor. All vapors readily in each other.

This is accomplished in the *injector*, where the analyte and mobile phase are combined. The analyte may be a solid, liquid, or vapor. If it is a solid, it is dissolved in a suitable solvent, put into a syringe, and injected into the injector. The high temperature in the injector evaporates the solvent and vaporizes the analyte, which is mixed with the mobile phase. The mixture is carried to the column containing the stationary phase where the components of the analyte are separated. As each component reaches the end of the stationary phase, it enters a detector. GC detectors are designed to create an electrical current when a component of the analyte is present. The strength of the current is proportional to the amount of analyte. This current is sent to a computer where it displays the analyte components as a series of peaks. Figure 4.9 is a one-component chromatogram of caffeine. There are many tiny peaks in the trace. These are noise and impurities. The peak at 5.141 minutes is caffeine. The solvent peak is suppressed because it is so large relative to the caffeine.

One important detector for GC is worth discussing. It is a mass spectrometer (MS). This instrument is attached directly to the gas chromatograph. Every component of the analyte that emerges from the GC enters the MS. In this instrument, the molecules of analyte are bombarded by a beam of electrons. These impart energy to the molecules, which makes them unstable and causes them to decay into more stable fragments and lose an electron from each fragment, forming

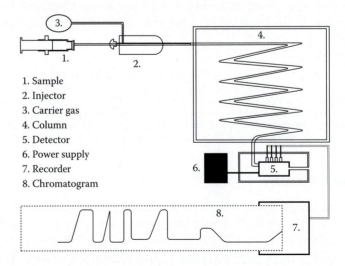

1. Sample
2. Injector
3. Carrier gas
4. Column
5. Detector
6. Power supply
7. Recorder
8. Chromatogram

Figure 4.8 Diagram of a gas chromatograph. Each peak in the chromatogram at the bottom represents a different substance. *Courtesy of* Meredith Haddon.

Chromatogram (All TIC)

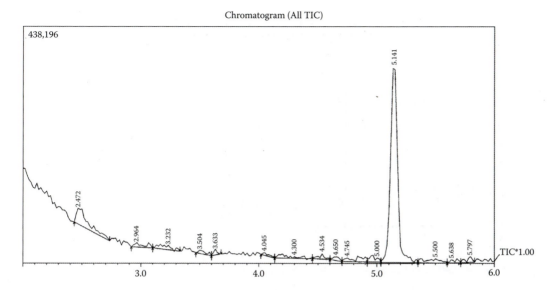

Figure 4.9 Chromatogram of caffeine. The beginning of the run is cut off. The huge peak represents the solvent. The rest of the small peaks are instrumental noise and minor impurities.

ions. These fragments are separated and displayed as a series of vertical lines arranged in order of increasing mass. Each substance has a unique pattern of fragments and this pattern can be used to identify the component with certainty. When a GC is connected to an MS, complex analytes can be separated into individual components and each can be identified. This is a great advantage of GC/MS and the vast majority of forensic science labs have these instruments. Figure 4.10 is the mass spectrum of cocaine.

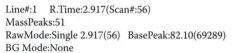

Line#:1   R.Time:2.917(Scan#:56)
MassPeaks:51
RawMode:Single 2.917(56)   BasePeak:82.10(69289)
BG Mode:None

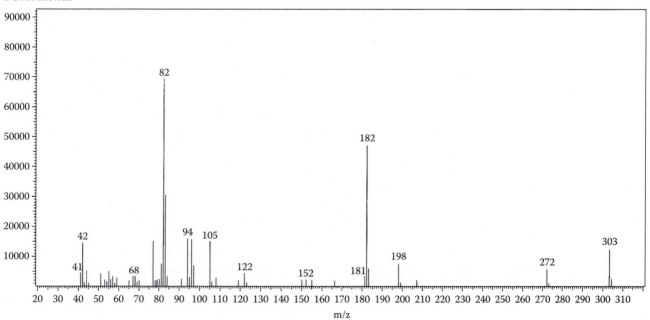

Figure 4.10 Mass spectrum of cocaine. The highest peak at 303 is the unfragmented cocaine molecule. The other peaks are stable fragments created during ionization of the cocaine in the mass spectrometer.

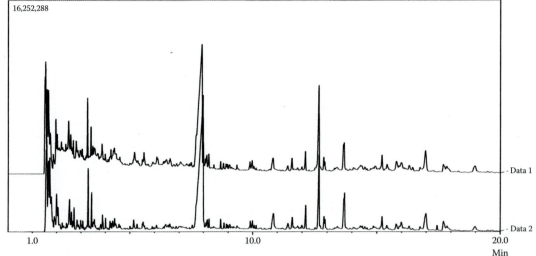

Figure 4.11 These are partially overlaid pyrograms of two fibers. The pyrograms are very similar and are clearly of the same chemical type, polyester in this case. Even though both fibers are of the same type that doesn't provide enough evidence to prove that they came from the same garment.

Pyrolysis Gas Chromatography (PyGC or PGC)

As versatile as gas chromatography is, there are many materials of forensic interest that it cannot handle, simply because they cannot be easily converted to a vapor, which is necessary for GC analysis. The practical limit of a GC instrument is about 300°C because the stationary phases and many analytes will decompose when the temperature is higher than this. Evidence such as fibers, paints, plastics, rubber, and other polymers cannot be vaporized at 300°. They require much higher temperatures, 700–1000°C. This can be achieved using an instrument called a *pyrolyzer*. This is essentially a furnace capable of heating up to 1000°. It is connected to the injector of the GC, filled with mobile phase and the analyte in its solid form is introduced. When the pyrolyzer is heated, the analyte vaporizes, mixes with the mobile phase and then is swept into the stationary phase. Since the pyrolyzer contains only the analyte and mobile phase, no air or oxygen is present and the analyte will not burn, but it does decompose into smaller, stable fragments which are characteristic of that material. These fragments are separated by the GC and displayed on a chart called a **pyrogram**. Each pyrogram is characteristic of the type of material present. Figure 4.11 is a pyrogram of two polyester fibers. All such fibers would produce similar pyrograms and these would be different from pyrograms for acrylic, nylon, etc.

With refinements such as **pyrolysis** and mass spectrometry, gas chromatography is perhaps the most versatile technique in the forensic science arsenal. Just about all forensic chemical evidence can be analyzed by GC. This includes drugs, poisons, fire residues, explosive residues, inks and paper, fibers, soils, glass, alcohol, plastics, paints, rubber, and many other materials. GC instruments can be outfitted with robot autosamplers, which permit the analyst to introduce many samples over time with minimal operator time and effort. The speed and value of GC/MS instruments have helped to revolutionize clinical and forensic toxicology. The ability to quickly determine which drugs a person has taken in an overdose case has saved many lives.

High Performance Liquid Chromatography

Recall the original chromatography experiments where plant pigments were separated by dissolving them in a mobile phase solvent and then pouring them through a solid bed of stationary phase. The mobile phase traveled through the stationary phase under the influence of gravity and this could take on the order of hours to complete. The columns were large and a lot of analyte was required in order to detect a single component on the column by its color. This was the first form of what we now call liquid chromatography, so called because the mobile phase is a liquid or liquid solution. Today, we use much smaller columns requiring much less sample and the mobile phase is pumped under pressure through the stationary phase resulting in experiments that take a few minutes rather than hours. Because of this dramatic increase in performance and efficiency, we call this technique high performance liquid chromatography (HPLC).

In **high performance liquid chromatography**, the stationary phase can be a viscous liquid such as used in GC and some of these are used in either technique. In addition, however, solid stationary phases are also used. The polarities of stationary phases in HPLC can vary from the very nonpolar to the very polar. The mobile phase is a liquid or a solution of two or more liquids. These can also vary in polarity from nonpolar to polar. This is an advantage over gas chromatography, where the mobile phase is always very nonpolar. With HPLC, a greater variety of substances can be separated. In addition, by incorporating two or more liquid pumps, the composition and polarity of the mobile phase can change on the fly during a run. This adds even more flexibility to the technique. HPLC is generally run at room temperature. The analyte must be soluble in the mobile phase. It is dissolved and then introduced into an injector where it is mixed with the mobile phase, which is then pumped through the column containing the stationary phase. The detectors used in liquid chromatography are different from those used in GC because they are detecting liquid solutions rather than vapor solutions but they work on the principle of converting a signal of the presence of an analyte component to an electric current. The output is a chart with each component of the analyte represented by a triangular peak as in GC. Thus these HPLC chromatograms can be used for quantitative analysis as with GC. Figure 4.12 is a photograph of an HPLC.

HPLC is widely used in forensic chemistry. It is useful for substances that cannot be heated without decomposing and for relatively nonvolatile liquids. Pyrolysis cannot be used but it is common now to incorporate a mass spectrometer as a detector for identification of the separated analyte components. Some of the types of evidence commonly analyzed by HPLC include, inks, dyes, pigments, drugs, alcohol in drunk driving cases, soil extracts, explosive residues, and some fire residues.

Thin Layer Chromatography

Gas and high performance liquid chromatography are similar in that they both employ a stationary phase housed in a hollow column, either coating the inside walls or filling the column with particles. These then require a sample delivery system (injector), a way to force the mobile phase through the stationary phase (pumps or pressure), and sophisticated detectors that permit the display of signals through a computer when an analyte component gets through the stationary phase. Although these types of chromatography are extremely versatile and sensitive, they are also expensive and, by necessity, can process only one sample at a time.

Figure 4.12 A photograph of an HPLC instrument. These instruments are generally quite modular so that a variety of pumps can be mounted into the system. There is also room for several detectors mounted in series.

One of the oldest chromatographic techniques was developed along different lines. Instead of a tubular column holding the stationary phase, certain types of paper could serve as the stationary phase. The analyte would then be dissolved in a small amount of solvent. Tiny spots of this analyte would be made at one end of the paper just above the bottom. The paper would then be dipped in the mobile phase, which would travel up the paper by a process known as capillary action, carrying the analyte with it. As the various components travel up the paper, they separate. This is called *paper chromatography*. It was developed nearly a hundred years ago. Over time it has undergone major enhancements. The paper has been replaced by a glass or plastic plate onto which a thin coating of a pure solid is coated. This is the stationary phase. There are a wide variety of solids of varying polarity that can be used, adding versatility compared to just having to use paper. This type of chromatography is called **thin layer chromatography**. It is widely used in forensic science laboratories for a variety of evidence. It is the most versatile type of chromatography because of the wide variety of stationary and mobile phases, its portability and low cost, and the ability to run more than one analyte at a time.

Running Thin Layer Chromatography

Figure 4.13 shows a typical TLC apparatus and set-up. The plastic or glass plate is usually the size of a microscope slide although sometimes much larger ones are used for preparative work. The stationary phase coatings are commonly pure, finely divided silica (sand) or alumina (aluminum oxide) or even any of several types of wax. The thickness of the coating can range from a few microns to 1 mm or more. The

Figure 4.13 A thin layer chromatography set-up. The filter paper in the beaker is there to keep the atmosphere inside the container saturated with mobile phase. This can greatly improve the quality and reproducibility of the chromatogram.

stationary phase is mixed with a binder that holds it onto the surface of the plate. The mobile phase is a liquid or liquid solution. The solution can contain various concentrations of polar and/or nonpolar liquids that determine its overall polarity. The analyte can be a mixture of solids or liquids, although solids are generally used.

A small amount of the solid is dissolved in a suitable, volatile solvent such as methanol or chloroform. This can be done in a spot or depression plate. A small capillary tube with an inside diameter of about 5 microns is dipped into the solvent which fills the tube. The end of the tube is then touched to the stationary phase about 1 cm above the bottom of the plate. This makes a small spot of analyte.

It may be necessary to over-spot an analyte to make sure that enough has been loaded onto the plate. This is usually a matter of trial and error. If over-spotting is done, the scientist should wait until the solvent in the spot evaporates to avoid making too large a spot. The goal is to make a spot that is as small as possible. It is possible to then load another analyte or standard next to the first one, leaving at least a couple of spot diameters between spots. Once the analytes have been loaded, the plate is placed into a chamber that contains mobile phase. The amount of mobile phase should not be so great as to cover the spots. Usually a piece of filter paper is used to line the inside of the chamber to saturate the chamber with mobile phase vapor. This improves the chromatography. Once the plate comes in contact with the mobile phase, the liquid travels up the plate by a process known as capillary action. This is the same process that carries water up through the roots of a tree all the way to the top leaves. As the mobile phase travels up through the stationary phase, it carries the analyte. Interactions of the analyte components with the stationary and mobile phases causes them to separate. When the mobile phase has reached the top of the plate, the plate is removed from the chamber and dried.

Detection of Analyte Components

There are several ways of detecting the presence of analyte component spots on the plate. One common way is to pretreat the stationary phase with a fluorescent dye. When the plate is put under an ultraviolet light, the dye fluoresces with a green color. In those places where analyte spots are present, the green color is masked and a dark spot appears. Another way to visualize some materials is to take advantage of their fluorescence. Illuminating them with an ultraviolet light will cause them to fluoresce. The most versatile way of visualizing spots is by spraying them with a reagent that reacts with the analyte to form a colored product.

Some of these spray reagents are specific for certain types of materials. Examples include *Fast Blue BB*, which colors the naturally occurring cannabinoids in marijuana red to orange depending upon which one(s) are present, and *Ehrlich's reagent*, which colors LSD and similar substances, purple. Other spray reagents are more general in their color reactions. *Greiss reagents* (a series of two) color all nitrate containing compounds bright red. Even more nonspecific is *iodoplatinate reagent*, which adds iodine across carbon–carbon double bonds and turns the analyte brown. These and other sprays are not completely specific for a single substance.

Interpreting TLC Plates

When the spots have been visualized, the **retention factor**, or Rf, is measured. The retention factor is the ratio between the distance that a given analyte component traveled up the plate from the point where the analyte spots are made to the distance that the mobile phase travels. An Rf is specific to a substance using a particular stationary phase and a particular mobile phase. It is a good way of comparing results between laboratories if the same conditions are used.

It is important to remember that the Rf of a substance is not unique. There may be many different substances that have the same Rf in a TLC experiment so this technique, like other chromatographic methods, is not used for absolute identification. TLC is often used to give presumptive or tentative information about the presence of a substance. For example, if an unknown white powder has a spot with the same Rf as the spot from a known sample of morphine, it can be presumed that morphine is present, but this still must be confirmed by other tests. Figure 4.14 illustrates the use of Rfs to make tentative identifications.

Thin layer chromatography is used on a wide variety of evidence types. These include drugs, inks and dyes, explosive residues, cosmetics such as lipsticks and nail polishes, and many other types. It is very quick, inexpensive, and versatile.

Something for You to Do

You can do some chromatography at home. It will be similar to thin layer chromatography, and you will end up with a custom T-shirt. You can also practice your technique on large pieces of blotter paper.

Take a clean white T-shirt (or piece of blotter paper). Get some liquid inks like the kinds that are used in fountain pens or ink refills for ink jet printers. Get a couple of different colors. To get the best results, you may have to dilute the ink with water. Make sure that you put something like blotter paper between the front and back of the T-shirt so the ink doesn't bleed through. Using an eyedropper, drip ink onto the shirt. You can overspot the same place to make the spots bigger and darker. You can drop the ink from several feet up to make splatters. When the ink hits the shirt, it will spread out away from the drop point in all directions like waves in a pond after a stone is dropped into it. The various dyes that make up the colorants in the inks will separate as the inks spread out. Depending on the complexity of the colorants, you may see several dyes in one ink. If you make several spots in different parts of the shirt, they will run together as they spread out, resulting in some interesting effects. While you are having fun designing your own clothes, remember that you are actually doing chromatography.

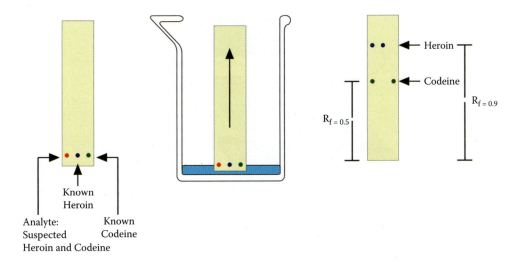

Figure 4.14 A TLC plate with R_fs of the various analyte components. *Courtesy of* Meredith Haddon.

Electrophoresis

One of the few drawbacks of chromatography is that these techniques do not result in absolute identification of the separated substances in an analyte. The peaks in a gas chromatogram or liquid chromatogram and the spots in a thin layer chromatogram are not unique to one particular substance. This is due to the concept of **resolution**. Resolution in chromatography is the ability of the technique to separate very similar substances. It frequently happens that two substances in an analyte are so similar that they won't separate and will show up as one peak or one spot. (Question: how do we know or find out whether a peak or spot is really one substance?) We can usually design a chromatographic system that will separate common mixtures that occur as evidence such as drugs or fiber dyes, etc., but sometimes it is not possible to separate components of a mixture by conventional chromatographic methods.

A prime example of evidence that cannot be separated by conventional gas or liquid or thin layer chromatography is DNA. DNA is analyzed by isolating pieces or fragments that differ from person to person. These fragments may differ only slightly in length or composition and cannot be separated and displayed as separate units by conventional chromatography. In such cases, the technique of **electrophoresis** can be used. Electrophoresis is a form of chromatography; it is used to separate components of a mixture and display them as spots or peaks. One type of electrophoresis is similar to liquid chromatography. Another type is similar to TLC. In both cases, there are, however, important differences. The stationary phases are somewhat different although both systems use solid materials. The mobile phase is very different. It is an electric current! There are two major types of electrophoresis used in forensic science—*gel* and *capillary*. They are described below.

Gel Electrophoresis

Gel electrophoresis is somewhat like thin layer chromatography, but there are important differences. The stationary phase in electrophoresis is a slab of a gelatin-like material, usually *agarose* or *polyacrylamide*. Instead of a thin layer, the slab is several millimeters thick. The DNA fragment mixture is mixed with a bit of liquid and put in wells made at one end of the gel. The entire gel slab is then immersed in

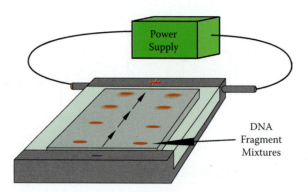

Figure 4.15 A gel electrophoresis apparatus. The power supply puts an electric charge onto the gel slab, positive on one side and negative on the other. The DNA fragments are loaded onto the negative side of the gel and they migrate toward the positive side, separating as they travel through the gel. *Courtesy of* Meredith Haddon.

a buffer solution that maintains a constant pH. A strong electric current (hundreds or even thousands of volts) is then put across the gel with the negative pole on the side where the DNA has been deposited. The other side of the slab has the positive pole. The buffer imparts a slightly negative charge to the DNA. When the current is turned on, the DNA will flow toward the positive pole because of its negative charge. The moving electric current is actually the mobile phase in electrophoresis. The current carries the DNA fragments through the gel. After a couple of hours, the current is turned off. The DNA fragments will have separated.

The principle of separation of DNA fragments by gel electrophoresis is essentially mass action. The lighter, smaller fragments travel faster and farther through the gel than the heavier, larger ones, so the fragments are separated by electrophoresis. There is almost no difference in the polarities of the DNA fragments. When the electrophoresis is finished, the DNA is stained with a fluorescent dye or treated with a radioactive material that will expose an x-ray film to visualize the DNA fragments. For most DNA typing applications, gel electrophoresis has been supplanted by capillary electrophoresis because of its higher resolution and ability to determine the quantity of DNA present as well as the types. Figure 4.15 is a diagram of a gel electrophoresis apparatus.

Capillary Electrophoresis

A diagram of a capillary electrophoresis instrument is shown in Figure 4.16. Instead of a slab of gel, a very thin column containing a stationary phase, often polyacrylamide gel, is used and both ends are immersed in a buffer solution. An electric charge is put across the column. When the analyte, such as DNA fragments, are introduced into the column, they travel through and are detected by its fluorescence. As in gel electrophoresis, the mobile phase is an electric current. The advantages of the gel column over the gel slab is that it is very efficient at separating DNA fragments and it is much more sensitive. In some experiments only a few nanograms of material are needed for separation. As with HPLC, the results of the analysis show a series of peaks, each of which represents a fragment of DNA. These peaks yield quantitative information as well as the size of each fragment. Figure 4.17 shows an *electrophorogram* of a DNA sample. Note that this electrophorogram shows peaks in several different colors. This is due to different fluores-

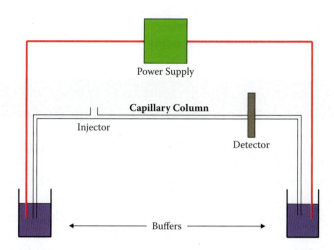

Figure 4.16 A capillary electrophoresis instrument. *Courtesy of* Meredith Haddon.

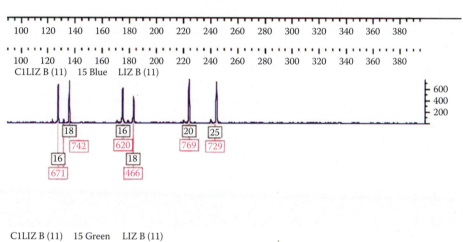

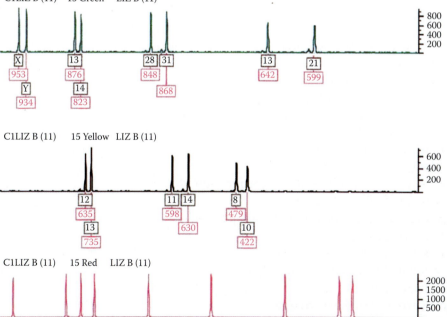

Figure 4.17 An electrophorogram of a DNA sample. The various DNA fragments are put in three groups, each with its own fluorescent dye. Each fragment shows up as one or two peaks, depending upon inheritance from the mother and father.

cent dyes that are applied to different categories of DNA fragments. The purpose of this process is to make interpretation easier.

Summary

Because very few types of chemical evidence are in a pure state, the material(s) of interest must be separated from the rest of the evidence. Most often, physical separation of the analyte is not possible or practical because of the amount of material and the time it would take to effect a separation. As a result, chemical separations are usually used to separate the evidence from the unneeded substances. The type of chemical separation employed depends upon the nature and amount of material present. For large amounts of materials (grams or more) liquid or solid phase extractions can be used. For smaller amounts of material one of several forms of chromatography are usually employed. If the analyte is stable at high temperatures and can be easily vaporized then gas chromatography is most often employed. If not, either high performance liquid chromatography or thin layer chromatography can be employed. For materials that are extremely similar such as DNA fragments, a variation of liquid chromatography called electrophoresis is used. The principle of separation in all types of chromatography is that different analyte components have a greater or lesser affinity for the stationary or mobile phase. An important characteristic of chromatography is resolution, the ability to separate two closely related substances.

Test Yourself

Multiple Choice

1. A solution whose pH is 9 has:
   a. An H^+ concentration of 9
   b. An H^+ concentration of -9
   c. An H^+ concentration of 10^9
   d. An H^+ concentration of 10^{-9}
2. A polar compound:
   a. Is insoluble in water
   b. Always has oxygen
   c. Has a positive side and a negative side
   d. Has a pH of less than 7
3. In gas chromatography, the mobile phase:
   a. Is an inert gas
   b. Is a liquid solution
   c. Is always polar
   d. Is located in a column
4. A mixture of four basic drugs:
   a. Cannot be separated
   b. Would show four peaks on a chromatogram
   c. Must be separated using a liquid extraction method
   d. Can only be separated using thin layer chromatography

5. In HPLC:
   a. The mobile phase is a solid
   b. A coated microscope slide is the stationary phase
   c. The mobile phase moves through the stationary phase by gravity
   d. The mobile phase is a liquid solution or pure liquid
6. All types of chromatography:
   a. Have a stationary phase and a mobile phase
   b. Have chromatograms with peaks on a chart
   c. Can be used to separate explosive residues from the debris of an explosion
   d. Have a liquid mobile phase
7. Gel electrophoresis:
   a. Cannot separate DNA fragments
   b. Is similar to gas chromatography
   c. Has a very thin column for the stationary phase
   d. Uses an electric current as the mobile phase
8. The first experiments that led to the development of chromatography:
   a. Used an inert gas as the stationary phase
   b. Showed that plant pigments could be separated and located by their color
   c. Used pumps to push the mobile phase through the column
   d. Were very much like today's thin layer chromatography
9. One of the major differences between GC and HPLC is that:
   a. GC has a liquid mobile phase
   b. GC uses columns to hold the mobile phase, whereas HPLC does not
   c. GC columns are heated, whereas HPLC columns are kept at room temperature
   d. HPLC always uses at least two liquids in its stationary phase
10. An ionic compound:
   a. Is more likely to dissolve in a polar solvent such as water than a nonpolar solvent
   b. Always has a pH greater than 7
   c. Generates excess OH^- when dissolved in water
   d. Cannot be separated from another ionic compound in a mixture

True-False

11. Chromatography techniques are used for separation and absolute identification of substances
12. In order to be analyzed by gas chromatography, an analyte must be thermally stable up to about 300°C
13. pH is a measure of the acidity of an aqueous solution
14. Electrophoresis is similar to liquid chromatography except for the nature of the mobile phase
15. In HPLC, the mobile phase is always a gas
16. In thin layer chromatography, the mobile phase is a liquid or solution

Matching

17. Retention time

18. Polarity
19. Adsorption

20. Electrophoresis

21. Thin layer chromatography

22. Mobile phase

a. Carries the analyte through the stationary phase

b. Mobile phase is electric current

c. More than one sample can be separated at the same time

d. Time it takes a sample to move through stationary phase

e. Process by which a solid grabs and holds an analyte

f. Property of a substance where it acts like a magnet

Short Essay

23. What is polarity? Give some examples of polar and nonpolar substances.
24. What is a mobile phase? What is its purpose in chromatography?
25. How is gel electrophoresis similar to thin layer chromatography? How is it different?

Further Reading

Saferstein, R. Forensic Applications of Mass Spectrometry. In *Forensic Science Handbook*. Vol. 1. 2nd ed. Ed. R. Saferstein. Upper Saddle River, NJ: Prentice Hall, 2002.

Staford, D. T. Forensic Capillary Gas Chromatography. In *Forensic Science Handbook*. Vol. 2. Ed. R. Saferstein. Upper Saddle River, NJ: Prentice Hall, 1988.

Suzuki, E. M. Forensic Applications of Infrared Spectroscopy. In *Forensic Science Handbook*. Vol. 3. Ed. R. Saferstein. Upper Saddle River, NJ: Prentice Hall, 1993.

On the Web

Outline of chromatography with illustrations: http://antoine.frostburg.edu/chem/senese/101/matter/chromatography.shtml

Diagrams of gas chromatography and thin-layer chromatography: http://antoine.frostburg.edu/chem/senese/101/matter/chromatography.shtml

Animations of gas chromatograpy and electrophoresis and how they work: www.shsu.edu/~chm_tgc/sounds/sound.html

Videos of solid phase microextraction: www.sigmaaldrich.com/analytical-chromatography/video/spme-video.html

Video of a liquid–liquid extraction: www.youtube.com/watch?v=vcwfhDhLiQU

5
Light and Matter

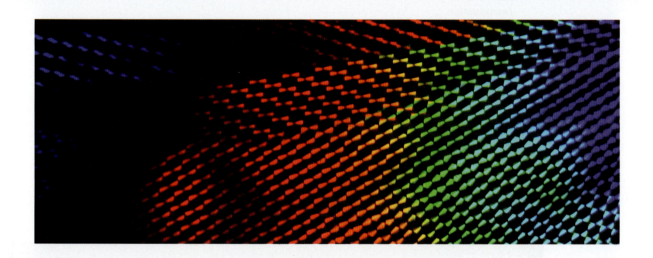

Learning Objectives

1. To be able to describe the wave nature of light
2. To be able to define and describe the properties of a wave: wavelength, frequency, period, and amplitude
3. To compute the wavelength and/or frequency of a wave using wave formulas
4. To be able to describe the particle nature (quantum nature) of the absorption of light
5. To be able to describe the major regions of the electromagnetic spectrum and their effects upon matter
6. To be able to describe the effect of UV/visible light on matter and the types of matter that absorb these types of light
7. To be able to describe the effect of infrared on matter and the types of matter that absorb these types of light
8. To be able to draw and label a typical spectrophotometer
9. To be able to define mass spectrometry
10. To be able to draw and label a diagram of a mass spectrometer
11. To be able to describe how substances are ionized and analyzed in mass spectrometry
12. To be able to define *parent peak* and *base peak*

Chapter 5
Light and Matter

Chapter Outline

Mini Glossary

Electromagnetic (EM) spectrum: A large range of wavelengths of radiation that can travel through a vacuum.

Frequency: A property of a wave, which is determined by the number of complete cycles of the wave past a given point in a time interval (usually a second).

Infrared (IR) radiation: An invisible wave in the electromagnetic spectrum characterized by lower frequency and longer wavelength and sensed as heat.

Longitudinal wave: A wave in which the individual particles move back and forth parallel to the direction of energy transfer.

Period of a wave: A property of a wave that indicates the time taken for one complete cycle of a wave.

Photon: A discrete bundle or quantum of electromagnetic energy in the form of light.

Transverse (sine) wave: A wave that oscillates perpendicular (at right angles) to the direction of energy transfer.

Ultraviolet (UV) radiation: An invisible wave in the electromagnetic spectrum characterized by higher frequency and shorter wavelength, falling between x-rays and visible light.

Visible light: Part of the electromagnetic spectrum that is discernable by the human eye.

Wavelength: A property of a wave determined by the linear distance between two successive identical parts of a wave

Introduction

Some shirts are red while others are blue. Exposing food to microwaves cooks it quickly and silently. X-rays can see the interior of a human body. All of these events occur because of the interaction between *electromagnetic radiation* and the atoms and molecules that comprise all matter. Electromagnetic radiation is energy in the form of waves. Some electromagnetic radiation is very energetic, such as x-rays and gamma radiation, while other types have relatively very little energy associated with them, such as microwaves and radio waves. Most forms of electromagnetic radiation are invisible to the human eye, whereas a small portion of the **electromagnetic spectrum** is manifested as **light energy**. Some of this light is visible to humans as color. This chapter describes the effects of some of the forms of electromagnetic radiation on matter. As we will see, certain materials can be characterized and even identified by measuring the changes they undergo when exposed to certain types of electromagnetic radiation. This can be significant forensically as part of the process of identifying unknown samples taken at a crime scene as evidence.

Many people use the term "light" to mean all electromagnetic radiation, whereas others refer to light as only the electromagnetic radiation we can see. In this chapter the two terms are used interchangeably.

What Is Light?

Light is radiant energy that comes to Earth via our sun. Visible light, that which we sense with our eyes, is only a small portion of the energy that travels through the vacuum of space to our planet. The sun's energy travels in the form of **electromagnetic waves**, which are fluctuations of electric and magnetic fields that transport energy from one location to another. See Figure 5.1. These waves are able to move through space, as they do not need a medium (particles) to transfer the energy.

Visible light exhibits what is called a "dual nature," meaning it can act as an electromagnetic wave and as a particle called a **photon**. Scientists make use of this dual nature in various instruments used in research and testing.

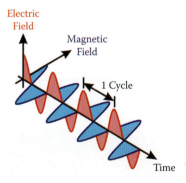

Figure 5.1 The magnetic and electric field orientation in an electromagnetic wave. http://inms -ienm. nrc-cnrc.gc.ca/i mages/research_ images/optical_co mb/COMBFIG1.gif.

Light as a Wave: The Electromagnetic Spectrum

Other forms of electromagnetic radiation are not visible to the naked eye and include radio waves, television waves, microwaves, **infrared waves**, **ultraviolet waves**, x-rays, and gamma rays. All of these waves have one property in common—they all travel at the same speed, the speed of light. But they also differ and are classified according to their **wavelength** and **frequency**.

The shortest wavelength waves that we normally encounter in our world are gamma rays. Because they have the shortest wavelength, they are the highest energy waves of those in the spectrum. We examine this relationship later in the chapter. The longest wavelengths are found in radio waves, which are lowest in energy. If the electromagnetic radiation is arranged in order of increasing wavelength (or frequency), it is known as the **electromagnetic (EM) spectrum**. This arrangement is shown in Figure 5.2.

Proceeding from left to right on the chart, the wavelengths go from longest to shortest and the frequencies from lowest to highest. The long radio waves have wavelengths that are in the range of 1–10 meters long. TV waves have slightly shorter wavelengths. Because these two types have long wavelengths, low frequency waves, they contain very little energy and are not harmful to humans. The next shorter wavelength region belongs to microwave radiation. Energy beams with these wavelengths cause molecules to spin. Microwaves are used to cook food by causing the water molecules in the food to rotate rapidly. These spinning water molecules come in contact with each other and generate heat by friction. The heat produced cooks the food.

One of the most important areas of the electromagnetic spectrum is the infrared (IR) region. **Infrared radiation** is invisible energy characterized by lower frequency and longer wavelength and sensed as heat. Radiation in this region causes the bonds in molecules to vibrate as if the bonds were springs. Every type of bond in every molecule will vibrate and there are many ways that a bond can undergo

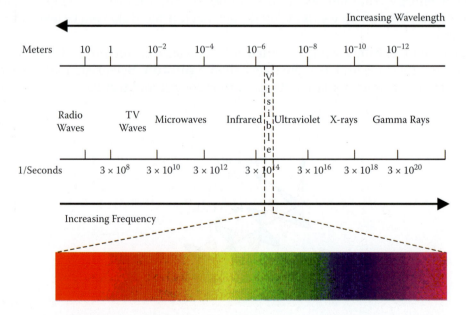

Figure 5.2 The electromagnetic (EM) spectrum. The visible region of light is a very narrow band between the infrared (IR) and the ultraviolet (UV) regions.

vibrations. Because of this, infrared spectra are very complex and unique. This is discussed in more detail later.

Light with higher frequencies than infrared are visible to the naked eye. The visible region is usually described by its wavelengths, which are measured in nanometers. Visible light ranges from about 400 to 800 nanometers (10^{-9} meters). Note in Figure 5.2 that visible light proceeds from red to violet as the frequency increases. This is why the region below the visible red light in frequency is called infrared. *Infra* means "below." The next higher frequencies comprise the ultraviolet (UV) region. The term *ultra* means "above." This region is above the frequency of visible violet light. Light in the visible and UV regions causes the outermost electrons in chemical bonds to absorb energy and move to higher atomic levels or orbitals. When they drop back to their ground state orbitals, they release energy in the form of visible or ultraviolet light. Ultraviolet light possesses enough energy to damage living cells. UV energy causes sunburn and can cause skin cancer.

Light with shorter wavelengths such as x-rays and gamma (γ) rays possess enough energy to severely damage living cells and can destroy them. Gamma rays are emitted by nuclear weapons in great quantities and are one reason exposure to a nuclear explosion is usually fatal.

Properties of Waves

There are two types of wave motion, longitudinal and transverse. Both wave types transfer energy from one place to another by repeatable motion of energy or particles. **Longitudinal waves** are sound waves and need a medium for the transfer of sound energy. The molecules in the medium move back and forth, creating regions of high and low pressure. As the molecules compress and expand, they collide and transfer the energy parallel along the wave. The basic structure of a longitudinal wave is shown in Figure 5.3. Although these types of waves are not used in the instrumentation discussed in this chapter, it is important to realize how sound waves are different from the waves of the EM spectrum. Radio waves are *not* sound waves, but are part of the electromagnetic spectrum and therefore do not need a medium for travel.

Light as a wave can be described as electromagnetic energy that oscillates in cycles (refer to Figure 5.1). It can be described as a **transverse wave** or sine wave. A transverse wave is shown in Figure 5.4. It is **periodic**, meaning that it oscillates back and forth repeatedly. The direction of its oscillation is perpendicular to the direction of energy propagation. There are several ways that a transverse wave can

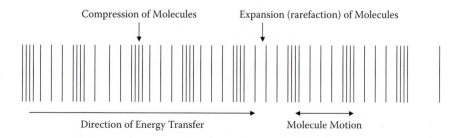

Figure 5.3 A longitudinal sound wave. The areas of high density of molecules are due to *compression* of the air and the areas of low density of molecules are due to *expansion* (called *rarefaction*) of the air. The motion of the molecules is parallel to the direction of energy transfer.

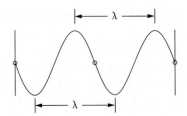

Figure 5.4 Light can be visualized as a series of transverse or sine waves. A given photon of light can be described in terms of its wavelength (λ), the distance between two adjacent peaks or valleys.

be described. The **wavelength** (λ) is the distance between any two adjacent peaks or valleys of the waves. It is measured in units of length that vary with the type of wave. For example, radio waves are very long and are measured in meters. X-rays, on the other hand, are very short and are measured in micrometers (μm or 10^{-6} meters), which are millionths of meters.

Another way of describing waves is by their frequency (f). The frequency of light is the number of cycles that pass a given point in one second. If you were standing on a street corner and could see and count the waves of red light emitted by a traffic signal, the number of waves that pass you in one second would be the frequency of that light. Frequency is measured in Hertz (Hz). One Hertz = one cycle per second. Its units are expressed as (1/sec or /sec).

The **period** (T) of a wave is a measure of the time taken for the wave to complete one cycle and is measured in seconds. Since both period and frequency have time in common, they are related to each other. The frequency (cycles/second) of a wave is the inverse of the period (seconds/cycle) of a wave. The Equation 5.1 shows this relationship.

$$f = \frac{1}{T} \qquad (5.1)$$

Additionally, frequency and wavelength are related to each other. They are also inversely proportional; as one gets larger, the other gets smaller. This is because the velocity of light is always the same (as it travels through air or a vacuum). The velocity of light (c) is approximately 3×10^8 meters/second. If you are back at that street corner counting waves, you would notice that waves from the red stop light have longer wavelengths than waves emanating from the green light. Further, you would count fewer red waves passing you in one second than green ones because they are both traveling at the same speed. The relationship between the speed of light, its wavelength and its frequency is expressed in Equation 5.2.

$$c = \text{speed of light in m/s}$$

$$\lambda = \text{wavelength in m}$$

$$f = \text{frequency in Hz or /sec} \qquad (5.2)$$

$$c = f\lambda$$

Note that the speed of light must have the same length units as the wavelength because in order for any equation to be valid, its units must be the same on both sides. This equation allows us to determine the wavelength of any beam of light if we know its frequency and vice versa.

Sample Problem

Suppose your favorite FM radio station is at 120 on the dial. We want to calculate the wavelength of this station. FM stations broadcast in the megahertz region of the electromagnetic spectrum. This station has a frequency of 120 megahertz or 120×10^6 Hz (/sec). Recall that the speed of light is 3×10^8 m/s.

Rearranging equation 5.1 we get: $\lambda = c/f$
Since $c = 3 \times 10^8$ m/s and $f = 120 \times 10^6$ /sec
Substitute in the equation and solve:

$$\lambda = \frac{3 \times 10^8 \text{ m/s}}{120 \times 10^6 \text{ /sec}} = 2.5 \text{ m}$$

The final wavelength is 2.5 m. Radio waves are very long indeed!

On Your Own

Go back to that street corner and look at the green light. Suppose you could measure its wavelength and found it to be 500 nanometers (nm). A nanometer is 10^{-9} meters. How many green waves would pass you in one second? (Answer: $f = 6 \times 10^{14}$ /sec)

The Energy of Light: The Photon

In restaurants, freshly cooked food is often kept hot until served by placing it under an infrared lamp. Clearly this type of light is hot. It contains energy. In fact, all radiation contains energy. Early in the twentieth century, a man named Max Planck deduced that radiation is made of discrete bundles of energy called quanta. He deduced that the amount of energy in these quanta is directly dependent on the frequency of vibration. From the work of Max Planck came the notion that light, a form of radiation, contains these bundles or quanta of energy, which we call **photons** of light.

The metric unit (SI unit) of energy is the joule (J). Another common unit of energy is the erg. The joule is a larger energy unit than the erg such that one joule is equal to 10^7 ergs. Equation 5.3 shows how frequency (f) and energy (E) are related.

$$E = hf \qquad\qquad (5.3)$$

In this equation, energy (E) is measured in joules (J) and frequency in 1/second. h is a constant of proportionality to get the units the same on both sides of the equation. It is called Planck's constant and its units are joules × seconds (J s). It has the value of 6.626×10^{-34} J s or 6.626×10^{-27} erg sec.

Sample Problem

Now let's see how much energy the waves that carry your favorite FM station have.

Recall that the frequency is 120×10^6 Hz.

By substituting in Equation 5.3, we get:

$$E = (6.626 \times 10^{-34} \text{ J s}) \times (120 \times 10^6 \text{ /sec}) = 7.95 \times 10^{-26} \text{ J}$$

On Your Own

Calculate the energy of that beam of green light from the traffic light on the corner.

$$(\text{Answer: } E = 3.98 \times 10^{-19} \text{ J})$$

Compare your value to the energy of the radio station. What does this tell you about how the frequency is related to energy?

If you have the wavelength of light instead of the frequency, substitute the wave equation (5.2) solved for frequency into Equation 5.3. The energy of the light can be calculated from the new Equation 5.4 shown below.

Since

$$f = c/\lambda \qquad E = hc/\lambda \qquad\qquad (5.4)$$

Interactions of Light Energy and Matter

Many types of electromagnetic radiation can affect materials. Forensic science is most interested in those interactions that help describe or identify particular substances encountered as evidence. These substances include drugs, explosives, fibers, paints, and others. The areas of the electromagnetic spectrum most important to forensic scientists are the infrared, the visible, and the ultraviolet regions. These will be discussed separately, but first it is necessary to learn how the interactions of light and matter are measured, recorded, and displayed.

The types of interactions that matter undergoes when exposed to light depend on the energy (and thus the frequency) of the light. The interactions with a particular substance are dependent on its chemical structure. Different substances interact with certain wavelengths of light but not others.

Infrared and UV/visible light interact with electrons and bonds in molecules. Normally these reside in their lowest energy state, which is closest to the nucleus of the atom. Electromagnetic radiation will cause the electrons and bonds to absorb energy from the light and move to a higher energy level further from the atomic nucleus. The amount of energy absorbed of a given frequency of light is measured. Quantum mechanics dictates that the packet or photon of light must contain the exact energy needed to promote an electron or bond to a higher level. The molecule cannot absorb half of the frequency (or energy) and reject the rest. If a photon has 10^5 joules of energy, a substance cannot absorb 10^2 and reject the rest. Think of climbing a staircase. You can be on one stair or another stair, but you cannot be between the stairs. So it is with electrons. They can be on one level or another but not between the levels. This is shown graphically in Figure 5.5.

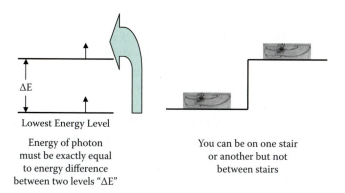

Lowest Energy Level

ΔE

Energy of photon
must be exactly equal
to energy difference
between two levels "ΔE"

You can be on one stair
or another but not
between stairs

Figure 5.5 Energy levels of electrons are quantized. An electron can only exist in a lower or higher energy state, but not between them. A photon of light must have energy exactly equal to the difference in energy between two electronic states in order for it to be absorbed by the molecule and promote an electron to a higher state. This is analogous to a shoe being on one stair or another but it cannot be between the stairs.

The Spectrophotometer

Each material will absorb energy from some photons and not others. An instrument called a **spectrophotometer** is used to measure which frequencies (or wavelengths) of light are absorbed and how much. A simplified diagram of a spectrophotometer is shown in Figure 5.6.

The source emits light of all of the wavelengths in that region of the spectrum. Different types of sources are used for each type of light. For example a **Nerntz glower** emits light in the infrared region. A **xenon lamp** is used to obtain visible light and a **deuterium lamp** emits ultraviolet light.

The **monochromator** is usually a prism or grating. It has the property of **refracting** (bending) light waves. Shorter wavelength light is refracted to a greater degree than long wave light. In the visible range, violet light is bent more than red light. The ability of a monochromator to refract light enables it to separate the light from the source into individual wavelengths. The monochromator can be turned slowly so that different wavelengths are exposed to the sample over time. During the course of a run, all of the wavelengths will reach the sample eventually. The type of sample holder used in a spectrophotometer depends on what type of analysis is being performed. In some cases, liquids or solutions are best, in others, solids are used.

As the light passes through the sample, some of it will be absorbed, the rest transmitted. The light that is transmitted reaches the detector. The type of detector

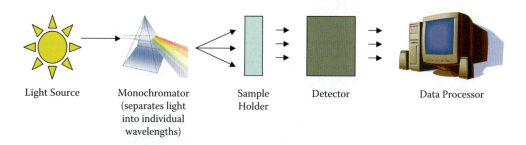

Light Source

Monochromator
(separates light
into individual
wavelengths)

Sample
Holder

Detector

Data Processor

Figure 5.6 A typical spectrophotometer. The light source will differ depending on the type of light (e.g., infrared or visible) studied. The monochromator separates the light into individual wavelengths using a prism. The detector design depends on the type of light being analyzed. For example, a UV light detector is a type of photocell.

used depends on the type of light being analyzed. For example, infrared light detectors are generally some type of **thermocouple**, a device that is able to convert heat into electricity. The more light that reaches the detector, the more electricity can be generated. For UV and visible light, a **photocell** is used. A photocell converts light to electricity and like the thermocouple, creates more electricity when it receives more light.

The monochromator and the detector are both controlled and monitored by a data processor, which is usually a computer. The data processor collects data about the wavelength of light and the response of the detector. It ultimately creates a plot of wavelength (or frequency) versus the amount of light transmitted or absorbed by the sample. This plot is called a spectrum.

Ultraviolet/Visible Spectrophotometry

One of the most important characteristics of evidence is its color. This is most useful in analyzing paints and fibers. For example, there are many red fibers and, although the human eye is a very good discriminator of color, it can be fooled. Scientific evidence analysis requires something more objective than a scientist's opinion that two fibers are the same color. There is also the problem of metamerism, the property that two objects may appear to be the same color in one type of light but different in another. See Figure 5.7.

In the end, the only objective means of determining the exact color of an object is to measure the amounts and wavelengths of visible light that it absorbs. This requires a visible spectrophotometer.

The absorbance of visible and ultraviolet light depends on the outer shell or valence electrons; those that participate in the covalent chemical bonds that bind atoms together in molecules. As it turns out, not all molecules absorb light in the ultraviolet/visible region. Only those molecules that have bonds of low enough energy will be UV/visible active. The best UV/visible absorbers are molecules with **conjugated carbon–carbon (or nitrogen) double bonds** that alternate with single bonds. Some examples are shown in Figure 5.8.

The structure of crystal violet, a common blue dye found in ballpoint pen inks, is shown in Figure 5.9. Note the large number of conjugated double bonds in

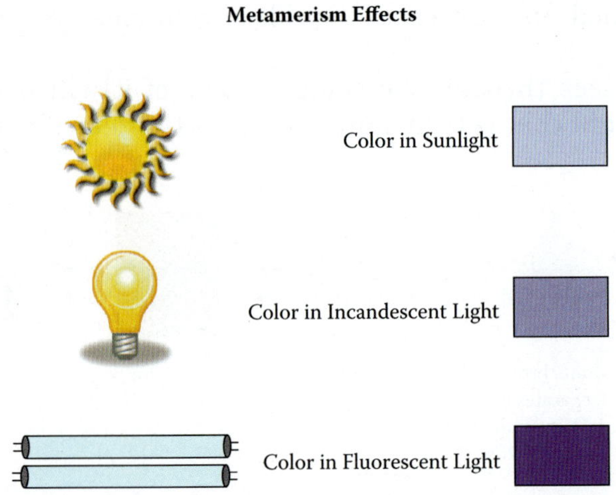

Metamerism Effects

Figure 5.7 Metamerism is the effect different light sources have on the color of an object. The hue of the color changes depending on the source of illumination.

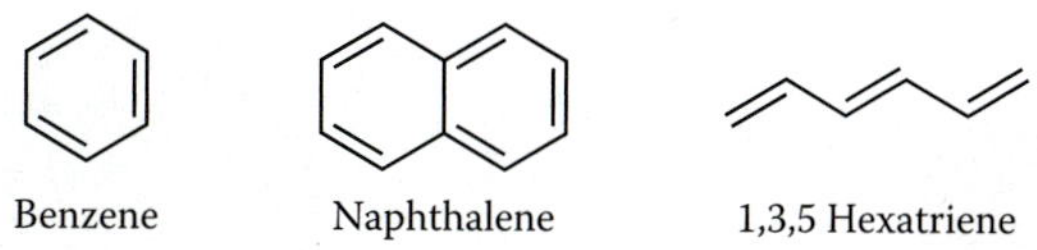

Benzene   Naphthalene   1,3,5 Hexatriene

Figure 5.8 These substances are examples of molecules that readily absorb UV light.

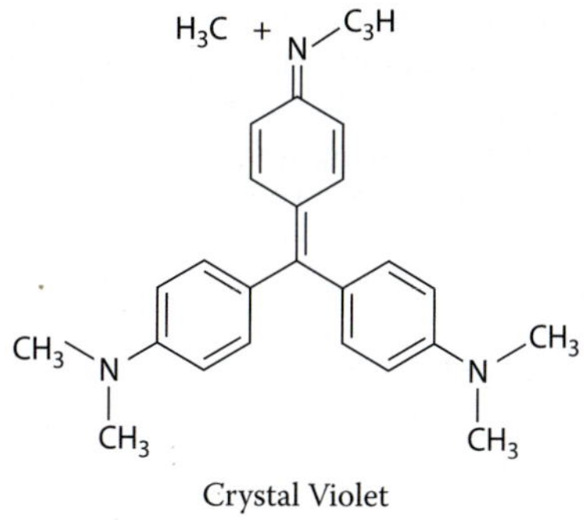

Crystal Violet

Figure 5.9 The structure of crystal violet.

this molecule. This explains its bright color. Most dyes and pigments are highly conjugated.

As mentioned previously, UV/visible spectra arise from the transition of valence electrons from a lower energy level to a higher one. In most molecules, spectra are relatively simple, with only one or two transitions. Because of the energy supplied by room temperature, the transitions tend to be very broad. The UV spectrum of heroin is shown in Figure 5.10. Note that there are two absorptions (peaks) that lie close to each other and are quite broad.

Sometimes it is necessary or desirable to obtain the visible and/or UV spectrum of a microscopic sample such as a single fiber. In such a case, a UV/visible microspectrophotometer is used. This instrument is a combination of a microscope and a spectrophotometer. It is explained in detail in Chapter 6: Microscopy.

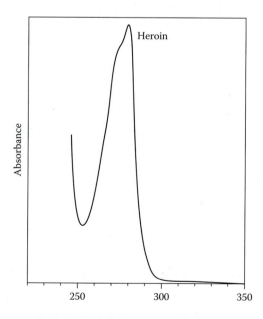

Figure 5.10 The ultraviolet spectrum of heroin.

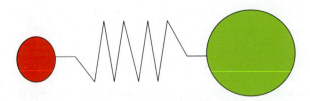

Figure 5.11 The absorption of infrared energy by a molecule can be visualized by considering a spring with weights at each end. In order to start the spring vibrating, energy of the exact magnitude must be available. The amount of energy depends on the strength of the spring and the masses of the two weights. Likewise, the photon of infrared light that will be absorbed by a bond depends on the strength of the bond and the masses of the atoms that are bonded.

Infrared Spectrophotometry

Every covalent chemical bond consists of one, two, or three pairs of electrons between two atoms. Each atom usually contributes half of the electrons in the bond. The best way to understand how infrared spectrophotometry occurs is to consider each bond as two weights connected by a spring. This is shown in Figure 5.11 where the red and green balls represent the two atoms and the spring represents the bond. Two weights connected by a spring are collectively called a **harmonic oscillator**. If the spring is stretched, it will vibrate back and forth at a constant frequency that depends on the strength of the spring and the masses of the two weights. Any change, however slight, in the mass of either weight or the strength of the spring, will change the harmonic frequency. So it is with atoms that are joined by chemical bonds. Each bond will absorb just the right energy (quantized) to start the bond vibrating. Every type of bond connecting every type of atom will have different frequencies of vibration. Also, each bond can undergo several different types of vibrations, each one requiring a different energy photon of light. Figure 5.12 shows some of the vibrations of the water molecule.

The more bonds there are in a molecule, the more vibrations there are and the more complex will be the infrared spectrum. Even very similar molecules can have different infrared spectra. Figure 5.13 shows the structures of amphetamine and methamphetamine. Figure 5.14 shows their infrared spectra. Even though the molecules are very similar in structure, their infrared spectra can be easily differentiated.

Infrared spectra are so complex that each molecule has a unique spectrum. This means that infrared spectrophotometry can be used to unequivocally identify a pure substance.

Sometimes it is necessary or desirable to obtain the infrared spectrum of a microscopic sample such as a single fiber, a bit of ink, or a small paint chip. In these cases, an IR microspectrophotometer can be used. This instrument is a combination of a microscope and in infrared spectrophotometer. It is explained in detail in Chapter 6: Microscopy.

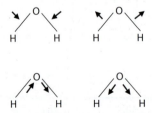

Figure 5.12 These are some of the vibrations that a water molecule can undergo. Some of these will appear as peaks in the infrared spectrum of water. Not all molecular vibrations are active in the infrared region.

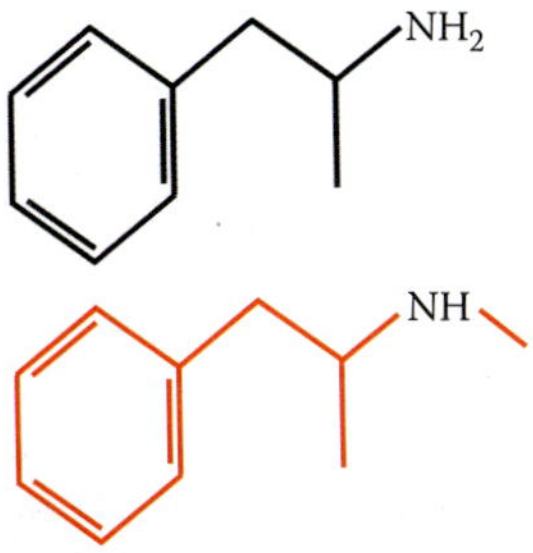

Figure 5.13 Structures of methamphetamine and amphetamine.

These basic principles of the spectrophotometer apply to UV/visible and infrared instruments. Today's infrared spectrophotometers work on a somewhat different principle. Instead of the monochromator that selects which wavelengths of light reach the sample, the source light is sent instead to a **Michaelson interferometer**. This apparatus converts the light beam containing all the wavelengths of infrared light into an **interferogram**, which is a set of all of the wavelengths of light formed into a pattern of added and subtracted intensities of light. The interferogram is then projected onto the sample, which absorbs and transmits the light as usual. The interferogram is then turned back into individual wavelengths using a mathematical process called the **Fourier transform.** The wavelengths and absorptions are then plotted as usual. This type of infrared spectroscopy is called **Fourier transform infrared spectrophotometry (FTIR).**

Mass Spectrometry

Until now we have been looking at the interactions of electromagnetic radiation and matter focusing on UV/visible and infrared light. Now the focus shifts to another type of interaction. Instead of using light as a means of delivering energy to matter, a beam of high-speed electrons can be used. A pure chemical substance is converted to a vapor and introduced into an evacuated chamber and then bombarded with a beam of high-speed electrons. The energy of the electrons is absorbed by the substance. This causes the substance to lose an electron of its own and form a positive ion. In mass spectrometry, this is called the **molecular** (M^+) **ion**. In some cases, the molecule will lose two electrons and will then have a +2 charge, but this relatively rare. The M^+ ion is usually unstable and will decompose, producing **daughter ions**. These are fragments of the original molecule that are also positive ions. Depending on their stability, the daughter ions may undergo further decomposition into smaller fragments. If a substance is subjected to bombardment with an electron beam under the same conditions each time, the number, amounts, and sizes of each fragment will be reproducible.

After the ionization step, the ions are accelerated down a tube and focused using magnets. This step separates the fragments by weight. A mass detector is used to arrange the fragments by increasing mass and displaying them as vertical lines from smallest mass to largest. A diagram of a mass spectrometer is shown in Figure 5.15. The mass spectrum of cocaine is shown in Figure 5.16. With few exceptions, the pattern of fragments and their relative amounts is unique to each substance, so mass spectrometry can be used to identify a pure chemical compound.

Strictly speaking, a mass spectrum does not show the masses of the fragments and shows the mass (m) divided by the charge of an electron (*e*) or m/*e*. This is because, as

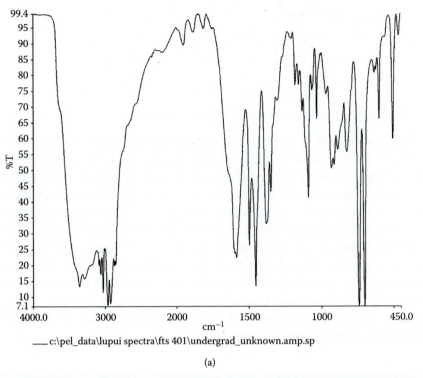

_____ c:\pel_data\lupui spectra\fts 401\undergrad_unknown.amp.sp

(a)

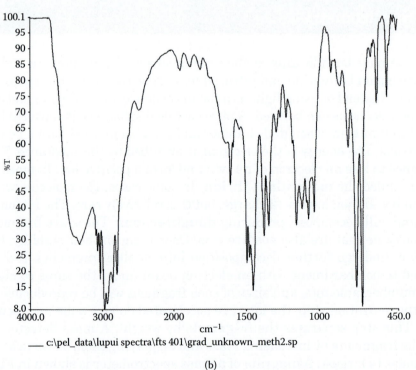

_____ c:\pel_data\lupui spectra\fts 401\grad_unknown_meth2.sp

(b)

Figure 5.14 Infrared spectra of (a) amphetamine and (b) methamphetamine. Even though the molecules are structurally similar, their infrared spectra can be used to differentiate them.

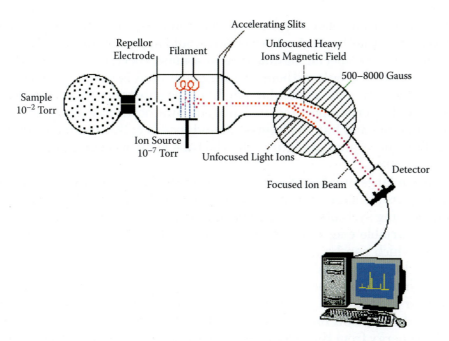

Figure 5.15 Diagram of a mass spectrometer. Reprinted with permission of William Reusch. www. cem.msu.ed u/~reusch/VirtualT ext/Spe ctrpy/MassSpec /masspec1.htm.

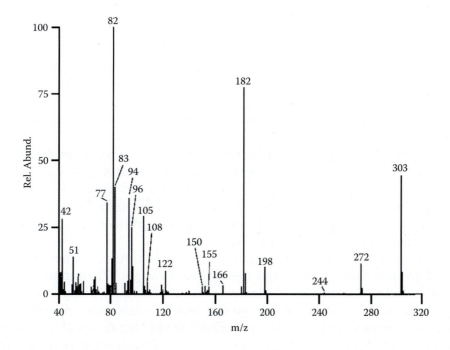

Figure 5.16 Mass spectrum of cocaine.

mentioned above, some molecules or fragments may lose two electrons. A fragment with a mass of 78 that has lost two electrons would appear at m/e 39 (78/2).

Certain ions have special significance in a mass spectrum. The ion that represents the original molecule without any fragmentation is called the **parent peak**. The mass of this ion is the molecular weight of the substance. Knowing the molecular weight can be very important in identifying unknown materials. The fragment that is most stable and has the highest abundance is called the **base peak**. In the mass spectrum of cocaine in Figure 5.16, the base peak of cocaine is 82 and the parent peak is at 303.

There are a large number of modifications of the basic mass spectrometer in use today. There are different types of sources, methods of ionization, sample chambers, and focusing systems. For example, instead of an electron beam as the source of energy, a variable energy laser beam can be used. The beam can be focused on the sample, which can be a solid or vapor. The laser ionizes the molecules in the sample, but does not contain enough energy to cause fragmentation. The only ion that is seen in the mass spectrum is the parent peak, making it easy to determine the molecular weight of an unknown substance. This type of mass spectrometry is called **laser desorption mass spectrometry (LDMS)**. Sometimes it is difficult to transfer the energy from the laser directly to the sample, so the sample is embedded in a conducting matrix that accepts energy from the laser and transfers it to the sample. This type of mass spectrometry is called **matrix-assisted laser** desorption/ionization (MALDI). LDMS and MALDI have been used on a number of types of evidence, most recently on inks. LDMS spectra of ink on paper can be generated directly, without removing the ink first.

Summary

Light has the unique characteristic of presenting as an electromagnetic wave or as a particle. Light waves are transverse waves consisting of oscillations of electric and magnetic fields that travel through space. Light as a particle is a packet of energy called a photon. Waves can be described by their frequency (the number of waves that pass by each second) or by wavelength, the distance between the same points on two adjacent waves. The energy associated with a photon of light is dependent on its frequency; the higher the frequency, the more energy. Light waves are arranged into the electromagnetic spectrum. Each region of the spectrum contains waves that have different effects on matter.

The interactions of light and matter are measured using a spectrophotometer. This instrument consists of a light source, a monochromator that selects the wavelengths of light that reach the sample, the sample compartment, a detector for determining which wavelengths of light were transmitted through the sample and a data processor that collects information about the wavelengths of light and the amount of light absorbed and transmitted by the sample.

The areas of the electromagnetic spectrum of most interest to forensic scientists are the ultraviolet/visible range and the infrared range. When matter is exposed to UV/visible light, it promotes electrons to higher orbitals. These spectra tend to be broad with only one or two major peaks. Not all substances absorb UV/visible light. Organic compounds that have conjugated double bonds are the most active in this region. Visible light is a narrow region of the UV/visible spectrum whose wavelengths of light can be seen by the human eye as color.

The infrared region causes the bonds between atoms in all substances to vibrate. There are several different types of vibrations that can take place in a chemical bond. Infrared spectra are so complex that the spectrum for each chemical substance is unique.

Mass spectrometry uses a beam of electrons to interact with light. The electrons cause the substance to lose one or sometimes two of its own electrons, forming a positive ion. This ion may undergo degradation to smaller ions. The ions are separated and detected by the mass spectrometer and displayed as a series of peaks of increasing mass-to-charge ratio. The mass spectrum for a pure substance is reproducible and unique to that substance.

Test Yourself

Multiple Choice

1. The velocity of light in a vacuum or air is approximately:
   a. 3×10^{10} meters per second
   b. 3×10^{8} meters per second
   c. 186,000 meters per second
   d. 186,000 miles per minute
2. The number of light waves that pass a point in one second is called its:
   a. Frequency
   b. Wavelength
   c. Period
   d. Quantum
3. As the frequency of light increases:
   a. Its energy increases
   b. Its wavelength increases
   c. Planck's constant increases
   d. Its energy decreases
4. Planck's constant:
   a. Is a measure of the speed of light in frequency units
   b. Is a measure of wavelength
   c. Relates the energy of a photon of light to its frequency
   d. Varies with the medium that the light is passing through
5. The part of the spectrophotometer that selects the wavelength of light that reaches the sample is:
   a. The Nernst glower
   b. The monochromator
   c. The photocell
   d. The thermocouple
6. If a spectrophotometer has a photocell detector and a xenon lamp source it is a
   a. Mass spectrometer:
   b. An infrared spectrophotometer
   c. A microwave instrument
   d. A UV/visible spectrophotometer
7. The type of spectrometry that measures the energy that is absorbed by molecules that causes bond vibrations is:

    a. UV/visible

    b. Infrared

    c. Mass

    d. X-ray

8. The type of spectrometry that uses electrons to bombard a sample is:

    a. Scanning electron microscopy

    b. Mass spectrometry

    c. Infrared spectrophotometry

    d. Microwave spectrometry

9. The parent peak in a mass spectrum refers to:

    a. A substance used to calibrate the instrument

    b. The most abundant ion

    c. An ion that has lost two electrons

    d. The molecular ion

10. The _____ spectrum is so complex it is considered to be unique:

    a. Visible

    b. Ultraviolet

    c. Infrared

    d. Microwave

11. Light has a "dual nature" which means that it can act as both:

    a. A transverse and longitudinal wave

    b. A wave and a particle

    c. A photon and a quanta

    d. An electric wave and a magnetic wave

12. The period of a wave is:

    a. The number of waves passing a point in a second

    b. The number of waves passing a point in a meter

    c. The time it takes for one complete wave to pass a point

    d. The distance it takes for one complete wave to pass a point

13. A photon is:

    a. An electromagnetic wave

    b. An object that splits light into its component colors

    c. The time for a complete wave

    d. A discrete packet of energy

14. As the wavelength of radiation increases, its energy:

    a. Increases

    b. Decreases

    c. Stays the same

15. All forms of radiation in the electromagnetic spectrum have what in common?

    a. Wavelength

    b. Frequency

    c. Period

    d. Velocity

Short Answer

16. Explain what happens to the electrons in an atom when they absorb a photon of energy.

17. Sketch the basic structure of the spectrophotometer.
18. Determine the wavelength of the transverse wave below.

Height (m)

1.0   2.0   3.0

Displacement (m)

Problem Solving

19. a. Green light has a wavelength of 510 nm. What is the frequency of the light?
    b. One possible frequency of x-rays is 3×10^{18} Hz. What is the wavelength of this x-ray?
20. a. Calculate the energy content in each of the radiation sources in problem 19.
    b. Another electromagnetic wave has an energy of 1.98×10^{-17} joules. Find the wavelength.
    c. What type of EM wave is this?

Further Reading

Skoog, D. A., F. J. Holler, and T. A. Nieman. *Principles of Instrumental Analysis*. 5th ed. Brooks Cole, 1997.
Humecki, H. J. ed. *Practical Guide to Infrared Microspectroscopy*. New York: Marcel Dekker, 1995.
Perkampus, H. H. and H. C. Griter. *UV-Vis Spectroscopy and Its Applications*. New York: Springer, 1992.

On the Web

For background on the dual nature of light: http://nobelprize.org/nobel_prizes/physics/articles/ekspong/index.html
Infrared radiation: www.gemini.edu/public/infrared.html
Plank's Constant and the Energy of a Photon: www.color ado.edu/ph ysics/2000/quantum-zone/photoe lectric2.html
Ultraviolet radiation: www.biospherical.com/nsf/student/page3.html

6
Microscopy

Learning Objectives

1. To be able to describe the light path through a simple lens
2. To be able to define a compound microscope and describe the light path through it
3. To be able to name the parts of a compound microscope
4. To be able to describe how a comparison microscope is constructed
5. To be able describe how a stereo microscope is constructed
6. To be able to define plane polarized light
7. To be able to describe how a polarized light microscope works
8. To be able to describe how a scanning electron microscope works
9. To be able to define and describe energy dispersive x-ray analysis

Chapter 6
Microscopy

Mini Glossary

Analyzer: A removable polarizer in a microscope that has a fixed plane of polarization.

Anisotropic: The property of matter whereby it reacts differently to light, depending on the direction the light strikes the specimen.

Backscattered electrons: Electrons form the primary beam that are reflected off the surface of a specimen in an electron microscope.

Binocular: A microscope with two ocular lenses.

Body (viewing) tube: The part of the compound microscope that holds the ocular and objective lenses.

Comparison bridge: A device in a comparison microscope that uses mirrors to focus light from two stages to oculars that are next to each other.

Comparison microscope: Two compound microscopes that are connected with a comparison bridge that enables the observer to view two objects at the same time, one with each eye.

Compound microscope: A microscope consisting of two convex lenses. The first magnifies the object, creating a virtual image, and the second magnifies this image to yield a further magnified image. The total magnification is the product of the magnification of each lens.

Condenser: A lens that focuses light from the illuminator to the specimen.

Depth of focus: A measure of how far inside the object the image will be in focus.

Diaphragm: A device in a microscope that eliminates extraneous light from the illuminator.

Electron microscopy: A type of high-resolution microscopy that uses a beam of electrons to magnify a specimen. The electron microscope is capable of magnifying an object more than 200,000 times.

Eyepiece (ocular): A convex lens placed at the top of the body tube of the microscope. The observer looks through the ocular at the object.

Field diaphragm: A device in a microscope that controls the intensity of light that reaches the specimen.

Field of view: The area of a specimen that is in view at any one time.

Focal length: There are points on each side of a lens where an object would be in exact focus. The distance between these two points is the focal length of that lens.

Isotropic: The property of matter whereby it reacts the same way no matter what direction light that strikes it is coming from.

Microspectrophotometry: A combination of a microscope and a spectrophotometer that permits the analysis of microscopic specimens.

Monocular: A microscope with a single ocular lens.

Objective lens: The second lens, located at the bottom of the body tube, usually on a turret, which contains several lenses of varying magnification.

Polarized light: Light that passes through a special filter that allows only light in a single plane to pass through.

Reflected light microscopy: A type of microscopy in which light is reflected from the surface of an opaque object and then passes through the lenses to the observer's eye.

Refraction: Bending and slowing of a light beam as it passes through a transparent medium. All transparent gases, liquids, and solids refract light.

Resolution: The ability of the human eye to see two closely spaced objects. It is the minimum distance between two objects at which they may still be seen as two distinct objects.

Scanning electron microscopy: A type of electron microscopy where electrons reflect from the surface of a specimen and are captured and magnify the specimen.

Secondary electrons: Electrons emitted by a specimen in an electron microscope when it is bombarded by a beam of primary electrons.

Simple magnifier: A device that employs a single convex lens to magnify an object.

Spectrophotometer: An instrument used to measure the interaction of light and matter.

Spectroscopy: The interaction of light and matter.

Stage: The platform on which the specimen is viewed.

Stereo microscope: A microscope made with two objective lenses that focus in slightly different places on the specimen so that the observer can see the specimen in three dimensions.

Transmission electron microscopy: A type of electron microscopy that uses thin sections of specimens that the electron beam can penetrate.

Transmission light microscopy: A type of microscopy where light passes through a transparent specimen to the observer's eye.

Trinocular: A microscope with two ocular lenses and a holder for a camera that can see what the observer sees under the microscope.

Virtual image: An image created by a convex lens on the other side of the lens from the observer. It is not a real image and a screen placed on that side of the lens will not show the image.

Working distance: The distance between the objective lens and the stage.

Energy dispersive x-ray analysis: Identification of a chemical element by the characteristic x-rays it emits when it is bombarded with a beam of electrons in an electron microscope.

Acronyms

EDX: Energy dispersive x-ray analysis
EM: Electron microscope
PLM: Polarized light microscope
SEM: Scanning electron microscopy
x: The amount of magnification of an image; 10x = ten times magnification.

Introduction

If there is such a thing as a universal instrument of science, it is the microscope, or perhaps we should say "microscopes," because there are many different kinds. Microscopes are so versatile that they have become indispensable in all types of scientific and technical laboratories; medical, environmental, pharmaceutical, geological and, of course, forensic science. Practically every forensic science lab in the world has at least one and usually several microscopes. Practically all types of forensic evidence are analyzed by at least one type of microscope. The reasons for the popularity of microscopes in a crime laboratory are numerous:

1. Sample preparation is often minimal. Usually the object of interest is placed under the microscope without preparation beyond using a microscope slide and cover slip. Sometimes thin sections of a material may be prepared or the object may be immersed in a liquid of particular refractive index to improve viewing, but that is usually the extent of preparation.
2. Microscopes can be used for separation and identification. A material of interest such as explosive residue may be mixed with debris such as that from an explosion. Individual particles of explosive can be picked out and physically separated and sometimes identified by their overall appearance and crystal structure.
3. In the majority of cases, microscopy is nondestructive. Little or no material is consumed during analysis by microscopy. This is very important in forensic science where the evidence often consists solely of a few particles of a material. If it is consumed during analysis, there is no way that re-analysis can take place or further work can be done on it. Microscopy can divulge much information about a substance without consuming it.

4. Microscopy is versatile. There are microscopes that magnify an object only a few times while the operator manipulates it in three-dimensional space, thus revealing important information about its surface characteristics. There are also microscopes that can magnify an object more than 200,000 times and, at the same time, determine its elemental composition. Some microscopes can magnify images while comparing two objects side-by-side and are equipped with high-resolution cameras that can photograph what the operator sees. Lenses, filters, and polarizers permit viewing of an object under various light conditions, thus increasing the amount of information available about it.

5. Microscopes can be combined with other analytical instruments such as spectrophotometers (Chapter 5) to extend the instrument's capabilities. For example, an infrared microspectrophotometer can isolate and magnify a single fiber and then collect its infrared spectrum.

In this chapter, we explore the roles that microscopy plays in forensic science. We will look at everything from a simple hand magnifier that magnifies an object two or three times to an electron microscope that is capable of magnifying an object more than 200,000 times. We will see how basic microscopes can be modified to compare two objects or illuminate them with polarized light or magnify an object in three dimensions.

Types of Microscopes

Microscopes are usually differentiated by the amount of useful magnification they can provide without distorting the appearance of an object. Several of the most useful microscopes in a forensic science laboratory are based on the compound microscope. Most of this chapter will be devoted to the compound microscope and its modifications. Compound microscopes normally can be used to magnify an object from about 40 to 1,000 times. Simple microscopes can be used to magnify an object 4 to 20 times. At the other end of the scale, electron microscopy can magnify an object more than 200,000 times.

Forensic Microscopy

Because of the versatility of microscopes, one type or another is used on nearly every kind of scientific evidence. In some types of evidence or some cases where evidence is limited, most or all of the analysis is done by microscopy. In the hands of a skilled microscopist, many objects and materials can be completely identified by using a microscope and no other analysis is needed. In most situations, however, microscopy is teamed with other techniques of analysis. For example, a microscope may be used to perform preliminary screening or analysis to learn about the general features, size distribution, purity, color, or other characteristics of the evidence at hand. Table 6.1 presents some of the common types of forensic evidence and the types of microscopes employed in their analysis. The last column indicates whether the microscope is the main tool for analysis or is used as part of a team of instruments or techniques.

TABLE 6.1
**Common Types of Forensic Evidence and Types of Microscopes
Employed in Their Analysis**

Type of Evidence	Type(s) of Microscopes	Level of Use
Bullets and cartridges	Comparison	Principal
Drugs	Stereo, simple compound	Ancillary
Dust	Basic compound, polarizing	Principal
Fibers	Basic compound, polarizing, microspectrophotemeter	Ancillary
Fingerprints	Magnifying glass	Principal
Glass	Basic compound	Principal
Hair	Basic compound	Principal
Paint	Basic compound, microspectrophotometer	Ancillary
Soil	Magnifying glass	Principal
Serology	Magnifying glass, basic compound	Principal
Tool marks	Magnifying glass, comparison	Principal
Gunshot residue	Scanning electron microscopy	Principal
Paint fragments, other microscopic particles	Scanning electron microscopy	Ancillary

The Lens: How Objects Are Magnified

Simple Magnifiers

A lens is usually a round, curved object made of glass or another transparent material. Glass lenses are the highest quality. For most microscopes, the lenses are convex. It is wide in the middle and then tapers around the edges. Convex lenses focus light that reaches it to a point on the other side of the lens. The bending of light by a lens is called refraction. A single lens can be used as a simple magnifier. If you take a magnifying glass and focus it on an object, you see an enlarged view of the object. The light rays from the object to the eye form a virtual image further away from the lens. This is called a virtual image because it is not real. If you held a white screen up in the plane where the image would be, it wouldn't show up on the screen. The formation of a virtual image by a simple convex lens is shown in Figure 6.1.

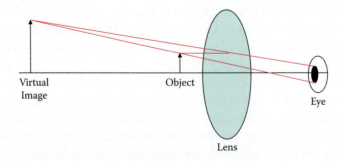

Virtual Image   Object   Eye   Lens

Figure 6.1 A simple convex lens. As light passes through the lens, it is refracted (bent) and forms an inverted, virtual image on the other side of the lens that is magnified according to the size and degree of curvature of the lens.

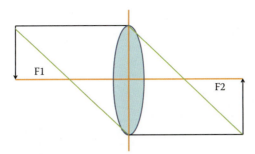

Figure 6.2 The focal length of a lens is the distance between two in-focus images on either side of the lens.

The size and shape of the lens determine the amount of magnification it can achieve. The main factor is the focal length of the lens. There are points on each side of a lens where an object would be in exact focus. The distance between these two points is the focal length of that lens. This is shown in Figure 6.2.

Another important characteristic of lens optics is resolution—the ability of the human eye to see two closely spaced objects. It is the minimum distance between two objects that can still be seen as two distinct objects. The human eye can distinguish two objects next to each other easily from a distance of about ten inches. At this distance, two objects can be separated by about twenty millimeters. If we want to see more detail in an object with better resolution, we need to magnify the object. As magnification increases, the light passing through the lens must be increasingly refracted. In order to do this, the lens diameter must decrease. If we want to magnify an object 100 times, we would need a simple lens about a half inch in diameter. This limits the practical magnifications of simple hand lenses to about 15×.

Compound Magnifiers

As explained above, the geometry of a simple lens limits its magnification. It is often necessary or desirable to magnify an object 100 times or more. This can be accomplished by using a **compound magnifier**. This employs two simple lenses arranged in a line. The first lens magnifies the object as shown in Figure 6.1. The other lens is placed at the location of the virtual image produced by the first lens. The virtual image is magnified by the second lens, producing a real image whose total magnification is the product of the magnification of each lens. Thus, if the first lens magnifies the object 10 times and the second lens magnifies it 20 times, the total magnification is 200 times. Figure 6.3 shows how two convex lenses magnify an object. It is normally possible to use 40× lenses in a compound magnification system for a total of 1,600×. With specialized lenses, it is possible to go even higher, but there are limits. As the magnification increases, the resolution of the system also increases. At some point, however, there will no longer be an increase in resolution with continued magnification. This empty magnification results in increasingly fuzzy images.

The Compound Microscope

The design of the basic compound microscope has been remarkably stable since it was invented over a hundred years ago. There have been improvements in virtually

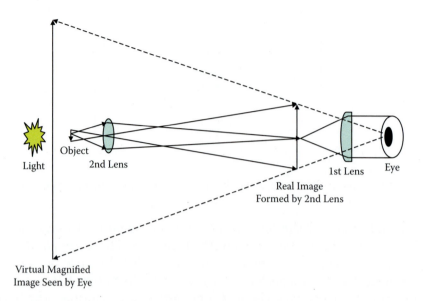

Light

Object
2nd Lens

1st Lens   Eye

Real Image
Formed by 2nd Lens

Virtual Magnified
Image Seen by Eye

Figure 6.3 Compound lenses. Two convex lenses will magnify an object equal to the product of the magnification of each lens. The first lens magnifies the object, creating a virtual image. The second lens is placed so that magnifies this image, creating a real image.

every part of the instrument so that even an inexpensive model can be suitable for many applications. A compound microscope basically consists of two convex lenses, a stage to mount the object, a system to project light through the lenses, and a system for focusing objects. Refer to Figure 6.4 as the various parts of a compound microscope are described.

At the top of the microscope, you look through the first convex lens—the **eyepiece** or **ocular**. If there is one eyepiece, it is referred to as **monocular**. In many microscopes, there are two identical eyepieces, one for each eye; both show the same field of view. This is called a **binocular** eyepiece. Increasingly, microscopes are even **trinocular**; there are the two ocular lenses and a tube for a video camera that can project an image into a computer where it can be viewed, printed, and saved. Most ocular lenses have 10× magnification. In binocular instruments, one or both of the oculars may be focusable independently to compensate for differences in vision in each eye. Oculars can be outfitted with fine cross hair lines so that an object can be centered in the field of view. Sometimes a measuring scale can be etched into an ocular. This can be used, along with a calibration slide, to accurately measure the size of an object. The ocular is at the top of the viewing tube. This tube contains both lenses.

Below the ocular, at the bottom of the viewing tube is the other convex lens, the **objective** lens (or just, objective), so called because of its proximity to the object. Most microscopes today have several objective lenses (e.g., 4×, 10×, 20×) mounted on a turret that can be turned, thus swinging a particular objective into place. Objective lenses have many special characteristics and may be chosen for particular applications. Their characteristics are etched into the body of the lens.

The **stage** of the microscope is a horizontal surface where the sample is mounted. It has a hole in the center where light emanating from beneath is passed through the sample. In some microscopes, the stage is circular and rotates 360 degrees. In other microscopes, the stage is fixed. There may be special holders or clips for microscope slides on the stage. The object to be viewed is mounted on the stage. Most often, the object is put on a microscope slide and held there with a cover slip.

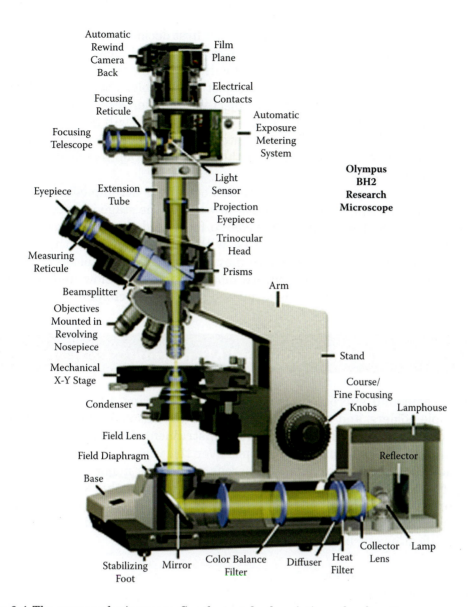

Figure 6.4 The compound microscope. See the text for descriptions of each part.

Stages can be rotated or moved up and down or left and right to center the object in the field of view. There are two types of illumination systems. If the object is thin and transparent, **transmitted light** microscopy is used. The light shines up from below the object and the light source is located underneath the stage. Light passes through the hole in the stage onto the object.

Between the light source and the stage is a **condenser**. This is a lens that focuses and condenses the light onto the object. It has its own **diaphragm** that is used to eliminate extraneous light. The microscope may also have a **field diaphragm,** which controls the intensity of light that reaches the object. Some microscopes magnify opaque objects such as bullets or cartridges. Light cannot pass through these objects, so light sources mounted beneath the object will not be of much use. Instead, **reflected light microscopy** is used. In this microscope, the light source is external and is aimed at the object from the top or the side. The light reflects off the surface of the object and then passes through the objective and ocular lenses. This concept is discussed later in this chapter in the section on comparison microscopes.

When viewing an object the examiner must first decide how much of it should be in view at one time. This is the **field of view**. The field of view is inversely proportional to the magnification. A microscopist will usually mount at object at low power magnification to survey as much of the object as possible. Then magnification can be increased to focus on one part of the object with higher resolution. The **depth of focus** is a measure of how far inside the object the image will be in focus. This can be useful when a transparent object is heterogeneous and the analyst wants to be able to see the different parts in focus at the same time. Depth of focus increases as magnification decreases.

Every microscope has a focusing system. Focusing is accomplished in one of two ways. Either the viewing tube is raised or lowered or the stage is raised or lowered. Two focusing knobs are used; one for coarse focus and the other for finer adjustments. Microscopes can also be outfitted with many accessories that help tailor them for particular applications. There may be light filters, interference filters, or most importantly, polarizers, which are mounted usually below and/or above the stage. Polarized light microscopy is discussed later in this chapter.

Modifications of the Compound Microscope

The basic compound microscope is very versatile, offering a variety of magnifications, sample holders, and types of illumination, and has achieved great popularity in forensic analysis. It is also a very flexible instrument. A number of modifications have been made to compound microscopes over the years to extend their capabilities. Some of these are quite simple whereas others are major overhauls that can multiply the cost of the microscope several times over. In this section, we discuss four major types of modifications of the basic compound microscope described above that extend its utility greatly, making it useful for most types of forensic evidence. These modifications include:

- Comparison microscope
- Stereo microscope
- Polarized light microscope
- Microspectrophotometer

The Comparison Microscope

Consider the following forensic situation: You have received two bullets (or two human hairs or two fibers) that you must compare microscopically. You have one compound microscope at your disposal, modified so it can use reflected light for the bullets as needed. How could you use this microscope to compare two similar objects to see whether they have the same or different microscopic characteristics? In some cases, you could mount both objects on the same slide, but then you cannot manipulate them separately—and you cannot do this with bullets. You could view one object at a time and try to remember or draw the characteristics you see, but that would be far from useful. If you had a binocular or trinocular instrument, you could mount a camera and take pictures of each object and compare the pictures. Unfortunately, no picture has the resolution of the human eye and some data is bound to be lost.

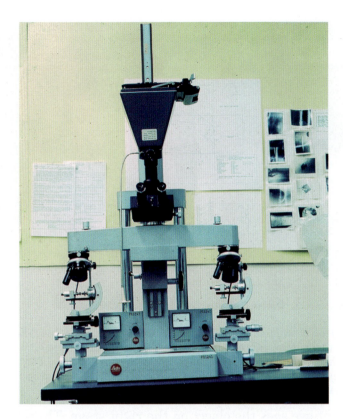

Figure 6.5 The comparison microscope. Specimens are mounted on each stage. The comparison bridge near the top directs each image to a separate ocular lens. Both specimens can be seen simultaneously, one with each eye.

Clearly, the best solution to the problem would be to be able to see both objects under the microscope at the same time and be able to manipulate them independently—and then even photograph the comparison. A compound microscope can be modified to accomplish this. Actually this requires two compound microscopes. The result is a comparison microscope. These microscopes are universally employed in crime laboratories for the analysis of bullets and cartridges and widely used for the comparison of hairs, fibers, glass, tears, and fractures.

The comparison microscope consists of two compound microscopes that are connected with a comparison bridge. A picture of a typical comparison microscope is shown in Figure 6.5.

There are two separate microscope bodies, each with its own stage and objective lenses. Some have transmitted light sources with all of the accompanying optics, including condensers and field diaphragms. Others have external light sources on each stage for reflected light microscopy. Some comparison microscopes have both transmitted and reflected light sources. Instead of oculars at the top of each microscope, the two viewing tubes are connected by a **comparison bridge** that culminates in a binocular or trinocular eyepiece. See Figure 6.6 for a photomicrograph of two cut wires.

The comparison bridge consists of a closed tube containing two sets of identical mirrors that direct the light from the objective lenses toward the center of the bridge. Additional mirrors then direct the light from each microscope up to a monocular eyepiece. The two eyepieces are mounted next to each other so that the examiner can look through them at the same time. The left eye sees the object on the left

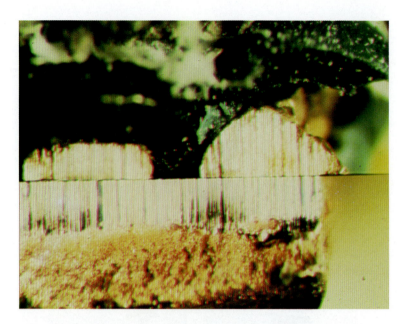

Figure 6.6 Comparison of two tool marks under a comparison microscope. The image at the bottom is a piece of metal cut by a large pair of wire cutters. The image at the top is two wires from a bundle of telephone cables that were alleged to have been cut by the wire cutters. The wire on the right is an excellent match from the wire cutters. The wire on the left is not lined up correctly with the part of the metal that was cut by the same part of the wire cutter blade.

stage and the right eye sees the object on the right stage. There is a line down the middle of the images from top to bottom that indicates how much of the combined image is from the left microscope and how much from the right. The comparison bridge mirrors can be manipulated so that only one of the two images is in view. Also, the two images can be overlaid one on top of the other. Virtually all modern comparison microscopes have a camera mounted on the eyepiece to capture the compared images. Figure 6.7 shows a photomicrograph of the stria (horizontal markings on the surface of bullets made by the inside of the barrel) on two bullets under a comparison microscope.

In addition to the standard flat stage, many comparison microscopes have specialized sample holders for objects such as bullets and cartridges. A bullet holder is shown in Figure 6.8.

Figure 6.7 Photomicrograph of markings on the sides of two bullets fired from same weapon. Note the vertical line in the middle of the picture. This demarks the field of view seen by each eye. The markings on the two bullets can be easily compared this way.

Figure 6.8 A bullet holder that fits on the stage of a comparison microscope. This type of holder permits manipulation of the bullet in all directions and, in addition, allows it to be rotated on its long axis. *Courtesy of* Leeds Forensic Systems, Inc.

The Stereo Microscope

As we have seen so far, hand magnifiers are used on flat objects and can magnify them up to about 15×. Basic compound microscopes can magnify images over 1,000 times but need transmitted light for high magnifications. Reflected light can be used on opaque objects with lower magnifications, but only surface characteristics can be examined. Sometimes a laboratory receives evidence that is three dimensional in nature. It is necessary to magnify and view all sides of the evidence and be able to manipulate the evidence while viewing it. In such cases, low magnification is required, usually 25 to 50×. For such applications, the stereo microscope was developed. Stereo microscopes are always binocular, usually have several objective lenses of varying magnification, and a long **working distance**, the space between the stage and the objective lens. In a stereo microscope, the stage is below the objective lens and in some models, there is no stage; the object is placed on the table. Working distances are often 6 to 12 inches. Another important point: because of the optics involved, compound microscopes always invert the object, but the stereoscope contains additional optics that orient the object as it is without the microscope, making manipulation easier.

A basic stereo microscope is shown in Figure 6.9. Notice that there is no stage in this model. The illumination source is a ring of light surrounding the objective and pointing down toward the table surface.

The light path through the microscope is shown in Figure 6.10. The stereo microscope consists of two monocular, compound microscopes mounted side by side and aligned so that the objective lenses are slightly offset so that they view slightly different parts of the object, resulting in a three-dimensional appearance. Today, many stereo microscopes have a trinocular head that permits the addition of a real time digital video camera that allows the examiner to view the object on a computer screen. The image can then be manipulated and enhanced and photographed.

As you might expect, there are many applications of stereo microscopy in forensic science. One common use is in the analysis of marijuana. The leaves and seeds of the plant have characteristic shapes and appearances. There are two different types of hairs on the top and bottom surfaces of the leaves. One of the major examinations of marijuana consists of viewing the various structures on the leaves and the appearance of the seeds under the stereo microscope at about 25× magnification. A photograph of marijuana leaves under a stereo microscope is shown in Figure 6.11.

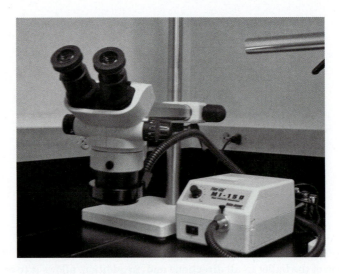

Figure 6.9 A stereo microscope. Note the absence of a stage. Specimens are mounted directly on the table. Light is supplied by a light ring below the objective lens.

Figure 6.10 The light path through a stereo microscope. Note that the two light paths converge slightly away from each other, thus creating the three-dimensional image.

The Polarized Light Microscope (PLM)

With some relatively minor modifications, a compound microscope can have polarized light capabilities. The PLM is easily the most powerful tool in the forensic science lab. Unfortunately many, if not most forensic scientists rely heavily on computerized instrumentation and do not take the time or effort needed to learn how to use this powerful tool. One can discover details about the structure of materials and their surface characteristics that can lead to identification.

With respect to optical properties, there are two types of materials. The first consists of substances such as gases, liquids, and some solids whose structure is

Figure 6.11 Marijuana leaf material under a stereo microscope at 40× magnification.

such that they react to light the same way no matter what direction it comes from or how it strikes the material. Such materials are designated **isotropic**. The other type of material, which includes most solids, reacts to light differently depending on its orientation and direction. These are designated **anisotropic**. Consider corduroy pants. The fabric has ribs that are aligned in one direction. The structure of many solids is such that they have a kind of alignment and they will react differently to light that is in the direction of the alignment than to light that is 90 degrees away from the alignment. When light is emitted from a source, it travels in waves that can be aligned in any direction. A polarizer is a kind of light filter. It blocks out all light except that which is traveling in a single plane, the one aligned with the **polarizer**. This is called **polarized light**. This can be seen in Figure 6.12.

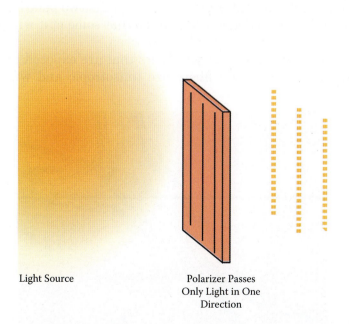

Light Source   Polarizer Passes
                                Only Light in One
                                   Direction

Figure 6.12 How light is polarized. Light normally travels in waves in all directions and planes. A polarizer is a filter that blocks out all light except that which is traveling in one particular plane. *Courtesy of* Meredith Haddon.

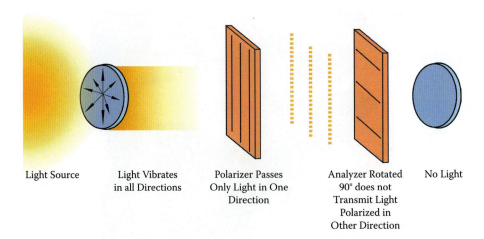

Light Source   Light Vibrates   Polarizer Passes   Analyzer Rotated   No Light
                    in all Directions   Only Light in One   90° does not
                                          Direction   Transmit Light
                                                                  Polarized in
                                                                  Other Direction

Figure 6.13 Crossed polarizers. If the two polarizers are oriented 90° from each other then no light will emerge from the second one. *Courtesy of* Meredith Haddon.

Anisotropic materials have a preferred directionality to their structure. Polarized light will have different optical effects on these substances, depending on how the light is aligned with the preferred direction. A PLM contains two polarizers. One, aptly called the polarizer, is located below the stage and is aligned east–west, so that the only light that gets through is aligned east–west. When it strikes the object on the stage, it will react in some way by showing a particular color. If the object is rotated, it will show a different color if it is anisotropic. The other polarizer is located above the stage. It is oriented north–south, the opposite of the orientation of the polarizer. It is called the **analyzer**. If east–west light from the polarizer tries to pass through the analyzer, none will get through. This is shown in Figure 6.13.

If an isotropic material is placed between the crossed polarizers, no light should emerge through the analyzer because the material doesn't affect the light at all. If, however, an anisotropic material is placed between the two polarizers, the material will slightly change the direction of the light so that some of it will get through the analyzer and the image of the material will be seen.

Figure 6.14 shows some white acrylic fibers that are exposed to polarized light. Because of their structure, many fibers are anisotropic and will show different

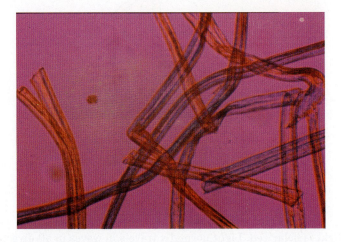

Figure 6.14 White acrylic fibers under polarized light. The orange and blue interference colors are due to the different interactions of the fibers owing to their orientation toward the polarized light.

colors, depending on the alignment of the polarized light. Some of the fibers in this figure appear blue while others are orange. This is due to the way they are aligned relative to the polarized light.

Microspectrophotometry

As we have seen in the discussion of polarized light above, it is clear that certain materials will react when exposed to some types of light. Light may be absorbed or reflected by the material. When light is absorbed by a transparent material, some of it may pass through, some may be scattered, and some may be affected to the extent that it changes wavelength. The behavior of light and its measurement when it interacts with matter is called **spectroscopy** and the measuring instrument is called a **spectrophotometer**. This is discussed in detail in Chapter 5. It is pretty easy to measure the effects of matter on light when there is a relatively large quantity of matter. In forensic science, however, we often receive only very small amounts of material such as a single fiber or tiny paint chip. We would like to know the exact color of a fiber and whether two fibers are exactly the same color, for example, but conventional spectroscopy cannot be performed because of the small amount of material available. To solve this problem, forensic scientists employ a **microspectrophotometer**, a marriage between a microscope and a spectrophotometer. In microspectrophotometry, a sample such as a fiber is mounted under a microscope. After the light passes through the sample and the image is magnified, it is sent to the spectrophotometer for analysis. Any transparent object that can be suitably magnified by the microscope is a candidate for microspectrophotometry.

There are two types of microspectrophotometers. One type is essentially a microscope where the light source may be ultraviolet, visible or infrared light. This passes through the sample, which is mounted on the microscope stage. After passing through the lenses, the light is channeled to a detector, as it is in a conventional spectrophotometer. A picture of a UV-visible–near-infrared microspectrophotometer is shown in Figure 6.15.

The size of the light beam that reaches the sample can be controlled either manually through an iris diaphragm or electronically through a computer. The size of the spot of light is seen as a "cursor" under the microscope or on a computer screen. The light cursor can be moved around the object to obtain a spectrum of a particular part. In some cases, the amount of sample within the cursor is controlled by changing the objective lens to increase or decrease magnification. In other cases, the size and shape of the cursor can be controlled from the computer. It is necessary to properly adjust the cursor because a correct spectrum can only be obtained if all of the light that reaches the detector has passed through the object. No stray light should reach the detector. A picture of pieces of cosmetic glitter under the microscope in Figure 6.15 is shown in Figure 6.16.

The other type of microspectrophotometer is shown in Figure 6.17. This is essentially a conventional infrared spectrophotometer that has a microscope mounted as an accessory. Under the control of a computer, the light from the spectrophotometer can be redirected so that it passes through the microscope where it interacts with the object mounted on the stage. In the instrument pictured in Figure 6.17 there is no ocular on the microscope. There is instead a digital camera connected to the computer. The magnified object is shown on the computer screen. The movement of the stage is controlled by a mechanical joystick.

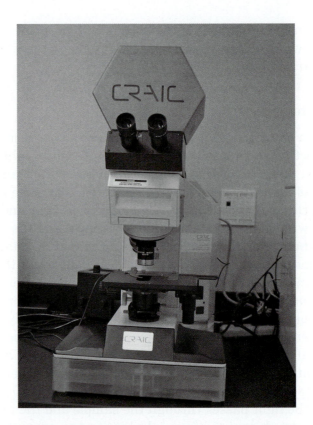

Figure 6.15 A microspectrophotometer. The large box on top of the microscope is the detector. Ultraviolet, visible, and near infrared light can be used as the light source.

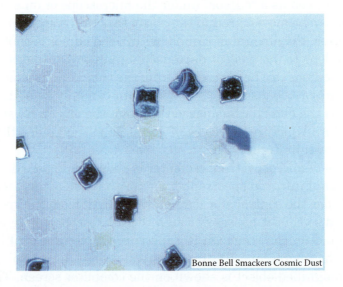

Figure 6.16 Cosmetic glitter particles under a microspectrophotometer.

Figure 6.17 An infrared microspectrophotometer. The infrared spectrophotometer is on the right side of the picture. This is connected by a light pipe to the microscope on the left. The infrared light travels from the bench, through the microscope and then to a detector mounted inside the microscope. There is no ocular lens. Instead, a video camera captures the images and sends them to a computer. The stage is controlled by a joystick.

Whether the microspectrophotometer is a modified microscope or a modified spectrophotometer is a matter of manufacturing choice. The same type of instrument (ultraviolet or infrared) can be configured either way.

Electron Microscopy

All of the compound microscopes discussed thus far suffer from the same limitation: they can achieve a maximum magnification of about 1,600 power. At magnifications over about 400 power, the object and objective lens must usually be immersed in a special liquid to alter the refractive index so that the object can be viewed clearly. This magnification limitation is due to the need to increase the curvature and decrease the size of the lens so much that it causes distortion of the light above these values. There is also a limit to the amount of resolution that can be obtained from this optical system of magnification.

In forensic science, however, there are many instances when it is necessary to magnify images higher than the maximum of a light microscope. An instrument that could accomplish this would have to use a magnification system other than light and lenses. The electron microscope uses electrons rather than light to magnify images. There are no lenses involved, so distortion of light is not an issue. Magnifications exceeding 200,000 times are easily achievable.

There are two types of electron microscope. If an image is made thin enough, then a beam of electrons can pass through a material and interact with it. This is called **transmission electron microscopy**. This type of electron microscopy is not commonly used in forensic science since most of the forensic applications require relatively thick particles that the electrons cannot pass through. The other type of electron microscopy is called scanning electron microscopy and the measuring instrument is called the scanning electron microscopy (SEM). An SEM can magnify an image from 10 to more than 200,000 times. A photograph of an SEM is shown in Figure 6.18. A simplified schematic of how an SEM works is shown in Figure 6.19.

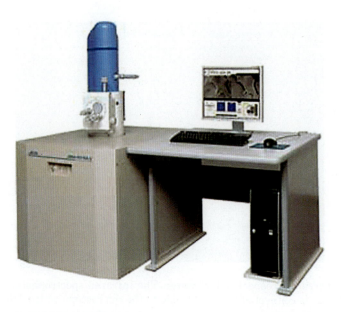

Figure 6.18 A scanning electron microscope.

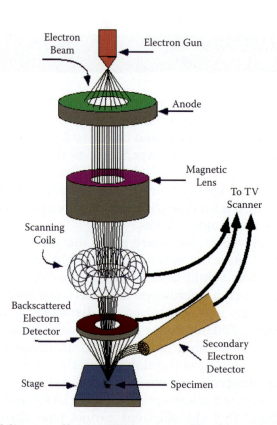

Figure 6.19 A simplified diagram of how an SEM operates. The electron gun produces electrons that are focused through a magnetic lens onto the specimen. Backscattered electrons are captured by a detector and sent to a cathode ray tube or computer screen where the object is visualized. Secondary electrons may also be captured and analyzed. *Courtesy of* Josh Klesel, Material Sciences Unit, Iowa State University.

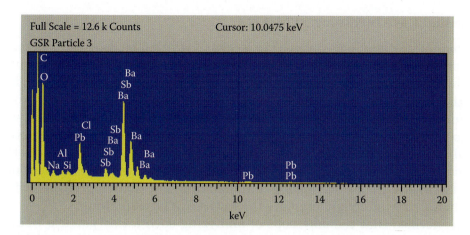

Figure 6.20 The printout from an energy dispersive x-ray analyzer focused on a particle of suspected gunshot residue. Note the presence of barium (Ba), antimony (Sb), and lead (Pb), which are characteristic of gunshot residue. C = carbon. O = oxygen. Cl = Chlorine. Al = aluminum. Na = sodium. Si = silicon.

A tiny object is usually mounted on a metal stub and put in an evacuated sample compartment. In order to get proper interactions between the electron beam and the object, it must be able to conduct electricity. A coating of carbon or gold is usually applied to the object to facilitate this. A beam of electrons is aimed at the object. Most of the electrons are absorbed by the object. Where the beam touches the object, it causes **secondary electrons** to be emitted from the chemical elements present in the object. In addition, some of the original electrons in the beam aimed at the object reflect off the surface. These are called **backscattered electrons**. Both the secondary and backscattered electrons are captured, amplified, and aimed at a cathode ray tube (CRT), which is essentially a television tube. The interior of the screen of the tube contains phosphorescent materials that glow when struck with electrons. The primary electron beam is scanned across the object and a magnified image of the object appears on the CRT.

When the beam of electrons from the SEM source strikes the material to be magnified, a great deal of energy is absorbed by the material from the beam. This causes the atoms that make up the material to be unstable and their nuclei will emit x-rays. Each chemical element has its own characteristic set of x-rays of particular frequencies. Some scanning electron microscopes have the capability of measuring these x-rays. This technique is called **energy dispersive x-ray analysis (EDX)**. An **x-ray analyzer** captures the x-rays and displays them by frequency and quantity. It also assigns element identities to each bundle of x-rays by their frequencies. For example, many samples of gunshot residue contain particles of the primer used to set off the propellant (see Chapter 9). Most common ammunition primers today contain barium, antimony, and lead. If gunshot residues are analyzed by SEM, they will emit x-rays whose frequencies are characteristic of these elements. The presence of these elements in spherical particles from suspected gunshot residue constitutes proof of the presence of a primer. Figure 6.20 shows the display from an x-ray analyzer of a suspected primer particle from gunshot residue. The presence of antimony, barium, and lead can clearly be seen.

SEM/EDX is one of the most versatile analytical methods in forensic science because it allows the microscopist to visualize and examine extremely small particles in three dimensions as well as determine the chemical compositions of many materials.

An Unusual Case Involving SEM/EDX

The author of this book was involved in a case in which a homeowner was installing a gas water heater in his home. He tried to ignite the pilot light using the automatic igniter built into the heater, but was unable to. He then lit a match to try and get the pilot light ignited and this caused an explosion. A forensic engineer was brought in to examine the remains of the water heater. He noted that an orifice that was supposed to carry gas to the pilot light assembly was partially clogged. The attorneys involved in the case wanted to know what was blocking the orifice. It was thought that, rather than a foreign material, the blockage was caused by improper machining or cleaning of the orifice during manufacture. The diameter of the orifice was approximately 20 μ, the approximate thickness of a human hair.

It was decided that the only hope of analyzing such a tiny particle would be to ream out the orifice with a fine wire while holding it over top of an SEM sample stub. This was accomplished; the particle landed on the stub and was held there by sticky tape. The particle was smaller than the size of a period (.) on this page. The stub was inserted into the SEM. The particle was clearly visible and EDX analysis indicated the presence of mostly zinc with some tin. The piece of metal that contained the orifice was made mostly of iron with some copper. Therefore, the blockage had to have come from the outside. It couldn't be a part of the metal left behind when the orifice was reamed out. The origin of the particle was never determined.

Summary

Microscopy is the most powerful tool in the analytical arsenal of forensic science. Much of the evidence received in a crime laboratory consists of microscopic particles. Microscopy enables the forensic examiner to see this evidence and in some cases, identify it without further analysis. Microscopes range from simple hand magnifiers to powerful electron microscopes. The simplest microscope is the convex lens. Two convex lenses constitute the optics of the compound microscope. The combined magnification of a multiple lens system is the product of the magnification of each lens. The compound microscope can be operated as a transmitted light system or a reflected light system. The major parts are the light source, condenser and iris diaphragm to control the light. The object sits on a movable stage. There are one or more objective lenses above the stage. They are at the bottom of the body tube. At the top is the ocular or eyepiece lens. Practically all microscopes have a coarse and a fine focus. The practical limit of magnification of a lens is measured by its numerical aperture. A microscope can magnify an image more than 1,000 times. Microscopes can operate in transmission or reflection mode. A transmission microscope is the most popular. It requires that the object magnified be transparent and thin enough to allow sufficient light through. Reflecting microscopes shine light on the surface of an opaque object and magnify it. It is useful for evidence such as bullets and cartridges.

The comparison microscope consists of two compound microscopes connected by a comparison bridge so that the examiner can see two objects at the same time, one with each eye. This permits direct observation of the microscopic characteristics of the two objects. The stereo microscope is a low power instrument that enables viewing of objects in three dimensions and allows the examiner to manipulate the object easily because of a long working distance. The polarizing light microscope has two polarizing filters that block out all light except that which propagates in a particular plane. This kind of light is useful for examining the characteristics of anisotropic substances, which behave differently, depending on how the light is aligned. Microspectrophotometers are a combination of a microscope and a spectrophotometer. These instruments allow the generation of ultraviolet, visible, or infrared spectra of a microscopic object whose size precludes analysis by conventional spectrophotometers. The scanning electron microscope uses a beam of electrons to magnify an object. The beam strikes a sample, causing it to emit secondary electrons that are captured, amplified, and displayed using a cathode ray tube. This enables magnifications of up to 200,000 times. At the same time, the elements in the object emit x-rays whose frequencies are characteristic of the elements in the object. Energy dispersive x-ray analysis displays the x-rays by frequency and determines which elements are present and in what relative concentrations.

Test Yourself

Multiple Choice

1. The ocular of a compound microscope has a magnification of 10× and the objective has a magnification of 10×. The total magnification of the microscope is:
   a. 10×
   b. 20×
   c. 100×
   d. 1,000×
2. The objective lens of a compound microscope has a numerical aperture of 0.4. The maximum useful magnification of the microscope is:
   a. 400×
   b. 1,000×
   c. 10×
   d. There is not enough information given to calculate this
3. The part of the microscope that focuses the light on an object is the:
   a. Iris diaphragm
   b. Coarse focus
   c. Condenser
   d. Body tube
4. The polarizing filter in a PLM that is located above the objective is called the:
   a. Polarizer
   b. Analyzer
   c. Abbe condenser
   d. Iris
5. A substance that reacts the same to light polarized in any direction is:
   a. An isotope
   b. Anisotropic
   c. Isotropic
   d. Divergent
6. The part of the comparison microscope that allows the examiner to view two objects simultaneously is called the:
   a. Comparator

   b. Comparison bridge
   c. Spectroscope
   d. Stage
7. A stereo microscope can best be described as:
   a. Two compound microscopes aligned so that they each see a slightly different part of an object
   b. Two compound microscopes aligned with a comparison bridge
   c. A compound microscope with two separate stages and a single ocular
   d. A compound microscope with two eyepieces and a camera mount
8. In SEM, secondary electrons:
   a. Strike the object, releasing other electrons
   b. Strike the object and then reflect off the surface
   c. Are emitted when a beam of primary electrons strikes the object
   d. Are emitted by the nucleus of the various elements when the object is struck by a beam of x-rays
9. In microscopy, resolution is a measure of:
   a. The ability of the lenses to separate two tiny details that are close together
   b. The total magnification power of the microscope
   c. The empty magnification of the microscope
   d. The ability of an electron microscope to determine the presence of a large number of elements

True or False

10. Empty magnification is magnification above the level where resolution is increased.
11. Two polarizers aligned 90 degrees from each other will block out all light.
12. A stereo microscope consists of two complete compound microscopes connected by a comparison bridge.
13. A simple convex lens creates a magnified real image of an object.
14. A trinocular microscope has three objective lenses mounted on a turret.
15. An electron microscope uses secondary electrons to magnify an image.
16. Liquids and gases are usually isotropic.

Matching

17. Compound microscope   a. Has a polarizer and an analyzer
18. Electron microscope   b. Permits viewing of two objects at once
19. Stereomicroscope   c. Consists of a single convex lens
20. Comparison microscope   d. Long working distance, three-dimensional
21. Simple hand magnifier   e. Basic two convex lens microscope
22. Polarizing microscope   f. Magnifies images more than 100,000 times

Short Essay

23. Show by diagram how a virtual image of an object is created by a convex lens.
24. Why is there a practical limitation of magnification by a compound microscope about 1600×? What causes this?

25. How does a comparison microscope work? What are its advantages over simply using two compound microscopes?

Further Reading

McCrone, W. C. Forensic Microscopy. In *Forensic Science*. 2d ed. G. Davies, ed. Washington, D.C.: American Chemical Society, 1986.

Palenik, S. Microscopy and Microchemistry of Physical Evidence, in *Forensic Science Handbook*. Vol. 2. R. Saferstein, ed. Upper Saddle River, NJ: Prentice Hall, 1988.

DeForest, P. R. Foundations of Forensic Microscopy, in *Forensic Science Handbook*. Vol. 1. 2nd ed. R. Saferstein, ed. Englewood Cliffs, NJ: Prentice Hall, 2002.

On the Web

Overview of all types of microscopy: http://en.wikipedia.org/wiki/Microscopy

An excellent resource for microscopy. Includes descriptions of various types of microscopy, virtual microscopy and even a museum of microscopy: http://micro.magnet.fsu.edu/primer/java/electronmicroscopy/magnify1/index.html

Homepage of the Microscopy Society of America: www.microscopy.org

Free online journal: Microscopy & Analysis: www.microscopyebooks.com

Beautiful photomicrographs: http://education.denniskunkel.com

PART III

Patterns and Impressions

7
Fingerprints and Other Impressions

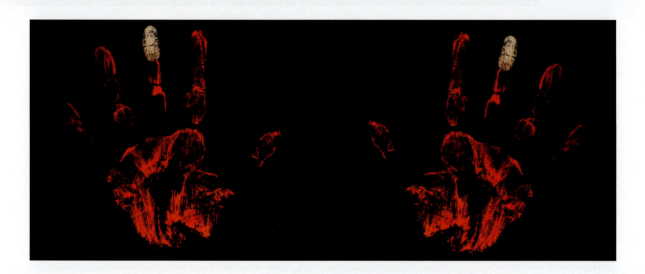

Learning Objectives

1. To be able to define dactyloscopy and ridgegology
2. To be able to describe the main events in the history of fingerprint science
3. To be able to name and describe the underlying principles that govern fingerprint examination
4. To be able to recognize the different types of fingerprint patterns
5. To be able to describe the three levels of data derived from fingerprint examination
6. To be able to name and describe the common methods for physical and chemical detection of fingerprints
7. To be able to describe Super Glue® fuming and the use of lasers in fingerprint development
8. To be able to describe how IAFIS works
9. To be able to describe some of the latest digital methods of fingerprint comparison and identification

Chapter 7
Fingerprints and Other Impressions

Chapter Outline

Mini Glossary

Anthropometry: A method of measurement of human body characteristics used to show variation or to differentiate between two individuals.

Arch: One of the three general types of fingerprint patterns that has no deltas.

Casting: Preservation of a three-dimensional impression by molding with dental stone.

Chemical fingerprinting: A method of enhancing latent fingerprints by reacting chemicals with the fingerprint residue.

Dactyloscopy: The science of friction ridge comparison.

Dermal papillae: The layer of cells in the skin between the dermis and epidermis.

Dermis: The innermost portion of the skin, which contains blood vessels, nerves, hair follicles and sweat glands.

Epidermis: The outermost portion of the skin, which contains five translucent layers of skin and no blood vessels.

Fingerprint dusting: A method of enhancing latent fingerprints by applying powders to the print residues, making them visible.

Fluorescence: The emission of electromagnetic radiation (usually light) from an atom that has absorbed energy from another source, causing electrons to shift energy levels in the atom.

Friction ridges: The raised portion of the epidermis that contain pores and allow skin to have gripping properties.

IAFIS: Integrated Automated Fingerprint Identification System, IAFIS is the National fingerprint database maintained by the FBI.

Impression: The remnant shape of one object after contacting another that is movable.

Latent fingerprint: A fingerprint that is not visible to the unaided eye.

Loop: One of the three general types of fingerprint patterns. A loop has one delta.

Minutiae: Minutiae are the various patterns friction ridges form as part of the fingerprint.

Patent fingerprint: A visible fingerprint deposited via a substrate such as blood, grease, or paint.

Plastic fingerprint: A visible fingerprint impression deposited by contact with a soft material.

Sublimation: A change of phase in which a solid material absorbs heat and transforms directly into a gas without going through a liquid phase.

Whorl: One of the three general types of fingerprint patterns. A whorl has two deltas.

National Institute for Standards and Technology (NIST) and the National Crime Information Center (NCIC)

Unfortunately, the companies that developed the hardware and software for conducting the searches did not use standard protocols and it was difficult to share data among users of different systems. In 1999, the FBI implemented a new automated system called the **Integrated Automated Fingerprint Identification System (IAFIS).**

Introduction

One of the major goals of the criminal and civil investigation process is to be able to identify people, especially victims and suspects, but also the owners of various objects and the authors of relevant documents. One of the best known and accepted methods of personal identification is by matching fingerprints and other friction ridges. **Friction ridges** are the raised portions of the outside layer of skin that form rows that curve and loop across the finger. The pattern these ridges make varies from one person to another and from finger to finger on a single individual. The science of comparison of friction ridge structures such as fingerprints is called **dactyloscopy**. Dactyloscopy employs the science of ridge analysis to analyze and compare fingerprints. Although the use of fingerprints for personal identification has been around for thousands of years, it is still evolving. Scientists are actively researching more objective methods of comparing fingerprints and new ways of visualizing them. To some extent, the principles discussed in this chapter also apply to other areas of the body that contain friction ridges. These include the palms of the hands, the soles of the feet, and even lip prints. However, these prints are much less commonly encountered than fingerprints and will not be discussed further in this chapter.

The Quest for a Reliable Method of Personal Identification

There is anecdotal evidence that Chinese people used fingerprints as a form of signature for legal documents more than three thousand years ago. It is not known whether this was done for the purpose of identifying the author of the document and there is no surviving evidence that any basic principles were developed that guided people in identifying fingerprints or comparing them.

The first organized use of friction ridges for identification occurred in the late 1870s when William Herschel, a British official posted in India, started requiring that any contracts involving indigenous people contain imprints of their entire hands. Again there is no evidence that he had developed any systematic way of linking these handprints to a particular person.

The first article that discussed the use of fingerprints for identification purposes was published in *Nature* in 1880 by Henry Fauld. He was a missionary in Japan working in a hospital when he discovered that there were unique patterns of human fingerprints. He tried to chemically alter his own fingerprints but the original pattern grew back. He demonstrated that fingerprint impressions could be taken by dipping the fingers in ink and suggested that they could eventually be collected from crime scenes. He even used fingerprints to help the Tokyo police in a burglary investigation. Fauld was interested in doing more research and eventually appealed for funds to the famous anthropologist, Charles Darwin. Darwin passed on the appeal to his nephew, Sir Francis Galton. Galton didn't fund Fauld, but did take credit for Fauld's discoveries.

During this same time period, in 1883, a French police expert, Alphonse Bertillion devised the first systematic method of personal identification. His system relied on a carefully constructed and detailed description of a person. This was called the portrait *parlé* and was accompanied by full-length photographs and precise measurements of the body called **anthropometry** (an-thro-póm-e-tree). Bertillionage, as the complete system was called, was based on the unproven premise that, after the age of about 18, the human skeleton stops growing. In addition, it was thought that all skeletons were different and this was reflected in the uniqueness of the body measurements that he prescribed. Bertillionage was considered a reliable method of personal identification into the beginning of the twentieth century. However, in 1903 the Will West affair signaled the demise of Bertillionage. Will West was sentenced to Leavenworth Prison in Kansas after being convicted of a crime. At that time, the prison system routinely collected portraits parlé on its prisoners to keep track of them. When West was being processed at the prison, officials found that there already was a William West serving time in Leavenworth. His body measurements were virtually the same as the incoming prisoner and in fact, the two men looked like twins. Their fingerprints were very different, however. This case showed that Bertillionage could not be relied upon as a means of personal identification and it quickly fell out of favor and was replaced by fingerprints.

Meanwhile Sir Francis Galton published a book titled *Finger Prints*. This book can be found online at the website www.galton.org. One of the major contributions of this book was that it proposed that all fingerprint patterns could be put into one of three categories: loops, arches, and whorls. Galton also asserted that all fingerprints were unique and that they didn't change throughout life.

Once Galton suggested that fingerprints fell into certain patterns, the next step was the development of a classification system. The goal of such a system was to put a set of fingerprints from one person into one of a small number of groups. This would make searching through many sets of fingerprints easier. If a person were fingerprinted and the police wanted to know if that person was already in a data base, the classification of fingerprint sets would make that feasible. As it turned out, two independent classification systems were developed at about the same time. Juan Vucetich, an Argentine police officer, became interested in Galton's work and developed the first classification system. It has been continuously refined and is still widely used today in South and Central America. In England, Sir Edward Henry developed a somewhat different classification system. It too has survived and, although it has been modified, is used today in the United States and much of Europe.

The original Henry system used five classifications to put a set of ten fingerprints into one of thousands of classes. This worked well until the number of sets of fingerprints in each class became so large that it ceased to be practical as a searching tool. In recent years, the FBI has added additional classifications to increase the number of classes. The classifications developed by Henry used certain characteristics of each fingerprint. These included designating which fingers had loops, arches, and whorls and how many ridges were in a particular pattern. The Henry classification system is discussed in more detail later in this chapter.

The Origin of Fingerprints

The purpose of fingerprints as well as the friction ridges on the palms and soles of the feet is to provide a textured surface for gripping and holding on to objects. Fingerprints arise from the skin, particularly the **dermal papillae**, the layer of cells between the **epidermis** (the outermost skin layer) and the **dermis** (the inner layer of the skin). These layers can be seen in Figure 7.1. Fingerprint ridges begin forming when the fetus is in the womb at about the eighth week of gestation and are fully formed by the seventeenth week. From that point on, barring artificial means of alteration, fingerprints do not change throughout life except to grow larger as the body grows.

As the friction ridges develop, perspiration glands are formed. These terminate in rows of sweat pores that form on the fingerprint ridges. As perspiration is discharged from the sweat glands, it exits through the pores onto the surface of the ridges. Perspiration residue along with sweat, skin cells, proteins, fats, and other

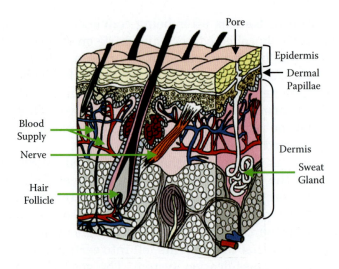

Figure 7.1 Cross section of layers of skin. *Courtesy of* Max Houck.

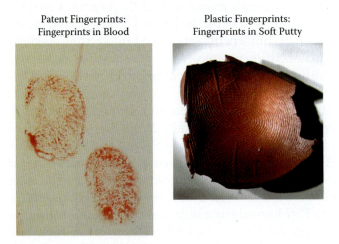

Figure 7.2 Examples of patent and plastic fingerprints.

materials is deposited when a finger touches a surface. Since these materials are normally invisible, this image is called a *latent fingerprint*. A fingerprint that is deposited in paint or blood on a surface and is readily visible is called a *patent print*. A fingerprint that is formed in a soft material such as putty is called a *plastic print*. Figure 7.2 shows examples of patent and plastic prints.

The Anatomy of Fingerprints

For the purposes of dactyloscopy, a fingerprint consists of the friction ridge skin of the last joint on each finger taken from cuticle to cuticle. Although other joints of the fingers as well as palms and foot soles may have unique ridge patterns, these have not been studied rigorously. Each fingerprint consists of a set of ridges of various shapes and sizes. The major types are:

Bifurcations: Ridges that split into two ridges
Ending ridge: A simple straight ridge

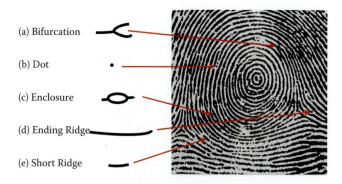

(a) Bifurcation

(b) Dot

(c) Enclosure

(d) Ending Ridge

(e) Short Ridge

Figure 7.3 Examples of ridge characteristics or minutiae.

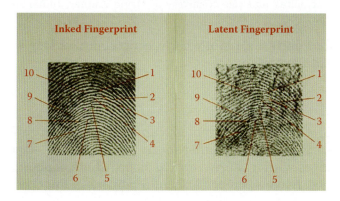

Figure 7.4 Comparison of an unknown latent fingerprint with an inked print taken from a suspect. The lines and numbers show some of the corresponding ridges in each print. *Courtesy of* David Zauner, Indianapolis–Marion County Forensic Services Agency.

Dot: Tiny round ridges
Short ridge: A small, isolated segment of ridge
Enclosure: A ridge that forks and forms a complete circle and then becomes a single ridge again
Trifurcation: A ridge that splits into three ridges

Figure 7.3 shows some of the major ridge characteristics.

Taken together, the ridge characteristics of a fingerprint are called **minutiae**. The types and locations of specific minutiae impart the uniqueness that is the basis for comparison of fingerprints. Figure 7.4 shows a point-by-point comparison between a fingerprint lifted from a crime scene and one taken from a set of inked prints of the suspect.

Fingerprint Patterns

The major ridges in each finger form a pattern. There are three major pattern types. These are the **loop**, the **arch,** and the **whorl**. Arches, loops, and whorls are categorized based on the presence or absence of deltas. Friction ridges that curve and change direction form a triangular intersection called the delta. An arch has no deltas, a loop has one, and a whorl has two. Figure 7.5 shows the delta and the center of the curve, called the core.

The three major pattern types are further subdivided into a total of eight patterns. Every fingerprint forms one of the eight patterns. Arches are divided into plain and tented arches. Radial and ulnar loops characterize the loop category.

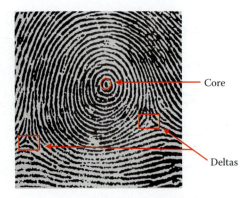

Figure 7.5 Fingerprint deltas and core. *Courtesy of* David Zauner, Indianapolis–Marion County Forensic Services Agency.

The whorls have four patterns; plain whorls, central pocket loop whorls, double loop whorls, and accidental whorls.

Arches

The two types of arches, plain and tented, can be seen in Figure 7.6 along with the other six patterns. These patterns differ in the severity of the slope of the arch. The tented arch has ridges with a nearly vertical slope, whereas plain arches have more gently sloping ridges. Arches comprise about 5 percent of fingerprints.

Loops

Figure 7.6 also shows examples of the two types of loop prints—loop patterns, radial loops, and ulnar loops. To prevent ambiguity and increase specificity, the direction that the loop opens refers to the major bones of the forearm—the radius and the ulna. See Figure 7.7. The radius is on the thumb side of the forearm and the ulna is on the little finger side. If a loop on a finger opens in the direction of the thumb, it is a radial loop. If it opens toward the little finger, it is ulnar. This means that a radial loop on a

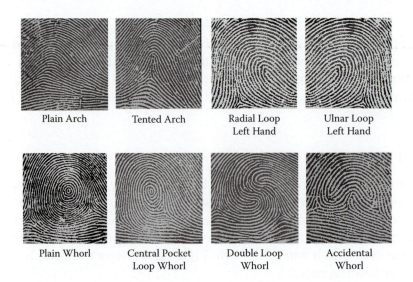

Figure 7.6 The eight fingerprint patterns; plain arch, tented arch, radial loop, ulnar loop, plain whorl, central pocket loop whorl, and accidental whorl. *Courtesy of* David Zauner, Indianapolis–Marion County Forensic Services Agency.

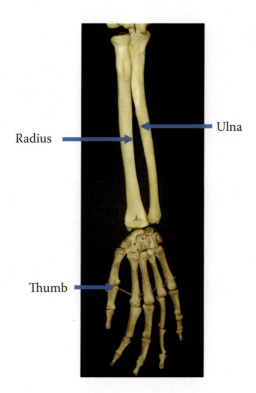

Radius **Ulna**

Thumb

Figure 7.7 The bones of the human arm. Website: http://content.answer s.com/main/content/im g/ ahd4/A4ulna.jpg.

finger on the left hand will open in the opposite direction of a radial loop on a finger of the right hand. The curvatures of the friction ridges that constitute a loop produce the triangularly shaped delta where the ridges change direction. Loop patterns have only one delta (see Figure 7.8) and make up nearly two-thirds of all fingerprints.

Whorls

Whorl patterns make up the other 30 percent of fingerprints. There are four types of whorl patterns: plain, double loop, central pocket loop, and accidental. Examples of these four patterns are shown in the second row of fingerprints in Figure 7.6. The plain whorl has many circular ridges and looks somewhat like a pond after a pebble has been dropped in it. A central pocket loop looks somewhat like a loop print with a small whorl in the middle. A double loop contains two overlapping loops that open in opposite directions. An accidental whorl is the catchall for patterns that don't fit any of the others or that are made up of two types of the other patterns (except for a plain arch). Characteristic of all whorls is that they have two deltas as part of the pattern, as illustrated in Figure 7.8.

Detection and Visualization of Fingerprints

Fingerprints can be deposited on a wide variety of surfaces at a crime scene. That is why fingerprint technicians spend so much time searching a scene to recover them. Even criminals who wear gloves at a crime scene may leave fingerprints. Gloves may slip off or be taken off for one reason or another. It may even be possible for a glove to leave an image of its outer surface on an object.

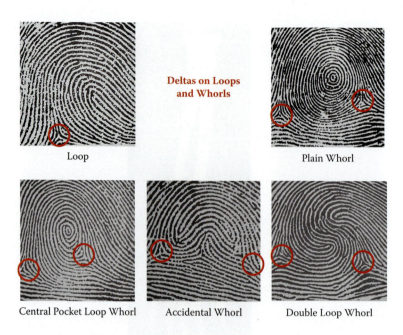

Deltas on Loops
and Whorls

Loop   Plain Whorl

Central Pocket Loop Whorl   Accidental Whorl   Double Loop Whorl

Figure 7.8 The location of the delta on fingerprint loops and whorls. The circles note the locations of the deltas formed by friction ridges that run parallel and then diverge and flow in separate directions, leaving a triangle shaped pattern. Loops can be identified by having one delta, whereas whorls characteristically have two deltas. *Courtesy of* David Zauner, Indianapolis–Marion County Forensic Services Agency.

Patent and **plastic fingerprints** are generally easy to discover as they have been either left in paint or some other medium or they have been impressed into a material such as putty. Thus, the major challenge for the fingerprint technician lies in discovering and visualizing latent prints. The science of visualization has been changing rapidly in recent years with many new chemical and physical methods being continually being developed and revised.

Locating and visualizing fingerprints may be done in one step or two. For example, a recent development in locating fingerprints takes advantage of the ability of fingerprint residues to reflect ultraviolet light in a manner that is different from the surrounding surface. The Reflected Ultraviolet Imaging System consists of a "gun" that aims UV light at a nonabsorbent surface such as glass or painted wood. UV light strikes the surface and then is reflected back to the receiver. The fingerprint image is then enhanced and converted to a visible image. This method is used only for locating prints. They will still have to be visualized using another method. Other methods such as **fingerprint dusting** using powders and cyanoacrylate (Super Glue®) fuming using chemicals are often used to locate and visualize latent prints in one step.

The method used to visualize a latent fingerprint depends on the type of surface. Smooth, nonporous surfaces can be easily dusted with fingerprint powders or cyanoacrylate fumed. There are a large number of commercially available fingerprint powders that come in a wide variety of colors. These are applied with camel's hair or nylon brushes that have very soft bristles. A powder will be chosen such that its color contrasts with the color of the surface being dusted. For surfaces that have fine texture such as some plastics and hides, magnetic powders are often used with magnetic brushes. The brush is moved across the surface of the object without touching it. This allows the powder to cling to the surface of the fingerprint residues without getting into the cracks in the surface.

Chemical Methods of Fingerprint Visualization

There are a large number of chemical methods used to visualize fingerprints on various surfaces. Developing new chemical methods is one of the most active areas of fingerprint research. These methods of **chemical fingerprinting** are based on reactions between latent fingerprint residues and certain chemical compounds. The oldest chemical method is iodine fuming. Iodine is a solid at room temperature. When heated, it **sublimes** (from the root word *sublimation*); it becomes a vapor without first becoming a liquid. When iodine fumes are exposed to fingerprint residues, specifically the lipids or fats in the residue, they react to form a reddish-brown image of the fingerprint. This image is only temporary due to the fact that the iodine will continually sublime and evaporate as a gas into the air. Therefore, the visualized prints must be photographed soon after exposure to iodine. Sometimes treatment with a starch solution will fix the iodine to the fingerprint to preserve it, but in any case a photograph should be made as soon as the iodine makes the print visible. Caution must be taken with iodine fuming as the iodine gas is extremely toxic. Exhaust fume hoods are used for iodine processing.

Another older method for developing fingerprints is silver nitrate. Silver ions in solution react with chloride ions present in the sweat residue from a fingerprint and form silver chloride as shown in Equation 7.1:

$$Ag^+ + Cl^- \rightarrow AgCl \qquad (7.1)$$

Silver chloride is a white, insoluble powder. It is unstable in the presence of light, which will reduce the silver ion to silver metal as shown in Equation 7.2.

$$2AgCl + light \rightarrow 2Ag + Cl_2 \qquad (7.2)$$

Silver metal is a grayish solid. Because silver nitrate originally had to be applied as an aqueous solution, it was not used where water could damage the surface. This limited its use as a fingerprint developer. A vast improvement to silver nitrate is physical developer. This is a silver-based product that contains a reducing agent. It can be used on similar surfaces to those used with silver nitrate, but can also be used on surfaces that had been wet at one time.

Perhaps the most popular chemical method of fingerprint visualization is ninhydrin. Ninhydrin is an excellent reagent for developing fingerprint images on porous surfaces such as paper. It reacts with amino acids present in the fingerprint to form a colored compound known as Ruhemann's purple. Ninhydrin is sprayed directly onto a surface. At room temperature, it may take a couple of hours for prints to appear and weak prints may take more than one day. Heating the surface to about 100°C will hasten the reaction. Figure 7.9 shows a fingerprint that was developed by ninhydrin.

Cyanoacrylate (Super Glue®) Fuming

In 1982, some Japanese scientists were experimenting with a cyanoacrylate ester that they had used to make a new type of glue. They heated some of the glue in a hood and when they came back later, they found that glassware in the hood had visible fingerprints. Furthermore, these whitish prints were very stable and virtually impossible to remove. The scientists determined that the cyanoacrylate fumes had condensed preferentially on the fingerprint ridges—and Super Glue fuming was born.

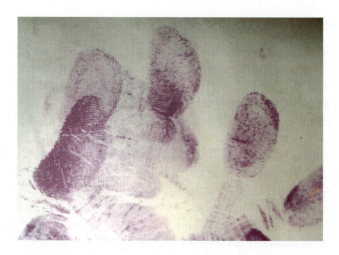

Figure 7.9 These fingerprints on paper were developed using ninhydrin.

Cyanoacrylate reacts with the trace amino acids, proteins, and fatty acids from fingerprint residue. When the liquid is gently heated in a humid environment, the gaseous form of cyanoacrylate will bond with the residues to form a white precipitate on the friction ridges of the print. The addition of moisture speeds up the process, so most Super Glue chambers have a water source present in the chamber.

Today many forensic science laboratories use tanks where Super Glue fuming can be done on many different types of objects. There are also small portable wands that can be used to fume small areas. Some kits have been developed that can fume the entire inside of an automobile. The prints visualized by cyanoacrylate are rock-hard and nearly impossible to remove. This is actually a great advantage over other chemical methods of fingerprint development because the fumed prints can be treated with powders or other chemicals to increase the contrast between the print and the surface on which it is found. If the secondary treatment doesn't work, it can be wiped away and another method can then be tried.

Fluorescence of Fingerprints

Around the time that cyanoacrylate fuming was being developed, it was discovered that fingerprint residues contain several substances that will fluoresce when exposed to certain wavelengths of light. **Fluorescence** is the emission of electromagnetic radiation (usually light) from an atom that has absorbed energy from another source, causing electrons to shift energy levels in the atom. This shifting from one electron level to another and back again involves first energy absorption by an electron, then energy emission, at a different wavelength, as it returns to its original state. The energy emitted can be detected as various colors of light in fluoresced fingerprints.

One problem with fluorescence is that the concentrations of fingerprint residues are sometimes low and thus, very strong light sources are needed to provide enough energy to induce fluorescence. The first attempts to observe native fluorescence from fingerprints employed an argon ion laser. Some components of fingerprints fluoresce when exposed to this greenish light. However, lasers cannot cause fluorescence in many fingerprints because the fluorescing materials are too sparse.

After cyanoacrylate fuming was developed, forensic scientists took advantage of the near indestructibility of the fumed prints. The images could be treated with

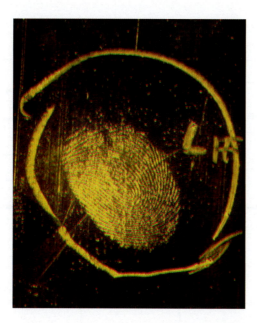

Figure 7.10 This print is on the butt of a rifle. It was first treated with Super Glue and then Rhodamine 6G, a dye. An argon laser was used to visualize the print. The dye caused the print to fluoresce with a yellow color.

liquid fluorescent dyes such as Rhodamine 6G. The dye is applied to the Super Glued image and then the excess is washed off. Green argon laser light is aimed at the print. The dye absorbs the light and then fluoresces, emitting yellow light. Figure 7.10 shows a fingerprint on the butt of a rifle. The rifle is fumed with Super Glue and then Rhodamine 6G added. A laser is aimed at the print and a picture is taken of the fluoresced print using a special filter on the camera that blocks out the laser light.

Since laser fingerprint development was pioneered by the argon laser and Rhodamine 6G, lasers have been replaced by alternate light sources. These are powerful lamps that use filters to shine one wavelength of light on a fingerprint. Rhodamine 6G remains the laser dye of choice in examining fluoresced prints. This has now become one of the most popular methods of fingerprint development in forensic science laboratories today.

Comparison of Fingerprints

The purpose of developing or visualizing latent fingerprints is to be able to compare them to fingerprint images taken from an individual who is a suspect in a criminal investigation. Known fingerprints are collected from a subject on a ten-print card. This card is used universally to gather known fingerprints. A ten-print card is shown in Figure 7.11. It has space for information about the subject. There is a block for the rolled print of each finger. To collect the print, each finger is rolled in printer's ink from cuticle to cuticle and then rolled out into the proper box on the card. The ten blocks start with the right thumb and proceed to the right little finger in the top row and then the left thumb through the left little finger on the bottom row. Below these ten blocks are spaces for tap prints. The four fingers of each hand are tapped in the printer's ink and then tapped into the proper block on the card. Tap prints are also made of each thumb.

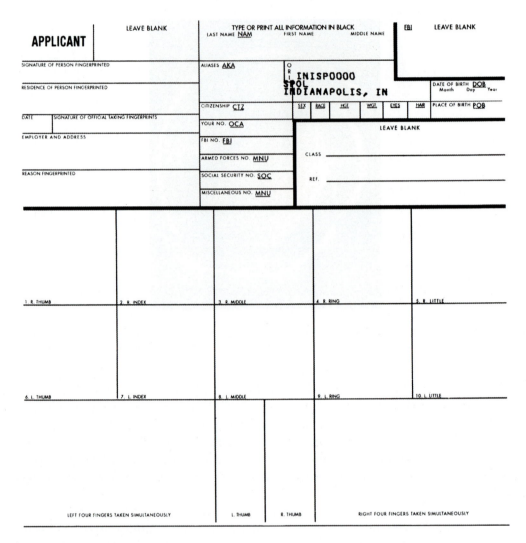

Figure 7.11 A ten-print fingerprint card. *Courtesy of* the Indiana State Police.

Beginning in the 1990s, many law enforcement agencies began replacing the inked ten-print card with computer images of fingerprints. The digital method called Live Scan compiles images of the friction ridges in a manner similar to the inking procedure, except that the fingerprints are "rolled" onto a scanning bed linked to a computer and a digital ten-print card is instantly compiled and downloaded to a fingerprint database. Obvious advantages of this modern method for storing fingerprint records are the virtually instantaneous recording of the fingerprints into the database and the absence of smudging and damaging of fingerprints rolled in printer's ink. See Figure 7.12.

Classification of Sets of Fingerprints

There are two types of fingerprint comparisons. The first is used when the goal is to identify a particular person from his or her fingerprints. In this case, a complete set of inked fingerprints is taken and sent to a database such as the one at the FBI, which maintains many millions of sets of prints. It would be impossible to manually compare the submitted set of prints to so many sets in the database. The way this is handled is by using a classification system. The one adopted and developed

Figure 7.12 Digital Fingerprinting using Live Scan fingerprint scanner. http://thelpgroup.com/liv-escan.html and www.fulc rumbiometrics.com/ images/live scan.jpg

TABLE 7.1
Henry Classification System

Finger	Right Hand					Left Hand				
	Thumb	Index Finger	Middle Finger	Ring Finger	Little Finger	Thumb	Index Finger	Middle Finger	Ring Finger	Little Finger
Digit Number	1	2	3	4	5	6	7	8	9	10
Henry Value	16	16	8	8	4	4	2	2	1	1

by the FBI is widely used by fingerprint laboratories in the United States today. It is based on the original Henry system. The Henry system used several methods of classifying prints. Each one was based on a different set of characteristics. Letter and number symbols were used to describe the type of each classification and the end result looked like a fraction containing a series of numbers and letters in the numerator and denominator. A description of the complete system is beyond the scope of this book, but the primary classification will be described to illustrate how the Henry system (and the FBI system) operates.

The Primary Classification

Take another look at the ten-print fingerprint card in Figure 7.11. Each of the ten boxes at the top is assigned a number. The boxes across the top containing the right hand fingerprints is given the numbers 1 through 5 and the ones below, containing the left hand prints are numbered 6 through 10. Each finger is examined and its type (arch, loop, or whorl) is determined. For the purpose of this classification, any print that is a plain whorl, double loop, central pocket loop, or accidental, is considered to be a whorl. In the primary classification, only whorls are counted. Each box that has a whorl print gets a value. If there is a whorl in boxes 1 or 2, the value is 16; in 3 or 4, the value is 8; in 5 or 6, the value is 4; in 7 or 8, the value is 2; in 9 or 10, the value is 1. See the Table 7.1 above.

To get the primary classification, the values of all of the even numbered boxes containing whorls are added together and then 1 is added to the total. This is the numerator of the fraction. The values of the odd-numbered fingers containing whorls are added together and then 1 is added to the total. This is the denominator of the classification. Note the formula below.

Henry Classification Formula

$$\frac{\text{Even Digits Henry Value} + 1}{\text{Odd Digits Henry Value} + 1} \quad \textbf{OR}$$

$$\frac{\text{R Index + R Ring + L Thumb + L Middle + L Little + 1}}{\text{R Thumb + R Middle + R Little + L Index + L Ring + 1}}$$

Example Problem:

Right thumb = radial loop
Right index = radial loop
Right middle = plain whorl
Right ring = tented arch
Right little = double loop
Left thumb = plain whorl
Left index = ulnar loop
Left middle = accidental
Left ring = ulnar loop
Left little = plain whorl

Whorl prints are on finger numbers 3, 5, 6, 8, 10. The even-numbered fingers containing whorls receive the following values:

6 = 4
8 = 2
10 = 1

The numerator of the fraction would be: 4 + 2 + 1 + 1 = 8
The odd-number fingers containing whorls get the following values:

3 = 8
5 = 4

The denominator of the fraction would be 8 + 4 + 1 = 13

$$\textbf{OR} \quad \frac{0 + 0 + 4 + 2 + 1 + 1 = 8}{0 + 8 + 4 + 0 + 0 + 1 = 13}$$

The primary classification would then be:

$$\frac{8}{13}$$

Careful examination of the Henry primary classification scheme shows that there are 1024 possible fractions. A 1 is added to both the numerator and denominator so that the computers that store and classify sets of prints do not have to deal with 0. Approximately 25 percent of all sets of fingerprints have a classification of 1 over 1; that is they have no whorls.

The other classifications within the FBI system also create hundreds or thousands of classes of prints. Using all of the classifications, there are many thousands of classes. When a set of ten prints is classified and the database is searched, there may be a few hundred sets that match that classification. It is a lot easier for a fingerprint technician to scan these relatively few sets of prints to see if there is a match.

Comparison of Single Fingerprints

Unfortunately, few crime scenes contain complete sets of fingerprints. More likely there are one or two and they may be partial prints; that is, part of the pattern is missing. Partial prints can be matched to a known print if enough ridges are present.

When the fingerprint examiner determines that there are sufficient points (friction ridge details) present in the unknown scene print and a known print, then a decision of identification of the unknown is made. Until a few years ago, many states and many countries had standards that set forth the number of points that a fingerprint examiner must find in a known and unknown print in order to declare that identification had been made. In some places, the minimum number of points was ten, while in others it was twelve or sixteen, etc. When there are many standards for the same identification, there is no standard. In 1990, the membership of the International Association for Identification, an umbrella group for experts including fingerprint examiners, declared that henceforth, there would be no standard minimum number of points for identification. Instead, each examiner would determine how many points would be necessary.

There are three levels of friction ridge details:

Level 1 details include the general features and pattern (e.g., ulnar loop) of the fingerprint. These cannot be used for individualization but can be used to exclude a print from comparison.

Level 2 details include particular ridges such as endings or bifurcations. These minutiae (characteristics) enable individualization of an unknown print. What is important here is not that the known and unknown prints contain the same number of each type of ridge, but that each detail is in the same position relative to other ridges in each print. In that sense, it is like comparing two samples of handwriting. The individual characteristics lie not in the fact that the known and unknown contain the same number of a and e letters, but that the specific shapes and sizes of each letter are the same in each exhibit. Recall that Figure 7.4 shows how a known and an unknown fingerprint are compared using levels 1 and 2 minutiae. This is the most familiar way of displaying fingerprint identifications in a court.

Level 3 details require a low-power microscope to uncover. These are the minute imperfections in a print such as cuts, scars, edge shapes, ridge contours, and even sweat gland pores. These minutiae are so unique that their presence in the known and unknown print virtually insures individuality. It should be noted, however, that the presence of many of these features depends on how good the image of the print is. Some methods of fingerprint visualization show level 3 details better than others and this must be taken into account

Fingerprint Pores

Figure 7.13 An inked fingerprint that shows the pores on the friction ridges. The pores appear as the white un-inked circles on the fingerprint.

when comparing prints. In Figure 7.13 sweat pores can be seen as tiny white holes in the ridges of the print.

Automated Fingerprint Identification Systems (AFIS and IAFIS)

The development of high-powered, easy-to-use, and readily available computers has had a profound effect on forensic science. One of the most dramatic advances facilitated by computers is the automated search process for fingerprints. Prior to the development of computerized searching systems, it was impossible for law enforcement agencies to search vast data sets of ten-print fingerprint cards. In the beginning, law enforcement agencies proceeded very slowly in using computers for this task. This was because computers with enough memory capacity to hold large databases of fingerprints were available only at great expense. In addition, the technology for faithfully capturing fingerprint images was rudimentary. When AFIS systems first came out, single fingerprints from crime scenes had to be enlarged and then the major ridges traced so they would be of high enough quality for the computers to scan them for searching.

A standard format for storing fingerprint data was developed by the FBI with the help of the National Institute for Standards and Technology (NIST) and the National Crime Information Center (NCIC). Unfortunately, the companies that developed the hardware and software for conducting the searches did not use standard protocols and it was difficult to share data among users of different systems. In 1999, the FBI implemented a new automated system called the **Integrated Automated Fingerprint Identification System (IAFIS).** This is an entirely digital system that compares a person's set of ten fingerprints against a database of millions of sets of prints in a matter of a few minutes. In addition, it can search the database for a single, latent print developed from a crime scene.

All scanned fingerprints can now be digitally enhanced to improve clarity. The problem of incompatibility among different searching systems is being solved by the development of a new generation of workstations that are able to input fingerprints from all the systems commercially available today. When these workstations are fully developed law enforcement agents can search local, state and national databases simultaneously.

AFIS systems operate by anchoring the position of a fingerprint and searching the database using two types of ridges: bifurcations and ridge endings. The database is queried to find prints with the same number of these ridges in the same relative positions. The most likely candidates can be displayed for direct comparison. Unlike what is seen in the media, AFIS rarely matches a suspect fingerprint to one individual. The computer system generates a list of possible matches for the fingerprint examiner to analyze and determine a probable match. The human element is still an integral part of fingerprint matching.

Common Questions about Fingerprints

1. Can you sand off your fingerprints?
   Yes, it is possible, but it will leave scars on your hands that will be permanent and unique, creating more individuality to your fingerprints. This would ultimately make your fingerprints *easier* to identify.
2. Can you surgically alter your fingerprints by cutting them off all the down to the dermal papillae?
   Yes, it is possible, but no documented successful cases have been noted.
3. Can you graft someone else's surgically removed fingerprints onto yours?
   Yes, it is possible, but again no documented successful cases in a criminal arena have been noted. A plastic impression of someone else's fingerprint can be made and then that piece of plastic can be laid over your fingerprint. This has been depicted on TV and the movies and it does work. The following episode of *Mythbusters* shows the casting and testing of fingerprints.
   www.youtube.com/watch?gl=BR&hl=pt&v=MAfAVGES-Yc

Other Impressions: Footwear and Tire Treads

When one object makes physical contact with another, it may leave some of its physical characteristics on the recipient in the form of an **impression**. If the recipient object is soft or pliable such as putty, mud, concrete, or soft dirt, the impression will be three-dimensional. If the recipient material is hard and the donor object has some material such as dirt, dust, blood, or ink on its surface, the impression will be left on the surface of the recipient and will be two-dimensional.

There are many examples of impression evidence. Fingerprints are the most familiar example. Oils and other materials on the surfaces of the fingers are deposited on surfaces as two-dimensional impressions. These are discussed in detail in this chapter. Firing pin impressions are made by guns on the backs of cartridges. These are discussed in Chapter 9. Automobile tires and footwear can leave tread or sole impressions in dirt. These types of impressions are the subject of this section.

Footwear Impressions

Many types of shoes have soles with distinctive tread patterns whereas others are smooth. Footwear evidence can be extremely valuable in associating perpetrators of crimes with the crime scenes. There may be footwear impressions at and near the entry points to a crime scene, at the scene, and at and near the exits. In fact, there are many more footwear impressions at and around crime scenes than are ever discovered or collected. It is reasonable to conclude that there are more potential footwear impressions at crime scenes than there are fingerprint impressions.

There are a number of reasons why footwear evidence is overlooked in crime scene investigations. The impressions are generally on the ground, which may be uneven or not conducive to holding impressions. They may be invisible or nearly so. They may have been tramped on by paramedics or other personnel before they can be preserved. Many crime scene investigators lack the necessary training to discover, preserve, and process footwear impressions. Police, detectives, judges, and juries often misunderstand or undervalue footwear evidence. They are often surprised to find that a footwear impression can be associated to the exact shoe from which it arose. This, in turn, discourages police investigators from collecting this potentially important evidence.

Some people believe that footwear impressions are very fragile and do not last very long. In fact, many impressions can last permanently and those that cannot, can be permanently recorded by a combination of photography and casting. There is no way to know, however, how much time has passed since an impression was made. Inferences may be made from circumstances surrounding the incident, but the impression itself contains no time markers. Impressions made in sand or snow may start to deteriorate very soon after being formed and the rate of deterioration is dependent on many environmental factors.

Individual or Class Evidence

As with other impression evidence, the conclusion that can be reached from a comparison of known and unknown footwear evidence depends on the number of unique details in the impression. When shoes are brand new, impressions of their soles will be pretty much the same as the impressions of all other shoes of the same type and size. Wear over time produces random markings and imperfections that begin to alter the impression, making it more unique as time passes. (See Figure 7.14.)

Figure 7.14 The bottom of this athletic shoe shows wear patterns that are unique to this shoe. The wear patterns, imbedded materials, and imperfections make this shoe individual evidence.

Eventually, there will be enough unique details present in an impression to permit a competent examiner to conclude that the impression arose from one particular shoe (or other type of footwear). There are no definitive standards that dictate how many points of identification must be present or what type or quality they must be. It is a matter of the experience and comfort level of the particular examiner that determines whether a conclusion of individuality will be made.

More than 1.5 billion shoes are sold annually in the United States. Given the large variety of types and sizes of shoes available, any one type and size of shoe will be worn by a very small fraction of people at any one time. The very fact that a footwear impression is the same type and size as a shoe worn by the suspect will eliminate a large portion of the population from consideration, irrespective of any unique wear patterns in the impression. The presence of some wear marks and manufacturing imperfections will add discrimination to the comparison even if they fall short of permitting individualization. This is an important concept that shouldn't be ignored by investigators.

Aside from the probable wearer of the shoe, other information can be determined from a footwear comparison. It can indicate the type and make of shoe and the approximate or exact size. From the number and types of impressions, the number of perpetrators as well as their entry and exit paths from the crime scene may be determined.

How Footwear Impressions Are Formed

Footwear impressions can occur in one of two ways. One impression could be three-dimensional (having length, width and depth) and another could be two-dimensional, showing only length and width. If the surface is soft enough to hold the impression, the shoe can deform the surface, leaving a permanent or temporary impression. Traces of material may be transferred from the shoe to the surface (positive impression) or from the surface to the shoe (negative impression). The transfer of material to and from the shoe can be aided by the buildup of static electricity that takes place when a shoe makes contact with the ground. Positive impressions are much more common than negative impressions because the latter requires that the shoe be clean and that is not a very common condition. Positive and negative impressions are most often two dimensional. Figure 7.15 shows a two-dimensional

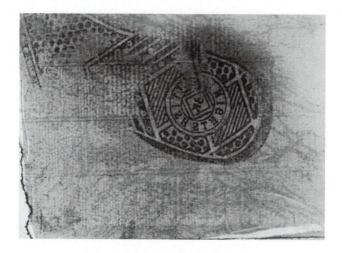

Figure 7.15 A two-dimensional inked footwear impression. Reprinted courtesy of Bodziac, W. T., *Footwear Impression Evidence, 2nd Ed.,* Taylor & Francis, 1996.

Figure 7.16 A three-dimensional footwear impression made in soil. *Reprinted courtesy of* Bodziac, W. T., *Footwear Impression Evidence, 2nd Ed.*, Taylor & Francis, 1996.

footwear impression and Figure 7.16 shows a three-dimensional impression that was made in soil.

How Footwear Impressions Are Preserved

All footwear impressions must be photographed at the scene. Today digital photography is widely used for this purpose. In all cases, a ruler or other measuring tool must be inserted in the photograph if it is to be used in court. A reference object such as a coin is not acceptable. In the case of two-dimensional impressions, the photograph will be used for comparison with the known footwear so it must be of the highest quality. The camera should be mounted on a tripod for the best results.

Three-dimensional footwear impressions can be preserved by **casting**. Casting is a process by which a three-dimensional impression is filled with a material that hardens and captures an image of the impression. Unlike a photograph, a casting captures virtually every important characteristic of the impression including surface texture, unevenness of the depth, and even microscopic details that differentiate one footwear impression from another. Castings do not have the perceptual or focus or lighting problems that sometimes accompany photography and they form a positive image so that raised ridges on the cast are the same as the raised ridges of the footwear and a direct comparison can be made.

Over the years, many casting materials have been used. Some of the most popular were various types of plaster including Plaster of Paris. None of these were really suitable for footwear casts because they were too soft. Attempts to remove debris such as soil from the cast resulted in the loss of significant detail from the cast. Today the universal product for making footwear casts is dental stone. This is a gypsum cement adapted for use by the dental industry to make high-quality teeth impressions. It is harder than plaster and captures detail to a much greater extent. Figure 7.17 shows a cast of a footwear impression made in soil. Half the cast is made with dental stone and the other with Plaster of Paris. The level of detail is greater in the dental stone.

Tire Tread Impressions

A tire tread is the part of an automobile tire that makes contact with the road. Today's tire treads have complicated designs in them that serve several functions.

Figure 7.17 A plaster cast of a footwear impression. *Reprinted courtesy of* Bodziac, W. T., *Footwear Impression Evidence, 2nd Ed.*, Taylor & Francis, 1996.

In some ways, tire treads are similar to footwear soles. They both serve to increase friction at the point of contact and this helps to minimize slippage. These functions are more important in tires than shoes because tires travel at much higher speeds in all sorts of weather on a variety of surfaces. They also must be able to start and stop rapidly while maintaining control. Tires also support more weight than does footwear so they must be made of durable materials. Like footwear, tires are mass produced and brand new ones bear few, if any, unique characteristics. With time and use, however, tire treads pick up increasing numbers of details that set them apart from all other tires. In such cases, a tire tread can be individualized to a particular tire.

Development of Tire Treads

The first air-filled (pneumatic) tire was developed by John Dunlop in 1888. His tires, manufactured by Dunlop Tires were bald—they had no tread. At first, this wasn't a problem because there were no roads and cars traveled very slowly, so the need for traction wasn't pronounced. By the beginning of the twentieth century, roads were developed and the need for friction-producing surfaces on tires became evident. In 1907, Harvey Firestone designed the first traction design for tire treads. The tread pattern wasn't scientifically designed. It consisted of the words "Firestone and non-skid" carved into the tread. Every time a Firestone tire left a tread print, it advertised the company. Today, computers are used to help design tire treads that not only provide gripping power, but also channel away water to prevent hydroplaning. Some tread elements also reduce road noise.

Identification Markings on Tire Sidewalls

Take a look at the tires on your family car. The sidewalls have several groups of numbers that have been stamped into the tire. A tire sidewall is shown in Figure 7.18.

Some of the markings indicate the make and model of the tire. Others are not so easy to interpret. Consider the following set of numbers and letters on a tire sidewall:

```
LT225/65 R 14
```

The "LT" indicates that the tire is made for a light truck such as a pickup truck or some SUVs. If the vehicle were a passenger car, the first letter would be a "P." The "225" is the cross section of the tire measured in millimeters. The cross

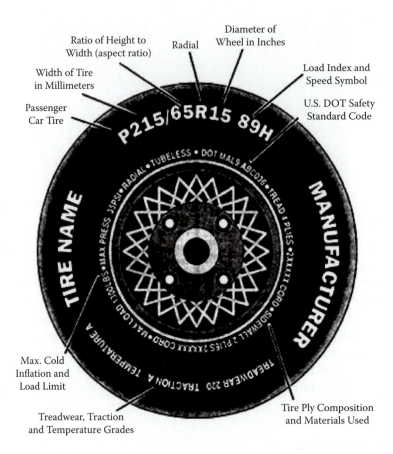

Figure 7.18 A tire sidewall. Tire Guides, Inc. Boca Raton, Florida, www.tireguides.com.

section is measured from sidewall to sidewall. A tire can be mounted on several different wheel rims and this would affect the measured cross section. The designated cross section is obtained when the tire is mounted on the wheel rim for which it was made. The "65" is called the aspect ratio and is measured from where the tire is sealed to the rim (the bead) to the top of the tread. The aspect ratio is actually the percentage of the height to the width. In this case, the height is 65 percent of the width and should measure 146 mm. The final R designates the type of tire. The most common type is radial although there are also diagonal bias (D) and belted (B). The last number is the diameter of the wheel rim for which the tire was developed in inches.

The Evidential Value of Tire Impressions

Even though an estimated two-thirds of major crimes in the U.S. involve automobiles, it is unfortunate that many crime scene investigators overlook this potentially important evidence. In some cases, the only way a vehicle may be identified is from tire impressions left at the scene. A properly prepared record (photograph or casting) of a tire impression can be associated with the exact tire that made it and can thus be individual evidence.

Capturing Tire Impressions

Tire impressions are similar to footwear impressions in some respects. They may both be two-dimensional or three-dimensional and two-dimensional impressions

Figure 7.19 A plaster cast of a part of a tire impression.

may be positive or negative, depending on how they are produced. However, tire impressions are usually much larger than footwear impressions, making them more difficult to collect and match to the tire. As is the case with all types of impressions, tire tread impressions should be photographed at the scene whether or not a casting will be made. In the case of three-dimensional tire impressions, castings must be made at the scene because the object containing the impression cannot be taken to the laboratory for casting or further analysis. Figure 7.19 shows a plaster cast of a tire tread impression.

With footwear impressions, dental stone casts of three-dimensional impressions are nearly always superior to photographs for comparison with known shoes. This is not always the case with tire tread impressions. Sometimes there are difficulties with making a good cast and the investigator is better served by photographs. For example, making a cast on a steep incline can be difficult because the casting material may flow downhill. The upper part of the cast may be too thin and will fall apart when the cast is lifted. In other cases, the tire impression may be several feet long resulting in very heavy and bulky casts. In such situations, a series of overlapping photographs may be a better way to record the impression. Finally, all three-dimensional casts of tires make negative impressions. It is never good practice to compare a negative impression with a positive tread surface or photograph. Instead, the tire is photographed and the negative of the picture is used for the comparison.

As with footwear impressions, dental stone is the preferred casting material for most surfaces. For tire impressions in snow, casting wax is used. In all cases, as with footwear, a suitable measuring instrument must be included in photographs of casts or impressions.

In addition to tread patterns and wear details, tire tread impressions can be used to derive other information about the tire and vehicle. For example, the Michigan State Police Forensic Science Division maintains a database containing measurements of wheelbase and stance. The wheelbase of a vehicle is the distance from the center of the front wheel hub to the center of the real wheel hub. The stance is the distance from the centerline of the right tire to the centerline of the left tire. Combining the wheelbase and stance data with the tread pattern of the tires (if original equipment), the make and model of a car or truck may be determined.

Summary

Fingerprints are among the oldest methods of personal identification. There is anecdotal evidence that the Chinese used fingerprints to help identify people thousands of years ago. It has only been in the past 150 years that it has been recognized that fingerprint science can be used reliably for personal identification. Fingerprints are created during gestation and once formed, do not change throughout life, except in size. It is believed that all fingerprints are unique and this is the underlying principle that allows fingerprints to be used for identification of a person.

All fingerprints form patterns. There are eight patterns in all. The major types are loops, arches, and whorls. Within these types are subtypes. There are radial and ulnar loops, tented and plain arches, plain whorls, central pocket loops, accidentals, and double loop whorls. These patterns are made up of fingerprint ridges. There are several types of ridge characteristics including dots, ridge endings, bifurcations, trifurcations, and enclosures. For comparison purposes, there are three levels of data. Level one includes the overall pattern of the print and general ridge characteristics. Level two includes the arrangements of various ridge types relative to each other. Level three data includes the details of the ridge characteristics including edges and sweat pores.

When a finger touches an object, it leaves an image of the ridge characteristics. The image is made up of sweat, skin cells, proteins, fats, and other materials. A **latent fingerprint** is one that must be visualized or developed using chemical or physical methods. Patent prints are those that are already visible because they have been made in fresh blood, paint, etc. Plastic prints are impressions made in a pliant material such as putty. One of the major breakthroughs in fingerprint visualization technology is Super Glue (cyanoacrylate) fuming, which forms a hard image of a fingerprint. This image can be treated with a fluorescent dye and then a strong light source can cause the dye to fluoresce, thus clarifying the image further.

There are several methods for classifying sets of ten fingerprints. The method used in the United States and in Europe was developed by Sir Edward Henry and today bears his name. It actually has five different classifications, each of which focuses on a different set of fingerprint characteristics. Together the system creates thousands of classes in which a set of prints can be placed. This makes searching for the right set out of millions fairly easy.

The development of computers and electronic imaging has made automated searching of fingerprint databases possible. These AFIS systems are being standardized so that local, state, and federal law enforcement agents can search the same databases and share information.

Table 7.2 lists common surfaces on which fingerprints may be successfully visualized and the type of reagents and conditions that are used for visualization.

Footwear and tire impressions can be two or three dimensional. Impression evidence can be individualized to one particular object if there are sufficient unique characteristics present. These characteristics arise from the random wearing of the shoeprint or tire tread.

Preserving impressions is very important because they often cannot be transported intact to the forensic science lab. Proper, high-resolution photography is commonly done, with digital photography becoming more popular. A suitable measuring instrument must be in the picture to facilitate scale determination. The measuring instrument must be a ruler or other device that actually measures distance. Ordinary objects such as coins or a cigarette pack that could provide perspective but

TABLE 7.2
Surfaces Where Fingerprints May Be Seen and Methods for Visualizing Them

Method	Surfaces	Preautions
Ninhydrin	Porous surfaces such as paper	Avoid contact with powder; avoid heat or sparks
Physical Developer	Porous objects	Numerous safety precautions
Iodine	Large surfaces like entire walls	Only visible for a few hours
Super Glue fuming	Almost any surface	Fumes are irritating but not toxic
DFO	Paper	None

not measurement should not be used. Dental stone has become the casting material of choice for many impressions because of its ease of use and high definition.

Mini Lab Activities

Mini Lab 1. Make your own Super Glue Fuming Tank

You can easily make your own cyanoacrylate fuming tank. The easiest way is to start with a discarded aquarium. Ten- to twenty-gallon tanks are best. It is OK if it leaks water—you won't be putting water in it. Make sure that the glass walls are not broken or cracked. It will need a tight-fitting top. This can be made from a piece of plywood and using Velcro around the top of the tank and around the piece of wood to hold it securely on the tank. Line three sides of the tank and the bottom with aluminum foil. This helps to catalyze the reaction. Leave the front side free for viewing. You will also need a source of heat to vaporize the Super Glue. This can be a hot plate or cup warmer or you can use a light bulb in a ceramic receptacle. If you use the latter, make a sleeve slightly taller than the light bulb from a soda can that has the top sawed off. The sleeve is then inverted over the light bulb. In either case, you can put the Super Glue in a small aluminum foil tray and lay it on the hot plate or on top of the sleeve. You should only need a few drops of Super Glue. Put the object that you want to obtain fingerprints from in the tank with a beaker or dish or glass of very hot water (to catalyze the reaction of the cyanoacrylate with the fingerprints). Leave the object in the tank until you see whitish fingerprint ridges. It should take about 30 minutes to develop prints. After the prints have been developed, take off the top and turn off the heat. (Be careful to let the fumes dissipate before getting too close to the top of the tank.) Super Glue fumes are irritating but harmless in small quantities. You should also be aware that the prints you have developed will be virtually impossible to remove from the object, so don't use anything expensive to develop prints on. Glass microscope slides or clear plastic disposable cups are good choices.

Mini Lab 2. Henry Classification of Your Fingerprints

Make an inked set of your own prints on paper using printer's ink or a similar medium. Another inexpensive way to get a good print is by using pencil graphite, cellophane tape and a transparency sheet. Rub a No. 2 pencil on paper to make a graphite square, roll finger into the graphite, tape the finger from cuticle to cuticle, pull off tape and put on the back side of transparency paper. Label and read. You will not get clear ridge characteristics, but you can at least classify the print as an arch, loop or whorl if done correctly.

1. Perform the Henry primary classification on your set of prints.
2. If a set of fingerprints has the primary classification of 17/8, which specific fingers must have whorls?

Test Yourself

Multiple Choice

1. Which of the following types of ridges are "counted" in the primary Henry classification of a set of prints?
   a. Loops
   b. Arches
   c. Whorls
   d. All of the above
2. The police official who developed a fingerprint classification system still used in Central and South America is:
   a. Henry Faulds
   b. Will West
   c. Juan Vucetich
   d. Juan Valdez
3. A radial loop
   a. Always opens toward the left
   b. Is a type of whorl pattern
   c. Comprises 50 percent of all fingerprints
   d. Opens toward the thumb side of the hand
4. IAFIS is:
   a. The International Association that sets standards for fingerprint analysis
   b. A type of automated searching system for fingerprints
   c. An abbreviation for a type of chemical that is used to cause fingerprints to fluoresce
   d. A federal agency that sets standards for forensic evidence analysis
5. Level 3 fingerprint data includes:
   a. The positions of sweat pores along fingerprint ridges
   b. The general pattern type of a fingerprint
   c. Only bifurcations and ridge endings
   d. Only ridges that can be seen with Super Glue fuming
6. Ruhemann's purple is:
   a. Formed from the reaction of cyanoacrylate with fingerprint residues
   b. Formed from the reaction of ninhydrin with fingerprint residues
   c. Formed from the reaction of silver nitrate and fingerprint residues
   d. The color that Rhodamine 6G emits when an argon laser is shined on it
7. Which of the following is *not* a type of whorl pattern:
   a. Tented arch
   b. Double loop
   c. Accidental
   d. Central pocket loop

8. If the primary Henry classification of a set of fingerprints is 1/1, which 2 fingers have whorls?
   a. Left index/right middle
   b. Left and right thumbs
   c. Left and right little fingers
   d. No fingers have whorls
9. If the primary Henry classification of a set of fingerprints is 17/1, which finger has a whorl?
   a. Right thumb
   b. Right index
   c. Right middle
   d. Left thumb
10. Alphonse Bertillion was famous for:
   a. Recognizing that fingerprints were individual
   b. Discovering Super Glue fuming
   c. Developing a system of body measurements to identify people
   d. Discovering ninhydrin
11. When AFIS searches its database of fingerprints it searches for which types of patterns:
   a. Arches and loops
   b. Ridge endings and enclosures
   c. Whorls and loops
   d. Ridge endings and bifurcations
12. Iodine fumes adhere to what type of fingerprint residue:
   a. Water
   b. Amino acids
   c. Lipids and fats
   d. Salts
13. Ninhydrin reacts with what type of fingerprint residue:
   a. Water
   b. Amino acids
   c. Lipids and fats
   d. Salts
14. Three dimensional footwear evidence can be preserved by:
   a. Fuming
   b. Dusting
   c. Casting
   d. Photography
15. Tire impressions are important because:
   a. They show direction
   b. They can be matched to a specific tire
   c. They match the type of vehicle
   d. They are permanent

Matching

16. Arch   a. One type of fingerprint that has two deltas
17. Loop   b. A fingerprint invisible to the naked eye
18. Whorl   c. The active ingredient in Super Glue which reacts with fingerprint residue forming a white precipitate

19. Plastic fingerprint   d. A visible fingerprint left behind due to residue on the finger such as blood, grease or paint.

20. Patent fingerprint   e. One type of fingerprint that has no deltas
21. Latent fingerprint   f. Change of phase from a solid directly to a gas
22. Rhodamine 6G   g. One of the oldest chemical methods of fingerprint visualization

23. Cyanoacrylate   h. One type of fingerprint that has one delta
24. Silver nitrate   i. A liquid fluorescent dye used to enhance fingerprints
25. Sublimation   j. A visible fingerprint impression in a soft solid

Short Answer

26. Look carefully at the footwear impression casts A to C. Match the inked shoeprints (P1 to P6) to the footwear casts. Identify individual points of match on the impression and the print.

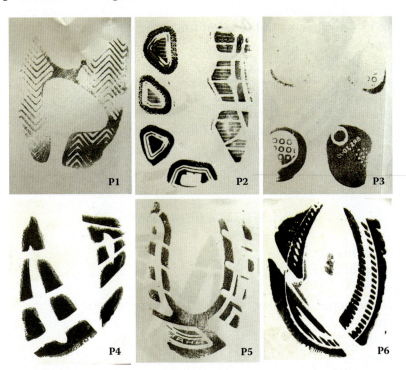

27. Look carefully at the tire impression casts A and B. Match the inked tire tread prints to the tire casts. Identify individual points of match on the impression and the inked tread.

Tire Impression Cast A   Tire Impression Cast B

28. Look carefully at the inked fingerprint. Which of the eight types of finger-prints does it represent?

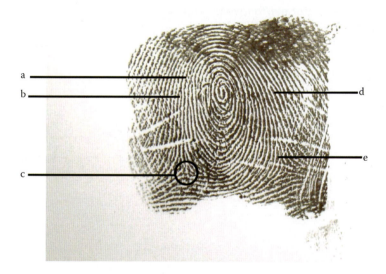

29. For the fingerprint shown in Question 28, identify the parts labeled a through e.

Short Essay

30. Construct a flow chart showing the development of the human classification system from the first attempts to differentiate individuals to modern day methods.

Further Reading

Lee, H. C., and R. E. Gaensslen, eds. *Advances in Fingerprint Technology*. 2nd ed. Boca
    Raton, FL: CRC Press, 2001.
Cowger, J. E. *Friction Ridge Skin.* Boca Raton, FL: CRC Press, 1992.

On the Web

www.fbi.gov/hq/cjisd/iafis.htm
www.forensic-evidence.com/site/ID/ID00004_2.html
www.forensicmag.com/articles.asp?pid=114
http://query.nytimes.com/mem/archive-free/pdf?_r=1&res=980CE5D81E3BEE3ABC4151D
    FB0668382609EDE
www.ccs.neu.edu/home/feneric/cyanoacrylate.html
www.galton.org
www.fbi.gov/hq/cjisd/takingfps.html
http://galton.org/fingerprints/books/henry/henry-classification.pdf
www.sciencedaily.com/releases/2005/03/050322135157.htm
www.sciencedaily.com/releases/2008/09/080915210509.htm
www.crime-scene-investigator.net/footwear.html
www.youtube.com/watch?v=9_6WyZXTaBo

8
Questioned Documents

Learning Objectives

1. To be able to define a questioned document
2. To be able to describe the training that a questioned document examiner must undergo
3. To be able to describe how handwriting is developed over time
4. To be able to describe the methods for analyzing and comparing handwriting
5. To be able to describe the proper methods for collection of handwriting exemplars
6. To be able to describe methods for uncovering erasures and other obliterations
7. To be able to describe ESDA and how it is used in questioned document analysis
8. To be able to describe the methods used for analysis and comparison of inks and papers
9. To be able to describe the methods of analysis of copier toners
10. To be able to describe how forgeries and tracings are detected

Chapter 8

Questioned Documents

Mini Glossary

Best evidence rule: Rule that governs the admissibility of document evidence. Generally, only the original document is admissible.

Exemplar: A sample of handwriting whose source is known. Used for comparison with questioned document.

Graphology (graphoanalysis): Determination of certain personality characteristics by examination of someone's handwriting.

Non-requested exemplar: Already-existing documents that are part of the suspect's everyday correspondence.

Palmer: A method of teaching hand printing and writing by copying letters. See Zaner-Bloser.

Pattern evidence: Consists of markings believed to be individual to each person.

Questioned document: Any written or printed communication between individuals whose source or authenticity is in doubt.

Requested exemplar: Samples of handwriting the author is asked to provide.

Zaner-Bloser: A method of teaching hand printing and writing by copying letters. Related to Palmer method.

Acronyms

ABFDE: American Board of Forensic Document Examiners
ASQDE: American Society of Questioned Document Examiners
ESDA: Electrostatic detection apparatus

Introduction

This chapter is all about questioned documents. This is a broad term that encompasses many types of evidence. Most people think of questioned document examinations as having to do with comparing handwriting samples, and many forensic cases involve handwriting. But, as we shall see, questioned document analysis involves so much more: charred and indented writing, paper and ink analysis, forgeries, watermarks, etc. Handwritten documents are a type of pattern evidence that consists of markings believed to be individual to each person. Like other types of pattern evidence such as fingerprints and firearms, questioned document examiners are largely trained by classical apprenticeship methods, where the trainee spends two to three years learning from a professional document examiner, mostly one on one.

Of all of the disciplines of forensic science, questioned document analysis is the one that is most utilized in civil cases. Many questioned document examiners spend as much time on civil cases as they do on crimes. Some of these civil cases are very famous and have helped give questioned document analysis much (but not always favorable) publicity.

On April 5, 1976, the reclusive billionaire industrialist Howard Hughes died on a plane that was bringing him back from Acapulco to Houston. He had been in a coma when he was put on the plane. At the time he died, Hughes was estimated to control a financial empire worth nearly $3 billion. In today's dollars, that would easily be twice as much. His empire included casinos, real estate, and a helicopter company. He had no wife, no children, no siblings, and no living parents. The last few years of his life, Hughes was a recluse and was rarely seen in public. For that matter, he was rarely seen even by his closest aides. Questions were raised about who would inherit his vast estate and where the estate would be probated. He had interests in Texas, California, and Nevada. Each of these states would receive inheritance taxes worth millions when the estate was probated.

There was a great deal of speculation in the media about the possible existence of a will, but none surfaced right away. Then on April 27, officials of the Mormon Church in Salt Lake City discovered what was purported to be a will of Howard

Hughes. The will was holographic (entirely handwritten) and three pages long. The papers had been left in an office of the church. Besides the will, there were two envelopes and a note requesting that the will be delivered to the Clerk of Clark County (Las Vegas), Nevada. The note was in the same handwriting as the will. Two other handwritten items were included, but they appeared to be written in a different handwriting.

A questioned document examiner made a preliminary determination that the will was authentic and so it was then filed in Clark County. A battle then ensued, resulting in a six-month trial over the authenticity of the will. This challenge to authenticity was triggered by a provision in the will that part of the estate, more than $150 million, was to go to Melvin Dummars. Dummars indicated that he met Howard Hughes in the southwestern desert during a trip to Los Angeles. Hughes had been injured in a motorcycle accident when Dummars came across him on the highway. He picked up Hughes and dropped him off at a casino in Las Vegas. The bequest in Hughes' will was a reward for Dummars' kind behavior.

During the trial, Dummars' story changed a number of times and several questioned document examiners from the U.S. and Europe pored over the will. Ultimately, the jury found that Dummars forged the will. One of the most prominent of the examiners, John J. Harris, was sure from the start of his examination that the will was probably a fraud. After his work, he had no doubt. He gave a number of reasons for the surety of his conclusions. These included that there was ample writing in the will and known samples of Hughes writing to make comparisons, that the writing in the will was forced and labored (unlike Hughes normal flowing writing style), and that the writing in the will lacked natural variation usually found in long passages of writing.

In this chapter, the main emphasis is on the analysis of handwriting, but we will also look at printing and copying as well as alterations to documents and the analysis of inks and papers. This field is changing rapidly because fewer people use handwriting, especially in formal documents, in favor of computer printers. The typewriter has all but vanished. The emphasis on printed documents has brought new challenges to this interesting field.

What Is a Questioned Document?

A **questioned document** is any written or printed communication between individuals whose source or authenticity is in doubt. The document doesn't have to be written on paper. Questioned documents have been written on the sides of houses, on mirrors, and on tables. They can be written in ink, blood, paint, or even lipstick. Questioned documents include forged passports, wills, currency, draft cards, and driver's licenses. Anytime there is commerce between people that involves a document, there is the potential for fraud, forgery, alteration, counterfeiting, or theft. Questioned document examiners must know a great deal about writing, printing, typewriting, inks, papers, and methods of altering or obliterating writing. Documents are unique in that they are subject to the **best evidence rule**. This means that the original document must be examined and admitted into court. With few exceptions, copies of documents are not permitted for identification and court purposes.

The Questioned Document Examiner

Document examiners compare unknown handwriting, typewriting, and other documentary evidence with known standards in an attempt to establish the origin or authenticity of the unknown materials. They also attempt to restore obliterated or damaged writings and analyze paper and inks. This field has, over time, become more dependent on chemical methods for the analysis of writing instruments and obliterated or altered writing. The educational trend among examiners is to require a college degree. There are few college-level and continuing education courses on questioned document examination. The path to the profession is generally through an apprenticeship. This is similar to the way people become fingerprint examiners or firearms examiners. In questioned document examination, the apprenticeship lasts two to four years. The training program consists of literature readings and research, lectures, examinations and practical problems. There are also mock trials toward the end of the training period. When a document examiner has completed the apprenticeship (s)he becomes a journeyman examiner. Then there is a voluntary certification process through the American Board of Forensic Document Examiners, ABFDE, www.abfde.org. This certification is a tremendous advantage to the questioned document examiner because it adds greatly to his or her qualifications as an expert, especially in court. The professional organization of questioned document examiners is the American Society of Questioned Document Examiners, ASQDE, www.asqde.org. A bachelor's degree in a natural science or a related field is highly desirable as is ABFDE certification.

Sometimes questioned document examination is confused with **graphology** (**graphoanalysis**). Graphologists claim to be able to discern certain personality characteristics by examination of someone's handwriting. For example, around the time that President Nixon was impeached, at least one graphologist published an article analyzing his handwriting and purporting to show that his handwriting indicated that he was dishonest. There is no scientific basis for linking personality traits to handwriting characteristics. Unfortunately, some judges have confused graphology with questioned document analysis and have permitted graphologists to testify in court concerning matters of questioned document identification and authenticity. Graphologists are not permitted to become certified by the ABFDE. Some attorneys facing the selection of a jury for a trial, will enlist the help of graphologists to aid in uncovering hidden biases in potential jurors that could help or hinder the attorney's case.

Handwriting Analysis

Handwriting and hand printing evidence analysis is the most common and most challenging of all of the examinations that document examiners are called on to perform. Even though computer printing is replacing handwriting in many applications, there are still many types of documents that are handwritten or that contain handwritten signatures that must be compared. Handwriting comparisons have been admissible in U.S. courts for more than a hundred years. The basis for handwriting comparisons and conclusions is that a person's handwriting contains a number of unique, reproducible characteristics so that it can be individualized to that person. There are no standards for the amount of handwriting samples that must be present in order to effect a comparison or the number of unique features that must be found in the known and unknown specimens. There is also no hard and fast definition of what constitutes a unique feature. Little has been reported in the scientific literature that would conclusively establish the basis for individualization of handwriting. In recent years, these issues have been brought up in courts during challenges to the identification of a writer from his or her handwriting. Increasingly, judges have ruled that there is not a sufficient scientific basis for the individuality of handwriting. See Chapter 21 for a discussion on admissibility of scientific evidence.

How Handwriting Develops

The methods used in schools to teach people to print and then write have changed little over the past century or more. Most schools use a variation of either the **Palmer** method or the **Zaner-Bloser** method of teaching handwriting. Each method uses a set of printing and writing fonts. Figure 8.1 shows a sample of Palmer fonts. The capital and lowercase letters are written on a large, lined piece of paper mounted atop the blackboard in the front of the classroom and each student spends many hours copying the letters and eventually making words. The students are initially evaluated by the teacher on the degree to which they are able to exactly copy the letters and words. Once students have achieved a measure of penmanship and dexterity so that their hand printing or writing can be read by someone else, the lessons shift toward what is being written rather than how it looks. At this point, students pay less attention to the appearance of their handwriting and the writing process becomes internalized and automatic.

Each person brings embellishments to handwriting to make it his or her own. It becomes such a habit that people don't even think about how their writing looks. They are generally not concerned about the characteristics of their handwriting. Ironically, this makes it more difficult for someone to deliberately disguise his handwriting because he is not aware of its nuances and traits. As we will see later, this can be exploited when collecting known specimens of someone's handwriting.

Even though handwriting becomes internalized with time, it is not static and unchanging like fingerprints. Handwriting changes as a person ages. This may be due to a matter of personal preference or to changes in dexterity brought on by advancing age or to infirmity or disease. Handwriting can also change, although less markedly, as the purpose of the writing changes. Depending on the circumstances, a person's signature may be very neat or practically illegible. A long, languid love letter will have different handwriting characteristics (it is usually readable) than notes scribbled during a physics lecture. In spite of these circumstantial changes,

Figure 8.1 Palmer fonts. These letter shapes are commonly used to teach young children to print.

a person's handwriting maintains its essential unique features regardless of the circumstances surrounding the writing.

Other factors can also affect handwriting on a short- or long-term basis. One of the most profound influences is health. Diseases can cause temporary or permanent weaknesses of muscles that control writing. Sometimes changes happen gradually and sometimes they may be quite abrupt, such as the case of a hand injury or arthritis. Tremors caused by advancing age or diseases such as Parkinson's may cause major changes in handwriting. Alcohol and drugs may cause temporary changes to writing. If a subject suffers from chronic alcoholism or drug abuse, these changes may become permanent.

Handwriting Comparison

Handwriting comparisons depend on two major factors—the presence of sufficient unique characteristics in the questioned specimen of writing and the proper collection of **exemplars**, which are the specimens of writing from the suspected author. Handwriting has natural variation and some of the characteristics of a person's handwriting depend on the writing instrument, paper, physical condition, and mental condition of the author at the time the document was written. Thus, the general rule of handwriting exemplars is that the exemplars should be as similar in all controllable aspects as the unknown. If the unknown is printed rather than cursive, the known must be printed. If the writing instrument used in the questioned document is pencil, the exemplars must also be collected in pencil. Because handwriting changes with time, known and unknown specimens must be of approximately the same age.

Exemplars can be **requested** or **non-requested**. Requested exemplars are samples of handwriting that the author is asked to provide. These samples are taken under conditions established by the document examiner. They are usually the preferred method of getting known handwriting specimens because of the high degree of control that the examiner has over their collection. Non-requested exemplars are already-existing documents that are part of the suspect's everyday correspondence. These are collected instead of requested specimens when the suspect is uncooperative, unavailable, incapacitated, or deceased. They may also be collected along with requested samples for additional comparison purposes when it is suspected that the suspect may be purposefully altering his handwriting. There are rules and guidelines for the collection of requested and non-requested writings. They are given below:

Requested Exemplars

Requested exemplars are sought by an investigator or may be ordered by a court. There is no question of authenticity in these circumstances so admissibility in court is usually not an issue. When exemplars are requested, the circumstances of the session are arranged so that the conditions are as similar to those of the unknown sample as possible. These include but are not limited to the following:

- Unless it is known for certain that the questioned document was made when the writer was in an uncomfortable position, the subject should be made as comfortable as possible. The chair, table, and lighting should be optimal.
- The same type and color of writing instrument should be used. This means that if the questioned document were written with a blue gel pen, for example, so should the exemplar.

- The paper should be the same type (lined or unlined) for both exemplar and unknown.
- The exemplar should always be taken by dictation. The subject is not shown the questioned document and is not allowed to copy it. Dictation reduces opportunities to alter handwriting. Remember that the act of handwriting is subconscious. Altering one's handwriting on purpose takes conscious effort. If a passage is dictated, the subject must listen to the words and write them down. This makes it harder to concentrate on disguising the handwriting.
- Sufficient exemplars should be taken. Requesting long passages of handwriting will ensure that a representative sample is gathered. It also helps to uncover attempts to disguise handwriting. As the length of the passage increases it becomes increasingly difficult to maintain deliberately altered writing. Eventually most people will lapse back into their habitual ways of writing.
- Although document examiners recommend that the subject not see the actual questioned document, it is often helpful to dictate some phrases and sentences from the document. This is especially important where there are misspellings or mistakes in grammar in the questioned document. The subject may repeat these same mistakes in the exemplar.
- Exemplars should be taken in context. If the questioned document is a check, then the subject should be asked to fill out a number of checks (ten to twenty) for various amounts. If the questioned document is a signature on a document, then the subject should be asked to write his or her signature many times on documents similar to the questioned document.

There are inherent disadvantages to requested writings. Foremost is that it calls attention to the fact that the subject's handwriting is at issue and the subject may then be tempted to alter her handwriting. This may also cause the subject to be apprehensive or nervous. These conditions may cause unintended alterations in handwriting. There are also times when it is obvious that the suspect is attempting to disguise his handwriting. In order to minimize this activity, there are a number of strategies that can be used. These include taking frequent breaks and even taking the requested writings over several days, challenging the suspect on the abnormal appearance of his handwriting, and using other requested and non-requested specimens.

Non-Requested Exemplars

Non-requested writing consists of documents written by the subject for purposes other than the questioned document case. They may be written in the normal course of business or correspondence or documents such as diaries. They are likely to represent the writer's true handwriting. The writer did not write the document with the idea that it might be used as an exemplar. No emphasis or attention is directed at the writing. Even though non-requested writings represent the writer's true penmanship, there are also disadvantages to this type of exemplar. First, unless these writings clearly identify the author, it may be difficult to have them introduced as evidence in court. Also, the non-requested writing will likely not bear any resemblance to the questioned document and may not contain a sufficient number of words or phrases from the questioned document, making comparison more difficult. It is also important that the exemplar and the questioned document be about the same age. Many questioned document examiners prefer that the exemplars consist of a combination of requested and non-requested samples.

Characteristics Used for Comparison of Handwriting

Handwriting comparisons can be complex and difficult depending on the characteristics of the unknown specimen and the circumstances surrounding the case. Nonetheless, there a few basic rules that guide examiners in their analyses. They should be kept in mind at all times:

- No two people have identical handwriting.
- There is natural variation in a person's writing in that he or she will not write the same letter or number exactly the same way twice. This is one reason why large samples of writings are needed for the examiner to learn the individual's range of variation in his or her writing.
- There is no one single writing characteristic that is so unique by itself that it will individualize handwriting.
- There is no set number of characteristics that must be present for an examiner to identify the author of a questioned document. As with any type of evidence comparison: There must be a sufficient number of similarities between the known and unknown and no unexplainable differences.

As with many types of evidence, handwriting contains class characteristics and those that can potentially be used in individualization. Document examiners must make sure that their conclusions about the authenticity or authorship of a questioned document are based on individual characteristics. For example, the **slant** of writing is generally a class characteristic, whereas **unusual flourishes** at the end of words or **ornate capital letters** are individual characteristics. When a questioned document examiner focuses on particular letters or letter combinations, he will generally create a chart that shows several instances of these letters in the known and unknown writing samples to demonstrate the natural variation in the writer's style and the similarity of the characteristic in both documents to the jury at a trial. This type of exhibit is shown in Figure 8.2.

Signatures can be especially problematic for a questioned document examiner. The questioned document may consist entirely of one signature. For example, a fraudulent check may have only the payee, the amount, and the signature on it. Although all of this writing can be used for identification, the key is the signature. The characteristics of a signature are very sensitive to context and the exemplars must be taken under conditions that approximate those under which the questioned document was made. Figure 8.3 shows how signatures are compared in a questioned document analysis. For example, if the questioned document is a check, the requested exemplars would normally consist of a series of blank checks that the suspect would fill out to various payees for various amounts.

Fraud and Forgery

There are numerous cases where a forger attempts to mimic or forge another person's handwriting. Forgers obtain authentic samples of handwriting from an author and then practice writing in the same style until they are proficient. Very often, this occurs with signatures. Unless the forger is an expert, attempts at forgery can usually be uncovered by careful examination of the writing by a questioned document examiner. Of course, when a document such as a check is forged, the merchant who

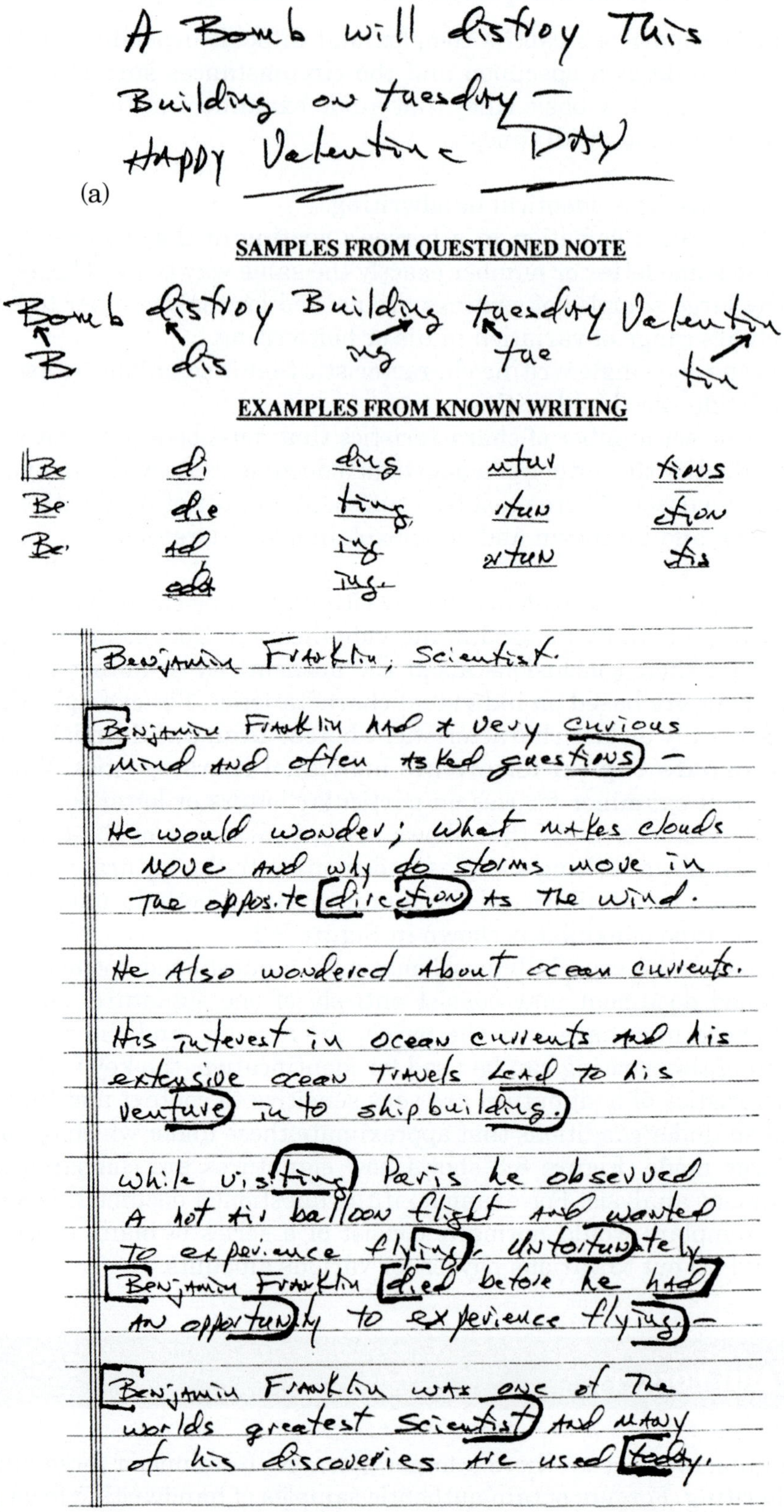

Figure 8.2 (a) Questioned document. (b) A court document prepared by a questioned document examiner showing the comparison of handwriting characteristics from the questioned document and a known sample of the subject's handwriting. *Courtesy of* Robert Kullman, Speckin Labs.

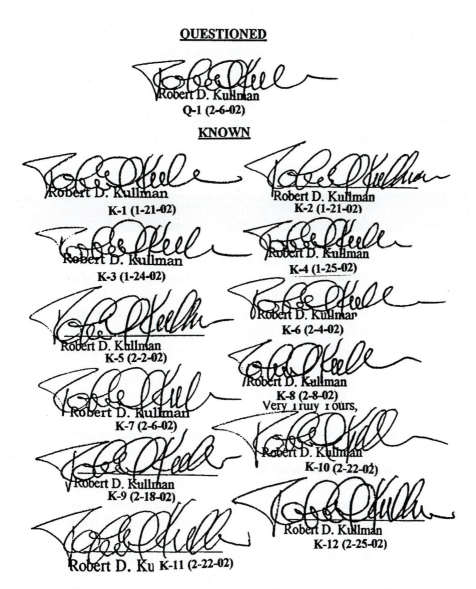

Figure 8.3 Comparison of a questioned signature with known signatures. Note that several specimens of the known signature are taken to allow for natural variation. *Courtesy of* Robert Kullman, Speckin Labs.

takes the check doesn't have authentic samples of the real author's handwriting and even if he did, he would most probably not be able to tell that the check was a forgery. Some of the signs of forgery include differences in line quality (e.g., thickness, smoothness), connecting strokes, pen lifts, starts and stops, and retouching. Figure 8.4 shows an analysis of a fraudulent document.

Sometimes, a document forger will resort to **tracing** a sample of someone else's handwriting. This may be accomplished in any of several ways. For example, the forger may put a piece of tracing paper over the document and trace the writing using a sharp object. This will be used as a template for the forged writing. Sometimes a new document will be placed over the original and the writing directly traced onto the new document. This is something that you could try. Take a document with your signature and then place a thin piece of paper over it and trace your signature on the top sheet. Then compare the signatures. When you trace handwriting like this you invariably do it slowly so that you can capture as many of the handwriting characteristics as possible. Unless you have an extremely steady hand, the line quality of the tracing will be uneven and will look like it has been drawn. These characteristics are very common and questioned document examiners usually have little problem in detecting tracings.

The third and least elegant type of forgery occurs when the forger forgoes any pretense of copying or tracing someone else's handwriting. Instead, he will use his own handwriting, usually disguised, to write the document. Since the merchant receiver of the document will not have ready access to the authentic handwriting of the victim of the forgery, he will not be able to tell this is a forgery until after the document has been passed.

Erasures, Obliterations, and Alterations

A large number of questioned document cases involve alteration of a document. There are several types of alterations. These include erasures, obliterations, additions, and charring. In addition, a questioned document may be written on the top sheet of a pad of paper and then that sheet is removed and is unavailable to the document examiner. In these cases, it may be possible to determine what was written by visualizing the indented writing that appears on the sheets below the top sheet. See the section on indented writing below.

Erasures

Erasure involves removing writing from a document through mechanical or chemical means. Mechanical erasures are accomplished by rubbing an abrasive material over the writing. If this is done thoroughly it will be impossible to determine what writing was erased. It is not difficult, however, to determine that an erasure has occurred. Mechanical erasures invariably disturb some of the fibers in the paper and this can be seen with a stereomicroscope. Figure 8.5 shows a mechanical erasure.

Chemical erasers are usually bleaching agents that destroy the dyes in the ink so they are no longer visible. The paper will often be discolored or bleached where the chemical has been applied. Sometimes the erased area will show up as a different color from the rest of the paper when exposed to infrared or ultraviolet light. Figure 8.6 shows a chemical erasure.

Obliterations

Besides erasure, there are other ways to render handwriting unreadable. It can be crossed out with another writing instrument or completely written over by another writing instrument such as a marking pen. In two cases examined by one of the authors of this book, a questioned document examiner brought some pages of computer printed contracts that had parts obliterated by a black marker. In both cases his clients wanted to be able to see what was under the obliteration. In one of the cases, the writing was visualized by immersing the document in methyl alcohol. This dissolved enough of the marker to show the writing underneath. The marker on the other document case was resistant to solvents. Instead, mineral oil was added to wet the document and then a strong light was applied to the marker. The obliterated printing could be seen (backwards) on the back side of the document. This was held up to a mirror and photographed. In some cases, writing that has been crossed out with another writing instrument can be successfully recovered using infrared

John Anderson agrees to pay Betsy Wilson
$300.00 per Month for A LOAN. Payments
start October 1, 2003 and The LOAN will be
PAID in full on March 1, 2006. LOAN MAY be
PAID off early. ——   John Anderson 9/10/03

                                    Betsy Wilson 9/10/03.

5:20 PM 2/16/2006 Lights=Side, Longpass=OFF, Bandpass=OFF, Mag=12.81
Integration=OFF,   Gain=Auto,   Brightness=40,   Contrast=54

5:32 PM 2/16/2006 Lights=Infra Red, Longpass=OFF, Bandpass=OFF, Mag=3.96
Integration=OFF,   Gain=Auto,   Brightness=40,   Contrast=54

Figure 8.5 The top figure is a questioned document concerning the payment of $300 per month on a loan. A close-up of the $300 indicates that the area where the 3 was altered by erasure. This was confirmed by an electrostatic detection test (ESDA) that clearly shows the area where the 3 was erased. *Courtesy of* Robert Kullman, Speckin Labs.

Laboratory Report: Direct Light

Laboratory Report: Ultra-Violet Light

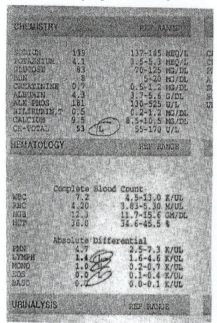

Figure 8.6 This is an altered medical laboratory report. On the right side of the report, shown under ultraviolet light, there are two chemical erasure spots. The small one was a 3 and the larger one was a H with a circle around it. *Courtesy of* Robert Kullman, Speckin Labs.

or ultraviolet light. If the ink used to cross out the document is transparent to the light, one can "see" through it to the writing below. This is shown in Figure 8.7, which is a draft card with the signature altered. The altered signature is transparent in the infrared light so that the real signature can be seen.

Another type of obliteration occurs when an attempt is made to destroy a document by burning. This can be done purposefully or accidentally as in the case of a house fire where documents are damaged. If the document is not completely burned up, it may be charred. This blackens the paper, making it difficult to see the writing. Fortunately, some inks and pencil leads will burn more slowly than paper and the writing may be preserved and viewed under a strong or oblique light. Some charred writing is shown in Figure 8.8.

Indented Writing

Indented writing occurs when someone writes a document on the top sheet of a pad of paper. If the pressure of the writing instrument on the paper is great enough, an image of the writing can be seen in the sheets underneath the top page. Sometimes TV shows or movies depict the restoration of indented writing by having someone lightly rub the indented writing with the side of a pencil lead. Not only does this not work—it also destroys the evidence so that tests that do work cannot be used. One way that sometimes works is to shine a desk lamp on the indented writing at an oblique angle. Then the writing can be photographed. Oblique lighting is shown in Figure 8.9.

Something for You to Do

Amaze your friends! Get a pad of notebook paper (lined or unlined). Have someone else (it's not fair to do it yourself) write a message in pen or pencil on the top page. Do not tell the person the purpose of doing this. Tell the person to tear off the top page and hide it from you. Take a gooseneck lamp or desk lamp if you have one or a large flashlight and hold

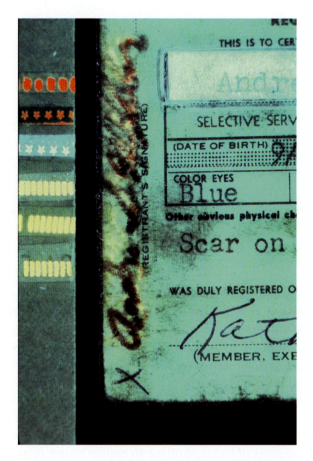

Figure 8.7 The altered signature in this draft card can be seen using ultraviolet light.

Figure 8.8 The lettering on this document can be clearly seen even though an attempt was made to burn the paper.

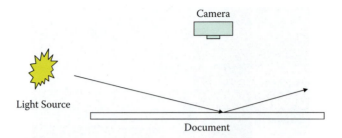

Figure 8.9 This shows how oblique lighting can be used to examine indented writing in a document.

it at a steep, oblique angle to the next sheet on the pad as shown in Figure 8.9. You should be able to read the indented writing on this page. It may help to turn out all of the lights in the room except for the one you are shining on the paper. You can then tell the writer what the message said. If the pen or pencil pressure was hard enough, you may be able to read the writing on the third page in the pad. Do not use heavy weight stationary or computer paper for this as the indentation may be too slight to read.

A great improvement in the detection of indented writing is the **electrostatic detection apparatus** (ESDA). This instrument is capable of recovering indented writing several pages below the original. ESDA takes advantage of the fact that a document that is charged with static electricity will build up greater charge within the furrows of the indentations in the paper, even microscopic ones. In practice, the document is laid on a flat platen on the ESDA. It is covered with a clear plastic sheet to protect it. The plastic is made to adhere tightly to the document by a vacuum applied from below. Next, a wand charged with high voltage electricity is passed over the plastic sheet, imparting a high static charge to the plastic sheet and the document. Then a fine mist of toner, similar to copier toner, is applied to the charged plastic sheet. Particles of the toner are attracted to the sheet in general, but more so to the furrows of the indented writing. Thus the toner forms an image of the indented writing. This can be photographed or a sticky sheet of plastic can be laid on top of the toner to capture it permanently. Figure 8.10 shows indented writing recovered by ESDA.

ESDA also has other uses besides reading indented writing. Sometimes a questioned document examiner may be confronted with a document that has two overlapping strokes usually made by two different writing instruments. The question here is which stroke was made first. One of the authors of this book has been asked to examine several such cases in connection with student cheating on exams. In a typical case, students would be called upon to do problems in a space provided below the question on an exam. If the student left the answer space blank then the grader was instructed to put a red ink slash through the empty space. The exam would be returned to the student who would then fill in an answer in that space and then question the instructor about why the answer wasn't acceptable. The cheating can be uncovered by determining whether that handwritten answer was written over top of the red ink slash. In a few cases, this could be determined by strong, oblique lighting and a stereo microscope. In all cases, ESDA can give a pretty much unequivocal answer and is the method of choice for such overwritings.

Additions

Sometimes, a person may wish to fraudulently alter the writing on a document by adding something later. For example, numbers may be added to a check to change

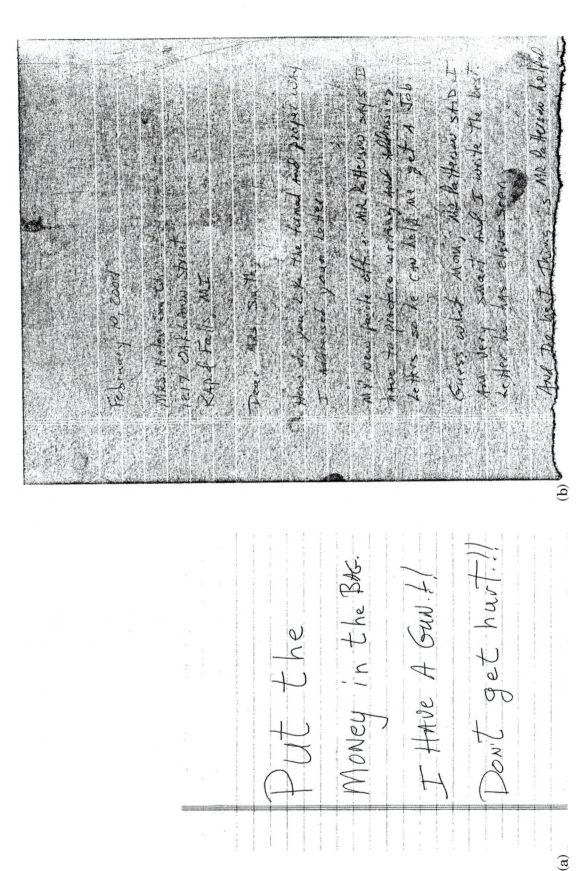

(a)

(b)

Figure 8.10 A much better way to examine indented writing is by ESDA. (a) This note was given to a bank teller during a robbery. (b) This is what was recovered on the paper that the note was written on. This writing was made on the sheet above this one in the pad and the writing was indented into the page containing the robbery note. *Courtesy of* Robert Kullman, Speckin Labs.

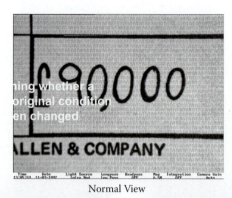
Normal View

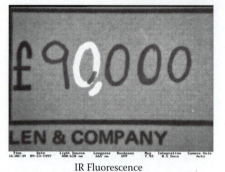
IR Fluorescence

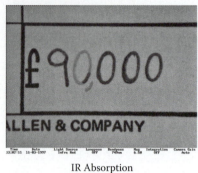
IR Absorption

Figure 8.11 Added writing. You can clearly see the extra zero with infrared illumination and fluorescence. *Courtesy of* Robert Kullman, Speckin Labs.

the amount. Even if the writer uses the same color pen as the original document, forgeries like this can often be detected. Many times, the amount of writing added is too small to determine whether the author of the addition is different from the author of the original document—however, the chemical characteristics of the ink in the pen may be different. One pen may appear to be a different color when the document is exposed to ultraviolet or infrared light. Of course, most forgers will not know this in advance. An example of this can be seen in Figure 8.11, which shows the addition of a number to a monetary figure.

Typewriters, Photocopiers, and Computer Printers

Today, many documents that would have been handwritten are now printed. Much correspondence that would have been mailed is now emailed and a high percentage of that is never printed. The computer printer has largely replaced the typewriter. Copy machines are still widely used but some computer printers can make copies of documents. Before the advent of computers, most printed documents were created on a typewriter. Mechanical printing machines (typewriters, computer printers, and copiers) produce printed (or sometimes cursive) letters. Questioned documents made by these machines must be analyzed by different means than handwriting. Unless the machine is malfunctioning in some way or is aging, its printing will look very much like printing from other machines of the same type and the printed material cannot be individualized to a particular machine. It is only when the machine develops unique quirks or characteristics that it becomes possible to associate a document with a particular printer or copier or typewriter.

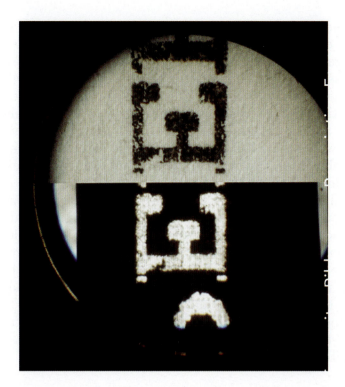

Figure 8.12 Characteristics of typewriter type. The flaws in the E from this typewriter can be clearly seen and are common to the document and the typewriter ribbon. *Courtesy of* Robert Kullman, Speckin Labs.

Typewriters

Typewriters work by having raised letters or numbers strike a piece of carbon film that then leaves an impression of the figure on the paper. Originally, each key on the keyboard was attached to a single figure. Then, typewriters were improved when IBM developed the Selectric® typewriter, which has a small ball with all of the letters, numbers, and symbols on its surface. When a key is pressed, the ball rotates so that the proper figure is in line with the carbon ribbon. In theory, it should be difficult to individualize a document to a particular typewriter because of mass production of the same make and model. In practice, typewriters sometimes develop individual characteristics over time. Figures may bend or chip or get filled in so that they produce unique characteristics on the page. This is less common with the ball type of instrument than with individual keys. In order to make determinations about the association of a questioned, typewritten document with a typewriter, the typewriter itself should be submitted as evidence. Figure 8.12 shows a magnified section of a typewriter ribbon with the letter E and a prescription form containing the same letter. Imperfections in the letter can be used to associate the prescription form to a particular typewriter.

Photocopiers

Photocopiers are routinely used today to make high quality copies of documents. In fact, some color copiers make such faithful copies that fraudulent documents are often made by making copies. Every year agents from the Department of the Treasury seize counterfeit money that was made using a high quality color copier and paper similar to that used to print real money. Most photocopiers work on a similar principle to ESDA. A cylindrical drum is coated with a light sensitive material.

The drum is charged with static electricity. Because the surface is light sensitive, the static charge dissipates when exposed to light. An image of the document is captured by a camera device and then transferred to the surface of the drum. Wherever the document has printing, it will be dark and the static charge will remain on the drum. Where there is no printing on the document, it will appear light and the static charge in those regions will dissipate. A toner, made of finely divided carbon particles, is then applied to the surface of the drum. The toner is attracted and held in those regions where there is a static charge. The rest of the toner falls away. The paper is then grabbed and run over the drum. The toner is transferred to the paper and heat is applied to fuse the toner to the paper.

Under normal circumstances, it is not possible to individualize a document to a particular printer. There may be circumstances where individual markings are deposited on paper when copies are made. For example, the device that feeds the paper into the machine leaves **grabber marks** on the paper. These may yield information about the make and perhaps the model of the copier. As the copier is used, toner may build up in areas of the cylinder or in some cases, there may be toner gaps. These can then leave unique markings on each copy made by that machine. Once the machine is cleaned, these will usually go away. There may also develop mechanical defects in the cylinder or camera that cause permanent unique markings to be deposited on copies.

Computer Printers

Computer printers come in a variety of types. The first were the **dot-matrix** types that deposited letters on paper in a similar fashion to typewriters except much faster. Today, computer printers are chiefly **laser printers** or **ink jet printers**. Laser printers work very much like photocopiers. They use similar toners and lasers to help with the deposition and fusing processes. They are very fast printers. Ink jet printers literally spray ink on the paper in the form of letters, numbers and symbols. The solvent in the ink evaporates rapidly, leaving the dyes behind. Modern technology has developed reliable printers that seldom have defects and seldom exhibit individual characteristics.

Paper Examination

There are some questioned document cases where the issue is whether a multipage document has had pages added to it after the original document was written. A will or contract falls into this category. If the document is handwritten then there may be differences in the characteristics of the writing or writing instrument. If the document is printed, there may not be any obvious differences in the printing but there may be differences in the paper. Even though papers may all look the same, there are chemical and physical differences. Some papers contain fillers that help improve color and appearance. Some are coated to facilitate printing. Sizing agents are added to help keep ink from penetrating into the paper. Chemical tests can be performed on paper to identify these additives, but they are mostly destructive and therefore cannot be done on questioned documents.

Nondestructive physical examinations may also be done on paper. Even though different papers may be nominally 8.5 × 11", there may be slight, but consistent differences from paper to paper that careful measurements can reveal. Likewise, the thickness of papers may be slightly different, although these differences are in the thousandths of inches and measurements must be made with a special paper micrometer.

Ink Examinations

Ink examinations may be used to help identify the writing instrument or even to help determine how old a document or a part of a document is. Identification of the writing instrument may be accomplished by analysis of the dyes in the ink. The United States Secret Service maintains a library of more than five thousand ink samples that can be compared to a sample from a questioned document.

The questioned document examiner must not deface the document when taking ink samples. There are tools available that can punch out a hole in a document that is smaller in diameter than the width of a pen stroke. This way, samples can be taken of the ink in a document without ruining the writing or unduly defacing the document. One of the more popular methods for analyzing ink samples is thin layer chromatography. Ink plugs from the questioned document can be compared against those from the writing instrument in question. A thin layer chromatogram of ink samples is shown in Figure 8.13.

Document dating using the characteristics of ink writing is becoming more common as methods of analysis have improved. There are basically two types of cases where this comes into play. The first involves a series of dated writings made on the same document at different times. An example of this is a patient's medical chart on which the doctor makes entries each time the patient is examined. In medical malpractice cases, the issue of when a particular entry was made in the record can be important evidence. The entry may have a date on it and the examiner would want to know whether this entry was made after the one before it in the record and before the one after it. In other cases, the age of the entire document may be at issue. This may be a matter of determining whether the dyes used in the writing ink existed at the time that the document was purported to have been written. For example, crystal violet dye was introduced into blue ball point pens about 1956. If a document was written with this dye and purports to be written in 1940, it is clearly a fraud. The United States Secret Service ink database contains starting and ending dates of manufacture for all of the inks in its library.

Recently, new methods have been developed for determining the age of ink by tracking the degradation of certain dyes as the ink ages. One method for doing

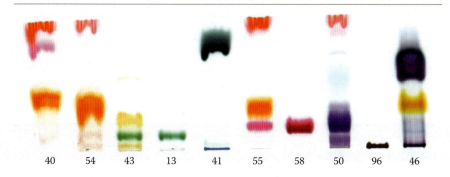

40   54   43   13   41   55   58   50   96   46

Figure 8.13 This TLC plate shows ten pens. All of the dyes in the pens are different and the pens can be easily distinguished.

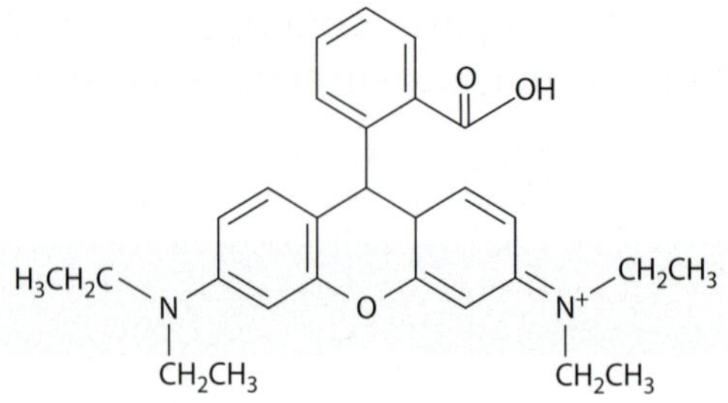

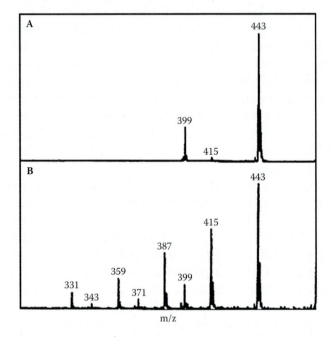

Figure 8.14 The structure of Rhodamine B, a common dye in blue pens.

Figure 8.15 The mass spectrum of partially aged Rhodamine B. Each of the major, lower weight peaks represents the replacement of successive ethyl groups (MW = 29) with a hydrogen (AW = 1). *Courtesy of* John Allison.

this is **laser desorption mass spectrometry (LDMS)**. In this technique, a laser is used to drive molecules of ink off the surface of a document. The molecules are ionized and separated in a mass spectrometer. As the dye ages due to exposure to light and oxygen, it degrades into smaller molecules. This process can be roughly correlated with time. One common example is the LDMS of Rhodamine B in ballpoint pens. The structure of this dye is shown in Figure 8.14. Note that there are four ethyl (–CH₂–CH₃) groups on this molecule. As it ages the dye successively loses these groups and they are replaced by hydrogen atoms (–H). The mass spectrum loses 28 mass units each time a methyl group is lost. Figure 8.15 shows the mass spectrum of this dye. The mass spectrum shows how this dye degrades.

Physical Matches on Torn Paper

In questioned document analysis, torn paper is evidence in a surprising number of cases. For example, a piece of paper may be torn in half and a document may

Perforation Match on Postage Stamps

Figure 8.16 Physical match with stamps. The way that the torn perforations in the stamps line up can be seen clearly. This is a very old case as can be seen by the postage (10 cents) on the stamps!

be written on one of the halves. A piece of paper may be torn out of a spiral notebook, leaving jagged edges on the torn paper and on the remnants that are often left enmeshed within the metal spirals. Papers such as rolls of stamps may contain perforations with irregular edges where the stamps have been torn off. One such case occurred many years ago when someone sent a series of threatening letters to a U.S. senator, who saved the letters and envelopes and turned them over to the FBI. The stamps on the letters were collected. When a suspect was identified, a search warrant was executed for his home and a roll of stamps was seized. The perforations on the stamp at the end of the roll and on the stamps on the letters were compared and it was determined that the stamps on the letters came from that roll of stamps. Figure 8.16 shows some of the physical matches made on the stamps. You can see that this is a very old case as the stamps cost only ten cents!

Summary

A questioned document can be almost any object that contains handwritten or printed characters whose source or authenticity is in doubt. Questioned document examiners are specially trained professionals who undergo multi-year apprenticeships to learn how to examine documents. The identification of handwriting is the single most common and important activity of a questioned document examiner. The key to being able to successfully compare handwriting is to have sufficient, high quality known samples (exemplars). These can be requested from the subject or be non requested samples taken from the subject's correspondence.

Handwriting is learned at an early age and quickly becomes an internalized, subconscious activity. At this point, people develop their own unique styles of handwriting. If a sufficient number of these characteristics are present in a questioned document and exemplar, the document examiner may conclude that the subject wrote the handwriting.

In addition to the comparison of handwritings, document examiners compare typed writings, photocopier copies, and computer printed documents. They also examine erasures and obliterations as well as indented writings. Besides writing and printing, questioned document examiners are called on to compare samples of paper and ink.

Test Yourself

Multiple Choice

1. Which of the following is not a good practice in taking requested handwriting exemplars?
   a. Collect a lot of writing samples
   b. Have the subject copy the questioned document
   c. Use the same type of writing implement and paper as the questioned document
   d. Dictate the requested exemplar

2. Which of the following is not an example of a questioned document?
   a. A forged passport
   b. A stolen traveler's check
   c. A copy of a ten dollar bill made in a photocopier
   d. A threatening message written in spray paint on the side of someone's house
   e. All of the above are examples of a questioned document

3. Which of the following is not true of questioned document examiners?
   a. They can learn their craft solely by getting a college degree in questioned document examination
   b. They usually perform a two- to three-year apprenticeship with a practicing questioned document examiner
   c. There is an opportunity for a questioned document examiner to achieve certification after training
   d. Questioned document examiners do not have to have a college degree to become certified.

4. Which of the following is not an acceptable method for revealing indented writing?
   a. Oblique lighting
   b. Intense lighting
   c. Rubbing with a pencil lead
   d. ESDA

5. Which of the following method is used for the comparison of ink samples?
   a. Gas chromatography
   b. Thin layer chromatography
   c. Infrared spectrophotometry
   d. Fluorescence spectroscopy

6. In the Mormon will case, discussed at the beginning of the chapter, one of the characteristics of the will that indicated that it was not Howard Hughes' writing was:
   a. It was written in a forced, halting manner
   b. It was written in pencil
   c. It was entirely handwritten
   d. It was not signed

7. Which of the following is not true of handwriting?
   a. It changes throughout life
   b. It is not affected by drugs or alcohol
   c. It is a subconscious behavior
   d. It can change with the context of the writing

8. Which of the following practices of collecting exemplars will help to minimize the chance of a writer deliberately altering his writing?
   a. Have the subject stand up while writing
   b. Always use lined paper to make sure that the subject writes in straight
       lines
   c. Dictate long passages
   d. Show the subject the questioned document
9. ESDA is used mainly for:
   a. Identifying ink
   b. Determining that a document is a photocopy
   c. Determining the age of a handwritten document
   d. Reading indented writing
10. Which of the following is most likely to develop individual characteristics
    when it is used over a long period of time?
    a. Typewriting
    b. Photocopying
    c. Dot matrix printing
    d. Laser jet printing

True or False

11. Overwriting can always be detected by oblique lighting.
12. Identification of the writing on a charred document depends on the observa-
    tion that ink and lead burn slower than paper.
13. The age of a document can be estimated by determining the degree of chemi-
    cal degradation of the ink used to write it.
14. It is not possible to determine whether writing has been mechanically
    erased.
15. Specialized lighting such as infrared or ultraviolet can be used to uncover
    attempts to alter a document by addition of extra numbers or letters.
16. A non-request exemplar is one that already exists at the time of the ques-
    tioned document case.

Matching

17. ESDA   a. Method of teaching printing
18. Chemical erasure   b. A type of angular lighting
19. Palmer method   c. A method for uncovering indented writing
20. Oblique lighting   d. A device that prints documents using mechanically
                             struck keys
21. Grabber marks   e. Obliterates writing by bleaching ink
22. Typewriter   f. Made on paper by copier

Short Essay

23. Explain the difference between requested and non-requested exemplars.
    When would one want to use non request exemplars?
24. What is indented writing? How is it analyzed?
25. Under what conditions, if any, can a document created on a typewriter be
    individualized to a particular machine?

Further Reading

Hilton, O. *Scientific Examination of Questioned Documents. 2nd* ed. New York: Elsevier, 1982.
Osborne, A. S. *Questioned Documents.* 2nd ed. Albany, NY: Boyd Printing Company, 1929.
Brunelle, R. L. Questioned Document Examination. *Forensic Science Handbook.* Vol. 1. 2nd
    ed. Ed. R. Saferstein. Upper Saddle River, NJ: Prentice Hall, 2002.

On the Web

A good overview of questioned document examination: http://en.wikipedia.org/wiki/
    Questioned_document_examination.
American Society of Questioned Document Examiners: www.asqde.org.
Classic typewriters: http://staff.xu.edu/~polt/typewriters/index.html.
Newspaper account of how the CIA used questioned documents in a case linking Iraq to
    uranium ore: www.commondreams.org/headlines03/0322-04.htm.
Use of stereomicroscopy and specialized lighting to detect overwriting: www.youtube.com/
    watch?v=qSF4ENiQeek.

9

Firearms and Toolmarks

Learning Objectives

1. To be able to define toolmark analysis and toolmarks
2. To be able to define firearms analysis and its scope
3. To be able to define rifling and how it arises in weapons
4. To be able to define and list the various types of weapons
5. To be able to define and give examples of stria
6. To be able to describe the various types of markings left on bullets and cartridges by weapons
7. To be able to describe how bullets and cartridges are matched to particular weapons
8. To be able to describe the various types of propellants and primers used in weapons
9. To be able to describe how distance-of-firing determinations are made with rifled weapons and shotguns
10. To be able to describe other types of toolmarks
11. To be able to describe how serial number restorations are accomplished and the principle behind them.

Chapter 9
Firearms and Toolmarks

Chapter Outline

Mini Glossary

Ballistics: The study of projectiles in motion.

Caliber: The bore diameter of a rifled gun barrel.

DRUGFIRE: A database of fired cartridge cases developed by the FBI in 2002.

Firearms identification: A category of toolmark identification in which the examiner matches fired bullets, cartridge cases or other ammunition components to a specific firearm.

Gauge: A way of measuring the bore diameter of a shotgun based on the number of solid spheres of a diameter equal to the inside diameter of the barrel that could be made from a pound of lead.

Groove: The curved track machined into the barrel of a firearm that causes the bullet to spin upon exit from the barrel.

GSR: An acronym for gunshot residue, which is the burned and unburned gunpowder that exits the firearm after the bullet.

IBIS: An acronym for Integrated Ballistics Identification System, a database developed by the Bureau of Alcohol, Tobacco, Firearms and Explosives to compare markings on fired bullets.

Land: The part of a gun barrel that is untouched by the machining process which cuts the grooves into the barrel.

NIBIN: An acronym for National Integrated Ballistic Information Network, a database that combined the FBI's DRUGFIRE database of cartridge casings and the ATF's IBIS database of fired bullets.

Rifling: The cutting of curved grooves in a firearm barrel during the manufacturing process. Rifled barrels impart spin on fired bullets which increases stability and accuracy in flight.

Stippling: Small, dry, reddish orange abrasions on skin or small, black specks on objects caused by unburned powder and small metal fragments from a firearm striking the object.

Toolmark: A scratch or other microscopic marking left by the action of a tool on an object when the two come into contact.

Twist: A term used in bullet identification which refers to the direction of the grooves impressed into the fired bullet by the lands in the gun barrel.

Case Study

Bartolomeo Vanzetti and Nicola Sacco handcuffed in 1923

On Friday, April 15, 1920, in South Braintree, Massahusetts, two men robbed two security guards who were delivering payroll money to the Slater and Morrill Shoe Factory. During the robbery, both guards were fatally wounded by gunshots from the robbers. The robbers then drove off in a black car with the payroll boxes containing $16,000. Later, police recovered the stolen getaway car and recovered six cartridges from the crime scene. These were later traced back to three ammunition manufacturers: Remington, Peters, and Winchester. Because the same car was implicated in an earlier robbery, the investigation focused on a known thug named Mike Boda. However, he had already fled to Italy by the time the payroll robbery took place. Police then arrested two of Boda's known associates, Italian laborers Nicola Sacco and Bartolomeo Vanzetti. At the time of their arrest, both were carrying guns and Sacco's was the same caliber, .32 Colt automatic, as the murder weapon. Sacco was also carrying ammunition made by the same three manufacturers.

Sacco and Vanzetti were tried for the payroll robbery and the murder of one of the security guards. Four bullets had been recovered from the dead guards and experts for the prosecution and defense were retained to determine whether Sacco's .32 Colt pistol was the murder weapon. Not surprisingly, the prosecution experts, though somewhat in disagreement, testified on the whole that Sacco's gun was the murder weapon. The defense experts testified that it was not. It is noteworthy that none of the experts based their opinions on any scientific analysis. None had any formal training in firearms examinations. Ultimately, the jury found Sacco and Vanzetti guilty. They based their opinion in large part on the fact that the bullets that killed the guard were so old and outdated that no one could locate any others except in the possession of Sacco. During the trial, the jurors were furnished with magnifying glasses so that they could view the markings on the bullets.

There was an immediate cry to have the verdict overturned and to set a new trial. The defense hired Albert Hamilton who stated that the murder weapon was definitely not Sacco's, but Hamilton had no real experience or expertise from which to draw these conclusions. Hamilton was a controversial character who had a reputation as someone who would testify to anything he was paid for: a hired gun. The prosecution's expert, Charles Van Amburgh, re-examined the bullet evidence and stuck to his opinion that Sacco's gun fired the fatal bullets. At a hearing to determine whether a retrial was needed, Hamilton brought another gun into court that was the same make and model as Sacco's and tried to exchange the barrels of the two weapons! He was caught by the judge who subsequently denied the motion for a retrial. In 1927, a committee of expert firearms examiners examined the bullet and cartridge evidence and concurred with the prosecution. Even the defense's new expert agreed. Sacco and Vanzetti were executed for the murder. The evidence was re-examined in 1961 and again in 1983 and both supported the conclusions of the 1927 panel. In 1977, however, the governor of Massachusetts issued a proclamation that Sacco and Vanzetti were innocent! The case remains controversial today.

Protests over the guilty verdict and death sentence for
Sacco and Vanzetti.

Introduction

This chapter is about toolmarks. A **toolmark** is a scratch or other microscopic marking left by the action of a tool on an object. Toolmarks are created when two metal objects come into contact with each other. Examples of toolmarks include the microscopic impressions left by the blade of a wire cutter on the end of a cut wire and the scrapings of the edge of a screwdriver left on a door jamb during an attempted break-in. A major part of the science of **firearms identification** also involves the analysis of toolmarks. In many weapons, a tool is used to ream out the barrel of a gun. These toolmarks are then transferred to the surface of any bullet fired through the barrel. Other markings are left on cartridge cases as a bullet is fired. These markings were originally made by tools that made the parts of the weapon. Each time a metal instrument scrapes metal, the instrument changes and becomes more unique. It may develop more scratches, nicks, or other wear patterns. These individual characteristics are then transferred to the subsequent metal object the tool contacts.

Firearms Identification

Trafficking of illegal firearms and the commission of crimes using firearms remain two of the most serious problems in American society today. In 2002, the Bureau of Alcohol, Tobacco, Firearms and Explosives reported that over 80,000 weapons were sold illegally in the U.S. and nearly 2,000 people were charged with selling guns illegally. As the population ages in the United States, the number of crimes has stabilized or been reduced and this is reflected in the stability in recent years in the number of offenses in which a firearm was used. It is currently about 350,000 per year.

The science of firearms identification covers a number of related disciplines. Most people are aware that bullets and cartridges can be traced back to a particular weapon under certain circumstances and this is a major part of the firearms examiner's job. Examiners also determine whether a particular firearm can be fired. This comes into play when a firearm has been deliberately disabled or modified or when a gun is fished out of a creek or lake. Firearms examiners may also be called upon to estimate the distance from which a gun shot or shotgun pellet was fired. **Serial number restorations** on firearms and other objects are often the jobs of a firearms examiner. Some firearms examiners also analyze gunshot residue from hands or other objects to determine whether that person recently fired a weapon. In many crime labs, this activity is carried out by the trace evidence section of the lab.

Ballistics is often used as a synonym for firearms examination. This is somewhat of a misnomer because *ballistics* is defined as the study of projectiles in motion. These projectiles can range from bullets to baseballs to rocket ships. Firearms examiners are interested in ballistics as part of their knowledge because they must understand the characteristics of bullets and shot gun pellets as they are fired by a weapon and reach their target. But, a firearm examiner additionally studies the toolmarks left behind on fired ammunition to match a weapon to a crime. Firearms examiners also work with forensic pathologists in the area of **wound ballistics**, the study of patterns of injury caused by firearm projectiles.

Types of Firearms

There are a bewildering variety of firearms on the market today and precise definitions are often elusive. Firearms examiners generally characterize weapons into one of five categories:

1. **Pistols.** These are also sometimes called **handguns** because they were originally designed to be operated with one hand. Pistols are in turn, divided into two subcategories:
   a. **Revolvers**: These are pistols that contain revolving cylinders with chambers that hold individual **live rounds** (bullets plus cartridge cases). As the weapon is cocked, the next chamber comes into line with the **firing pin** and barrel. After the bullet is fired, the cartridge case remains in the cylinder and must be manually removed.
   b. **Self-loading**: These pistols are usually loaded with a **magazine** that contains a number of bullets. The magazine is loaded into the grip of the gun and the bullets are fed into the firing chamber by a spring load. The cartridge casings are extracted and ejected from the chamber automatically after firing.

2. **Rifles:** Rifles are similar to pistols but are made to be operated with two hands. There are a large number of different types that range from single shot to automatic rifles.

3. **Machine guns:** These are fully automatic weapons that obtain their ammunition from magazines or belts. These weapons produce heavy recoil when fired and cannot be safely fired by holding with two hands. They must have a fixed mounting.

4. **Submachine guns:** These weapons are like machine guns but are meant to be hand held.

5. **Shotguns**: Shotguns differ from the other four types of weapons in that they do not fire bullets. Instead, they fire a range of ammunition, such as shotgun shells or single slugs. Shotgun shell ammunition, such as buckshot and birdshot, consists of plastic cartridges which contain small, usually round, pellets. Because shotguns do not fire bullets, they are not rifled.

Rifling

When a quarterback throws a football to a receiver, he lets the ball fall from his fingertips as he throws. This imparts a spin to the ball along its long axis. This spinning motion imparts angular momentum to the ball, which keeps the ball on its intended trajectory. The consequences of the failure to impart spin to a projectile are put to good advantage by a knuckleball pitcher in baseball. The pitcher throws the ball purposefully without spin, using his knuckles to grip the ball. Without the spin the ball is subject to air resistance and will travel toward the batter with an unpredictable trajectory. This makes the ball much harder to hit because the batter doesn't know where the ball is going. Neither does the catcher who often will be unable to catch a knuckleball.

When someone fires a weapon at a target, he would like to ensure that the bullet has the best chance to hit where it is aimed. This means that the bullet must be made to spin on its long axis as it emerges from the barrel of the weapon. This is accomplished by manufacturing the barrel of the weapon so that rifling is incorporated. The rifling process bores the inside of a gun barrel from one end to the other,

Figure 9.1 Lands and grooves in a rifled barrel. This view looks through the barrel toward the trigger. Note the spiral shapes of the lands and grooves. *Courtesy of* David Brundage, Marion County, Indiana Forensic Services Agency.

Figure 9.2 Rifling broach for gun barrel. Note the downward path to the notches that carve the grooves in the barrel. This imparts the twist in the bullet. *Courtesy of* www.precisionforensictesting. com.

producing a series of **lands** and **grooves**. When the barrel is manufactured a tool such as a rifling button or gang broach is used to dig grooves into the inner surface of the barrel. Figure 9.1 is a diagram of the barrel of a weapon showing the lands and grooves. Figure 9.2 shows one of the metal tools used by a gun manufacturer to make the grooves in a gun barrel.

The grooves are dug in a spiral fashion. Each groove spirals as it travels through the barrel. Between each groove is a raised area called a land. **Rifling** is similar to a series of hills and valleys. The valleys are grooves in the earth and between each valley is a hill (land). There may be an odd or even number of lands and grooves. The numbers range from two to nine of each.

The *number* of lands and grooves, the *direction* of their **twist** through the barrel and the *angle* of twist are all class characteristics that can give valuable information to the firearms examiner about the manufacturer and model of the weapon. The twist of the lands and grooves is noted as a right twist (clockwise) or left twist (counterclockwise). Figure 9.3 shows some of these class characteristics. Note that the *groove* in the barrel makes a *land* in the bullet and a *land* in the barrel makes a *groove* in the bullet. Also note that the number and letter in the bullet drawing represent the number of lands or grooves and the direction of twist. For example, 4R means 4 lands or grooves with a right twist.

The broach or button that makes the lands and grooves is a tool. Its cutting surfaces contain microscopic imperfections made by the tools used to manufacture them. These microscopic markings are transferred to the surfaces of the lands and grooves during the manufacture of the barrel. When the bullet is fired it will pick up not only the lands and grooves but the microscopic imperfections. These usually appear as tiny striations or stria in the lands and grooves and are shown in Figure 9.4 and in Figure 9.5, which is a comparison of the stria in two bullets under a comparison microscope. Striations impart individuality (individual characteristics)

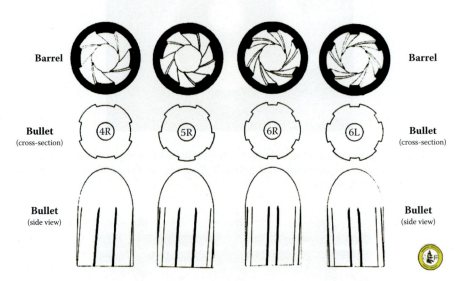

Figure 9.3 Some class characteristics of firearms. The barrel imparts lands and grooves to the sides of the bullets. The number of lands and grooves as well as the angle and direction of twist are class characteristics. *Courtesy of* David Brundage, Marion County, Indiana Forensic Services Agency.

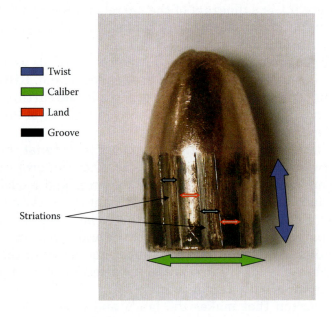

Figure 9.4 Class and individual characteristics of a fired bullet. *Courtesy of* www.precisionforensic testing.com.

Figure 9.5 A photomicrograph showing comparison of bullet stria. The vertical line near the left side of the picture is the dividing line between the two bullets. *Courtesy of* David Brundage, Marion County, Indiana Forensic Services Agency.

to the bullet and aid in the identification of a match between a test-fired bullet and one taken from the crime scene.

If the proper size ammunition is used in a rifled weapon, the bullet expands due to the heat of the gunpowder being ignited. The bullet expands into the grooves and follows them like tracks as it exits the barrel. Because the grooves spiral through the barrel, the bullet spins as it leaves the barrel. Each land in the barrel will dig a groove in the side of the bullet. Each groove in the barrel will become a land in the bullet. Thus the number of lands and grooves, the angle and direction of twist can all be determined by examining the fired bullet. The lands and grooves of the bullet contain the stria that are present in the barrel's lands and grooves.

The Size of Ammunition and Barrels

The size of rifled firearms is described by their **caliber** or bore diameter. To find the bore diameter of a rifled barrel, the distance from opposing lands is measured. If there is an odd number of lands and they don't oppose each other, the bore diameter is the diameter of a circle that touches the tops of the lands. Caliber is no longer used to describe the size of a barrel. It is now used to describe the size of a particular cartridge case or the base of a fired bullet. In the United States, this is the diameter of the base of the cartridge case or bullet measured in hundreds or thousandths of inches (millimeters in Europe). Figure 9.6 shows typical gun calibers in both metric and English system measurements.

Because shotguns do not use bullets, the size of the barrel and the ammunition are measured differently. Many shotgun barrels are constricted by the maker to produce a choke. This narrows the barrel so that the pellets are kept in a tight grouping as they leave the barrel. As they travel toward the target, the pellets will naturally tend to spread out in a cone pattern. The choke reduces the diameter of the cone at any given distance so that the pellets will form a smaller pattern at the target. The

Gun Barrel Caliber	English System Measurement	Metric System Measurement
22	0.223 inches	5.6 mm
25	0.257 inches	6.5 mm
30	0.308 inches	7.8 mm
32	0.321 inches	8.1 mm
38	0.357 inches	9.0 mm
9 mm	0.355 inches	9.0 mm
40	0.400 inches	10.0 mm
45	0.451 inches	11.6 mm

Figure 9.6 Common calibers of guns with the bore diameters in inches and in millimeters.

Figure 9.7 Shotgun ammunition. *Courtesy of* www.precisionforensictesting.com.

diameter of the shotgun barrel is called its **gauge**. The gauge is a measure of the number of pellets weighing one pound that would have the same diameter as the barrel if they were grouped in a circular pattern. For example, twelve lead pellets that together weigh one pound would have the same diameter as a twelve-gauge shotgun. Figure 9.7 shows a typical shotgun cartridge with lead pellets.

The Anatomy of a Live Round (Cartridge)

Figure 9.8 is a diagram of a live round or cartridge. A cartridge is made up of a bullet that fits into the top of a cartridge case. It is held in place by a series of small grooves that circle the bullet near the base. These are called cannelures. Bullets come in three types:

1. **Lead (or lead alloy):** Originally, all bullets were made of nearly pure lead. When the technology of propellants improved to increase velocity, bullets

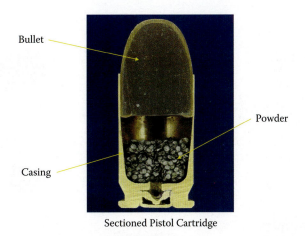

Sectioned Pistol Cartridge

Figure 9.8 A diagram of a live round, also called a cartridge. *Courtesy of* David Brundage, Marion County, Indiana Forensic Services Agency.

became hotter and the soft lead had a tendency to foul the inside of the barrel, so antimony is usually added as an alloy to harden the lead.

2. **Fully jacketed bullets:** These bullets have a layer of copper, brass, or steel that completely girdles the base. This hardens the bullet but reduces its expansion upon firing. Jacketed bullets will also usually not pick up as much detail in the lands and grooves as lead bullets.

3. **Half-jacketed bullets:** These bullets have a jacket around only half the bullet. Usually this is the base of the bullet. The nose is exposed.

Figure 9.9 shows some common types of bullets for comparison.

There are many variations on the above including hollow points, Teflon-coated (armor piercing), and exploding bullets. Cartridge cases are made of brass, nickel-plated brass, or aluminum. They come in a variety of shapes to accommodate different types of firearms. Like bullets, cartridge cases may have cannelures impressed into their surfaces. These keep the bullet from being pushed too far down into the casing. Figure 9.10 shows the three types of cartridge cases.

The heads of some cartridge cases contain markings stamped into the surface. These can reveal the manufacturer and/or the caliber. Other markings on cartridge cases can be imparted by extractors and ejectors in the case of self-loading pistols as well as firing pin impressions and breech face markings. Some of these markings on a cartridge cases are shown in Figures 9.11a and 9.11b.

Propellants

The oldest recorded propellant is black powder, invented by the Chinese around the tenth century. It was used for signals and fireworks. Black powder is a physical mixture of finely divided particles of charcoal (C), sulfur (S), and saltpeter (KNO_3 or potassium nitrate). Formulations vary but saltpeter is always the major component. Saltpeter furnishes the oxygen while the charcoal and sulfur are the fuels that react with the oxygen. See Chapter 21 for a discussion of how explosives work. Even though black powder has been entirely replaced as a commercial propellant by smokeless powders, it is still used by battle reenactors and fans of old weapons.

Smokeless powder was developed in the late nineteenth century to replace black powder as a propellant in weapons. Black powder produces a great amount of smoke

Bullet Reference Chart

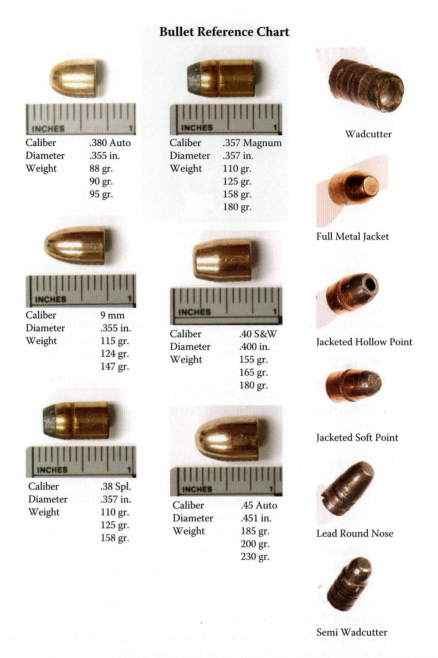

Caliber	.380 Auto
Diameter	.355 in.
Weight	88 gr.
	90 gr.
	95 gr.

Caliber	.357 Magnum
Diameter	.357 in.
Weight	110 gr.
	125 gr.
	158 gr.
	180 gr.

Caliber	9 mm
Diameter	.355 in.
Weight	115 gr.
	124 gr.
	147 gr.

Caliber	.40 S&W
Diameter	.400 in.
Weight	155 gr.
	165 gr.
	180 gr.

Caliber	.38 Spl.
Diameter	.357 in.
Weight	110 gr.
	125 gr.
	158 gr.

Caliber	.45 Auto
Diameter	.451 in.
Weight	185 gr.
	200 gr.
	230 gr.

Wadcutter

Full Metal Jacket

Jacketed Hollow Point

Jacketed Soft Point

Lead Round Nose

Semi Wadcutter

Figure 9.9 Common types of bullets for comparison. Courtesy of www.precisionforensictesting.com.

that could easily reveal the position of the shooter. Smokeless powder emits much less smoke. Smokeless powders come in two varieties: single base and double base. Single base smokeless powder consists of cotton lint or wood pulp that has been titrated by a nitric acid/sulfuric acid mixture. The nitrate ions combine with the hydroxyl groups on the cellulose. This is a chemical mixture of the oxygen and fuel that produces a potent propellant. Double base smokeless powders consist of about 70 percent ± 10 percent cellulose nitrate and about 30 percent ± 10 percent nitroglycerine. These make for more energetic propellants per unit weight, in part because the nitroglycerine lowers the amount of water present in the mixture from about two percent to less than one percent. Water adversely affects the power of the propellant by acting as a heat sink. It is important to note that smokeless powders do not explode inside a cartridge; but instead, they combust. Since the combustion occurs in a closed space, it can have the force of an explosion.

Figure 9.10 Cartridge cases: (L to R) aluminum, brass, and nickel-plated brass. *Courtesy of* www. precisionforensictesting.com.

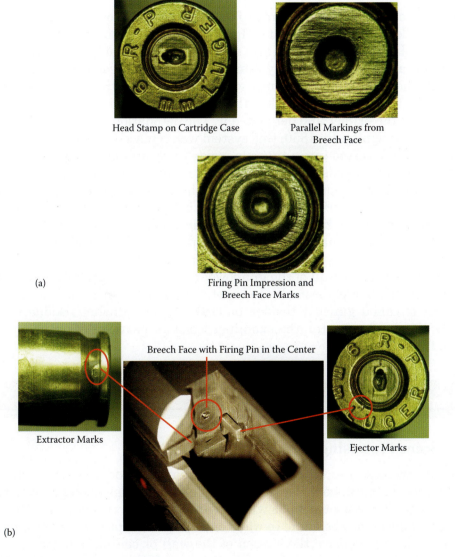

Figure 9.11 Diagrams showing some of the markings made on cartridges by firing a weapon. *Courtesy of* www.precisionforensictesting.com.

Figure 9.12 The nickel center of this cartridge case is the primer cup (shown circled). The firing pin strikes this part of the cartridge in the gun chamber to initiate the explosion. *Courtesy of* www. precisionforensictesting.com.

Primers

In 1807, a Scottish clergyman named James Forsythe discovered the shock-sensitive explosive called mercury fulminate [$Hg(ONC_2)$]. This type of explosive detonates if it is struck or shocked. A spark will also set it off. By 1850, cartridges were being manufactured that contained mercury fulminate inside the head of the cartridge as the primer. At the beginning, the primer was inserted inside the rim of the cartridge. A small pin protruded from the back of the rim. When this pin was struck by the hammer, it struck the primer and detonated it. The detonation caused the powder inside the cartridge to ignite. By 1850, this system was replaced by a simpler one in which the primer was inserted into a tiny cup inside the center of the cartridge head. This portion of the cartridge is commonly referred to as the primer cup.

The firing pin was mounted on the end of the hammer. When it struck the primer cup it compressed the primer and detonated it. The flame produced by the detonation escaped through a hole in the cup and ignited the propellant. Over time, the composition of primers has changed, first by potassium chlorate ($KClO_3$) and today, by a mixture of lead styphnate, antimony sulfide, barium nitrate, and tetracene. When a gun is fired, not all of the gunpowder is burned completely and that burned powder exits the barrel as smoke and soot. This material that leaves the gun with the bullet is called gunshot residue or **GSR**. When gunshot residue is analyzed from the hands of a shooter, the examiner looks for particles of antimony, lead and barium from the primer.

Examination of Firearms Evidence

Crime Scene Processing

As with all crime scenes, those that contain firearms evidence must be clearly documented and photographed. Because bullets and cartridge casings are small, they must be identified in photographs with labels or markers of some type. Often bullets or shotgun pellets may be found in walls or ceilings. The preferred collection method in such cases is to remove the section of the wall or ceiling and send it to the lab where the bullet or pellets can be safely removed. If this is not possible, rubberized tools must be used to remove the bullets.

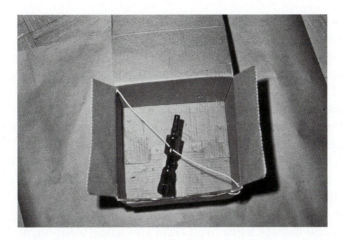

Figure 9.13 A proper method for packaging a weapon for shipment to the crime lab. The gun is suspended in the box by the trigger guard.

Bullets and cartridge casings must never be marked for identification anywhere on their surfaces where there might be forensically significant markings. Many crime scene investigators do not mark them at all but put them in small vials or boxes and then mark the containers. Likewise weapons should never be marked in places were there might be evidence. Sometimes tags can be used. Guns should never be handled by inserting a pencil or anything else in the barrel. This could change the markings in the barrel and render test firings useless. Figure 9.13 shows one way that a weapon can be packaged for shipment to the laboratory.

In many cases, firearms are coated with a thin layer of lubricating oil. This makes them unsuitable surfaces for retaining fingerprint images. Nonetheless, weapons should always be packaged in such a way that fingerprints could be collected if present.

Preliminary Examination

Firearms examiners should always keep in mind that weapons may be sources of significant trace evidence and the examination of the weapon may have to be put off until trace evidence is processed. As previously mentioned, fingerprints are unlikely but not impossible to recover. Blood, fibers or paint flecks may be on the weapon. Bits of tissue from a close-in or contact shot may be present on the weapon or inside the barrel. If the weapon were in the owner's pocket, it may have picked up trace evidence such as lint, fibers, dirt, etc.

Once recovered, as much information as possible should be gathered from the weapon in hopes of identifying the owner or user. The serial number is especially important. Criminals also know this and in many cases they will grind down or file off the serial number. As we see at the end of this chapter, there are methods for restoring obliterated serial numbers.

Bullet and Cartridge Case Comparison

Bullets

At the heart of bullet and cartridge case identification is the need to correctly collect known samples for comparison. For bullets, this means test firing the weapon into a trap. The same type of ammunition must be used as the questioned type. All test firings must be done into the same type of trap. Cotton or other cloth wadding has been used as a trap, but it may cause abrasions on the bullet from the cloth or may partially obliterate markings from the barrel. A better solution is a large water tank. These tanks are made of stainless steel and are long, narrow and deep. The weapon is usually fired through a short pipe into the water. The bottom of the tank is in the shape of a cone in the middle so that all fired bullets will fall into the cone where a small basket is used to retrieve them.

Once the bullets are recovered, their *class* characteristics should first be determined. These include caliber, the number of lands and grooves, and their angles and directions of twist. If these all match the crime scene bullets, the examiner can proceed with the comparison of *individual* characteristics. This is always done with a comparison microscope as described in Chapter 6. If matching stria are found in a pair of land or groove impressions, the bullets should be rotated together to the next land or groove. If the bullets were fired from the same weapon, stria from all of the intact lands and grooves should match.

Just because two bullets were fired from the same weapon doesn't mean that the stria will always match. For example, rust may build up inside the barrel of a weapon and the stria in a bullet may be due mainly to rust. As bullets are fired through such a gun, rust particles are removed and the stria change. Even if rust isn't a problem, repeated firings of a weapon will cause changes in the stria pattern, especially with metal-jacketed bullets. Imperfections in the surface of the jacket can impart stria to the barrel of the gun and remove some that are already there. After fifty firings or so, the stria of the fiftieth bullet may not match the first. Some weapons have interchangeable barrels. This will clearly cause problems if the barrel has been changed between the time the crime scene bullet was fired and the time that the weapon was test-fired.

Cartridge Cases

Cartridges cases can yield the same types of information as bullets. The examiner will attempt to determine the type of weapon used. If a suspect weapon is present, it can be determined whether the cartridge case was fired by that weapon. There are a number of markings on cartridge cases that help make these associations. Stria are present in firing pin impressions, extractor and ejector markings (except in revolvers), breech face markings, and sometimes chamber markings. Figure 9.14 shows a firing pin impression. The pin on the end of the hammer strikes the head of the cartridge case, detonating the primer. There are a few stria on the surface of the firing pin which are then transferred to the casing.

When a bullet is fired, the cartridge case recoils back toward the shooter. A block of metal, called the breech, stops the cartridge case from hitting the shooter. This block contains stria that are transferred to the surface of the head of the casing. A comparison of breech face markings on two cartridge casings is shown in Figure 9.15.

After the bullet is fired from the cartridge, the casing must be removed so that another round can be loaded into the gun. The metal extractor grabs the cartridge so that it can be expelled from the chamber by the metal ejector. Extractor marks can be found on the lip of the cartridge case and extractor marks on the headstamp. Examples of both markings are shown in Figure 9.10b.

Striations on the sides of the cartridge case called chamber marks aid in identification. Chamber marks are produced by the expansion of gases and heat when the cartridge is fired. The casing is pressed tightly against the gun chamber and marks

Figure 9.14 Stria created by a firing pin impression. The line dividing the two cartridges is just to the left of the center of the picture. *Courtesy of* David Brundage, Marion County, Indiana Forensic Services Agency.

Figure 9.15 Stria created by the action of the cartridge slamming up against the breech as the bullet is ejected. Two cartridges shown here were fired by the same weapon. *Courtesy of* David Brundage, Marion County, Indiana Forensic Services Agency.

are impressed as it expands and moves. Figure 9.16 shows chamber marks on a cartridge case and the portion of the gun barrel that made the marks.

Digital Imaging Systems for Ammunition

In 1993, the FBI began the **DRUGFIRE** system. This system is a database of firing pin and primer impressions on spent cartridge cases recovered from crime scenes. A computer network was set up so that firearms examiners could search the database for impressions. The examiner determined whether a crime scene cartridge casing or one test-fired from a seized weapon matched any of the impressions in the database.

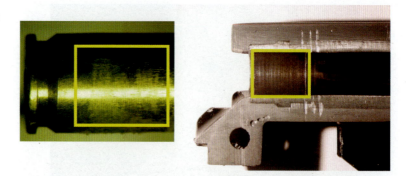

Figure 9.16 Chamber marks on a fired cartridge case and the gun barrel chamber. These fine striations can aid in identification. *Courtesy of* www.precisionforensictesting.com.

If a match was found then arrangements were be made to procure the actual cartridge casing so that a physical, microscopic comparison could be completed.

At the same time that the FBI was developing DRUGFIRE, the Bureau of Alcohol, Tobacco, Firearms and Explosives (BATF) developed the Integrated Ballistics Identification System (IBIS) to capture and rapidly compare bullet stria. Unfortunately, IBIS and DRUGFIRE were not compatible. In order to be able to search both databases, an examiner had to have two different computer workstations. As a result, in 1997, the FBI and ATF established the National Integrated Ballistic Information Network (NIBIN) that permits searching of bullets or cartridge cases using the same computer system. It can be found online at http://dci.sd.gov/lab/nibin.htm.

The development of the bullet and cartridge case databases led to the concept of ballistic fingerprinting. Under this program, each new weapon is test fired at the factory and the cartridge case is recovered. Breechface marks and firing pin impressions are stored in a computer database. If cartridge cases are recovered at a crime scene and no weapon is found, the breechface markings and firing pin impressions can be compared to those in the database. Although this may seem like an effective program, it has been fraught with problems. First, it is expensive to implement. Second, it is often hard to substantiate a paper trail of a gun purchase. False identification documents may be used. Sales may be made illegally. Weapons can be stolen from original owners. Finally, if many rounds are fired between the time the gun is manufactured and the time it is used in a crime, firing pin impressions and breechface markings, like bullet stria, may change enough so that they can no longer be matched to a test-fired sample. Presently, only two states require ballistic fingerprinting of handguns sold.

Distance-of-Fire Determinations

Gunshots

When a bullet is fired from a gun, hot gases containing residue from the primer and smokeless powder will be expelled from the barrel and will travel for short distances in a roughly conical pattern. This residue is composed of soot from the burned powder and **stippling**, which is unburned gunpowder and barrel residue. Depending on the distance from the weapon to the target, some of this residue may be deposited on the target. The size of the gunshot residue (GSR) pattern can be used to determine

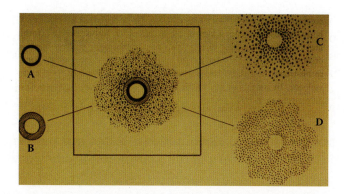

Figure 9.17 The anatomy of a bullet hole in a target. *A* is a contusion ring caused by friction. *B* is a ring of dirt that is deposited on the target by the bullet. *C* is stippling, or unburned and partially burned particles of gunshot residue. *D* is soot from the gunpowder.

the approximate distance between the weapon and the target when the bullet was fired. There are a number of limitations to this test that must be kept in mind when distance-of-firing measurements are made.

Gunshot residues do not travel far before being dispersed. It is rare to find gunshot residue on a target that is more than eighteen inches from the weapon. If no residues are found on the target, the range is called a distance shot. If gunshot residues are found on the target, the range is called a close range shot. In a contact shot the muzzle of the barrel is in direct contact with the target and no gunshot residue will be found on the target. If the target is a human head, gunshot residue may be injected into the soft tissues of the head and will be found inside the wound.

A distance shot produces a bullet hole that is roughly round. The edges of the hole may be burned or singed owing to friction from the bullet as it passes through the target. This contusion ring may be partially or totally obscured by a ring of dirt made up of lubricant, dirt and dust, and metal shavings. The size, shape and other characteristics of the bullet hole do not change with distance so these characteristics cannot be used to estimate the distance of firing.

Gunshot residue will be deposited in a close range shot. The residue consists of large and small particles of burned or unburned propellant and some primer particles. The largest are easily seen as discrete particles and are called stippling or tattooing. The smaller particles appear as soot.

Distance-of-firing determinations are done by test firing the same weapon and ammunition at various distances and then comparing the size of the stippling and soot pattern on the target. Not even another weapon of the same exact type will reproduce gunshot patterns and serious errors can occur in interpretation if the exact same weapon is not used. Figure 9.17 shows the various characteristics of a bullet hole in a target.

Shotgun Shots

As a shot leaves the barrel of the shotgun, it tends to spread in a conical pattern. When the shot strikes the target, the pellets form a roughly circular pattern. The size of the pattern increases as the distance of firing increases. Although this sounds straightforward, a number of problems can arise in determining the distance of firing.

Humans are usually the targets of shotgun firings. The human body is a relatively small target and unless the target is fairly close to the firing, some of the pellets will miss the body altogether. This means that it may be difficult or impossible to establish an accurate pellet pattern.

If there is an intermediate target such as a window screen, the pattern on the final target may be distorted because the leading pellets will be slowed by the intermediate target and may be hit from behind by the trailing pellets, thus causing scattering. This is not predictable and not reproducible.

As with gunshot distance-of-firing determinations, test firings of shotguns must be done with the same weapon and ammunition in order to make proper interpretations

Normally, distance-of-firing determinations of shotgun patterns are performed by comparing the size of the pattern of the known and unknown shots.

Toolmarks

At the beginning of this chapter, a toolmark was defined as a scratch or other microscopic marking left by the action of a tool on an object. The discussion of firearms analysis showed that the markings left on bullets and cartridges as a gun was fired are all the results of toolmarks. The analysis of toolmarks takes advantage of the observation that no two toolmarks, even those left by the same type of tool, are identical. This implies that, in general, toolmarks should be individualizable. This is borne out in part by the observation that even consecutively manufactured guns whose parts are machined by the same tool will be distinguishable by their toolmarks. There has been almost no research, however, into the toolmark characteristics left by brand new tools, such as wire cutters, that were consecutively manufactured. Thus, care must be taken when extending the observations about bullets to all tools. The criterion of a match of known and unknown toolmarks: *that there be a sufficient number of similarities and no unexplainable differences*, must be applied cautiously, since there have not been sufficient studies to determine a *standard* number of similarities in toolmark identification.

Virtually any tool can leave markings and these markings may be used to help determine the source of the evidence. Take, for example, the evidence shown in Figure 9.18. This case involved a breaking and entering into a remote country house. The perpetrator cut the telephone lines with a wire cutter so the occupants couldn't call for help. When he was arrested, the wire cutters were still in his possession with his fingerprints all over the handles. Test cuts were made on a metal sheet to get the entire cutting blade surface. The photo shows how the some of the toolmarks in the cut wires match the test cuts in the metal sheet. These matches are shown as photomicrographs taken with a comparison microscope.

Figure 9.19 shows a fairly common toolmark examination. Here a screwdriver was used to attempt to pry open a door. The blade left markings on the doorjamb. Test scrapings were made into sheet metal. Once again, the stria in the knowns and unknowns can be seen to match.

Figure 9.20 shows a comparison microscope photo of a tip of a screwdriver on the left scraping across a surface. The photo on the right shows a scrape by the same screwdriver tip along a similar surface. Notice how the abrasion lines match left to right.

Serial Number Restoration

One of the more interesting toolmarks is a serial number that is stamped into an object, usually metal. When the machine stamps the serial number into the metal, the area below the stamped letter becomes strained. The metal bonds are

Figure 9.18 A match and non-match. A comparison of two cut wires with a piece of sheet metal, all cut by the same wire cutter. The two wires are in the top photo and the piece of sheet metal is in the bottom photo. Note that the striations on the *right* wire line up perfectly with the striations on the sheet metal whereas the striations on the *left* wire do not match. This is because the wire on the left was cut by a *different* part of the wire cutter.

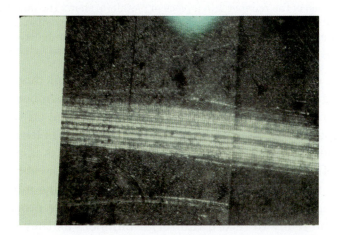

Figure 9.19 Stria made by a screwdriver on a piece of metal. Two scrapings were made by the same tool. The stria are virtually the same with each scraping.

Figure 9.20 Toolmark comparison. This is a comparison microscope photo of toolmarks made by the same metal tool. Notice how the individual striations line up left to right. *Courtesy of* www.precision forensictesting.com.

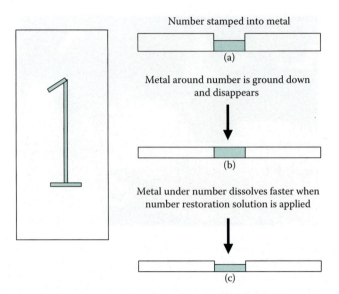

Figure 9.21 A diagram showing how a serial number that is stamped into metal can be restored. (a) shows the indentation of the number 1 in a piece of metal; (b) shows the metal around the number being scraped off using a grinder. Although the number is no longer visible, the metal is deformed where the number was stamped; (c) shows how the metal under the number dissolves more rapidly than the surrounding metal. The number reappears for a short time and can be read.

weakened. Often a thief will attempt to remove the serial number from a stolen object such as a gun by filing or grinding off the serial numbers. He will usually stop when the number disappears, that is when he has filed off the metal that surrounds the stamped serial number until the whole surface is level. What he doesn't realize is that the strained metal below the serial numbers is a sort of "memory" of the numbers. If a solution that dissolves the metal is swabbed on the ground surface, the area where the serial number was will dissolve much faster and the number will reappear, at least temporarily. The swabbing process must be done with camera at the ready to record the serial numbers as they appear. Once they disappear again, they will be gone forever. Figure 9.21 is a series of diagrams of a serial number stamped into a metal surface. The first figure shows the top view of the letter 1 stamped into a piece of metal. Figure (a) shows this as viewed from the side as a cutaway. The shaded area is where the number is stamped into the metal. In (b), the surface has been ground down until it is level and the serial number disappears. In (c), the dissolving solution has been applied and the area beneath the serial number dissolves much faster than the surrounding metal and the number reappears.

Figure 9.22 shows the restoration of an actual serial number obliteration. Photo (a) illustrates the sanding process to smooth the surface for chemical treatment. In Photo (b), the serial number begins to appear when chemicals are added to the prepped surface, and in Photo (c) the number is visible and photographed.

There are a number of recipes for solutions suitable for recovering serial numbers. These solutions are specific for different types of metals. Most serial numbers are applied to an iron or steel surface. One of the more popular solutions consists of 100 mL each of concentrated hydrochloric acid and water and 90 g of cupric chloride ($CuCl_2$). This solution acts as a reducing agent that dissolves iron and deposits copper.

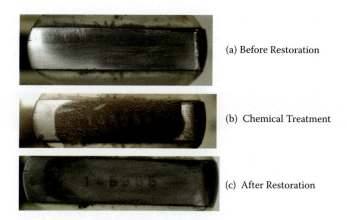

(a) Before Restoration

(b) Chemical Treatment

(c) After Restoration

Figure 9.22 Serial number restoration. The surface which contains the obliterated serial numbers is first sanded smooth (*a*), then treated with chemicals (*b*), and then wiped clean to reveal the numbers (*c*). Recovered serial numbers are then photographed before they fade from view. *Photos courtesy* of www.precisionforensictesting.com.

Summary

Toolmarks are scratches made by tools that are used to fabricate objects such as guns and wire cutters. The tools leave microscopic markings on the surface of the object. These markings are unique to each tool and can be used to individualize the object. Firearms analysis is a major area of toolmarks. Tools are used to put the **grooves** and lands in rifled barrels that make bullets spin as they leave the barrel. The tools that dig the grooves leave microscopic markings called stria or striations on the inside of the barrel. These are transferred to the surface of the bullet as it passes through the barrel. Other parts of the weapon, also manufactured by tools, leave markings on cartridge cases. These include extractor and ejector markings and chamber marks as well as breech face and firing pin impressions. All of these are potentially individual markings. The number of lands and grooves in a bullet as well as the angle and direction of twist are class characteristics. The striations within a groove in a bullet are individual characteristics. There is no set number of individual characteristics that must be present in order to declare that a bullet or cartridge casing was fired from a particular weapon.

Shotguns fire pellets rather than bullets and the barrels of these guns are not rifled. The pellets cannot be traced back to the individual weapon, but markings on the cartridge such as firing pin and breech face impressions can individualize the cartridge.

Distance-of-firing determinations can be estimated if the same weapon and ammunition are available. For bullets, the distance of firing is determined by the pattern left by propellant and primer that follows the bullet out of the barrel. The stippling and soot are only deposited on the target for a short distance. Beyond that, there is no reliable way of making distance of firing determinations. With shotguns, the diameter of the pellet pattern on the target can be used to determine the distance-of-firing if the same weapon and ammunition are used.

Other tools such as screwdrivers and wire cutters also leave stria or striations on the surface of objects. These markings may also be traceable back to the particular tool.

Serial number restoration is related to toolmark analysis except the goal is to identify the serial number that was ground off the metal surface of an object such as a gun. The metal bonds beneath the stamped serial number are weakened. When a dissolving or etching solution is used, this weakened metal dissolves faster than the surrounding metal and the serial number will be temporarily visualized.

Mini Lab Activities

TOOLMARKS

Materials:

> Six to eight *different suspect* screwdrivers (ends are worn, different shaped tips, different types of grooves in the tips)
> Unknown cast of one of the screwdrivers—the *evidence*
> Unknown scrape by one of the screwdrivers—the *evidence*
> Heavy duty aluminum foil (cut into 3-inch squares)
> Modeling clay
> Set up by the instructor

Procedure:

1. Make casts of the entire tip of each screwdriver using the modeling clay. Do this by taking a small piece of clay and smoothing it out into a 2-inch square. Gently press one side of the tip of the screwdriver into the clay, leaving room for an impression of the other side of the tip. Flip the tip over and make a second impression in the clay piece. Additionally, make an impression of the end of the screwdriver tip. Your clay piece should look *something* like the diagram below. Label your cast. Repeat for all suspect screwdrivers.

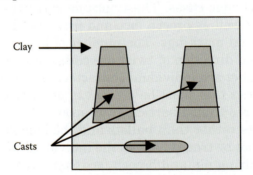

2. Using your suspect casts, determine which matches the cast of the evidence. Be prepared to support your claim with details about the match.
3. Using the same screwdrivers, gently scrape them across the aluminum foil sheet, using both sides of the tip. Label your suspect scrapes.
4. Compare your test scrapes to the evidence. Determine which matches the cast of the evidence. Be prepared to support your claim with details about the match.

Test Yourself

Multiple Choice

1. Rifling of a barrel refers to
   a. The grooves made in the barrel
   b. The stria in the barrel
   c. The lands and grooves in the barrel
   d. The firing pin impression
2. Which markings will not be found on a cartridge casing fired from a revolver?
   a. Lands
   b. Extractor markings
   c. Firing pin impressions
   d. Breechface markings
3. Which of the following is a class characteristic of a fired bullet or cartridge casing?
   a. Number of lands and grooves
   b. Ejector markings
   c. Breechface markings
   d. Bullet striations
4. Which of the following is true of distance-of-firing determinations of shotguns?
   a. Distance of firing cannot be determined with shotguns
   b. When a human being is the target, distance-of-firing determinations are easy because all of the pellets usually hit the target
   c. Intermediate targets have no effect on distance-of-firing determinations
   d. The same weapon and ammunition must be used to determine the distance of firing
5. Which of the following is true about the stria in a barrel of a gun?
   a. They are present in all weapons
   b. They are class characteristics
   c. They never change as the weapon is fired repeatedly
   d. They are initially made by the tool that makes the barrel
6. The major propellant used in firearms today is:
   a. Smokeless powder
   b. Sodium azide
   c. Black powder
   d. Mercury fulminate
7. Which of the following is not a rifled weapon?
   a. Pistol
   b. Shotgun
   c. Machine gun
   d. Submachine gun
8. Today, "caliber" is defined in the United States as:
   a. The diameter of the base of the cartridge in thousandths of inches
   b. The distance from the top of opposite lands in the barrel
   c. The distance from the bottom of opposite grooves in the barrel
   d. The length of the bullet in inches

9. Which of the following is true about serial number restoration?
   a. Serial numbers can be restored on any surface
   b. The metal below a stamped serial number is more dense than the surrounding metal, making it slower to dissolve in an etching solution
   c. The metal below a stamped serial number is strained, making it faster to dissolve in an etching solution than the surrounding metal
   d. Once restored, serial numbers remain visible permanently
10. In the Sacco–Vanzetti case discussed at the beginning of the chapter, the jury based its guilty finding mainly on:
   a. The matching striations on the bullets to Sacco's gun as determined by a firearms examiner
   b. The fact that the type of ammunition used in the killings was very rare and only the defendants had any of it
   c. The fact that all of the firearms examiners for the defense and prosecution agreed that the bullets taken from the dead guard matched Sacco's weapon
   d. Sacco's admission of guilt on the stand in his trial
11. Determining the path of a bullet is considered to be part of the study of _____.
   a. Trajectories
   b. Firearms identification
   c. Ballistics
   d. Toolmark identification
12. Which of the following weapons does *not* have rifling in the barrel?
   a. Revolver
   b. Shotgun
   c. Pistol
   d. Handgun

True or False

13. When a manufacturer rifles a barrel of a gun, it uses a broach tool to cut grooves into the metal barrel.
14. Once a toolmark has been impressed upon a surface, the tool making the mark never changes.
15. If a perpetrator sands down a serial number to the point where it is no longer visible, it is beyond the point of restoration.
16. Chamber marks on cartridge cases are considered individual characteristics.
17. Stippling on a surface is caused by metal shavings exiting a gun barrel.
18. Chemicals dissolve the unstamped area of a metal more rapidly than the stamped area, causing obliterated serial numbers to appear.
19. Extractor marks, breechface marks, striations, and serial numbers are all examples of toolmarks.

Short Answer

20. Bullet diagram. Name the labeled parts. Is the twist left or right?

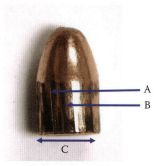

21. When a bullet is found at a crime scene imbedded into a material, the crime scene technician should use rubberized tools to extract the bullet. What is the reasoning behind this?

22. A weapon is recovered from a crime scene. What types of evidence might the firearms examiner retrieve from the weapon and in what order, if any, should the evidence be processed?

23. List the class characteristics of a fired bullet. How can a fired bullet become individualized to a weapon?

24. Describe an instance when a fired bullet would *not* match the weapon from which it was fired?

25. If ballistic fingerprinting can create a database of manufactured weapons, why do more states not enlist such a program?

Further Readings

Heard, B. J. *Handbook of Firearms and Ballistics.* Chichester, England: Wiley & Sons, 1997.

Rowe, W. F. Firearms Identification. *Forensic Science Handbook.* Vol. 2, Ed. R. Saferstein. Upper Saddle River, NJ: Prentice Hall, 1988.

Davis, J. E. *An Introduction to Toolmarks, Firearms, and the Striagraph.* Springfield, IL: Charles Thomas, 1958.

On the Web

National Integrated Ballistic Information Network (NIBIN) http://dci.sd.gov/lab/nibin.htm
Stippling: www.fbi.gov/hq/lab/fsc/backissu/april2004/research/2004_02_research02.htm
Sacco & Vanzetti: www.youtube.com/watch?v=C3SuTTcj2u8
Firearms:www.ct.gov/dps/cwp/view.asp?a=2155&q=315176
www.fbi.gov/hq/lab/fsc/backissu/april2000/schehl1.htm#Introduction
www.firearmsid.com
www.nibin.gov/
http://library.med.utah.edu/WebPath/TUTORIAL/GUNS/GUNINTRO.html
Toolmarks
www.fbi.gov/hq/lab/fsc/backissu/april2000/schehl2.htm#Toolmark
Case solved using firearms database
www.saf.org/USAtoday102799.html

PART IV

Forensic Biology

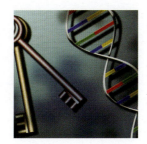

PART IV

Forensic Biology

10
Forensic Pathology

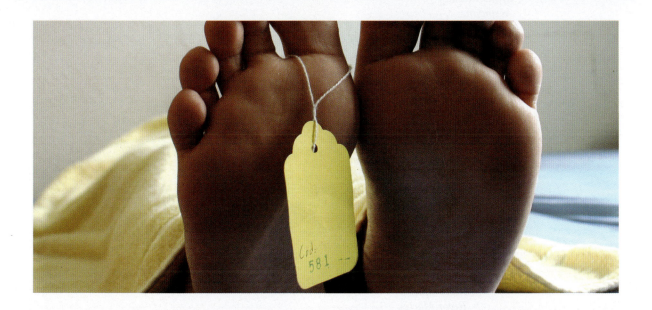

1. To be able to define pathology and forensic pathology and explain the differences
2. To be able to describe the coroner and medical examiner systems and describe their differences and similarities
3. To be able to define and distinguish between the cause of death and the manner of death
4. To be able to define and describe the medicolegal autopsy and explain when a coroner or medical examiner must perform an autopsy
5. To be able to describe the patterns of injury and characteristics of mechanical, electrical, thermal and chemical types of death
6. To be able to define the postmortem interval and explain how the short- and long-term PMIs are estimated

Chapter 10
Forensic Pathology

Chapter Outline

Mini Glossary

Algor mortis: Cooling of the body after death.

Anatomic pathology: The study of the structural and morphological changes to the body as the result of a disease state.

Autopsy: Internal and external investigation of a body to determine cause and manner of death.

Cause of death: The trauma or injury or the disease (or combination of both) which resulted in cessation of life.

Clinical pathology: The analysis of various materials removed from the body including blood, saliva, spinal fluid, urine, etc. for the purpose of determining the presence of drugs and/or poisons and their role in illness or death.

Coroner: Elected official whose function is to determine the cause and manner of death in cases that are statutorily mandated.

Crowner: Chief tax collector in medieval England. Functions included determining cause and manner of death.

Embalming: Addition of a preservative chemical to the body shortly after death.

Exhumation: Removal of a body after burial.

Hyperthermia: Extreme heat.

Hypothermia: Extreme cold.

Livor mortis: Tendency of the blood to pool at the lowest part of the body under the influence of gravity after death.

Manner of death: The set of circumstances that existed at the time the death was caused. There are only four manners of death: homicide, natural causes, accidental, or suicide.

Mechanism of death: The actual physical, physiological or chemical event that brings on cessation of life.

Medical examiner: Appointed official whose function is to determine the cause and manner of death in cases that are statutorily mandated. Must be a physician.

Medicolegal autopsy: Part of postmortem investigation of the body. Same as autopsy.

Pathology: The medical specialty concerned with the determination of the causes and manners of disease and death.

Postmortem interval (PMI): Time since death.

Rief of the shire: Local official appointed by the Crowner to help with determination of cause and manner of death.

Rigor mortis: Stiffening of the joints within hours after death.

Stippling: Particles of burned and unburned gunshot residue that is deposited on the surface of the target of a gun shot.

Acronyms

PMI: Postmortem interval

Introduction

Forensic pathology is one of the most important of the forensic applications of biology. Although **pathology** is a medical specialty that involves both the living and the dead, forensic pathology is involved only with the dead. Pathology originally involved the study of the structural and morphological changes to the body as the result of a disease state. Today this is called anatomic pathology. In modern times, pathology has been expanded to include the study of disease by analytical laboratory methods. This includes the analysis of various materials removed from the body including blood, saliva, spinal fluid, urine, etc. for the purpose of determining the presence of drugs and/or poisons and their role in illness or death. Today, this branch is called clinical pathology. The difference is the purpose for which the pathology is being carried out. Most clinical pathology today is done by forensic toxicologists who work with forensic pathologists in helping determine the cause and

manner of death in postmortem cases. Forensic toxicology is discussed in detail in Chapter 17. Both anatomic and clinical pathology are used in the practice of forensic pathology. Forensic pathology is the determination of the cause and manner of death in cases of suspicious or unexplained death. In this chapter we will study the role of the forensic pathologist in the investigation of death and will learn a bit about how the cause and manner of death can be determined and who has the responsibility for making these determinations.

How to Become a Forensic Pathologist

After high school, it takes approximately fourteen years to become a fully trained, board-certified forensic pathologist. First, one must obtain a college degree (at least four years) and apply to medical school, since pathology is a medical specialty and practitioners must first obtain a medical degree. This takes four more years after obtaining a college degree. After completing medical school, many physicians desire to become specialists in a specific type of medicine such as pediatrics, internal medicine or pathology. This requires a residency in a specialty. This generally takes three to four additional years after medical school. After a four-year residency in pathology, a physician can become board certified as a general pathologist. However, to obtain certification in forensic pathology, the pathologist must spend an additional year or two in a residency and can then apply for certification from the American Board of Forensic Pathology.

The major duties of a forensic pathologist are:

- To determine the apparent cause of death
- To determine (estimate) the postmortem interval (PMI) or time of death
- To ascertain the manner of death
- To determine the identity of the deceased

Investigation of Death: Coroners and Medical Examiners

Every country and, in the United States, each state, has a system in place to investigate deaths. This system includes one or more officials who are in charge of the death investigation process and one or more pathologists who assist in the investigation by conducting a medicolegal autopsy or postmortem investigation of the body. Today in the United States and some other countries, there are two systems of death investigation—the **coroner** and the **medical examiner**. Before explaining these, a bit of history is necessary.

The first system for the investigation of death in the Western world was developed around 1000 B.C. in England. Officials called **crowners** were named by the king to collect taxes from around the country. At some point, landholders would die and a decision had to be made as to the disposition of their land holdings. This was a very important function to the king because much of his wealth derived from goods and taxes that were given by the landowners as a condition of continuing in possession of the land. Thus, if a landowner committed suicide, his land and wealth would be forfeited to the crown because by the act of taking his own life he had in a way, deprived the king of a taxpayer. By the same token, someone who killed a landowner would likewise be removing a taxpayer from the rolls and would forfeit his land as part of his punishment. The process of determining how and why someone died fell to the crowner because of the goods and taxes implications of the death. In a far-flung empire this was a complicated system and the crowner would enlist help by appointing local officials in each county (shire), the **rief of the shire** (or shire rief) to help with death investigations. The shire rief would investigate the crime, often by enlisting the help of local upstanding citizens who would view the body and the evidence from witnesses and help reach a conclusion as to the cause and manner of death. There were no physicians, let alone pathologists at the time who could provide expertise to this process. That wouldn't happen until much later.

When the American colonies were founded, citizens imported much of the English legal system, including the system of death investigation. The crowner became the coroner who is responsible for the determination of cause and manner of death. Most states had a coroner for each county and, in some cases, for major cities. The Shire Rief became, of course, the sheriff whose job became one of law enforcement and jail management rather than having a specific role in the investigation of death. As time passed, it became evident that there are some problems with the coroner system. First, for the most part, coroners didn't have to be pathologists or even physicians. They didn't have to have any medical training whatsoever. Some coroners were, and are today, funeral home directors. This means that a coroner could steer business to his own funeral home after completing examination of a body. This has led to some abuse of the system. As medical education developed in the United States and pathology became a recognized medical specialty, coroners began to enlist pathologists help in investigating deaths. In recognition of these problems, a medical examiner system was developed. Under this system, the official who is responsible for the determination of the cause and manner of death must be a physician (although usually not a pathologist) and is appointed by the government of the county or state. If the medical examiner is not a pathologist he or she will enlist the aid of one or more of them to help with death investigations. Massachusetts was the first state to have a medical examiner, in 1877. Today about half of the states use the medical examiner system and the other half use a form of the coroner system. Some have mixed systems and employ both medical examiners and coroners.

Death Investigation Process

When a body is found under suspicious or unexplained circumstances, a medical examiner or coroner (or deputy) is called to the death scene. At that time the official determines that the person is, in fact, dead and makes some preliminary observations about the cause and manner of death by noting the position of the body and the surroundings of the death, as well as obvious wounds or trauma. In addition, data is collected that can be used to estimate the **postmortem interval (PMI)** or time since death. This is often a critical piece of information in solving a homicide. When the pathologist is finished with this examination, the body is often turned over to a special death investigation scene team, which is specially trained to examine a body so as to be able to spot, document and collect important trace and other evidence before moving the body to the morgue. Improper handling of a body at a death scene can cause the loss or compromise of critical evidence of the cause and manner of

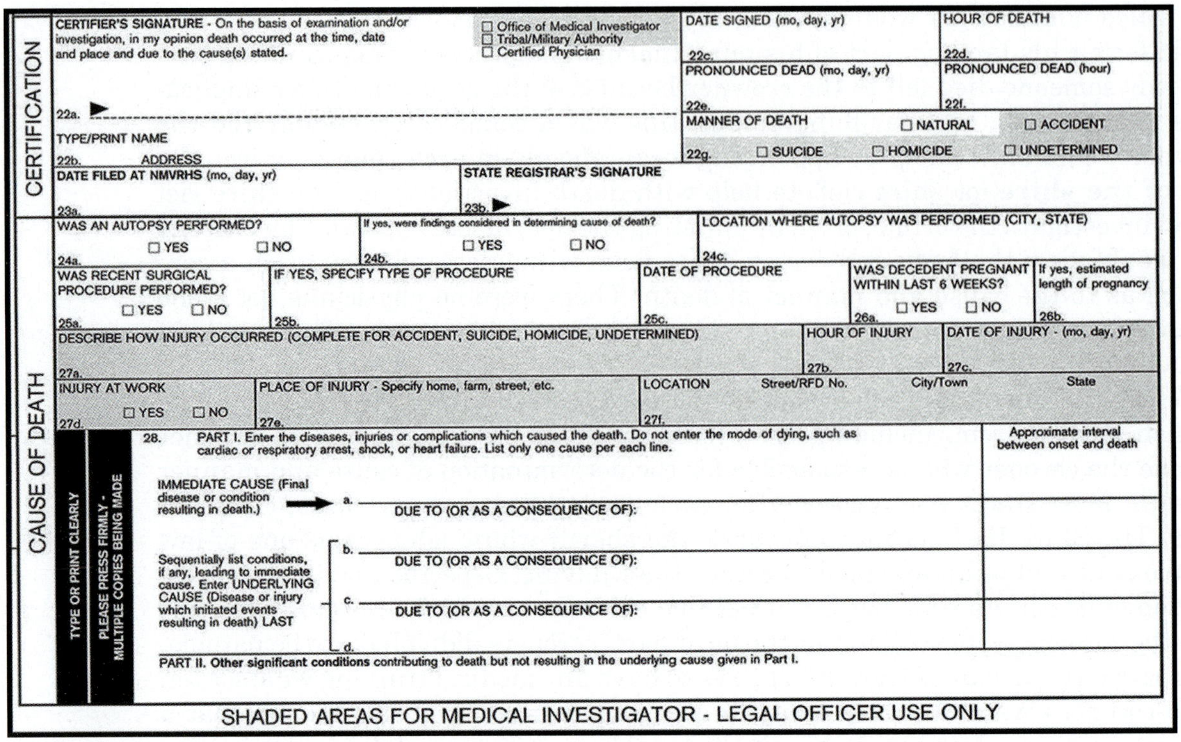
CERTIFICATION
CERTIFIER'S SIGNATURE - On the basis of examination and/or investigation, in my opinion death occurred at the time, date and place and due to the cause(s) stated.
☐ Office of Medical Investigator
☐ Tribal/Military Authority
☐ Certified Physician
22a.
TYPE/PRINT NAME
22b. ADDRESS
DATE SIGNED (mo, day, yr) 22c.
HOUR OF DEATH 22d.
PRONOUNCED DEAD (mo, day, yr) 22e.
PRONOUNCED DEAD (hour) 22f.
MANNER OF DEATH ☐ NATURAL ☐ ACCIDENT
22g. ☐ SUICIDE ☐ HOMICIDE ☐ UNDETERMINED
DATE FILED AT NMVRHS (mo, day, yr) 23a.
STATE REGISTRAR'S SIGNATURE 23b.
CAUSE OF DEATH
WAS AN AUTOPSY PERFORMED? ☐ YES ☐ NO 24a.
If yes, were findings considered in determining cause of death? ☐ YES ☐ NO 24b.
LOCATION WHERE AUTOPSY WAS PERFORMED (CITY, STATE) 24c.
WAS RECENT SURGICAL PROCEDURE PERFORMED? ☐ YES ☐ NO 25a.
IF YES, SPECIFY TYPE OF PROCEDURE 25b.
DATE OF PROCEDURE 25c.
WAS DECEDENT PREGNANT WITHIN LAST 6 WEEKS? ☐ YES ☐ NO 26a.
If yes, estimated length of pregnancy 26b.
DESCRIBE HOW INJURY OCCURRED (COMPLETE FOR ACCIDENT, SUICIDE, HOMICIDE, UNDETERMINED) 27a.
HOUR OF INJURY 27b.
DATE OF INJURY - (mo, day, yr) 27c.
INJURY AT WORK ☐ YES ☐ NO 27d.
PLACE OF INJURY - Specify home, farm, street, etc. 27e.
LOCATION Street/RFD No. City/Town State 27f.
TYPE OR PRINT CLEARLY
PLEASE PRESS FIRMLY - MULTIPLE COPIES BEING MADE
28. PART I. Enter the diseases, injuries or complications which caused the death. Do not enter the mode of dying, such as cardiac or respiratory arrest, shock, or heart failure. List only one cause per each line.
Approximate interval between onset and death
IMMEDIATE CAUSE (Final disease or condition resulting in death.) a.
DUE TO (OR AS A CONSEQUENCE OF):
Sequentially list conditions, if any, leading to immediate cause. Enter UNDERLYING CAUSE (Disease or injury which initiated events resulting in death) LAST
b.
DUE TO (OR AS A CONSEQUENCE OF):
c.
DUE TO (OR AS A CONSEQUENCE OF):
d.
PART II. Other significant conditions contributing to death but not resulting in the underlying cause given in Part I.
SHADED AREAS FOR MEDICAL INVESTIGATOR - LEGAL OFFICER USE ONLY

Figure 10.1 A portion of a death certificate showing the possible manners of death. The medical examiner or coroner must choose one of these for each death. Note that the area under "cause of death" permits several entries.

death. Only after this careful search for evidence and documentation of the scene, is the body removed.

Death Certificate

Every state requires that a death certificate be issued for every death that occurs within each jurisdiction. State law provides what the death certificate must contain and who may fill it out and sign it. The law also describes those situations where a death must be investigated by the coroner or medical examiner and signed by him or her. Although these laws vary somewhat, they require that suspicious or unexplained deaths and those of people who haven't recently been under the care of a physician must be investigated by the medical examiner or coroner. Typically this will involve about one-third of all deaths. These deaths will usually, but not always, involve a medicolegal autopsy as part of the death investigation process. The two critical pieces of information on the death certificate are the cause and manner of death. Figure 10.1 shows a portion of a typical death certificate.

Cause of Death

There are many **causes of death**. The trauma or injury or the disease (or combination of both) which resulted in cessation of life is the cause of death. Normally a pathologist will determine the primary or immediate cause of death and, if present, secondary or contributing cause(s) of death. For example, consider the case of a man who is driving his car on a highway. He suddenly has a stroke, which causes the loss of sight in his eyes and loss of motor control of his arms and legs. He loses control of his car and crashes into a tree. The impact forces the steering column into his chest, causing fatal trauma to his heart. The primary cause of death is the injury sustained in the crash. The stroke would be a contributing cause of death. If the man had high blood pressure, it may have contributed to causing the stroke and could be viewed as a contributing cause of death. In other cases the injury or disease itself causes death quickly and there are no other secondary causes. An especially lethal snakebite would be an example of this.

Some pathologists also speak of the **mechanism of death**. This is the actual physical, physiological, or chemical event that brings on cessation of life. Here the pathologist must carefully examine the organ or system that failed due to the application of the cause of death and describe exactly what changes occurred that were incompatible with life.

Occasionally, determination of the cause of death can be tricky. For example, suppose that someone suffered a nonlethal gunshot wound when being robbed at gun point. The bullet became lodged in an inoperable location in the man's head, but did not cause him to die or even be ill. Years later, he gets into a fight with another man in a barroom brawl. The other man hits him in the head with a chair, but not hard enough to kill him. The blow dislodges the bullet from its location and its movement causes trauma to the brain that causes uncontrollable bleeding that causes death. What was the actual cause of death? It can be difficult to determine years after the first contributing factor.

Manner of Death

The manner of death is the set of circumstances that existed at the time the death was caused. There are only four manners of death and thus, all deaths must be attributed to one of them. These are homicide, natural causes, accidental, or suicide. There is a space on the death certificate that requires the coroner or medical examiner to list the manner of death. See Figure 10.2. In some states the official must put one of the four, even if he or she has to make an educated guess. In most states, however, the official can put "undetermined" if there is not enough information to reach a definite conclusion about the manner of death.

In many cases, the manner of death is evident. If someone dies after a massive heart attack in his home, the manner of death will be listed as *natural causes*. If a person is driving a car while talking on a cell phone and accidentally drops the phone and then loses control of the car while trying to retrieve the phone, and then has a fatal crash, the manner of death will be *accidental*. About thirty years ago there was a poisoning case in Michigan where a housekeeper, angry at not getting a raise in salary, set out to kill her employer by putting ant syrup (a combination of honey and arsenic used to attract and poison ants) in the employer's coffee. Instead, the employer's visiting sister drank the coffee by mistake and died. The manner of death was a *homicide* even though the housekeeper didn't mean to kill the sister.

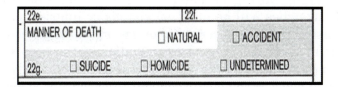

Figure 10.2 A close up of the manner of death portion of a death certificate. This certificate permits a conclusion of "undetermined." In some states, this is not permitted.

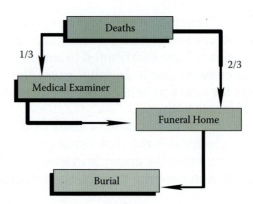

Figure 10.3 This chart shows the distribution of deaths and the fraction sent to a medical examiner or coroner for autopsy. *Courtesy of* Meredith Haddon.

Medicolegal Autopsy

One of the most critical parts of the investigation of death is the **autopsy** (also called medicolegal autopsy). In medicolegal cases, it is hard to imagine how one could accurately determine the cause and manner of death without probing the exterior and interior of the body. The term *autopsy* means to "see with one's own eyes." This doesn't seem like an appropriate term to describe the examination of a dead body. The term *necropsy* or "looking at the dead" is a better descriptor. Many religions throughout the world forbid or limit autopsies. Certain Middle Eastern religions forbid them. The religions of Judaism, Christianity, and Islam put limitations on when autopsies can be performed. Under the English Common Law, the kin of the deceased must give permission for an autopsy to be done. This has carried over to the United States and is the policy in most states today. The exceptions occur when the law states that the medical examiner or coroner must perform an autopsy. The number of autopsies that are performed in this country has declined greatly since World War II. Today hospital autopsies are performed in less than 5 percent of deaths. There are several reasons for this. First, autopsies can be expensive and the cost must be borne by the hospital. Second, a hospital autopsy is usually only done with the consent of the family and there may be personal or religious reasons when the family objects. Autopsies present a great learning opportunity for pathologists. Many of the most important advances in medicine have occurred as the result of knowledge gained by autopsies, so it is a shame that these opportunities are decreasing. As shown in Figure 10.3, medicolegal autopsies make up about one-third of all autopsies.

Autopsy Process

Any type of autopsy—medicolegal or a routine examination performed in a hospital—proceeds in a logical manner from the outside in. In many cases, the pathologist will dictate findings during the autopsy. These will later be reduced to written notes. Sometimes sketches will be made of wounds or injuries but photography is more commonly used. One of the most important characteristics of a medicolegal autopsy is that it involves not only an examination of the body to determine the cause and manner of death, but also requires a search of the body for physical evidence that can yield clues to the identity of the deceased if it is not known, or perhaps the identity of the perpetrator in the case of a homicide. Pathologists who are not trained in forensic pathology often overlook or compromise significant physical evidence. Types of evidence that are often overlooked by non-forensically trained pathologists include trace evidence such as hairs and fibers, dirt and skin under nails, gunshot residues and small wounds that might have forensic significance. Also, forensic pathologists are specially trained to recognize patterns of injury and associate them with particular causes.

External Examination

The external examination of the body can be very important. It can yield clues about the cause and manner of death, provide identifying markings such as tattoos or unusual clothing and can, of course provide trace evidence that can help associate the deceased with the crime scene and/or perpetrator. A detailed examination of the entire body is made. The body is extensively photographed clothed and unclothed. Wounds and trauma are noted such as entry and exit gunshot wounds or defensive wounds.

Internal Examination

After the external examination is made and properly documented, standard incisions are made in the torso and the internal examinations are done. Body fluid samples including blood, urine, and other fluids are usually removed and sent to a forensic toxicologist for examination to determine whether there are drugs or poisons in the body that could have caused or contributed to death. All of the major organs are removed, weighed, and measured. They will also be examined to determine if there are characteristic wounds or injuries that can give clues as to the cause and manner of death. Wounds or injuries that appeared on the outside of the body and travel inside are traced. These would include gunshot wounds and knife wounds. If there are bullets or shotgun pellets still in the body, they will be located and removed. The body may be x-rayed so that this can be compared to antemortem x-rays in case the identity of the deceased is an issue.

Patterns of Injury and Classification of Violent Deaths

The major purpose of the autopsy is to determine the cause and manner of death, especially in the case of violent death. The most important evidence of the deceased is the pattern of injury evidenced by certain types of violent deaths. Forensic pathologists are trained to recognize these patterns and relate them to the cause of death. A pathologist who is not forensically trained may not spot the patterns or may misinterpret them. Patterns of injury in violent deaths fall into one of four classes; mechanical, thermal, electrical or chemical. Some types of death may overlap two or more of the classes. For example, asphyxiation (oxygen deprivation to the brain that causes death) can be mechanical, chemical or electrical in nature.

Deaths due to Mechanical Causes

The most common mechanical types of violent death are gunshots and stabbing. Other types include motor vehicle incidents and falls. Sharp force injuries include knives and other implements. The type of wound produced by a sharp implement is called an incised wound. It has relatively sharp edges. A blunt force injury, on the other hand, causes lacerations. These have rougher edges than incisions. Figure 10.4a is a drawing of an incision and 10.4b is a laceration. Forensic pathologists can examine a wound and generally tell the type of weapon used. If a knife has serrations in it,

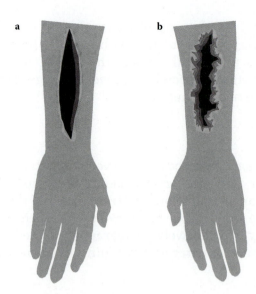

a   **b**

Figure 10.4 a) an incision; b) a laceration. Note the ragged edges on a laceration. *Courtesy of* Meredith Haddon.

these can show up in the margins of the wound. If the knife strikes bone, the serrations can be detected on the surface of the bone. It is generally not possible to determine the exact size of the weapon that causes a laceration or incision. In order for a sharp implement to cause death, it must damage a major artery or the heart or brain or spinal cord. Blunt force injuries can cause death by a variety of means.

Firearm injuries are a type of blunt force injury. Different injury patterns arise from bullet wounds than shot gun pellet wounds. High-speed bullets from hunting and military rifles cause more damage to a body than do lower speed bullets from hand guns. Some gunshots penetrate the body but do not exit. They become lodged in bone or an organ. Gunshots that enter and exit the body are called perforating wounds.

In the case of gunshot wounds, pathologists often attempt to determine how far away from the victim the gun was when it was shot. Gunshots can be divided into three types: contact, intermediate and distant. In a contact shot the gun is pressed against the body and discharged. The entry wound will show blackening and swelling. The swelling is due to the injection of hot, escaping gases from the barrel of the gun (see Chapter 9 for a discussion of firearms) under the skin. This swelling often causes lacerations in the skin. Figure 10.5 is a drawing of a contact shot.

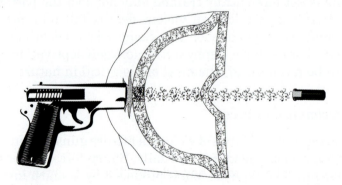

Figure 10.5 Diagram of a contact shot. Hot gases escaping from the muzzle of the gun are injected into and underneath the skin, causing it to bulge out. If there is any stippling, it is confined to a narrow circular area. There will usually be burns at the point of contact with the skin. *Courtesy of* Meredith Haddon.

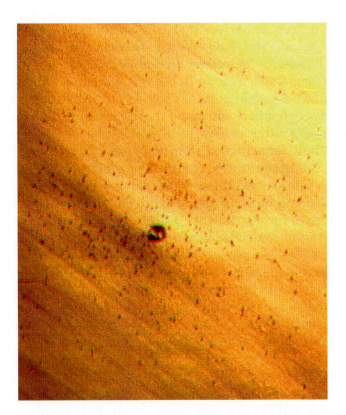

Figure 10.6 Stippling around a bullet hole in cloth. This consists of partially burned and unburned particles of gunshot residue. These can be enhanced by chemical treatment.

In an intermediate shot, particles of unburned and partially burned propellant (usually smokeless powder) lodge in the skin. This effect is called **stippling**. The diameter of the ring of stippling around the wound is proportional to the distance of firing. For most weapons, stippling appears only when the gun is discharged within a few feet of the target. Beyond that distance, the stippling either doesn't reach the target or falls off when it hits. These are called distance shots. Figure 10.6 shows stippling on a target.

Deaths due to Chemical Causes

The fate of drugs and alcohol in the body is discussed in detail in Chapter 17: Forensic Toxicology. Drugs and alcohol are contributory factors in death far more often than they are the cause of death. This is because it generally takes a good deal of a drug to cause a fatal overdose and many people will pass out before they can ingest a fatal dose. Also, certain drugs and alcohol cause detrimental changes in motor coordination and functions that can lead to death if the victim takes part in activities that require these functions. Drunk or drugged driving is an example of a situation where death may occur because a driver is intoxicated and loses control of the car and dies in an accident.

Drugs that cause death are most commonly depressants. A high overdose of alcohol, for example, can cause a person to lapse into a coma and respiration will slow so much that the victim ceases to breathe and dies. The cause of death is lack of oxygen owing to the slow breathing rate. In many cases, a person who has taken a large quantity of alcohol over time will start to vomit. This will bring up the alcohol in the stomach and no more will be absorbed. If the overdose occurs rapidly, the vomiting reflex may be depressed and the person will not vomit and death will ensue.

The amount of a drug or alcohol that can cause death depends in part on the person's history of taking the drug. With most drugs, a tolerance builds up that allows the person to tolerate increased levels before death ensues. As discussed in Chapter 17, synergism is also a factor in the role of drugs in causing death. Alcohol and barbiturates are both depressants. They do not work in exactly the same way but they do magnify each other's effects so that a person can die from a combination even though the dose of either one by itself wouldn't be lethal. Entertainers such as Janis Joplin and Jimi Hendrix died from accidental overdoses of alcohol and barbiturates. Besides the barbiturates, opiates and diazepam (e.g., Valium) overdoses cause death by the same mechanism. There have been no known death overdoses from marijuana. Cocaine has been reported to cause overdose deaths but by a different mechanism than for depressants. Cocaine is a stimulant. At very high doses it causes seizures and uncontrolled heart beating, both of which can cause death.

Carbon monoxide (CO) is a product of incomplete combustion of hydrocarbon fuels such as natural gas and gasoline. (Complete combustion results in the formation of carbon dioxide.) CO is a colorless, odorless, tasteless gas. When ingested, it attaches to hemoglobin in the blood. Hemoglobin is the substance in blood that carries molecules of oxygen to each cell in the body. Carbon monoxide ties up the hemoglobin, forming carboxyhemoglobin so there is less of it for oxygen to attach to. As a result the victim dies of asphyxiation. Carboxyhemoglobin is bright red and victims of CO poisoning have characteristic red coloration. Blood levels of CO as low as 20 percent can kill. Level's as high as 90 percent are common among people trapped in fires.

Hydrogen cyanide (HCN) can also cause death. It is highly poisonous and has the characteristic odor of almonds. It acts by interfering with oxygen delivery to the brain, causing asphyxiation. It has been used as an instrument for executing felons sentenced to death in the *gas chamber*. In such cases, potassium cyanide tablets or powder are mixed with a strong acid. This forms HCN, which the prisoner then inhales, causing death. Swallowing potassium cyanide has the same effect because it is converted to HCN by stomach acid.

Deaths due to Electrical Causes

Electrical deaths can occur in any of several ways, depending upon the type and magnitude of the electrical current that the victim is exposed to. Alternating current of moderate voltage (less than about 1,000 volts) causes the heart to quiver uncontrollably. This is called ventricular fibrillation, and can cause death within a few minutes. The person may not even be burned by the electrical energy at these levels. At higher levels of voltage, the heart stops beating because the electrical current disrupts the nervous impulses that keep the heart in rhythm. Also, voltages of this magnitude can cause severe burns in seconds and destruction of cellular material in the body.

Deaths due to Burns or Extreme Cold

Extreme heat is called **hyperthermia**. Extreme cold is called **hypothermia**. In order for the body to function normally, it must maintain a temperature very close to 37°C (99°F). Significant deviations from this temperature for even a few minutes can cause injury and can lead to death. Because of this, a person who dies from hyperthermia or hypothermia may not show outward signs of the cause of death unless there are visible burns or signs of frostbite on the body. The determination of the cause of death is often made by noting the environment where the body was found. Alcohol can be especially dangerous when a person is exposed to low temperatures. Alcohol dilates (expands) blood vessels which can increase heat loss and, as a person's intoxication level increases, sensitivity to heat and cold decreases so that the person may not perceive the dangerous temperature levels.

The Postmortem Interval (PMI)—Time of Death

Determination of the PMI is very important in death investigation. It can help establish or refute the alibi of a suspect. It can be a key piece of evidence in determining the manner of death. Unfortunately, the PMI cannot be determined exactly because the modern methods of determination do not result in sufficiently accurate data. In addition, the environment surrounding a corpse can greatly affect changes in the body that are used to determine PMI. For example, if someone dies and the body is left outside in cold weather, the rate of body cooling slows markedly. Because of this uncertainty, pathologists always express the PMI as a range of hours or even days, reflecting the uncertainty of measurement of the relevant factors. The investigation of the PMI begins at the death scene. The temperature and physical environment are noted. The amount of clothing or other covering of the deceased is also important. The attending pathologist will usually take the core temperature of the deceased to develop a preliminary estimation of **algor mortis**, the tendency of a body to cool after death. Preliminary observations of the pooling of blood at the lowest part of the body caused by gravity (**livor mortis**) are also made. The degree of stiffening of the body (**rigor mortis**) is also estimated. All of these factors help the pathologist estimate an early PMI, up to 48 hours. If the deceased has been dead for several days, or weeks, or sometimes longer, then the above factors are no longer present and other methods must be used to estimate the PMI. These include the degree of decomposition of the body and the activities of insects on the body. The latter is covered in Chapter 12: Forensic Entomology.

Early Postmortem Interval

Rigor, livor, and algor mortis all take place during the first forty-eight hours after death has occurred. There are well established guidelines of the time intervals for each of these actions. These must be tempered, however, by the temperature and environment where the deceased died. High or low temperatures and/or humidity can affect the rates at which these activities take place as will the degree of protection (clothing, indoors versus outdoors, land or water) of the body.

Algor Mortis

A good rule of thumb for the cooling of a body after death is that, under moderate conditions of temperature, an adult clothed appropriately for that temperature will cool 1°C each hour after death. It will thus take the better part of a day for a body to cool from its normal temperature of 37°C to a room temperature of 20°C (70°F). The ambient temperature can have a great effect upon this assumption. If the body is found in the desert in the summer where the temperature can be over 40°C, the body may actually warm up after death! If the temperature is very cold, the body will cool faster than 1° per hour. There are numerous diseases that cause fever so that the body temperature is higher than 37°C at death and this will affect PMI determinations.

Generally speaking, pathologists will only use algor mortis as a method of estimating PMI if the death took place within twelve hours of being discovered.

Rigor Mortis

When a person dies, his or her joints and muscles are relaxed. After two to five hours, the muscles begin to contract, causing stiffening of the joints. The process is complete between twelve and twenty-four hours after death. Then, over the next two or three days, the rigor mortis disappears. These times are subject to the same variations that affect algor mortis. Rigor mortis is accelerated by heat and by strenuous physical activity shortly before death.

Livor Mortis

When a person dies, blood stops circulating. When this occurs, the blood tends to pool at the lowest part of the body under the influence of gravity. If for example, the deceased is lying on his back at death, the blood will pool toward the floor. This area of the body will become pinkish to purple. The upper parts of the body will become pale. The surface that is in contact with the body may leave an impression on the skin as livor proceeds. This may indicate whether a body has been moved since livor mortis began. The livor mortis pattern may be disrupted if the body is resting on a floor or other surface because the pressure exerted by the body's weight prevents blood pooling in that area. Livor mortis onset is fairly rapid, appearing as soon as thirty minutes after death. After a few hours the livor mortis becomes fixed; the blood pressure has ruptured the vessels and the blood starts to permeate the surrounding tissues. Once this happens, the area where livor mortis has taken place changes from reddish to greenish and then to brown. Sometimes livor mortis can be confused with bruises or contusions, especially after several hours have elapsed. Figure 10.7 is a drawing of how livor mortis looks.

Other Methods of Estimating PMI

Some chemical levels may be related to the PMI. These include potassium levels in eye fluids and metabolites in the brain. The appearance of a film over the eye is also related to PMI. Cardiac pH, ultrasound tests in muscles, electrical activity of skeletal muscles and the appearance of wounds are all methods that have been evaluated as contributors to the estimate of PMI. Examination of stomach contents has been a standard part of an autopsy for many years because the presence of chemicals or undigested drugs can be important evidence in determining the cause and manner of death. Stomach contents may also be used to help estimate PMI. It takes about two to four hours for the stomach to digest a meal. If there is evidence of food in the stomach at death, then a presumption is that the person must have died no more than two to four hours earlier. Stomach emptying may only be used as a corroborative test however, because there is great variation in the time of digestion owing to the condition of the deceased at the time of death. Some digestion also takes place after death and during putrefaction.

Late PMI

After one or two days have passed, other activities take place on and in the body that can help in establishing the PMI. For example, decomposition of a corpse begins

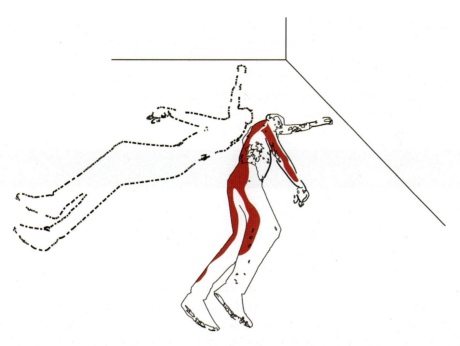

Figure 10.7 Diagram showing *livor mortis*. In this drawing, the body is found face up in the area where the outline is drawn. The body is turned over face down to show how the blood collects on the parts that are in contact with the floor. The dark area is the *livor mortis*. *Courtesy of* Meredith Haddon.

soon after death and putrefaction may be evident within two or three days. The body becomes discolored with the skin turning greenish near the abdomen and hips. The action of anaerobic bacteria from outside the body and in the intestinal tract begin to cause decomposition. This results in the production of copious quantities of gas that cause the body to bloat. If a person has drowned and sunk to the bottom of the water, the gas formation can actually cause the body to rise and float. The decomposition of the body depends upon the availability of oxygen. If the body is submerged in water or is buried, the decomposition process takes place much more slowly. High temperatures accelerate decomposition. When a body is discovered several days or weeks after death, the action of insects on and in the body can provide valuable information about the PMI. This subject is discussed in detail in Chapter 12: Forensic Entomology.

Embalming and Exhumations

Throughout history, human beings have developed myriad ways of dealing with death and especially the body after death. In some cultures, there have been attempts to preserve bodies for as long as possible. Mummification is an example of this and it is very effective at long-term preservation of bodies. One of the most common burial traditions in the United States is embalming of the dead before burial in a vault or casket. **Embalming** is a process whereby a chemical such as formaldehyde is added to preserve the body tissues and retard decomposition so that the body will be in a presentable condition for viewing prior to the funeral. Unlike mummification, embalming is a temporary preservation process whose effects wear off in a matter of months. From a forensic death investigation viewpoint, embalming presents serious problems that arise if and when a body must be removed from the vault or casket after burial because of questions concerning cause or manner of death. If there is a drug or poison in the body at the time of death, embalming will usually dilute it, replace it in the body or react chemically with it to alter or destroy it. It is sometimes possible to detect the presence of certain drugs or poisons even if they have been exposed to embalming agents.

The Teamwork Approach

Death investigation can be very complex and usually requires the talents and skills of a number of individuals to be successfully concluded. The medical examiner's office or chief coroner's office is often the epicenter for these investigations. Sometimes the local crime laboratory is located within the ME's office or the coroner's office. These laboratories may have one or more forensic anthropologists, entomologists or odontologists on staff or under a consulting arrangement to assist with death investigations. This arrangement is common in large metropolitan areas or in jurisdictions that span a large geographical area. We will discuss the role of forensic anthropology and odontology in more detail in Chapter 11, and forensic entomology in Chapter 12.

Summary

Pathology is the medical subspecialty that studies the changes that a body undergoes as the result of injury or disease. There are two major branches to pathology—anatomic and clinical. **Anatomic pathology** involves the study of the body and its organ and tissue systems whereas clinical pathology involves the analysis of blood and body fluids for drugs and poisons and their role in the cause of death. Forensic pathology involves both anatomic and clinical pathology in the determination of the cause and manner of death in cases of suspicious or unexplained death.

Each state has a system for the practice of forensic pathology. Approximately half of the states use the medical examiner system whereby the administrator is an appointed physician, although not necessarily a pathologist. The other states use the coroner system, whereby the administrator is elected on a county wide or statewide basis. In most states the coroner does not have to be a physician. Each state has laws that determine the types of cases that must go to the medical examiner or coroner. They generally fall under the categories of unexplained or violent deaths or those where the deceased was not under the care of a physician.

The medicolegal postmortem examination or **autopsy** involves a careful exterior and interior examination of the body for injuries, wounds or disease, as well as any trace or other evidence that might link the death to a perpetrator. The autopsy should be done by a forensically trained pathologist. The pathologist must determine a cause and manner of death as well as estimate the postmortem interval (PMI) or time since death. The PMI can be estimated in a number of ways including core temperature, livor mortis or rigor mortis, and other changes to the body. Longer term PMI can be estimated by observing decomposition or insect activity on the body.

The manner of death can be by accident, suicide, homicide, or natural causes. The cause of death refers to the actual incident or condition that is incompatible with sustaining life. There are certain patterns of injury that are usually present in various types of death.

Test Yourself

Multiple Choice

1. Which of the following is *not* a manner of death?
   a. Accidental
   b. Homicide
   c. Heart attack
   d. Suicide
   e. Natural causes
2. The original function of the coroner in medieval England was:
   a. Surgeon
   b. Tax collector
   c. Legal advisor to the King
   d. Pathologist
   e. Town crier
3. Today, the medical examiner:
   a. Must be a physician
   b. Determines cause and manner of death
   c. Signs the death certificate
   d. Is appointed
   e. All of the above
4. If a body has been discovered several days after death, the PMI may be determined by:
   a. Insect activity
   b. Bloating
   c. Livor mortis
   d. Rigor mortis
   e. None of the above
5. Settling of the blood to the lower parts of the body after death is called:
   a. Rigor mortis
   b. Algor mortis
   c. Livor mortis
   d. Bloating
   e. None of the above
6. Analysis of blood and body fluids to determine whether drugs or poisons contributed to the death is part of:
   a. Anatomic pathology
   b. Clinical pathology
   c. Systemic pathology
   d. Coroner's responsibility
   e. None of the above
7. Which of the following is not a duty of a pathologist who attends a crime scene when a body is discovered?

    a. Making sure that the person is dead

    b. Collecting data concerning the PMI

    c. Supervising the search for trace evidence around the body

    d. Beginning the autopsy

    e. Authorizing transport of the body to the morgue

8. When someone has been poisoned by carbon monoxide, the main pattern of injury is:

    a. Red coloration of the skin

    b. Blue coloration around the eyes

    c. Hemorrhaging in the eyes

    d. Bleeding around the mouth

    e. Accelerated rigor mortis

9. When someone has been killed by a contact shot, the area around the wound shows:

    a. Lots of stippling

    b. A large entry wound

    c. Blackening and swelling

    d. Little if any bleeding

    e. A wound the size of the caliber of the bullet

10. Which of the following circumstances surrounding a death would be least likely to be investigated by the medical examiner or coroner?

    a. A death in a two-car auto crash

    b. A heart attack suffered by an elderly woman while at home

    c. A body hidden under some brush in the woods

    d. A boy killed while deer hunting

    e. A death in a hospital during major surgery

True-False

11. All accidental deaths are investigated by the coroner or medical examiner.

12. The only difference between a coroner and a medical examiner is that the coroner is elected.

13. Autopsies consist of both external and internal examinations of the body.

14. Death by a gunshot through the heart is an example of a manner of death.

15. It takes at least 12 years of education beyond high school to become board certified as a pathologist.

Matching

16. Livor mortis	a. Stiffening of the joints after death
17. Rigor mortis	b. Autopsy
18. Algor mortis	c. Cooling of the body after death
19. PMI	d. Time since death
20. Examination of the body after death	e. Pooling of blood into lower body parts after death

Short Essay

21. What is the difference between the cause of death and the manner of death?

22. Briefly explain the history of the coroner system.

23. What are some of the ways that a pathologist can estimate the PMI? What are their advantages and disadvantages?
24. Briefly describe how a forensic pathologist is educated and trained.
25. Under what conditions would a medical examiner or coroner be required to receive a body for autopsy?

Further Reading

DiMaio, J. M. and M. D. DiMaio. *Forensic Pathology*. Boston: Elsevier, 1989.

Spitz, W., ed. *Medicolegal Investigation of Death*. Springfield, IL: Charles Thomas, 1993.

Fisher, R. S. and C. S. Petty. *A Handbook of Forensic Pathology for Non-Forensic Pathologists*. National Institute of Law Enforcement and Criminal Justice. U.S. Department of Justice. Washington, DC, 1977.

On the Web

John Ydstie talks with Dr. Ryan Parr, an anthropologist at Ontario's Lakehead University, about a four-year effort to determine the identity of a thirteen-month-old child who died in the *Titanic* disaster. The child was buried in Halifax, Nova Scotia. Parr coordinated the work of over fifty scientists, genealogists, and *Titanic* researchers, using DNA to trace the child to living family members: www.npr.org/templates/story/story.php?storyId=835398.

Exercises and materials for a game in which students analyze forensic evidence from a fictitious murder. The evidence is used to formulate hypotheses and open up avenues of investigation: www.ableweb.org/volumes/vol-22/minor/index.htm.

Frequently asked questions about forensic pathology careers: http://web2.airmail.net/uthman/forensic_career.html.

Home page of the National Association of Medical Examiners: www.thename.org.

Forensic pathology on the famous Shroud of Turin: www.shroudofturin4journalists.com/pathology.htm.

11
Anthropology and Odontology

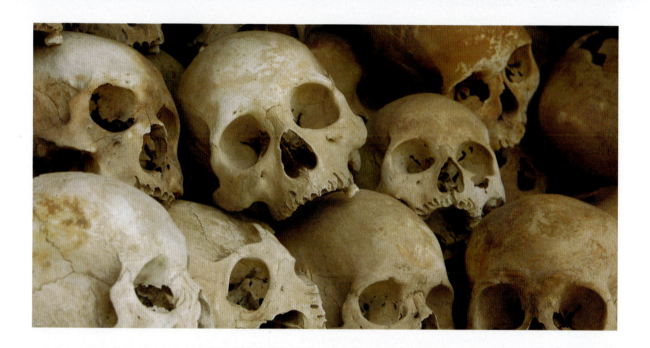

Learning Objectives

1. To be able to define anthropology and forensic anthropology and give examples of each
2. To be able to describe the functions of the forensic anthropologist
3. To be able to describe the development and structure of bones
4. To be able to describe the various components of the biological profile
5. To be able to describe how bones are individualized
6. To be able to describe the various anthropological tests that can be done on skulls to help identify them
7. To be able to define forensic odontology and describe the functions of the forensic odontologist

Chapter 11
Anthropology and Odontology

Chapter Outline

Mini Glossary

Antemortem: This term is used to describe an occurrence prior to death.
Anthropology: The study of the human race, including life style, culture and physical traits, throughout time.
Deciduous teeth: The first set of teeth, commonly called the "baby teeth."
Diaphysis: This term is used to identify the mid-section or the shaft of the bone.
Epiphyseal line: This line toward the ends of the long bones, marks the location of the childhood epiphyseal plate and is found between the diaphysis and the epiphysis in adult bones.

Epiphyseal plate: Found in the metaphysis, this part of a long bone is a hyaline cartilage plate in children who are growing, but matures into bone in adults and is replaced by the epiphyseal line.

Epiphysis: A term used to identify the rounded ends of a long bone.

Forensic anthropology: A specialty area within physical anthropology that uses characteristics of bone structure (osteology) to determine the identity of human remains and present findings in a court of law.

Forensic odontology: Examining human dentition for forensic purposes, such as determining identity of human remains, approximating the age of a person, analyzing bite marks, and examining dental structure of a person suspected to be a victim of abuse.

Greater sciatic notch: Located on the posterior portion pelvic bone between the ilium and the ischium, this notch is an important trait used by forensic anthropologists in the determination of the sex of the decedent.

Metaphysis: The part of a long bone that lies between the diaphysis and epiphysis, and is the growth area of the bone that produces an increase in stature in children.

Odontology: The scientific study of human dentition.

Osteology: This is the scientific study of bones.

Permanent teeth: The second set of human teeth which replace the deciduous teeth.

Physical anthropology: The study of the biological traits and evolution of those traits in humans throughout time.

Postmortem interval (PMI): PostMortem Interval. This term is used to describe the amount of time since death occurred.

Pubic symphysis: The right and left pubic bones of the pelvis come together at this cartilaginous joint called the pubic symphysis.

Introduction

Anthropology is the study of humans. It includes their cultures and their biology. The latter is usually called **physical anthropology,** although the term "bio-anthropology" is more accurate. **Forensic anthropology** is a specialty within physical anthropology. It involves applications of **osteology** and *skeletal identification* to matters involving the law and the public. Osteology is the study of bone. Forensic anthropologists work with skeletal remains to determine the identity of the deceased. They often work with forensic pathologists and forensic odontologists (dentists) to help determine the cause and manner of death and the **postmortem interval (PMI)** or length of time since death.

The underlying principle of skeletal identification is that the human skeleton is unique in some ways. Most bones have unique characteristics that arise from genetics, growth, use, injury, or trauma. A forensic anthropologist identifies these characteristics in skeletal remains and compares them to **antemortem** (before death) evidence. If enough of these unique characteristics exist in an unknown skeleton and a suspected person, an identification can be made and possibly the determination of the cause and manner of death.

Forensic anthropologists not only identify skeletal remains, but are the principal investigators who collect the remains that are discovered. This process is akin to an archeological dig, where artifacts (often skeletal remains) are discovered. The proper collection of skeletal remains is crucial to a successful identification and must always be done under the watchful eye of an experienced forensic anthropologist.

In recent years the role of the forensic anthropologist has extended beyond the identification of skeletal remains. In mass disasters such as the destruction of the World Trade Center or plane crashes, forensic anthropologists are routinely called in to help recover bodies. Some forensic anthropologists are experts in constructing facial features over a skull in the hope that someone will be able to identify the person. In other cases, forensic anthropologists can superimpose a face on a skull using a computer or digital camera to determine whether a skull belonged to a particular person. Forensic anthropologists help with facial and body recognition of people in crowds and even analyze characteristics such as *gait* (the visual characteristics of walking or running) as a means of identification.

The Human Skeleton

The central focus of the work of forensic anthropologists is the human skeleton. Before describing how the skeleton is used in this work, it is important to understand some features of the skeletal system. Diagrams of a human skeleton are shown in Figure 11.1, showing the bones from the front (anterior or ventral) and the back (posterior or dorsal).

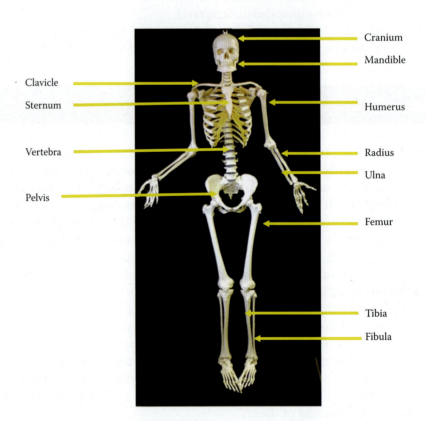

Figure 11.1 Anterior and posterior views of the human skeleton. http://hes.ucfsd.org/gclaypo/skelweb/skel04.html.

Long Bone

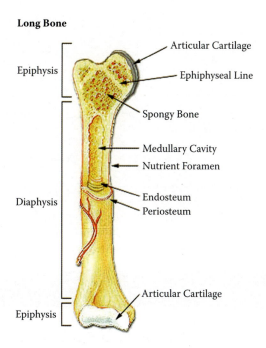

Epiphysis

Articular Cartilage

Ephiphyseal Line

Spongy Bone

Medullary Cavity

Nutrient Foramen

Diaphysis

Endosteum

Periosteum

Articular Cartilage

Epiphysis

Figure 11.2 Structure of bone. http://en.wikipedia.org/wiki/Bone.

The basic unit of the skeleton is the bone. There are 206 of them in the normal human skeleton. Bones are living, functioning entities and the skeleton is considered an organ system. Bones grow and change over time, as they can alter and repair themselves as needed. The interiors of many larger bones contain *marrow*, which, among other things, is responsible for the production of red blood cells. Bones serve a number of functions in the body. First, they provide support for the other organs and tissues. Muscles attach at bones and their contractions make motion possible. Bones also serve a protective function for some of the more delicate soft tissues. The rib cage protects the heart and lungs. The skull protects the brain from shock. Bones are also the bodies' center for growth. They begin to grow at birth and continue until early adulthood.

Bone Structure

Bone is a complex material with several layers. Figure 11.2 shows the structure of bone. The outermost layer is called *compact bone*. It is hard and smooth. In long bones, there is an internal layer called *trabecular bone,* which is light and spongy. It adds strength to bone without adding much weight. The bone marrow is contained in the centers of long bones in a *medullary cavity.*

In many forensic anthropology cases, there are only fragments of bone present and the macrostructure described above may not be present in sufficient quantity or quality to identify the bone. It may be necessary to identify the material as bone using its microstructure. A thin cross section of a bone sample is prepared and would look similar to Figure 11.3. There are special growth units in bone called *osteons*. They are deposited in layers and eventually form chambers. The chambers contain canals that blood vessels travel to reach each cell in the bone. This network of canals is called the *Haversian system*. The individual cells in the bone are called *osteocytes* and make up most of the compact bone. Osteocytes are connected by a microscopic canal system called the *canaliculi*. Even if bone is burned, it can usually be identified by the presence of Haversian canals.

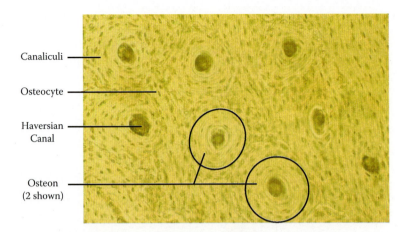

Canaliculi

Osteocyte

Haversian
Canal

Osteon
(2 shown)

Figure 11.3 The Haversian system in long bones. *Courtesy of* Norman Sauer.

Identification of Skeletal Remains

The ultimate goal of the identification of skeletal remains is to determine the identity of the bones. Whose are they? This process requires individual features of the bones to enable exact identification. Individual features include antemortem (before death) injury or trauma to the bone, facial reconstruction, and photographic superimposition. Unusual shapes or features in bone can also be used for individualization. Absolute identification is often not possible and in such cases, the forensic anthropologist will resort to class or general feature identification to determine age, gender, race, stature, cause of death, and other factors. In doing this, the forensic anthropologist will develop a *biological profile* of the remains.

Before the biological profile and individual characteristics are determined, three questions must be answered about submitted specimens:

1. Is the material bone?
2. If so, is it human?
3. Does the age of the bone make it useful for forensic purposes?

Is the Specimen Bone?

In cases where whole bones or large pieces of bone are present, identification is usually straightforward. In those cases where there are only fragments of bone or it has been burned or bleached or otherwise damaged, then microscopic analysis must be used. In these cases, the presence of Haversian canals is proof that the material is bone.

Is the Specimen Human Bone?

Depending on the size and condition of the bone, the species may be determined macroscopically by comparing its features to those of various animal species. This sometimes presents a challenge because some pig and sheep bones and some bear paws can appear very similar to human bones. Sometimes there will be tissue and/or hairs clinging to the bone and these can be observed and analyzed to determine their species. If the bones are too small or too damaged to be examined macroscopically, then microscopic analysis can be undertaken. In such cases, the exact species may not be determined, but human bone may be ruled out. A type of bone not found in humans but present in many animals is called *plexiform*. In plexiform bone, the Haversian canals are arranged in geometric patterns and packed tightly together with little or no bone between them. In human bone, the Haversian canals are evenly spaced and there is bone between them. Even so, it is not always possible to make a definitive determination that tiny fragments of bone are human in origin.

The Significance of Age

Other than radiocarbon dating (measuring the remnants of the carbon-14 isotope), there are no reliable methods for dating skeletal remains. Other clues as to the age of skeletal remains may make an estimation of age possible. There are practical, criminal justice considerations about the age of bone. If skeletal remains can be reliably shown to be more than about fifty years old, its forensic value is questionable. Suppose someone was murdered and the body buried and then discovered fifty years later. The chances are that the murderer is also dead or at least so elderly that prosecution would be useless. This means that, when reliable knowledge about the age of bone remains, this must be taken into account when deciding if it is forensically significant.

The Biological Profile

After it has been determined that the bone is human and of fairly recent origin, the process of identification begins. First, class characteristics will be determined as part of a biological profile. Then, if possible, individual characteristics will be determined that could lead to absolute identification. The class characteristics will enable the anthropologist to classify the skeletal remains in a subgroup such as males or a member of a particular race. Other factors such as stature, socioeconomic status, and time since death may also be determined. Because there is variation in skeletal characteristics among individuals within the same subgroup, it is sometimes necessary to consult databases or collections of skeletons that belong to a particular subgroup so that the range of variation within a subgroup can be known. The more common *class characteristics* that are determined as part of a biological profile are *age, sex, race* and *stature*.

Age of Death

Although bones change throughout life in response to activity or inactivity, aging, disease, and injury, there are definite intervals during which bones are actively growing. Once they have reached maturity, the bones will not grow except for repairs and reactions to aging. Thus, the mechanisms by which the age at death is estimated are different for people who die while their bones are still growing (subadults) compared to those whose bones have stopped growing (adults).

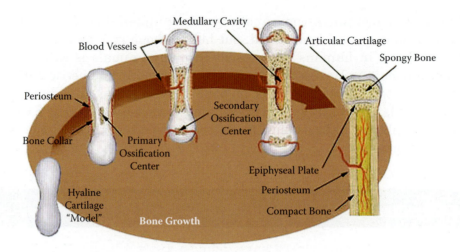

Figure 11.4 Bone growth. http://en.wikipedia.org/wiki/Bone.

Using Dentition to Determine Age

One of the most reliable ways of determining the age of a sub-adult is by assessing the formation of teeth and their eruption through the gums. In most cases, temporary teeth (deciduous teeth) are formed and then permanent teeth form and erupt in a fairly predictable time period. There are many available charts that list the timetables for the formation of temporary and permanent teeth for various populations. Males and females exhibit significant differences in the rates at which certain teeth mature and some of the charts reflect these differences. See the following websites for timelines of tooth development: http://en.wikipedia.org/wiki/Tooth_development and www.3dmouth.org/6/6_1.cfm.

Using Bone Development to Determine Age

Bones also have definite phases of growth that are age dependent. When the long bones start to grow, they consist of the shaft or **diaphysis** and the end(s) or **epiphysis**. As the individual develops these two fuse together at the growth area, called the **metaphysis**. Within the metaphysis is the **epiphyseal plate** or growth plate, which lengthens as the immature bones grow. When the union is complete, growth ceases and what remains is a thin line at the growth area called the **epiphyseal line**. The union is not an event; it takes place over years. Figure 11.4 shows the three stages of union of the diaphysis and the epiphysis. In general, union of individual bones takes place earlier for females than males. For example, the clavicle in the shoulder has an epiphysis that fuses in women between the ages of 17 and 21 but in males the union takes place between the ages of 18 and 22.

Using Pubic and Rib Bones to Determine Age

After a person has reached adulthood (approximately 25 to 30 years), bones have stopped growing. Changes to the bones are more subtle and there are fewer places on the skeleton where changes can be directly related to age. The main areas in the body where age determinations are made in adults are the *pubic bones* and *rib bones*. Many researchers have spent years of careful measurement to refine the data that can be derived from changes in these bones and improve the accuracy of age-at-death determinations.

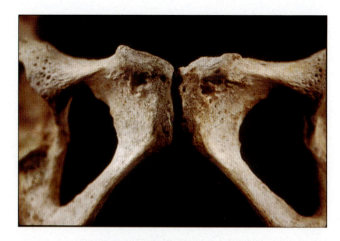

Figure 11.5 Female pubis. *Courtesy of* Norman Sauer.

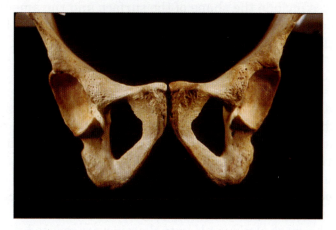

Figure 11.6 Male pubis. *Courtesy of* Norman Sauer.

The Pubic Symphysis

In adults, there are several ways of determining age at death. One of the most common methods is the macroscopic observation of the condition of the **pubic symphysis**. The left and right hip (pelvic) bones join at the *pelvis*. Where these join there is a symphysis or space that has a small amount of cartilage. When the cartilage is removed and the bones are separated, the shape and surface texture on the medial (inner) surfaces can be examined. These portions of the pelvic bone change in a predictable way as a person ages. The surface is rough and billowed in younger adults, but by age 35 the surface becomes increasingly smoother and develops a rim. After age 35, the symphysis steadily degenerates and the surface begins to erode.

Figure 11.5 shows a female human pubis. Figure 11.6 shows a male pubis. The space in the middle of the photo is where the cartilage of the pubic symphysis would be and the inside edge of the exposed area in the middle is what is examined to help determine approximate age.

Although male and female pubic symphyses undergo similar changes with age, the age ranges are different for each phase of change.

Changes in the Ends of the Ribs

In addition to the pubic symphysis, the ends of the ribs that meet in the front of the body (the *sternal ends*) also change as a person gets older. The rib ends change in

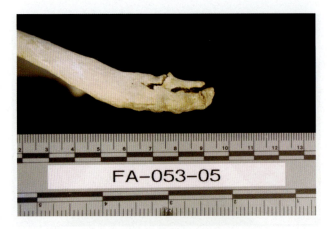

Figure 11.7 Sternal rib in older person. *Courtesy of* Norman Sauer.

several ways. These include the shape of the surface and the amount of pitting, the type and quality of bone and the presence of projections from the bone. Figure 11.7 shows the sternal rib area of a human being.

Gender

In general, human males are larger than females, but this is more obvious in life than when only the skeleton remains. In some cases, there is little difference in size between male and female skeletons and the examination to determine gender must focus on certain regions of the skeleton. These differences are not unequivocal until after puberty and it may be hazardous to try to determine the sex of a skeleton younger than about eighteen. Most commonly, the skull and the pelvis are the areas that are most diagnostic of gender.

The pelvis is the most obvious place to discover sex related differences. This is largely because the pelvis has different functions in males and females. In females the pelvis region must support a fetus during development and delivery. The male pelvis is generally larger than the female while the female pelvis is broader. The most obvious locations on the pelvis where gender differences can be seen is the **greater sciatic notch** and the area below the **pubic symphysis** which forms the sub-pubic angle. Figures 11.5 and 11.6 show the location of the sub pubic angle on a male and female pelvis, with Figure 11.8 showing the angle in more detail. Generally the angle is less than 90 degrees in males.

The greater sciatic notch is located in the posterior end of the pelvis; one notch on either side of the coccyx or tailbone. See Figure 11.9. In females the notch is quite broad with an angle greater than 60 degrees, whereas in males, the angle is much smaller. This is a very reliable test for determining gender of skeletal remains.

In the absence of pubic bones, certain features of the skull are good indicators of sex. A number of skull bones differ in males and females. These include the prominence of brow ridges, the shape of the mastoid process of the temporal bone, the absence or presence of the external occipital protuberance, and other areas. Figure 11.10 shows a male skull with a large mastoid process, prominent brow ridges, an external occipital protuberance, and a gently sloping forehead—all generally male characteristics.

Race

The determination of a person's race or ancestry can be difficult. The skeleton does not contain many obvious characteristics that define racial characteristics. Certainly

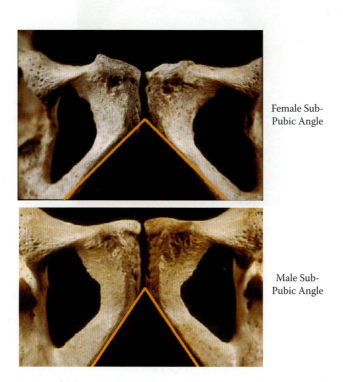

Figure 11.8 The sub-pubic angle is much greater for females (top photo) than for males (bottom photo). *Courtesy of* Norman Sauer.

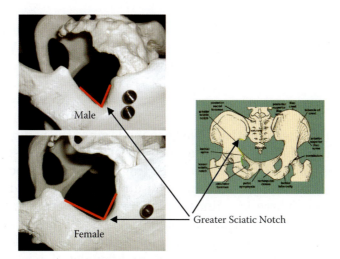

Figure 11.9 The greater sciatic notch is larger in females, generally exceeding 60 degrees. The top photo shows the notch in a male pelvis whereas the bottom photo illustrates the notch in a female pelvis.

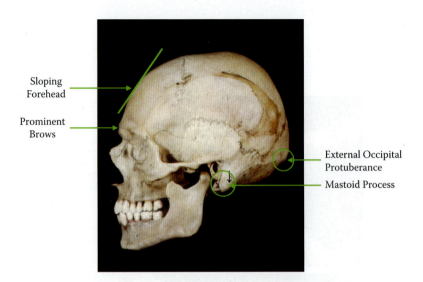

Figure 11.10 Some of the skull traits that help determine the sex of the remains. *Courtesy of* Norman Sauer.

today, there are no pure ethnic or racial groups and there may never have been any. There are also popular perceptions of what a given person's race is and how some people self define their own race. There are also a number of different ways of defining ancestry. A typical scheme is used by the United States Department of Commerce in its census every ten years. The categories are Caucasian, Black, Asian, Native American, Hispanic, and Other.

The most reliable means of determining race in the skeleton are centered on the skull and can be based on either gross morphological examination or mathematical analysis of various morphological features. There are a number of skull characteristics that are racially distinct. For example, eye orbits vary from round to triangular or rectangular. Other variations occur in the nasal apertures, the palate, and the mouth region.

The femur in the leg also exhibits racial characteristics, specifically the curvature of the diaphysis, which varies from straight in people of African-American ancestry to curved with Caucasian ancestry.

Stature

Attempts at stature determination have been made since the beginning of the twentieth century. Today, the most practical method for determining stature uses measurements of long bones. Sometimes a large fragment of a long bone may be used. The long bones are the humerus, radius and ulna of the arm and the femur, tibia and fibula of the leg. There is a linear relationship between the lengths of these bones and the overall stature of the individual. When estimating stature, the more long bone measurements that can be obtained, the better. Table 11.1 shows the equations used to estimate stature for males and females of various ethnic groups. The stature is measured in centimeters.

Of course, in order to use this table, one must know the gender and ethnic origin of the bone. An example of how this would work is as follows.

Suppose that a femur of length 54 cm has been recovered from an excavation of skeletal remains. The biological profile indicates that the skeleton is a male and is most likely Caucasian. The proper formula from the table above is:

TABLE 11.1
Stature for Males and Females of Various Ethnic Groups

Race/Sex	Formula (cm)	Standard Deviation
Caucasian Male	2.89 * humerus + 78.10	±4.57
	3.79 * radius + 79.42	±4.66
	3.76 * ulna + 75.55	±4.72
	2.32 * femur + 65.53	±3.94
	2.42 * tibia + 81.93	±4.00
	2.60 * fibula + 3.86	±3.86
Caucasian Female	3.36 * humerus + 57.97	±4.45
	4.74 * radius + 54.93	±4.24
	4.27 * ulna + 57.76	±4.30
	2.47 * femur + 54.10	±3.72
	2.90 * tibia + 61.53	±3.66
	2.93 * fibula + 59.61	±3.57
African Male	2.88 * humerus + 75.48	±4.23
	3.32 * radius + 85.43	±4.57
	3.20 * ulna + 80.77	±4.74
	2.10 * femur + 72.22	±3.91
	2.19 * tibia + 85.36	±3.96
	2.34 * fibula + 80.07	±4.02
African Female	3.08 * humerus + 64.47	±4.25
	3.67 * radius + 71.79	±4.59
	3.31 * ulna + 75.38	±4.83
	2.28 * femur + 59.76	±3.41
	2.45 * tibia + 72.65	±3.70
	2.49 * fibula + 70.90	±3.80
Asian Male	2.68 * humerus + 83.19	±4.16
	3.54 * radius + 82.00	±4.60
	3.48 * ulna + 77.45	±4.66
	2.15 * femur + 72.57	±3.80
	2.39 * tibia + 81.45	±3.27
	2.40 * fibula + 80.56	±3.24

Source: Forensic Anthropology Training Manual, Karen Ramey Burns, 2007.

$$2.32 * \text{femur} + 65.53 \pm 3.94$$

Inserting 54 cm for the femur length into the formula gives the result of 194.75 to 186.87 cm or 76.67 to 73.57 inches (2.54 cm = 1 inch). This translates to a height range of 6 feet 4 inches to six feet 1 inch.

Individualization of Human Bone

The elements of the biological profile described above are all class characteristics of bone. It would obviously be useful to be able to individualize bones or a skull to a particular individual. In the case of bones, this can only be done by comparing unique features of the bone with one from a known source. Typically, this would involve taking postmortem and antemortem x-rays of the bone. In the case of a skull, superimposition of a face on the skull using computer- or camera-based techniques can lead to a more positive identification.

Bone Trauma and Individual Features

Most people receive some injuries to bones during a lifetime. If a bone is broken, it will show signs of the break as it heals. These signs usually remain throughout life and will show in x-rays. A postmortem x-ray can be compared with an antemortem x-ray and this may provide positive evidence of the identity of a person.

Even if a bone is not injured during life, there are many instances where a bone exhibits enough variation among individuals that x-rays of these bones can be used for identification. There are several bones in the skull including the frontal sinuses and places where arteries and veins enter and leave the skull that can be individualized. In cases where these bones are to be used for identification, comparisons are made between postmortem and antemortem x-rays and also with x-rays of the same bones of other individuals of the same sex and race to ensure that the features are in fact unique.

Analysis of Skulls

If all or most of a skull is recovered there are at least two ways that identifications may be made. The most reliable method is *photographic superimposition*. This involves the comparison of the skull with a photograph of the suspected owner. One of the newer methods of accomplishing the comparison is to use video cameras to capture the image of the skull and of the actual photo and then superimpose the two. Videography has the advantage of permitting manipulations of the images including fading and using various sizes and angles. Computers can also be used to superimpose images and analyze them to determine whether they came from the same individual. Figure 11.11 shows the superimposition of a face on a skull.

The other method of analysis is used when a skull is recovered and there are no clues as to its origin. A three-dimensional reconstruction of the soft tissues of a face is built onto the skull. Compilations of tissue thicknesses for various parts of the face have been compiled for various races of males and females. A proper reconstruction

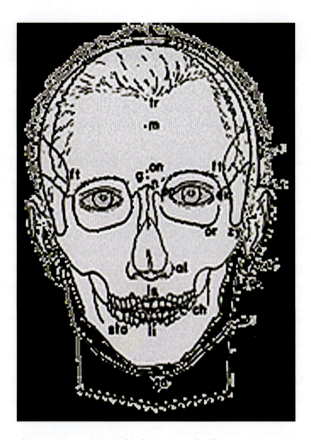

Figure 11.11 Drawing of superimposition of a face on a skull.

requires that the race and sex of the skull be known. Using the measurement tables, the anthropologist uses pegs and clay to build the face. See Figure 11.12.

Some guesswork is involved in choosing lips, nose, eyebrows, etc. Prosthetic eyes and wigs are also used. This method is not used for identification of a particular individual. Sometimes facial reconstructions are prepared and photographed. The picture is distributed to the news media and broadcast in the hopes that the family of a missing person will recognize it.

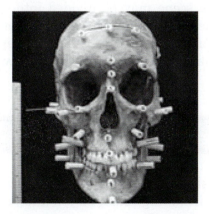

Figure 11.12 Facial reconstruction using a recovered skull. The pegs determine the depth of the tissue. Clay will then be added to the peg depth creating the final facial image. www.uof aweb.ualber ta.ca/expressnews_temp late/images/6939.001.jpg.

Collection of Bones

Most physical evidence at crime scenes is discovered and collected by crime scene technicians or investigators. On the other hand, skeletal remains are seldom discovered this way. Most often, bones are happened upon by hikers, hunters, or other people in a wooded or remote area, often near a lake or stream. Because such scenes are unbounded and unsecured when discovered, it is especially important for law enforcement agents to seal off and protect such scenes. The search for and collection of skeletal evidence in outdoor scenes must be left to professional anthropologists trained in recognition and collection of such material above ground and buried. If the remains retain decomposing flesh, the search may be aided by the presence of flies or other arthropods (See Chapter 12: Forensic Entomology) or by specially trained dogs. In some cases where there is evidence that bodies may be buried in shallow graves, military planes with ground-penetrating radar may be used to help locate the remains.

Something Extra: An Australian "Body Farm"

In Western Australia, the Departments of Anthropology and entomology of the University of Western Australia maintain a sort of body farm. Unlike the United States body farm in Tennessee, Australian researchers are prohibited from using human cadavers for the study of decomposition and insect activity. Instead they use very large pigs (up to three hundred pounds). The decomposition of pigs proceeds in a similar manner to humans. The pigs are euthanized and then placed in various locations in a remote plot of ground near the university. Some are dressed in clothes, some are covered by brush or branches, and some are buried in shallow graves. The pigs spend about forty days in this field and are visited daily by researchers. The Australian Air Force also uses the body farm to train pilots in the use of ground penetrating radar. The pilots perform regular fly-overs to see whether they can find the buried pigs with their radar.

Collection of bone evidence from an outdoor crime scene is somewhat like an archaeological dig. The perimeters of the scene are located and marked off. Depending on its size, the scene may be divided into quadrants to organize the search. The entire scene is carefully photographed before any search takes place. Each piece of bone is carefully marked with a flag or other marker and documented. After the surface bones have been collected, then excavation will be employed to discover buried bones.

Forensic Odontology

Forensic odontology (dentistry) is a part of forensic medicine. It deals with the examination of dental evidence including teeth, mouth and jaws and the presentation of expert evidence in a court of law. There are a number of aspects of forensic odontology. They include:

- Identification of human remains in crimes and mass disasters
- Estimation of the age of a living or dead person

- Analysis of bite marks found on the victims of an attack and in foods or other substances including wood and leather
- Examination of the dentition and face of a person suspected to be the victim of abuse

Structure and Development of Teeth

Teeth are unique in the human anatomy for a number of reasons. First, the outer part of a tooth is made of a substance called *enamel*. This is the hardest substance produced by the human body. Because of this, it can leave impressions in a wide variety of materials from wood to flesh. These impressions can, under certain conditions, provide a means of identification. When a person dies and is interred, the teeth are among the longest surviving structures and may provide a means of identification long after all of the soft tissues have decayed away. Teeth also interact directly with a person's environment and thus his or her condition may reflect elements of lifestyle and experiences.

Dentists describe teeth using a numbering system shown in Figure 11.13. Each time an individual visits a dentist, a chart is kept of the condition and treatment of each tooth by number. When a skull is recovered from a crime scene or disaster scene, this chart can be extremely helpful in identifying the dental remains. Each tooth is made up of three parts: the *crown*, the *body*, and the *root*. The anatomy of a tooth is shown in Figure 11.14.

Teeth are also oriented by their sides. The chewing surface of the tooth is the occlusal surface.

Humans develop two sets of teeth as they grow. The first set is the "baby" teeth. Dentists refer to this set as the **deciduous teeth**. They are gradually replaced by the **permanent teeth**. Different teeth develop at different rates. Dentists can estimate the age of a person by the conditions of development of various teeth. For example, the first *deciduous* incisor tooth erupts through the gums at about nine months of age. The first *permanent* tooth is a molar that erupts at about six years. The third molar or "wisdom" tooth erupts between seventeen and twenty-

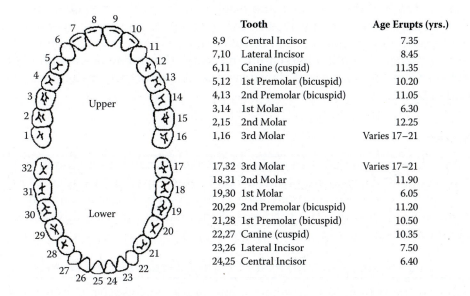

	Tooth	Age Erupts (yrs.)
8,9	Central Incisor	7.35
7,10	Lateral Incisor	8.45
6,11	Canine (cuspid)	11.35
5,12	1st Premolar (bicuspid)	10.20
4,13	2nd Premolar (bicuspid)	11.05
3,14	1st Molar	6.30
2,15	2nd Molar	12.25
1,16	3rd Molar	Varies 17–21
17,32	3rd Molar	Varies 17–21
18,31	2nd Molar	11.90
19,30	1st Molar	6.05
20,29	2nd Premolar (bicuspid)	11.20
21,28	1st Premolar (bicuspid)	10.50
22,27	Canine (cuspid)	10.35
23,26	Lateral Incisor	7.50
24,25	Central Incisor	6.40

Figure 11.13 A dentist's chart showing how the teeth are numbered with a chart of the teeth names and average ages of eruption.

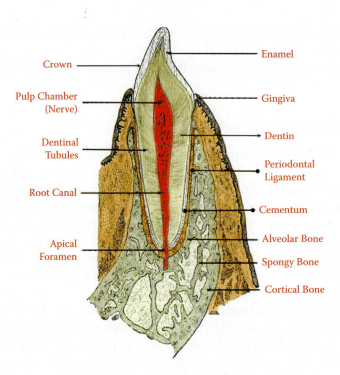

Figure 11.14 The anatomy of a tooth. *Courtesy of* Martin S. Spiller, D.M.D., www.doctorspiller.com.

one years. The wisdom teeth often erupt irregularly and have to be removed by a dentist.

Identification of Dental Remains

Although there is usually sufficient evidence to identify a dead body, sometimes dentition is the only way of achieving a positive identification. Cases aided by dental record checks include burning, drowning, fire or explosion, and decomposition. All mouths and dentition are different and a trained forensic odontologist may be able to provide enough information for a positive identification. This is normally done by charting the teeth of the deceased and comparing the chart with dental records of persons who may have been involved in the incident. If a suspected person is identified, comparison of postmortem and antemortem dental x-rays can be used to confirm the conclusion. Even if a person has no teeth, there may be enough identifying information from the analysis of dentures and the structure of the jaws and skull as revealed by x-rays.

Bite Marks

There have been a number of cases in recent years where a bite mark impression made on a person's body by an attacker has been compared with a cast of the suspect's teeth. This is a controversial area of analysis at this point and insufficient research has been done to settle the issue of whether bite mark analysis constitutes individual evidence.

Case Study: Bite Marks as Crucial Evidence: Ted Bundy

Probably the most famous case where a bite mark was positively associated with an attacker involved the convicted serial killer, Theodore Bundy. Bundy was suspected of killing more than forty young women during his spree that started in

Washington state and spread to other states in the western U.S. He was briefly captured and jailed in Colorado but escaped and traveled to Florida where he continued his murderous spree. In the space of a few weeks, he attacked at least five women in the Tallahassee area. Among the victims was Lisa Levy who, along with her roommate, Martha Bowman, was murdered on January 15, 1978. Bundy wiped the area clean of fingerprints and took the murder weapon (a wooden club). Some traces of blood, a few smudged fingerprints and some sperm samples were recovered from the crime scene but could not be conclusively matched to Bundy. Officers at the crime scene inspected Levy's body and found two bite marks on her body: one on her breast and a more distinct one on her left buttock. The one on her buttock was photographed at the scene. A ruler was put into the photograph for measuring purposes. By the time Bundy went on trial, the actual tissue samples containing the bite mark had been lost. After obtaining a warrant to get a bite mark impression from Bundy, Dr. Richard Souviron, a Florida dentist, took detailed photographs of Bundy's dentition. At Bundy's trial, Dr. Souviron showed the jury the photographs of Bundy's teeth and the bite mark from Levy's body. His testimony was bolstered by Dr. Lowell Levine, a forensic dentist from New York affiliated with the New York City Medical Examiner's Office. On the basis of the bite mark testimony and that of a witness, Bundy was convicted of Lisa Levy's murder and sentenced to die in the electric chair.

Forensic Odontology in Abuse Cases

Each year, many thousands of children and adults are physically abused by parents, spouses and others. In the case of child abuse, it may be necessary to remove the child from the home pending an investigation. In order for local social service agencies or law enforcement agents to remove a child, they must have evidence that the child is being or has been abused. In many cases, a child or adult victim is brought to the emergency room of a hospital for treatment. If an emergency room physician suspects that the victim has been abused as evidenced by facial injuries, she may ask for an opinion of a forensic odontologist. If she is able to determine that the injuries were sustained as a result of blunt force such as a fist, this may provide enough evidence to investigate the case as abuse.

Summary

Forensic anthropology is a part of physical anthropology. This, in turn, is a part of anthropology, the study of man. Forensic anthropologists work with skeletal remains to help determine the cause and manner of death and the postmortem interval in cases of suspicious death. They also help search death scenes to recover skeletal evidence. This can be similar to an archaeological dig.

In working with skeletal remains, the forensic anthropologist attempts to identify the individual to whom the remains belong. This often involves determining the biological profile of the skeleton. Before determining the biological profile, the anthropologist must determine whether the remains are human and of an age that makes them useful for forensic purposes. The biological profile consists of determining the age at death of the bones, sex, race, and stature. After the biological profile is determined, attempts may be made to individualize the bone. This can involve comparison of post- and antemortem x-rays to uncover bone trauma or unusual features. The analysis of skulls can also be important. Photographic superimposition of a face on a skull can identify it. It is also possible to build a face on a skull to determine whether it matches a missing person.

Forensic odontology (dentistry) is an important area often performed along with anthropology. Forensic odontologists help with the identification of human remains, estimate age, analyze bite marks, and help determine whether abuse has taken place.

Mini Lab Activities

MINI LAB 1: PELVIC BONES AND AGE

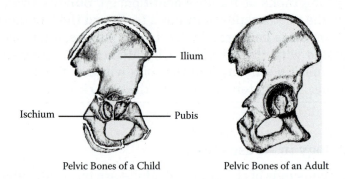

Pelvic Bones of a Child   Pelvic Bones of an Adult

The drawing shows the pelvic bones of an adult and a child. How are they different? Why are they different?

On the adult pelvis show the points of fusion of the ilium, ischium, and pubis bones. Are there eipiphyseal lines present? If so, show with a colored line where they are located.

MINI LAB 2: BITE MARKS

Cut the base from a disposable foam drinking cup. Then cut the cup in half vertically so that you have two equal halves with no base. Sandwich the two halves together. Place the narrow end into your mouth as far as possible. (It might be necessary to make the end narrower to fit your mouth by cutting the outside edges.) Bite down gently on the foam cup making a bite mark impression of your upper and lower teeth. Be careful not to bite through the foam, as you are only making an impression in the foam.

Have your classmates make their bite mark impressions. Then make a few "crime scene" bite marks using clay, soft cheese, chewing gum, or candy bars.

Be careful to use gloves when handling the evidence and exemplars and try to match the unknown crime scene bite marks to the known exemplars.

Test Yourself

Multiple Choice

1. The following bones are helpful in determining the sex of human skeletal remains:
   a. Femur, pelvis
   b. Humerus, skull
   c. Pelvis, skull
   d. Pelvis, tibia
2. The determination of age of skeletal remains is aided by
   a. Analysis of the dentition
   b. Measuring the curvature of the femur
   c. Measuring the nasal cavity
   d. Measuring the angle of the greater sciatic notch
3. The determination of the sex of skeletal remains is aided by
   a. Analysis of the dentition
   b. Measuring the curvature of the femur
   c. Measuring the nasal cavity
   d. Measuring the angle of the greater sciatic notch
4. The determination of the possible racial ancestry of the skeletal remains is aided by
   a. Looking for the presence of deciduous teeth
   b. Measuring the curvature of the femur
   c. Observing the presence of epiphyseal lines on the femur
   d. Measuring the angle of the greater sciatic notch
5. If the sub pubic angle of an intact pelvis is less than 90 degrees, then the remains are
   a. Caucasian
   b. Asian
   c. Male
   d. Female
6. If a human lower jaw bone has been recovered from a wooded area and shows evidence of permanent teeth with the absence of second molars, second premolars and third molars, then the approximate age of the decedent can be best estimated to be under
   a. 5 years old
   b. 8 years old
   c. 21 years old
   d. 11 years old
7. Which portion of a long bone contains the growth plate or epiphyseal plate?
   a. Epiphysis
   b. Metaphysis
   c. Diaphysis
8. The cells that make up bone are called
   a. Osteocytes
   b. Osteons
   c. Canaliculi
   d. Haversians

9. A human skull has a subtle brow ridge, the mastoid process is small, the forehead is rounded, not slanting and the external occipital protuberance is absent. This skull is *most* likely
   a. Male
   b. Female

10. What is the circled area of the base of the human skull called?
    a. Sub-pubic arch
    b. Sciatic notch
    c. External occipital protuberance
    d. Mastoid process

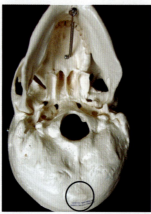 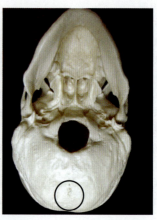

       Base of Male Skull   Base of Female Skull

Short Answer

11. Define forensic anthropology. How does it differ from osteology?
12. What are some of the techniques that are used in the proper recovery of skeletal remains? How is this like archaeology?
13. How do forensic anthropologists help determine the postmortem interval?
14. What is the significance of the pubic symphysis in the determination of age of skeletal remains?
15. Explain how the length of long bones such as the femur can be used to estimate the stature of a person?
16. What is the biological profile? What are its components?
17. What is photographic superimposition? How is it used in skeletal identification?
18. How does knowledge of the development of teeth help determine the age of a person?
19. How are bite marks used in the identification of a person? Why is this type of analysis controversial?
20. A bone is found in a wooded area that resembles a human adult's femur by maturity of the bone, but it is unclear if it could be human or animal. Quick measurement of the length reveals that it is 19.5 cm long. What is your conclusion?

Problem Solving

21–25. Measure your height in feet and inches. Determine the length range of each of your long bones using Table 11.1 for your gender and race.

Further Reading

Sauer, N. Manner of Death in T. Rathbun, J. and Buikstra. *Human Identification: Case Studies in Forensic Anthropology*. Springfield, IL: Charles Thomas, 1984, pp. 176–184.

Ubelaker, D. *Human Skeletal Remains*. Washington, D.C.: Taraxacum, 2000.

Ubelaker, D. H. and H. Scammell. *Bones: A Forensic Detective's Casebook*. Edward Burlingame Books, New York, 1992.

White, T. D. *Human Osteology*. London: Academic Press, 2000.

Burns, K. *Forensic Anthropology Training Manual*. 2nd ed. Upper Saddle River, NJ: Pearson-Prentice Hall, 2007.

On the Web

Forensic Anthropology

www.pbs.org/saf/1203/teaching/teaching2.htm
http://biology.clc.uc.edu/courses/bio105/bone.htm
http://scienceblogs.com/afarensis/2006/06/17/lessons_from_kennewick_fitting/
www.anthro4n6.net/forensics/
www.forensicanthro.com/
http://whyfiles.org/192forensic_anthro/
http://facstaff.unca.edu/cnicolay/BIO223-F08/HO-forensic.pdf
www.forensicanthro.com/resources.html
www.mnsu.edu/emuseum/biology/humananatomy/skeletal/terms.html
www.mnsu.edu/emuseum/biology/forensics/
www.anthro4n6.net/forensics/report.html#Inventory

Forensic Odontology

www.3dmouth.org/6/6_1.cfm
http://en.wikipedia.org/wiki/Tooth_development

Facial Reconstruction

www.forensicartist.com/reconstruction.html
www.karenttaylor.com/

Tennessee Body Farm: University of Tennessee Forensic Anthropology Center

http://web.utk.edu/~fac/

12
Forensic Entomology

Learning Objectives

1. To be able to define entomology and forensic entomology and give examples
2. To be able to describe the contributions that forensic entomology can make in solving death cases
3. To be able to describe the ways that forensic entomology can help determine the postmortem interval
4. To be able to list and describe the various types of arthropods that invade a body after death
5. To be able to describe the contributions of forensic entomology to the determination of the presence of drugs and poisons in a body
6. To be able to describe the five stages of decomposition of a body after death

Chapter 12
Forensic Entomology

Chapter Outline

Mini Glossary

Entomology: Generalized study of insects and related arthropods (crustaceans, spiders, etc.).

Forensic entomology: The application of entomology to civil and criminal incidents.

Instar: Developmental stages of the larva of a fly.

Medicolegal forensic entomology: This type of forensic entomology is used in the investigation of death, abuse, and neglect cases.

Necrophage: Insects that feed on the tissue of a corpse.

Omnivore: Arthropods that feed not only on the body, but on other insects that have been attracted to the corpse. Omnivores include mainly wasps and beetles.

Postmortem interval (PMI): Time since death. In the context of forensic entomology, it is the time interval between when the body is first exposed to insects and when it is discovered.

Urban forensic entomology: The analysis of the presence of arthropods in homes, businesses, gardens, and farms.

Introduction

The earliest record of the use of entomology in a criminal investigation is described in a book published in China in the thirteenth century. The book, called *His Yuan Lu* ("The Washing Away of Wrongs"), contains a description of a murder investigation in a rice paddy. The incident involved a homicide committed by one of the workers. The investigator lined up the workers and told them to lay their sickles on the ground. One of the implements contained very faint traces of blood. Although this could not have been identified as blood scientifically at that time, it almost immediately attracted flies. Since the only implement that could have caused the murder was a sickle and the murderer had to be one of the workers, the flies "identified" the guilty worker's sickle as having blood on it. The perpetrator of the crime was, in effect, caught red-handed and he confessed.

This incident is a textbook example of the use of insects in solving crimes and is the subject of this chapter. We will see that forensic entomology is not only is a useful science in crime investigation, but can also be helpful in civil incidents in rural areas and cities alike.

Entomology is the generalized study of insects and related arthropods (crustaceans, spiders, etc.). **Forensic entomology** is the application of entomology to civil and criminal incidents. The most important and noteworthy applications of forensic entomology involve its use in criminal cases, but it has very important applications in the civil area. For example, **urban forensic anthropology** involves the analysis of the presence of arthropods in homes, businesses, gardens, and farms. There have been a number of cases where the indiscriminate use of pesticides has killed many arthropods. The location and quantity of these dead animals provide strong evidence that the pesticides were used improperly or without proper cautions taken against their spread. There are also cases where insects invade food and other consumer products such as soft drinks, salad dressings, and even candy. These situations often lead to litigation because of improper storage of food materials. Forensic entomologists are often called into such cases to provide testimony about how and why these insects were able to invade food storage containers and facilities.

Medicolegal forensic entomology is the most visible and common application of entomology. This type of forensic entomology is used in the investigation of death, abuse, and neglect cases. Although most noteworthy for its contribution to estimation of the **postmortem interval (PMI)** or time since death, there are many other types of information that can be gleaned from the study of arthropods at crime scenes. These include the climatic and temperature conditions at death, the location of a body and determination of whether a body had been moved shortly after death, how a body was stored, the location of antemortem (before death) injuries, whether a body had been buried or submerged in water, and sometimes the presence of drugs and poisons in a body. Suspects have been linked to a scene by the presence of arthropods. The extent of abuse or neglect of infants and elderly persons can be established by insect activity.

Considering all of these situations, the role of the forensic entomologist in a crime investigation can be a major one. His or her principal role is to collect and identify arthropod specimens and interpret these findings in relation to environmental variables. Arguably the most important contribution of medicolegal forensic entomology to crime investigation is in the estimation of the PMI in cases where a body is discovered days after death. The contribution of forensic entomology in late postmortem interval determination is discussed in detail in Chapter 10: Forensic Pathology. The basis for estimation of the PMI by forensic entomologists is that many different types of insects will invade a corpse at predictable intervals after death, some very soon after a body has been deposited. These arthropods have predictable developmental stages and parts of the body that they will inhabit. Forensic entomologists examine the insects on and in a body when it is discovered. From the types of insects present, their developmental stages, and the degree of activity on the body, entomologists can sometimes make remarkably accurate and precise determinations of the PMI, even days after death. Insect behavior may also yield information about how, or even if, a crime occurred.

With all of these valuable uses of entomology, it is interesting to note that this type of evidence is underused in homicide investigations. Insects are often ignored as evidence and are treated as a gross nuisance by investigators at crime scenes and by pathology personnel at autopsies. There are several reasons for this. Crime scene technicians who collect evidence are seldom trained to recognize the significance of the presence of arthropods on a body. They don't realize the importance of this evidence and are not trained in the proper methods of collection of insects. Investigators are told that this evidence is unreliable and that entomologists can only give an estimate of the PMI, not an exact determination. In fact, there are no methods that can give an exact PMI at any time after death. Finally, there are only a few dozen forensically trained entomologists in the whole United States. If untrained entomologists are called to crime scenes, mistakes are often made and the value of the evidence is diminished or lost, further contributing to the lack of regard for this science.

Becoming a Forensic Entomologist

To become certified as a Diplomate in the American Board of Forensic Entomology (ABFE/ http://research.missouri.edu/entomology), one must first obtain a Ph.D. in entomology. There are a number of universities nationwide that offer this degree. Some universities also offer bachelor's or master's degrees in forensic entomology. There is a formal organization of professional entomologists who are board certified. This is the American Registry of Professional Entomologists (ARPE).

The PMI: The Life Cycle of the Blowfly

The key evidence presented by arthropods in determining the PMI is the determination of what types are present in and around a body and what stages of life are exhibited. Many species of arthropod invade a body and they normally arrive at predictable intervals in particular order. Of course, all of this is highly dependent on the environmental conditions surrounding the corpse. Like most life activities, cold conditions slow insect activity. If a body is heavily clothed or partially or totally buried, it will take insects longer to reach the body. Many insects are inactive at night, so if a body is left at an outdoor sight at night, there may be no activity until dawn. It generally takes insects longer to find a body that is indoors or under water. Even with all of these environmental variables, there are a remarkable number of constants and consistencies about insect behavior at the site of a

Figure 12.1 An adult blowfly. *Courtesy of* Dr. Richard Merritt.

dead body. It is also important to note that, with respect to forensic entomology, the PMI is not the same as the time since death, but is the time interval since the body was put into an environment where interaction with insects is possible. For example, if someone is killed and the body is put into the trunk of a car that is then driven 8 hours to a location where the body is dumped, insect activity can only begin at that time and determination of the PMI will not reflect the time that the body spent in the car.

In many situations, the common blowfly is the first insect to reach a dead body. Flies are able to find and invade a corpse long before the police or crime scene unit arrives. They can squeeze into the tightest of spaces to get to a body. In cases where bodies are buried in the rubble of a fire or explosion, it is sometimes possible to follow the flies to the bodies in the rubble. This method was used to help locate bodies in the rubble of the Murrah building in the Oklahoma City bombing. Once female flies find the body, they will immediately lay eggs and the life cycle of the fly begins as described below.

Egg laying begins in naturally moist areas of the body such as the mouth, eyes, and nose and around open wounds. Generally egg laying takes place only in daylight, so if a death occurs at night, egg laying will be delayed. One female blowfly can lay hundreds of eggs in a short period. Another common carrion fly, the flesh fly, deposits live larvae in the same areas as blowfly eggs. Figure 12.1 is a picture of a blowfly. Figure 12.2 is a picture of an adult flesh fly.

Fly larvae go through three developmental stages called **instars**. During each instar, the maggot increases in size dramatically. By the time a maggot reaches the third instar, most of the flesh of the body has been consumed. Under moderate dry conditions, the first instar of the blowfly forms from the egg about 8 hours after the egg is oviposited. The second instar forms around 20 hours later and the third about 20 hours after that. After about 5 days, the larva stops feeding and rests. After a few more days, the larva becomes a pupa. The adult fly emerges about 3 weeks after the eggs are laid. Figure 12.3 shows blowfly maggots and Figure 12.4 shows pupae of a number of species of flies.

Using the time intervals given above, an entomologist can begin to develop clues that will help determine the PMI. Again, it must be stressed that the time intervals of some of the stages given above depend somewhat upon the environmental

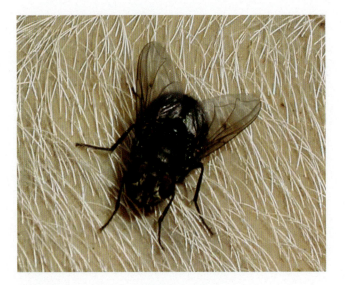

Figure 12.2 An adult flesh fly. *Courtesy of* Dr. Richard Merritt.

Figure 12.3 Blowfly maggots. *Courtesy of* Dr. Richard Merritt.

Figure 12.4 Pupae of several species of flies. *Courtesy of* Dr. Richard Merritt.

conditions present. There are also other artifactual situations that can affect the entomologist's estimation of the PMI. One forensic entomologist (Richard Merritt in a private communication) tells of a case where an entomologist encountered unusually large maggots in a body. His conclusion was that the maggots had been feeding at the body for some time and his determination of the PMI was based on this long interval. However, other measurements of insect activity were at odds with the PMI determination based on the data from the maggots. Forensic toxicology of the remains of the body showed that the victim had ingested cocaine shortly before death. Some of this was transferred to the maggots as they fed on the body tissues. The stimulant effect of the cocaine caused the maggots to eat much more rapidly than normal, accelerating their growth greatly and leading to the incorrect data. This raises two interesting points: First, if possible, the entomologist must not rely on only one piece of life cycle or insect data in reaching conclusions about PMI. Corroborating evidence should always be obtained where possible. Second, if there is insufficient tissue remaining on a dead body for drug screening, maggots can be collected and tested for the presence of drugs. Another important point about making observations from insect activity is that the act of eating and digesting tissues by insects releases a great deal of energy. Temperatures around a body being consumed by insects can reach nearly 120°F at times. This, in turn, accelerates decomposition of the body and insect activity.

The life cycle of the fly described above is only one example of the use of arthropod life cycles to estimate PMI. Other types of insects invade bodies and lay eggs on a predictable schedule. Still others will attack and eat the eggs and larvae of other insects, also on a predictable schedule. This way, entomologists usually have several data points from which to draw conclusions concerning the PMI.

Decomposition of a Body after Death

When a person dies, decomposition of the tissues and organs begins to take place almost immediately, although outward evidence may not be seen for hours depending on the temperature and moisture conditions. Much of this decomposition is carried out by bacteria inside and outside the body, but when they are available, arthropods can speed up this process remarkably. Catts and Goff (Forensic Entomology in Criminal Investigations, in *American Review of Entomology*, Annual Reviews of Entomology, 1992, 37:253–72) describe four roles that arthropods play in decomposition of bodies.

1. **Necrophages:** These insects actually feed on the tissue of the corpse. Many of them are flies. Entomologists study the life cycles of these insects on the body to help determine PMI.
2. **Omnivores:** Some arthropods feed not only on the body, but on other insects that have been attracted to the corpse. **Omnivores** include mainly wasps and beetles. It is interesting to note that if omnivores are present in large quantities, they may deplete the population of necrophages, thus retarding decomposition
3. **Predators and parasites:** Some categories of arthropods, including some flies and mites, act as parasites on other insects and some may start out as necrophages, becoming predators of other insects at a later stage.

Figure 12.5 Carrion beetles. *Courtesy of* Dr. Richard Merritt.

4. **Incidentals:** These are arthropods including some spiders, centipedes, mites, and others that used the corpse as part of their normal habitat. They move into the corpse and make it their home, at least for a time.

Figure 12.5 shows carrion beetles.

Stages of Decomposition

There is great variability in the time it takes for a body to decompose. The major determinant is temperature. Warm temperatures will accelerate the decomposition process and cold weather will depress it. A level of decomposition that might take 18–24 hours in cool weather can take only a few hours in tropical weather. Another factor is the amount of protection that the body has. Clothing slows decomposition, as does burial or immersion in water. A forensic entomologist who uses the life cycles of various arthropods to help determine the postmortem interval must take these variables into consideration.

Even with this great variability, there are common patterns to the decomposition process. There are several distinct stages to decomposition and they occur in the same order each time. The environment of the body will determine the duration of each stage and the local arthropod population will also have some effect. Forensic entomologists generally identify five stages of decomposition. The first three comprise one phase in which the arthropods feed on the body and their life cycle proceeds increasing the biomass greatly. Maggots are the major arthropods in this phase. Under moderate environmental conditions, this phase takes about 10 days. The three stages in this phase are listed below along with their average durations and some of the insects that are commonly found on the carcass during each stage:

- Fresh (1–2 days): Adult blowflies, flesh flies, yellow jackets
- Bloated (2–6 days): Blowflies and other flies, some beetles, yellow jackets
- Decay (5–11 days): Some flies and beetles, cockroaches

When this phase is complete, the maggots leave the body and the decomposition fluids have mostly seeped away. At this point, there has been a drastic decrease in biomass at the scene. The second phase of decomposition has 2 stages and takes 2 weeks or more. The stages are as follows:

- Post-decay (10–24 days): Some beetles, fruit flies, gnats, some flies
- Dry stage (24+ days): Some beetles, ants, and flies

Factors That Affect PMI

In this chapter, we've briefly mentioned some of the factors that can affect the determination of the PMI. This section organizes these factors and they are discussed in a bit more detail.

Physical Factors

A body buried in a vault or casket will be much more resistant to attack by insects than one that is dumped into a hole which is then filled with dirt. Even burying a body in soil will affect the rate of attack by arthropods. The temperature a few feet underground will generally be more constant than on the surface. It will be dark which inhibits egg laying by insects. It may be difficult for many insects including flies to reach the body. There is also generally less air if the body is tightly compacted by soil. Anaerobic bacteria are much more active in deep soil and this may affect decomposition of the body. There is also generally more moisture in soil a few feet below ground. If a body is submerged in water, especially if it is trapped in a car or other container, decomposition due to insects is very different than on land. The temperature is usually more constant, there may be less light depending on how deep the body is, and the variety and types of arthropods available to feed on the body will be very different than on land. All of these factors make determination of the PMI more difficult for the forensic entomologist.

Chemical Factors

In Chapter 10: Forensic Pathology, the role of embalming on the determination of the presence of drugs or poisons in a body when a body was exhumed was discussed. Embalming chemicals also affect insect attack on dead bodies. These agents are generally poisonous to most arthropods, so their activity will be greatly retarded by the presence of embalming fluids. As the body decomposes, the embalming agents may leak or evaporate and some insect activity can then take place, but it is retarded. If a body is placed or buried on land where insecticides are used to control pests that attack crops, these poisons will also affect arthropods that feed on bodies. Again, the usual effect is to greatly retard insect activity and reproduction, thus making the normal entomological data suspect. It was also previously mentioned that drugs present in a body at death may be consumed by arthropods. The drugs will, in turn, affect these animals. Stimulants such as cocaine will accelerate insect activity, whereas depressants can retard activity. There has been little attention paid to the effects of hallucinogens such as LSD or marijuana on insect activity.

Climate

It was previously mentioned that high temperatures accelerate virtually all biological activity. Likewise, cold weather will have the opposite effect, so it is not surprising that temperatures will affect the rate of activity and reproduction of insects that have invaded a body. In addition, high winds may cover or uncover a body with debris and make it harder for flying insects to find and land on a body. Heavy rains can wash insects off a body and if the body becomes partially submerged, the water can dramatically affect insect activity.

Animals

Arthropods are not the only animals that take an interest in corpses. Larger animals such as rodents, dogs, cats, and scavengers will attack and feed on bodies. They may also carry parts of a body such as arms and legs to another location where they may eat or bury them. If the activity of these larger animals is significant enough, there may be little left at the scene for insects to be much of a factor. Such situations make death scene investigation and PMI determination much more difficult than would otherwise be the case. Even if a person dies indoors and there are family pets trapped in the house with the victim, the pets will eventually attack the body, especially if hunger becomes a problem.

Entomological Investigation and Evidence Collection

Although some arthropods are collected at crime scenes by technicians, the majority of this type of investigation is carried out by forensic entomologists who have the training and knowledge to properly collect evidence, make ecological observations, and properly interpret the data.

At the Death Scene

The function of the forensic entomologist at a death scene is to catalogue and collect arthropod evidence from the body and surrounding area. Insects may be coming and going from the body at any time so it is important to collect specimens around the body as well as on and under it. The entomologist must also make careful observations about the temperature and condition of the body at the time of recovery and must determine, to the extent possible, what the ecological conditions have been since the corpse was discovered. One important contribution that arthropods can make to the determination of cause of death is that they may pinpoint the sight of trauma. Flies will deposit their eggs in openings in the body and especially those where blood is present such as a gunshot or knife wound. It should be noted however, that insect activity on a body can also cause artifacts. For example, insects can enlarge or distort a knife or bullet wound. They can also cause what appear to be blood spatters, but are actually transfers of blood by the insects or larvae to another surface.

Summary

Forensic entomology is the part of entomology that involves how insects invade a body after death. Various types of arthropods such as flies, ants, beetles, wasps, yellow jackets, etc. will invade a body and sometimes lay their eggs or hatch their larvae. Different species of insects will invade at different intervals after death. This insect succession helps forensic entomologists determine the time since death. Entomologists must also understand the life cycles of various insects and recognize which form is present on a body as an aid to determining the PMI. The most common insects to reach a body after death are blowflies and bottle flies. They have definite life stages that occur at reliable intervals after a body dies although environmental conditions can greatly affect the timing of these stages.

A body will decay over time in fairly well-defined stages and these stages are accompanied by arthropod activity of various types. There are five identifiable stages of decay. In addition to determining the postmortem interval, forensic entomologists can help in determining where wounds occurred, if a body has been moved since death, the presence of drugs or poisons in the body and other types of information.

Test Yourself

Multiple Choice

1. The major contribution of forensic entomology to death investigation is:
   a. Determination of the cause of death
   b. Determination of the PMI
   c. Determination of the manner of death
   d. Determination of the presence of drugs in the victim
2. The first insects to reach a body in the outdoors are generally:
   a. Spiders
   b. Carrion beetles
   c. Blow flies
   d. Centipedes
3. Insect activity is useful in which of the following situations:
   a. Abuse or neglect of the elderly
   b. Presence of drugs or poisons in the body
   c. Linking of suspects to a crime
   d. Determination of PMI
   e. All of the above
4. Insect evidence is often neglected by crime scene investigators because:
   a. It is disturbing to many people
   b. The evidence is unreliable and entomologists can only estimate the PMI from insect evidence
   c. Insects only attack a body that has been deposited outdoors
   d. Entomology is useless if the body has been buried
   e. The PMI cannot be estimated in very cold weather
5. The proper order of the fly's life cycle is:
   a. Egg, maggot, pupa
   b. Egg, pupae, maggot
   c. Instars one, two, three, egg, pupa
   d. Egg, instar three, maggot pupa
6. Which of the following is not a role that arthropods play in the decomposition of a body?
   a. Omnivore
   b. Instar

     c. Predator

     d. Necrophage

7. Which of the following is the correct order of decomposition stages of a body?

     a. Fresh, bloated dry, decay

     b. Bloated, dry, decay, fresh

     c. Fresh, dry, decay, bloated

     d. Fresh, bloated, decay, dry

8. Which of the following is *not* a factor that affects decomposition of a body and insect activity?

     a. Cold

     b. Wind

     c. Rain

     d. Embalming fluid

     e. All the above are factors

True or False

9. The only application of forensic entomology is determination of the PMI.

10. Urban entomology involves the analysis of the presence of arthropods in homes and businesses.

11. Forensic anthropology can be used to link a suspect to a crime scene.

12. The life cycle of a fly will slow down in very cold weather.

13. The blowfly is usually the first insect that will discover a dead body.

14. Insect evidence is often treated as a nuisance by investigators and pathologists.

15. If temperatures are moderate, a forensic entomologist can determine a PMI to within one hour of death.

16. Fly larvae go through four instars before becoming adults.

17. Some arthropods such as spiders will actually move into a corpse for a time and make it their home.

Matching

18. Instar	a. Fly larva
19. Omnivore insect	b. Chemical that retards insect activity
20. Insecticide	c. Eats other insects as well as flesh
21. Bloated stage	d. Developmental stage of a fly
22. Maggot	e. A stage of decomposition

Short Essay

23. What contributions can forensic entomology make in the investigation of death?

24. How do forensic entomologists determine the postmortem interval? What time frames are involved?

25. How does insect behavior help pinpoint the locations of wounds on a body?

Further Reading

Catts, E. P. and M. L. Goff. Forensic Entomology in Criminal Investigations. *Annu. Rev. Entomology*, 1992.

Goff, M. L. *A Fly for the Prosecution: How Insect Evidence Helps Solve Crimes*. Cambridge, MA: Harvard University Press, 2001.

Byrd, J. H. and J. L. Castner, eds. *Forensic Entomology: The Utility of Arthropods in Legal Investigations*. Boca Raton, FL: CRC Press, 2001.

On the Web

Homepage of the American Board of Forensic Entomology: http://research.missouri.edu/entomology.

A comprehensive bibliography on forensic entomology: www.forensicentomology.com/literature.htm.

Excellent introductory site for forensic entomology: www.forensicentomology.com.

Case studies in forensic entomology: http://research.missouri.edu/entomology/casestudies.html.

Video showing decomposition of a pig: http://lubbock.tamu.edu/ipm/AgWeb/videos/Forensic/Forensicvideos.html.

Many images of insects: http://entomology.unl.edu/images.

13
Serology

Learning Objectives

1. To be able to define and describe the components of blood
2. To be able to describe preliminary tests for blood
3. To be able to describe confirmatory tests for blood
3. To be able to define semen and describe its components
5. To be able to describe the preliminary and confirmatory tests for semen
6. To be able to describe the common tests for vaginal secretions
7. To be able to describe the common tests for saliva
8. To be able to describe the role of bloodstain pattern analysis in crime scene reconstruction
9. To be able to describe the physical properties of blood and how they contribute to the various types of bloodstains
10. To be able to describe the various types of bloodstains

Chapter 13
Serology

Chapter Outline

Mini Glossary

Agglutination: The joining or clumping of antigen-bearing red blood cells and the antibodies specific to that antigen.

Altered bloodstains: Shed blood that has been changed physically or physiologically.

Antibodies: Antibodies are found in the blood serum and are specific to a blood type. They serve as protection from noncompatible blood types.

Antigen: Antigens in blood are inherited substances on the erythrocyte (red blood cell), which are responsible for eliciting a blood group reaction to specific antibodies.

Blood: A solution of various materials important for sustaining life.

Bloodstain pattern analysis (BSPA): An area of forensic science that interprets the patterns seen in deposited blood and relates them to the actions that could have caused the pattern.

Confirmatory test: A test used to identify the specific fluid or material present.

Erythrocytes: Components of the solid part of the blood responsible for carrying oxygen and removing carbon dioxide from the cells, commonly called red blood cells.

Forensic serology: The examination and identification of body fluids as they relate to a crime scene.

Leukocytes: Components of the solid part of the blood responsible for fighting infection, commonly called white blood cells.

Passive bloodstains: Bloodshed that travels under the influence of gravity only.

Plasma: The liquid portion of the blood that contains, in suspension, the blood cells and platelets along with water, glucose, proteins, and other chemical compounds.

Screening (presumptive) test: A test that establishes the *possibility* that a specific type of fluid or substance is present in a sample.

Serology: The examination and identification of body fluids.

Spatter bloodstains: Blood that moves due to a force in addition to gravity and will exhibit directionality and specific distribution patterns.

Thromobocytes: Components of the solid part of the blood that assists in the clotting process. They are commonly called platelets.

Viscous: A property of a liquid that imparts resistance to flow.

Introduction

One of the first blood spatter cases in the United States took place in Utah. The case involved the admissibility of blood spatter evidence. A man was seen entering the home of his girlfriend and then, a few minutes later, exited carrying her in his arms. He put her in the back seat of his car and drove off. A neighbor witnessed this and called police, who stopped him. He claimed that he had found her lying on the floor and picked her up to take her to the hospital. The police were suspicious and arrested him. The girl died as the result of stab wounds. As part of the investigation, the accused's bloodstained clothes were sent to the crime laboratory for analysis. The serologist examined his shirt and pants and determined that the bloodstains were the result of blood spurting under pressure from a source in front of him and landing on his clothing. At his trial for murder, the defendant sought to exclude the blood spatter evidence on the grounds that its underlying basis had not been proven. The court rejected the argument and admitted the blood spatter evidence and the defendant was convicted. He appealed to the Utah Supreme Court, which upheld the admissibility of the evidence.

In recent times, DNA testing has received a great deal of attention. The pulse of this attention has been quickened by media publicity. The public has been informed of DNA's ability to identify someone from traces of biological material left at crime scenes—and of cases where imprisoned people have been set free by post-conviction DNA typing that proves that they were wrongly convicted. Many people, including some law enforcement personnel, believe that the only test necessary for blood analysis is DNA typing. People are not aware of how blood was analyzed in a crime lab before DNA typing and what tests are still necessary to fully characterize blood and other body fluids. This information is of much more than historical or academic interest. Many of these tests are still used in modern crime labs. These older techniques are still valuable in cases where DNA typing cannot be done or is of limited use for one reason or another. In those cases where DNA typing has caused the

Figure 13.1 Bloodstains produced by a bullet traveling through a blood-soaked sponge. *Courtesy of Forensic Science Educational Consulting, LLC.*

reversal of a conviction, pre-DNA serological testing was done at the time of the crime. In most cases, this testing was done properly and proper interpretations were made concerning the likelihood that the evidence came from the suspect or victim. The problem is that the serological evidence is not as powerful as DNA evidence and cannot *individualize* blood to a particular person. If a case is reopened because of DNA typing, testimony may be required concerning the serological analysis performed before the original trial. Thus, a good working knowledge of forensic serology can be very important to a forensic biologist

This chapter has three parts: the analysis of blood, the identification of other biological fluids and stains, and the analysis of bloodstain patterns. All of these areas of inquiry constitute the science of **forensic serology**. Serology is defined as the examination of body fluids. These include blood, saliva, seminal fluid, vaginal secretions, urine, feces, and even tissues and organs. The majority of serological evidence consists of blood and the body fluids generated by sexual assault cases: semen, saliva, and vaginal secretions. Bloodstain pattern analysis is an emerging forensic science that has become quite common in the past twenty years or so. Figure 13.1 shows an impact pattern bloodstain due to gunshot.

Blood

Before discussing the analysis of blood, it is important to understand the basics. Blood is a solution of various materials in water. It is also a suspension whereby insoluble materials are carried through the body by the water. The liquid portion of blood is called **plasma**. It comprises about 55 percent of the total volume of blood. The substances dissolved in the plasma include proteins, carbohydrates, fats, salts and minerals, and antibodies. In addition, plasma contains materials that are responsible for blood clotting.

The suspended materials in blood make up the other 45 percent and include red blood cells, white blood cells, and platelets. Red blood cells (**erythrocytes**) are formed

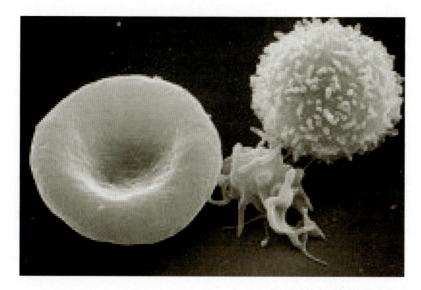

Figure 13.2 These are single examples of the solid parts of the blood as seen under an electron microscope. The red blood cell (erythrocyte) is on the left, the white blood cell (leukocyte) is on the right, and the platelet (thrombocyte) is in the middle. As a group, these solid materials constitute 45 percent of human blood. Produced by Electron Microscopy facility at the National Cancer Institute at Frederick, MD.

in bone marrow and are primarily responsible for transport of oxygen to cells and carbon dioxide away from them. They have no nucleus (and no nuclear DNA). White blood cells (**leukocytes**) are normally formed in the lymph nodes and are primarily involved in the body's immune system. Leukocytes possess nuclei and can therefore contain nuclear DNA. Platelets (**thrombocytes**) handle a major part of the blood clotting process. Figure 13.2 is an electron microscope image of these components of blood.

Analysis of Blood

The purpose of analyzing blood at a crime scene is to determine its source. The blood may be on the floor, wall, or an object at the scene. It may be on clothing worn by the victim or the suspect of the crime. It may be wet or dry. Blood may be partially degraded or putrefied. Depending on the conditions of the scene, there may be a very small amount of blood present, limiting the types of analysis that can be done or, in some cases, may not permit any analysis. Blood is a perishable biological material and failure to properly collect and preserve it may result in spoilage, inability to analyze it, or inadmissibility of the analytical results in court.

Preliminary Considerations

Most people think a bloodstain is easy to spot. Nothing else could look like wet or dried blood. Many believe that visual identification should be enough. The fact is, however, that scientific and legal requirements make a positive identification of the blood through scientific means a necessity. Good laboratory practice requires that properly validated protocols be employed for the positive identification of blood. Varying the protocol is permissible as long as there are sound reasons for doing so. The protocols for the chemical analysis of blood follow the same protocols as any other types of evidence and have at least the following elements:

1. Careful preliminary physical examination of the item to spot potential evidence
2. Careful recording of the evidence (photos and videotaping) and its exact location
3. Preliminary or *screening tests* that permit a *presumption* of the presence of certain types of evidence
4. Sensitive and specific *confirmatory tests* of the chemical identity of the evidence

In the case of serological evidence, additional tests are done after confirmation that the evidence is or contains blood or another body fluid. These include the determination of the species of the blood and analysis of the markers in the blood that serve to limit the number of people from whom the blood could have been taken. Today that test is usually DNA typing.

Locating Blood on Objects

The fact that a stain is dark red or black may mean that it is blood. Sometimes these stains are very small or are on dark surfaces that mask their presence. In some cases, blood has been washed off the surface. Some tests can help locate bloodstains. These also serve as preliminary tests for blood. The two major tests for this purpose are *Luminol* and *fluorescein*. Both of these tests use luminescence techniques to locate faint or small bloodstains on objects at a crime scene.

Luminol

Luminol is a very sensitive reagent that undergoes oxidation by hydrogen peroxide in alkaline solution in the presence of the *heme* fraction of *hemoglobin*, a molecule in red blood cells that carries oxygen and carbon dioxide to and from cells. The structure of heme is shown in Figure 13.3.

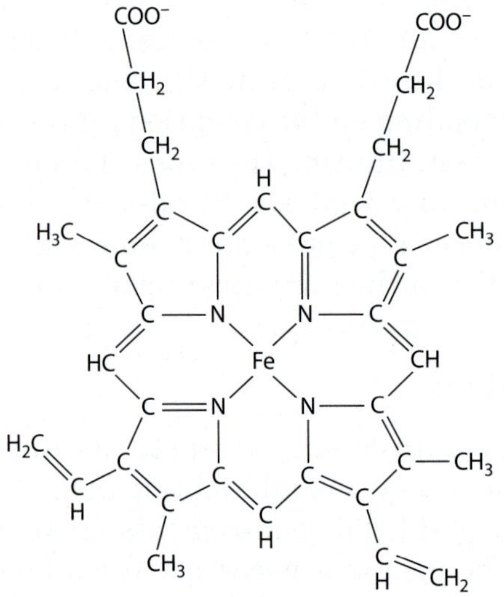

Heme
(Fe-protoporphyrin IX)

Figure 13.3 The structure of heme.

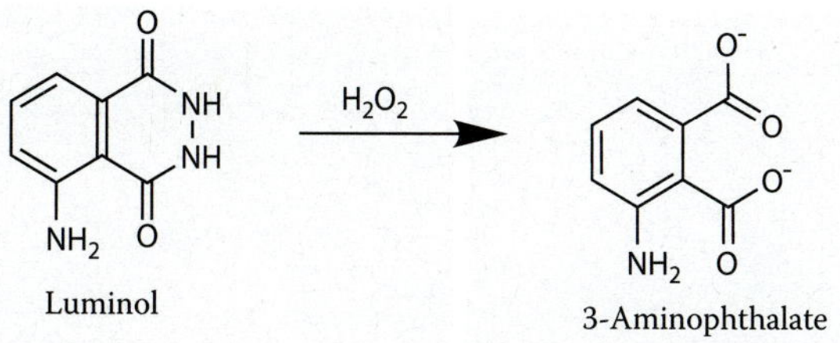

Figure 13.4 The Luminol reaction.

The reaction of Luminol with hydrogen peroxide is shown in Figure 13.4. It is catalyzed by heme, but heme doesn't take part in the reaction. The product of the reaction, 3-aminophthalate, undergoes *chemiluminescence*. When the product is formed it emits light on its own. No additional light is needed. At a crime scene the area is darkened and the Luminol reagent is applied. The appearance of a bright blue to yellow-green color is indicative of the possible presence of blood. The color should appear immediately and last for at least 30 seconds before another application of reagent is needed.

Some research has been done to determine whether Luminol can contaminate a blood sample and render it unusable for further analysis. For the most part, Luminol doesn't affect blood, at least as far as DNA testing goes. In any case, Luminol, like other reagents, should only be used when necessary to avoid possible contamination of the blood sample.

Fluorescein

Fluorescein, like Luminol, emits light when exposed to an oxidant and heme. Unlike Luminol, however, fluorescein undergoes fluorescence rather than chemiluminescence. It is applied to a suspected bloodstain along with hydrogen peroxide. A strong, short-wave light is then used to induce fluorescence. The structure of fluorescein is shown in Figure 13.5.

Commercial fluorescein preparations contain a thickening agent that allows them to be used on vertical surfaces. Luminol solutions do not. Research has shown that fluorescein does not interfere with DNA typing. The luminous effects of both reagents are shown in Figure 13.6.

Confirmatory Tests for Blood

Luminol and fluorescein are very useful for locating blood on large surfaces, but they are not specific for blood. Other substances, including certain vegetable extracts, can give false positive tests for blood. At times, it may be useful or

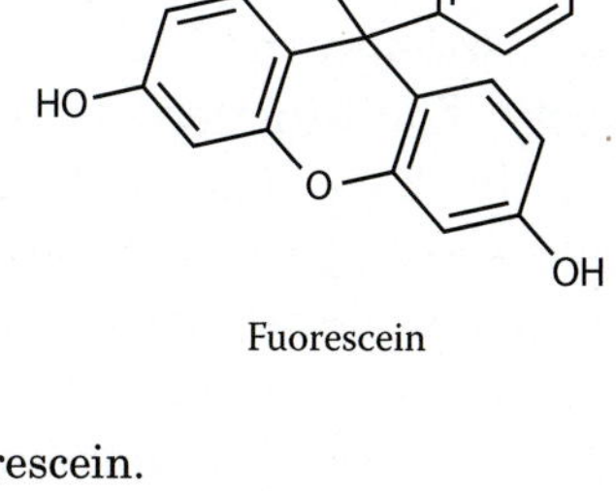

Fuorescein

Figure 13.5 The structure of fluorescein.

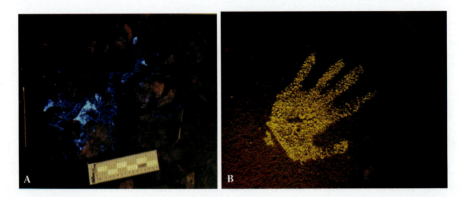

Figure 13.6 Chemical enhancement of blood to visualize a bloodstain. (A) shows the addition of Luminol to show the presence of blood. (B) shows the addition of fluorescein showing a bloodstained handprint.

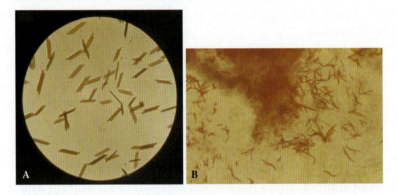

Figure 13.7 (A) shows Teichmann crystals obtained from the reaction with blood, while (B) shows Takayama crystals obtained from the reaction with blood. Reprinted courtesy of J. J. Nordby and S. H. James, *Forensic Science: An Introduction to Scientific and Investigative Techniques,* CRC Press.

necessary to confirm the presence of blood. The two most popular chemical tests for the confirmation of blood are the *Teichmann* and *Takayama* tests. Both are *microcrystal* tests. A crystallizing reagent is added to suspected blood. The formation of characteristic shaped crystals formed by the reaction of the reagent and heme is confirmatory for blood. Figure 13.7 shows results of the two microcrystal tests—photomicrographs of Teichmann crystals and of Takayama crystals.

Species Determination

After determining that a stain is blood, the next step is to determine whether it is human or if not and/or what type of animal it comes from. Most common tests that determine the species of origin of blood are of the *immunoprecipitation* type. A test animal, usually a rabbit, is injected with human blood serum that contains proteins called **antigens**, which define the blood as human. The rabbit's immune system will determine that the serum is foreign (not rabbit) material and will produce a substance known as an **antibody**. The function of an antibody is to attack foreign materials so they cannot harm the host. The rabbit's blood is now an *antiserum* for human antigens and can be used to test for their presence. Some of the rabbit antiserum is added to a suspected sample of human blood, either in a test tube (*precipitin ring test*) in solution or in a gel (*Ouchterlony double diffusion test*). If the blood is human, there will be a reaction between the anti-human antibodies in the rabbit

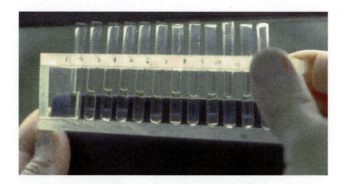

Figure 13.8 The precipitin ring reaction. Note the whitish rings in many of the culture tubes indicating a positive reaction. Reprinted courtesy of J. J. Nordby and S. H. James, *Forensic Science: An Introduction to Scientific and Investigative Techniques,* CRC Press.

antiserum and the human antigens in the blood. The reaction will be seen as a *precipitate*. In the precipitin ring test, a brownish ring is seen where the antiserum and blood meet. See Figure 13.8.

In the Ouchterlony test, the antigens and antibodies diffuse through the gel toward each other. They form a brownish precipitate where they meet. This is shown via a diagram in Figure 13.9a. If the bloodstain is not human, no precipitation will take place. In the diagram, there is precipitate formation in front of stains 2, 3, and 5, but not in front of stains 1 and 4. Therefore, it can be deduced that the human blood is only in samples 2, 3 and 5.

Figure 13.9b shows an Ouchterlony precipitate test with positive results shown in three of the four samples. The only negative result is the sample in the lower left-hand portion on the plate in the photo.

In the field (at the crime scene), investigators can perform portable tests. The **presumptive** or **screening** test to determine whether the reddish brown substance found at the scene is blood is called the Kastle–Meyer test. This test can be packaged for field use or done in the lab. The major compounds used in the test are phenolphthalein (a color indicator) and hydrogen peroxide (combines with the *heme* in hemoglobin), and, in the presence of blood containing hemoglobin, yields a vivid fuchsia or pink color. This, however, only indicates that the substance contains

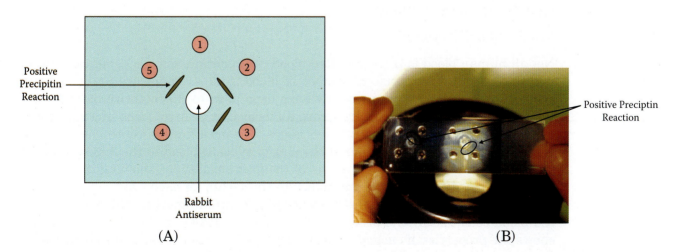

(A) (B)

Figure 13.9 Diagram A shows how the Ouchterlony test works. Photo B is an actual Ouchterlony test. Note the whitish streaks in all but the lower left corner around the center well. Reprinted courtesy of J. J. Nordby and S. H. James, *Forensic Science: An Introduction to Scientific and Investigative Techniques,* CRC Press.

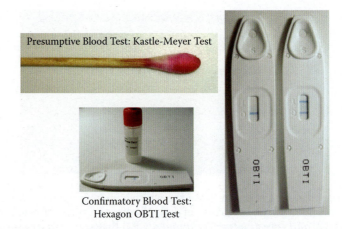

Figure 13.10 Presumptive and confirmatory blood tests that can be done in the field. Top photo shows a positive result for blood with the Kastle-Meyer Test. The other photos show the Hexagon OBTI test. A positive result for human blood is the strip with two blue lines; the top line is positive human, the bottom is the positive control for the test. The left strip is a negative test, the right is positive. Photo courtesy of Forensic Science Educational Consulting, LLC.

hemoglobin, a component of human and animal blood. See the cotton swab on the left in Figure 13.10, showing a positive presumptive test for blood.

The confirmatory field test for human blood is called the Hexagon OBTI test. This testing device looks similar to that used in a home pregnancy test and works in a similar manner, with blue lines as indicators of positive results. In the absorbent strip are blue particles and monoclonal anti-human Hb antibodies. When the sample blood (hemoglobin) is mixed with the OBTI reagent (in the bottle) and dropped into the well on the end, the solution migrates up the strip to the position that contains the anti-human antibodies and forms a thin blue line, indicating a positive result for human blood. The second blue line is a control and must register as a blue line in every test or the strip is deemed defective and the test is invalid. Figure 13.10 shows the Hexagon OBTI kit components and a positive human test result (blue line at T) alongside a negative for human blood result (notice the C or control is positive, indicating a valid test).

Genetic Markers in Blood

Red Blood Cell Antigens

Not all human blood is the same. Red blood cells contain various genetically inherited antigens that comprise a number of blood groups. There are many different types of blood groups, but only a few have been used to characterize blood forensically. The antigens in a blood group are all formed at a single locus in a single gene and are formed independently of other genes. The most familiar of the blood groups is the *ABO group*. There are four subgroups or types of blood in the ABO system, A, B, AB and O. Figure 13.11 is a model of the four blood types showing the antigens on the red blood cells and the antibodies in the serum for each type.

Each is characterized by the presence of certain antigens on the surface of the red blood cells and by the presence of certain antibodies in the serum. Table 13.1 shows the properties of each of the subgroups of the ABO group and information on donating and receiving blood according to blood type.

When antibodies and antigens of the same type (e.g., anti-A and A) come together, **agglutination** takes place. This is a process in which the antigens and antibodies

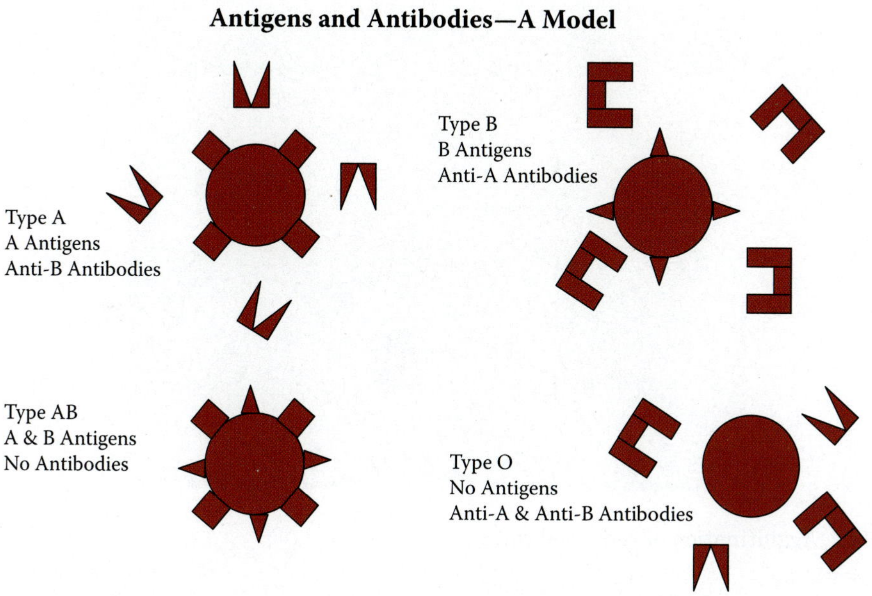

Antigens and Antibodies—A Model

Figure 13.11 A model of the four ABO blood types showing the erythrocytes, antigens, and antibodies. *Courtesy of* Forensic Science Educational Consulting, LLC.

TABLE 13.1
Properties of Blood Types of the ABO Group

Type	Antigens	Antibody	Can Give Blood To	Can Receive Blood From	Population Percentage
A	A	Anti -B	A, AB	O, A	42
B	B	Anti - A	B, AB	O, B	12
AB	A, B	None	AB	A, B, AB, O	3
O	None	Anti-A and	A, B, AB, O	O	43

attach together. The antigens are on the red blood cell surfaces and the antibodies come from a foreign serum or other source. To the naked eye or under a microscope it appears as if the red blood cells have become stuck together. Agglutinated cells are shown in the slide in Figure 13.12.

Note from Table 13.1 that a person's blood does not contain antibodies that are the same type as the antigens on the red blood cells. Before blood systems and agglutination were discovered, many blood transfusions caused injury and death because the transfused blood contained antibodies that attacked the host's antigens, causing massive agglutination. Karl Landsteiner won the Nobel Prize for his discovery of the different types of blood in the ABO system.

Human blood can be typed in the ABO system by adding a serum containing antibodies of known type. For example, if anti-A antibodies are added to a blood sample and agglutination occurs but it does not occur when anti-B antibodies are added, the blood must be type A. Table 13.2 shows agglutination and blood typing for all four blood types.

Another blood group system inherited genetically is the *Rh factor*, which is also expressed as an antigen on red blood cells. All humans are either Rh positive (Rh⁺) or Rh negative (Rh⁻), depending on whether they possess the antigen or not. The Rh factor is usually written along with the blood type, for example A⁺ or A⁻, the former has a gene for the Rh factor and the latter does not have the Rh gene.

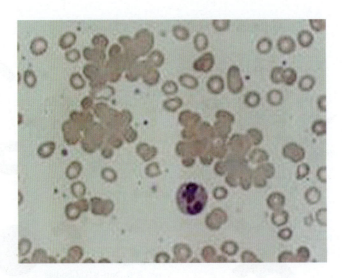

Figure 13.12 Agglutination of red blood cells.

TABLE 13.2
Agglutination Reaction of Blood Typing Sera

Anti-A Serum	Anti-B Serum	Blood Type
Agglutination	No Agglutination	A
No Agglutination	Agglutination	B
Agglutination	Agglutination	AB
No Agglutination	No Agglutination	O

There are other blood group systems in human blood that have different antigens and antibodies associated with them. Examples of these are *Lewis and MN* blood systems.

Blood Enzyme Markers

As seen in Table 13.1, the ABO blood type is not very discriminating. Even the rarest blood type still includes 3 percent of the human population. Therefore, blood type is considered to be *class* evidence, and blood typing of crime scene evidence is used to exclude suspects. During the 1970s and early 1980s, scientists searched for tests that included fewer people in a given classification. One of the important constraints on markers was that they had to survive the drying process. In many if not most of the cases where blood was found, it was dried. Most of the blood antigen systems, except for ABO, could not be used when the blood dried because the antigens were destroyed.

One viable solution involved the so-called *polymorphic enzymes*. These are enzymes found in human blood. They have the property of polymorphism; they exist in several forms. Each person has one of the forms of each enzyme. Databases were built that determined the population frequency of each form of each enzyme. If several enzymes are analyzed, the odds of a person having a particular set of enzyme forms would be very rare. Many of these enzymes also survive the drying process and are thus forensically useful where dried stains are found as evidence. This type of analysis is seldom used, having been replaced by DNA typing, which is much more specific.

Other Biological Fluids and Stains

A number of other biological fluids besides blood serve as evidence in crimes. Three of the most important are *seminal fluid*, *vaginal secretions* and *saliva*. All may constitute prominent evidence in *criminal sexual conduct (CSC)* crimes. Saliva may be found on or in evidence in many other types of crimes. Biological fluids can be very important evidence in cases where the perpetrator is a stranger to the victim. In most cases, there are no witnesses to CSC crimes. It may be crucial to associate physical evidence with a suspect. In some cases, locating biological evidence may be important so that it can be DNA typed. In other cases, confirmation of the type of evidence may be necessary to establish that CSC has taken place.

Seminal Fluid

Seminal fluid or semen is a mixture of cells, sperm, and a variety of organic and inorganic materials. It is a gelatinous material produced in males by the seminal vesicles, prostate, and Cowper's glands. In a normal male, about 5 mL of semen is ejaculated and contains about 100 million sperm. Some males have low sperm counts (*oligospermic*) or may have no sperm in their semen (*aspermic*). Sperm consists of a head that contains the DNA from the male and a flagellated tail that helps it move.

Preliminary Tests for Semen

Seminal fluid contains large concentrations of an enzyme known as *seminal acid phosphatase (SAP)*. There are other forms of acid phosphatase in some body fluids and the presence of SAP is considered to be *presumptive*. Over the years, the SAP test has emerged as the only acceptable presumptive test for seminal fluid throughout the world. The *Brentamine Fast Blue B* reagent is the major test for seminal fluid. An intense purple color that appears within 2 minutes is considered positive for SAP. The reagent is carcinogenic and must be handled with care.

Confirmatory Tests for Semen

Identification of Sperm

The only unambiguous test for seminal fluid is the identification of sperm cells. In most cases, the sperm analyzed in a crime lab are no longer motile and a stain is used to identify the sperm in the presence of other cellular material in the stain. A pair of dyes, *picroindigocarmine* (PIC) and *Nuclear Fast Red*, collectively called Christmas tree stain, have been developed for the specific purpose of visualizing sperm cells. See Figure 13.13.

Prostate-Specific Antigen

As mentioned previously, some males are oligospermic or aspermic and sperm may not be present in a suspected semen stain. In 1978, George Sensabaugh demonstrated that seminal fluid may be confirmed if a stain reacts positively for the presence of seminal acid phosphatase and if *prostate-specific antigen* (PSA or p30) is identified. P30 is secreted into semen by the prostate gland and is found mainly in semen. P30 may be found in other body fluids but the concentrations are below the

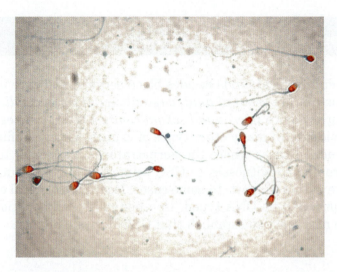

Figure 13.13 Sperm stained with Christmas tree stain. Reprinted courtesy of J. J. Nordby and S. H. James, *Forensic Science: An Introduction to Scientific and Investigative Techniques,* CRC Press.

limits of detection of the test. A special antibody–antigen test kit for PSA was developed in 1999, and is used in crime labs today.

Vaginal Secretions

The analysis of vaginal secretions can be important when a foreign object has been inserted into the vagina. The major test for vaginal secretions is to identify *glyco-genated epithelial cells*. These cell types are formed during menstruation and their quantity depends on the stage of the menstrual cycle, with ovulation producing the highest concentrations of glycogenated cells. The test consists of staining the glycogen using *periodic acid-Schiff reagent (PAS)*. It stains glycogen a bright magenta color. It is not a specific test since glycogenated epithelial cells may be found in other parts of the bodies of males and females, although in lower concentrations.

Saliva

Saliva is produced in the mouth to aid the preliminary digestion of food. More than one liter of saliva is produced each day by normal humans. It consists of water, proteins, enzymes, and salts. There are no specific tests for saliva. The generally accepted test for saliva is the *alpha amylase test*. Alpha amylase is an enzyme that is used to help break down starches in foods. Although it is found in many other body fluids, its concentration in saliva is many times higher than in any other fluid. The *starch-iodide* test is commonly used to identify alpha amylase.

Bloodstain Pattern Analysis

Bloodstain pattern analysis (BSPA) is a growing field of crime scene analysis and forensic technology. It has become an important tool in helping a forensic investigator determine what happened in a violent incident where blood has been shed. It can be used to provide evidence against a suspect or to exonerate an accused person. It can also be an invaluable tool in reconstructing an incident.

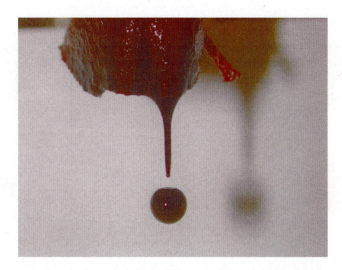

Figure 13.14 A blood droplet dripping from blood-soaked cloth. Note the spherical shape. Reprinted courtesy of J. J. Nordby and S. H. James, *Forensic Science: An Introduction to Scientific and Investigative Techniques,* CRC Press.

Physical Properties of Blood

In order to understand how blood spatter patterns are formed and how to interpret their characteristics, it is necessary to know something about the physical properties of **blood**. Although the majority of blood is water, blood doesn't act like water when it is dripped or projected. Blood has a fairly high surface tension that tends to cause a decrease in its surface area and makes it difficult to penetrate. This means that blood droplets tend to adhere to an external surface. Blood will only separate and spatter when sufficient external forces overcome surface tension. When a droplet of blood separates from a larger quantity and falls toward the earth it will form a *spherical drop*, not a teardrop as is commonly depicted. Figure 13.14 shows the shape of a blood droplet as it falls from a blood-soaked article. A blood drop in flight will oscillate from this oval or elliptical shape to a circular shape and back again until it contacts a surface and collapses.

The size of the spherical blood droplet depends on the size of the surface from which it falls. A larger surface will produce a larger blood droplet. Blood is also very **viscous**. This means that it will flow more slowly than water. It has also been shown that the longer the distance a blood droplet falls, the larger the diameter of the stain on the floor or other surface, although there is a physical limit to the size that a falling droplet will achieve. Blood falling under the influence of gravity will accelerate like any other falling object. At some point, the force of gravity will equal the frictional force of the air on the droplet. When this happens, the falling blood drop will no longer accelerate and will reach a stable condition called *terminal velocity*. The terminal velocity is dependent on the volume of the drop, but generally the average terminal velocity is approximately 25 ft/sec for a blood drop of 0.05 mL volume. At heights greater than the height at which terminal velocity is reached, the diameter of a blood drop will not increase. Studies have shown that the average sized blood drop will reach terminal velocity at a height of approximately 7 feet.

When water falls to the floor it tends to spatter—it breaks up into smaller droplets. This is due to surface tension and viscosity. In contrast to water, blood droplets will not break up into smaller droplets if they hit a hard, smooth surface such as tile. Blood molecules have cohesive properties that hold them together and increase the surface tension in the blood. If a surface is rough like concrete, then the jagged edges will break

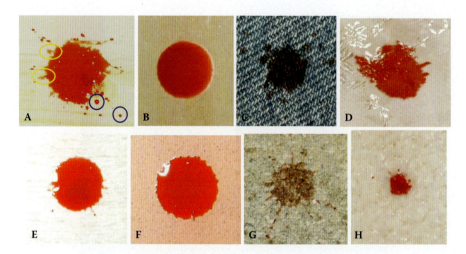

Figure 13.15 These photos show one blood drop released from a height of 36 inches onto various target surfaces at 90 degrees. Notice the difference in size and shape and the absence or presence of spines and satellite spatter. The yellow ovals in A designate spines and the blue circles show satellite spatter. The target surfaces are as follows: (A) raw wood; (B) smooth plastic; (C) cotton jean; (D) polyester; (E) painted wood; (F) tile; (G) cement; (H) carpet. *Courtesy of* Forensic Science Educational Consulting, LLC.

up the surface tension of the blood and cause it to spatter, creating *satellite spatter* and *spines*. Figure 13.15 shows blood dropped at right angles or 90 degrees onto various surfaces from a height of 36 inches. The circled projections in photo A designate the spines (projections of blood that extend beyond the parent drop of blood) and satellite spatter (small droplets that leave the parent blood drop and land near it).

Geometry of Bloodstains

When blood is thrown or cast onto a surface at an angle, the leading edge of the droplets will be elongated relative to the back or trailing edge. The shape of the droplet can be used to determine the direction from which it came as well as the approximate angle relative to the surface it strikes. If there are a number of bloodstains, the *area of convergence* can be determined by drawing lines from the leading edges of the stains through the long axis. These lines come together in a general area where the blood emerged. This can be seen in Figure 13.16.

The angle of impact can be determined by measuring the length and width of the stain in millimeters as shown in Figure 13.17, being careful only to measure the *original* shape of the stain and not the projections (spines and tails). The arcsin (inverse sin or sin^{-1}) of the ratio of the width (W) to the length (L) is equal to the angle of impact. See Equation 13.1.

$$\Theta = \arcsin \frac{\text{width (mm)}}{\text{length (mm)}} \tag{13.1}$$

where Θ = angle of impact.

For example, if the width of a bloodstain is 1.3 mm and the length is 2 mm, then:

$$\Theta = (\arcsin) \frac{1.3 \text{ mm}}{2.0 \text{ mm}} = (\arcsin)0.65 = 40.54 \text{ degrees}$$

Therefore, The angle of impact would be about 41 degrees.

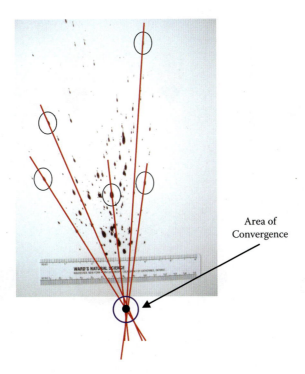

Figure 13.16 Diagram showing how the area of convergence of an impact blood spatter pattern is determined. *Courtesy of* Forensic Science Educational Consulting, LLC.

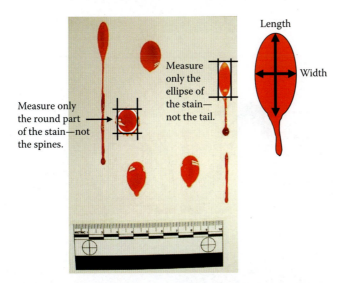

Figure 13.17 Measuring width and length of bloodstains to determine impact angle. *Courtesy of* Forensic Science Educational Consulting, LLC.

The shapes of the angled bloodstains give the investigator a general idea of the point of origin. The "tail" of the stain and any spines visible indicate which direction the blood came from. Figure 13.18 shows blood dripped at 10 degree angle increments. Notice the how the elliptical nature of the stain increases with the angle of impact to the surface.

Figure 13.19 demonstrates actual bloodstains being analyzed. Step one is to measure the bloodstain length and width, and then use the formula to determine impact angles. Lines are drawn lightly through the stain to determine the area of convergence on the target surface (or strings can be used in place of pencil lines to

Figure 13.18 Blood drops at various angles of impact. *Courtesy of* Forensic Science Educational Consulting, LLC.

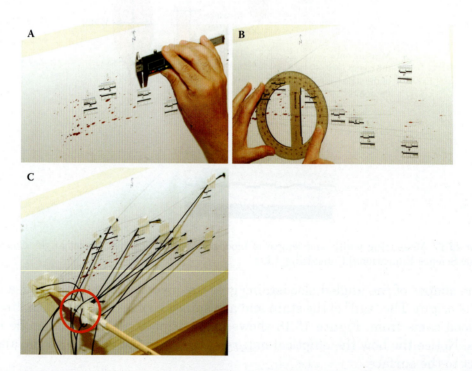

Figure 13.19 Locating an area of convergence in space using impact angles of a bloodstain. (A) measuring length and width of small bloodstains. (B) Drawing the area of convergence on the contact surface. (C) "Stringing" the angles of impact into three-dimensional (3D) space to locate the origin of the blood. The circle shows 3D area of convergence. *Courtesy of* Forensic Science Educational Consulting, LLC.

preserve the stains). Finally, strings are projected based on the measured impact angled out into space to determine the area of convergence or origin of the blood. Another method that can be used in place of the last stringing step is to use a second trigonometry formula to mathematically calculate the distance from the target surface. (See graphic in Appendix A.)

Bloodstain Pattern Categories

There are many types of bloodstain patterns. Bloodstains can be divided into three basic categories: passive, spatter, and altered. **Passive** stains are created due to the force of gravity acting on the blood. Examples of passive bloodstains are *vertical* blood drops (blood dripping at 90 degrees to the surface), *transfer* stains (blood on an object that contacts another object and leaves a bloody pattern—swipes, footprints, etc.), *large volume* bloodstains (blood exiting in mass from a person or object), and *flow* (large pool of blow moving down a wall or incline). Examples of passive bloodstains can be seen in Figures 13.20 and 13.21.

Spatter stains involve a force in addition to gravity, and bloodstains in this category show directionality and distribution to the blood. Included in this group of bloodstains are *impact spatter due to blunt force* resulting from a bloody object receiving a blow. This type of stain must first have blood on its surface to create this type of pattern from subsequent spatter. In most cases, the first blow will not produce an impact stain. Subsequent blows will result in impact spatter. *Impact stains due to blunt force* range in length from 1 to 4 mm in size and are usually the type of stains that are "strung" by law enforcement. *Impact stains due to gunshot* are smaller in size, usually less than 1 mm in length, and have a misty appearance. Spattered stains also include those *projected* away from the body. One of these patterns is called a *cast-off*, which is a pattern produced from a bloody object such as a

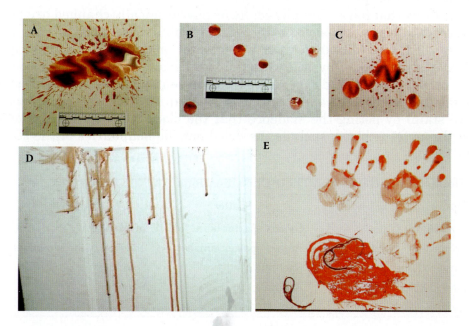

Figure 13.20 Passive bloodstain patterns. (A) large volume; (B) vertical drips; (C) multiple vertical drips; (D) flow; (E) transfer.

Figure 13.21 A swiped bloodstain pattern in which a bloodied object contacted the surface and deposited blood in a sweeping motion. Reprinted courtesy of T. Bevel and R. M. Gardner, *Bloodstain Pattern Analysis: With an Introduction to Crime Scene Reconstruction*, 2nd ed., CRC Press.

knife, baseball bat, or bloody hand. These stains form a linear pattern, often on a ceiling. Figure 13.22a shows these types of spatter stains.

Other spatter-type bloodstains are *arterial* spurts and *expirated* blood. Arterial spurts are easily recognized by an arc pattern due to the rise and fall of blood pressure and indicate that a major artery (carotid, femoral) has been breached. This is shown in Figure 13.22b. Expiratory blood is ejected with force from the mouth or the nose. Individuals with injuries to the face or chest will commonly cough or sneeze blood, a natural reaction to fluid in the breathing passages. The pattern from expiratory blood looks similar to impact spatter, but sometimes air bubbles can be seen in the blood drops.

Bloodstains that have been physically or physiologically changed are placed in the **altered** category. Physiologically altered stains arise when insects interact with the blood, when blood clots, or when water or other foreign materials mix with the existing blood. Physically altered blood examples are *voids* (blood should be present, but it is not) and *wipes* (blood was present, but a person or object moved through it and changed its appearance). A wipe can be distinguished from a swipe (passive stain) by noting the evidence that the blood was deposited prior to the motion through the blood, such as the dried outside boundaries of the stain. See Figure 13.23.

Bloodstain Patterns and Their Classifications

Passive	Spatter	Altered
Vertical drips	Impact spatter blunt force	Insect activity
Prints (shoe, hand, hair, etc)	Impact spatter gunshot	Addition of foreign material
Large volume	Cast-off	Void
Flow	Arterial	Wipe
Swipe	Expirated	

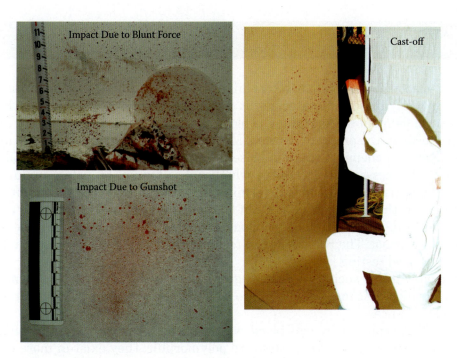

Figure 13.22a. Spatter bloodstains. *Courtesy of* Forensic Science Educational Consulting, LLC.

Figure 13.22b Arterial (left) and expired bloodstains.

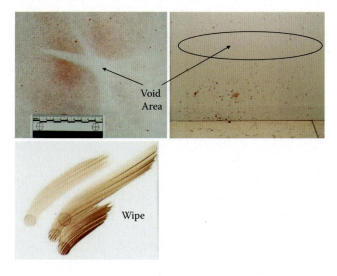

Figure 13.23 Altered bloodstains.

Summary

Blood is a suspension of solid, mostly cellular material in a fluid that consists of water containing many dissolved materials. It is often necessary to determine whether a reddish stain found at a crime scene is blood. There are several preliminary and confirmatory tests for the presence of blood. Most of these tests involve the heme molecule as a catalyst in a chemical reaction or series of reactions. After a stain is identified as blood, it is necessary to determine whether it is human by using immunological tests. Rabbit antiserum is used to determine whether human blood is present by demonstrating that the human antibodies in the rabbit's blood will agglutinate red blood cells in the blood. Field testing can be done on suspected stains to determine whether they are blood or not. The Kastle–Meyer test and Hexagon OBTI are tests that can be packaged for field testing.

Other body fluids such as saliva, vaginal swabs, or secretions and semen must also be identified at crime scenes. There are also screening and confirmatory tests for these substances.

Before DNA typing there was blood typing. Blood contains proteins such as antigens as well as certain enzymes that are polymorphic; they exist in more than one form. These substances can be used to subdivide a human population according to which forms of these materials are present. Groups of associated antigens (proteins on the surfaces of red blood cells) provide one means of differentiating blood samples. These antigens form blood groups such as ABO or Rh. In addition to blood groups, there are enzymes associated with red blood cells and white blood cells that are also polymorphic. Electrophoresis is used to separate and identify these enzymes in a blood sample. Several blood groups and enzymes used to be typed in a typical blood case. Even though these substances are all independent of each other, the cumulative population frequencies were not as discriminating as DNA typing. In addition, many of these substances do not survive the drying process and cannot be typed on dried stains.

The physical properties of blood give rise to spatter patterns that occur by several mechanisms. It is possible to determine the angle and direction of a blood spatter by measuring the size and shape of the spatter. It is also possible to determine the point of origin of a series of related blood spatters using triangulation. Different types of blood spatter mechanisms give rise to characteristic patterns. Three general categories of bloodstain patterns are passive, spatter, and altered. Bloodstains found at crime scenes can be classified into one of these groups.

Appendix A

Trigonometry calculation for locating a bloodstain.

Finding the Third Dimension

$$Tan(\theta) = P/D$$
$$P = Tan(\theta)*D$$

Blood Droplet

P

θ

From Area of Convergence

D

Mini Lab Activities

MINI LAB 1: THE GENETICS OF BLOOD TYPING

A child's blood type is inherited from the parents. One allele (code for blood type on the chromosome) comes from the mother and one allele comes from the father. The possible combinations of alleles (genotype) and resulting blood type (phenotype) are listed below. The allele for type O is recessive and the alleles for A and B are co-dominant.

Blood Type A	Blood Type B	Blood Type AB	Blood Type O
A, A	B, B	A, B	O, O
A, O	B, O	B, A	

Using a Punnet square allows one to see the possible progeny of a genetic cross (parents). The *genotype* of each parent is entered into the top and side of the square. The combinations of alleles give the *genotype* of the offspring. For example:

Parent Genotype	A	O
A	A, A	A, O
B	A, B	B, O

The *phenotype* (what trait is expressed) of the parents combines blood types A and AB. The *phenotype* of the offspring combines blood types: A, AB, and B. The chances are approximately 50 percent that their children will be type A, 25 percent will be type B, and 25 percent will be type AB.

Your turn:

1. Complete the following crosses of parents using the Punnet square method.
2. Predict the genotype and phenotype of the offspring.
3. What are the percent chances for each type?

Group 1: Dad is AB, Mom is AB
Group 2: Dad is OO, Mom is AB
Group 3: Dad is AA, Mom is BO
Group 4: Dad is BO, Mom is AO

Extension. The Rh factor can also be added to the crosses. Rh⁺ is dominant and Rh⁻ is recessive.

MINI LAB 2: ANALYZING VERTICAL BLOOD DROPS

For this exercise, the author recommends simulated blood products for bloodstain pattern analysis: *Introduction to Blood Spatter* (36V4407) and *Simulated Drip and Projected Blood* (37V5310) from Ward's Natural Science, www.wardsci.com.

Test Yourself

Short Essay

1. What are the two major components of blood?
2. What parts of blood are forensically important for typing?
3. Name two preliminary and two confirmatory tests for blood.
4. What is the most common test for identifying saliva?
5. What is the only test that is absolutely confirmatory for semen?
6. Describe briefly how a blood sample is determined to be human?
7. What are the two major mechanisms that give rise to blood spatter patterns?
8. Give an example of a type of spatter bloodstain.
9. Give an example of a type of altered bloodstain.
10. Give an example of a type of passive bloodstain.
11. What is a cast off blood spatter?
12. What is the difference between a wipe bloodstain pattern and a swipe pattern?
13. What are the parts labeled A and B in the graphic below?

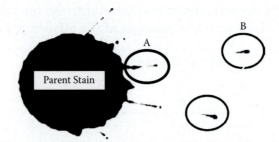

14. Describe how the parts in question 13 can be produced.
15. The photo below shows blood dropped at various angles. For each labeled stain, find the impact angle, using the formula from the chapter. Show your work.

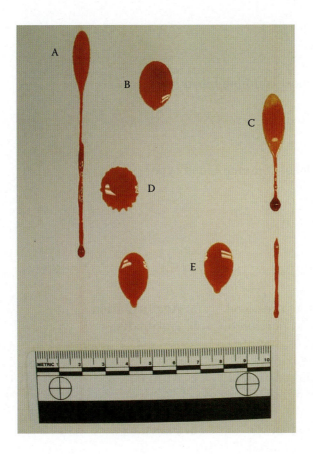

Multiple Choice

16. The person responsible for ABO blood typing was:
    a. Landsteiner
    b. Mendel
    c. MacDonell
    d. Takayama
17. A person with O blood can give to:
    a. Another O
    b. A person with B
    c. An A
    d. Any blood type
18. A person with O blood can receive from:
    a. Another O
    b. A person with B
    c. An A
    d. An AB
19. Type B blood contains type ___ antibodies.
    a. AB
    b. A
    c. B
    d. None
20. One parent is type AB; the other is type O. A possible genotype for an off-spring is:
    a. AB

    b. OO

    c. AO

    d. All of these

21. Which is the most common blood type?

    a. AB

    b. O

    c. A

    d. B

22. Which is the least common blood type?

    a. AB

    b. O

    c. A

    d. B

Matching

23. Liquid portion of the blood	a. Agglutination
24. Part of the solid portion of the blood that oxygenates the cells of the body	b. Antibodies
25. Part of the solid portion of the blood that fights infection	c. Antigen
26. Substance found on the outside surface of a red blood cell	d. Plasma
27. Substance found in the plasma of the blood that reacts with an antigen	e. Red blood cells
28. Clumping in the blood as a result of mixing two incompatible blood types	f. White blood cells

Short Answer

29. For phenotype A blood, what are the genotype possibilities?

30. What is genotype for a homozygous B person?

31. Draw and complete a Punnet square that crosses type O blood with type AB blood. Give percentages for the blood types.

32. Anti-A serum, anti-B serum, and anti-Rh serum are added to a blood sample. There is agglutination in the anti-B and in the anti-Rh. What is the complete blood type?

33. Anti-A serum, anti-B serum and anti-Rh serum are added to a blood sample. There is no agglutination in the anti-A and the anti-B, but there is agglutination in the anti-Rh. What is the complete blood type?

34. A mother has type O⁻ blood and the father is heterozygous B⁻. What are all the possible blood types of the offspring?

Practice Exercise in Impact Angle Studies

35. Example stains: The long axes and short axes of the following bloodstains were measured and the values are listed below. Measure the lengths of the stain axes in millimeters using calipers and compare your measurements to the example measurements. If you are measuring correctly, your values should be close to the example impact angles, ±2 degrees.

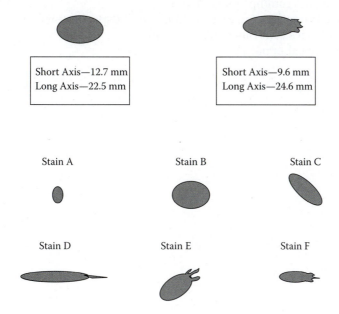

Short Axis—12.7 mm
Long Axis—22.5 mm

Short Axis—9.6 mm
Long Axis—24.6 mm

Stain A   Stain B   Stain C

Stain D   Stain E   Stain F

Find the impact angle of the stains labeled A to F using the same procedure as done in the example stains above.

Further Reading

MacDonell, H. L. *Interpretation of Bloodstains: Physical Considerations.* Ed. C. Wecht. New York: Appleton, 1971.

James, S. H. and W. G. Eckert. *Interpretation of Bloodstain Evidence at Crime Scenes.* 2nd ed. Boca Raton, FL: CRC Press, 1999.

Shaler, R. C. Modern Forensic Biology. In *Forensic Science Handbook.* Vol. 1, 2nd ed. Ed. R. Saferstein, ed. Upper Saddle River, NJ: Prentice Hall, 2002.

James, S. H., Kish, P. E., and T. P. Sutton. *Principles of Bloodstain Pattern Analysis: Theory and Practice.* CRC Press, Boca Raton, FL, 2005.

Bevel, T. and R. M. Gardner. *Bloodstain Pattern Analysis: With an Introduction to Crime Scene Reconstruction,* 3rd ed., CRC Press, Boca Raton, FL, 2008.

On the Web

Agglutination and Blood Typing

http://nobelprize.org/educational_games/medicine/landsteiner/readmore.html
http://waynesword.palomar.edu/aniblood.htm
http://anthro.palomar.edu/blood/blood_components.htm

Blood Testing

www.geocities.com/a4n6degener8/bloodintro.htm
http://anthro.palomar.edu/blood/blood_components.htm

BSPA

http://christmanforensics.com/bp_analysis.php
www.nfstc.org/links/animations/images/blood percent20spatters.swf
www.crimescene-forensics.com/Blood_Stains.html
www.pbs.org/wgbh/nova/sheppard/

14
DNA Typing

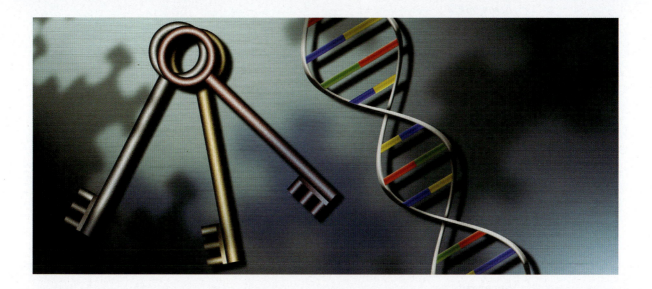

Learning Objectives

1. To be able to define DNA and describe its structure
2. To be able to describe the precautions necessary when collecting biologic evidence
3. To be able to describe how RFLP DNA typing is carried out
4. To be able to describe how PCR is carried out and how DNA can be typed by PCR
5. To be able to describe how STRs are measured
6. To be able to describe how population frequency statistics are used to describe the significance of a DNA match
7. To be able to define mitochondrial DNA and describe how it is typed
8. To be able to define CODIS and describe its structure and how it is used in criminal investigation

Chapter 14
DNA Typing

Chapter Outline

Mini Glossary

Allele: One of the forms of a gene.

Amelogenin: A piece of DNA found in the X and Y chromosome that determines gender.

Annealing: Addition of DNA primers in PCR to begin the replication process.

Denaturation: Unzipping double-stranded DNA to single strands under the influence of high temperature.

DNA: A large, polymeric molecule found in virtually every cell in the body.

DNA polymerase: An enzyme used in PCR to add bases one at a time.

DNA primers: Short strands of DNA used to begin the replication process of PCR.

Elimination samples: Samples of DNA from someone who might have handled biologic evidence during collection and analysis.

Extension: Addition of individual bases to a single strand of DNA to replicate it in PCR.

Gene: Part of a chromosome consisting of a sequence of base pairs. These sequences ultimately tell the cell what proteins to manufacture that result in expression of characteristics such as eye color, gender, height, etc.

Hypervariable region: A locus of DNA that is highly polymorphic.

Length polymorphism: A type of polymorphism whose forms differ in the length of a repeating segment of DNA.

Mitochondria: Structures present in every cell in the body without exception. They are in the cytoplasm, outside the nucleus. Mitochondria are responsible for energy production in the cell and they contain DNA, which helps in this function.

Polymerase chain reaction (PCR): A method for replicating DNA using temperature and bases under the influence of an enzyme.

Polymorphic: A gene or other part of DNA that exists in more than one form.

Population frequency: How often a particular type of DNA occurs in a given population.

Restriction enzyme: An enzyme that cuts DNA strands at predetermined loci.

Restriction fragment length polymorphism (RFLP): DNA typing that uses long length polymorphs to characterize DNA.

Sequence polymorphism: A type of polymorphism whose forms differ in one or more base pairs.

Short tandem repeats: Method of DNA typing using short length polymorphs.

Substrate control: A piece of a material on which biologic evidence has been deposited. A form of negative control.

Y-STR: A short tandem repeat found only on the Y chromosome.

Acronyms

CODIS: Combined DNA indexing system
DNA: Deoxyribonucleic acid
PCR: Polymerase chain reaction
RFLP: Restriction fragment length polymorphism
STR: Short tandem repeat

Introduction

In 1992, The Innocence Project (IP) was founded by attorneys Barry Scheck and Peter Neufeld. It is affiliated with the Benjamin N. Cardozo School of Law at Yeshiva University in New York. The IP was set up to provide assistance to persons who had been convicted of a serious crime where post-conviction DNA typing could be used to prove claims of innocence. Several types of cases are examined by the Innocence Project. These include challenges based on a claim of ineffective counsel, mistakes by crime laboratory scientists, or cases where the conviction was based in part on pre-DNA typing blood analysis that falsely associated the accused with the victim or put him at the crime scene. These situations often occurred because blood typing, as it was practiced before DNA typing, could not associate someone to biological evidence with the level of certainty that DNA typing does today. In several cases investigated by the IP, the accused was included in a population of possible owners of biological evidence (e.g., blood, hair, semen) by blood typing procedures and convicted partly because of this. Post-conviction DNA typing proved conclusively that the accused and convicted person could not have been the source of the incriminating biological evidence. To date, more than 260 falsely convicted people have been exonerated by post-conviction DNA testing. Of these, more than a dozen were sentenced to death!

The Innocence Project has not only obtained the release of many innocent people, but has served to illustrate that wrongful convictions are not isolated, once-in-a-lifetime occurrences in the United States. Because of the high numbers of wrongful convictions discovered by the IP, at least one state has suspended its death penalty until more safeguards are put into place to ensure that all death penalty convictions have been arrived at properly. There are now Innocence Projects in practically every state in the U.S.

One of the early Innocence Project cases was *Bloodsworth v. Maryland*. Kirk Bloodsworth was convicted of the rape and murder of a nine-year-old girl in Maryland in 1984. The police received an anonymous tip that Bloodsworth had been seen with the victim on the day of the crime. Five eyewitnesses helped with a composite police sketch. Bloodsworth was identified from that sketch. All five eyewitnesses identified him at the trial. Some statements made by Bloodsworth concerning something terrible that he had done were also admitted at trial.

After his conviction, his attorney appealed based on police conduct concerning a supposedly bloody rock that was used to kill the girl that Bloodsworth was linked to. The terrible conduct by Bloodsworth turned to be a false lead. The defense was also never told that the police were investigating another suspect. The conviction was overturned and Bloodsworth was retried, convicted, and sentenced to two consecutive life terms.

In 1992, the Innocence Project intervened and obtained biological evidence that was reexamined with the prosecutor's agreement. Testing of the victim's undergarments against Bloodworth's DNA excluded him as the murderer/rapist. He was pardoned in 1993 after serving eight years in prison. He was the first inmate on death row who was released from prison owing to the Innocence Project efforts.

In Chapter 13: Serology, we learned the concept of polymorphism. Some biologic evidence such as blood contains substances that occur in several forms distributed throughout the human population. Many of these factors have been extensively studied and population frequencies have been determined for them. This gives forensic scientists hard data on which to base conclusions concerning the degree of association of biological evidence to a victim or suspect. This approach, although helpful in determining whether a person left biological evidence at a crime scene, suffers from three major deficiencies. First, many polymorphic enzymes and antigens do not survive the drying process and cannot be measured in dried blood stains, which are more commonly encountered at crime scenes than fresh blood. Second, even if many of them are measured in a particular person, there is not enough total variation from one person to the next to be able to use these blood groupings to definitively associate a person with biological evidence. Finally, these polymorphic substances are present mainly in blood. If the perpetrator or victim of a crime left other biologic material such as skin, saliva, or hair, these substances wouldn't be of any help.

In the early 1980s, a revolution in forensic biology occurred. Scientists demonstrated that certain parts of the DNA structure were different enough to divide human populations into many groups. Using DNA has enhanced the potential for matching a suspect or victim to biological evidence from the crime scene. It has also been shown that DNA measurements can be achieved on almost any type of biologic evidence from blood to hair to skin to saliva. DNA can be typed on fresh or old evidence, even on ancient preserved mummies! In this chapter, we explore the chemical nature of DNA and how it varies from person to person. We show how DNA can be typed, how databases of DNA types can be constructed and searched, and how databasing can help solve old, cold cases.

What Is DNA?

Deoxyribonucleic Acid (DNA) is a large, polymeric molecule found in virtually every cell in the body. Two significant exceptions are red blood cells and nerve cells. Red cells are produced in bone marrow and have no need of DNA for replication and nerve cells do not generally regenerate. DNA can be found in two regions of a cell—the nucleus and the mitochondria. Mitochondrial DNA has a different structure from nuclear DNA and is inherited differently. We'll discuss this later in this chapter.

Nuclear DNA is a unique type of molecule. Its shape is called a *double helix*. See Figure 14.1. Consider a very long ladder. This ladder has two poles connected by many rungs. Each rung consists of two complementary pieces joined together. Now take the ladder and twist it many times throughout its length until it resembles a spiral staircase. This is the geometry of the DNA molecule. The poles of the DNA molecule (called the backbone) are not forensically significant. They are exactly the same in all people. The rungs are special, however. Each rung is made up of two *bases* or *nucleotides* joined together in the middle as well as to the poles, so each rung is made up of a base pair. These base pairs are comprised of two of the following:

Adenine (A)
Thymine (T)
Guanine (G)
Cytosine (C)

Because of the complex chemical structure of the bases, only certain pairs can join together. The rule is that adenine can only bond to thymine and guanine can

Figure 14.1 DNA double helix. The four bases are adenine, thymine, guanine, and cytosine.

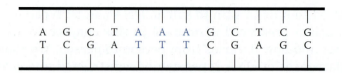

Figure 14.2 A base pair sequence. Only *A* can pair with *T* and only *C* can pair with *G*.

only bond to cytosine. No base can join with itself. A strand of DNA contains millions of base pairs and the rules can never be violated. Figure 14.2 shows a portion of a DNA strand with some representative base pairs.

Notice that base pairs will often repeat themselves. This is illustrated by the T–A pair repeating three times in the DNA strand in Figure 14.2. The order of the base pairs seems to be random, but in most cases, it is not. The repeats are important and the overall order of the base pairs throughout DNA is very significant. It comprises a genetic code that directs the body to ultimately build proteins that are the building blocks for all human organs and tissues. This code literally makes us who and what we are. Since the DNA comes equally from both parents, we inherit their characteristics according to certain rules of inheritance or laws of genetics.

Cellular DNA

Nuclear DNA is arranged in structures called *chromosomes*. Human beings have 46 chromosomes. They are arranged in 23 pairs. Each parent supplies one member of each of the 23 pairs. It is through the chromosomes that each person inherits physical, mental, and emotional characteristics from both parents. These characteristics are defined within a *genetic code* contained within portions of the chromosomes called **genes**. A gene is a part of a chromosome consisting of a sequence of base pairs. These sequences ultimately tell the cell what proteins to manufacture that result in expression of characteristics such as eye color, gender, height, etc. The location where a gene (or other sequence of interest) is found on a chromosome is called its *locus*. The human *genome* contains more than 100,000 genes. For example, there are genes that determine the color of one's hair. Since different people have different hair colors, there must be some variations within the hair color genes that result in the different hair colors in a population. These variations in characteristics are due to differences in the genetic code caused by differences in the order of the base pair sequences. A gene that exists in more than one form is referred to as **polymorphic**. The different forms of genes are called **alleles**. Thus, there is an allele for brown hair, red hair, etc. Some hair colors are intermediate between pure colors because a person inherits different alleles from each parent. If an individual inherits the same allele for a particular characteristic from both parents, he is said to be *homozygous* with respect to that gene. If he receives a different allele from each parent then he is *heterozygous* with respect to that gene. Figure 14.3 shows how both parents contribute one chromosome of each of the 23 pairs to the offspring.

If a person inherits a gene from a parent that codes for brown hair and one from the other parent that codes for blond hair, she will usually have brown hair. This is because the allele for brown hair is *dominant* and the allele for blond hair is *recessive*.

There are two types of polymorphism in genes. The first is called **sequence polymorphism**. This occurs when there is a difference in one or more base pairs within a gene. Examine the base pair sequence in the short strand of DNA shown below. Note the difference in the base pair at the position marked by the arrow. The two sequences are identical except for that single base pair.

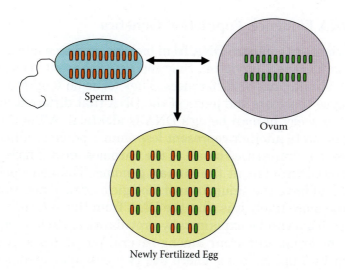

Figure 14.3 The sperm contains 23 chromosomes from the father. The egg (ovum) contains 23 corresponding chromosomes from the mother. When the sperm fertilizes the egg, the chromosomes and the new cell contain 23 pairs of chromosomes.

```
C T C G A T T A A G G   C T C G G T T A A G G
: : : : ▲ : : : : :  and  : : : : ▲ : : : : : :
G A G C T A A T T C C   G A G C C A A T T C C
```

The other type of polymorphism is called **length polymorphism**. This occurs in strands of DNA in which repeating sequences of base pairs are encountered. Examine the DNA strands below.

```
C A T G T A C - C A T G T A C
: : : : : : : : : : : : : :
G T A C A T G - G T A C A T G
```

```
C A T G T A C - C A T G T A C - C A T G T A C - C A T G T A C
: : : : : : : : : : : : : : : : : : : : : : : : : : : :
G T A C A T G - G T A C A T G - G T A C A T G - G T A C A T G
```

```
C A T G T A C - C A T G T A C - C A T G T A C - C A T G T A C - C A T G T A C
: : : : : : : : : : : : : : : : : : : : : : : : : : : : : : : : : : : :
G T A C A T G - G T A C A T G - G T A C A T G - G T A C A T G - G T A C A T G
```

All three of the strands contain the base pair sequence:

```
C A T G T A C
: : : : : : :
G T A C A T G
```

In the first strand, the sequence repeats twice. In the second strand, the same sequence repeats four times, and in the third strand, five times. Because the repeats occur right next to each other without any intervening base pairs, they are referred to as **tandem repeats**. Length and sequence polymorphism are very important in distinguishing one person's DNA from another because certain strands of DNA may differ from one person to the next only by a small sequence or length polymorphism.

Interpreting DNA Evidence: Population Genetics

When forensic scientists compare DNA from biologic evidence at a crime scene with known DNA from a suspect or victim, they compare many sites on several chromosomes to look for similarities or differences. They focus on length or sequence polymorphisms because these are the parts of the DNA that differentiate people. More than 99 percent of every human being's DNA is identical. All of the differences in DNA from one person to another represent less than 1 percent of his or her DNA.

Scientists look for similarities on all of the chromosomes. There are many polymorphisms scattered throughout the human genome. The more polymorphic sites that are located and have the same form of biologic evidence and the DNA of a suspect or victim, the more likely it is that the DNA from the evidence came from that victim or suspect. This can be explained by probabilities. Probability measures the likelihood that one event will occur among several possibilities. A common example can be found in flipping coins. There are two possible outcomes from flipping a coin—heads (H) or tails (T). Since they are equally likely of occurring, the probability of getting heads is ½ or 0.5. Suppose a coin is flipped twice. What are the odds that it will come up heads both times? There are four possible outcomes from flipping a coin twice: H–H, H–T, T–H, and T–T. Each of these possibilities has an equal likelihood of occurring since a coin has no memory of how it lands on each flip. Thus, the probability that it will come up heads both times (H–H) is ¼ or .25. This number can be arrived at using the *product rule*. This rule states that the probability of two or more independent events occurring is the product of the probabilities of each event. Thus the probability of two coin flips coming up heads is ½ x ½ = ¼ because the probability of heads coming up on one flip is ½ and on the other flip, ½. Likewise, the probability of getting heads three times in a row is ⅛ or 0.125. This is because there are eight possibilities that can occur when a coin is flipped three times: H–H–H, H–H–T, H–T–H, T–T–H, H–T–T, T–H–T, T–H–H, T–T–T. Only one of these possibilities (H–H–H) results in getting heads all three times. The more times a coin is flipped, the less chance that any particular outcome will occur. It is very important that each event is independent of the others or the rule will not apply.

Something for You to Do

Take a deck of 52 cards. How many different cards are there and how many of each card are there in a full deck? What is the probability that a card drawn at random will be an ace? Now what is the probability that the next card you draw will also be an ace? Remember how many cards are left and how many aces are left in the deck if you draw an ace on the first try. Using probabilities, you can calculate the chances of getting dealt any poker or blackjack hand.

The proprietors of gambling casinos determine their payouts on various games of chance by the probabilities of your drawing each kind of hand and the chances that you will beat the house on each type of game. For example, a roulette wheel contains the numbers 1 through 36 plus a 0 and 00. If you bet $1 on any number and the payoff for hitting that number is $36, you will eventually lose your money because the probability of hitting a given number on a spin of the wheel is 38 to 1. If you bet $1 on the number 7 every time, it should come up once on the average of every 38 spins. If it comes up on the 38th spin, you have bet $38 and you finally get back $36 for hitting the number. Over time, you have to lose.

Going back to the coin flip, what are the odds of getting a tails ten times in a row? It is more than a 1000 to 1. One way to visualize this is that you would have to make more than 1000 tries at flipping a coin 10 times to ensure on the average that one of those tries would give 10 straight tails.

Forensic scientists use probabilities in a similar way when interpreting the likelihood that a sample of DNA came from a particular person. At each locus (the base pair sequence) where the DNA type is to be analyzed, scientists have determined the **population frequency** of that allele. If there are, for example, fifteen possible alleles at a particular locus, the percent of the human population that has each of these types will be known. Unlike with coin flips, the probability that any one of those fifteen alleles will occur is not the same as for the other alleles. Some are more common than others and scientists have to determine the population frequency of all of them. Today, the major worldwide protocol for the analysis of DNA for comparison purposes utilizes a set of thirteen loci for which the frequency of each allele at each site is known. The product rule can be used to determine the overall probability of having all of these alleles. As will be explained later, these probabilities are extremely small.

Collection and Preservation of DNA Evidence

It has been said many times that forensic evidence is only as good as the skills of the people who collect it. Some people describe this as "garbage in, garbage out". This is especially true with biologic evidence, which can be highly perishable. Even though DNA is an amazingly hardy substance, its degradation can be a problem. Improperly preserved DNA can be rendered useless in a short time. Today, traces of DNA are sufficient to obtain a complete profile. Stamps and envelopes that have been licked with saliva contain enough cells to be DNA typed. Tooth brushes, pillows, the inside of a hat, discarded chewing gum—all are potential sources for DNA.

Special care must be taken in collecting biologic evidence. It should always be assumed to be infectious; it could be a carrier for diseases such as hepatitis or AIDS. There should be minimal contact with the evidence. Contamination of biologic evidence is a real problem, especially since so little DNA is necessary to type. All precautions against contamination must be taken. These include wearing protective clothing that minimizes the loss of hair or dandruff or other biologic material from the person collecting the evidence, wearing gloves and changing them every time new evidence is collected, using tools such as tweezers to collect evidence, and making sure that positive and negative controls are collected as well as **elimination samples**. These are known samples of DNA collected from all personnel at the scene who could possibly have contributed DNA.

Biologic evidence must never be packaged in airtight containers because moisture can build up which promotes the growth of bacteria that can degrade DNA. Paper bags or other breathable containers should be used. Wherever possible, if a garment or other material is suspected to contain blood, the whole article should be submitted. If that is not possible, samples can be removed and sent to the lab. These must always be accompanied by a sample of the article that doesn't contain any biologic material. This is called a **substrate control**. It is a type of negative control. See Chapter 3 for a discussion of positive and negative controls and their importance in chemical analysis of evidence. Although most cellular material in humans contains DNA, known samples are usually collected from gently scraping the inside of the cheek. These *buccal samples* contain more than enough DNA for typing and are obtained easily with a minimum of invasion of the person's body. If blood samples are taken, they should be put in tubes that already contain a preservative such as *EDTA* (ethylenediamine tetraacetic acid).

DNA Typing

The process of DNA typing involves discovering which alleles are present at each locus being measured of one or more of the 46 chromosomes. Today's protocols call for determining the DNA type at 13 specific loci. The population frequency for various populations of people is accurately known for each allele. The populations include Caucasians, African Americans, Hispanics and others. There is no difference in the way males and females are treated with respect to population frequencies. There is one chromosome (X,Y) which determines whether a person will be a male or female. In virtually all forensic biology labs in the U.S. and in most of the rest of the world, one particular type of DNA typing, called **short tandem repeats (STRs)** is used. Some laboratories still use older methods for DNA typing. In the sections that follow, there will be a short description of these older methods for historic purposes, followed by a discussion of STRs.

Restriction Fragment Length Polymorphism (RFLP)

Restriction fragment length polymorphism (RFLP) was the first commercial technique for DNA typing. Like many techniques in forensic science, RFLP grew out of a technology that was developed for other purposes.

For many years, biologists have sought ways to improve certain desirable characteristics in plants and animals such as increasing resistance to disease or accelerating growth. One modern technology for accomplishing this is called *recombinant DNA methodology*. The gene for a desirable characteristic present in one organism is isolated and spliced into the DNA of a different organism so the second organism now has that trait. This is done by splicing the gene first into bacteria that are then introduced into the new organism. An example of recombinant DNA methodology is the introduction of the growth hormone gene from humans into certain species of fish, which then grow much faster than normal. This provides a vital source of protein for people who do not get enough protein in their diets. In the laboratory, the gene that codes for the desirable trait is spliced out of a DNA strand by **restriction enzymes** (or *endonucleases*). Restriction enzymes are designed to cut DNA strands at specific base pair locations. For example, a restriction enzyme can be made to cleave DNA between a C–G and an A–T sequence. The RFLP technique employs restriction enzymes to cut DNA at certain known polymorphic locations. These DNA fragments exhibit length polymorphism. The core repeating sequence is between 15 and 40 base pairs long. These repeat locations are called **hypervariable regions**, which means that they contain a large number of alleles. The first hypervariable site was a gene known as D14S1. Over the next few years additional sites were discovered.

Some of these loci are not genes but lie between genes on a chromosome. Their function is not well understood. Once a hypervariable region is discovered, its base pair sequence is determined and a specific restriction enzyme is developed that will splice out the entire tandem repeat. If more than one region is to be analyzed at the same time, several restriction enzymes can be introduced. Because some hypervariable regions can occur in several locations on a chromosome, the splicing process may result in hundreds of DNA fragments produced. The fragments must be separated so that the repeat can be isolated and its length determined and compared to other DNA samples. Traditionally, RFLP separations are accomplished using gel electrophoresis. (See Chapter 4.) This process also results in the DNA strands becoming *denatured*. This means that the double helix breaks apart where each member of a base pair connects with the other one. This is shown in Figure 14.4.

Once the DNA fragments have been separated, they are transferred to a nylon membrane using a technique known as Southern blotting. The gel is fragile so a nylon membrane is used because it is much more stable. In the next part of the

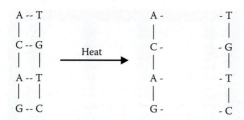

Figure 14.4 Heat will denature DNA. The double stranded DNA unzips into two single complementary strands. If the heat is taken away, the strands recombine.

RFLP process, the repeating unit fragments are labeled so they can be seen amidst the many other DNA fragments that are also created during the splicing process by the restriction enzymes. To accomplish this, a *probe* is added to the DNA on the nylon membrane. A probe is a short piece of DNA that is complementary to the repeating unit to be labeled. For example, the section above on length polymorphism showed three strands of DNA made up of repeating units. Each repeat consisted of a number of the sequence:

```
C A T G T A C
: : : : : : :
G T A C A T G
```

If the chains of this unit were subjected to electrophoresis, the units would denature leaving two pieces: C A T G T A C and G T A C A T G. A probe could be made up of either of these two sequences. When the probe is added to the fragments of DNA it will seek out its complementary strand and attach itself. If the probe is labeled either radioactively or with a fluorescent substance, the new piece of DNA will thus be labeled. If the probes are radioactively labeled, then the gel plate with all of the fragments can be exposed to a photographic plate. It will expose the film only where it is in contact with radioactively labeled DNA. Thus the fragments of interest will be shown on the plate. If the probes are fluorescently labeled, then they can be visualized by an ultraviolet light. The labeled fragments on the gel plate will glow and can be photographed using ultraviolet-sensitive film. This is shown graphically in Figure 14.5.

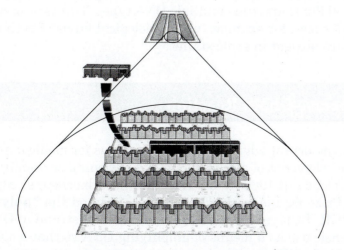

Figure 14.5 Probe hybridization. The black pieces are radioactive or fluorescent probes engineered to be complementary to the VNTRs. The result is that the VNTRs become radioactively or fluorescently labeled.

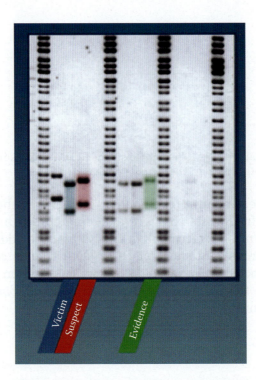

Figure 14.6 The black bands with many pieces of DNA are ladders. They are used to calibrate the plate so the lengths of the strands of evidentiary DNA can be measured accurately.

The resultant fluorescent nylon membrane or exposed film contains spots where the labeled strands of DNA are located. An exposed photographic film with DNA spots is shown in Figure 14.6. The lanes that have many spots exposed are strands of known length DNA that are prepared for calibration purposes. These are called *DNA ladders*.

RFLP suffers from some significant problems. First, the repeating DNA strands are quite long, often thousands of base pairs. When DNA degrades, the long strands tend to cleave in unpredictable locations into smaller pieces. If the degradation is advanced enough, there may not be sufficient long strands to type by RFLP. In addition, RFLP requires a relatively large amount of material for successful typing. One of the strengths of RFLP is its ability to resolve samples containing more than one person's biological fluids and thus multiple DNA types. This is a common occurrence in sexual assault cases, for example, where biological fluids of both the perpetrator and the victim are present in some stains.

The Polymerase Chain Reaction

One of the most important advances in DNA analysis for medical and forensic purposes was the development of a reliable method of cloning or amplifying DNA. This process was developed in 1983 by Dr. Kary Mullis, a biochemist who subsequently won the Nobel Prize for his work. He called his method the **"polymerase chain reaction"** or **PCR**. PCR can be used to clone part of a strand of DNA. It was first adapted for forensic use as a means of amplifying DNA so that a sufficient amount would be available for RFLP analysis. Later, a method for direct typing of DNA that had been amplified by PCR was developed. Today, the STR method is most widely used. It combines features of both PCR and RFLP.

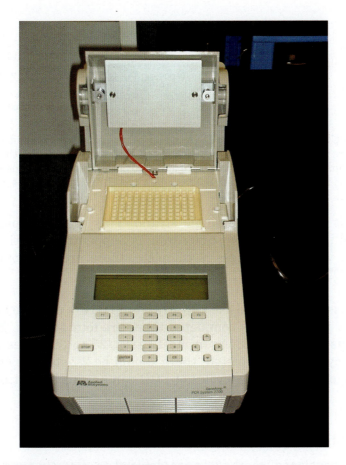

Figure 14.7 A thermocycler. *Courtesy of* Richard Li.

How DNA Is Amplified

DNA is amplified through the action of *DNA polymerase*, an enzyme present in all living organisms. As a cell divides, DNA is replicated so the exact same type and amount are present in the new cell. During cell division, the DNA first denatures, becoming single-stranded. DNA polymerase catalyzes the addition of complimentary base pairs to the DNA, thus forming new double helix strands. Dr. Mullis developed a *thermal cycler*, an instrument that can be heated to various temperatures under controlled conditions. Figure 14.7 shows a thermal cycler.

The PCR process takes place in the thermal cycler. The DNA to be replicated is mixed with a solvent, the DNA polymerase, as well as short pieces of DNA called *primers*, and a supply of the four bases (C, T, A, G) that will be added to the DNA one by one to replicate it. The amplification process takes place in three steps. The process is shown in Figure 14.8.

1. **Denaturation:** The mixture is heated close to boiling, causing the strands of DNA to denature and become single-stranded. Each piece of complementary single-stranded DNA becomes the template for the formation of a new strand.
2. **Annealing:** The temperature of the mixture is lowered. The primers then add to one end of each of the single-stranded DNA. These will be the starting points for the formation of new double-stranded DNA.
3. **Extension:** In the presence of DNA polymerase as a catalyst, a base (nucleotide) adds to the first open position next to the primer according to the

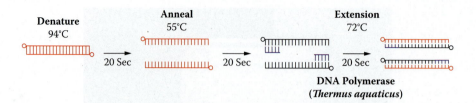

Figure 14.8 The PCR process. The target DNA is first heated to 94°C causing it to denature. In the second step, primers are added to one end of each of the strands. Then, under the influence of DNA polymerase, individual complementary bases are added to each strand one by one until a new double strand is built. Then the DNA is reheated to 94°C again and the process repeats, each time doubling the amount of DNA.

base that is already on the single strand. This process repeats until the new strand is complete. The same thing is happening to both of the single strands so, when the process is complete, there are two complete double strands of DNA.

The mixture is reheated and the two strands denature and the process repeats. The second time the process is completed there are four strands. Each cycle doubles the previous amount of DNA. In most cases, 25 to 30 cycles are completed. In theory, if 30 cycles are completed, there should be 2^{30} strands of DNA or about 1 trillion pieces of DNA! Thirty cycles of PCR can be carried out in a matter of a few hours.

How PCR-Amplified DNA Is Typed

Once PCR was developed, methods were devised to directly type the DNA that had been amplified. Certain polymorphic loci were chosen that could be amplified and then typed in one operation. The first locus chosen for typing was a gene that functions in the creation of white blood cells (leukocytes). This gene is called *HLA DQ*α where (HLA stands for *human leukocyte antigen*). DQα exhibits sequence polymorphism. The method for determining which allele is present is called the *reverse dot blot*. The amplified DNA is put in several places on specially treated nylon strips that contain all of the alleles and color-forming reagents. Where there is a match with one of the known alleles, the color changes. The reverse dot blot process has been used on a number of genes besides DQα. The main problem with typing PCR products is that the genes and other sites that are best are not very polymorphic and even the rarest types have high population frequencies. This means that, even if several genes are typed, the forensic scientist must give a qualified conclusion of association because many people could have the same DNA type determined by PCR. Another problem is that PCR cannot distinguish separate DNA types in mixtures.

Short Tandem Repeats (STRs)

In the middle 1990s, a method of DNA typing was developed that combined the strengths of PCR and RFLP while minimizing their disadvantages—and STRs were born. STRs are loci on chromosomes that repeat like those used in RFLP, but the repeating sequence is much shorter, about 3 to 7 base pairs long. The entire repeat sequences are normally a few hundred base pairs long, compared to the thousands used in RFLP. This gives rise to one big advantage of STRs over RFLP: the shorter repeating sequences are much less prone to damage from degradation. STRs are also very plentiful in the human genome so that there are many to choose from.

STR analysis starts with PCR. The locus of interest is identified and amplified by PCR. The amplified fragments are separated and displayed using capillary electrophoresis. Figure 4.20 in Chapter 4 shows a capillary electrophorogram. Currently, thirteen STR loci are commonly amplified and analyzed in forensic cases. Notice in Figure 4.20 that for most of the loci there are two peaks indicating that two alleles were present. Remember that this is because we inherit one allele from each parent and they are often different forms. When thirteen independent loci are analyzed and the population frequency of each allele at each locus is known, the product rule will yield probabilities of an overall frequency in the population that are staggeringly small. Table 14.1 below lists the thirteen loci and their population frequencies for a hypothetical African American male.

The first column is the locus where the STR is found. The second column (genotype) lists the particular alleles that this individual possesses. Note that he is heterozygous at 10 loci and homozygous at D13S317, D8S1179 and FGA. The third column (allele frequencies) shows the allele frequencies for each allele. For example in CSF1PO, the 10 allele is found in 271 out of every thousand people in the black population. The fourth column (match statistic) is 2 times the product of the allele frequencies when the locus is heterozygous and the square of the allele frequency in homozygous cases. To find the random match statistic, all 13 match statistics are multiplied (rule of multiplication). The final number, just short of 7 septillion,

TABLE 14.1
Population Statistics for 13 Loci in Hypothetical African American Male

Locus	Genotype	Allele Frequencies	Match Statistic
CSF1PO	10, 12	0.257; 0.298	0.153
D13S317	11, 11	0.306	0.09036
D16S539	11, 12	0.318; 0.096	0.125
D18S51	14, 18	0.072; 0.123	0.0177
D21S11	27, 37	0.078; 0.002	0.000831
D3S1358	15, 17	0.302; 0.205	0.123
D5S818	8, 12	0.048; 0.353	0.0338
D7S820	8, 10	0.236; 0.331	0.156
D8S1179	12, 12	0.141	0.0199
FGA	22, 22	0.196	0.0384
THO1	6, 9	0.124; 0.151	0.0374
TPOX	10, 11	0.089; 0.219	0.0389
vWA	15, 16	0.236; 0.269	0.127

Note: Random match statistic: 2.327×10^{-18} or 1 person in 427,800,000,000,000,000 chosen at random from the black population would be expected to match by chance.
Source: Courtesy of Orchid Genescreen, East Lansing, Michigan.

is astronomic. As a point of reference, it is estimated that no more than 100 billion (100,000,000,000) people have ever lived on Earth.

How does one interpret this final number? It is sometimes called "the odds of a chance occurrence." Suppose that the evidence at a crime scene has DNA of the exact type shown in Table 14.1. Further, suppose that a suspect in the case has the exact same DNA type. A very important question for the trier-of-fact at a trial would be: What are the chances that the owner of the DNA could be someone else other than the suspect? If the trier-of-fact is going to assume that the suspect is the owner of the DNA, it would be disturbing to find out later that someone else coincidentally had the same DNA. The huge final match statistic, 5.422×10^{-19} shows that the chance of a coincidental match is extremely remote. The statistic indicates that only 1 out of every 1,837,000,000,000,000,000 people in the black population should have this same DNA type. This doesn't mean that no two black people have this same DNA type. These population frequencies for each allele are drawn from a sample of the black population, not the entire population. It would never be possible to conclude that no one else has this same DNA type without testing the entire population, a practical impossibility. Thus the idea of individualizing even DNA evidence is controversial.

It is not possible to prove individuality and it shouldn't be inferred from statistical arguments. One must be very careful about making inferences from so called rare events, such as a particular DNA type. Consider birthdays—there are 365 possible birthdays. One would suppose that, in a room containing 100 people, the odds of two of them having the same birthday would be small. In fact, it is nearly a 50 percent chance! Nonetheless, consider that people who become suspects in crimes are suspects for a reason or multiple reasons. There will always be multiple types of evidence that make that person a suspect. The DNA type is only one of those pieces of evidence. The conclusion that the DNA type in question is very rare and the chances of a coincidental match between evidentiary DNA and a suspect is very small should be sufficient in a criminal trial.

Determination of Gender

In many cases, especially those involving sexual assault, it is important to know whether the biological sample belongs to a male or a female. There are two approaches taken in gender determination. The first involves analysis of the locus called **amelogenin**. Amelogenin is found in one region of the chromosomes that determine gender. These are the X and Y chromosomes. Amelogenin is not an STR, but is commonly analyzed along with STRs by capillary electrophoresis. At one region of the amelogenin locus, males have six more base pairs than do females. Females always receive an X chromosome from each parent, whereas males receive one X chromosome and one Y chromosome. Females will thus show only one band for amelogenin whereas males will have two bands, one of which is six base pairs longer than the other. Even if the stain is mixed with a male fraction and a female fraction, it will be possible to determine that both are present using amelogenin.

The other method of gender determination is to analyze the STRs present only on the Y chromosome. These are called **Y-STRs**. This type of analysis is also useful in mixed stains, even those that are badly degraded or contain a large female fraction, as would be expected in vaginal swabs in a sexual assault case.

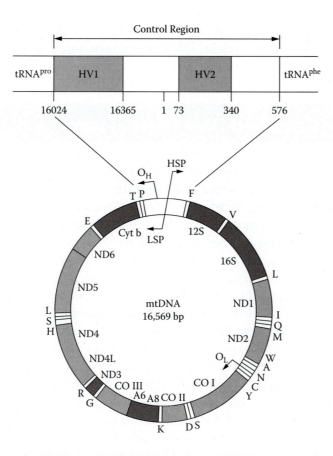

Figure 14.9 Mitochondrial DNA, showing the two variable regions.

Mitochondrial DNA

Sometimes it is not possible to obtain nuclear DNA for analysis or it may be so degraded that analysis is not possible. This is sometimes the case with skeletal remains. Fortunately there is another kind of DNA present in the body, although it makes up only about 1 percent of the DNA. This DNA is located in the **mitochondria**. Mitochondria are structures present in every cell in the body. They are in the cytoplasm, outside the nucleus. Mitochondria are responsible for energy production in the cell and they contain DNA that helps in this function. There are thousands of mitochondria in each cell and thus thousands of copies of DNA, whereas there are only a few copies of nuclear DNA in each cell.

Mitochondrial DNA differs from nuclear DNA in important ways. First, it is not arranged in a double helix but instead, is circular as is shown in Figure 14.9. There are 37 genes in human mitochondrial DNA that direct energy production, but the forensically important part consists of about 1100 base pairs within two regions that do not have a genetic code function. These regions are highly variable (*hypervariable*) and are very useful in DNA comparisons. The two regions are called *HV1* and *HV2*.

Mitochondrial DNA is inherited only from the mother. There is no contribution to mitochondrial DNA from the father. This makes mitochondrial DNA typing a useful vehicle for tracing one's parentage back through the maternal line. Siblings in a family have the same mitochondrial DNA as do their mother and maternal grandmother, etc. Although there is a great deal of variability in mitochondrial

DNA among unrelated people, only two regions exhibit this variability so that the match probabilities in mitochondrial DNA typing are much lower than those of cellular DNA.

CODIS: The Combined DNA Index System

One of the most important advances in DNA typing has been the development of local, state, and national databases that contain DNA types of many people who have been involved in crime. When DNA from an unknown suspect is found at a crime scene, it can be typed and the type sent to a database that contains thousands of DNA types from people convicted of felonies or, in some cases, arrested for felony crimes. There have been many cases where blind hits have been made even in cases where the perpetrator committed crimes in a different state.

The set of DNA databases is called **CODIS** or **Combined DNA Index System**. CODIS was begun in 1990 and is arranged in three layers. The first is the local level where all DNA profiles are first entered. These local databases feed into a statewide database. The 50 state databases feed into a national CODIS database. This system allows crime laboratories to search a particular case at the appropriate level for that case, saving time and resources. Every state in the United States participates in the CODIS and each state has passed legislation that mandates which offenders must contribute samples of DNA for inclusion in the database. The only thing that has held back development of CODIS is the lack of funding to crime laboratories for processing the samples. Active cases are the top priority of every crime lab and samples that are collected just for entry into CODIS must take a backseat. As a result, there are hundreds of thousands of cases backlogged in crime labs nationwide. It is important to get this data entered into CODIS because law enforcement agencies are going back to old cases where they have biologic evidence but no suspect, and are processing the evidence and entering the data into CODIS for search purposes. There have been hundreds of hits nationwide in these so-called *cold cases*.

In order to make CODIS work, all of the data entered for each case must be of the same type. The thirteen loci that are described in Table 14.1 are the standard loci for CODIS and each sample must have a DNA type at those thirteen loci. According to the FBI, more than 27,000 investigations have been aided in 49 states, two federal labs, and Puerto Rico through August of 2005. An investigation in this context is a case where a match for DNA was produced by CODIS that would not have otherwise occurred. (See www.fbi.gov/hq/lab/codis/aidedmap.htm.)

CODIS Success Stories

The FBI periodically describes CODIS success stories on its website. Three examples are given below. (See www.fbi.gov/success.htm.)

Solving a Double Murder in the Deep South

In the summer of 1992, Rita Baldo and her daughter, Lisa, were murdered in their Florida apartment. Both had gunshot wounds to the head and Lisa had been raped. Investigators found DNA in the saliva of three cigarette butts at the scene (neither of the women smoked). The DNA profile was compared with those taken from various suspects in the case, but none matched. The profile was uploaded to CODIS in 1998.

Three years later, a Wisconsin forensic scientist matched a profile from that state's convicted offenders' database with the DNA from the Florida case. The profile came from convicted felon James A. Frederick, who was serving time in Wisconsin. A later, more sophisticated test of hairs in the apartment also matched Frederick's DNA. Frederick was indicted in May 2003.

Putting a Rapist on Parole Behind Bars for Good

In September 2000, Carol Shields was found suffocated and murdered in a friend's apartment in north Kansas City. Her clothes were missing and the killer had meticulously cleaned the scene. Still, investigators managed to find DNA underneath the victim's fingernails. The following June, that DNA was linked to a profile in the National DNA Information System (NDIS) from paroled Arkansas rapist Wayne DuMond, who had not been a suspect in the case. DuMond was arrested, tried, and convicted—largely on the strength of the DNA evidence. He was given a life sentence without parole.

Cracking a 1968 Murder Case

In 1968, a fourteen-year-old girl named Linda Harmon was raped and murdered in San Francisco while babysitting for a neighbor. A semen sample from the autopsy was collected and stored by the San Francisco medical examiner. The case went unsolved, but last year the sample was tested for DNA. It matched that of William Speer, a convicted rapist who had been confined to an Arizona mental hospital. It is believed to be the oldest cold case solved by CODIS. Speer was arrested and pled not guilty to Harmon's murder. He was ultimately convicted of murder.

Summary

DNA is the building block of life. It directs all cellular functions. More than 99 percent of human DNA is identical in all people. Less than 1 percent makes us different. Parts of this DNA are polymorphic; they exist in more than one form. By typing this DNA, or describing the forms that are present in biologic evidence and in suspects or victims, such evidence can be associated with one particular person in some cases.

There are several ways DNA typing can be done. Restriction fragment length polymorphism was the first type developed. It separated and identified long chains that contain shorter repeating units of DNA that have different numbers of repeats in different people. RFLP requires a relatively large amount of DNA that has not been significantly degraded. PCR was developed to replicate DNA through a heat-controlled process that duplicates single-stranded DNA and makes more double strands. Each cycle doubles the amount of DNA present. Today, DNA is typed using short tandem repeats, which combine the advantages of RFLP and PCR. STRs are short strands of DNA with many repeats. They are highly variable in the human population and are many of them in the human genome. PCR is used to amplify them and capillary electrophoresis is used to separate them by size. Currently 13 loci are used in STR DNA typing. The same thirteen loci are used to compile the

CODIS database, which contains DNA from offenders in all 50 states. The database can be searched for possible suspects in crimes where the perpetrator has left DNA but is unidentified.

Test Yourself

Multiple Choice

1. Which of the following is *not* a nucleotide used to make up DNA?
   a. Adenine
   b. Guanine
   c. Arginine
   d. Thymine
   e. Cytosine
2. Which of the following is *not* a step in PCR?
   a. Addition of primers to ends of DNA strands
   b. Denaturation
   c. Addition of individual nucleotides
   d. Southern blotting
   e. All the above are steps in PCR
3. Which of the following is true about RFLP?
   a. The repeat strands are very short
   b. It analyzes only mitochondrial DNA
   c. It involves amplifying DNA
   d. Restriction enzymes are used to cut the DNA at the ends of the repeat sites
   e. None of the above is true
4. Which of the following is true of mitochondrial DNA compared to nuclear DNA?
   a. There are many more variable regions in mitochondrial DNA
   b. There are longer repeats in mitochondrial DNA
   c. There are many more copies of mitochondrial DNA in cells
   d. Mitochondrial DNA comes only from the father
5. Which of the following is a method used to determine the gender of a biologic sample?
   a. Mitochondrial typing
   b. RFLP typing
   c. PCR
   d. Amelogenin typing
6. Two strands of DNA having the same repeating base pair sequence but different numbers of repeats of that sequence are an example of:
   a. Length polymorphism
   b. Sequence polymorphism
   c. Hypervariability
   d. Hyperventilation
   e. Number polymorphism
7. Which of the following is *not* a component of the CODIS system?
   a. Local database
   b. National database

   c. Convicted felon samples

   d. Convicted misdemeanor samples

   e. State database

8. Which of the following best describes a gene?

   a. A physical characteristic

   b. A repeating sequence of base pairs

   c. A part of a human chromosome that gives rise to a particular characteristic such as hair color

   d. A sequence polymorphism

   e. None of the above

9. STRs are:

   a. Length polymorphisms

   b. Sequence polymorphism

   c. Genes

   d. PCR products

   e. Found only in mitochondria

10. In restriction fragment length polymorphism DNA typing:

   a. DNA is fragmented by restriction genes

   b. Fragments are made up of length polymorphs

   c. The fragments are 4 to 7 base pairs long

   d. Capillary electrophoresis is used to visualize the fragments

True or False

11. Because random match probabilities for DNA typing by STRs are so low, DNA can be associated reliably with one and only one person in the world.

12. Biological evidence should be stored in breathable containers to prevent degradation.

13. RFLP fragments are more susceptible to degradation than short tandem repeats.

14. Mitochondrial DNA is passed from generation to generation by the father only.

15. Mitochondrial DNA has only two regions that are polymorphic.

16. There is only one CODIS database that covers the whole country.

17. There is no DNA in hairs.

Matching

18. PCR   a. Analyzes DNA by fragmentation of long length polymorphs

19. DNA   b. Short gender determining repeat

20. RFLP   c. Clones DNA

21. STR   d. Analyzes DNA at 13 loci

22. Y-STR   e. Deoxyribonucleic acid

Short Essay

23. Briefly describe how the PCR process works.

24. Briefly describe the precautions that must be considered when collecting potential DNA evidence.

25. Briefly describe the differences between STR and RFLP analysis.

Further Reading

Butler, J. M. *Forensic DNA Typing*. San Diego, CA: Academic Press, 2001.
Inman, K. and N. Rudin. *An Introduction to Forensic DNA Analysis*. 2nd ed. Boca Raton, FL: CRC Press, 2002.

On the Web

Excellent primer on DNA typing: http://www.ornl.gov/sci/techresources/Human_Genome/elsi/forensics.shtml.

A brief history of DNA typing with graphics: http://www.cstl.nist.gov/div831/strbase/ppt/intro.pdf.

Videos that explain DNA typing:

http://video.google.com/videosearch?hl=en&q=dna+fingerprinting&revid=1171294260&ei=I5mtSbWLAouINbag_OUE&resnum=0&um=1&ie=UTF-8&ei=YJqtSfi_GciLngeClty5Bg&sa=X&oi=video_result_group&resnum=4&ct=title#.

15
Hair

1. To be able to define and describe hair
2. To be able to explain the origin and growth patterns of hair
3. To be able to describe the microscopic structure of human and nonhuman hairs
4. To be able to explain how to differentiate human from nonhuman hair
5. To be able to explain how hairs are compared
6. To be able to explain how known hair samples are collected
7. To be able to explain the role of mitochondrial DNA typing of hair in the analysis of hair from a crime scene

Chapter 15
Hair

Mini Glossary

Anagen growth phase: Active growing period of hair.
Catagen growth phase: Transition phase between growth and rest phases of hair growth.
Cortex: Middle and thickest layer of hair in humans. Contains color granules.
Cortical fusi: Small bubble-like structures in cortex of hair.
Cuticle: Outermost layer of hair. Consists of overlapping scales of keratin.
Epidermis: Outer layer of skin.
Follicle: Structure from which hairs originate and grow.
Keratin: Substance that makes up the cuticle of the hair.
Medulla: Inner layer of hair.
Melanin: Pigment responsible for hair color.
Melanocyte: Cells that produce melanin, the pigment responsible for hair color.
Ovoid bodies: Structures in cortex. Their function is unknown.
Telogen growth phase: Rest phase when hair stops growing completely.

Introduction

On March 20, 1987, an eight-year-old girl was attacked in her home in Billings, Montana by an intruder who had broken in through a locked window. She was repeatedly raped and then the intruder left after stealing a purse and jacket from the girl's room. The victim was examined the same day. Police collected her underwear and the bed sheets on which the rapes were committed. Several hairs were collected from the bed sheets and semen was identified on her underwear. After a description by the victim, police produced a sketch of the intruder. An officer who had seen the sketch thought it looked like Jimmy Ray Bromgard. Eventually, the victim picked him out of a lineup, but was unsure he was the perpetrator. In court, she expressed some doubt of the identity of Bromgard, but his assigned counsel didn't object to the identification.

At the trial, the entire case against Bromgard revolved around the hairs found in the bed sheets. The semen on the underwear could not be typed to determine what blood group it belonged to. The forensic expert testified that the head and pubic hairs found on the sheets were indistinguishable from Bromgard's hair samples. He then told the jury that the chances that the crime scene head hairs came from someone else where 100 to 1. He also reached the same conclusion concerning the pubic hairs. He then concluded that the chance that someone else was the owner of the hairs was 10,000 to 1, which is $1/100 \times 1/100$. The statistics used by the expert were not scientific.

There is no credible data that would permit a hair examiner to determine the likelihood that a particular person was the owner of shed hairs. The 100 to 1 statistic had no scientific basis. In addition, had these statistics been valid, the only way that the overall odds of 10,000 to 1 that Bromgard was the perpetrator would be valid, was if the head hair and pubic hair statistics were totally independent of each other. Clearly, this cannot be the case if the head and pubic hairs came from the same person. This testimony was extremely damning to Bromgard and yet went virtually unchallenged. He was convicted of rape and spent years in prison. His conviction was finally vacated when the New York Innocence Project had the semen re-analyzed years later and compared it to Bromgard's DNA and found no match. The semen could not have been deposited by Bromgard.

In 2007, an expert review panel condemned the forensic hair examiner's testimony as being without scientific foundation and concluded that there is no way that statistics can be applied to determine the likelihood that a crime scene hair matched a particular individual.

The same hair examiner who analyzed the hair in the *Bromgard* case also analyzed hair in many other cases and offered similar scientifically flawed conclusions. There have also been other hair examiners who have reached unsupportable conclusions concerning hair analysis. Some of these cases, like the *Bromgard* case, have been reversed due to the work of the Innocence Project. This has called into question the practice and value of hair analysis. This is unfortunate because hair has a number of characteristics that make it valuable as a source of evidence. Hair is very stable. It can be found years after someone is buried in a casket. It is very inert to chemical attack. It contains DNA, so it can be used for identification. It is easily lost from a person's body and transferred to another person or an object, and thus can help track a person's location and movement. It is also a repository for anything including foods, minerals, drugs, and poisons that a person has ingested. The average head hair remains on the head for around three months, so this repository characteristic can be very useful.

What was wrong with the conclusions reached by the hair examiner in the *Bromgard* case and in other similar cases? Hair shares some of the same issues as fingerprints, bullets, shoe prints, etc. It is basically pattern evidence. As we will see, hair consists of a number of layers that can exist in any of a number of configurations. There is no classification system for hair structure—no way to classify it into a finite number of classes. Thus, there is no data that would reveal how rare or common a particular configuration of hair structure is. Because of this, there is no way a hair examiner can calculate the probability that a hair came from a particular person. This is complicated by the fact that there is a good deal of variation in hair structure within a person's head or other area of the body. Sometimes this variation exceeds that which occurs between two different people. It is important to be aware of these limitations of hair analysis. There are no circumstances where a hair can be matched to a particular individual by comparing the hairs visually, microscopically and/or chemically. Thus, hair is class evidence. It is possible for a degree of association to be made between hairs from a crime scene and those taken from a suspect or victim. If there are sufficient physical and chemical characteristics common to both, it is permissible to conclude that the crime scene hairs *could have come from* the suspect or victim. As stated above, there are no statistics available to determine the certainty with which the association can be made. It is of course, quite proper to reach a conclusion that crime scene hairs could not have come from a particular person.

In recent years, DNA typing has added a great deal of information to the analysis of biological evidence because there are a finite number of DNA types and a DNA classification scheme has been developed that permits conclusions about how rare or common a particular DNA type is. The role of DNA in hair analysis is discussed later in this chapter.

What Is Hair?

Hair is an outgrowth of the **epidermis**, or outer layer of the skin. It is found only in mammals. Figure 15.1 is a diagram of the cross-section of human skin including the layers of the skin and hair **follicles**. Follicles are the structures from which hairs originate and grow. When hair begins to grow, its outer covering is soft. When it

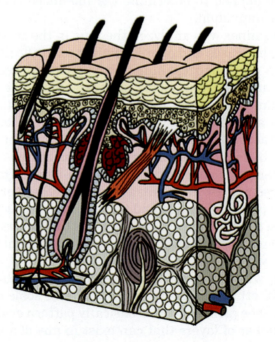

Figure 15.1 Cross-section of dermis and epidermis of human skin. *Courtesy of* Max Houck.

reaches the top of the skin, the outer layer begins to harden into **keratin**. Keratin is made of proteins. It is the same material that makes up fingernails and toenails in humans and horns in other animals.

The follicle where the hair grows is enervated by blood vessels that provide nourishment and exchange materials between blood and the inside of the hair. Anything that is ingested by the person, such as food, drugs, or poisons, is eventually incorporated into the growing region of the hair. When the hair reaches the surface of the skin and keratinizes, it is essentially dead. It is no longer in contact with blood vessels and doesn't exchange anything with its biologic environment. This means that whatever substances were absorbed by the growing part of the hair will remain there. In this regard, the hair is a sort of filing cabinet that one cannot remove files from. Thus, when hair grows it is really being pushed up by the growing part of the hair in the follicle. It is analogous to the size of a stack of dinner plates growing taller by continuously adding more plates to the bottom of the stack. The plates on the top aren't getting bigger, they are being pushed out and up by the ones being added from below. If a person smokes marijuana, for example, some THC and other substances present in the plant will be absorbed into the growing region of the person's hair. As this section gets pushed up and out from the follicle, the THC remains in that section of the hair until the hair is cut or falls out. This is why drug analysis is increasingly performed on hair. The hair retains some of the drug each time the person uses it. Unlike urine analysis, which provides only a snapshot of the drugs in a person's body, hair analysis provides a history. Head hair grows approximately one-half inch per month. This can be used to estimate the time when a drug or other substance was ingested. The average head hair falls out after about ninety days.

Hair Growth

Most tissues grow in a smooth, regular fashion. Anyone who observes hair growing out after cutting it would assume that hair also grows like this, but such is not the case. In fact, there are three distinct stages of hair growth. These are depicted in Figure 15.2.

The active growing period of hair is called the **anagen** phase. The follicle produces new hair cells that are added to the shaft of the hair, thus pushing the hair up the follicle toward the surface of the skin. This is the most active phase of hair growth. At any given time, the majority of hairs are in the anagen phase.

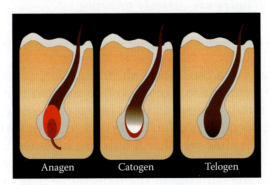

Figure 15.2 Growth stages of hair. They are the anagen, catagen, and telogen from left to right. *Courtesy of* Meredith Haddon.

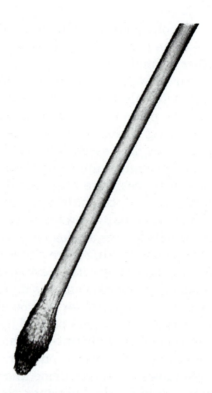

Figure 15.3 A human hair root in the catagen phase. *Courtesy of* Max Houck.

After the anagen phase is complete, the next phase begins. This is the **catagen** phase. It is a transition between growth and rest. Cell production in the follicle declines and the root of the hair shrinks into a bulb-like shape. Figure 15.3 shows the bulbous root of human hair associated with the catagen phase of growth.

In the **telogen** phase, the hair has stopped growing completely. It will stay this way until the hair is lost by pulling (combing or brushing) or shedding. Hairs lost in one of these ways will contain the root. The loss of the hair triggers the end of the telogen phase and the resumption of the anagen phase and a new hair begins to grow. Normally a person will naturally shed a few dozen hairs per day. This number can increase with frequent and vigorous brushing or combing. It takes about six months to grow a completely new scalp of hair. Some people believe that hair growth can be stimulated by cutting or shaving hair. There is no evidence that this happens. Cutting off a hair above the root does not stimulate the resumption of the anagen phase of growth. Hair will continue to grow at its normal rate if shaved or cut and if the hair is in the anagen phase at the time. At any given time, about 85 percent of human scalp hairs are actively growing.

Forcible Removal of Hair

Remember that humans are constantly shedding hair, especially from the scalp. This is one reason why hairs are found so often at even nonviolent crime scenes. Sometimes hairs are forcibly removed by yanking or tearing or by violent contact and are also left at the scene. It is often important to know whether a hair was shed or removed. Can we determine whether a hair has been forcibly removed? It is not as easy as it sounds. There are obvious cases. Some but not all forcibly removed hair will have follicle cells clinging to the hair. Some may actually have blood on the root. This would be especially true if the hair were still growing (anagen phase). If the hair was in the resting phase when pulled, it may not have any of the follicle sheath on it because bulbous roots of the hair in this phase are not tightly held in the follicle. The amount of cellular material on the root depends on how fast the hair was pulled. If the hair is pulled quickly, the chances of finding cells from the follicle are increased.

Something for You to Do

Get a hairbrush and brush your hair as you normally do. Do not use any extra force. Brush until you have about a dozen hairs on the brush. Remove them and examine them with a magnifying glass or low-power microscope. Concentrate on the roots of the hairs. Are the roots all the same shape? How would you describe the shape of the roots? Do you see cellular material clinging to any of the roots? (You may need a higher power microscope to see this.) The presence of cellular material clinging to the root of a hair may indicate that the hair was forcibly removed as opposed to merely falling out. Now look at the hairs from someone else in your family or a friend. Are their roots the same shape as yours? You can also compare the color of your hairs and compare those to the others. Check out the average length of the hairs and the presence of damage such as split ends. Look for variation between the hairs from your head. Some people have significant differences in structure and appearance in hairs taken from the same head.

Hair Color

Look around you. There seems to be a wide variety of head hair colors, from very light to black. Of course, some of these colors result from artificial coloring agents that grow out with the hair and fade with time, but naturally colored hair also comes in various shades that are under the control of our genetic inheritance. As hair grows, special cells called **melanocytes** produce granules of **melanin**. Melanin is the pigment that gives hair its color. There are two types of melanin. One is dark brown and the other is lighter, almost blond. Under the influence of genetic instructions, these two types of melanin are present in various combinations, densities, and distributions, giving rise to the natural hair colors in the human population. These granules are dispersed throughout the middle layer of the hair (the cortex). When hair is dyed, the melanin does not take up the dye. Instead, the dye coats the surface of the hair. Various colored human hairs are shown in Figure 15.4

The Structure of Human Hair

Scalp hairs are more often found at crime scenes than any other type, so they will be used to illustrate the structure of human hairs. Hairs from other parts of the body differ in systematic ways from head hair and a competent hair examiner can distinguish among hairs from various parts of the body.

Look at the human head hair in Figure 15.5. It has three regions. The **root** is at the widest end of the hair and is attached to the follicle and is the growing area. The second region is the **shaft**. From the root to the tip, the shaft tapers. The **tip** is the end of the hair away from the root. The hair is narrowest at the tip. This means that one must be careful in describing the diameter of a hair. It depends upon where it is measured.

From the outside, hairs appear to be homogeneous throughout and one cannot tell whether the hair is solid like a steel rod or hollow like a garden hose. In fact, hair is neither. Its structure is quite complex and can be related to that of a lead pencil. Like a pencil, a hair has three layers, but they differ in relative thickness and structural characteristics from the layers in a pencil. The relative thickness of the layers in human hair differs somewhat depending on its location on the body.

Light   Medium   Dark

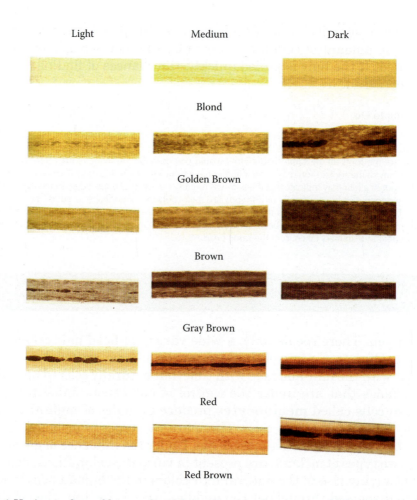

Blond

Golden Brown

Brown

Gray Brown

Red

Red Brown

Figure 15.4 Various colors of human head hair. Reprinted courtesy of Ogle, R. R. and M. J. Fox, *Atlas of Human Hair: Microscopic Characteristics,* New York: Taylor & Francis, 1996.

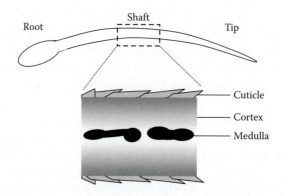

Figure 15.5 A complete human head hair from root to tip. *Courtesy of* Max Houck.

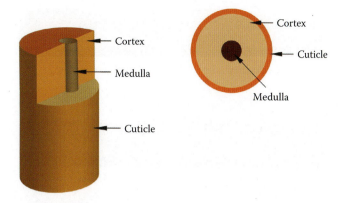

Figure 15.6 The three layers of hair. *Courtesy of* Meredith Haddon.

Figure 15.7 A human head hair showing the cortex and the medulla. The hair is mounted in a liquid with the same refractive index as the cuticle, so it cannot be seen.

They are also quite different from the layer thickness in animal hairs. A diagram of the three layers of a human hair is shown in Figure 15.6. An actual human head hair is shown in Figure 15.7.

The outermost layer of the hair is the **cuticle**. It is made of keratin, the same material that makes up fingernails and toenails, and is responsible for the stability and inertness of hair. Although keratin is transparent, the structure of the cuticle is such that it is difficult to see through. The hair in Figure 15.7 is mounted in a liquid that makes the cuticle more transparent so that the inner layers of the hair can be seen. The cuticle is not a smooth layer like the painted outer surface of a pencil. Instead, it consists of a series of overlapping scales arranged much like the shingles on a roof. The cuticular scales are very small and hard to see even with a microscope. The best way to see the scales of a cuticle is to make a cast of them, sort of like making a cast of a shoe in cement. One way to do this is described below.

Something for You to Do

You can easily make a scale cast of a human hair. You need some clear nail polish, a microscope slide, and some hairs. Deposit a thin layer of nail polish on the surface of the slide and lay one or more hairs across the slide. Leave them there until the nail polish dries (about ten minutes) and then pull them off. A cast of the scale patterns will be visible in the nail polish. You will need at least a low power microscope to clearly see the pattern. Try this on some of your own scalp hair and some hair from your friends and family. Do all of the scale casts look similar? In a shingle roof, the shingles are arranged in a neat pattern. Is that the case with human hair cuticular scales? If you can get hairs from animals such as a cat and/or dog, make scale casts of them. How are the scales arranged compared to human scales?

The middle layer of hair is the **cortex**. In humans, this is the most prominent and thickest layer. The cortex is made up of spindle-shaped cells and is also transparent. Pigment granules are dispersed throughout the cortex. These granules are generally not spaced in an even pattern, but instead are often found in clumps. They vary from person to person, in size and shape, and in distribution. The cortex

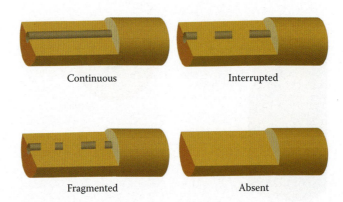

Continuous   Interrupted

Fragmented   Absent

Figure 15.8 Four types of medullae found in human hair. *Courtesy of* Meredith Haddon.

also contains **cortical fusi**. These are small bubble-like structures. Their appearance may be related to the transition from the anagen to catagen growth phase of hair. **Ovoid bodies**, which look like large pigment granules, may also be present in the cortex. Their function is not known. They do not exhibit a pattern, but appear irregularly within the cortex.

The innermost layer of the hair is the **medulla**. It consists of cells that form a shaft through the middle of the hair. In human head hair, the medulla may be totally absent, present in a few areas of the hair, or mostly present except for a few gaps. In some cases, the entire shaft may be visible. This gives rise to a classification system for human hair medullae. Figure 15.8 shows a diagram of the four types of human medullae.

Human versus Nonhuman Hairs

Human hairs differ from animal hairs in several important ways. This is due, at least in part, to the function of hair in many animals, which is protective and for camouflaging. In humans, hair has lost its protective function through evolution and is mostly decorative. In many animals, hair has evolved to perform different specialized functions. Many animals possess three different types of hair. The first are called *guard hairs*. These are firm hairs with a protective function. They have distinct features that make them useful for forensic purposes. They are most often used for microscopic comparison. The rest of the animal's coat consists of *fur hairs*. These are relatively featureless and do not provide much information about the type of animal. Finally, there are *whiskers*. Whiskers are sensitive to touch and are used by the animal for sensory purposes. Even though animal hairs differ from human hairs, they still mostly contain the same three layers—cuticle, cortex, and medulla. There are, however, a number of microscopic characteristics that can be useful in distinguishing human from nonhuman hairs.

- The cuticular scales of human hairs tend to be unorganized and overlap like roof shingles. Other animals have more organized, patterned scales. The cuticle is usually thicker relative to the rest of the hair in other animals. You can observe this when you make scale casts of human and animal hairs as directed above.
- The medullae of other animals tend to be thicker relative to the rest of the hair. In humans, the medulla is less than one-third of the hair diameter,

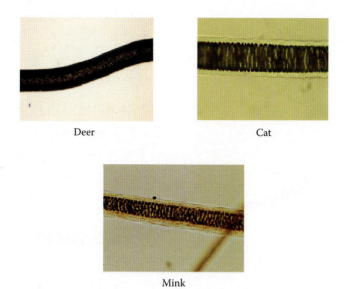

Deer   Cat

Mink

Figure 15.9 Deer, cat, and mink fur hairs. *Courtesy of* Max Houck.

whereas in other animals, it is more than half. Many animals have thick, continuous medullae. Animals do not have the same classification system for medullae as do humans. Animal medullae are always continuous. Interrupted, fragmented, and absent medullae are present only in humans. Some animals such as cats and mice have *ladder* or *stacked* medullae that resemble a stack of dinner plates or a string of pearls. Members of the deer family have medullae that look like fine latticework. Figure 15.9 shows the interior structures of some animal hairs.

Hair Treatment and Damage

Humans subject their hair to many types of treatments and these can help in the comparison of known and unknown hairs. For example, razor cutting of hairs leaves angled tips whereas scissor cut hair has straight tips. Bleaches oxidize the cortical hair pigment granules, thus removing their color. When hair is dyed, it has a painted appearance and there is an abrupt color change between the natural color and the dyed color. Hair is also subject to disease and degradation from drying out or chemical treatments. These conditions can have forensic value in hair comparisons because they are relatively unusual and they give the affected hairs a unique appearance. Figure 15.10 shows hairs that have been damaged by treatment or disease.

Comparison of Human Hairs

Hair evidence is found in a great variety of crimes. Most commonly, it is evidence at scenes of crimes of violence such as criminal sexual assault. In these types of crimes, pubic hairs from the victim and perpetrator will often be found on their bodies on the surface where the attack took place and in surrounding areas. This is especially

Burned Hair   Split Ends

Crushed Hair

Figure 15.10 Various types of damage to human hairs. *Courtesy of* Max Houck.

powerful evidence, as it demonstrates the transfer of two types of evidence between perpetrator and victim. This is often accompanied by the transfer of fibers, making the hair even more probative evidence. Hairs are shed naturally and may be found at scenes. During a violent incident, hair may be pulled and found at the scene. In all of these incidents, hair is good class evidence and can provide information about the identity of the perpetrator and the victim as well as the circumstances of the incident. Hair is easily transferred from one surface to another and may undergo several transfers after being shed. One of the authors of this book once did a study about the mass transfer of fibers to clothing at a large forensic science meeting. One of the findings was quite unexpected; a large number of dog and cat hairs from the owners' pets were found on clothing worn at the meeting.

As with other types of evidence, the collection of known samples is important. In the majority of cases, either head or pubic (or both) hairs are left as evidence at crime scenes. It is important to obtain a sufficient number of known hairs and they must represent the head or pubic area as a whole. At least two dozen hairs are needed for comparisons. Fifty is better. They must be combed and (gently) pulled to ensure hairs in all stages of growth are represented. The known sample must contain hairs from areas that have been treated. This includes dyeing, braiding, bleaching, graying, etc. There are natural variations of morphological characteristics of hairs within the same head or other area of the body. There must be enough known samples present so that the hair examiner is aware of the degree of variation.

Hairs are mounted on microscope slides and immersed in a suitable liquid that enables the examiner to see through the cuticle into the inner layers of the hair. The cuticle has a refractive index of about 1.50. Suitable Cargill liquids can be used as can glycerin (RI = 1.475). The microscope should be able to provide magnification of 25 to 200 power. A comparison microscope is ideal so that known and unknown hairs can be viewed together. Scale casts should also be taken of some of the hairs from the crime scene as well as the samples from the suspect and/or victim. Various charts are used by hair examiners to record the data about the known and unknown hair. There is no standard set of data that must be collected. The examiner typically collects data about the hair as a whole, including length, diameter, coloring, disease, and treatment. In addition, specific information is noted for the root, shaft,

Figure 15.11 Comparison of human hairs. The pair of blond hairs on the left are very similar in color and in fragmented medulla and diameter. They could have come from the same head of hair. The pair on the right are different in color, diameter, and distribution of color particles in the cortex. This would be an exclusion. *Courtesy of* Max Houck.

and tip. Characteristics of the medulla are noted including its diameter, continuity, and color. The cortex is examined for the presence and distribution of color granules, ovoid bodies, and cortical fusi.

On the basis of the comparison of unknown hairs, there are three possible conclusions a hair examiner can reach. If there are sufficient common characteristics between the knowns and unknowns and there are no unexplainable significant differences, the hair examiner can conclude that the unknown hairs could have originated from the person who provided the known samples. If the known and unknown samples exhibit significant differences that exceed the range of variation within a set of hairs, the conclusion would be that the known donor could not have been the source of the unknown hairs. If there are some similarities between the known and unknown but there are also some slight variations, no conclusion about the association can be given. Figure 15.11 shows a comparison of two hairs that came from the same source and two that came from a different source.

What Can Be Determined from the Structure of Hair?

As we have seen, a great deal can be determined from the structural analysis of hair. These include the following:

- **Human or animal:** It is easy to determine whether a hair is human or animal, especially head hair. Recall that humans have fragmented or absent medullae in their head hair, whereas animals have continuous medullae. The medulla in human hair is generally less than one-third of the diameter of the hair, whereas in animals, it may be more than half. In humans, the cuticular scales are irregular, whereas in animals they are arranged in a much more regular fashion.
- **Part of the body:** For human hair, it is usually not difficult to determine what part of the body hairs came from. Most crime scene hairs are either from the head or the pubis. Pubic hairs tend to be shorter, curlier, stiffer, and contain more pronounced medullae than head hairs.
- **Color:** Hair that has been colored has more of a painted look than hair with a natural color. The natural color is due to clusters of melanin, whereas dyed

hair has a coating on the surface. As hair grows, the line of demarcation between the dye and the natural color becomes more pronounced. If hair is bleached, the melanin particles have a washed out appearance.

- **Disease, mistreatment:** Diseased, teased, or artificially straightened or curled hair can usually be detected under a microscope.

There are also a number of characteristics that some people believe hair can reveal. This, however, is generally not true. Some of these are listed below.

- **Age:** Age cannot be determined from the examination of hair. The fact that hair is gray doesn't mean that the person is old. The only hair that can be differentiated by age is the very fine hair called *lanugo* which is found on newborns.
- **Gender:** At one time, perhaps fifty years ago, people may have concluded that long hair was female. If hair spray was present, it must be female. One would be tempted to say that only females dyed their hair. None of these are true today, if they ever were. The only reliable determinate for gender in hair is a DNA analysis to see whether the Y (male) chromosome is present.
- **Race:** There are some racial characteristics of hair that show up if the person has fairly pure racial ancestry. These include different hair diameters, cross-sectional shapes, thickness of cuticle, and distribution of pigments. As interracial marriages take place, these characteristics tend to become less pronounced.

DNA Analysis of Hair

Except for the roots, hair does not contain sufficient nucleated cells to perform genomic DNA analysis, but hair cells do contain mitochondria and mitochondrial DNA typing is now routinely done on hair samples. DNA typing is explained in Chapter 14. Mitochondrial DNA is inherited only through the maternal line. One's father does not contribute mitochondrial DNA. As a result, all people have the same mitochondrial DNA as their mothers. Because of this, mitochondrial DNA is not suitable for individualization. In cases where mitochondrial DNA typing narrows down the possible suspects to siblings, the microscopic analysis of DNA may distinguish among the hair of the siblings and perhaps the techniques taken together may provide individualization. In other cases, there may be insufficient DNA to perform complete analysis.

It is becoming clear that microscopic analysis and mitochondrial DNA analysis are complementary techniques valuable in the analysis of hair. Since the maturation of mitochondrial DNA, many hair examiners, including those of the FBI, have developed a protocol for the analysis of hair that employs both structural analysis and mitochondrial DNA analysis. The hairs are first compared microscopically. If there are neither unexplained differences nor sufficient similarities that provide evidence of an association between the known and unknown hairs, mitochondrial DNA analysis is done. If the DNA types are the same, an association is made, but this is not an individualization. It just narrows down the population that could have been the source of the hair.

Hair as a Source of Drugs

Earlier in this chapter, it was noted that as hair grows, it has a blood supply to nourish it. Anything in the blood will appear in equilibrium with the growing part of the hair. This means that, if the person were taking a drug such as cocaine, some of it would end up in the hair. Remember also that when hair stops growing, it ceases to exchange materials with the blood stream and becomes a repository for whatever substances were introduced into it during the growing phase. This has implications for testing someone for illicit drugs. When a person is to be tested for the presence of illicit drugs (controlled substances) as is the case in many workplaces or pre-employment drug screens, the conventional sample is usually urine, although blood may also be used. The problems with urine drug screening include the ability to tamper with the sample, flushing the urine with diuretic drugs, and the fact that the urine test yields only a snapshot of what drugs are present in the body, but provides no information about how often the person has taken the drugs or for how long.

Hair testing for drugs overcomes all of these problems. The subject cannot tamper with the hair, diuretics have no effect (in fact, the diuretic will show up in the hair), and the hair provides a kind of memory of drug use. Each time the drug is taken, it will show up in the hair—so for as long as the hair is on the head (ninety days on the average), it will provide a history of drug use. Drug testing in hair is also less invasive than taking a urine or blood sample—the hair is simply combed out or snipped off. Although drug testing in hair is a bit more expensive than urine testing, the cost has decreased and continues to decrease as more laboratories are doing this type of testing and there is demand for it.

Summary

Hair is an appendage that grows out of the skin or dermis. It has three growth stages—anagen catagen, and telogen. Hair consists of three layers. The outermost is the cuticle. The middle layer is the cortex. It contains the color granules that define the color of the hair. The inner layer is the medulla, a shaft that runs the length of the hair. The cuticle is made up of overlapping scales like shingles on a roof. Human and nonhuman hairs differ in all three layers. The scales in the cuticle of human hairs tend to be less organized than those of other animals. The medullae in human hairs are generally less continuous than those of animals and may be absent altogether. At least a couple dozen known hairs are collected for comparison with unknowns because of the large amount of variation in the structures of hairs from a single subject.

Hairs are compared by noting the microscopic characteristics of the hair as a whole and of the individual layers. If there are sufficient characteristics in known and unknown hairs that match, the donor of the known hairs could be the source of the unknowns. Hair is virtually always class evidence. Mitochondrial DNA typing can be performed on hairs. It is a complementary technique to microscopic analysis of hairs. Many laboratories now use both structural analysis and mitochondrial DNA analysis in tandem. Hair is also a good source of tracing illicit drugs. Unlike urine tests, there are no problems with tampering with the sample or flushing the drugs and hair provides a memory of how often the subject took the drugs instead of providing only a one-time snapshot.

Test Yourself

Multiple Choice

1. Which of the following is not a type of medulla found in a human hair?
   a. Fragmented
   b. Continuous
   c. Stacked
   d. Interrupted
   e. Absent

2. Which of the following is not a layer of hair?
   a. Medulla
   b. Root
   c. Cortex
   d. Cuticle
   e. All the above are layers of hair

3. Which of the following is not found in the cortex?
   a. Color granules
   b. Ovoid bodies
   c. Cortical fusi
   d. Scales

4. In which of the following growth stages of hair does active growing take place?
   a. Catagen
   b. Anagen
   c. Telogen
   d. Antigen

5. If a hair falls out on its own, without any combing or pulling, it is likely in which growth stage?
   a. Catagen
   b. Anagen
   c. Telogen
   d. Antigen

6. A hair with a thick cuticle and regular scales and a continuous medulla is:
   a. Animal other than human
   b. Human
   c. Could be animal or human
   d. Neither human or other animal

7. If a known and unknown hair have very similar microscopic characteristics and no unexplainable differences, then:
   a. The unknown had to have come from the known source
   b. The unknown could have come from the known source
   c. The unknown could not have come from the known source
   d. There is a 95 percent probability that the unknown came from the known source

8. Which is true about DNA typing of hair?
   a. Genomic DNA typing can be done on the shaft of the hair
   b. Only mitochondrial DNA typing is commonly done on human hair
   c. No DNA typing can be done on human hair
   d. Only hair in the anagen growing phase can be DNA typed
9. Which of the following is an advantage of drug testing using hair rather than urine?
   a. It is cheaper
   b. It gives a short-term drug use history
   c. It can detect more drugs
   d. It doesn't require confirmation
10. Hair is individualizable evidence when:
   a. Mitrochondrial DNA typing is done
   b. When the known and unknown both have a continuous medulla
   c. When all three layers of hair are similar in the known and unknown
   d. Hair evidence is not individualizable

True or False

11. Hair continuously grows all along its shaft.
12. In the case described at the beginning of the chapter, instead of multiplying the 100:1 odds for the head and pubic hairs, the hair examiner should have added the two together.
13. There are three stages of growth in hair.
14. The average lifetime of head hair is about three months.
15. The chances of two individuals having a fragmented medulla in their hair is about 100 to 1.
16. Human head hairs seldom have a continuous medulla.
17. Cuticular scale patterns in human head hairs tend to be very regular.

Matching

18. Catagen stage   a. Middle layer of the hair
19. Continuous medulla   b. Transition stage in hair growth
20. Cortical fusi   c. Small cells located in cortex
21. Melanin   d. Rapid growth stage of hair
22. Cortex   e. Substance that makes up hair pigment
23. Anagen stage   f. Found mainly in animals

Short Essay

24. Describe how hair grows. What are the stages of growth?
25. Describe the major differences in the structure of hair in humans and animals

Further Reading

Bisbing, R. The Forensic Identification and Association of Human Hair. Ed. R. Saferstein. *Forensic Science Handbook*. Vol. 1. 2nd ed. Englewood Cliffs, NJ: Prentice Hall, 2002.

Robertson, J., ed. *Forensic Examination of Hair.* New York: Taylor & Francis, 1999.

Hicks, J. W. *Microscopy of Hairs: A Practical Guide and Manual.* Washington, D.C.: U.S. Government Printing Office, 1977.

On the Web

Introduction to hair analysis by FBI: http://www.fbi.gov/hq/lab/fsc/backissu/july2000/deedric1.htm.

Presentation to National Academy of Sciences on hair analysis by McCrone Associates: http://www7.nationalacademies.org/stl/April%20Forensic%20Bisbing.pdf.

Powerpoint presentation on hair analysis: a-s.clayton.edu/shornbuckle/CHEM4204/2008%20presentations%20and%20objectives/...-

PART V

Forensic Chemistry

PART V

Forensic Chemistry

16
Illicit Drugs

Learning Objectives

1. To be able to define a drug and distinguish licit drugs from illicit ones
2. To be able to describe the characteristics of the federal schedules for controlled substances
3. To be able to describe the classification of drugs by major effect
4. To be able to classify common illicit drugs
5. To be able to describe how an illicit drug is analyzed correctly by a forensic chemist

Chapter 16
Illicit Drugs

Chapter Outline

Mini Glossary

Confirmation test: Test used to conclusively identify a pure drug substance.

Depressant: A drug prescribed to relieve anxiety, nervousness, and restlessness.

Drug: A substance designed to have specific physical and/or emotional effects on people or in some cases animals.

Hallucinogen: A drug that causes people to see and hear things that aren't there.

Illicit Drug: Sometimes called *abused drugs* or *controlled substances* in the United States, these drugs are of two types. The first consists of **licit drugs** that are abused or taken for purposes other than those for which they were originally developed. The other type of illicit drug is a substance that has no recognized medical purpose.

Narcotic: Powerful sleep-inducing central nervous system depressant.

Screening test: The most general tests for drugs, also sometimes called spot test or field test.

Separation test: Test used to separate a drug from a mixture of cutting and diluting agents.

Stimulant: A drug that elevates a person's mood and causes euphoria.

Withdrawal: A syndrome of symptoms that occur in drug addicts when they stop taking a drug.

Acronyms

DEA: Drug Enforcement Administration

FDA: Food and Drug Administration

LSD: Lysergic acid diethylamide. The most powerful hallucinogen.

MDMA: Methylenedioxymethamphetamine. A derivative of methamphetamine and a powerful hallucinogen.

PCP: Phenylcyclohexylpiperidine. A powerful hallucinogen.

SWGDRUG: Scientific working group on the analysis of illicit drugs.

Introduction

In April, 1976, one of the authors of this book was working as a drug chemist with what was then called the Virginia Bureau of Forensic Sciences. The Arlington County Virginia Police Department received a tip that some people were manufacturing drugs in a subdivision home in the county. The tip came from a neighbor who saw several suspicious-looking people carting boxes and drums of what appeared to be chemicals into the house. The police department, in cooperation with U.S. Drug Enforcement Agents, staked out the house to see whether further activity was taking place. They ascertained that the inhabitants were probably making PCP (phencyclidine, sometimes called "angel dust"). The police department narcotics agents contacted the Virginia lab and asked for a chemist to help them ascertain how far the PCP preparation had gone. It was proposed that one of the agents along with the chemist (the author of this book) would walk slowly by the house and sniff the air. The idea was that an odor of benzene and/or ethyl ether would indicate that the clandestine drug manufacturers would be in the last step of the synthesis of the PCP. In prosecuting drug manufacturers, it is much easier for the prosecution if the target drug is actually present. It is much easier to prosecute someone for "manufacture" of an illicit drug than it is for "attempted manufacture." As a result of this reconnoiter, the police and DEA raided the house and uncovered a major clandestine PCP lab. The entire floor of the two-car garage was covered with six inches of parsley, and the PCP had been dissolved in camp stove fuel and poured on the parsley. Had the house not been raided, the fuel would have been allowed to evaporate and the PCP treated parsley (called "wobble weed" on the street), would have been bagged and sold for smoking. The narcotics agents estimated the haul to be worth more than $1M.

The recreational use of illicit drugs is one of the most serious societal problems in the United States. The use of illicit drugs costs many millions of dollars in lost productivity and medical expenses and many more millions in efforts by law enforcement agents to stem the flow of drugs into the country and arrest users and distributors of drugs. Crime laboratories are swamped with illicit drug cases and American crime labs have a collective backlog of thousands of drug cases. Many drug cases go to court and forensic drug chemists spend many hours testifying or waiting to, while new cases pile up back in the lab. Since the presidency of Ronald Reagan, beginning in 1980, the federal government has been waging a war on drugs. The thrust of the government's activities has been to try and interdict the drugs on their way into the U.S. This has yielded mixed results because the U.S. borders are relatively open and drugs come from Mexico and South and Central America (cocaine, marijuana, **MDMA**—known as ecstasy, methamphetamine) and from Europe and Asia (heroin, Fentanyl). In addition, there are many large and small laboratories that manufacture methamphetamine, MDMA, PCP and LSD, and many recreational marijuana growers in the U.S. The government has also spent money on treatment and drug prevention programs but not nearly as much as has been spent on interdiction. There have been joint task forces involving U.S. personnel that attempt to destroy drug growing and lab operations in the countries of origin. Because illicit drugs can be such major cash crops, local government cooperation has been mixed also. In this chapter, we discuss the history of illicit drugs, how they are controlled by federal and state laws and how they are used and abused.

Illicit Drugs

Most people think of the term "drug" as a substance prescribed to treat a disease or other illness. In fact, a **drug** is a substance designed to have specific physical and/or emotional effects on people or, in some cases, animals. The vast majority of drugs are produced by pharmaceutical companies for a particular disease or disorder. These are called **licit drugs**. Under this definition, ethyl alcohol, which is used in beer, wine, and spirits, is not a drug. It may have some benefits in moderate quantities, but it is not prescribed for that purpose. Alcohol is covered in Chapter 17: Forensic Toxicology. From a legal standpoint, all licit drugs in the United States must have a recognized medical use as defined by the **United States Food and Drug Administration (FDA)**. If the FDA doesn't recognize a drug as having a legitimate use, it isn't a licit drug.

Illicit drugs, sometimes called *abused drugs* or *controlled substances* in the United States, are of two types. The first consists of licit drugs abused or taken for purposes other than those for which they were originally developed. Methamphetamine is a good example of this. For many years, methamphetamine was legitimately marketed as a **stimulant** to counter feelings of fatigue or depression and as appetite suppressants. It even played a role in controlling hyperkinesia, which is a nerve disorder manifested by hyperactivity. Today, however, methamphetamine is hardly used for these purposes. Instead, tablets and capsules that have been diverted from legitimate channels (stolen), and powdered forms made in clandestine laboratories are ingested by people for the purpose of getting high. It is also possible to use a licit drug for the purpose it was developed, but to use it fraudulently or inappropriately. An example of this would be the use of steroids by Olympic and other athletes to give them an unfair competitive advantage.

The other type of illicit drug is a substance that has no recognized medical purpose. It could be a synthetic substance, like phencyclidine (PCP) or it could be derived from a plant, like cocaine and morphine (which is then made into heroin). In some cases, part of the plant is ingested, as in the case of marijuana or opium. These types of illicit drugs are far and away the most popular throughout the world. Because these two categories of drugs do not have any legitimate medical purpose, it is illegal to possess, use, grow, or sell them. Why is this so? What harm is there in a person smoking marijuana, for example, in his own home, not bothering anyone else? Many people believe that this kind of behavior is a detriment to our society. It is wasteful, perhaps harmful behavior that does not advance society and may cost a good deal of money for treatment of drug disorders such as addiction. Others believe that it is hypocritical of the government to control and penalize the use of such substances for recreational purposes when an additive substance such as ethyl alcohol is freely available and heavily abused by a large segment of the adult population. This argument has been waged for many years and for now, comes down on the side of controlling illicit drugs and keeping alcohol more or less freely available.

The Control of Illicit Drugs in the United States

The possession, use, and sale of illicit drugs have been the subject of governmental control since the early part of the twentieth century. During this time, the issue of drug control has been affected by research and popular culture and, as a result, the laws and regulations have been somewhat disjointed and uncoordinated. Prior to the beginning of the twentieth century, drugs like marijuana, opium, heroin, and cocaine were used in the U.S. but there was little in the way of control over their use. In many cases, these drugs were mixed with flavorings and/or alcohol and sold as elixirs from the backs of traveling wagons. They were sold as medicinals that could cure practically every disease. Of course, they had little or no effect and represented fraudulent advertising. In the early twentieth century, the federal government began to exert some control over many of these drugs. In part, the government intervention was prompted by public reaction to opium smoking among Chinese immigrants, the rise of cocaine use, and increased activity by purveyors of patent medicines. In 1906, the *Pure Food and Drugs Act*, which prohibited interstate commerce in mislabeled or adulterated food and drugs, was passed by Congress and signed into law. Among the substances targeted by the law were marijuana, cocaine, heroin, and opium. This act was administered by the Department of Agriculture.

In 1914, Congress passed a major tax and control bill, the Harrison Act, which is properly known as "An act to provide for the registration of, with collectors of internal revenue, and to impose a special tax upon all persons who produce, import, manufacture, compound, deal in, dispense or give away opium or coca leaves, their salts, derivatives, or preparations, and for other purposes." This law was enforced and administered by the Bureau of Internal Revenue in the Treasury Department. It gave the federal government broad control over cocaine and narcotics traffic in the U.S. Much of the Harrison Act was aimed at controlling the rise of drug addiction. At first, the attitude of government officials was that it was best to permit the addicts continued access to the addicting drugs while, at the same time, trying to remove the supply by putting the pushers out of business. A few years later, in the late 1920s, the public sentiment changed and it was felt that addiction to drugs could be cured by abstinence—taking the supply of drugs away from the addicts. This meant cracking down on physicians who were supplying addicts with their drugs by writing prescriptions. Clearly, the emphasis on drug control was changing from viewing addiction as a medical problem to a law enforcement issue.

By 1930, law enforcement of drugs had become a major issue and Congress passed legislation that formed the Bureau of Narcotics within the Treasury Department. This moved control of drug abuse from the Agriculture Department to Treasury, again because of the tax issue. The Bureau of Narcotics stepped up law enforcement against illicit drugs, particularly opium, heroin, cocaine, and marijuana. At this time, anyone who wanted to buy, import, or sell any of these drugs had to register and pay a tax. Because marijuana was included, it was labeled a narcotic in all relevant federal laws, a label that stuck until the early 1970s. In 1956, the Narcotic Drug Control Act was passed by the Congress in reaction to testimony that indicated that postwar drug use had exploded and that half of all crime in cities in the U.S. was related to illegal drug use. Penalties for use and sales of drugs greatly increased. Stiff jail sentences went to all but first-time offenders and anyone who sold drugs to a minor faced the death penalty. This law also had another important feature. If a new drug came into the marketplace that had a potential for abuse, a recommendation to control it could be made by the Food and Drug Administration to the Secretary of Health, Education, and Welfare. Drugs such as amphetamines, barbiturates, and LSD were brought under control during this time. Rather than labeling them narcotics, they were referred to in the law as "dangerous drugs." The Bureau of Narcotics was changed to the Bureau of Narcotics and Dangerous Drugs and became the chief enforcer of the new laws. Congress passed the Comprehensive Controlled Substances Act of 1970. This law put all controlled substances in the federal realm. This meant that the federal government could prosecute anyone for a drug offense regardless of whether interstate trafficking was involved and irrespective of state laws. The **Comprehensive Controlled Substances Act** resulted in a number of major changes in drug enforcement in the U.S.:

- Control of drugs became a direct law enforcement activity, rather than registration and taxation.
- Enforcement was moved from the Treasury Department to the Justice Department and the Bureau of Narcotics and Dangerous Drugs became the **Drug Enforcement Administration (DEA)**.
- The decision on which drugs should be controlled rests with the Secretary of Health and Human Services, which delegates to the FDA the determination of which drugs should be controlled. In making decisions about whether a drug should be controlled, the FDA evaluates such factors as pharmacological effects, ability to induce psychological dependence or physical addiction, and whether there is any legitimate medical use for the substance (as defined and recognized by the FDA).
- Under this law, tobacco and alcohol products are excluded. Controlled drugs are put into five schedules. See Table 1 for a summary of the schedules and the drugs that are found in each one. More comprehensive information about the federal schedules can be found on the DEA website at: www.dea.gov/concern/abuse/chap1/contents.htm.

Today, the federal laws that regulate illicit drugs are in the Federal Code, Title 21 - Food and Drugs: Chapter 13: Drug Abuse Prevention And Control: www.deadiversion.usdoj.gov/21cfr/cfr/. Under these laws, many of the illicit drugs are termed controlled substances and are put in one of five schedules or categories. Most of the substances we define as illicit drugs are categorized in one of these schedules. With a few exceptions, all of the drugs that are in the same schedule have the same penalties for possession or distribution (sale). In some cases, penalties increase as the amount of illicit drug increases. So if someone possesses 50g (about 2 ounces) of cocaine, he or she gets a stiffer penalty than someone who possesses only one gram.

Determination of a Drug Schedule

Since the 1970 law put the responsibility of controlling drugs in federal hands, it became the responsibility of the U.S. Congress to determine which drugs fall into the five schedules and which schedule a particular drug should be in. In order to make these decisions, the Congress relies on experts to answer two questions:

1. Does the drug have a legitimate medical use in the United States?
2. What is its potential for abuse?

The first question is pretty easy to answer. Remember that the United States Food and Drug Administration decides whether a drug has a legitimate medical use, so Congress looks to that agency for guidance. The second question is a bit more difficult to answer. Several factors go into determining the potential for abuse of a particular drug. Is the drug addictive? Many drugs cause physical changes to take place in the body and after a time, the person becomes physically dependent on the drug. There is a constant craving that can only be satisfied by having the drug. After a while, *tolerance* builds up and it takes more and more of the drug to satisfy the craving. Heroin and a form of cocaine called *crack* are examples of physically addictive drugs. If you become addicted to a drug and then try and stop taking it, you will become sick. This sickness is called **withdrawal** and it can be very dangerous to the addict. Most people eventually recover from withdrawal, but the craving for the drug may last for years. Some illicit drugs don't cause physical dependence but do cause psychological dependence. The craving for the drug is there, but there is no withdrawal if the person suddenly stops taking the drug. Drugs that cause either physical or intense psychological dependence are said to have a high potential for abuse. Please see Chapter 18: Toxicology for a more detailed discussion of the issues of drug addiction, tolerance, and dependence. Other factors that contribute to the potential for abuse have to do with availability of the drug. If a drug is relatively cheap and easy to get or manufacture with minimal risk of getting caught, it tends to have a high potential for abuse. The way these two factors come into play in putting illicit drugs in particular schedules is summarized in Table 16.1.

As might be expected, drugs in Schedules I and II carry the most severe penalties. Possession or sale of one of these drugs can result in several years in prison and heavy fines. Once an illicit drug is placed in a federal schedule, it generally stays there. Movement in and out of the schedules is very rare and Congress must consider each action separately.

State Modifications of Controlled Substance Laws

Part of the Comprehensive Drug Control Act of 1970 provided that federal laws supersede state laws when controlling drugs. Nonetheless, states are permitted some latitude in fashioning their own drug control laws. For example, there is variation in what schedule a particular drug may be put in. This is common with marijuana.

TABLE 16.1
Federal Drug Schedules

<hr>

Schedule I

- The drug or other substance has a high potential for abuse.
- The drug or other substance has no currently accepted medical use in treatment in the United States.
- Some Schedule I substances are heroin, LSD, and marijuana.

Schedule II

- The drug or other substance has a high potential for abuse.
- The drug or other substance has a currently accepted medical use in treatment in the United States or a currently accepted medical use with severe restrictions.
- Abuse of the drug or other substance may lead to severe psychological or physical dependence.
- Schedule II substances include cocaine and methamphetamine.

Schedule III

- The drug or other substance has a lower potential for abuse than the drugs or other substances in Schedules I and II.
- The drug or other substance has a currently accepted medical use in treatment in the United States.
- Abuse of the drug or other substance may lead to moderate or low physical dependence or high psychological dependence.
- Anabolic steroids, and aspirin or Tylenol® containing codeine, are Schedule III substances.

Schedule IV

- The drug or other substance has a low potential for abuse relative to the drugs or other substances in Schedule III.
- The drug or other substance has a currently accepted medical use in treatment in the United States.
- Abuse of the drug or other substance may lead to limited physical dependence or psychological dependence relative to the drugs or other substances in Schedule III.
- Included in Schedule IV are Darvon®, Equanil®, and Valium®.

Schedule V

- The drug or other substance has a low potential for abuse relative to the drugs or other substances in Schedule IV.
- The drug or other substance has a currently accepted medical use in treatment in the United States.
- Abuse of the drug or other substance may lead to limited physical dependence or psychological dependence relative to the drugs or other substances in Schedule IV.
- Some over-the-counter cough medicines with codeine are classified in Schedule V.

In other cases, some states have more or fewer schedules. Penalties for possession, manufacture, and distribution also vary from state to state. When states have tried to legalize certain drugs or decriminalize them, however, the federal government has stepped in to prevent it and the courts have sided with the federal government over the states.

Classification of Illicit Drugs

Besides putting drugs in federal schedules, there are other ways to classify them that are more organized and that put similar drugs in the same class. For example, drugs can be classified by their origin. In this system, all illicit drugs would fall into one of three classes:

- Naturally occurring substances (e.g., marijuana, cocaine, morphine)
- Derived from a naturally occurring substance (heroin, made from morphine; LSD, made from lysergic acid)
- Synthetic (methamphetamine, PCP)

The most common method of classifying illicit drugs is by their major effects on a human being. This is the system used in this chapter. Under this scheme, there are four major classes of illicit drugs:

- Stimulants
- Depressants
- Narcotics
- Hallucinogens

Each of these classes will be discussed and some common examples will be given.

Stimulants

Central nervous system stimulants have the effects of elevating a person's mood, temporarily increasing energy levels, relieving some symptoms of depression, and stimulating people who are tired or lethargic. Their "street" or slang name is *uppers*. For the most part, stimulants are not physically addictive, but there are some exceptions. Many of them have powerful effects and can cause strong, intense psychological dependence. Two of the best examples of illicit stimulants are cocaine and methamphetamine.

Cocaine

The stimulant properties of cocaine have been known for centuries. It is a naturally occurring substance, derived from the *Erythoxylon coca* plant. Note that this is not the same as the *cocoa* plant from which chocolate is derived. The coca plant grows mainly in only one part of the world—the Amazon slopes of the Andes Mountains in South America. The epicenter of cocaine production in recent times has been Colombia. Figure 16.1 shows coca leaves.

Medically, cocaine is a topical anesthetic. This means that it causes numbness of any area of the body with which it comes in direct contact. It is still used in some

Figure 16.1 Coca leaves. Cocaine can be extracted directly from the leaves by chewing. Bits of seashell will enhance the extraction. Chemical extractions are done on a commercial basis.

medical procedures as an anesthetic, but has largely been replaced by other drugs. As a topical anesthetic, cocaine is similar to other drugs such as procaine (novocaine), which is used to numb the teeth and gums in dental procedures, and benzocaine, which is used to treat the pain of sunburn. Clearly, people don't abuse cocaine because it numbs their skin. For thousands of years, the indigenous farmers in the mountainous regions of South America have known that they could increase their energy and endurance by chewing on the leaves of the coca plant. Their saliva served to extract some of the cocaine from the leaves and this gave them a temporary stimulant high to enable them to do the arduous work of farming the hilly land. Later, many of these people chewed on bits of seashell with the coca leaves. This provided an alkaline environment in the mouth that made the extraction of the cocaine more efficient so the effects of the cocaine were increased and lasted longer. In the latter part of the nineteenth century and the early part of the twentieth, cocaine use as a stimulant increased in the United States. It was used in many elixirs, which are liquids that contain various medicinal and flavoring ingredients sold for particular medical purposes. In the early part of the twentieth century, some people sold these concoctions out of the backs of wagons and represented them as miracle cures. It is interesting to note that, when the federal government cracked down on elixirs containing cocaine and made the producers remove it, they substituted another legal stimulant, caffeine. Today, most cola soft drinks have caffeine in them—some used to have cocaine.

Preparation and Ingestion

Since cocaine is a naturally occurring substance, all that is necessary to abuse it is to extract it from coca leaves. The leaves are chopped up and dissolved in hot, alkaline water or an organic solvent. The cocaine is extracted from the leaves. Then another solvent containing hydrochloric acid is added that precipitates the purified cocaine. The powder that is produced is *cocaine hydrochloride*. This flaky white powder is sometimes called *snow* because it is so white and fluffy. It is also called *flake* or *blow*.

Cocaine is almost always diluted when sold to users. Typically, it is cut with an inert powder like sugar so that the final product is 20 to 50 percent pure. The most

Figure 16.2 (a) Cocaine flake (hydrochloride); (b) Crack cocaine. Crack is made from cocaine flake by treatment with an alkaline substance such as sodium bicarbonate.

common way of ingesting cocaine flake is by *snorting*. A line of cocaine is laid down on a flat surface such as a mirror. Then, using a tiny spoon or a straw, the cocaine is drawn up into the nose. The first sensation one gets from snorting coke is numbness in the nose—remember that cocaine is a topical anesthetic. After that, the cocaine high will occur within about thirty minutes and last an hour or so, depending on how much was snorted and user's experience with the drug. Because the cocaine has to pass through the nasal passages to the blood stream in order to be effective, some of it is blocked or chemically changed and never gets through, thus reducing the potency of the drug.

In the 1980s, a form of cocaine called *crack* became popular. Crack can be made from cocaine flake using household chemicals such as lye and cleaning fluid. Unlike cocaine flake, which is a fluffy powder, crack comes in the form of small rocks that are easily cracked or broken (hence the name). Also, unlike cocaine flake, crack is smoked using a small pipe. In this form, cocaine can be physically addictive because so much more of it gets into the blood stream through the lungs. For this reason, the federal government and many states attach more severe penalties for the possession of crack than for the same amount of flake. Interestingly, some people believe that the term "crack" comes from the Gaelic word *craic* which means "have a good time." Figure 16.2 shows crack and cocaine flake.

Methamphetamine

Methamphetamine and its cousin, amphetamine, have been popular illicit drugs for more than forty years. Both drugs have had legitimate medical uses in the United

Figure 16.3 A clandestine methamphetamine laboratory. Such a laboratory is very dangerous because of open, toxic chemical containers and flammable gases.

States and continue to do so. They are legally marketed as stimulants to relieve lethargy, drowsiness, and depression. Both have also been prescribed for hyperkinesia (over activity) and both have been used as appetite suppressants. Because they are so frequently abused, they are rarely produced for licit purposes any longer. For many years, methamphetamine and amphetamine were obtained by theft from pharmacies and warehouses, but today, these sources are so tightly controlled that most of the drugs, especially methamphetamine, are produced in home-made (clandestine) labs. In some places in the United States, "meth labs" have become practically an epidemic. Methamphetamine was nicknamed "speed" on the streets because of its powerful stimulant properties, especially when pure. High doses of this drug can cause death and, in the 1960s, the warning on the street was that "speed kills."

Preparation and Ingestion

The most popular method of preparation of methamphetamine uses an over-the-counter cold remedy called *pseudoephredine*. This drug is a very popular decongestant. In some places, people buy huge quantities of cold remedies and extract the pseudoephedrine so they can make methamphetamine. In some states, laws have been passed that require that cold remedies be kept behind a counter and that only small amounts can be sold to a person and that everyone who buys any quantity must show identification and sign for the drug. A second major ingredient for this method of preparation of methamphetamine is ammonia. Many farmers use pure, liquid, anhydrous ammonia as an ingredient in fertilizer and they keep large tanks on their property. Reports of thefts of large quantities of ammonia are on the rise all over the country. The other chemical needed for the synthesis is lithium, which can be extracted from some batteries. Methamphetamine production is becoming so popular in some areas of the country that law enforcement agents are at a loss to control it. Figure 16.3 shows a clandestine methamphetamine lab.

Depressants

In the 1960s and 1970s, **depressants** were much more popular illicit drugs than they are today. By far, the most popular depressants were the *barbiturates*. These are a whole family of drugs that have been prescribed to relieve anxiety, nervousness, and restlessness. They range from the very mild drug, such as phenobarbital, which was, at one time, an ingredient of some allergy medicines, to the very powerful types, such as pentobarbital and pentothiobarbital. The former is used to put very sick animals to sleep and has also been used as the lethal injection for some criminals who are sentenced to die. Pentothiobarbital, or sodium pentathol, is used as a general anesthetic that puts people to sleep during major surgery. The barbiturates are highly addictive drugs and are unusual in that sudden withdrawal, sometimes called "cold turkey withdrawal," can be fatal. Some people have gotten into vicious cycles with amphetamines and barbiturates where they take increasing doses of one to counteract the effects of the other. Some of the more potent barbiturates can cause death when taken with liquor. Accidental overdoses of alcohol and barbiturates caused the deaths of some celebrities including Janis Joplin and Jimi Hendrix. For the most part, barbiturates are not prescribed anymore because of their addictive nature and overdose danger. They have been replaced by other drugs such as Valium.

Hallucinogens

The most notorious of the illicit drugs are **hallucinogens**. These drugs cause audio and visual hallucinations, which mean that they cause people to see and hear things that aren't there. Some of the more popular hallucinogens are marijuana, LSD, mescaline, and psilocybin.

Marijuana

Marijuana has been called by many colorful names over the hundreds of years that it has been used. These include weed, hop, Mary Jane, toke, and many others. Marijuana is classified as a hallucinogen mainly because it doesn't fit in the other categories. It doesn't cause hallucinations to the degree that the other members of this group including LSD, some mushrooms, and some cactus extracts do. The effects are usually more of a mellowing out but there can be a wide range of effects depending on the person and how experienced he or she is with the drug. One of the more interesting effects of marijuana that has been widely reported is the munchies. Smoking marijuana apparently makes some users ravenously hungry.

Preparation and Ingestion

Marijuana is a plant belonging to the genus *Cannabis*. It grows virtually anywhere although warm and sunny conditions are favored. The leaves and flowers of the plant contain a number of naturally occurring substances that cause its psychological effects. The most important member of this group of chemicals has the tongue-twisting name of tetrahydrocannabinol or THC. The leaves and flowering parts are usually separated from the plant and dried in an oven. Then they are chopped up and rolled into cigarettes and smoked. Marijuana can also be ingested by baking it into a number of foods. Marijuana brownies have been popular for more than forty years. The higher the THC content, the more potent are the effects. Marijuana cigarettes may range from 1 percent THC on up. Genetically engineered marijuana with a THC content of nearly 40 percent has been reported! The stems, roots and seeds do not contain any appreciable quantities of THC. Figure 16.4 shows some marijuana leaves.

A number of preparations of marijuana have been made. Sometimes the pure resin is harvested from the flowering parts of the plant. This thick, sticky liquid has the highest THC content of any part of the plant. It is called hashish oil or hash oil. This is smoked in small pipes designed for this purpose. It is also common to take chopped up marijuana and extract it with a solvent. When the solvent is evaporated,

Figure 16.4 Marijuana leaf. These leaves always have an odd number of fronds.

Figure 16.5 Marijuana exhibits. The chunks in the dish on the right are pieces of hashish. The pipes are mostly home-made and are used to smoke the hashish.

a semisolid, cake-like material called hashish is left. This is formed into bricks and sold. To use it, a small piece is broken off and smoked it in a hash pipe or a "bong." Figure 16.5 shows some of the various forms of marijuana and devices used for smoking hashish. The large, brown chunks in the dish on the right side of the figure are pieces of hashish. Sometimes marijuana leaves are mixed with or coated with another drug such as **PCP.** This is called "wobble weed." PCP is itself a powerful hallucinogen. When mixed with marijuana and smoked, the effects are similar to strong, high quality marijuana. Many times marijuana buyers will pay for high quality weed, but get garden-variety marijuana laced with PCP.

Medical Marijuana?

In recent years, there have been reports that marijuana may be beneficial in treating certain diseases. For example, marijuana has been used to treat glaucoma, a progressive eye disease that eventually leads to blindness. It is caused by excessive pressure in the eye. There is some evidence that marijuana may stop the progress of the disease, but doesn't reverse it. Some cancer patients are treated with powerful drugs that seek to arrest the progress of the disease (chemotherapy). These drugs can destroy cancer cells but they also have serious side effects such as hair loss and extreme nausea. Because of this, many people on chemotherapy don't eat enough food. This causes them to become weaker and less able to cope with the disease. There is some evidence that marijuana may relieve the nausea symptoms for a short time, thus permitting the patients to eat. It is important to know that the Food and Drug Administration has not approved either of these medical uses for marijuana, in part because marijuana has not been subjected to the usual long, involved clinical testing necessary to establish that a drug has a legitimate use. People who want to use marijuana for medical purposes usually have to go to court to get an order that allows them to obtain it. Tablets containing the marijuana extract are then supplied by a federal government contractor.

LSD

Lysergic acid diethylamide (LSD) is probably the most potent hallucinogen. One small droplet (approximately fifty micrograms) can cause visual and auditory hallucinations that can last up to twelve hours. Because of its potency, it is taken in some unusual dosage forms. The most common form of LSD is called "blotter acid." LSD is diluted with a solvent and dripped onto blotter paper or other absorbent paper. The paper is cut into tiny squares that are then eaten. LSD has also been made into tiny tablets called "microdots" or other colorful names such as "orange sunshine" or "purple haze." It has even been mixed with gelatin and cut into small squares called "window panes." It has also been found on decals that kids lick and stick on their bodies. LSD can be absorbed through skin, so law enforcement agents and forensic chemists must be careful when handling it. See Figure 16.6 for various forms of blotter acid LSD.

Figure 16.6 "Blotter acid" forms of LSD. The LSD is dissolved in a liquid and poured on a paper that has been previously treated with the designs.

Figure 16.7 Peyote cactus buttons. These were seized in a raid in Virginia. More than three hundred buttons were found in a house.

Mescaline and Peyote

The peyote cactus can be found in the Southwestern part of the United States as well as parts of Mexico and other desert areas. For hundreds of years, some Native American tribes have used the buttons from this plant in their religious rites. The buttons contain a hallucinogenic drug called *mescaline*. The buttons are eaten and hallucinogenic symptoms start shortly thereafter. Because the buttons contain lots of plant material, they are often not well digested. The author of this book was once involved in a clandestine drug lab raid where more than two hundred buttons were found along with a blender and some cocoa powder. The perpetrator was apparently making mescaline milk shakes to try to avoid the nausea that comes from eating raw cactus buttons. Figure 16.7 shows some of the peyote cactus buttons that were seized in this raid.

Psilocybin

Remember *Alice in Wonderland* when Alice eats some mushrooms and grows really, really big and some other mushrooms make her really small? There are more than a dozen types of mushrooms that grow in the United States and can cause hallucinations. These mushrooms contain *psilocybin* and *psilocin*. These are relatively mild, short-acting hallucinogens. If one is not absolutely sure about what to look for, gathering and eating these mushrooms can be a bit like Russian roulette. Many mushrooms are very poisonous and attempts to get high could easily be fatal if the wrong ones are eaten. Figure 16.8 shows varieties of psilocybin mushrooms.

Narcotics

The term **narcotic** is often associated with illicit drugs and generally has a bad connotation in the United States. The word comes from the root *narco,* which means

Figure 16.8 Psilocybin mushrooms. At least fifteen varieties of mushrooms contain psilocybin. There are many poisonous look-alikes.

"sleep." All narcotics are powerful sleep-inducing, central nervous system depressants. In legal circles, the term "narcotic" refers to substances derived from the *opium poppy (Papaver somniferum)*. Remember *The Wizard of Oz*? On the way to Oz, Dorothy and her friends fall asleep while tramping through the poppy fields. This is because at the top of the poppy plant is a large pod that contains a gooey resin. For centuries people have been harvesting the dried resin and smoking it in opium dens. About 10 percent of this resin consists of *morphine* (named for Morpheus, the God of sleep). Morphine is a powerful narcotic. In addition to causing sleep, it exhibits the other major characteristic of narcotics; it relieves pain. Morphine is sometimes used as a pain reliever for people who have had major surgery or trauma. Another naturally occurring narcotic found in opium is *codeine*. It is less powerful than morphine. It is used mainly in treating coughs by depressing the nerves that trigger coughing. It is also mixed with Tylenol® for treatment of pain after minor surgery and toothaches.

Heroin

The most famous (or infamous) narcotic is *heroin*. Heroin is a semisynthetic substance made from morphine. Poppies grow mainly in the Far East and the raw opium is shipped to France where the morphine is extracted and converted to heroin, which is distributed all over the world. The movie *The French Connection* tells the story of the heroin trade in New York. The same dose of heroin is ten times stronger than morphine and is used in some countries for the same purpose as morphine. In this country, heroin has no accepted medical use and is in Schedule I. All narcotics are physically addictive, heroin especially so, and withdrawal symptoms can be quite severe, but seldom fatal.

Preparation and Ingestion

Heroin is sold on the street as a white or brown powder that is about 3 to 10 percent pure. The rest consists of cutting agents like sugars. Heroin is commonly ingested by injection with a syringe. This can cause problems beyond the heroin itself. Addicts have a habit of sharing needles and this is a good way to transmit blood-borne diseases such as AIDS and hepatitis. Typically, some of the powder is put in a small container such as a discarded bottle cap and water is added. The mixture is heated to dissolve the heroin and then the liquid is pulled into a syringe, filtering it through a small wad of cotton or similar material. Heroin addicts have telltale needle tracks on their arms and often find other places on their bodies to inject the drug to avoid detection.

In addition to morphine and codeine, there are other narcotics in opium, but they occur only in trace quantities. In recent years, many synthetic narcotics have been developed. These have similar properties to some of those naturally occurring, but with fewer side effects. The best known of these is methadone, which is used as a substitute for heroin for people who are trying to kick the habit. In the past few years, oxycontin has returned to the scene as a "rave" drug, used at large parties where lots of drugs and alcohol are consumed.

Analysis of Illicit Drugs

Agents of the United States **Drug Enforcement Administration (DEA)** as well as state and local police have personnel dedicated to lessening the flow of drugs into the United States and arresting people who possess or sell them to others. When these drugs are seized, they are sent to a crime lab where forensic drug chemists analyze them. A number of considerations determine how the drugs will be analyzed. These include:

- What the drug is and what form it is in.
- Is there a large amount of the drug in one package or in many packages?
- Is there a very small amount of the drug?
- Is the weight of the drug mixture a consideration?

Requirements for Analysis of Drugs

Any conclusion presented by a forensic scientist in a court or on a lab report must be scientifically reliable and defendable. This means that if a scientist identifies a white powder as containing cocaine, he or she must prove this *to a degree of reasonable scientific certainty*. This is the standard of proof in a court. There must be no reasonable alternative to the conclusion reached by the scientist. For this reason, most drug samples must have at least one confirmatory test performed. There are a number of protocols for the analysis of drugs. The one employed by a particular chemist depends on the lab, the caseload, and the instrumentation available. The international **Scientific Working Group on Drug Analysis (SWGDRUG)** (www.swgdrug.org) has developed standards and protocols for the analysis of common illicit drugs.

Schemes for Analysis for Drugs

In general, tests for drugs proceed from the general to the specific. Each test serves to give more information about the possible identity of the drug and either the scheme as a whole or a confirmatory test will positively identify the drug.

Screening Test

The most general test for drugs is called a **screening test**, sometimes called a spot test or a field test. There are screening tests for most of the common illicit drugs. Most of these tests consist of adding one or more chemical reagents to a pinch of the suspected drug and then observing one or more color changes. For example, the common screening test for marijuana involves three chemicals and the final color is purple. For cocaine, the test uses three chemicals and the final color is turquoise. The purpose of these tests is to narrow the possibilities for a drug sample. This can be especially important if the submitted sample is a white powder, which could be any of a number of things. Screening tests can be very important in leading the chemist toward the actual drug. It is important to emphasize that screening tests are never used to confirm the presence of a specific drug. For each screening test, there may be many substances that could give a positive reaction.

Separation Test

Very few illicit drug samples, especially powdered samples, are sold on the street in a pure form. Virtually all of them are diluted with one or more materials. This is done to maximize profits and minimize overdoses. Cocaine, for example, is often cut with sugars or other white powders. The same is true for heroin and methamphetamine. In order to eventually positively identify a drug, it must be separated from the cutting agents using a **separation test**. This can be done on a large scale using liquid solvents to extract the drug away from cutting agents. On a small scale, where only a small amount of the drug may be present, gas chromatography is used. For some drugs, liquid chromatography may be used. These techniques are discussed in Chapter 4. Figure 16.9 is a chromatogram of two drugs, caffeine and cocaine.

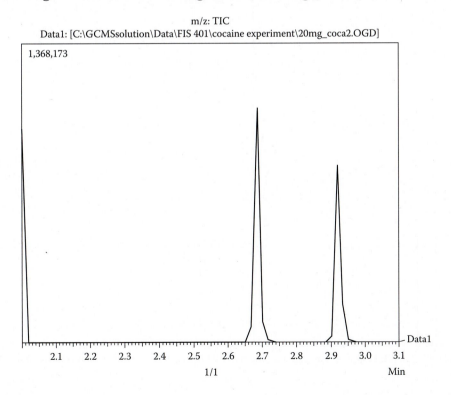

Figure 16.9 Gas chromatogram of caffeine (first peak) and cocaine (second peak). These are common stimulant drugs.

Confirmation Test

As mentioned above, most drug samples must be confirmed by a single test so that there is no uncertainty about the identity of the drug. In most crime labs, the **confirmation test** is mass spectrometry. This test is explained in Chapter 5. Figure 16.10 is a mass spectrum of cocaine.

One of the few drugs that doesn't normally require a confirmatory test is marijuana. This is because it is a plant that is easily recognized. The visual recognition of parts of the plant under a microscope is part of the protocol. Other tests, such as a screening test and perhaps a separation test, are usually done to isolate the THC and the protocol as a whole is considered to be confirmatory for marijuana.

Sometimes it is not possible to confirm the presence of a drug when there is so little drug present that there is not enough to complete the analysis. Examples of this might be testing the residue in a syringe for heroin or the dust in a straw for cocaine. In such cases, nondestructive tests are done first. Other tests would only be performed if enough of the drug was left to test further. Sometimes this partial scheme results in a report that gives only a qualified identification of the drug. Other times, the opposite problem arises when there is a very large amount of the drug in many packages. Decisions must be made as to how the packages will be

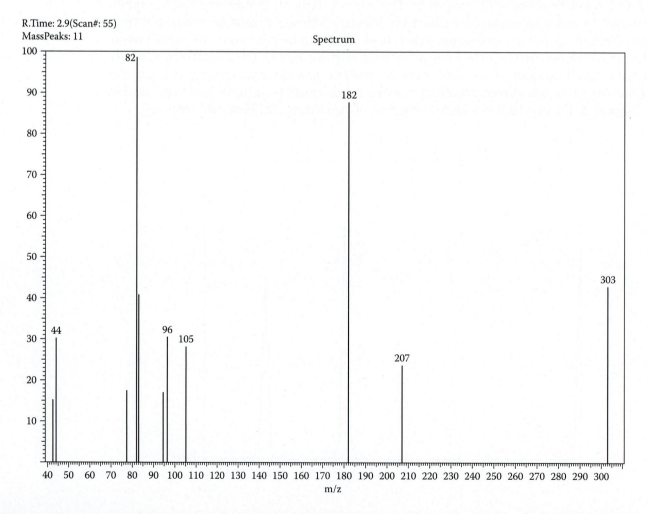

Figure 16.10 Mass spectrum of cocaine. The parent peak of m/e = 303 is the molecular weight of unfragmented cocaine. The base peak (most intense) is at m/e = 82.

sampled and tested and how many packages will be opened and tested. The author once had a case that consisted of 16,000 pounds of marijuana in 50-pound bricks. Samples of each of the 320 bricks were taken and tested. In another case, the author received 535 small packets containing suspected cocaine. All of them were opened and weighed and screened. All were about the same weight and responded the same to the screening test for cocaine. A portion of the packets were subjected to further testing to confirm the presence of the cocaine. This is permissible as long as representative samples are tested.

Summary

Illicit drugs are those that are either legitimately manufactured drugs taken for purposes other than what they were made for, or drugs that have no medical use and are taken solely for abuse purposes. Illicit drugs fall into four classes by major effects—stimulants, depressants, narcotics, and hallucinogens. The federal government controls many illicit drugs through laws that create five schedules that organize the drugs. These schedules regulate drugs by the presence or absence of a legitimate medical use and by their potential for abuse. Illicit drugs are analyzed by forensic chemists who develop protocols for analysis that take into account the form and quantity of the drug present as well as its purity. In most cases, a confirmatory test must be done on a drug sample to unequivocally identify it.

Test Yourself

Multiple Choice

1. Which of the following is *not* be an illicit drug?
   a. Aspirin
   b. Cocaine
   c. Heroin
   d. Tylenol with codeine
   e. LSD
2. A drug with a high potential for abuse and a legitimate medical use would most likely be put in federal schedule:
   a. 1
   b. 2
   c. 3
   d. 4
   e. 5
3. Heroin is classified as a:
   a. Stimulant
   b. Narcotic
   c. Steroid
   d. Hallucinogen
   e. Over-the-counter medicine
4. Marijuana:
   a. Comes from a plant

    b. Is totally synthetic

    c. Is chemically made from another drug

    d. Is a plant

    e. Is usually injected with a syringe and needle

5. If a forensic chemist receives only a very small amount of a drug:

    a. She won't analyze it at all

    b. She will do nondestructive tests first

    c. She will do only the confirmatory test

    d. She will do only one test and then stop

    e. She will analyze the drug but won't write a report of her findings

6. SWGDRUG is:

    a. A confirmatory test for illicit drugs

    b. A liquid form of cocaine

    c. An international committee that set standards for the analysis of drugs

    d. The federal agency with the responsibility for arresting drug traffickers.

7. Which of the following is *not* classified as an hallucinogen?

    a. Marijuana

    b. Methadone

    c. Psilocybin

    d. LSD

    e. Mescaline

8. If a new drug were discovered that had a high potential for abuse and no accepted medical use, it would most likely be put in schedule:

    a. 5

    b. 1

    c. 2

    d. 6

    e. It wouldn't be in a schedule

9. If a chemist received a case that contained 1,000 small baggies of a tan powder, all in the same type of packaging and with all about the same weight of powder, which scheme should she use to test these?

    a. Run all tests on all 1,000 packets

    b. Run a field test on all 1,000 packets and then confirm the identity of one sample

    c. Combine the powders from all 1,000 packets and run one set of tests

    d. Take a representative sample of the packets and run the tests on them

    e. Pick out one sample of the 1,000 at random and run all tests on it

10. Which of the following drugs does not require a confirmatory test:

    a. Cocaine

    b. Heroin

    c. Marijuana

    d. PCP

    e. None of the above

True or False

11. Mass spectrometry is a confirmatory test for drugs.

12. Most street drugs are relatively pure and separation tests are seldom needed.

13. Prescription drugs are not put in any federal schedule.

14. State drug laws must be exactly the same as federal drug laws.

15. LSD is considered to be the most powerful of the hallucinogenic drugs.
16. Cocaine is a naturally occurring substance found in the poppy plant.
17. Marijuana analysis does not normally require a confirmatory test.

Matching

18. Hash oil	a. Naturally occurring drug from poppy plant
19. Mescaline	b. Synthetic hallucinogen
20. Morphine	c. Synthetic narcotic
21. PCP	d. Preparation of marijuana
22. Methadone	e. Naturally occurring drug from cactus

Short Essay

23. Name and describe the two criteria used for the classification of drugs into a federal schedule. Who has the ultimate responsibility for adding drugs to a schedule?
24. Go to the following website: www.dea.gov/pubs/abuse/index.htm. Use the information in the publication *Drugs of Abuse* published by the DEA to find the following information:
    a. What schedule is marijuana in?
    b. What schedule is cocaine in?

Further Reading

Siegel, J. *Analysis of Illicit Drugs*. Ed. R. Saferstein. Handbook of Forensic Science. Vol 2. 2nd ed. Upper Saddle River, NJ: Prentice-Hall, 2004.
Liu, R. H. and D. E. Gadzala. *Handbook of Drug Analysis: Applications in Forensic and Clinical Laboratories*. Washington, DC: American Chemical Society, 1997.
Smith, F. *Handbook of Forensic Drug Analysis*. San Diego, CA: Academic Press, 2004.

On the Web

SWGDRUG, the scientific working group on drug analysis: www.swgdrug.org.
Careers in forensic drug analysis: www.forensiccareers.com/index.php?option=com_content &task=view&id=27&Itemid=30.
Powerpoint presentation on forensic drug analysis www7.nationalacademies.org/stl/ April%20Forensic%20Bono.pdf.

17
Forensic Toxicology

Learning Objectives

1. To be able to define forensic toxicology
2. To be able to define and give examples of absorption, metabolism, elimination, metabolite
3. To be able to describe the major effects on the rate of absorption of alcohol from the stomach into the blood stream
4. To be able to describe the major metabolites of alcohol
5. To be able to describe the major effects on the rate of elimination of alcohol from the bloodstream
6. To be able to draw and describe a Widmark curve
7. To be able to describe the major effects of alcohol on the body
8. To be able to describe the major methods of measuring blood and breath alcohol

Chapter 17
Forensic Toxicology

Chapter Outline

Mini Glossary

Addiction: Physical effects of a drug on a person manifested by an extreme craving for the drug. If deprived of the drug, withdrawal will set in.

Deciliter: One-tenth of a liter or 100 mL.

Dependence: A psychological phenomenon. Any physical changes that may accompany regular use of a drug are insufficient to cause addiction. There may still be a powerful craving for the drug, but failure to take the drug does not cause withdrawal.

Enteric dosage form: Form of a drug that is made to be released over time in the bloodstream.

Forensic toxicology: The legal application of toxicology as well as other scientific disciplines such as analytical chemistry and clinical chemistry to criminal and civil cases, including drug use, medicolegal investigation of death, and poisoning.

Half life: The time it takes for the concentration of a drug in the body to be reduced by 50 percent.

Horizontal gaze nystagmus: Movement of the eyeball as an object is passed slowly in front of the eyes horizontally.

Implied consent: Permission to submit to a drunk driving alcohol test that you give when you sign your driver's license.

Metabolite: The action of the liver on a drug to change it into a different substance that is generally less harmful and easier to eliminate from the body.

Oxidation–reduction reaction: Electrons are moved from one substance to another, changing the valence state of one or more atoms.

Pharmacology: The study of drugs and all of their harmful and beneficial effects on living things.

Proof: A measure of alcohol concentration in hard liquors. It is equal to twice the percentage of alcohol in the drink.

Synergism: Magnified effects from a combination of similarly acting drugs.

Tolerance: Occurs when increasing doses are required to maintain the same level of effect as the original dose.

Toxicology: The study of the harmful effects of drugs and poisons on living things.

Withdrawal: A syndrome; a set of reactions to the lack of a drug. The symptoms include sleeplessness, restlessness, nausea, hallucinations, headaches, and other pain. Withdrawal can last for days or even weeks.

Acronyms

BAC: Blood alcohol concentration
Redox: Oxidation–reduction reaction

Introduction

Janis Joplin, a famous 1960s and 1970s rock star, died of an overdose of heroin, possibly complicated by alcohol. Jimi Hendrix, another famous rock star of the same era, died of an accidental overdose of barbiturates. The website **www.av1611.org/rockdead.html** lists forty rock stars who died from drug overdoses. The website **http://en.wikipedia.org/wiki/List_of_drug-related_deaths** has an alphabetical list of noted people from all walks of life who died from drug-related causes.

In some of these cases, drugs were combined with alcohol to cause death, often accidental. In Chapter 16: Illicit Drugs, we learned that central nervous system depressants are one of the four major types of abused drugs. Alcohol is also a central nervous system depressant, although it works somewhat differently than the drugs. It is not too difficult to accidentally overdose on this combination, when someone takes depressants that, by themselves, wouldn't be lethal and drinking an amount of alcohol that, likewise, wouldn't be lethal by itself. As we shall see in this chapter drugs can combine their effects to cause overall effects that are greater than the sum of the individual effects. This can result in an accidental (or deliberate) overdose.

Chapter 16 covered illicit drugs seized from drug users and sellers on the street. The major categories and effects of these substances were discussed. Of course, the effects that drugs have on a particular person depend on the physical and emotional traits of the person as well as the amount and strength of the drug and the frequency it is taken by the user. This chapter is concerned with the fate of these drugs when they are ingested. First, the general principles of pharmacology are covered. These include the methods of ingestion of drugs, how they get into the blood stream and then to the various organs in the body, how they are treated chemically in the body, and how they are eliminated. Then the particular example of ethyl alcohol (spirits) will be used to illustrate these principles. Although alcohol is not classified as an illicit drug, its behavior in the human body provides an excellent example of how drugs in general are handled. In addition to the toxicology of alcohol, its chemical analysis for the purpose of drunk driving enforcement is also discussed. More than half of the cases that forensic toxicologists receive in public crime laboratories are concerned with drunk driving, so it is appropriate that we focus on alcohol.

Forensic Toxicology

Toxicology is the study of the harmful effects of drugs and poisons on living things. It includes the study of symptoms, mechanisms, treatment, and detection of these drugs and poisons. If the use of drugs and poisons results in death under suspicious circumstances, it becomes **forensic toxicology**. Toxicology is a branch of the science of **pharmacology**. Pharmacology is the study of all of the interactions of drugs and similar substances on living beings. Pharmacology involves the administration of drugs, absorption into the body, actions and interactions, metabolism and elimination. The relationships between toxicology, pharmacology, and forensic toxicology are illustrated in Figure 17.1.

Becoming a Forensic Toxicologist

A great deal of what forensic toxicologists do is to measure the concentrations of drugs and poisons in various body fluids and substances such as blood, urine, and breath. This is done in some cases on living humans, as in drunk driving cases, or on people who have died under circumstances when the coroner or medical examiner has to determine the cause and manner of death. These measurements are a type of analytical chemistry and so much of what forensic toxicologists have to know is chemistry. A good preparation for becoming a forensic toxicologist is a bachelor's degree in chemistry. Some universities also offer bachelor's degrees in clinical chemistry or in toxicology, although these are more often offered at the graduate level. With a bachelor's degree, a scientist is qualified to make measurements of drug, poison, and alcohol levels in a body, but not qualified to interpret these levels in terms of their contribution to a death. In order to make these determinations, a scientist must be educated in pharmacology and toxicology. This normally requires a Ph.D. in one of those fields. A Ph.D. in chemistry is normally not specific enough, unless it

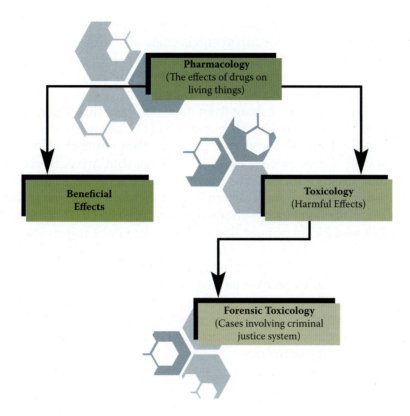

Figure 17.1. Relationships between pharmacology and toxicology and forensic toxicology. *Courtesy of* Meredith Haddon.

is in clinical chemistry. A forensic toxicologist with a Ph.D. may be certified by the American Board of Forensic Toxicology (www.abft.org). A bachelor's level toxicologist may be certified as a forensic toxicologist specialist.

Principles of Pharmacology

In Chapter 16, the term "drug" was defined as a substance designed to have specific physical and/or emotional effects on living things. Licit drugs are manufactured to have beneficial effects. Poisons, by definition, have harmful effects. Some drugs, if taken inappropriately or in combination with other drugs or in high doses, can have harmful effects and a person can be poisoned by them. Pharmacologists study all sorts of drugs and poisons. They learn what happens to a drug when it is taken and what effects it has on organisms.

This chapter is concerned mainly with what happens to a drug when it is taken. This branch of pharmacology is called *pharmacodynamics*. It includes methods of ingestion of a drug, how it is absorbed into the bloodstream and other parts of the body, how it is distributed throughout the body, how it is changed (metabolized) into other substances, and how it is eliminated.

Drug Intake

Drugs can be administered in a number of ways. These include swallowing a powder, tablet, or capsule, or dissolving a powder in water and then drinking it. Liquids and vapors may be inhaled through the nose. Sometimes drugs are taken via an intramuscular, subcutaneous, or intravenous injection with a syringe and needle. The best method of ingestion for a particular drug depends on how it interacts with organs such as the stomach and how quickly the drug needs to be absorbed and distributed. If a drug is destroyed by stomach acids, the oral route of ingestion must be avoided. In order to prevent a drug from dissolving too quickly in the stomach or small intestine, it may be coated with a material that slows dissolution of the drug or it may come in the form of tiny coated particles that enter the blood stream over a long period of time (timed release capsules). Drugs that are protected in this way are called **enteric dosage forms**. The route of ingestion will also affect the rate the drug enters the blood stream. As is shown later, this has a profound influence on the effects of the drug. Intravenous injections directly into the blood stream provide the fastest route, followed by intramuscular and subcutaneous injections. Oral administration is normally the slowest means of getting a drug into the blood stream. Occasionally drugs enter the body via unusual routes. One of the most popular ways of ingesting cocaine used to be by snorting or inhaling through the nose. Now the most popular method of taking cocaine and some other drugs such as marijuana is by smoking it in a pipe or, in the case of marijuana leaf, by rolling it into cigarettes. Some drugs that are designed to act on the digestive system or intestines are administered anally (suppositories).

Absorption

Once the drug as enters the body, it is absorbed into the blood stream. If the drug is a vapor and is inhaled into the lungs, it will eventually enter the blood through tiny capillaries that are in contact with the smallest sacs in the lungs, known as *alveoli*. Figure 17.2 shows the structure of a human lung, including alveoli.

Drugs introduced via intramuscular or subcutaneous injection enter the blood stream through capillaries present in muscle or skin tissue. If the drug is taken orally, it will first enter the stomach. It may then pass through the stomach through the *pyloris* (a valve that connects the stomach to the small intestine and then into the small intestine). Some drugs are absorbed into the blood stream from the stomach, some from the small intestine, and some are absorbed in both places. Figure 17.3 shows the stomach and small intestine.

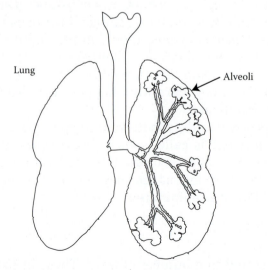

Figure 17.2 The human lung showing alveoli. *Courtesy of* Richard Li.

As an example, a 140 lb female wants to know how many ounces of liquor she can drink so that her BAC will just reach 0.08, the level at which she would be considered intoxicated in most states.

$$Wgt = 140, \quad BAC = 0.08$$

$$Volume = \frac{140 \times 0.08}{4.67}$$

$$Volume = 2.4 \text{ oz}$$

One shot of whiskey contains about 1.25 oz, so this woman will be intoxicated after two drinks. If she is drinking wine, 10 oz would do the job, assuming that the wine contains 12 percent alcohol. If she is drinking beer, with an alcohol concentration of about 6 percent, she could drink 20 oz of beer and her BAC would be 0.08. That is not even two beers!

Something for You to Do

Using the above equations, calculate how much 100 proof liquor, wine, and beer a man would have to drink in order to reach a level of 0.08 BAC. Then do the same calculation for yourself, using your own weight. You don't have to hand this in so be honest about your weight!

Drunk Driving Laws

Every state has a set of laws that seek to control drunk driving and punish people who drive while intoxicated. This starts when a person applies for a driver's license. When you sign your license, you are giving **implied consent** that you will submit to a blood or breath test if you are stopped for drunk driving. Refusal to submit to the test when requested by a law enforcement agent may result in your losing your license to drive, whether or not you are subsequently found to be intoxicated. The action to take your license is handled by the Bureau of Motor Vehicles or Secretary of State as an administrative procedure. The length of time you lose your license is usually between 90 and 180 days.

Testing Alcohol Levels

Most states use a breath-testing instrument to obtain an alcohol level in the field. The venerable breathalyzer is still used in many places, although it is being gradually replaced by portable breath testers. Breathalyzers work by a type of chemical reaction called oxidation–reduction (redox). In this type of reaction, electrons are moved from one substance to another, changing the valence state of one or more atoms. In the redox reaction that is the heart of the breathalyzer, alcohol participates in the reaction. The major reaction is given below:

$$2K_2Cr_2O_7 + 3CH_3CH_2OH + 8H_2SO_4 \rightarrow 2Cr_2(SO_4)_3 + 2K_2SO_4 + 3CH_3OOH + 11H_2O$$

potassium dichromate (orange)   ethanol   sulfuric acid   chromium sulfate (green)   potassium sulfate   acetic acid   water

The solution without alcohol starts out orange owing to the potassium dichromate. As alcohol is added, it changes the potassium dichromate to chromium sulfate, which is green. A spectrophotometer is used to measure the loss of the orange color. This loss is proportional to the amount of ethanol present. The subject introduces the alcohol into the instrument by breathing into a tube connected to the breathalyzer.

Newer breath testing instruments use fuel cell technology whereby the alcohol is part of a fuel cell that produces electricity. The more alcohol that is present, the more electricity is produced. Other instruments measure the amount of infrared light absorbed by alcohol. In most cases, the breath alcohol concentration measured by these instruments can be converted to BAC internally using the experimentally determined 210:1 ratio (210 liters of breath contain the same amount of alcohol as one deciliter of blood).

Once a BAC level is determined in the field, how is it interpreted? How does the police officer or toxicologist know where on the Widmark curve the measurement is? This can be an important consideration in many drunk driving cases as can be seen in the following example.

A driver is stopped for operating a vehicle while intoxicated. The officer administers a breath test and determines that the BAC is 0.06. The driver was seen leaving a bar two hours prior to the stop. If the toxicologist uses the rate of elimination, figure of 0.015 percent per hour and back-calculates two hours previously, the driver's BAC must have been 0.09 when he left the bar. (How did he arrive at this number?) That means that the driver was intoxicated when he left the bar and got behind the wheel because the law defines intoxication as a BAC of 0.08 or above.

Can the driver be prosecuted for operating a motor vehicle while intoxicated? There are some prosecutors who will prosecute this as an intoxication case if they can get a toxicologist to testify to this back-calculation. Most toxicologists are wary of doing this because of the assumptions that have to be made. The most important one is that the rate of elimination is exactly 0.015 percent in every person. This is known to be not accurate. It could be higher or lower in a particular case. The only way to find out would be to take a series of BAC or breath alcohol measurements over time on that particular person. In some states, there is a provision for charging a driver with being *impaired* rather than intoxicated in cases where the BAC is over 0.05 percent but less than 0.08 percent when the driver is stopped.

Field Sobriety Testing

Although drunk driving laws in most states require only that the driver's BAC be over the limit in order to sustain a charge of operating a vehicle while intoxicated, sometimes officers want to document the impaired behavior of the driver when the driver is stopped. Many states have adopted a field sobriety testing program that was first developed in California. Officers who administer the suite of tests are specially trained and certified. The suite includes three tests and all must be taken.

- **Walk and turn:** The subject must walk in a straight line putting one foot directly in front of the other with the toe of one foot touching the heel of the other. People who are intoxicated will not be able to walk in a straight line and may lose their balance.
- **Stand on one foot:** The subject must lift one foot and stand on the other for a period of time. People who are intoxicated will not be able to keep one foot off the ground or will lose their balance

- **Horizontal gaze nystagmus:** The officer holds a pencil or similar object about 12 inches in front of the subject's face at eye level. The officer then moves the pencil across the field of view of the subject, instructing the subject to keep his head still and follow the pencil only with his eyes. The eyes of a sober person will move smoothly as he follows the pencil back and forth. The eyes of an intoxicated person will travel with jerky movements when trying to follow the pencil.

In states that recognize the field sobriety testing program, the results of the tests are admissible in court as evidence of impairment. Many illicit drugs will also elicit similar responses to those of ethanol. If a person is driving erratically and stopped for drunk driving and a breath-testing instrument indicates that the subject wasn't drinking, the field sobriety testing program can show that the subject was under the influence of an illicit drug.

Measurement of BAC

Drunk driving cases represent more than half of the case load of forensic toxicologists nationwide. Even though the results of a breath test may be admissible in court as evidence of intoxication, many prosecutors require that a blood test be done to directly measure BAC. Some forensic science labs get dozens of blood samples each day from people suspected of driving while intoxicated. These people are taken to a hospital or clinic and have their blood drawn by a professional phlebotomist. The blood is then sent to the crime lab. The most popular method of BAC analysis in a forensic science lab is by gas chromatography using headspace analysis. The tube containing the blood is heated slightly and a gas-tight syringe is inserted and a sample of the vapor above the blood is withdrawn and injected into a gas chromatograph. An internal standard is also put in the tube to help in the quantitative analysis of the alcohol in the blood. An automatic sampler is often used so that many blood samples can be run automatically overnight. A computer calculates the amount of ethanol present. The next day the toxicologist interprets the findings and writes the reports.

Summary

Pharmacology is the study of the effects of drugs and poisons on living organisms. Forensic toxicologists determine the presence and amounts of drugs and poisons in people and interpret their effects. They study the ingestion, absorption, and elimination of drugs from the body. They also have to be aware of synergistic effects and tolerance. In order to properly interpret findings about drugs, the toxicologist must know the subject's drug history including any addictions or drug dependencies. The most commonly abused substance is ethyl alcohol, or ethanol. More than half of the caseload of forensic toxicologists is in drunk driving cases. The blood alcohol concentration is affected by the type of drinks, the amount of alcohol, how fast it is ingested, and what is in the stomach at the time of ingestion. Ethanol is a central nervous depressant and neurotoxin. It is eliminated from the body mainly by metabolism and excretion in the urine. The concentration of ethanol can be measured either in blood or breath. Field sobriety testing is also used as additional evidence of impairment.

Test Yourself

Multiple Choice

1. Which of the following is not a metabolite of ethanol?
   a. Acetaldehyde
   b. Acetone
   c. Acetic acid
   d. All of the above are metabolites of alcohol
2. Most drugs and ethanol are eliminated from the body mainly by:
   a. Breathing
   b. Sweating
   c. Metabolism followed by excretion in the urine
   d. Decomposition by the kidneys
3. Synergism takes place when:
   a. Someone becomes addicted to a drug
   b. A person has to take larger doses of a drug to get the same effects
   c. A drug is metabolized into two different substances
   d. Two drugs are taken at once and their effects magnify each other
4. When a person builds up tolerance to a drug it means that:
   a. He must take larger doses to continue to realize the same effects
   b. He will undergo withdrawal if he stops taking the drug
   c. He will no longer be affected by the drug
   d. He must stop taking the drug right away
5. Which of the following is not used in field sobriety testing?
   a. Walk and turn
   b. Count backward from 100
   c. Horizontal gaze nystagmus
   d. Stand on one foot
6. Which of the following would not affect the rate of absorption of ethanol into the blood stream?
   a. How fast you drink
   b. The concentration of alcohol in the drink
   c. What is in the stomach at the time of drinking
   d. How soon before drinking you exercised
7. The Widmark curve displays:
   a. The relationship between absorption and metabolism
   b. The blood alcohol level as a function of time
   c. The blood alcohol level as a function of metabolic rate
   d. The ratio between the amount of alcohol eliminated by metabolism to the amount eliminated by respiration
8. Synergism is:
   a. A form of metabolism in the liver
   b. The buildup of drugs in fatty tissue

   c. The travel of drugs from the stomach to small intestine

   d. The magnification of the effects of two or more drugs that have similar actions

9. Tolerance is:

   a. The need for ever-increasing amounts of a drug

   b. The elimination of a drug directly through the urine without passing through the liver

   c. A measure of the activity of a drug on the brain

   d. Slowing absorption of a drug into the bloodstream by the presence of food in the stomach

10. The most common surrogate for brain alcohol measurement in drunk driving cases is:

   a. Blood

   b. Breath

   c. Urine

   d. Vitreous humor

True or False

11. Stopping use of an addictive drug will bring on symptoms of withdrawal.

12. If you are stopped for driving while intoxicated and you refuse to take a sobriety test you can lose your drivers' license anyway.

13. The LD_{50} of alcohol is about 0.4 g/dL.

14. Marijuana is believed to exhibit a reverse tolerance effect at times.

15. The half life of a drug is the time it takes to reduce its concentration in blood by 50 percent.

16. The LD_{50} of a drug is the concentration of the drug that causes death in half the people who take that amount.

17. The amount of alcohol in the bloodstream that constitutes being under the influence in drunk driving cases is 1.0 g/dL.

Matching

18. Toxicology   a. Time it takes to decrease drug concentration by 50 percent

19. Pharmacology   b. Substance that liver converts alcohol into

20. Metabolism   c. Study of harmful effects of drug and poisons

21. Acetaldehyde   d. Study of all effects of drugs

22. Half-life   e. Action of liver on drugs

Short Essay

23. What is the Widmark curve? What does it tell you about blood alcohol concentration?

24. What are the major methods for analyzing alcohol in blood? Which one(s) can be used at the scene?

25. What is synergism? How does it work?

Further Reading

Garriott, J. C., ed. *Medicolegal Aspects of Alcohol*. 3rd ed. Tucson, AZ: Lawyers and Judges Publishing Co., 1996
Levine, B, ed. *Principles of Forensic Toxicology*. Washington, DC: AACC Press, 1999.

On the Web

Overview of forensic toxicology http://en.wikipedia.org/wiki/Forensic_toxicology.
Comprehensive list of forensic toxicology web sites http://home.lightspeed.net/~abarbour/vlibft.html.
Society of Forensic Toxicologists www.soft-tox.org.
American Board of Forensic Toxicologists, which offers certification of forensic toxicologists www.abft.org.

18

Fibers, Paints, and Other Polymers

Learning Objectives

1. To be able to define a monomer and polymer
2. To be able to describe the types of evidence that are polymer based
3. To be able to define paint
4. To be able to describe the different types of paint by end use
5. To be able to describe how paint evidence is encountered, collected, and preserved
6. To be able to describe the common methods of analysis of paint
7. To be able to describe the different types of fibers
8. To be able to describe the common types of natural fibers
9. To be able to describe the common types of synthetic fibers
10. To be able to describe how fiber evidence is encountered, collected, and preserved
11. To be able to describe the common methods of analysis of fibers
12. To be able to describe how other types of polymer-based evidence are analyzed

Chapter 18

Fibers, Paints, and Other Polymers

Chapter Outline

Mini Glossary

Clearcoat: The final layer of paint applied to an automobile that adds durability and ultraviolet protection to the colored paint layer.

Dye: Generally organic substances that bind to fiber and absorb various wavelengths of light, producing a colored appearance.

Fracture match: Matching broken objects to the original source.

FTIR: Acronym for Fourier transform infrared spectrophotometry. FTIR microscopy is used to analyze the composition of small objects.

Metamerism: The quality of some colors that causes them to appear differently under different light sources. For instance, two color samples may look identical in natural light, but not in artificial light.

Monomer: Single repeating units of molecules.

Natural fiber: A fiber that exists in nature. Natural fibers can come from animals, plants, or minerals.

Pigment: Mostly inorganic particles, small in size and insoluble; they suspend in the chemical mixture of a fiber and absorb different wavelengths of light.

Polymer: Long chains of repeating molecular units or long chains of monomers.

Primer: The primer layer is the coating layer applied to the unpainted automobile—the first layer applied after the bare metal has been treated for rust.

PyGC: An acronym for pyrolysis gas chromatography, an instrumental technique used to analyze the chemical compositions of small amounts of evidence.

Refractive index (RI): A number that represents the ratio between the speed of light in air to the speed of light in the medium analyzed.

Semisynthetic fiber: A fiber that is sourced to a natural, nonfibrous material but undergoes chemical processing to produce a fiber.

Synthetic fiber: Fibers that are man-made chemical compounds formed into predetermined fiber shapes by extrusion from a machine.

Tear match: Two materials that have been ripped in pieces that can be shown to match based on examination (usually microscopically) of the patterns.

Topcoat: The coating layer for an automobile that imparts the color to the vehicle.

Introduction

On July 28, 1979, a woman hunting for empty cans and bottles along an Atlanta, Georgia roadside stumbled upon a pair of dead African American males. One had been shot and the coroner later determined that the other had been choked to death. Both had been reported missing for about a week. Thus began the investigation of a string of homicides of young, black males in the Atlanta area. Ultimately, Wayne Bertram Williams was blamed for 23 of 30 homicides. He was convicted of the deaths of two of them—both adult ex-convicts. Williams became a suspect when officers starting staking out bridges over the Chattahoochee River because several of the victims had been dumped into the river. On May 22, 1981, an officer heard a splash in the water. At the same time, a car drove across the bridge near where the officer was stationed. He radioed to FBI and police nearby who stopped Williams and then interrogated him for over two hours and then released him. On June 21, Williams was arrested and charged with the murders of Nathaniel Carter and Jimmy Payne.

Since there were no witnesses to the killings, no fingerprints on the bodies, and DNA typing had not yet been developed, trace evidence became very important in this case. Dog hairs that matched Wayne Williams' dog and carpet fibers that matched known fibers from his car and office were found on a number of the victims. The FBI took great pains to research the fibers from Williams' office.

They traced the fibers back to the manufacturer and followed the trail to carpet manufacturers who used the fibers to make carpets. They determined how many yards of carpeting were made from this type of fiber and estimated how many yards were sold in Atlanta. They also made estimates of the number of rooms in homes and apartments in the Atlanta area and, from that, estimated the likelihood that a room contained a carpet of the same type as Wayne Williams' office. They were able to testify that the fibers in Wayne Williams' office were rare and that the fibers of this type found on the victims were likely to have come from his office. Williams was subsequently convicted of the murders and is currently serving a life sentence in prison.

This chapter covers several types of forensic evidence. They may seem to be different from each other, but they share a common characteristic; they are all **polymers**. This means that they have a special chemical structure that dictates how they will be analyzed. The major types of polymer evidence are paints, other coatings, and textile fibers. There are also less frequently encountered polymers such as plastics, rubbers, and paint-like products such as varnishes, shellacs, stains, and even some types of inks. Human and animal hairs are also polymers, but they are different enough from the other types of polymer evidence that they will be covered in a separate chapter.

What Is a Polymer?

Most substances are arranged in relatively small, discrete molecules. They tend to have relatively low boiling and melting points (except for metals). There is a class of materials that exist as long chains of repeating molecular units. These chains are called polymers. The repeating units are called **monomers**. The general structure of polymers is shown in Figure 18.1.

Figure 18.2 a shows a substance called styrene. When it polymerizes, it forms long, repeating units called polystyrene, also shown in Figure 18.2. The part of the molecule inside the parentheses is the repeating unit. Polystyrene is a common plastic and also a member of a subclass of polymers called *homopolymers*. These are

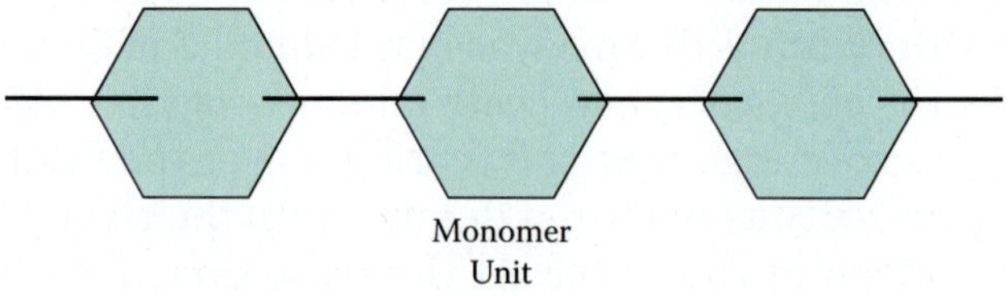

Monomer
Unit

Figure 18.1 General chemical structure of a polymer.

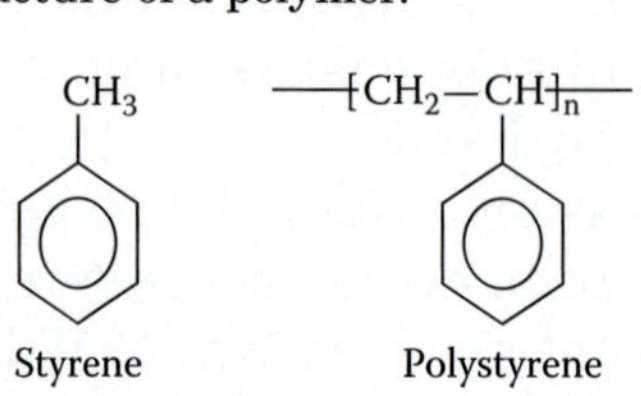

Styrene   Polystyrene

Figure 18.2 The chemical structure of styrene and polystyrene.

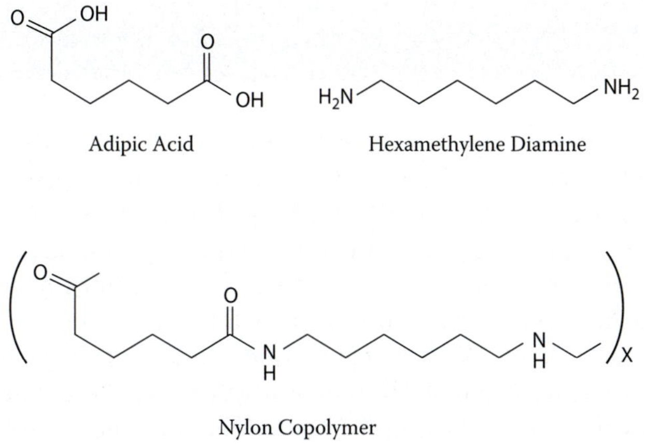

Adipic Acid   Hexamethylene Diamine

Nylon Copolymer

Figure 18.3 The chemical structure of one of the nylon polymers.

polymers with only one repeating unit. Because of this, few modifications can easily be made to the polymer and therefore, few subgroups are possible.

Some polymers use two (or more) monomers to construct a polymer. These are called *copolymers*. An example of a copolymer is *nylon*. The term nylon actually refers to a family of polymers. There are currently more than forty different types of nylon being commercially manufactured. One of the common types of nylon is nylon 66. This is made up of alternating monomers. One of them is *adipic acid*, a diacid containing six carbons. The other monomer is *hexamethylene diamine*, a diamine containing six carbons. The two monomers react by a process known as condensation. A molecule of adipic acid loses an OH group and the diamine loses an H. Water is formed and the two molecules combine to form an *amide*. This is shown in Figure 18.3.

Finally, there are *block polymers*. These contain blocks of similar monomers that repeat. Polymers form long chains of monomers and are fibrous in shape. They are ideal for use as textile fibers. If the polymer is to be used to make sheets as in plastics, rubber, or paints, the polymer strands are *cross-linked*. These cross-links are small molecules that attach two strands together as shown diagrammatically in Figure 18.4.

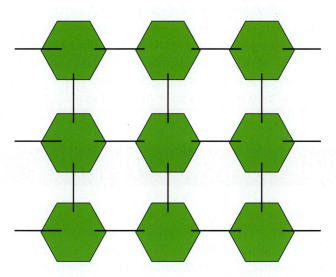

Figure 18.4 Cross-linking of polymers to form two-dimensional films.

Textile Fibers

Textile fibers are very common in our environment. They are used in the manufacture of clothing, automobile seats and carpets, home furnishings, and a host of other items. Depending on the characteristics of the fabric, fibers may be easily shed. When people make contact with other people or with objects, fibers may be deposited on the object or exchanged between the people. Once fibers are transferred, they may remain on the recipient for a short time or for many hours.

With today's emphasis on DNA, trace evidence such as fibers has become all but ignored. This is a mistake because there are many cases in which DNA is not found or no suspect has yet been identified for comparison of recovered DNA. Fibers can be very important evidence for a number of reasons:

- They may be easily transferred.
- There may be multiple transfers, thus helping determine how a series of events occurred.
- They are often produced with a specific end use in mind, like wrapping a body for disposal. Certain objects such as carpets are made from fibers with particular properties that best suited for this use. Thus, finding particular types of fibers can lead to the specific type of source.
- Fibers come in a huge variety of colors and thousands of dyes and pigments are used to produce them. There are literally millions of hues and colors available. This means that it is rare to find fibers at random that have the same microscopic and color properties.

One of the drawbacks of fiber evidence (and trace evidence in general) is that it is difficult to make quantitative interpretations about them. For example, if a few red, acrylic fibers are found on the victim of a crime and the suspect was known to have been wearing a red, acrylic sweater made of microscopically and optically similar fibers at the time of the crime, it would be very useful at trial for the jury to know how common these fibers are in the general population. If they are rare, then the fact that the fibers found at the scene match the sweater worn by the suspect takes on potentially great significance. There have been a few studies that attempt to assess the prevalence of certain fiber types in the environment. One type of research is the "target fiber study." A crime lab will pick a fiber—red acrylic, for example—and then determine how often such a fiber occurs in casework over a long period of time. In general, these studies show that the chances of finding any particular fiber at random are very small. However, there is little data that shed light on exactly how common a fiber type is and numerical probabilities are not calculated for fiber evidence.

Types of Fibers

In order for a polymer to be classified as a fiber, its length must be at least one hundred times its diameter. There are two major types of fibers: **natural** and **synthetic**. A natural fiber exists in nature as a fiber. Natural fibers can come from animals, plants, or minerals. A synthetic fiber is manufactured from materials that are not fibers.

TABLE 18.1
Common Fibers and Their Origins

Natural	Synthetic	Semi-Synthetic
Cotton—Plant—Cotton plant	Nylon	Rayon—Wood pulp
Wool—Animal—Sheep	Polyester	
Linen—Plant—Flax plant	Olefin	
Silk—Animal—Silkworm	Acetate	
Asbestos—Mineral—Asbestos	Acrylic	
Cashmere—Animal—Goat	Spandex	
Mohair—Animal—Rabbit	Fiberglass	

Some people also designate **semi-synthetic** as a separate type of fiber. This is a fiber made from a naturally occurring substance. For example, *rayon* is manufactured from wood pulp residue from the manufacture of paper. Table 18.1 lists common fibers by category, and in the case of the natural fibers, their sources.

Synthetic fibers must adhere to particular naming conventions. The Federal Trade Commission publishes a list of the approved names for fibers and their chemical contents.

Fiber Morphology

One of the key examinations in the comparison of fibers is the morphology or structure of the fiber. Certainly, if a fiber from a crime scene arose from a particular fabric, the structures of the known and unknown fibers must be the same. The following are the most important characteristics of fiber morphology:

- **Type:** This is the most important characteristic. The examiner must be able to classify a fiber according to the FTC-approved name or some other standard system for describing fibers. There are a number of tests that can help determine fiber type. In addition to microscopy, fibers can be burn tested, tested for solubility, or chemically treated to determine their affinity for dye. Some of these methods, however, are destructive to the evidence and therefore should be the last method of typing a fiber. Figure 18.5 shows different

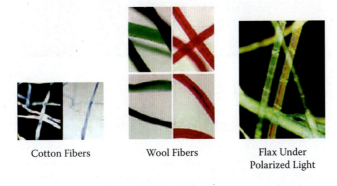

Cotton Fibers   Wool Fibers   Flax Under
                                                Polarized Light

Figure 18.5 Microscopic examination of fibers. Note the twisting of the cotton fibers and the presence of a medulla in the wool fibers. The structure of flax is enhanced using polarized light microscopy. www.fbi.gov/hq/lab /fsc/backis su/july2000/deedric 3.htm#Index (Fibers)

types of fiber using microscopic methods and Figure 18.6 shows a comparison chart for dye matching.

- **Size:** Fibers range in diameter from 10 to 50 μm or from 2×10^{-3} to 4×10^{-4} inches. Naturally occurring fibers are measured in μm. Synthetic fibers are usually measured in denier. This is a measure of the weight of a bundle of fibers that is 9,000 meters long. More dense fibers will have higher deniers.
- **Cross-section:** Not all fibers are round. Their cross-sections may give a clue to their end use. For example, many carpet fibers are trilobal or bilobal. Synthetic fibers can have any of hundreds of cross-sectional shapes.
- **Color:** Many natural fibers are white or some shade of brown. They are usually bleached before they are dyed. Fibers are colored by either dyeing them or printing a pattern directly onto the fabric. An individual fiber that has been dyed will usually have a uniform appearance under a microscope, whereas a fiber that has been printed may be uneven in color.
- **Crimp:** Some fibers have a natural wave or twist. Cotton is an example as shown in Figure 18.7. Synthetic fibers must have a wave mechanically applied. The crimp value is the number of crimps per unit length.

Figure 18.6 T.I.S identification key for dye stain testing of fabric.

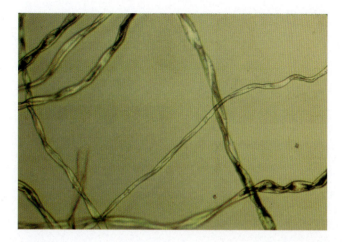

Figure 18.7 Photomicrograph of cotton fibers. Note the natural twist in the fibers.

Analysis of Synthetic Fibers

There are a number of physical and chemical tests for individual fibers. No amount of testing will result in individualization of a fiber to a particular fabric. If the evidence consists of a piece of torn fabric and the possible source is also available, then it may be possible to individualize the torn piece by way of a **tear match**. This is illustrated in Figure 18.8. In such cases it is helpful if the tear is irregular and/or if there is a pattern to the fabric.

Microscopy

A great deal can be discerned from microscopic analysis of fibers. General characteristics of the fiber such as color, length, diameter, and cross-sectional shape can be viewed.

Cross-Section

Many fibers are manufactured with particular shapes optimized for end use. For example, many carpet fibers are trilobal because this shape helps to hide dirt and

Figure 18.8 A fabric tear match.

Figure 18.9 Cross-section of trilobal synthetic fibers using a scanning electron microscope (left) and regular microscope (right). www.fbi.gov/hq/lab/fsc/backissu/july2000/ deedric3.htm#In dex (Fibers).

gives the carpet a desired feel and texture. Figure 18.9 shows some trilobal fibers in cross-section.

Diameter

Measurement of the diameter of a round fiber is straightforward. However, many fibers are not round. They may be oval, elongated, bilobal, or trilobal. The method for determining the diameter of a fiber depends on the shape. For example, oval and elongated fibers have two diameters and both are recorded. Figure 18.10 shows some fibers and how their cross-sections are measured.

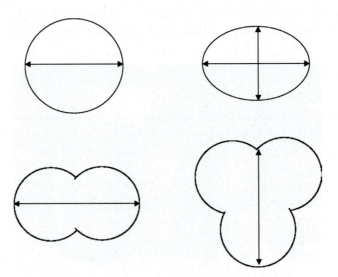

Figure 18.10 How diameters of various fiber shapes are measured.

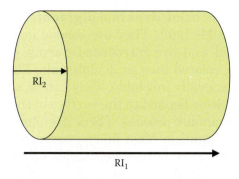

Figure 18.11 Two refractive indices of a round fiber.

Delusterants

Many synthetic fiber polymers are shiny when exposed to light. This may give an undesired sheen to the fabric. Delusterants are finely ground materials, usually titanium dioxide, introduced into the chemical mixture from which the fiber is made. They scatter light and reduce the luster of the fabric. Different manufacturers use different delusterants as well as different shapes, sizes, and distributions of delusterant particles. These characteristics help in determining the degree of association of known and unknown fibers.

Refractive Index

A discussion of how refractive indices are measured in liquids and solids is presented in Chapter 19: Glass and Soil. Like glass, fibers are transparent and also exhibit the property of **refractive index**. (Refractive index is a measure of the speed light travels through a transparent substance as compared its speed in air.) One difference, however, is that the shape of a fiber may cause it to have more than one refractive index. Many fibers have two refractive indices because light will travel at a different speed depending on whether it is traveling the length of the fiber or through the diameter of the fiber. This is shown in Figure 18.11. Even if a fiber is not round, there will not be enough of a difference in refractive indices between the various diameters of the fiber to be detected.

Color

A microscope isn't needed to examine the colors of fibers. The human eye is a remarkable instrument for discerning colors and shades of differences in color when known and unknown fibers are viewed under the same light conditions. There are two problems with this method in examining scientific evidence: first, examination by the eye is qualitative and subjective. There is no objective or numerical measurement that would confirm that two fibers are the same color. The other problem is called **metamerism**. It is possible for two fibers or other objects to appear to be exactly the same color to the eye under one set of light conditions, but actually be different colors when measured under a different set of conditions. To guard against this, a visible microspectrophotometer should be used to obtain the visible spectrum of the fiber. This will objectively determine the exact color of the fiber and will prove that two fibers have or do not have the same color. Microspectrophotometry is discussed in Chapter 5: Light and Matter, and Chapter 6: Microscopy.

Color is imparted to fibers using **dyes** and **pigments**. Dyes are generally organic substances that absorb visible light. They are soluble in the chemicals from which the fiber will be produced and are introduced during production. Pigments are generally, but not always, colored inorganic materials. They are finely divided into small particles that are generally insoluble. They can be suspended in the chemical mixture as the fiber is made or bonded to the surface of the fiber after manufacture. Coloring fibers can be a complex process. There are more than a dozen ways that dyes and pigments can be applied. Most fabrics are dyed with more than one dye and are dyed in batches rather than in a continuous process. Because of this, there will virtually always be slight differences in dye colors and concentrations from batch to batch of the same fabric. This can be a useful characteristic when comparing fibers.

Fibers may also be colored by printing colored patterns onto the surface of the fabric. This is more akin to painting than dyeing.

Chemical Analysis of Fibers

Fibers contain a polymer backbone and one or more dyes or pigments. There may also be delustering agents added during manufacturing. Some chemical examinations are performed on a fiber as a whole. It is also possible to extract dyes from the fibers and analyze them separately.

Analysis of Fibers as a Whole

There are two major methods for analyzing the chemical composition of fibers.

1. **Fourier transform infrared spectrophotometry (FTIR)** microscopy is widely used in crime labs. It is nondestructive and can determine not only what broad class the fiber belongs to, but can also identify the subclass. For example, nylon 66 can be differentiated from nylon 6-12 by FTIR. The microscope permits the analysis of one single fiber. FTIR microscopy is discussed in Chapter 5: Light and Matter.
2. **Pyrolysis gas chromatography (PyGC)** is also used to analyze fibers. A pyrogram can be generated from as little as 1/8 inch of fiber, but it is a destructive technique. It is superior to FTIR in distinguishing closely related fibers because it is sensitive to small differences in chemical makeup of the fibers. PGC is discussed in Chapter 4: Separation of Complex Mixtures.

Examples of FTIR and PyGC testing results will be illustrated in the next section about paints.

In addition to the above analytical tests, other examinations may be employed on fibers. Different classes of fibers are soluble in different solvents. Although this test is destructive, *solubility* can be accomplished using very little fiber and can be a quick way of determining the class to which a fiber belongs.

Dye Analysis

Dyes can be extracted from fibers using organic solvents. The particular solvent used depends on the type of fiber and dye. Once extracted, dyes are usually analyzed by thin layer chromatography. The dyes are not identified. Dyes from known and unknown fibers can be compared by this method. More recently, liquid chromatography/mass spectrometry has been employed in the analysis of fiber dyes. This method can be used to both separate and identify the individual dyes.

Interpretation of Fiber Evidence

As mentioned previously, target fiber studies show that most fibers occur infrequently in the environment. The main exception would be indigo-dyed cotton (blue jeans). This means that, if known and unknown fibers are similar in all physical and chemical respects, the degree of association is likely to be high. This is not the same as individualizing the evidence. *Only a tear match can individualize fibers.*

In addition to the above, fibers (and also hairs) share the common trait of being easily transferred from one fabric to another or from a fabric to another surface such as a chair seat. Once transferred, the fibers may persist on the recipient object or be easily transferred again (secondary transfer). Analyzing the journey of fibers from one place to another can help determine whether the wearer of the source of the fibers was at the scene of the crime. There have been a number of recent studies concerning primary and subsequent transfers of hairs and fibers as well as the ease of transfer and persistence of fibers.

Paints and Other Coatings

In 1996, a man was injured when driving his motorcycle through the downtown streets of Detroit, Michigan. He claimed that he was sideswiped by a white Detroit Police Department car. This caused him to lose control of his motorcycle and careen into another police car that was parked on the street. The man was arrested for reckless driving, drunk driving, and for damaging the parked patrol car. As part of the investigation, the police submitted evidence to the Detroit Police Department Crime Lab. The evidence included painted parts of the motorcycle as well as paint from the parked police car and paint from the police car that the man alleged had hit him. The motorcycle had been painted dark purple. There were some white smears of paint on parts of the motorcycle and some purple paint smears on the parked police car.

Even though both law enforcement vehicles were white, they had been painted at different times and some of the chemical characteristics of the paints were dissimilar so the paint from both cars could be differentiated. The white paint smears on the motorcycle were found to be chemically and physically similar to the paint on the parked police car and different from the paint on the other car. The purple paint on the parked police car was found to be similar physically and chemically to the paint on the motorcycle. No purple paint was found on the other car. On the basis of this evidence and a breath alcohol test, the motorcycle driver was found guilty of reckless driving and drunk driving.

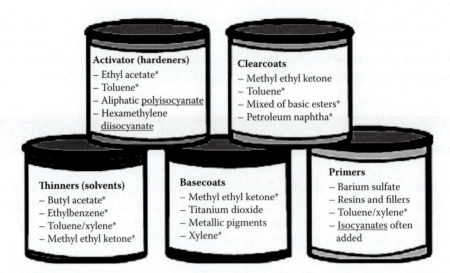

Figure 18.12 Chemical compositions of typical paints. Components followed by * are solvents. www.dispersion.com/paints.

What Are Paints?

Paints have something in common with fibers. They both contain polymers. In some cases, the polymers in paint are the same type of polymers found in fibers. Whereas the polymers in fibers are manufactured into long strands, in paints they are formed into sheets when they dry. Paint is a type of coating designed to cover a surface for the purposes of imparting color and/or protection. Paint chemistry is extremely complicated. Hundreds of compounds are used in the manufacture of a huge variety of paints. The interactions of these substances are so complex that a paint chemist can easily spend an entire career learning to understand just a few different types of paint chemistry. This great variation in paints is beneficial to forensic chemists because careful analysis and comparisons of paint evidence can lead to a high degree of association between known and unknown samples.

Chemically, the major components of paint are a binder and one or more pigments. Pigments are generally colored, inorganic substances ground into a fine powder and suspended (not dissolved) in the binder. The binder is mixed with other additives such as drying agents, delusterants, surfactants, etc. and then dissolved in a solvent. Sometimes the binder, solvents, and additives are collectively called the vehicle or film former. The solvent imparts liquidity to the paint so that it can be easily applied to the surface. The amount and nature of the solvent can be varied to accommodate brushing, rolling or spraying the paint. When the solvent evaporates, the binder polymerizes and forms a film that traps the pigment particles and smoothly covers the surface. Figure 18.12 shows the composition of typical automotive paint coatings.

There are some common terms used to describe particular kinds of paint. The word "enamel" is used to describe any paint that dries to a high gloss. Lacquers are fast-drying paints that dry by solvent evaporation.

Other Coatings

There are other materials besides paint designed to protect or impart color to surfaces. *Shellac* is a very old coating made from an insect extract (the *lac*) dissolved in methyl alcohol. It is mainly used to protect wood, although it has been largely replaced by varnishes. *Varnish* is a solution of film formers and resins dissolved in a solvent. It is used to protect wood. When a solvent evaporates, the film formers polymerize, leaving a hard, protective coating. Varnishes usually do not contain pigments or dyes. A *stain* contains soluble dyes or suspended pigments in a solvent. Stains will color a wood surface but will not coat it and offer no protection for the wood.

Types of Paint

For forensic purposes, paints are categorized by their use. There are three basic types.

1. **Automotive paints:** This is the most important type of paint in forensic work. Automobiles are widely used in crimes and many accidents involve cars and trucks.

2. **Structural paints:** These are used to paint buildings such as houses as well as objects such as mail boxes. They are used for protection as well as to impart color. The first house paints were oil based. These were very slow drying paints that usually contained linseed oil as the film former. The solvents were often toxic organic compounds. People could not safely remain inside a house right after it was painted. Today, homes are painted with latex-based paints that use water as the solvent. House paints are sometimes found as evidence in burglary cases and thefts.

3. **Artistic paints:** These are the oldest types of paints. They are designed to last a long time. Most are made from naturally occurring oils and pigments. Forgery is the most common forensic application of these paints.

There are also special purpose paints used for protection, color, or other purposes. For example, special paints are used to color and seal concrete floors. Fluorescent paints are used on some road and warning signs. Skid-resistant paints are used in public places where there is heavy foot traffic.

Automotive paints are, by far, the most commonly encountered paints in forensic science. Automobiles are always painted with several layers of paint, each one of a different type. The layer structure of automotive paints presents some interesting analytical challenges and evidentiary opportunities that are not usually found with other types of paint. For this reason, the remainder of the chapter focuses on automotive paints, although the sections on collection and analysis could be generalized to the other types (structural and artistic).

How Cars Are Painted

Most cars have four coats within the paint finish when they are first manufactured. The exception would be some luxury cars that have more than one topcoat layer (see below). Two coats of rustproofing are first applied to the car by bathing it in a pool of liquefied zinc and then an electroplate process is used. After this, the **primer** is applied. This is also done by electroplating. The pigments in this paint are designed to minimize corrosion of the body of the car. The color of the pigments is similar to that of the topcoat layers.

The next layer is the topcoat. This is the layer that imparts color to the car. It may contain metallic or pearlescent pigments that provide unique color effects. Traditionally, topcoats have been lacquers or more expensive enamel paints that use organic solvents. Today, water-based systems are more environmentally friendly. Topcoats usually dry by heat (thermosetting).

The final layer of paint is the **clearcoat**. At one time, only the most expensive cars received clearcoating, but today, all new cars have this top layer. The clearcoat is acrylic- or urethane-based and has no pigments. It imparts extra durability and ultraviolet light resistance.

Each coat of paint imparts a layer to the overall paint job. A cross-section of the paint on a car would show each layer. Many cars are repainted after an accident or simply because the owner wants to spruce up the car. Depending on the circumstances, different parts of the car may have different layer structures. This has implications on how paint evidence is collected from cars suspected of being involved in crashes or crimes.

Collection of Paint Evidence

Paint evidence comes in two types: *chips (flakes)* and *smears*. Paint chips contain most or all of the layers in the paint. Figure 18.13 shows paint chips from two different colored cars in a cross-sectional view. During a crash, paint chips may fall from the car and be transferred to a person or another object and even another car. Because the layer structure is intact, paint chips provide the most information from analysis. There are a number of methods of removing chips of paint from a car surface. If the chips are loose, they can be pried off. If not, a sharp scalpel or knife must be used to cut the chips out. The knife must cut all the way down to the surface on which the paint was applied to make sure that all the layers are collected.

Paint smears are much more difficult to handle. Paint smears usually consist of just the top layer of paint. When the top layer is a clearcoat, it may be difficult to see the transferred paint. Smears are often transferred when an automobile sideswipes another object. When the other object is a car, it is even more difficult to interpret a smear since it may be mixed in with other layers of paint.

Proper collection of known samples of paint from an automobile is critical to successful analysis. Like most forensic evidence, paint analysis is most valuable when the unknown can be compared with the known. It is important to collect all of the layers of paint in the known sample. Where the paint is collected from is just as important. In general, known paint samples should not be collected from the damaged area of the car, such as the driver's side of the car as shown in Figure 18.4. It is likely that foreign materials from the object that the car hit or that hit the car have gotten into the paint. Paint from the other object may have become intermixed with paint that is original to the car. The best practice is to gather known samples from *undamaged* areas as near as possible to the damaged area. Taking paint far away from the damaged area can be misleading. Parts of cars may have been repainted or even replaced and the characteristics of the paint in those parts may be very different from those in the damaged area.

Paint smears should not be removed from the surface of the object at the scene. The entire object or car part should be sent to the laboratory where the smear can be removed.

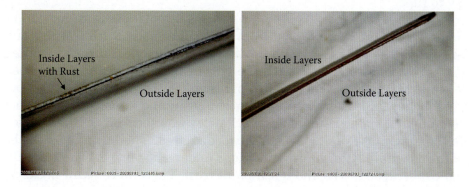

Figure 18.13 The photos are cross-sectional views of paint chips taken from a black car (left) and a red car (right). The black vehicle was an older car and showed evidence of rust on the inner coating of the paint chip.

Figure 18.14 The impact site of a two-car automobile crash. Known paint samples should be collected near this site, but not along any portion of the crushed area.

Paint chips should never be taped to a card or other object. The chip may be difficult to remove from the tape and the tape adhesive can contaminate the paint chip, and perhaps rendering chemical testing ineffective.

The Malcolm Fairley Case

In 1984, England was stricken with a series of crimes from an unknown assailant. The perpetrator began the crime spree by breaking and entering homes in quiet neighborhoods and stealing money and various items from the homeowners. As time passed, the criminal nature of his crimes escalated from robbery, to assault, and finally to rape. Nicknamed "The Fox" by law enforcement, Malcolm Fairley would break into homes, sometimes while the owners were away, watch videos under tents made from blankets and furniture, and eat food from the kitchen. Due to this type of behavior, the police coined his nickname. When the homeowners returned to their residence, he would tie them up and rob and/or assault them.

During one of his later robberies, Fairley recovered a shotgun from his victim. He used the gun to intimidate others during subsequent crimes. Although he claimed it was not loaded and he had no intent of shooting anyone, the possession of the gun was enough impetus to intensify the severity of his crimes from robbery to rape.

Fairley could not be identified by his victims because he wore masks during his crimes. One mask was a leg cut from a pair of trousers with two slits cut into the pant leg for the eyes. Although he did not kill anyone, Fairley assaulted the females, threatened the males with the gun in their faces, and then raped the female while the male watched. He would then leave with some of their possessions and money. This continued for almost a year, and at one point the shotgun went off and hit a male victim in the leg. Fairley was shocked by this and decided to hide the gun, mask, and gloves in a wooded area. The burial was the beginning of his downfall. After hiding the items under some brush, The Fox's British Leyland car scraped a tree and left a paint trail. There were paint flecks on the branches.

Police found the mask, gloves, and gun, and then happened on the tire tracks that led them to the scraped tree. They took samples, analyzed them, and identified them as the Harvest Yellow color of a British Leyland vehicle. The task then was to question the thousands of owners of that class and color of car. Upon questioning various owners, one office located Malcolm Fairley washing his scraped Harvest Yellow vehicle. They searched his property and also found the trousers with a leg missing, the match to his mask. The Fox, Malcolm Fairley, was apprehended, put on trial, and sent to prison for this crime spree. He was sentenced in London to six life sentences, but has been released under a new identity after serving twenty years.

Analysis of Paint

Paint possesses a number of physical and chemical properties that can be exploited in the analysis and comparison of paint. Some focus on the pigments while others target the binders. Others are performed on the paint sample as a whole.

Physical Properties

The most important characteristic of paint as evidence is the **color layer sequence**. Automotive paints and some structural paints contain layers. In the case of automotive paints, each layer may have a different composition and color. If an unknown paint sample and a known sample have different color layer sequences, then the known can be eliminated as a source for the unknown. It is well known that the weakest bond in an automotive paint job is the bond between the bottom layer of paint and the bare metal. Even so, paint chips may break off between layers of paint and not all layers may be present. In this case, the known and unknown may still have a common source, even if all of the layers are not present. This is shown in Figure 18.15 where A is an unknown paint chip and B and C are knowns. Note that B can be the source of A even though it has extra layers. A could have sheared off between the top layer of rust proofing and the primer layer whereas B was collected all the way down to the metal.

The exact colors of each layer of the paint can be confirmed using visible microspectrophotometry. In this case, the layers will have to be analyzed separately. This can be done by making "peels," peeling each layer off using a sharp scalpel. A cross-section of the paint can also be made using a microtome and each

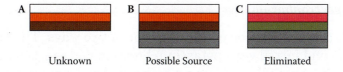

Unknown   Possible Source   Eliminated

Figure 18.15 Color-layer analysis of paint. Note that the only difference between the paint in A and B is that there are two more layers in B. In a real case, this could mean that a paint chip could have sheared off between the third and fourth layer, giving a chip such as A. Thus the automobile painted with paint B could still be the source of the unknown A. The paint chip C cannot be the source of the unknown because the second layer (topcoat) is clearly a different color.

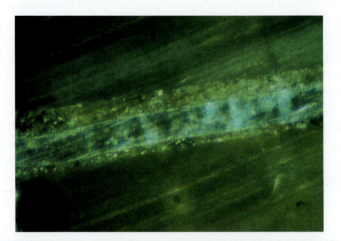

Figure 18.16 A cross-section of a real paint chip showing three layers.

layer can then be analyzed separately. Figure 18.16 shows a cross-section of a paint sample.

Chemical Properties

Solubility

Automobile paints may contain different binders. This can be a function of the manufacturer (General Motors used to employ only acrylic lacquers) or the cost of the car. Different binders may be soluble in different solvents or not soluble in any common solvent. The acrylic lacquers used in GM cars were the only automobile paints soluble in acetone. A tiny paint chip is put in a white spot plate under a stereomicroscope. A drop of solvent is added. The paint may be insoluble, soluble, or partially soluble. The pigments almost never dissolve.

Chromatography

Paints must be pyrolyzed if they are to be chromatographed. Typically a paint chip is analyzed intact and pyrolyzed at about 600 to 800°C. The resulting pyrogram will be a composite of all of the binders present in the paints. In general, the pigments will not appear in pyrolysis if they are inorganic. Figure 18.17 shows a pyrogram of an automobile paint sample. Figure 18.18 depicts sample pyrograms of two types of paint.

Infrared Microspectrophotometry

Infrared spectra of paints can be obtained in one of two ways. The entire paint chip can be ground up and mixed with potassium bromide and pressed into a pellet. The transmission spectrum of the paint as a whole can then be obtained. This spectrum will be a composite, which contains peaks for all of the binders and dyes, if any, that are present in the paint. This is useful for comparing one paint chip with another, but is not used to determine the nature of a single binder. Another way to obtain a spectrum of paint is to make peels and run the transmission spectrum of each layer. Finally, a cross-section can be made of the paint chip, and each layer can be viewed and analyzed under the microscope attached to the FTIR. Figure 18.19 shows the

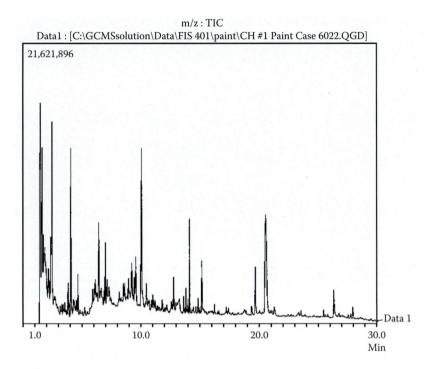

Figure 18.17 Pyrogram of an automobile paint.

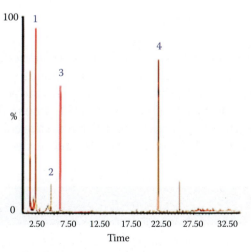

Sample vehicle touch-up paint.
Peak #1 methyl methacrylate, #2 styrene,
#3 butyl methacrylate, #4 benzylbutyl phthalate

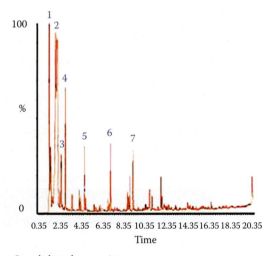

Sample latex house paint.
Peak #1 benzene, #2 acetic acid, #3 methyl
methacrylate, #4 toluene, #5 styrene, #6 indene,
#7 naphthalene.

Figure 18.18 Sample pyrograms of vehicle touch-up paint and house paint. www.pcimag.com/PCI/Home/Images/ pci0209-CDS-F3-4-lg.jpg.

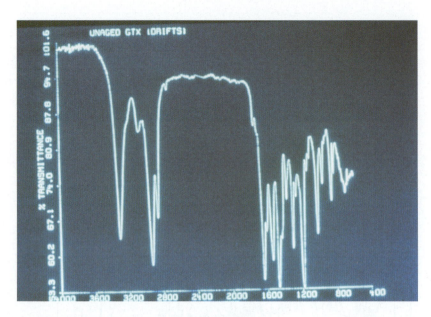

Figure 18.19 Infrared spectrum of an automobile paint.

infrared spectrum of a paint chip. The sample was prepared by pressing the chip into a pellet with potassium bromide (KBr).

Pigments

Most pigments are inorganic. Many are colored minerals. One of the best ways to analyze pigments is by scanning electron microscopy with energy dispersive x-ray analysis (SEM/EDX). This will show what elements are present and in what relative concentrations. This method is quick and practically nondestructive. It is a good complement to color analysis. As mentioned previously, peels or cross-sections of paint chips can be analyzed for color by visible microspectrophotometry.

Paint Smears

Paint smears can present significant problems. If they are transferred to another surface by impact they may be practically fused to the paint on that surface. They can be very difficult to remove. In many cases there is mostly pigment present in the smear, and SEM/EDX may be the best way to characterize the smear. If it can be removed, visible microspectrophotometry can be used to determine the colors. If there is sufficient binder present, then FTIR and PyGC can be utilized in the analysis.

The Evidentiary Value of Paint

With few exceptions, paint is class evidence. Mass production of automobiles at a single factory using robots means that many car paint jobs will be chemically and physically too similar to distinguish. Thus, paint analysis can easily eliminate a car from consideration but cannot individualize it. There are rare cases when a large paint chip is broken off a car and it can be **fracture matched** back to the original spot, but these occurrences are extremely rare.

With structural paints, the situation is the same. Usually, homes or objects will have only one layer of paint and the color layer sequence will be absent. Many structural paints are applied by brush or roller and the layers tend to be thicker than with automobiles. This means that the chance of finding a large enough paint chip to fracture-match is increased, although this situation is still relatively rare.

Summary

Paints and fibers are examples of polymers, which are long chain molecules made up of repeating links or monomers. Fibers can be natural or synthetic. Natural fibers can be of plant, mineral, or animal origin. There are many varieties of synthetic fibers. Fibers are normally class evidence, except when large pieces of fabric can be fit together in a tear match. Fibers are long molecules with a variety of cross-sectional shapes. These are often designed for particular end uses, and knowing the cross-sectional shape can give a clue to the possible source of the fiber. Fibers are analyzed using microscopy to describe the cross-section, diameter, color, and refractive indices. FTIR and PyGC are used to characterize the polymers in the fiber. Dyes can be extracted and chromatographed for comparing known and unknown fibers. Fibers are easily shed and transferred to other objects. This can help in showing that a particular garment may have been worn to a crime scene.

Paints are also polymers, but the strands are cross-linked so that the polymer forms sheets. Paints are made up of binders that hold the pigments on the surface. Pigments impart color to the paint. There are other additives in paint that give it desirable characteristics. Automotive paints are the most commonly found types of paint evidence. Each automobile is painted with several layers of different types of paints, including rustproofing layers, primer, topcoat, and clearcoat. Physical properties of paint, including color-layer sequence, are measured. The pigments in paint are analyzed using SEM. The binders are analyzed using FTIR, solubility, and PyGC. Paint is normally class evidence unless it can be fracture matched back to a source—a rare occurrence.

Mini Lab Activities

MINI LAB: BURN TESTING FIBER ANALYSIS

Obtain samples of the following fabrics (100% content is preferred):

Cotton
Linen
Wool
Cashmere
Silk
Nylon
Polyester
Rayon

Other materials needed:
Candle
Metal forceps
Safety goggles
50 mL beaker
Fabric (fiber) samples (from above list)

1. Using a small candle (tealights work well) as a heat source, analyze the reaction of each type of fiber to heating and burning.
2. Cut small 1 cm squares of each fabric (fiber) type.
3. Half fill the beaker with water to use as an extinguishing source.
4. Analyze each type of fiber using the method below and recording precisely what is observed via sight, smell, and touch.
    a. Using forceps, bring each fiber square NEAR, BUT NOT TOUCHING the flame. Note how the fiber reacts to the presence of heat. Record in the table.
    b. Place the fiber IN the flame and note how quickly it burns and describe the appearance of the flame.
    c. Quickly pull the fiber OUT of the flame, note whether it self-extinguishes or not. If not, blow out the flame. Note the SMELL of the burnt fiber and record in the chart what it resembles.
    d. After cooling, examine the RESIDUE of the burnt fiber (is it black, brown, white, flakey, sooty, hard, brittle, etc.) and describe it in the chart.

MINI LAB CHART
Burn Testing Fibers

Fiber	Near Flame	In Flame	Out of Flame	Smell	Residue
Cashmere					
Cotton					
Linen					
Nylon					
Polyester					
Rayon					
Silk					
Wool					

Additionally, small fiber strands, like yarn, rope, etc. can be tested. Other fabrics can be added to the table, including blended fabrics, such as 50/50 cotton polyester (t-shirts).

Test Yourself

Multiple Choice

1. Which of the following fibers does *not* have a natural origin?
    a. Wool
    b. Rayon

    c. Silk

    d. Nylon

2. Which of the following fibers is animal in origin?

    a. Cotton

    b. Silk

    c. Asbestos

    d. Linen

3. Which of the following fibers is partially natural and partially artificial?

    a. Wool

    b. Rayon

    c. Silk

    d. Nylon

4. Which of the following fibers is *not* animal in origin?

    a. Cashmere

    b. Silk

    c. Linen

    d. Wool

5. Which of the following tests can individualize fiber evidence?

    a. Burn testing

    b. Solvent testing

    c. Refractive index

    d. Tear matching

6. Which of the following tests can individualize paint evidence?

    a. SEM analysis

    b. FTIR analysis

    c. Fracture matching

    d. Color layering

7. A fiber is examined under the microscope and it has a twisted appearance. The class of this fiber could be:

    a. Cotton

    b. Wool

    c. Polyester

    d. Rayon

8. A polymer constructed with two or more monomers is called:

    a. Homopolymer

    b. Copolymer

    c. Cross-linked polymer

    d. Block polymer

Short Answer

9. What is a polymer? A monomer?

10. Define and give an example of a homopolymer and a copolymer.

11. What is paint? What are the major ingredients?

12. What is a fiber? What are the major types?

13. Why do some fibers have more than one refractive index?

14. Name and briefly describe the different layers of automobile paint.

15. What is a paint "peel"? What purpose does it have in paint analysis?

16. What is denier? What does it measure?

17. What does thermosetting mean?

18. What is color layer sequence? Why is it important in paint analysis?

Short Essay

19. Using the data from the Mini Lab Activity, construct a flow chart for fiber identification.

20. A three-vehicle accident occurs. The three vehicles involved are different colors; blue, silver, and red. The investigator wants to take evidence from the crash to substantiate victim's stories of what happened in the crash. It is noted by the investigator that all three cars have paint transfer marks on them, and the colors seem similar to the vehicles involved. Describe in detail the proper procedure that should be followed to obtain evidence from the scene.

Further Readings

Caddy, B., Ed. *Forensic Examination of Glass and Paint.* New York: Taylor & Francis, 2001.

Robertson, J. and M. Grieve, eds. *Forensic Examination of Fibres.* 2nd ed. New York: Taylor & Francis, 1999.

Thornton, J. L. Forensic Paint Examination, in *Forensic Science Handbook,* Vol. 1. 2nd ed. Upper Saddle River, NJ: Prentice Hall, 2002.

On the Web

www.enotes.com/forensic-science/paint-analysis
http://science.howstuffworks.com/forensic-lab-technique3.htm
www.forensic.santoshraut.com/physics.htm
www.fbi.gov/hq/lab/fsc/backissu/july2000/deedric3.htm#Index
http://pslc.ws/macrog/lab/lab01.htm

19
Glass and Soil

Learning Objectives

1. To be able to define and classify glass
2. To be able to define soil
3. To be able to define fracture match
4. To be able to sequence multiple fractures
5. To be able to determine direction of force on a piece of glass
6. To be able to define refractive index
7. To be able to describe the Becke line method for determining refractive index
8. To be able to describe the common methods for the analysis of soil

Chapter 19
Glass and Soil

Chapter Outline

Mini Glossary

Amorphous: Having no definite shape, form, or structure.

Becke line: The white line or "halo" around a solid object (in this case, glass) that has been immersed in a liquid medium, visible when viewed under a polarized light microscope.

Concentric fracture: The lines of fracture that tend to form a circle around the point of impact on a piece of glass.

Conchoidal lines: Curved stress lines along the side of a fractured piece of glass.

Fracture match: Fitting a piece of evidence into the source, like fitting a puzzle piece into a jigsaw puzzle, individualizing that piece of evidence.

Hot stage microscope: A special type of microscope in which the stage or platform for the slide changes temperature, heating the slide mounted on the stage.

Humus: The organic material in soil comprised of decayed plant and animal material.

ICP/MS: Inductively coupled plasma mass spectrometer, an instrument used to analyze the chemical composition of a sample material.

Radial fracture: The lines of fracture that extend outward from the point of impact on a piece of glass.

Refraction: The bending of light due a change in speed as it travels from one medium to another of different density.
Refractive index: A measure of how the speed of light is reduced as it travels through a medium as compared to its speed of light in a vacuum.
Soil: A mixture of crushed rock, minerals, and decayed plant and animal materials.

Introduction

Newspaper headlines after Coors' disappearance.

http://www.rockymountainnews.com/photos/2009/jan/21/118215/

On February 9, 1960, Adolph Coors III, an heir to the Coors beer company and fortune, was kidnapped and killed on a bridge near his home near Morrison, Colorado. Murdering Coors was not the original intent of his killer, a man named Joseph Corbett. Corbett had devised a scheme to kidnap Coors and demand a sizable ransom. Planning his moves for months, Corbett took a position at the Coors brewery so he could stalk Coors and determine his habits. Prior to the kidnapping, Corbett bought a 1951 four-door Mercury car under the name of Walter Osborne. Residents near the site of the kidnapping, a bridge on a road between the Coors residence and the brewery, had seen the car parked there several times prior to the incident. A few days before the kidnapping, Corbett quit his job at the Coors brewery.

On the morning of February 9, Coors left his home for the brewery. Parked on a bridge along the route to the brewery were Corbett and his car. Knowing that Coors would come to aid the "disabled" vehicle, Corbett waited. Sure enough, Adolf Coors approached the car. Corbett took this opportunity to grab his victim, but Coors overpowered him and tried to run back to his own car. This is when the kidnapping turned into a murder. As Coors fled, Corbett shot and killed him. He then put Coors' body in the trunk of his Mercury car and sped away.

Residents in the area reportedly heard shouting and a crack that sounded like a gun. Later, a witness saw Coors' truck parked with the engine running on a bridge at the kidnapping site. Later that day, Corbett mailed a $500,000 ransom note to Adolf Coors' wife. The next day, he drove up into the Rocky Mountains near Pike's Peak and dumped the body in a trash dump near a religious retreat. He then drove to New Jersey. The FBI traced the name Walter Osborne to Corbett and found that he had escaped from prison in Washington State in 1955. They tracked him to Atlantic City, New Jersey, where his car was spotted on fire. But, there was no sign of Corbett. Corbett had fled to Canada, where he was captured a few months later.

Even though the truck had been burned, investigators were able to locate soil under the wheel wells. There were four layers of soil in total under each well. From the outer to inner layer, the soils were as follows:

- Fourth (outer) contained material from the New Jersey dump where he burned car
- Third contained pink feldspars of Pike's Peak granite near where body was found
- Second had materials from the Morrison hogback formation around the Coors ranch
- First (inner) had pink feldspars of other front range granites generally related to the Rocky Mountain front range

The soils told the story of where the car had been since Corbett purchased it. The innermost layer was soil picked up from his routine trips around his home in Denver and the Coors Brewery. The second indicated that his car was near the Coors ranch. The third was similar to soil near the burial site and the fourth from the area near where the car was burned. Although soil is not individual evidence, the evidence was clearly convincing that the Mercury was the right car.

This chapter is about glass, soils, and similar materials. Although they are distinct types of evidence, glass and soils have some common characteristics. Forensic analysis involves primarily the physical properties of glass and soil, although some chemical analysis is performed on this evidence. Another common characteristic is that most laboratories do little testing on this evidence. A large portion of crime labs do no testing on soils directly. Examiners concentrate on soil analysis when soil at a crime scene contains a shoe print or tire tread. In many glass cases, the only analysis done is the refractive index test, which is covered in some detail in this chapter.

Glass

In school, everyone is taught the three states of matter—solid, liquid, and gas. Later, the concepts of plasma and fluid may be introduced. Glass is an example of yet another form of matter: an **amorphous solid**. Most solids have an ordered

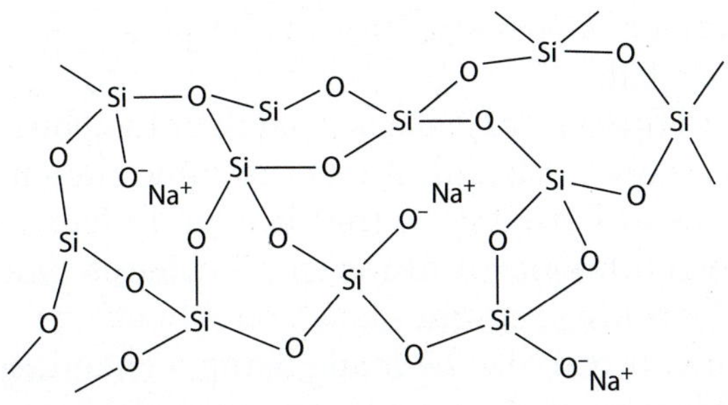

Figure 19.1 The chemical structure of glass.

structure and many have definite crystal habit. Table salt (sodium chloride) is made of cubic crystals, for example. Even metals have an ordered structure, described as *metal–metal bonding*. Glass has no ordered structure and no crystal habit, making it an amorphous solid. In its purest form, glass is made of silicon and oxygen molecules in the ratio of 2:1. All glass has as a common base the compound *silicon dioxide*. Its chemical formula could best be described as $(SiO_2)_n$. The chemical structure of glass is shown in Figure 19.1. Because of its properties, glass has also been referred to as a *supercooled liquid*.

Glass has properties of both a solid and a liquid. It has a high melting point, in excess of 2000°C, and is very hard and brittle like a solid. It is colorless and transparent and has no regular order to its chemical bonds, like a liquid. There have been some reports that glass can flow, albeit very slowly. These are the result of observations that glass windows that have been hung for many years seem to be thicker at the bottom than the top indicating that the glass sagged under the influence of gravity. There is no evidence that this happens and is likely due to poor quality manufacturing of the glass.

Types of Glass

The basic ingredient in glass is silicon dioxide. It comes from very pure sand that is heated until it melts and then allowed to cool. Very few types of glass are made of pure silicon dioxide. The majority of glass types contain additives and/or they vary in the way they are made so that they have certain desirable properties. Some of the common types of glass are:

- **Float glass or soda lime glass:** This is a type of glass that is used to make windows and other flat glass objects. Added to the silicon dioxide main ingredient are calcium carbonate (Na_2CO_3), the "soda" and calcium oxide (CaO), the "lime." The ingredients are heated to 1,500°C and poured onto a bath of molten tin. The glass is viscous and the tin is fluid so the two do not mix. As the glass cools, it forms a flat surface because the surface of the molten tin bath is flat.
- **Borosilicate glass:** This type of glass is made by "doping" molten glass with boron. The atoms of boron fit in holes in the glass structure and alter its properties. This type of glass has a high coefficient of thermal expansion. This means that it will not break easily when its temperature is rapidly increased or decreased. If you take a regular glass object, cool it, and then plunge it into hot water, it will break. Borosilicate glass (sometimes called Pyrex, which is a proprietary name) will not break. It is used in cookware

and other applications where stability in the presence of rapidly changing temperatures is needed.

- **Tempered glass:** This type of glass is used in automobile windows and plate glass windows in stores. Although it has the same chemical makeup as soda lime glass, it is specially treated so that it is up to four times stronger than regular glass. When it breaks, it forms small spheres that do not have sharp edges. It is made by taking regular glass and reheating it to about 700°C and then cooling rapidly. It can also be made using a chemical treatment.
- **Tinted glass:** This type of glass contains colorants. It is used for decoration or sometimes to reduce glare or heat penetration. The colorants in tinted glass are minerals of various colors. They are melted and mixed with the raw materials of the glass during the manufacturing process.
- **Leaded glass (crystal stemware):** This type of glass has become rare in today's society, due to the lead oxide additive. Crystal wine glasses, figurines, and paperweights are examples in this category. The lead additive gives the glass a higher refractive index, causing light to bend more as it passes through, ultimately resulting in the sparkle of crystal glassware and figurines. A characteristic *ping* sound is produced when leaded glass is lightly tapped, a resonant property caused by the bonding of the additives.

Glass as Forensic Evidence

There are more than seven hundred types of glass, but only about seventy are in common use today. Glass is widely used in consumer and commercial products and therefore is found just about everywhere. It isn't surprising that it shows up at many crime scenes, especially those that involve automobiles. Broken glass on many city streets may result from an accident or debris from any action that could cause broken glass. This glass may be incidental to a crime or other some incident. It is very important to collect proper known samples so incidental glass can be eliminated from consideration.

Glass is forensically important because

- It is frequently found at most crime scenes due to its plentiful nature and activities commonly involved in a crime (broken windows and doors, bottles and drinking glasses, auto windows, etc.).
- It can be carried away undetected from a scene.
- It does not decay under normal circumstances; it is stable evidence.
- It can contribute as class evidence in the pool of evidence linking a suspect to a crime.

Fracture Match

Because glass is mass-produced, there are few characteristics that are unique to a particular piece. For this reason, glass is generally considered to be *class* evidence and a piece of glass cannot normally be matched to a particular source. There is one exception when broken pieces of glass large enough to manipulate can be fitted together like pieces of a jigsaw puzzle. This is called a **fracture match** and is considered an *individual* characteristic. In some cases, there are several pieces of

Figure 19.2 A Molotov cocktail.

glass and the fracture match is fairly easy. Figure 19.2 is a broken Molotov cocktail, which is a device for starting fires. The glass container has been reassembled.

Other fracture matches are not so easy to interpret because they involve only two pieces of glass and the broken edge may be fairly straight. Fortunately, there are microscopic characteristics that can help in making a decision about a suspected match. When glass breaks, the applied forces cause the glass to stretch first. Glass is not especially malleable so it won't stretch far, but microscopic stress marks will form in the glass at the break. Since the application of the breaking force is randomly applied (not easily reproducible), the pattern of stress marks on either side of the break is unique. This can be seen in Figure 19.3, which is a photomicrograph of the broken edges of a piece of glass. Note the numerous stress marks and how they all correspond to each other. It would be virtually impossible to break the same type of glass the same way and get the same pattern of stress marks. This means that if the two

Figure 19.3 Stress marks in glass. The two edges at a break in an eyeglass lens are shown. The white lines are stress marks in the glass caused by the break.

sets of stress marks match, like the ones in Figure 19.3, the pattern is an individual characteristic.

It is relatively rare to find pieces of glass from a crime scene that are large enough to be fit back into a possible source. The majority of cases involve pieces of glass that are too small to fracture match and are thus class evidence.

Analyzing Broken Glass

Sequencing Glass Fractures

When a force is applied to a glass object, it will bend until it reaches its elastic limit. When the limit is reached, the glass splits in two. The portion of the glass that fails first will have a stress mark at right angles to the plane of the glass—whereas the remaining portion of the glass will stress to the breaking point. This results in a curved pattern of lines on the edge of a broken piece of glass called **conchoidal lines**. The edge of a broken piece of glass is shown in Figure 19.4 with visible conchoidal lines.

The point of impact is usually obvious and can also yield information to the glass examiner. The first task is to determine what type of object caused the damage to the glass. Examination of the hole (if there is one) or point of impact can help identify whether the object was a low-velocity or high-velocity projectile. A bullet or other projectile traveling at high velocity produces a hole on the entry side that is smooth and of similar diameter as the bullet. The exit side will be cratered around the hole, producing a much larger circle than the bullet. Figure 19.5 shows entry and exit holes in the glass.

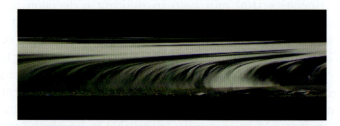

Figure 19.4 The edge of a piece of broken glass. The curved lines are called conchoidal lines. They are formed as a result of the transfer of energy from force of impact from one side of the glass to the other.

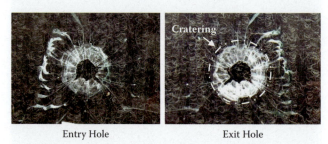

Entry Hole   Exit Hole

Figure 19.5 Entry and exit holes produced by the same bullet going through a glass window. The hole on the left is entry, characterized by a smoother hole and no cratering on the entry side. The hole on the right is exit, characterized by the cratering around the entry hole (whiter areas around the hole highlighted by the dotted circle).

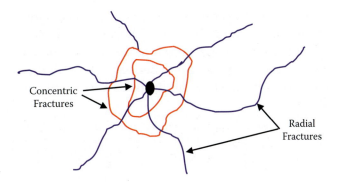

Figure 19.6 The lines of fracture due to impact on glass. The fracture lines that originate at the point of impact and move outward are *radial fractures*. The circular lines of fracture around the impact point are *concentric fractures*.

A low-velocity bullet hole will exhibit more shattering around the hole and the hole may be irregular in shape. Sometimes stones at high speed (coming off a tire) may cause damage to glass that mimic bullet fracture patterns. Therefore, it is important to carefully search the area of the crime scene for other evidence in order to determine what caused the breakage.

Two different lines of fracture are usually present near the impact site. These fracture lines can be helpful when determining the sequence of impacts when glass is impacted multiple times. For example, if a window has multiple gunshots, the shapes of the entry and exit holes point to the direction the shots were fired (inside or outside of the residence). But, by reading the fracture lines, it is possible to determine the order of impacts. The two types of fracture lines are **radial** and **concentric fracture lines**. (See Figure 19.6.) Radial fractures extend outward in a line from the point of impact origin on the glass. Concentric fractures make relatively circular patterns around the point of origin of the force.

Radial fractures stress first on the opposite side of the force, causing the glass to break there first. The side adjacent to the impact snaps next. The opposite is true of concentric fractures. The action of the radial break causes the side of impact to fail first and the opposite later. This is illustrated in Figure 19.7.

In the case of multiple impacts, the radial fracture lines give indication of which impact preceded another. No radial fracture can extend through an existing fracture

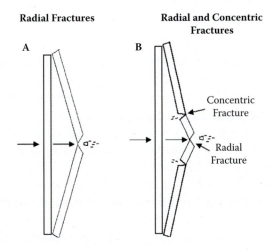

Figure 19.7 Diagram A shows the path of a projectile through a window, first when it impacts the window from the left, and then upon exit, producing radial fractures. Diagram B shows the path of a projectile upon entry (arrow at left) and then exit, producing radial and concentric fractures.

line. The glass has already been compromised, and the secondary fracture must end when it intersects a previous radial fracture. Therefore, it is possible to speculate a series of impacts. For example, in the sketch below of a window with three impacts, A, B, and C, impact A had to occur first, because B's radial fractures terminate in A's. C must have occurred after B, as its lines terminate in B's. Therefore the sequence is: A–B–C.

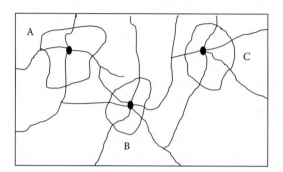

It is not, however, always this easy. For instance, if the window had one more impact, D, nestled between A and B, the order is not as definite. Possible sequences could be: A–B–C–D or A–B–D–C. The only sequence that can be certain is that A was first and B after A, then *either* C or D.

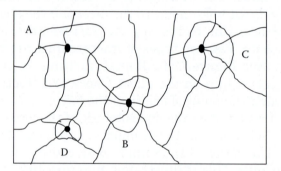

Sequencing fractures and analyzing holes in glass can be important contributions in reconstructing a crime.

Direction of Force

The stress lines (or conchoidal lines) formed as a result of impact and breakage (as seen in Figure 19.4) are useful tools in the determination of the direction of impact (force) on the glass. This information may be useful to corroborate statements or reconstruct the incident. Remember that the radial fractures break first on the opposite side of impact and then stress until they fall apart on the side of impact. Conchoidal lines are the results of this two-step occurrence. The first side of the glass to fail forms a perpendicular (right angle) line to the surface, as seen on the edge of the glass, and the side that fails last has lines that curve obliquely to its surface. The rule, commonly referred to as the 3R rule, is: when looking at the side edge of a RADIAL fracture line, there is a RIGHT angle on the REVERSE (opposite) side of the impact force. Figure 19.8 shows the same conchoidal lines, but the right angles and force are labeled.

The opposite of the 3R rule applies to concentric fracture lines. In this case, the right angle is formed on the *same* side as the impact force. This again is because

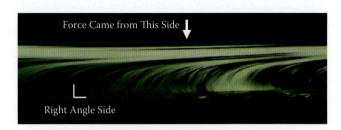

Figure 19.8 Direction of force using the 3R rule for a radial fracture piece of glass. Radial fractures have a right angle on the reverse side of the force.

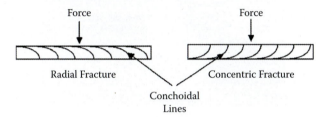

Figure 19.9 Using conchoidal lines on the edge of a piece of glass to determine direction of impact.

the concentric fractures break first on the side of impact and last on the opposite side. Figure 19.9 illustrates how force is determined using these lines of fracture. Mini Lab 1 at the end of this chapter explores the properties of broken glass and force of impact.

Class Characteristics of Glass

The number of class characteristics of glass is very limited because glass is so inert, and thus difficult to dissolve in any common solvents. This limits the chemical properties that can be described. A few crime labs have access to an **inductively coupled plasma mass spectrometer (ICP/MS)**. This instrument is capable of digesting glass and performing elemental analysis to determine its chemical composition. These instruments are expensive and require a good deal of skill to operate, and thus are not commonly used in crime labs. As a result, most forensic scientists concentrate on physical characteristics of the glass in making comparisons of glass from known and unknown sources. Some of the more common physical properties are as follows:

- Size, shape, dimensions, thickness
- Color
- Density
- Refractive index

Of these properties, one of the most discriminating is refractive index. This will be explained below.

Refractive Index

The speed of light in a vacuum is about 186,000 miles/second or about 3×10^8 meters/second. When light travels through any other transparent medium, it slows down. The effect that a particular medium has on the speed of light roughly correlates to its density. Just as you cannot walk as fast through water as you can through air (because water is denser than air and offers more resistance to your movement), so

Figure 19.10 Refraction of a plastic straw partially immersed in water. The straw appears to bend because of refraction.

it is with light passing through water. The magnitude of the decrease in the velocity of light as it passes through a transparent medium is called the **refractive index (RI)**, expressed as a ratio as shown in Equation 19.1.

$$RI = \frac{\text{The velocity of light in a vacuum}}{\text{The velocity of light in the transparent medium of interest}} \qquad (19.1)$$

The term **refractive index** comes from the term **refraction**. The varying speed of light when it passes from one medium to another causes the light to refract, change its direction, or bend. This is shown in Figure 19.10. A straight straw is partially immersed in water. When viewed from the side, the straw appears to have been bent. This is an example of refraction.

Refraction has several interesting properties that are exploited in the analysis of glass.

- If two transparent materials, such as a liquid and a transparent solid, have the same refractive index, light beams that pass through them will be refracted the same amount and light will not bend as it passes from one material to the other. The two materials will therefore look like one and cannot be distinguished. If the solid is immersed in the liquid, it will essentially disappear. Figure 19.11 is an example of a solid that has a refractive index similar to water. In the series of photos, the transparent solid, a cross-linked polyacrylamide called "ghost crystals," is immersed into distilled water and it seems to disappear.
- If a transparent material is heated, its refractive index will decrease. This is because, as a material is heated, it becomes less dense and more gas-like. This means that light passing through it will encounter less resistance and bend to a lesser degree. This effect is much more dramatic in liquids than solids. Glass, being solid material, barely changes its refractive index as it is heated.
- The amount of refraction light undergoes depends on its wavelength. The longer the wavelength of light, the less it bends as it travels from one medium

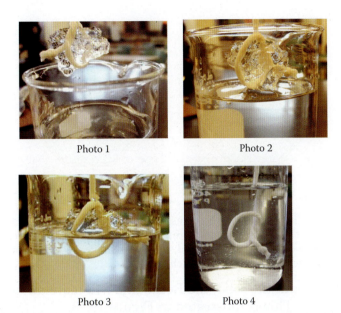

Photo 1   Photo 2

Photo 3   Photo 4

Figure 19.11 Immersion of a solid, transparent material into a liquid of the same refractive index. In photo 3, half of the solid still in air is visible, while the other half in water, is not. The solid is "invisible" in photo 4.

to the next. For example, red light (wavelength approximately 700 nm) bends less than blue light (wavelength approximately 400 nm).

- If a transparent solid is immersed in a transparent liquid of a different refractive index, a bright halo of light will be seen around the solid. This is called the **Becke line**. Since it is formed at the boundary between two different refractive indices, it will disappear if the solid and liquid have the same refractive index. Figure 19.12 shows the Becke line around a piece of glass immersed in a liquid at 100× magnification.
- If a transparent solid is immersed in a transparent liquid of different refractive index and viewed under a microscope, the Becke line will move as the ocular-to-objective lens distance is increased. If the liquid has a higher

Becke Lines

Figure 19.12 The white halo around the glass is the Becke line. It follows the exact contours of the glass.

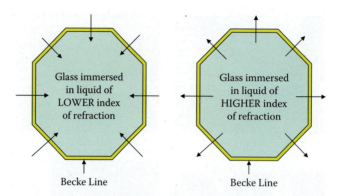

Figure 19.13 The Becke line moves as the focus of the microscope is changed. As the stage and objective are moved apart, the Becke line moves toward the medium of higher refractive index. If the glass has a higher refractive index than the liquid, the Becke line would move toward the glass as the objective lens and stage are moved away from each other.

refractive index than the solid, the Becke line will move away from the solid toward the liquid. This is illustrated in Figure 19.13.

Refractive Index Determination of a Small Glass Fragment

In many cases, glass recovered as evidence is in the form of very small fragments. Figure 19.14 shows a very small piece of borosilicate (Pyrex®) glass being tested in two liquids of known indices of refraction.

In a similar fashion, the refractive indices of small pieces of glass can be determined using a set of commercially available liquids whose refractive indices are known. Each liquid also has printed on its label the amount of refractive index change with each rise in temperature of one degree Celsius (1°C). Crime labs also use a **hot stage microscope**. This is a microfurnace that fits on top of the stage of a microscope. It can be heated under controlled conditions. A fragment of glass is immersed in a liquid whose refractive index is slightly higher than the glass and mounted on the hot stage. As the hot stage is heated, the temperature of the liquid and the glass will increase. The refractive index of the liquid will start to decrease. The refractive index of the glass will barely change because it is a solid. At some point, the refractive index of the liquid will drop until it is the same as that of the glass and the Becke line will disappear. If the glass is thin enough, it too will disappear. The hot stage monitors the temperature and how much it increases. The increase is noted at the time the Becke line disappears. From the data on the decrease of the refractive index with each degree rise in temperature, the refractive index of the glass can be determined. Figure 19.15 is a microscope with a hot stage mounted on the stage.

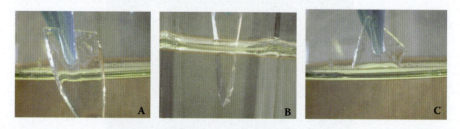

Figure 19.14 A shows a small piece of Pyrex glass not immersed in a liquid. B shows the same piece of glass immersed in water. C shows the piece immersed in vegetable oil. Pyrex and vegetable oil have similar indices of refraction as evidenced by the disappearance of the glass in the oil.

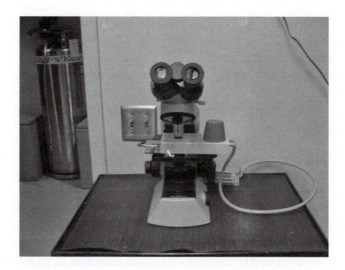

Figure 19.15 A compound microscope with a hot stage mounted on the stage.

The refractive indices for known and unknown glass particles can be determined in this way. Some forensic scientists go a step further and use special filters on the microscope that select particular wavelengths of light that are shone on the glass. This way several refractive indices can be determined. If two pieces of glass are similar, all their refractive indices taken at various wavelengths of light will have to agree. Remember, however, that even if two pieces of glass have the same physical properties such as refractive index, this is still *class* evidence.

Soil

Soil is found almost anywhere outdoors. It is very familiar to most people, who sometimes disparagingly call it "dirt." **Soil** is made up of crushed rocks and minerals mixed with decayed plant and animal material (**humus**). It can range from almost all crushed rock (beach sand) to almost all humus (peat bog). Except for water and man-made structures, soil covers the entire surface of the earth. Soil can be difficult to categorize and it takes a good deal of skill to identify its components. For these reasons, most forensic science laboratories do not analyze soil evidence except to the extent that someone left a shoe print or a car left a tire tread in the soil. This is unfortunate because the presence of soil evidence can tell a good deal about where a person or object has been. A good example of how important soil can be in solving crimes is exemplified in the Coors kidnapping case discussed at the beginning of this chapter.

Soil as Forensic Evidence

Soil evidence presents a number of challenges to forensic scientists. These may be the reasons why few laboratories take the time to analyze it.

- Soil varies in its chemical and physical properties from place to place, even within the same plot of ground. Studies have shown that soil profiles may differ markedly within a few meters of each other horizontally and vertically.
- There is no forensic classification scheme for soils. This means that there are potentially an infinite number of soil types, making it difficult to reach meaningful conclusions about associations among soil samples.

- It takes a good deal of skill to characterize the minerals present in soil. One must be familiar with crystal shapes and with polarizing light microscopy to analyze the inorganic fractions of soils.
- Soil is always *class* evidence. It has no unique characteristics that enable individualization.

Color Analysis of Soils

Sometimes it is possible to characterize soils by their color. The color is due to its mineral distribution and moisture content. Many minerals have characteristic colors. For example, copper-based minerals are green or blue. Iron minerals tend to be red or brown. In the early 1900s, a professor named Albert Munsell developed a color chart of all the various color hues. The Munsell Color Chart for Soil, an offshoot of the master color chart, is used today by forensic geologists to analyze soil. Soils can be examined visually for color or sometimes it is helpful to mix the soil with water, dissolving component minerals. If there are enough colored minerals in the soil, they will impart a tint to the water.

Physical Analysis of Soils

A soil sample's physical attributes can be analyzed microscopically. Equally sized samples of soil can be viewed under magnification and the percent of humus versus mineral materials can be estimated. The color, size, and shape of rock and mineral grains can be compared.

The sample can then be filtered using a sieve, which separates the organic (plant and animal) material from the soil, leaving the inorganic, crushed rock, and mineral grains. The density of the sample can be determined using a density gradient, a column of various liquids of varying density. Soil components will settle out in the liquid layer of the same density, forming a visual column for comparison. Mini Lab 2 is an exercise that utilizes a simpler version of this type of soil analysis.

Analysis of Humic Fractions of Soils

Some laboratories use HPLC to separate and display some of the common humus components of soils. The soil is extracted with acetonitrile and filtered. The filtrate is analyzed by HPLC. Figure 19.16 shows a liquid chromatogram of a soil sample.

Summary

Glass and soil are generally characterized by their physical properties. Glass is an amorphous solid made from pure silicon dioxide (beach sand). It contains various additives that alter its properties to make particular products. Glass is very inert and difficult to dissolve. The major tests performed on glass include color, dimension and thickness, density, and refractive index.

Direction of force and determination of sequence can be inferred by analyzing the radial and concentric fracture lines, entry and exit holes, and the conchoidal lines along the broken edges of a piece of glass.

As a transparent material, glass will bend and slow the velocity of light passing through the glass. This is called refraction. Different types of glass have different refractive indices. The refractive index of a tiny piece of glass is measured by

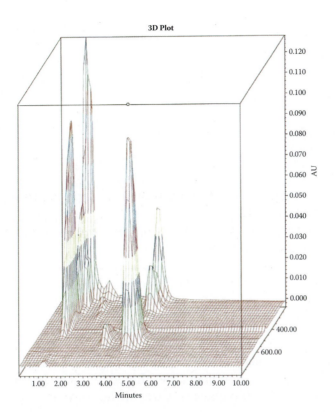

3D Plot

Figure 19.16 A liquid chromatogram of a soil sample. This is a pseudo-3-dimensional chromatogram. The x-axis is time in minutes. The y-axis is absorbance of light by the UV detector. The z-axis is the wavelength of light that exposes the soil sample. The wavelength range is 200 to 800 nanometers (nm).

immersing the glass in a liquid of known refractive index. If the refractive index of the liquid is different from the glass, a bright halo called the Becke line will appear around the glass. If the refractive index of the liquid and glass match, the Becke line will disappear. Refractive index varies with temperature and wavelength of light. These properties help in determining the refractive index of glass. Glass can be individualized if there are large enough pieces that can fit together like pieces of a jigsaw puzzle. In such cases, a microscope is used to visualize the stress marks formed when glass breaks.

Soil contains inorganic crushed rocks and minerals and organic decayed plant and animal material called humus. There is no forensic classification system for soils and soil content can differ markedly among samples taken a few meters from each other vertically and horizontally. This makes it difficult to successfully compare known and unknown soils. The inorganic fraction of soils can be analyzed by identifying the minerals present or by examining the color of the soils. Density of the inorganic portion of the soil can be visualized with a liquid density column. The organic humus fraction can be analyzed by liquid chromatography. Soil evidence is class evidence.

Mini Lab Activities

MINI LAB 1: DIRECTION OF FORCE ON GLASS

Materials:
Safety goggles
Lab gloves

Document glass (8 × 10)
Masking tape
Hammer
Clear tape
Two disposable storage bags (gallon size)
Hand lens
Small piece of cardboard (8 × 10 size or greater)

Procedure:

1. Outline the document glass edges with making tape to protect it and yourself. Be sure to cover both sides.
2. Using the clear tape, crisscross strips on one side of the glass vertically and horizontally. See diagram below.

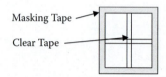

3. Place the taped glass piece into two storage bags and seal.
4. On a cardboard protected surface, use the edge of the hammer (or a hammer and a nail) to gently hit the glass in three different places, being careful not to dislodge the broken pieces.
5. Analyze the three impact patterns. Can you tell the order by looking at the radial fractures produced?
6. Identify radial and concentric fracture lines.
7. Carefully open the storage bags to access the broken glass.
8. Locate a large piece that has both concentric and radial fractures and dislodge it from the parent piece of glass.
9. Using a hand lens, analyze the conchoidal lines in the sides of the glass. Can you find the right angle of intersection and therefore the direction of force?

Note: Edge pieces of glass can be held under a stereo (dissecting) microscope under low power instead of using the hand lens.

MINI LAB 2: SOIL ANALYSIS DENSITY COLUMN

Materials:

Multiple soil samples from different locations
30–45 mesh sieve
Test tubes
Vegetable oil
Glycerin
Isopropanol
Distilled water
Corn syrup

Procedure:
For each soil sample, complete the following.

1. Prior to preparing your density column, be sure your soil sample has been allowed to dry thoroughly. If not, place it in an oven-proof container and heat on the lowest temperature for approximately ten minutes.
2. Make a density column using the test tube. Layer the liquids in the test tube from most dense at the bottom to least dense at the top. Allow to settle.

   Corn Syrup   1.360 g/mL
   Glycerin   1.261 g/mL
   Water   1.000 g/mL
   Vegetable Oil   0.890 g/mL
   Isopropanol   0.786 g/mL

3. Filter the organic materials by placing the sample though the mesh sieve and collect the filtered soil. Discard the organic material, as it will not be part of the density column.
4. Carefully place a small amount of the filtered soil into the density column and allow it to settle for twenty-four hours.
5. Sketch the results and estimate the percentage of each sample in each layer.

Note: Further comparative analysis can be easily done on the original soil sample by massing the sample first, then sieve and mass the organic and inorganic materials. Compare samples by amounts of organic versus inorganic materials.

Test Yourself

Multiple Choice

1. When the temperature of a liquid is raised
   a. Its refractive index increases
   b. Its refractive index decreases
   c. Its refractive index disappears
   d. Its refractive index doesn't change
   e. None of the above
2. A piece of glass has a refractive index of 1.53 when measured with 400 nm wavelength light. If the same piece of glass is analyzed with 600 nm light its refractive index
   a. Doubles to 2.06
   b. Increases
   c. Decreases
   d. Stays the same
   e. Cannot be measured
3. If a beam of light travels through a piece of glass at 90,000 miles per second, the refractive index of the glass is:
   a. 0.5
   b. 1.0
   c. 2.0
   d. 90,000
   e. 0
4. Most labs do not analyze soil because
   a. There is no forensic classification system for soils
   b. It is almost never individual evidence

    c. Chemical composition of soil samples vary within a few meters of area

    d. Analysis of soils requires a good deal of skill

    e. All of the above

5. Adding boron to molten glass

    a. Makes it more stable to rapid temperature changes

    b. Adds a greenish tint to the glass

    c. Makes the glass much harder

    d. Makes the glass more liquid like so that it flows

    e. Has no effect on glass

Short Essay

6. What is the definition of glass?
7. What properties does glass have in common with a liquid? A solid?
8. Define refractive index and refraction?
9. What is a Becke line and what causes it to form?
10. What is soil? What are the two major fractions of soil?

Problem Solving

11. A tiny fragment of glass is immersed in a liquid at 25°C on a microscope slide and then mounted in a hot stage furnace placed on a microscope stage. The Becke line is clearly visible and moves toward the liquid as the ocular-to-objective distance is increased, indicating that the liquid has a higher refractive index than the glass. The label on the bottle of the liquid indicates that the refractive index of the liquid at 25°C is 1.52. The hot stage is heated and the Becke line disappears when the temperature of the liquid has reached 45°C. The label on the bottle of the liquid indicates that the refractive index of the liquid decreases 0.005 for each degree rise in temperature. From this data, determine the refractive index of the glass.

12. A beam of light passes from air through Plexiglas, which has an index of refraction of 1.43. By what amount does the speed of light change?

13. Light traveling into an aquarium slows to a speed of 2.26×10^8 m/s. Calculate the index of refraction of water.

14. Sequence the impacts for the glass fractures in Photo 1 and Photo 2. Explain your reasoning.

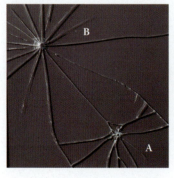
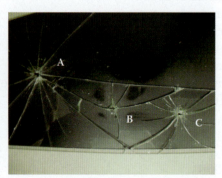

Glass Photo 1   Glass Photo 2

15. Photo A shows a piece of glass in water, index of refraction 1.33 and Photo B shows the same piece of glass in oil, index of refraction 1.47. Explain the results.

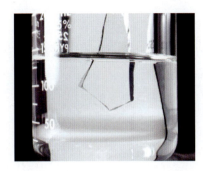

Photo A

Photo B

Further Reading

Miller, E. T. *Forensic Glass Comparisons*. Ed. R. Saferstein. Forensic Science Handbook. Vol. 1. Englewood Cliffs, NJ: Prentice Hall, 1982.
Caddy B., ed. *Forensic Examination of Glass and Paint: Analysis and Interpretation*. London: Taylor & Francis, 2001.

On the Web

Glass

http://micro.magnet.fsu.edu/optics/timeline/people/becke.html
www.brocku.ca/earthsciences/people/gfinn/optical/becke4.htm
www.edinformatics.com/inventions_inventors/glass.htm

Soil Analysis

http://en.wikipedia.org/wiki/Munsell_color_system
http://soil.gsfc.nasa.gov/pvg/munsell.htm
http://soil.gsfc.nasa.gov/index.html
http://soil.gsfc.nasa.gov/forengeo/secret.htm

Fires and Explosions

Learning Objectives

1. To be able to define fire and explosion
2. To be able to define and give examples of arson and incendiary fires
3. To be able to define combustion and give examples of combustion reactions
4. To be able to describe how fire and explosion scenes are investigated and what evidence is sought
5. To be able to describe methods for the laboratory analysis of fire and explosion debris

Chapter 20
Fires and Explosions

Chapter Outline

Mini Glossary

Accelerant: A fuel used to start a fire that will not start on its own or to speed up a fire.

Adsorption–elution: A method of recovery of accelerant vapors from fire debris that employs a material that adsorbs the vapors, which are then removed (eluted) and concentrated for analysis.

Black powder: A low power explosive made from potassium nitrate, sulfur, and carbon.

Bomb seat: The point of origin of a bombing.

Combustion: A type of chemical reaction whereby a fuel reacts with oxygen to release energy.

Deflagration: A type of explosion whereby the oxygen is mixed with the fuel in a form where the O is bonded to other atoms that form weaker bonds than in O_2, and thus require less activation energy to break.

Detonation: An instantaneous explosion. Produces escaping gases that travel in excess of the speed of sound.

Dynamite: An explosive containing nitroglycerine that is impregnated in paper and other absorbent materials.

Exothermic: A chemical reaction that gives off heat.

Fire tetrahedron: A diagram that shows the four factors that must be present for a fire to start and maintain. These are: fuel + oxygen + activation energy + combustion.

Fire trail: An accelerant is poured on a floor from room to room and then ignited. This is an efficient way to carry a fire from one place to another inside a building.

Greiss test: A chemical test used in the analysis of explosive. It gives a positive reaction to all substances that contain nitrate or nitrite.

Headspace: The airspace above a closed container that contains debris from a fire.

Hydrocarbon: A compound combining hydrogen and carbon atoms. Many are fuels used to accelerate fires.

Incendiary fire: A fire started deliberately with the intention of committing or hiding a crime.

Initiating (primary) explosive: A high explosive that is sensitive to detonation.

Low explosive: Explosions that produce escaping gases of velocities below the speed of sound.

Molotov cocktail: A bottle or other breakable container filled with an accelerant such as gasoline. A wick, usually a length of rag, is inserted in the top. The wick is ignited and the bottle is thrown into the building or other place where the arsonist wants to start the fire.

Non-initiating (secondary) explosive: An explosive that requires a booster charge.

Plastique: An explosive impregnated with a clay-like material so it can be shaped.

Point of origin: The location where fire started.

Solid phase microextraction (SPME): A method of adsorption–elution where the adsorbing medium is a small, coated needle.

Spalling: Blistering of concrete by exposure to extreme heat.

Acronyms

Δ: The Greek letter *delta* that stands for heat or energy
ANFO: Ammonium nitrate and fuel oil
PETN: Pentaerythritol tetranitrate
TNT: Trinitrotoluene

Introduction

On November 28, 1942, one of the most destructive fires in U.S. history occurred at the Coconut Grove nightclub in Boston. The club was supposed to have a capacity of five hundred people, but that night, the crowd exceeded a thousand. The club was formerly a speakeasy (an illegal bar that operated during Prohibition) during the 1920s. Some of the entrances and exits had been boarded up since then. The only working entrance was a revolving door in the front. The club also used flammable decorations such as cloth curtains and palm trees throughout. The refrigeration system used methyl chloride as the refrigerant. Methyl chloride is very flammable. It was a substitute for freon, which was in short supply owing to World War II.

Fire scene investigators traced the **point of origin** of the fire to the Melody Lounge in the basement. A lightbulb had burned out and a busboy was using a match for light while he changed the bulb. He apparently dropped the match. Within five minutes, the entire lounge was engulfed in flame. Many people tried to escape through a stairway to the main floor, but the door at the top was locked. Several people died in the stairwell from asphyxiation. The fire spread quickly to the main floor and engulfed it within another five minutes. Many people were trapped in the revolving door. Others were trampled to death and some died at their tables of asphyxiation from poisonous fumes. As a result of the fire, 490 people died and the owner was convicted of involuntary manslaughter and sentenced to three and a half years in prison.

This fire was set by accident, but the conditions in the night club were such that it should have been foreseen that any fire, deliberate or not, had the potential to kill and injure many people. Even as far back as 1942, there were fire codes in place that, had they been enforced, could have prevented many deaths. You can probably name a number of issues in this situation that caused the damage and loss of life. Many destructive fires occur by accidental causes and some by natural causes, such as lightning strikes. Still other fires are deliberate.

There are two types of deliberate fires. The first does not involve any criminal activity or an attempt to cover a crime. In some communities, it is permissible to burn leaves or trash or other debris on one's own property, although a license may be necessary. In other cases, however, a fire is set with the intent to commit a crime or cover up another crime. Such fires are called **incendiary** and the crime is *arson*. For example, someone may burn down a failing business in an attempt to collect fire insurance money. In other cases, a murderer may burn a house where he has killed the owner in the hopes of destroying the body and any incriminating evidence. In still other cases, an accountant may destroy documents in a fire to hide evidence of embezzlement. As we will see later, the determination of whether a fire was incendiary may boil down to eliminating the other causes; natural or accidental.

What Is a Fire?

Fire is the evolution of energy in the form of light, heat, and smoke as the result of combustion. **Combustion** is a type of chemical reaction whereby a *fuel* reacts with oxygen to release energy. Reactions that give off energy are termed **exothermic**. When a fuel substance reacts with oxygen, the reaction is always exothermic. Equation 20.1 is the simplest combustion reaction. It is the reaction of natural gas (methane) with oxygen to form carbon dioxide and water and heat energy. This is the reaction that heats homes or stoves that use natural gas.

$$CH_4 + O_2 \xrightarrow{\Delta} CO_2 + 2H_2O + \Delta \tag{20.1}$$
methane oxygen carbon dioxide water

The symbol Δ (the Greek letter **delta**) is the symbol used for heat energy in chemistry and physics. Notice that the Δ also appears over the reaction arrow. In chemistry, a symbol over a reaction arrow means "in the presence of." This means that heat is being put into the reaction. This heat is called the activation energy. In order to get methane and oxygen to react, it is necessary to break up the oxygen molecule as shown in Equation 20.2. As long as the energy produced by the reaction is greater than the *activation energy*, the overall reaction is exothermic

$$O_2 \xrightarrow{\Delta} 2O \qquad\qquad (20.2)$$

The atomic oxygen now reacts with the methane in the combustion. The amount of activation energy needed to start the reaction is very little compared to the energy that is emitted by the reaction. The activation energy can be in the form of a spark or small flame. Exothermic reactions like methane and oxygen produce energy because the energy stored in C–H bonds is greater than that in C–O or O–H bonds. The excess energy is given off in the form of heat and flame and smoke.

Gasoline is a petroleum distillate that contains more than three hundred substances. Most of them are **hydrocarbons**, which are substances made up of carbon and hydrogen. Methane is also a hydrocarbon. These are all potent fuels that combust with oxygen. A common combustion reaction takes place inside the internal combustion engine. Here, gasoline is compressed into a small space and ignited with a spark plug. This provides the activation energy for the reaction. The gasoline combusts in the air present in the engine cylinders and the energy produced causes the pistons to move and propel the car. One of the compounds in gasoline is *octane*, C_8H_{18}. It combusts with oxygen, as shown in Equation 20.3. The activation energy needed for this reaction serves two purposes. It breaks the oxygen molecule into oxygen atoms (Equation 20.2) and it vaporizes the octane, which is a liquid at room temperature. In general, fuels must be in the vapor phase to undergo combustion. Activation energy is partly used to convert liquid and solid fuels to vapor.

$$2C_8H_{18} + 25O_2 \xrightarrow{\Delta} 16CO_2 + 18H_2O + \Delta \qquad\qquad (20.3)$$

Note: This equation is balanced. All chemical equations must have the same number of each type of atom on both sides of the equation.

There are many more bonds in this reaction than in the one involving methane, so much more energy is given off by the combustion of octane. This reaction, along with many others in gasoline, can be put to work inside an internal combustion engine in a car. There are many other substances that can act as fuels in combustion reactions. Wood, plastic, natural and synthetic fibers and fabrics, carpeting, tile, drywall, and most building materials undergo combustion as long as there is sufficient activation energy available to vaporize the fuel. Once sufficient activation energy is available and the combustion reaction gets going, it will produce enough energy to provide additional activation energy to vaporize more fuel so that the reaction can continue. The reaction will continue perpetually until the fuel or the oxygen is spent or the temperature falls below that needed to continue to vaporize the fuel.

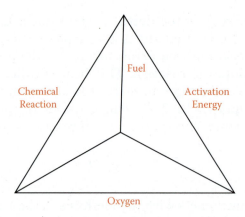

Figure 20.1 The fire tetrahedron.

Extinguishing a Fire

Fire experts use the concept of the **fire tetrahedron** when describing the materials and conditions needed to sustain a fire. Figure 20.1 shows a diagram of a fire tetrahedron. At each apex of the tetrahedron is one of the elements that must be present for a fire to be sustained—fuel + oxygen + activation energy + combustion.

All four of these elements must be present to have a fire. If any one of them is removed, the fire goes out. Fire extinguishers are based on this principle. They remove one or more of the elements of a fire. For example, water makes a good extinguisher for some fires. It cools the fire so that there is insufficient activation energy to split oxygen molecules and/or vaporize the fuel. Fire blankets smother a fire by preventing oxygen from getting to the fuel. Foam extinguishers work like the blanket in that they prevent oxygen from reaching the fire. See Figure 20.2 for a picture of a foam extinguisher. Carbon dioxide extinguishers blow out the fire like blowing out a candle. The carbon dioxide is sprayed at the fire under pressure and it blows away the oxygen. Carbon dioxide will not support combustion so the fire goes out.

Something for You to Do

Go to various buildings such as your school, a department store, and a gas station and ask if there any fire extinguishers. If so, look at the labels on them. The label will usually indicate what types of fires the extinguisher is designed to put out. Particular types of extinguishers are designed for different types of fires. You can also see a variety of fire extinguishers at building supply stores. Fire extinguishers do not contain water because water is available at most homes and businesses in large quantities. Besides, water is not a good extinguisher for certain types of fires such as electrical or grease. Why?

Incendiary Fires

Fire experts and the legal system use two closely related terms to describe fires that are deliberately set. The term **incendiary fire** means a fire that is willfully and intentionally set. The National Fire Protection Association recently changed from using the term "incendiary" to "intentionally," but "incendiary" is still widely used. When an incendiary fire is set in order to commit a crime or destroy evidence from a previous crime, the crime of *arson* has been committed. Arson is one of the most serious and costly crimes in the United States. Statistics from the United States Department of Homeland Security for the past ten years and the costs of these fires are shown in Table 20.1.

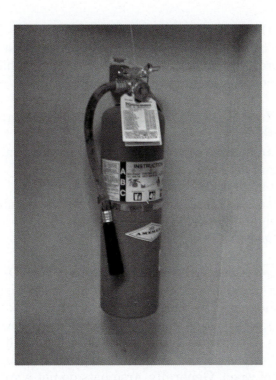

Figure 20.2 A chemical fire extinguisher. Different extinguishers are rated for different types of fires and are clearly marked with a lettering and symbol system that indicates which types of fires they are suitable for.

TABLE 20.1
Arson Fire Statistics

Year	Fires	Deaths	Direct Dollar Loss (in Millions)
1994	86,000	550	$1,447
1995[a]	90,500	740	$1,647
1996	85,500	520	$1,405
1997	78,500	445	$1,309
1998	76,000	470	$1,249
1999	72,000	370	$1,281
2000	75,000	505	$1,340
2001[b]	45,500	330	$1,013
2001[c]	45,500	2,451	$33,440
2002	44,500	350	$919
2003	37,500	305	$692

Source: National Fire Protection Association Fire Loss in the U.S. during 2003.

[a] Includes 168 civilian deaths that occurred in the explosion and fire in the Federal office building in Oklahoma City on April 19, 1995.

[b] Excludes the events of September 11, 2001.

[c] These estimates reflect the number of deaths, injuries, and dollar loss directly related to the events of September 11, 2001.

Table 20.1 shows that, although the number of arson fires has been decreasing, there were still more than 37,000 arson fires in 2003 that cost almost $700 million.

In 2001, the Federal Emergency Management Agency published the results of a research study on arson. A summary of their findings included the following:

- Arson is the leading cause of fires in the United States and the second leading cause of death.
- Fifty percent of arson fires occur outdoors, 30 percent occur in buildings, and 20 percent occur in vehicles.
- Half of all arson arrests are juveniles.
- Poorer neighborhoods experience fourteen times the number of arson fires as more affluent neighborhoods.
- Church arsons have increased since 1996.

There are a number of ways to start an incendiary fire. One could use a match, lighter, or blow torch to get something burning and then just leave the premises. This may not be as easy as it sounds. Have you ever tried to start a fire in a fireplace by lighting a large log with a match? It usually doesn't work. You have to light small twigs or pieces of paper with the match and gradually add larger pieces of wood until enough energy is put out by the fire to provide enough energy to vaporize parts of large pieces of wood. Generally, arsonists do not want to be at a fire scene any longer than necessary for fear of being seen. They want to start the fire as fast as possible and get out. In many cases, fires can be started remotely using a time delay to supply the activation energy. Figure 20.3 shows how matches can delay the start an incendiary fire.

For a moment, think of what an arsonist would want to accomplish if he were going to deliberately start a fire without being present when the fire started and without being caught. First, he would want to delay the start of the fire until he was out of the vicinity. Second, if complete destruction of the building is the goal, then fires need to be started in several places at once or there must be a method of causing the fire to spread rapidly. There must also be a continual source of air in the premises or the fire will extinguish after the oxygen present at the time of the fire is consumed. It is difficult to start fires in several places in a building simultaneously, so arsonists often use accelerants to spread a fire rapidly throughout. An **accelerant** is a fuel that is used to start a fire that otherwise couldn't be easily started or to make a fire burn faster. Accelerants are generally liquids that require

Figure 20.3 A fire was started in the carpeting in a car using a smoldering cigarette and a book of matches.

low activation energy so they can be readily combusted. They undergo highly exo-thermic reactions so there is plenty of energy to keep the fire going and to involve harder-to-burn materials. Accelerants can generally be obtained without calling attention to the purchaser. This is why gasoline, charcoal lighters, paint thinners, and other similar consumer products are widely used as accelerants. Gasoline is the accelerant of choice in more than half of all arson fires. Unfortunately, for the arsonist and fortunately for forensic scientists, even burned accelerants leave residues that can be detected and identified as to type. In most cases, a forensic chemist can determine if an accelerant was used in a fire and if so, whether it was gasoline or some other type of product. If this evidence is located and collected by the fire scene investigator, a forensic chemist can usually determine what type of product (e.g., gasoline, kerosene) it is, but cannot determine whether the accelerant came from a particular source such as a container found in a suspect's garage.

Investigation of a Fire

Investigation of fires is normally carried out by trained fire scene investigators. Most are trained first as firefighters and come to fire scene investigation from a career as a firefighter. Some have college degrees. A few universities and community colleges offer classes and even degrees in fire science, where students learn about the chemistry of fire and how fires start and spread, how they are suppressed, and how to investigate a fire and properly collect and preserve evidence.

It is the responsibility of the fire scene investigator to determine the cause of the fire. This is done by a physical inspection of the fire scene, discussion with the firefighters and witnesses, support of the forensic science laboratory in the analysis of fire residues, and perhaps even the use of dogs that are specially trained to detect common accelerants. This process is made more difficult by what happens to the structure when a fire occurs and when the fire department responds. When a fire is discovered, the fire department will respond as quickly as possible. They have two major duties. The first is to remove everyone who may be trapped in the fire and the second is to extinguish the fire. The latter is normally accomplished with thousands of gallons of water. After the fire is put out, the electricity and gas are turned off if they weren't already knocked out by the fire. After the fire is out and the firefighters have left, the fire scene investigator takes over.

Fire scene investigation can be very difficult. As mentioned above, there may be no light, heat, or air conditioning. The entire site will be drenched in water. The structure of the building may have been weakened by the fire and walking through it can be hazardous. There may be hazardous chemical fumes or residues present that were formed from burning materials. Figure 20.4 shows an indoor kitchen fire started by a defective coffee maker.

If a fire in a multistory building is severe enough, the upper floors may collapse on top of the lower floors. If the point of origin is on a lower floor, it may be buried in tons of material from upper floors. Heavy moving equipment may be needed to remove the debris layer by layer. This must be done carefully, as important evidence may be found in any of the layers.

Causes of a Fire

From the standpoint of the fire scene investigator there are only three causes of fires:

Figure 20.4 A fire in a kitchen. Note the V pattern of burning on the wall on the left side. *Courtesy of* James Novak.

- **Natural:** This could be a fire that is started by a lightning strike
- **Accidental:** Someone accidentally drops a match in bed or an electrical circuit becomes overloaded
- **Deliberate:** Arson

There are two ways a fire scene investigator determines that a fire is arson. The first is to find compelling evidence at the scene. This could be a fire-setting device such as a **Molotov cocktail**, a bottle, or other breakable container filled with a accelerant such as gasoline. Then a wick is inserted in the top. This is usually a length of rag. The wick is ignited and the bottle is thrown into the building or other place where the arsonist wants to start the fire. The Molotov cocktail contains three of the legs of the fire tetrahedron: activation energy, fuel, and heat. Another piece of evidence that strongly suggests arson is a **fire trail**. This is when an accelerant is poured on a floor from room to room and then ignited. This is an efficient way to carry a fire from one place to another inside a building. A picture of a Molotov cocktail can be found in Chapter 19: Glass and Soil, Figure 19.2.

The other way a fire scene investigator determines a fire is arson is to eliminate all possible natural or accidental causes of the fire. If this is done, then the only cause that is left is arson. Eliminating accidental causes of a fire can be difficult. Suppose, for example, a furnace explodes during the course of a fire. This could have happened because it was rigged to explode and actually caused the fire; it could have gotten involved in a fire that started elsewhere in the building; or it could have accidentally malfunctioned and caused the fire. Often a fire scene investigator calls in a heating contractor to examine the remains of the furnace to try and determine what happened. Other appliances such as water heaters, dryers, toasters, and ovens may also be involved in fires or cause them. Electrical system overloads can also be hard to interpret. It is possible to create an electrical overload that causes overheating of wires and can cause a fire. Many fires are caused by accidental overload, especially in older buildings.

The Point of Origin

By far the most important piece of information that a fire scene investigator needs to determine the cause of a fire is the **point of origin**. This is the location where the fire started. If an accelerant was used to start a fire, its residue will be most likely found at the point of origin. If an appliance malfunction caused the fire, the point of

Figure 20.5 A fire trail in a mobile home. *Courtesy of* Charles Hughes.

origin will be near the appliance. In a multistory building, arson fires are generally started on the first floor so the arsonist can escape easily without getting trapped in the fire. As mentioned above, this means that locating the point of origin may mean moving tons of material that could have collapsed on it.

The point of origin is generally where the most extensive burning takes place and is often gets the hottest. Some of the characteristics that fire scene investigators look for in searching for the point of origin include V-patterns of burning, **spalling** (blistering) of concrete, the beginning of a fire trail, the obvious presence of accelerants, and the apparent gathering or piling up of fuel materials.

It was mentioned before that arson fires are often characterized by fire trails and the presence of accelerants. Another clue that a fire may be arson is the presence of multiple points of origin. If an arsonist wants to make sure an entire building becomes involved in the fire, he will start fires at multiple points in the building. This can also be accomplished by the use of a fire trail. An accelerant is poured in a trail from room to room. Then the accelerant is ignited at one point and the ensuing fire travels along the trail. The result is that it appears as if multiple fires were started in each room. If the burning is not too severe, the fire scene investigator can see remnants of the fire trail. Figure 20.5 shows a fire trail.

Other Evidence at Fire Scenes

In their zeal to find the point of origin of a fire and determine its cause, fire scene investigators sometimes overlook other important evidence. Even though fires normally destroy much of the trace evidence found at other types of crime scenes, sometimes the fire doesn't reach some of the evidence. Fingerprints, hairs and fibers, shoe prints, blood, and documents can survive a fire under the right circumstances and these should not be overlooked. It is normally not difficult to determine if a fire is arson, but it can be very hard to determine who did it. Trace and other evidence can be crucial in making these determinations.

The Role of Accelerants

The presence of residues from a fuel such as gasoline can be strongly indicative of an arson fire. It should be kept in mind, however, that finding such residues doesn't necessarily mean the fire was deliberate. Many people keep cans or bottles of gasoline, charcoal lighter, paint thinner, or other accelerants in their homes or businesses. Any fire could reach these stored liquids and they could easily accelerate the fire. It can sometimes be difficult to determine if these accelerants were used to start the fire or were innocently involved. Accelerants can also greatly increase the damage of a fire because they give off so much heat. Such increased damage can destroy evidence that would otherwise have survived the fire. An example of this was a fire aboard an aircraft carrier that was docked at the Norfolk, Virginia Navy Yard. The damage to some of the rooms below decks on the ship was horrific because the heat from the fire ruptured overhead lines that carried hydraulic fluid used in the elevators that moved the planes up to the flight deck. This hydraulic fluid emitted copious heat energy when it burned, resulting in a great deal of damage. Metal beams that might otherwise have been weakened, deformed, or twisted, actually melted and collapsed.

Detection and Collection of Accelerants

Fire scene investigators are well trained to spot signs that accelerants were used in a fire. Evidence includes extreme heat and damage, sooty V-pattern burning, and fire trails. Hydrocarbon "sniffer" instruments can detect the presence of small quantities of common accelerants. In recent years, live sniffers called *arson dogs* have become popular among fire scene investigators. These dogs are specially trained to detect minute quantities of common accelerants.

Some materials are better than others for trapping and holding accelerants. The best materials are those that can easily absorb liquids. These include bedding, furniture with cushions, carpeting, clothing, and soil. Substances like tile, wood, wall board, and other building materials do not absorb and trap liquids very well and are less suitable candidates for containing accelerant residues. The more absorbent a material is, the better it is for accelerants. If some of the accelerant can penetrate the material, it may be protected from the fire and some unburned liquid may be trapped. This is the best evidence for analysis by forensic chemists.

Once evidence of an accelerant has been located, the debris must be collected and packaged for delivery to the crime lab. Since accelerants are volatile and evaporate easily, they must be packaged in airtight containers. Forensic chemists strongly recommend unused paint cans for packaging fire scene evidence. They can be made airtight but, at the same time, the tops can be easily removed in case access to the debris is needed. They come in various sizes up to five gallons to accommodate various amounts of evidence. Some fire scene investigators use empty glass jars with screw caps. These are not as useful as paint cans because they are breakable and because they cannot take heat, which is sometimes used in the analysis of fire residues. Large pieces of fire debris can be packaged in plastic bags, but only the type that doesn't breathe (can be made airtight). Care must be taken to seal these bags tightly. From the analytical standpoint, it is better to use several paint cans than one large plastic bag because large bags are difficult to manipulate in the laboratory.

Analysis of Fire Scene Evidence

The biggest challenge facing forensic chemists in the analysis of fire scene evidence is separating and concentrating the accelerant residues from the fire debris. This

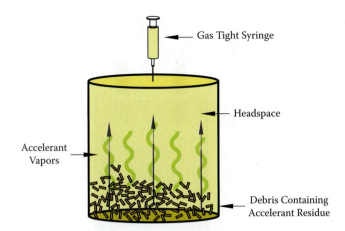

Figure 20.6 Diagram showing how the headspace in a sealed container of fire debris is sampled with a gas-tight syringe. The container is usually heated to drive more of the fire residue into the vapor phase. *Courtesy of* Meredith Haddon.

can be a real challenge because of the amount of debris present (sometimes too much, sometimes too little), the way it is packaged, and the nature and concentration of the accelerant. Over the years, there have been a number of ways of separating and concentrating accelerant residues. The methods used today are designed so that once the concentration step has been done, the identification of the accelerant type can be performed by gas chromatography. This method is practically universal in crime labs. The concentration methods that are commonly used today are described below.

Passive Headspace

The most popular method of concentration of accelerant residues, this method is shown in Figure 20.6. The container is airtight. It is gently heated so that some of the accelerant will evaporate into the air space above the debris (**headspace**). Eventually, the amount of accelerant in the headspace will be in equilibrium with the amount in the debris. The higher the temperature, the more accelerant will be in the headspace. The container can only be heated a small amount because heating raises the pressure in the can and it could rupture. After the container is heated, the headspace can be sampled with a gas-tight syringe, which can then be used to introduce the headspace vapor directly into a gas chromatograph.

Adsorption–Elution

Adsorption–elution is a modification of the passive headspace method. Two small holes are punched in the top of a can and a tube containing *activated charcoal* (fine carbon powder) is put in each hole. A vacuum pump is then connected to one of the tubes. When the vacuum is turned on, it pulls the air out of the headspace of the can. The air is pulled through one of the tubes containing the charcoal. Instead of a vacuum, the accelerant can be removed by pumping an inert gas such as nitrogen through one of the tubes. This pushes the accelerant vapors out of the other tube. The charcoal traps the accelerant vapors. This apparatus can be seen in Figure 20.7. As the headspace becomes evacuated, air rushes in from the outside through the second tube. More of the accelerant will evaporate from the fire debris into the headspace to re-establish the equilibrium. But this air is continuously pulled out of the can

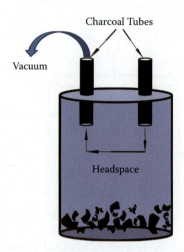

Figure 20.7 Absorption–elution method of concentrating fire residue. The debris is heated, driving more of the residue into the vapor phase. A vacuum is drawn on the container, which pulls the headspace vapors out, trapping them in the charcoal strip. Air rushes in through the other tube. *Courtesy of* Heredith Haddon.

Think about "negative controls" (Chapter 3)

Figure 20.8 Answer to quiz question.

by the vacuum pump, and more air continually rushes in through the other tube. Eventually, practically all of the accelerant will be trapped (adsorbed) onto the charcoal. Then the charcoal tubes are removed and a small amount of solvent is poured through the charcoal. This dissolves and elutes the accelerant off the charcoal. The dissolved accelerant can then be injected into a gas chromatograph for analysis.

Something for You to Do

Why are there two holes in the top of the can? Why not simply put one hole in the can and insert a charcoal tube and then apply a vacuum to that tube? If you can figure out why there must be two holes in the can, then why is there a charcoal tube in each hole? If you cannot figure it out then, see the hint shown in Figure 20.8.

Solid Phase Microextraction (SPME)

Solid phrase microextraction is the newest technique in accelerant concentration. It takes advantage of the sensitivity of today's modern GC/MS instruments that require only a few micrograms of analyte. The SPME apparatus consists of a syringe whose needle is coated with charcoal or another polymer efficient at adsorbing accelerant molecules. The needle is inserted into the headspace in a container of fire residue. The residue is heated and the accelerant will adsorb onto the surface of the coated needle. After about thirty minutes, the needle is withdrawn and inserted into a gas chromatograph. The heat from the GC will elute the accelerant from the coating on the needle.

Solvent Extraction

Solvent extraction used to be a popular method of accelerant concentration. It is performed by opening a can of fire residue and adding a suitable solvent, usually carbon disulfide (CS_2) or pentane (C_5H_{12}) and mixing well. Then the mixture is filtered and the solvent evaporated to a small volume and injected into a gas chromatograph.

The main drawback to solvent extraction is that many materials found in a home or business contain substances made from petroleum that dissolve in the solvent and interfere with the gas chromatography used to analyze the accelerant. Carbon disulfide is very volatile and flammable, has a disagreeable odor, and is toxic. Pentane is flammable and is sometimes found as a component of some accelerants.

Analysis of Accelerants

As mentioned above, the universal method for the analysis of accelerant residues is by gas chromatography, usually coupled to a mass spectrometer. The most common accelerants are gasoline and other consumer products such as charcoal lighter, paint thinners, and lamp oils. Fuels used in camping lanterns and stoves are also popular accelerants. Each of these products contains many components. Gasoline contains more than three hundred substances. The purpose of gas chromatography is not to identify each component, but to display the pattern of peaks obtained from a sample of fire debris. Figure 20.9 is a gas chromatogram of gasoline and Figure 20.10 is a gas chromatogram of charcoal lighter made from kerosene.

Interpretation of gas chromatograms of accelerants can be difficult. The chromatograms of gasoline and kerosene shown in Figures 20.9 and 20.10 are obtained from pristine materials, right out of the can. Accelerants subjected to the heat from a fire undergo physical and, to a lesser extent, chemical changes that affect their

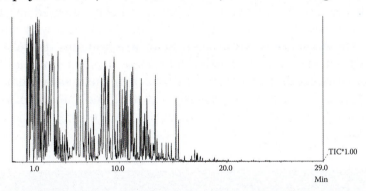

Figure 20.9 Capillary gas chromatogram of neat gasoline. There are more than three hundred substances in gasoline. Most of them are displayed as discrete peaks.

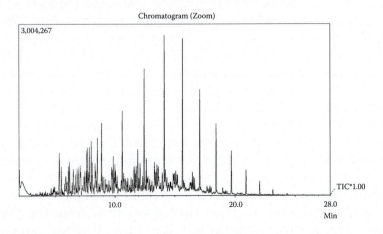

Figure 20.10 Gas chromatogram of charcoal lighter made from kerosene.

chromatograms. Some of the components of all accelerants are volatile and evaporate if exposed to heat. In the chromatograms in the figures, the most volatile substances are shown first (on the left). If they have evaporated, their peaks will be reduced and the chromatograms will be distorted. In extreme cases, an accelerant will evaporate or combust significantly and the associated chromatogram will look very different from the ones in Figures 20.9 and 20.10. Forensic chemists who analyze fire residues will prepare chromatographic libraries of common accelerants that have undergone various amounts of degradation due to partial combustion and/or evaporation. These can be used to compare against casework samples from a fire.

On the basis of laboratory analysis of fire residues, a forensic chemist can reasonably conclude that accelerant residues are present in fire debris. If there is enough present, the chemist may be able to determine the type of product. One must be careful here. A number of commercial products are made from the same material. For example, kerosene is used not only as a fuel for heating homes and businesses—it is also the main ingredient in many charcoal lighters and paint thinners. Thus, finding a kerosene pattern in a chromatogram of a fire residue does not justify naming what type of product it is—and, of course, there are no circumstances where a chemist would be justified in reaching a conclusion that fire residue came from a particular container. There is nothing unique about a gas chromatogram of one sample of gasoline compared to another.

No matter what conclusion the forensic scientist reaches about the presence and type of accelerant in fire residues, this information is only advisory to the fire scene investigator. The absence of an accelerant in fire residues does not mean the fire was not deliberately set. The wrong evidence may have been collected or there may have been insufficient accelerant present in the evidence because it was consumed by the fire. Likewise, the presence of an accelerant in fire residues doesn't mean the fire was deliberately set. As was previously mentioned, it is not unusual for accelerant materials such as gasoline to be stored in homes or businesses that may be innocently involved in a fire. It may be possible to determine the role of such materials in a fire if they are found some distance from the point of origin or are, in fact, used to make fire trail.

Explosions

If a fuel such as gasoline is confined to a closed space and then set on fire, gaseous products are produced (CO_2, H_2O, and others) along with energy. This causes the pressure to build up in the container until it ruptures. Most people would refer to this as an explosion, but it is actually only a fire that has been confined. To someone standing nearby, this is a distinction without a difference. It sure looks and sounds like an explosion. Most people think of an explosion as a violent release of energy, but a confined fire can also fit this definition.

When a gun is fired, it looks like there has been an explosion inside the cartridge that expels the bullet, but this is also a confined fire because smokeless powder (the propellant) burns rather than explodes. To a forensic chemist, however, there are important differences between a confined fire and an explosion. The major difference between an explosion and a fire is the amount of energy released and how fast the products of the explosion travel as they move away from the point of origin. Chemical explosions are combustions just like fires. Nuclear explosions operate on different principles and are not included in this discussion. The difference is in how much energy is emitted by a given amount of fuel and how intimately the oxygen is mixed with the fuel. There are two types of explosions: **deflagration** and **detonation**.

Deflagration

Recall that the source of oxygen in a fire is in the air that surrounds the fuel in the form of O_2—and that activation energy is needed to break the oxygen bonds before the fire can take place. This is partly responsible for the relatively slow speed of the combustion in a fire relative to that in an explosion. In a deflagration, the oxygen is physically mixed with the fuel and is in a form in which the O is bonded to other atoms that form weaker bonds than in O_2, and thus require less activation energy to break.

An example of an explosive that deflagrates when activated is **black powder**. Black powder is one of the oldest known explosives. It is composed of potassium nitrate (KNO_3), charcoal (a form of carbon), and sulfur in a weight ratio of 15:3:2. The ingredients are all powders and are finely divided and mixed together. The activation energy to begin the combustion is supplied by a match or a spark. When ignited, the reaction produces gases that escape at velocities up to the speed of sound (740 miles per hour—or about 1,100 feet per second). The bonds between the nitrogen and oxygen atoms in potassium nitrate are broken by the activation energy and these atoms then react with the carbon and sulfur, forming many products.

A great deal of energy is produced by these reactions. Explosions that produce escaping gases of velocities less than the speed of sound are referred to as **low explosives**. Another low explosive used in terrorist attacks such as the Murrah Federal Building in Oklahoma City (see Figure 20.11) is *ANFO*, is ammonium nitrate (NH_4NO_3) and fuel oil, a hydrocarbon fuel used to heat buildings. Ammonium nitrate is a pelleted fertilizer widely used by farmers. To make ANFO, these pellets are soaked in the fuel oil. This provides in intimate physical mixture of the fuel and the oxygen, but the velocities of the gases produced by the reaction are still slower

Figure 20.11 The Murrah Federal Building in Oklahoma City shortly after the 1996 bombing. Picture by Associated Press. Reprinted with permission of Oklahoma Bombing Investigation Committee (www.okbombing.org).

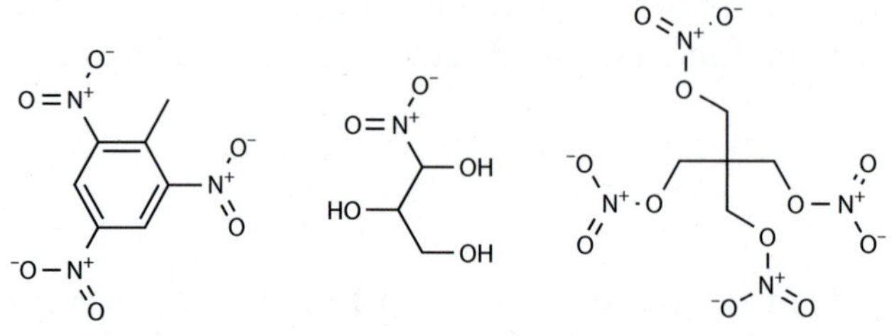

Figure 20.12 Chemical structures of some high explosives.

than the speed of sound. Low explosives produce much more energetic products than fires, but are still slow relative to high explosives, which are discussed next.

Detonation

A detonation is essentially an instantaneous explosion. It is so powerful that escaping gases travel at speeds greater than the speed of sound. Explosives that detonate are termed *high explosives*. The tremendous forces produced by high explosives push the surrounding air with such power that it can collapse buildings and move huge amounts of earth. In a high explosive, the oxygen is actually incorporated into the fuel molecules. When the activation energy is applied, the bonds connecting the oxygen atoms to the explosive molecule break as do all of the other bonds and then recombination takes place forming lower energy products. Since the oxygen is so intimately combined with the fuel, the combustion reaction is essentially instantaneous. Examples of some high explosives are given in Figure 20.12.

Notice that all of these explosives have oxygen incorporated as NO_2 or COH. Oxygen in this form is readily available to react with the other atoms in the fuel to release large amounts of energy very quickly. Some high explosives have very low activation energy and can detonate after only a small disturbance. Others are very stable and need another explosive to cause detonation.

Initiating and Non-Initiating High Explosives

There are two types of high explosives: **initiating** and **non-initiating**. These are also called **primary** and **secondary** high explosives. The relationships between these types of high explosives and some examples are given in Figure 20.13.

Initiating explosives are relatively sensitive to detonation. The extreme example of this is nitroglycerine, a syrupy liquid so sensitive that a small shock such as shaking or dropping it can cause detonation. Non-initiating explosives such as **dynamite** or TNT require a *booster charge* such as PETN (pentaerythritol tetranitrate). See Figure 20.13. There have been a number of modern modifications of explosives so they can be adapted to specialized uses. One of the more important of these advances has been the development of **plastique** explosives. These generally contain PETN and/or RDX mixed with a polymer plastic that has the consistency of clay. These explosives can be shaped or molded so their blast can be directed in particular directions. These explosives are highly popular in demolitions, especially where a large building is to be destroyed with a minimum of debris scattering. The charges are set in various locations and timed to detonate at particular intervals so that the building seems to implode. A picture gallery of the Seattle, Washington Kingdome stadium can be seen at: **http://seattlepi.nwsource.com/kingdome/gallery.asp**

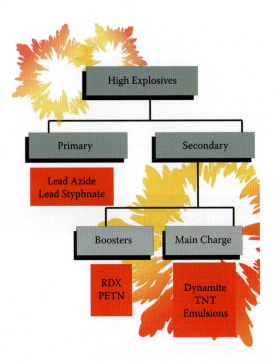

Figure 20.13 The relationships among different types of high explosives. *Courtesy of* Meredith Haddon.

Did You Know: Dynamite and the Nobel Prize?

One of the most potent and popular of all chemical high explosives is dynamite. The fuel in dynamite is nitroglycerine (Figure 20.12), but this is too unstable in its pure, liquid form, so it is mixed with *diatomaceous earth* and calcium carbonate (kieselguhr) and then rolled into tubes. In this form, it is much more stable and easy to handle and is considered a secondary explosive. It needs a blasting cap or primer cord to detonate it. Dynamite is widely used as an earth mover because of its high pushing force. It has also been used as a military explosive.

The inventor of dynamite was *Alfred Nobel*. He was born in Sweden in 1833 and rose to be one of the most influential industrialists in the world. As a young man, he was fluent in five languages and was more interested in literature than chemistry. He wrote plays, poetry, and novels in his spare time on his extensive travels. In the 1860s, Nobel began experimenting with nitroglycerine in a factory owned by his father. He concentrated on making the sensitive explosive easier to handle and more stable. He mixed it with many different substrates and finally settled on kieselguhr. He obtained a patent on the mixture and called it "dynamite." He sold dynamite all over the world and became very wealthy. He continued his chemical research throughout his life, ultimately making contributions to the development of artificial rubber and silk. As he grew older, Alfred Nobel became more interested in fostering the works of other inventors, especially those whose inventions or work benefited humanity. By the time he died in 1896, he had endowed a fund to make awards to people who exhibited great examples of human ingenuity. His first prize was awarded in 1901. Today, the most famous prize is the *Nobel Peace Prize*.

Ironically, Alfred Nobel thought that his invention of dynamite would banish war forever as man could see what terrible destruction it could wreak. He expressed this sentiment in a statement he made after receiving the patent on dynamite: "My dynamite will sooner lead to peace than a thousand world conventions. As soon as men will find that in one instant, whole armies can be utterly destroyed, they surely will abide by golden peace."

One may reflect on this statement and note that the same sentiments were expressed when the atomic bomb was developed by the United States. The real irony of course, is that the Nobel Prize for Peace is given to a person or organization that promotes the cause of peace and this prize is endowed with profits from the manufacture and sale of an explosive used in war.

Investigation of Bombing Scenes

The investigation of the scene of a bombing can be one of the most difficult types of crime scenes. The majority of criminal or terrorist bombings take place outdoors and debris (and evidence) can be scattered over a wide area. Access to the scene after a bombing may be relatively uncontrolled and very difficult to seal off. People may enter the scene or leave it bringing in extraneous materials or carrying off evidence. There may be human remains and dead bodies that could present problems and health hazards. If buildings are involved, there could be secondary effects such as further collapse, dust, and hazardous debris.

In some ways, investigation of bomb scenes is similar to that of fire scenes; the most important aspect is to locate the point of origin. In bombing scenes, the term **bomb seat** is often used but it means the same thing. The bomb seat will most likely be the best spot for locating and recovering unexploded residues of the explosive and/or parts of the bomb device. If the bombing takes place in the lower levels of a building, the upper floors may collapse onto the bomb seat, making its detection and recovery more difficult. In the first attempt to destroy the Twin Towers of the World Trade Center in New York in 1993, a truck loaded with explosives was parked in the garage on the fourth level below ground. Although the buildings didn't collapse, there was a great deal of damage to the parking garage. Upper levels of the garage, including many cars, crashed down onto the bomb seat. It took many weeks and heavy equipment to remove the rubble and expose the bomb seat, where parts of the truck, bomb parts, and unexploded and partially consumed explosive urea nitrate were found.

In the Oklahoma City bombing, a truck filled with ANFO was parked in front of the Murrah building and the explosive was detonated remotely. There is evidence that the fasteners holding up the wall of the truck that faced the building were loosened so that the escaping energy and gases would be directed toward the building. The truck was not entirely destroyed and evidence of its identity was an important clue in this case.

Consider what happens when a bomb goes off. When the detonation takes place, very hot gases are formed that race away from the bomb seat at high velocities, creating a *blast pressure* front and carrying debris and explosive residues along. The air around the explosion is pushed away, creating a partial vacuum at the site. As the blast pressure subsides, air rushes back toward the bomb seat to fill the vacuum, carrying debris with it and causing more destruction in the vicinity of the bomb seat. The actual location of the blast may be buried under tons of rubble. The progression of an explosion is depicted in Figure 20.14.

Finding parts of the explosive device can be very important, especially in terrorist bombings. The vast majority of terrorist bombs employ home-made devices

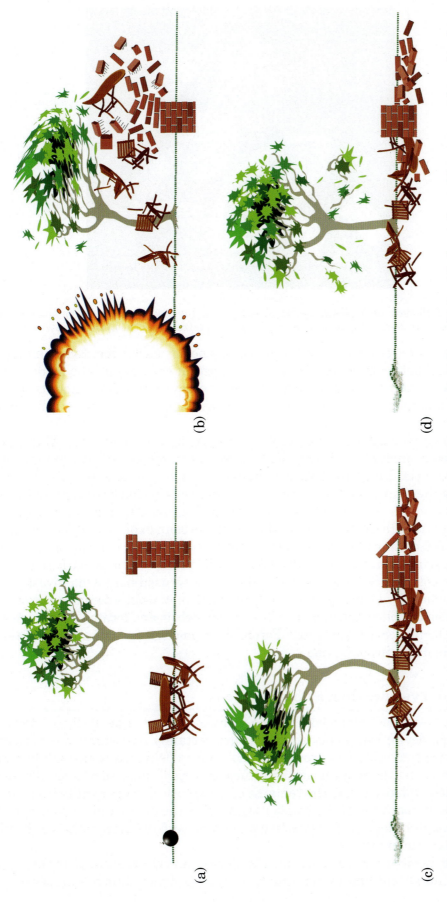

Figure 20.14 The progression of an explosion; Figure 14a is the condition of the scene before the explosion; 14b shows the positive pressure phase; 14c shows the damage after the negative pressure phase. 14d shows the condition of the scene after the explosion is over. *Courtesy of Meredith Haddon.*

Figure 20.15 Homemade explosive device. The can was filled with smokeless or black powder to make a bomb. Both were made in a prison workshop and seized from one of the inmates.

and terrorist groups tend to use the same technology each time. Even small pieces of the device that set off a bomb can yield important clues about who made it or how it was made and detonated. Finding pieces of a device in large amounts of rubble can involve painstaking searching and sifting. Figure 20.15 shows a home-made bomb device.

Locating unburned explosive material can also be very important. This material can be directly analyzed by instrumental and other methods and the exact explosive can then be identified easily. Exploded material leaves behind ions such as nitrite or nitrate, but these are generally components of soil anyway and finding them is not certain evidence of the presence of an explosive. Explosive-sniffing dogs can help here.

It is important to locate people in the wreckage of an explosion. Of course, finding survivors and getting them treated is the first responsibility of bomb scene responders. It is also important to locate dead bodies and remove them as early in the investigation as possible. So-called "cadaver dogs" can be used here. One investigator at the Oklahoma City bombing case indicated that they used a forensic entomologist who was able to "follow the flies" into the tons of debris and located dead bodies that attracted the flies. See Chapter 12: Forensic Entomology for a discussion of the role of insects in death investigation.

Analysis of Evidence from a Bomb Scene

The obvious evidence from a bomb scene includes burned or partially burned explosive and the device that exploded. These are certainly important, but are not the only evidence that scientists process. If the bomb is delivered to the site in a car or truck, identifying the remains of the vehicle can yield important clues. There may also be trace evidence inside the remains of the vehicle or fingerprints that can help identify the perpetrator. If the bomber is carrying the device and explodes it, there may be enough biological evidence to get DNA or perhaps even make an identification from his remains.

In most bombing cases, parts of the device survive the blast. If they can be recovered, important information can be had. A relatively limited number of people repeatedly assemble bombs for major terrorist groups and, like everyone else, are creatures of habit. Assuming that they can obtain parts in a regular fashion, they will assemble bombs pretty much the same way each time and the type of device provides a kind of signature of the bomb maker. There are a few investigators in major law enforcement agencies worldwide who are so knowledgeable about bombs that they may be able to identify the assembler from a few bomb fragments.

In most bombing incidents, some of the explosive material remains unexploded or partially exploded. How much of this remains depends on the amount of explosive, how it is confined, the location of the explosion, and the type of bomb seat. If particles of unexploded material are located, it is relatively easy to identify the type of explosive used, but even exploded debris can yield clues about the type of explosive. Intact particles of organic explosive can be analyzed by infrared spectrophotometry. Gas chromatography is generally not used with explosive residues because the heat inside the instrument can detonate the residue particles, causing damage to the column or instrument. One of the most important tests for explosive residues is called the **Griess test**. Many explosives contain nitrate or nitrite groups as part of the explosive because the N–O bonds are easily broken and provide lots of energy. The **Greiss test** detects the presence of nitrates and nitrates. If a particle is suspected of being an explosive residue, it will usually test positive for Griess because most explosives have nitrates or nitrites in them. The residue can be spotted on a thin layer chromatography plate and, after development, can be sprayed with the two reagents that make up the Griess test. The result will be an orange or red spot on the plate.

Summary

Both fires and explosions arise from a combustion; the reaction of a fuel with oxygen to produce energy. The reaction generally needs a boost of energy to get it started. This is called the activation energy. The differences between a fire and an explosion are the amounts of energy produced by the combustion and how the oxygen is made available for the reaction. In the case of fires, the oxygen is supplied by the surrounding air. Explosives are either of the low or high variety. Low explosives produce escaping gases whose velocities are less than the speed of light. High explosives produce gases that travel faster than the speed of light. In the case of low explosives, the oxygen is physically mixed with the fuel. In high explosives, the oxygen is part of the chemical structure of the explosive.

In fires and explosions, it is critical to find the point of origin (bomb seat, in the case of explosions). This is where evidence of how the fire or explosion started is most likely to be. In fires, this is the place where the hottest burning usually takes place and where fire trails or accelerants may be found. At the bomb seat, there is generally a great deal of debris and perhaps a crater. Accelerant residues are generally hydrocarbon fuels. There are various methods for removing the accelerant from the debris and concentrating it. The accelerant can be identified by gas chromatography. Explosive residues include unburned or partially burned explosive and parts of the explosive device. Hand sifting is generally necessary to recover these materials. Chromatography and spectroscopy are used to identify explosive residues.

Test Yourself

Multiple Choice

1. Which of the following is *not* necessary to have a fire?
   a. Fuel
   b. Activation energy
   c. Accelerant
   d. Oxygen

2. Which of the following is *not* evidence of the point of origin of a fire?
   a. Beginnings of fire trails
   b. Burned bedclothes
   c. Presence of accelerants
   d. Most intense burning

3. Which of the following is *not* a method of removing accelerant residues from fire debris?
   a. Gas chromatography
   b. Heated headspace
   c. Solvent extraction
   d. Absorbtion–elution
   e. Solid phase microextraction

4. In a low explosive, oxygen is:
   a. Physically mixed with the fuel
   b. Chemically part of the fuel
   c. In the air surrounding the fuel
   d. Not needed

5. Secondary explosives:
   a. Are types of low explosives
   b. Are non-initiating
   c. Require a booster
   d. Always contain oxygen in the form of O_2 molecules

6. ANFO is:
   a. A high explosive
   b. A mixture of a fertilizer and a commercial heating oil
   c. Burns rather than explodes when ignited
   d. Is very sensitive to detonation

7. Dynamite
   a. Is an initiating explosive
   b. Is a mixture containing nitroglycerine
   c. Deflagrates when ignited
   d. Produces escaping gases whose velocities are less than the speed of light

8. Solid phase microextraction:
   a. Is a method for detecting explosive residues
   b. Is the same thing as absorption–elution but on a micro scale
   c. Uses a coated wire inserted into the headspace of a container of fire debris, to adsorb accelerant residues
   d. Is a method for the identification of fire residues

9. The Griess test:
   a. Is used in the analysis of accelerants
   b. Detects the presence of oxygen in any form

   c. Reacts with nitrates and nitrates

   d. Reacts with all explosives

10. The activation energy needed to start a fire is used to:

   a. Break up molecular oxygen into atoms

   b. Decompose the fuel into carbon dioxide and water

   c. Extract accelerant residues from fire debris in a closed can

   d. Convert liquid oxygen to a vapor

True or False

11. The bomb seat is the same thing as the point of origin.

12. If a fire scene investigator can eliminate natural and accidental causes of a fire, then the fire must be arson.

13. A low explosive creates gases that escape at velocities up to the speed of sound.

14. Nitroglycerine is an initiating high explosive.

15. The presence of a fire trail always means that the fire was arson.

16. The presence of an accelerant in fire residues always means that the fire is arson.

17. The most important evidence of the cause of a fire can usually be found at the point of origin.

Matching

18. Detonation	a. Requires initiation by another high explosive
19. Incendiary	b. Damage to concrete by fire
20. Accelerant	c. Instantaneous combustion
21. Secondary high explosive	d. Deliberate fire
22. Spalling	e. Starts or speeds up a fire that otherwise wouldn't start on its own

Short Essay

23. Briefly describe and give an example of the three causes of a fire.

24. What is the fire tetrahedron? What are its parts? What relation does it have to putting out a fire?

25. What are the types of high explosives? How do they differ?

Further Reading

DeHaan J. *Kirk's Fire Investigation.* 3rd ed. Englewood Cliffs, NJ: Prentice-Hall, 1991.

Redsiker, D. and J. O'Connor. *Practical Fire and Arson Investigation.* 2nd ed. Boca Raton, FL: CRC Press, 1997.

Siegel, J., ed. Fire Investigation. In *Encyclopedia of Forensic Science.* London: Academic Press, 2000.

Urbanski, T. *Chemistry and Technology of Explosives*, Vols 1–3, Oxford: Pergamon Press, 1964

Yinon, J. and S. Zitrin. *The Analysis of Explosives.* Oxford: Pergamon Press, 1991.

Yinon, J. and S. Zitrin. *Modern Methods and Applications in Analysis of Explosives*: New York: John Wiley & Sons, 1993.

On the Web

Story and pictures of London, England bombing: http://en.wikipedia.org/wiki/7_July_2005_London_bombings.

Story and pictures of Madrid bombing: http://news.bbc.co.uk/1/hi/in_depth/europe/2004/madrid_train_attacks/default.stm.

Story and pictures of Oklahoma City Bombing: http://en.wikipedia.org/wiki/Oklahoma_City_bombing.

Helpful website on fire and arson investigations: http://www.interfire.org.

YouTube arson videos: http://www.mashget.com/topic/arson-fires.

PART VI

Legal Aspects of Forensic Science

21

Forensic Science and the Law

Learning Objectives

1. To be able to define admissibility of evidence
2. To be able to define and give examples of relevance of evidence
3. To be able to define and give examples of competence of evidence
4. To be able to describe the contributions of *Frye v. U.S.* to the admissibility of scientific evidence
5. To be able to describe the contributions of *Daubert v. Merrell Dow* to the admissibility of scientific evidence
6. To be able to describe the main features of a good forensic science laboratory report
7. To be able to define expert witness and distinguish an expert witness from a lay witness
8. To be able to describe the procedure of offering expert testimony
9. To be able to define *voir dire* and discuss its importance in expert testimony

Chapter 21
Forensic Science and the Law

Mini Glossary

Bench trial: A trial where the trier-of-fact is the judge.

Competence: A condition of admissibility of evidence. A set of legal constraints on the admissibility of evidence.

Expert witness: A witness who is qualified by knowledge, skills, or education to offer expert testimony and inferences or opinions that the average person could not provide.

General acceptance: A standard for the admissibility of scientific evidence. It means that the underlying scientific principle of the evidence is agreed on as true by the scientific community that would be most informed about the evidence.

Hearsay: A statement made outside of a court by someone who is not under oath that is used in court to assert the truth of a statement.

Jury trial: A trial where the trier-of-fact is the jury.

Lay witness: A witness who is not an expert and can only testify what he or she experienced with his or her five senses.

Materiality: The evidence has something to do with the case being tried here and now.

Peer review: A process whereby a research manuscript is reviewed by experts in the relevant scientific field.

Probativeness: Tendency to prove a fact.

Relevant: A condition of admissibility of evidence. It is made up of materiality and probativeness.

Statistically significant: A statistical test that determines whether differences between two measurements are real or products of the samples or other issues.

Subpoena: A command to appear in court for a hearing or trial at a set date.

Subpoena *duces tecum*: A command to appear in court and produce all reports and records concerning the case.

Trier-of-fact: The party that makes the decision of guilty or not guilty in a trial.

Introduction

In 1923, James Alphonso Frye was convicted of murder in Washington, D.C., in the Supreme Court of the District of Columbia. During his trial, he sought to have the results of a systolic blood pressure deception test admitted to help prove that he was not guilty of the crime. This test was a forerunner of today's modern polygraph test. The test measured changes in the subject's systolic blood pressure. The underlying principle is that when someone speaks the truth, he does so without any conscious effort, but that telling a deliberate lie requires conscious effort and is stressful and results in an involuntary change in systolic blood pressure. The prosecutor objected to the admission of this test, claiming that it was controversial and that scientists didn't agree whether the test was reliable and therefore the jury shouldn't have to speculate about its reliability and whether to put any weight on the results. The judge agreed with the prosecutor and Frye appealed to the United States Circuit Court of Appeals. The judges in the appeals court affirmed the lower court ruling and sustained the guilty verdict. In their written opinion, the judges claimed that the systolic blood pressure deception test was not generally accepted by the relevant scientific community and was therefore not admissible.

The *Frye* decision is one of the most important in U.S. law and in the field of forensic science. It set out the standard for admissibility of scientific evidence for more than a half century.

This chapter is about the relationship and interface between law and science. The reason forensic science exists is to provide evidence and answer legal questions such as who committed a crime, who is responsible for illegal acts that can harm society, and who should be blamed when a person is harmed. This book is mostly about the criminal justice system, but it is important to know that there is a parallel civil justice system for people or institutions that are the victims of harmful or illegal acts that do not amount to a crime, but for which damages may be paid. Although there are significant differences in how justice is carried out in these two systems, the way that forensic science is viewed and employed is the same.

Where does forensic science fit into the criminal justice system? Once a crime is reported or discovered, the police will launch an investigation. In large police departments, crime investigation is performed by detectives. They take overall charge of the investigation. Part of the investigation will be a search of the crime scene. This is a critical phase because much or all of the physical evidence of the crime will be found at the scene. As explained in Chapter 2: Crime Scene Investigation, part of the search of the crime scene is carried out by crime scene investigators. They collect, preserve, and package the evidence and have it sent to the forensic science lab for analysis. As the investigation proceeds, this may be a continuing process. Before a trial, witnesses may be *deposed*. This is an evidence-gathering process for the attorneys who question witnesses outside the courtroom. In this setting, witnesses are under oath and the questions and answers are recorded. If there is a preliminary hearing and/or trial, forensic scientists may be called to testify as an **expert witnesses**. In some cases, reports written by forensic scientists that set out their findings may be admitted in lieu of actual testimony. This process gives rise to three important considerations that affect the use of forensic science in the criminal justice system:

- The admissibility of scientific evidence
- Forensic science laboratory reports and their legal status
- The role of the expert witness in court

Of these, the most important and most studied is the admissibility of scientific evidence. Our adjudicative system operates by a series of rules. Some of these rules govern the admissibility of evidence in general and still others, the admissibility of scientific evidence in particular.

Admissibility of Evidence

In the U.S. adjudicative system, the party that determines guilt or innocence of the accused is called the **trier-of-fact**. In a **bench trial**, the trier-of-fact is the judge. In such cases, the judge presides over the trial and makes the final decision as to guilt or innocence. In a **jury trial**, the trier-of-fact is the jury. The jury can be as few as six people and as many as twelve (plus alternates). They listen to the evidence presented during the trial and are instructed by the judge as to the applicable law that governs the case. They apply the law to the facts and evidence of the case and reach a decision of guilt or innocence. In some cases, the jury may have a role in determing the punishment although this is usually the purview of the judge. During the trial, either or both parties (prosecutor or defendant) will present evidence that supports that side's theory of what happened in the incident. This evidence can take a variety of forms, including testimony involving eye witnesses, police, or experts, as well as physical evidence such as drugs, blood, or bullets. All evidence must conform to rules governing its admissibility and it is up to the judge to make determinations of admissibility even in a jury trial.

Admissibility of evidence is the determination of what matters may come before the trier-of-fact. There are many rules of evidence that seek to protect the jury from hearing evidence that is contaminated. Examples include evidence that is prejudicial, irrelevant, time wasting, unconstitutional and unreliable. The major rule that applies to *all* evidence, scientific or not, is that evidence must be **relevant** and **competent** in order to be admitted at trial. Otherwise relevant evidence may be inadmissible if it is not competent. Each of these concepts will be discussed in turn. Please keep in mind that there are many exceptions to the rules that follow. The explanations of the rules below are generalities that apply in the majority of basic situations. Also keep in mind that legal terms such as *competence* may have different meanings than they would otherwise have in a nonlegal setting.

Relevance

Relevance is made up of two components: **materiality** and **probativeness**. In order for evidence to be relevant, it must be both material and probative. **Material** means that the evidence has something to do with the case being tried here and now. It cannot refer to evidence that arose from some previous incident. For example, assume that a person is on trial for sexual assault. The fact that he may have committed previous sexual assaults is not material to this trial and is generally not admissible. Juries are not permitted to hear of a defendant's previous criminal record because it is not material and may also be prejudicial. **Probativeness** means that the evidence must prove something. In legal parlance, it means that the evidence must make a proposition more or less likely than it would be without the evidence. Probative evidence can help prove or disprove a proposition, accusation, or set of facts. For example, suppose a person is accused of killing another person by shooting him. When arrested, the suspect is found to be carrying a large knife. Since the death was by shooting, the knife is not probative. It doesn't help prove or disprove that the defendant shot the victim.

To summarize: if evidence tends to prove or disprove a proposition about the case being tried here and now, it is probative and material and therefore relevant.

Competence

Competence doesn't mean the same thing in the context of admissibility of evidence as it does in other situations. Here **competence** can mean a number of things having to do with the law. These include:

- **Prejudice:** Evidence cannot unduly prejudice the trier-of-fact for or against the accused. Highly inflammatory, gory color pictures of an autopsy or the dead victim may be inadmissible because their probativeness is outweighed by prejudice. The jury may become so horrified by the pictures that they can no longer be objective about the guilt or innocence of the defendant. Prior criminal activity and evidence of bad character are also generally inadmissible on the grounds of prejudice (and perhaps relevance).
- **Constitutional constraints:** The Fourth Amendment of the Constitution prohibits unreasonable searches of people and places and usually requires that a search warrant be issued by a judge or magistrate before a search can take place. The warrant and supporting affidavit (statement) must specify the location and persons to be searched and the items sought. If evidence is seized in violation of these requirements, it may be inadmissible no matter how relevant it is.
- **Statutory constraints:** The common law provides for a number of *privileges*—protected types of speech between doctor and patient, lawyer and client, marital partners, cleric and penitent, etc. For example, if husband makes potentially incriminating statements to his wife in the course of private communication, the wife cannot be compelled to testify against her husband and the husband can prevent the testimony even if the wife wants to testify. These are the marital privileges. These privileges are designed to foster communications that are deemed necessary without placing the speaker in danger of prosecution. You can see for example, how you would want private communications with your attorney to remain private. Many

people would not go to a doctor for treatment if they thought that information about their medical conditions could show up in a workplace or court.

- **Hearsay:** Hearsay refers to a statement made outside of a court by someone who is not under oath that is being used in court to assert the truth of the statement. Hearsay evidence can be dangerous because the person who repeats the statement in court can only testify as to what he heard or saw and not the truth of the statement. For example, if person A overhears a conversation between two people in which person B tells C that he robbed a bank, person A's retelling of what he overheard in a courtroom would be inadmissible hearsay. Person A could only testify that he heard the statement but could not answer questions about its truth. Even written documents can be considered statements and may be inadmissible. For example, a laboratory report by a forensic scientist is a form of hearsay but still may be admissible in court as an exception to the hearsay rule. There are many exceptions to the hearsay rule in modern jurisprudence. The hearsay rule was originally developed in medieval England as a way of keeping unreliable statements out of court.

Remember that in order for any evidence to be admissible in court, it must pass both the relevance and competence tests. Sometimes it is hard for the public to understand this. Have you ever heard of a situation where someone is found not guilty of a crime even though there existed incriminating evidence that couldn't be admitted because it was obtained illegally by a police officer who was executing an improper search warrant? Such cases are said to be decided unfairly because the defendant "got off on a technicality." The fact is that the rules of evidence are all technicalities; hurdles that must be surmounted if the evidence is to be admitted into court. These rules apply to *all* evidence, including testimony and physical evidence. In general, once evidence has been deemed to be relevant and competent, the trier-of-fact has enough knowledge to make judgments about the truth of the evidence and how much weight to give it.

Admissibility of Scientific Evidence

Have you ever seen a TV commercial for a product such as a new medicine? The spokesperson sometimes wears a white lab coat and perhaps even a stethoscope. The idea is that the viewer is supposed to believe that the speaker is a doctor or scientist and, as such, should be believed. This is the aura of truth that accompanies scientific matters simply because they are scientific. The problem is that much of the scientific and technical evidence presented in court is complex and often beyond the ability of jurors and judges who are not trained in science to understand. This opens the door for unreliable, unvalidated testimony that masquerades as science to be offered in court to unsuspecting judges and juries. There must be legal safeguards in place to ensure that the evidence that the trier-of-fact hears is reliable and scientifically valid. Therefore, in addition to all of the other rules of evidence discussed above, some special rules apply only to scientific and technical evidence.

Development of the Rules for Scientific Evidence

Prior to 1923 in the United States, scientific evidence was treated like any other evidence. If a witness could vouch for and explain the evidence and it was otherwise relevant and competent, it was admissible and the trier-of-fact could put whatever weight on it that they wanted. This is called the relevance standard for the admissibility of evidence. The *Frye* case described in the introduction to this chapter changed all that. A new standard for admissibility of scientific evidence arose from this case. It is called the **general acceptance** standard. It means that, whenever a party seeks to introduce a new scientific test or technique, it must first be generally accepted by the relevant scientific community. In the case of the systolic blood pressure deception test mentioned in the *Frye* case, the relevant scientific community would be psychologists and neurophysiologists. One of the problems with the *Frye* decision was that the Appeals Court never defined what it meant by "general acceptance." Over the intervening years since *Frye*, general acceptance has grown to mean that the technique has been published in a **peer-reviewed** book or journal.

Did You know: The Peer-Review Process

When a scientist makes a discovery, she will seek to publish it in a reputable book or journal so that she can claim credit for the discovery and so that other scientists can use her technique and build on it and make other discoveries. That is how science progresses. How does a reader of the journal know that the articles are reliable? One way is to engage in a peer-review process. Before the publisher and editor of the book or journal accept the manuscript, they send it to experts in the same field as the author (peers). They read the manuscript carefully and may even try to replicate some of the methodologies to make sure that they work properly. If they agree, the article is published. Although the peer-review process is very helpful in determining whether new methods and techniques are reliable and scientifically valid, it is not perfect. Very often the peers only read the manuscript and do not attempt to replicate the experiments or procedures because of lack of resources and time. Another problem is that a group of people who advocate the use of a scientifically questionable or invalid technique might set up their own journal and accept manuscripts from like-minded people. The manuscripts undergo a kind of peer review and the article gets published in the journal, but its methods are still suspect. This is called "junk science." Sometimes it is difficult to discredit or stamp out this practice.

Once the *Frye* decision was announced, it became the rule for federal courts in the United States. Federal court decisions generally do not apply to individual state court systems, but about half of the states eventually adopted the *Frye* standard while the other half continued to use the old relevancy standard. For more than 50 years, new scientific techniques were subjected to a *Frye* test in court in an effort to ensure they were scientifically sound. Even DNA typing survived a number of *Frye* tests in several states before being accepted nationwide.

Federal Rules of Evidence

It is the responsibility of the Congress to make rules that govern court procedures. This is done by enacting a set of rules called the *Federal Rules of Evidence (FREs)*. Many of these rules arose from the common law that came down from medieval England when the U.S. was founded. Others have developed over time from court decisions. Some of these rules refer to scientific evidence. In 1975, the Congress decided, after many hearings, to overhaul and modernize the rules of evidence. These changes included the rules that applied to scientific and technical evidence. An extensive discussion of these changes is beyond the scope of this book, but one new rule, FRE 702 warrants discussion. It reads as follows:

> If scientific, technical, or other specialized knowledge will assist the trier of fact to understand the evidence or to determine a fact in issue, a witness qualified as an expert by knowledge, skill, experience, training, or education, may testify thereto in the form of an opinion or otherwise, if (1) the testimony is based upon sufficient facts or data, (2) the testimony is the product of reliable principles and methods, and (3) the witness has applied the principles and methods reliably to the facts of the case.

Essentially, this rule hearkens back to the old relevancy standard. The judge decides whether the proposed scientific testimony will help the jury understand the evidence. Then the judge will permit an expert witness to testify about the scientific issue if the testimony is based on reliable scientific methods and principles. Nothing in this rule requires that the scientific principles be generally accepted by the relevant scientific community.

Once Congress passed these new rules, they became the law for all federal courts. Although they did not apply to state judicial systems, most states adopted many of these rules in whole or in part for their own courts. It is interesting to note that many federal courts ignored the FREs when making decisions about the admissibility of novel scientific evidence, instead continuing to rely on the *Frye* standard. This lasted until 1993 when the *Daubert* case was decided.

Daubert v. Merrell Dow

The *Daubert* case is an example of a *toxic tort*. A tort is a type of civil infraction. It is harm to a person or group by another person, group, organization, or company. A toxic tort is a harm that is alleged to have been caused by a dangerous or poisonous substance. The movie *Erin Brockovich* depicted a toxic tort caused by a company that dumped toxic substances into a water supply, leading to many illnesses and deaths. In the *Daubert* case, Mrs. Daubert was a pregnant woman whose doctor prescribed *Bendectin*, a drug commonly prescribed to relieve nausea among women in their first trimester of pregnancy. Mrs. Daubert took Bendectin during two successive pregnancies resulting in two babies that had birth defects. She sued the manufacturer of Bendectin, the Merrell-Dow company in federal court, claiming that the drug was the cause of the birth defects in her children. (The case was heard in Federal Court rather than state court because the Merrell-Dow company engages in interstate commerce and Federal courts have jurisdiction in such situations). The Merrell-Dow company denied that their drug caused the birth defects and a trial ensued.

The biochemical mechanisms that result in birth defects are not well known and there was no way at that time to prove medically that Bendectin caused birth defects. As a result, the plaintiff, Mrs. Daubert, had to use *epidemiology*, the study of disease that occurs in a large population, to prove her case. This is the same type of strategy used in court to establish that cigarettes cause cancer. Essentially, her epidemiologists had to gather data about the number of women who gave birth to babies with birth defects, the number of women who took Bendectin while pregnant, and the number of women who took Bendectin while pregnant and gave birth to babies with birth defects. They then took this data and used statistics to determine whether there was a **statistically significant** increase in the number of birth defects in babies from women who took Bendectin over the number in women who did not. The statistically significant requirement is very important in statistics. It is a test that determines whether a difference between two measurements is a real difference or a trivial one. For example, statistics may show an increase in birth defects with Bendectin but that increase may be due to the type and size of the sample of cases studied and may not be a true difference. Mrs. Daubert's statisticians determined that there was an increase and that it was statistically significant. Merrell-Dow's statisticians determined from approximately the same data that there was no statistically significant difference in birth defects with Bendectin.

When Mrs. Daubert's epidemiologists were going to offer their testimony, the defense objected on the grounds that her scientists did not use *generally accepted* methods of statistics in order to reach their conclusions and, because of that, their testimony should not be admitted. In raising this objection, the defense was invoking the *Frye* rule. The judge agreed with the defense and disallowed the plaintiff's testimony. Since her statisticians could not testify about their data, the defense had no case and the judge directed the jury to return a verdict for *Merrell-Dow.* (This outcome of a case is called a "directed verdict.") Mrs. Daubert's lawyers appealed the decision on the grounds that the trial judge used the wrong standard of admissibility of the scientific evidence and should have allowed the statisticians for the plaintiff to testify. They claimed that the judge should have used the standard set out in FRE 702 and not the *Frye* standard.

The United States Supreme Court agreed to hear the appeal and ultimately agreed with Mrs. Daubert. It remanded the case back to the trial court for a re-hearing and directed the judge to use the Federal Rules of Evidence to make his determination on the admissibility of the plaintiff's statistical evidence. The Supreme Court decision stated that the *Frye* standard no longer applied to the Federal courts and that it was too restrictive. It determined that FRE 702 put the responsibility on the judge to act as a "gatekeeper" and determine the admissibility of scientific evidence on broader grounds. The justices indicated that there were many possible tests of scientific validity beyond general acceptance and, in their decision in the *Daubert* case, listed a few:

- **Falsifiability:** This concept refers to testing a new theory or method. When a new scientific theory is proposed, it is subjected to rigorous experimentation that attempts to prove that the theory is false or doesn't work. If repeated attempts to prove it false fail, this provides evidence that the theory is valid. An example would be the theory that gravity on Earth pulls all objects toward the center of the Earth. If someone drops a hammer on Earth, it should fall. Repeated tests of this theory show that a dropped hammer will always fall down and not up. Since no examples of the theory being false have been shown, it must be true.
- **Known error rates:** During the development of a new technique or method, a scientist will determine or estimate the frequency of errors and their types when the method is used. All scientific tests and methods are subject to errors. Knowing the frequency of these errors will help the trier-of-fact determine the validity of the method.
- **Peer review:** The Supreme Court recognized the value of publishing and peer review of scientific methods and techniques and included peer review in their suggested means of assessing scientific validity.
- **General acceptance:** The Supreme Court didn't say that the *Frye* standard wasn't a valid means of assessing scientific validity, only that it cannot be the sole means of doing so. The court recognized that scientific consensus has significant value in evaluating a new scientific technique.

Since the Supreme Court ruling in *Daubert,* most states have adopted the decision in whole or in part. There are still a few *Frye* states and a few that rely on the old relevance standard, but *Daubert* has essentially become the law of the land. Further court decisions have clarified and extended *Daubert* since 1993 and test cases are still being prepared to determine whether *Daubert* should be extended to "soft" sciences such as psychology and whether it can be applied to old scientific techniques that have already been accepted in court. For example, there have been challenges recently to fingerprint and handwriting testimony on the grounds that they have not been proven to be scientifically valid. These challenges would not have been possible under the *Frye* standard since that decision referred only to new or novel scientific evidence and did not apply to evidence such as fingerprints, which had been accepted in courts for more than a hundred years.

Laboratory Reports

All scientific examinations, especially those meant for public consumption, culminate in a scientific report. This is always true in forensic science. Every case examined in a crime laboratory must include a written report that goes to the attorneys and to the court. The forensic scientist may be called to court to authenticate, substantiate, and explain the report to the trier-of-fact. The report is based on notes taken by the scientist during the evidence examination. These notes may also be required to be produced in court along with the report. There is no standard reporting system for forensic science in the U.S. Some laboratories use a brief report format, reporting only the evidence received, demographic data, and the results of the tests. Other labs use formal scientific reports that include a description of the examinations, their limitations, error rates, etc. Figure 21.1 is a specimen of a brief laboratory report issued by a crime laboratory.

Laboratory reports are examples of hearsay. They contain statements made outside of court by a person (the forensic scientist) who was not under oath at the time he or she wrote the report. Clearly, the opposing attorney cannot cross examine the report so, unless the scientist who wrote it is present in court, the report would have to stand on its own. Many states have provisions in their laws that permit the admission of lab reports if both sides stipulate (agree). Other states require the

---

REPORT OF LABORATORY EXAMINATION

IUPUI Forensic and Investigative Sciences

Date: 24 January 2005   **IUPUI case number:** 41-960

Contributing agency: Police Department   **County:**

Agency case number: PD.05.932   **Submitting official:**   Police Officer

Item #   **Description of items received**

One sealed plastic bag containing two plastic ziplock bags each containing green-brown plant material. Weight, item 1 = 23.3g
item 2 = 64.7g

Results of Examination

The green-brown plant material in items 1 and 2 were subjected to microscopic analysis, the modified Duquenois Levine test and thin layer chromatography, and were identified as marijuana, a schedule I controlled substance.

Figure 21.1 This is a specimen of a brief laboratory report issued by a forensic science laboratory. Note that the only information presented about the evidence is a description, weight, and the identity of the controlled substance. There is little information about what tests were done and their results.

author of the report to be present in court if the report is to be admitted as evidence. In some states, lab reports are admissible as a *business records* exception to the hearsay rule. This exception provides for the admission of records made in the regular course of business. They are deemed to be reliable because accurate records are essential to the functioning of a business.

Sometimes a laboratory report can play a crucial role in a trial. Over the course of a year, a forensic scientist may perform thousands of examinations on hundreds or thousands of cases. It is not unusual for a drug chemist to analyze more than a hundred cases per month. Many are routine cases involving cocaine, marijuana, or heroin, etc. Most of these cases will never be called to court and those that do may not be tried for one to two years. When an old case does come to trial, the scientist may not remember working on that specific case. The only evidence that she analyzed the case consists of her notes and the laboratory report. In such situations, the best evidence of the analysis of the evidence is not the scientist, but the lab report! This situation is illustrated below.

Past Recollection Refreshed

Consider the case where a forensic scientist is in court to testify about a case involving the possession of cocaine. She analyzed this evidence eighteen months ago and has since analyzed hundreds of other cocaine cases and other types of drug cases. She wrote a report detailing her findings in this case and has the notes she took at the time she did her analysis. During direct examination, the prosecutor shows her a bag containing the drug evidence and he asks her whether she can remember analyzing this evidence. She answers that she cannot remember working on this specific bag of white powder. The prosecutor then shows her the lab report that she wrote that details her work on the case, and he asks her if she can now remember working on this case. If the lab report triggers her memory, she can testify about the case. This is called "past recollection refreshed." The report and notes trigger her memory of the particular case and then she can remember analyzing it. Sometimes having the report and notes is still not enough to refresh the scientist's memory. This gives rise to another possible remedy.

Past Recollection Recorded

If the scientist cannot remember working on a case even after looking at her report and her notes, she cannot testify about the case but her lab report and notes can be admitted as proof of the facts therein. The report is clearly the most reliable evidence about the case. This is called "past recollection recorded." This means that, at the time of the analysis, the scientist took notes and wrote the report. As long as the notes and report can be linked unequivocally to the evidence in court, the report can be used as evidence that the evidence was analyzed even if the scientist cannot remember doing that analysis.

Expert Testimony

So far in this chapter you have learned that there are two types of real evidence: scientific and non-scientific. There are also two types of witnesses who can offer testimony in court: **expert** and **lay** (nonexpert) **witnesses**. Different rules govern the types of testimony these witnesses are permitted to offer. A lay witness can only testify to matters that he or she witnessed. In this sense, the term "witnessed" means that a person can testify to what he or she experienced with his or her five senses (as long as the evidence is relevant and competent). In general, lay witnesses are not permitted to offer opinions except those that any juror would understand and agree with. For example, a lay witness is permitted to testify that it was cold outside when she saw the suspect leave the bank. She could not, however, testify that a man who was driving erratically was drunk because that would require an expert opinion.

Federal Rule 702, which is reproduced earlier in this chapter defines an expert witness as follows: "a witness qualified as an expert by knowledge, skill, experience, training, or education." This statement has several implications. First, the witness must be *qualified as an expert*. This is the judge's responsibility. In a trial, either party can decide that he or she wants to offer testimony by an expert. The witness is brought into court and the party offering the expert will ask questions about his or her qualifications to be an expert and the areas of expertise. The other party will then have the opportunity to *voir dire*, or challenge the witness. This is a French term that means "to speak the truth." After this, the judge will accept or reject the witness as an expert and indicate the areas of expertise. Note that FRE 702 doesn't require an expert to be a Ph.D. or to be qualified solely by education. Consider the following scenario:. A man is killed in an automobile crash when he loses control of his car on a steep mountain road. A witness who was following the victim's car noticed that its brake lights were on most of the time, but the car did not appear to be slowing down. After the crash, the car is taken to a repair facility for inspection.

Suppose an acquaintance of the victim were accused of tampering with the brakes so that the man would be killed. If there were a trial then an important issue would be what caused the brakes to fail. How would this be determined? It would do little good to have the jury inspect the car's brakes because the average juror does not possess the knowledge needed to determine if and how the brakes failed. An expert would be needed to examine the brakes and *offer an expert opinion* about the condition of the brakes. This expert would be a brake mechanic who has many years of experience repairing brakes and may have taken classes that specifically addressed how to diagnose and repair malfunctioning brakes. Experience can be just as important as formal education in qualifying an expert. Notice that the expert's testimony in this case consists of opinions about the condition of the brakes. The expert examines the brakes and then draws inferences (conclusions) about what caused them to fail. These inferences are beyond the knowledge of the average person. Therein lies another way of defining an expert witness: a person who is qualified to draw inferences from facts that the average person cannot.

This discussion has highlighted two important differences between expert witnesses and lay witnesses:

- Expert witnesses must be qualified as an expert every time they testify in court.
- Expert witnesses are permitted to offer opinions whereas lay witnesses generally cannot.

Sometimes an expert witness is required to offer an opinion even if she would rather not. This is often accomplished in the form of a *hypothetical question*. This tactic is used when an attorney wishes to ask a question that would ordinarily not be permitted. Consider the following situation. A forensic pathologist is testifying about the death of a young child. The father has been charged with homicide, specifically for beating the child. The father claims that the child accidentally fell down the stairs. The prosecutor would like to ask the pathologist if the father beat the child, but that question is for the jury to decide and would not be permitted. Instead, the prosecutor will ask the witness to assume (hypothetically) certain facts, in this case, the exact pattern of injuries that the child sustained. Then the prosecutor would ask for an opinion about whether these injuries are consistent with the child being beaten by a strong adult or likely arose from the child falling down the stairs. The prosecutor is counting on the jury to make the connection between the hypothetical set of circumstances and the real circumstances of the case.

The Expert Witness in Court

Being an effective witness in court requires that one follow certain guidelines about behavior and comportment in court. A few of the more important rules are given below. Some of them apply to all witnesses whereas others are for expert witnesses.

- All witnesses are called to a trial with a subpoena. This is an order to appear in court for a specific matter on a specific date. It is signed by a judge. Ignoring a **subpoena** can put one in contempt of court and result in a jail sentence. For an expert witness, a **subpoena *duces tecum*** is usually issued. This commands the witness to produce all documents that are relevant to the case. This would include all reports, charts, graphs, and notes produced by the witness during the analysis of the evidence.
- When not testifying, all witnesses are usually sequestered and are not permitted in the courtroom until they are called to testify. This is accomplished by one party or the other invoking the *rule on witnesses*. Witnesses are instructed not to discuss the case or their testimony while in the waiting room.
- Court testimony by any witness consists of *direct examination* conducted by the party who has requested the witness and *cross-examination* conducted by the other party. This may be followed up by redirect and then recross and so on until both parties have finished asking questions.
- Expert witnesses may consult their notes or reports during testimony, but any documents they refer to in court may be inspected by either attorney.
- In a jury trial, it is good practice to look at the attorney when being asked a question, but one should focus on the jury when answering the question. If it is a bench trial, the witness should look at the judge when answering. This is especially important for expert witnesses. Their testimony is most effective when they have established a rapport with the trier-of-fact.
- Expert witnesses are often called on to explain complicated scientific or technical matters. It is easy to slip into the language or jargon of the trade. This language would be understood by other experts in the field, but not by the average person. It is very important that an expert witness explain difficult concepts using language that the average person would understand.
- All witnesses would do well to remember that a jury or judge is free to give whatever weight they choose to witness testimony. Just because someone is qualified by the judge to be an expert doesn't mean that the jury is required to believe what the witness says.

Something for You to Do: A Mock Trial

A mock trial is an excellent class project. The class can be divided into teams. The project may begin with a mock crime scene where members of the team collect evidence and perhaps even analyze it. Then the team is divided up for the trial. There will be a prosecutor, a defense attorney, one or more government expert witnesses, and one or more defense expert witnesses. The prosecution team will prepare expert testimony about the evidence that was collected and analyzed and the defense team will prepare to cross-examine the government's expert(s) and counter with expert testimony of their own. Someone can be appointed to be the judge and other members of the class can be the jury. At the end of the trial, the jury can vote to determine whether the defendant is guilty.

Summary

Scientific and technical evidence is treated differently from nontechnical evidence in our courts because it is difficult to understand by lay persons and because it has an aura of reliability by its very nature. The rules of evidence determine how and when evidence shall be admitted into court. Scientific evidence must obey all of these rules plus additional rules developed by court cases such as *Daubert* and *Frye* as well as the federal and state rules of evidence. Laboratory reports of forensic scientific analysis can be important evidence in criminal and civil cases. They are the written record, along with the scientist's notes, of how a case was analyzed. If a scientist cannot remember the case, the report may be the best evidence.

Expert witnesses are treated differently in court than are nonexpert or lay witnesses. An expert must be qualified every time he or she testifies by reciting his or her qualifications. He or she is then subject to cross examination on those qualifications (*voir dire*). The judge decides whether that person can testify as an expert in that case. A person can be an expert by any appropriate combination of knowledge, skills, experience, and education.

Test Yourself

Multiple Choice

1. *Voir dire* is:
   a. A French court
   b. A type of cross-examination about witnesses' qualifications
   c. A set of expert witness qualifications
   d. A famous case that helped shape the rules for the admissibility of scientific evidence
2. A person can be qualified as an expert on the basis of:
   a. Experience
   b. Education
   c. Knowledge
   d. Skills
   e. All of the above
3. In *Daubert v. Merrell Dow*, the United State Supreme Court set out criteria for testing the scientific validity of a scientific method or technique. Which of the following is *not* one of those criteria?
   a. Peer review
   b. Whether anyone has ever offered testimony in a federal court on this topic

    c. General acceptance of the scientific principle

    d. Error rates of the technique

    e. Falsifiability of the underlying theory

4. Which of the following applies to all types of testimony?

    a. Relevance

    b. *Frye v. U.S.*

    c. *Daubert v. Merrell Dow*

    d. FRE 702

5. Relevance consists of:

    a. Competence + admissibility

    b. Materiality + probativeness

    c. Materiality + competence

    d. Hearsay + Constitutional constraints

6. Which of the following is not a type of competence (criterion for admissibility of evidence)?

    a. Relevance

    b. Obedience to the Fourth Amendment of the U.S. Constitution

    c. Prejudice

    d. Priveleges

7. In *Daubert v. Merrell Dow:*

    a. Mrs. Daubert prevailed because Merrell Dow's experts failed to prove that Bendectin doesn't cause birth defects

    b. Merrell Dow prevailed because Daubert's epidemiologists didn't use scientifically valid methods for applying statistics to their data about Bendectin

    c. The U.S. Supreme Court refused to hear the appeal of the trial court

    d. The U.S. Supreme Court reversed the trial court's decision and awarded Mrs. Daubert damages for Bendectin's harm to her baby

8. In *Frye v. United States:*

    a. The trial court judge admitted the results of the systolic blood pressure deception test, but he was reversed by the appeals court

    b. Frye was found not guilty of murder

    c. The appeals court set a standard of "general acceptance by the relevant scientific community" for the admissibility of scientific evidence

    d. The U.S. Supreme Court ruled that the results of the deception test were inadmissible because of the decision in *Daubert v. Merrell Dow*

9. Scientific laboratory reports:

    a. Are never admissible in court

    b. May be admissible in some states if both sides agree

    c. Cannot be included in a subpoena of a witness

    d. Cannot be viewed in court by anyone other than the scientist who wrote it

    e. Are always admissible in court as a "business records exception" to the hearsay rule

10. There are extra rules that govern the admissibility of scientific and technical evidence because:

    a. Juries must be protected from junk science and unreliable or invalid science

    b. Only Ph.D.s can offer expert testimony

    c. The U.S. Supreme Court ruled in *Frye v. United States* that scientific evidence requires extra rules

    d. Courts ruled as far back as medieval times in England that scientific evidence must be accorded special treatment.

True or False

11. If evidence is probative, it is always admissible.
12. Properly signed laboratory reports are always admissible in court without the author's presence.
13. If a client makes a guilty admission to his attorney in private, the attorney cannot be compelled to testify against the client.
14. *Daubert v. Merrell Dow* is an example of a toxic tort case.
15. The "general acceptance" rule was developed in the *Frye* case.
16. An expert witness must have a college degree to be qualified to testify in court.
17. A judge can never be the trier-of-fact.

Matching

18. Federal rule 702	a. Legal constraint on admissibility of evidence
19. *Daubert v. Merrell Dow*	b. Congressional rule concerning scientific evidence
20. *Frye v. U.S.*	c. Probativeness + materiality
21. Competence	d. Set out general acceptance rule
22. Relevance	e. Set out scientific validity standard for evidence

Short Essay

23. What are the two major criteria for the admissibility of evidence? Give an example of each.
24. How does an expert witness differ from a lay witness?
25. Why are there special rules for the admissibility of scientific or technical evidence?

Further Reading

Giannelli, P. C. *Snyder Rules of Evidence Handbook: Ohio Practice.* New York: West Information, 1996.

Moessens, A. A, J. E. Starrs, C. E. Henderson, F. E. and Inbau. *Scientific Evidence in Civil and Criminal Cases.* 4th ed. New York: Foundation Press, 1995.

Kiely, T.F. *Forensic Evidence: Science and the Criminal Law.* Boca Raton, FL: CRC Press, 2001.

On the Web

A brief analysis of the *Frye* case: www.daubertontheweb.com/frye_opinion.htm

The complete U.S. Supreme Court opinion in *Daubert v. Merrell Dow:* http://supct.law.cornell.edu/supct/html/92-102.ZO.html

Excellent explanation of expert qualifications and testimony by Paul C. Giannelli: www.scientific.org/distribution/law-review/giannelli.pdf

Complete Federal Rules of Evidence: www.law.cornell.edu/rules/fre

Index